SAILORS GU

TO THE

WINDWARD IS

Welcome to 19th edition. This guide has now been in poduction for 38 years!

I would like to introduce Lexi Fisher. Lexi has been working with me for well over a year, and we are now equal partners in Chris Doyle Publishing. Lexi brings youth, energy and a fresh perspective to the guide. I am the old guy, and references to "I" in this book refer to me, wheras "we" refers to both of us.

Lexi is Grenadian and she loves sailing, freediving, suba diving, snorkeling, kayaking, and cruising.

We will both work hard to make sure this is the best guide available, and would like to thank you, our readers, for buying and using our guides and making this possible. Without you, our guides would not exist.

Chris Doyle

SAILORS GUIDE TO THE

Chris Doyle	Text, charts, layout
Lexi Fisher	
Sally Erdle	Illustrations
Chris Doyle	
Lexi Fisher	Photos
Scott Wilks	
Polly Philipson	
Shaid Rambally	

DISTRIBUTION

USA AND WORLDWIDE
Cruising Guide Publications
P.O. Box 1017
Dunedin, Florida 34697-1017
Tel: 727-733-5322
Fax: 727-734-8179
info@cruisingguides.com

ST. VINCENT & THE GRENADINES
Heather Grant, Erika's, Union Island,
St. Vincent and the Grenadines
Tel: 784-485-8335,
vip@erikamarine.com

ST. LUCIA
Anne Purvis,
Cap Estate, St. Lucia
Tel 758-488-5477/721-2846
anne.purvis6@gmail.com

GRENADA
Jeffrey Fisher, Mt. Edgecombe
Springs, St. George's, Grenada
Tel: 473-407-6355/419-3548
Jeffofisher@yahoo.com

Cover photos: Sunset. Prickly Bay,
Racing a Carriacou Sloop in Bequia Regatta,
Free diving with dophin

AUTHORS' NOTES

In the text we give a very rough price guide to the restaurants in the form of dollar signs.

$ cheap and cheerful
$$ below average
$$$ average priced
$$$$ above average
$$$$$ top of the line

We are happy to include advertising. It gives extra information and keeps the price of the book reasonable. If you wish to help us keep it that way, tell all the restaurateurs, service technicians and shopkeepers, "I read about it in the Sailors Guide." It helps us no end.

If you like, tell us about your experiences, good or bad. We will consider your comments when writing the next edition.

Chris Doyle
email: sailorsguide@gmail.com
or: c/o Cruising Guide Publications
P. O. Box 1017, Dunedin
FL 34697-1017
Fax: 727-734-8179

ACKNOWLEDGEMENTS

To everyone who helped; those who sat us down in their bars and shops to explain what they are trying to achieve; those who tapped us on the shoulder and said "know what you should say..."; to all those who have emailed us in suggestions and information – a big thank you to all of you! A special thanks to Ciarla Decker, for her help in Martinique.

This book would not be the same without your input. Chris Doyle & Lexi Fisher

Please check for updates at
www.doyleguides.com and on
Facebook "doyleguides"

WINDWARD ISLANDS

Published by
CHRIS DOYLE PUBLISHING
in association with
CRUISING GUIDE PUBLICATIONS

ISBN_978-0-9978540-7-7

First edition published.............1980
Second edition published 1982
Third edition published...........1984
Third edition revised 1985
Third edition revised 1986
Fourth edition published 1988
Fifth edition published............1990
Sixth edition published 1992
Seventh edition published.......1994
Eighth edition published 1996
Ninth edition published...........1998
Tenth edition published...........2000
Eleventh edition published......2002
Twelth edition published.........2004
Thirteenth edition published ...2006
Fourteenth edition published...2008
Fifteenth edition published 2010
Sixteenth edition published.....2012
Seventeenth edition published ...2014
Eighteenth edition published...2016
Nineteenth edition published ..2018

Printed in China by Four Colour Print Group, Louisville, Kentucky

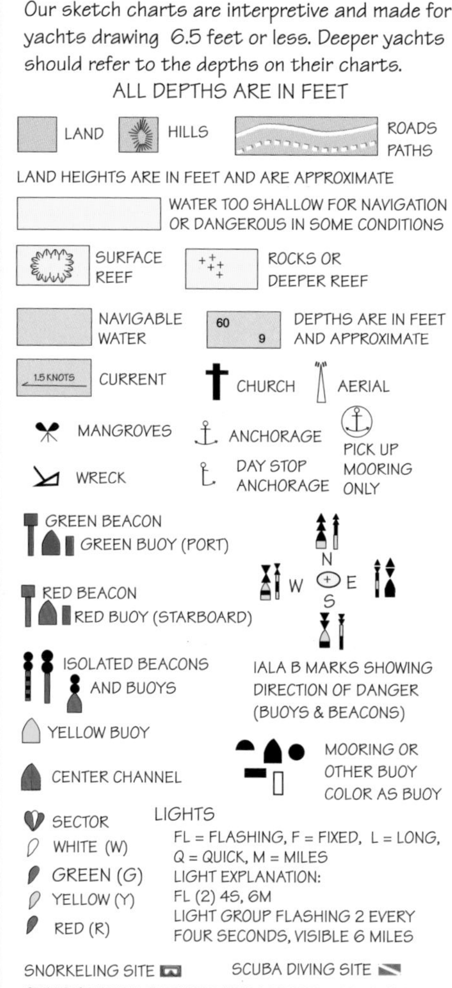

NOTICE

No warranty, expressed or implied, is made by the publisher and authors with respect to accuracy. This guide and these charts are the work of individuals. There may be errors and omissions, so undue credence should not be placed on this guide. This guide should be used with navigational charts and other navigational aids. This guide should not be used for navigation.

SAILORS GUIDE

TO THE

by Chris Doyle
& Lexi Fisher
19th edition

CRUISING GUIDE TO TRINIDAD, TOBAGO PLUS BARBADOS AND GUYANA
By Chris Doyle
2013
ISBN 978-0-944428-96-2
6 x 9, 256 pp. **$27.95**

This updated edition has been expanded to include Guyana. Including 55 sketch charts, aerial photographs, dazzling scenic photography throughout, unsurpassed onshore information with sections on exploring, provisioning, services and restaurants. The guide is linked to the author's website where you can download town maps, GPS waypoints given in the sketch charts and much more.

CRUISING GUIDE TO VENEZUELA & BONAIRE
By Chris Doyle
2006
ISBN 0-944428-78-9
6 x 9, 290 pp. **$27.95**

This is the latest updated version of the only seriously researched guide to this area. The book includes color aerial photos of many anchorages, clear and concise navigational charts, with information on things to do and places to go while on shore. The guide is linked to the author's website where you can download updates, town maps and much more. A few of these are still available as a printed version, when these run out it will be available as a digital dition only

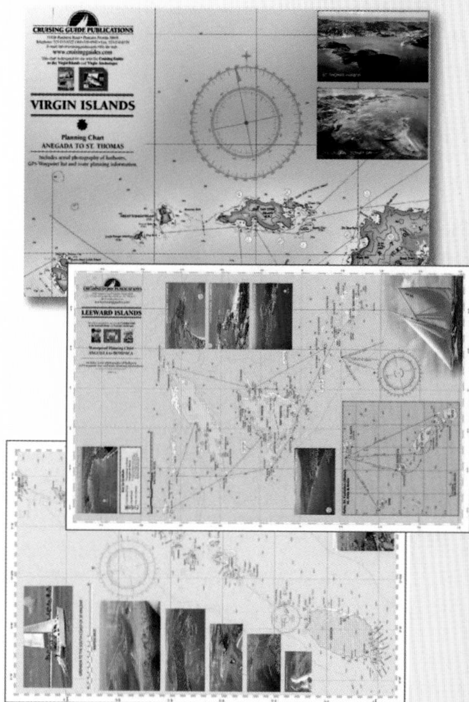

WATERPROOF PLANNING CHARTS OF THE VIRGIN, LEEWARD & WINDWARD ISLANDS COLOR WITH AERIAL PHOTOS

COLOR, FOLDED, DOUBLE-SIDED 17 X 27 $9.95 EACH

BUY OUR GUIDES ON OUR NEW APP!

Search for Cruising Guide Publications on Google Play or iTunes!

Cruising Guide Publications
P.O. Box 1017, Dunedin, FL 34697-1017 • phone 800-330-9542
International Orders 727-733-5322

Advertisers Index

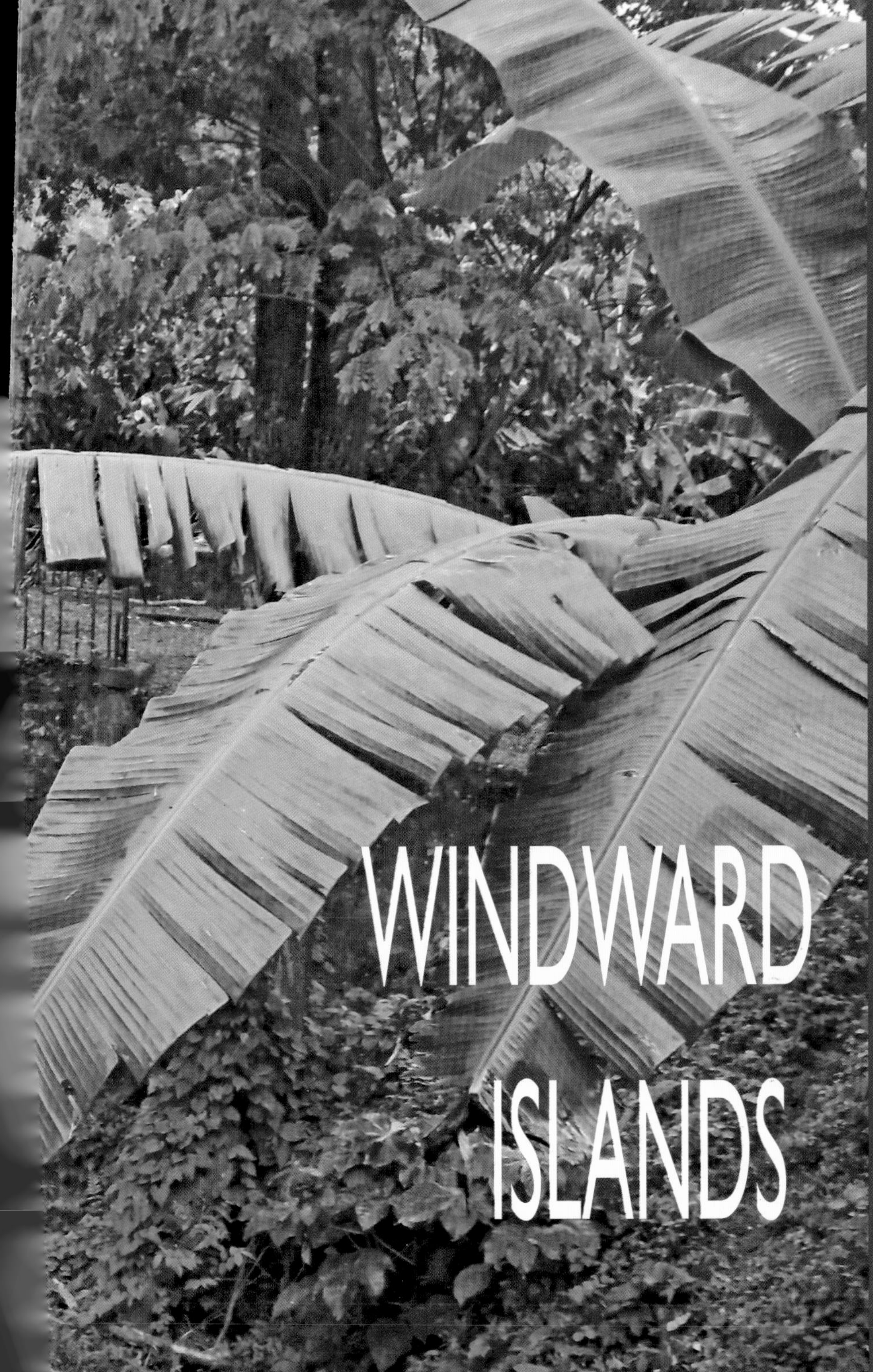

WINDWARD ISLANDS

Oldest bridge in Grenada at the Crayfish Bay Chocolate Factory estate

TABLE OF CONTENTS

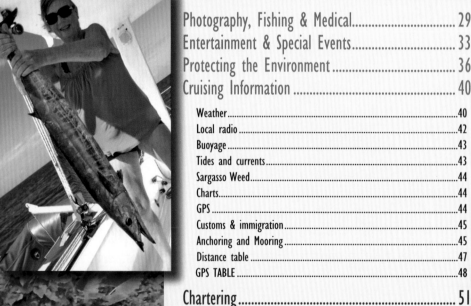

ANCHORAGES IN THE WINDWARD ISLANDS........................60

ONTINUED ON NEXT PAGE

SKETCH CHARTS

CONTINUED PAGE 9

SKETCH CHARTS

ST. VINCENT & THE GRENADINES (continued)

GRENADA & CARRIACOU

PLANNING &

CRUISING

Union Island Market

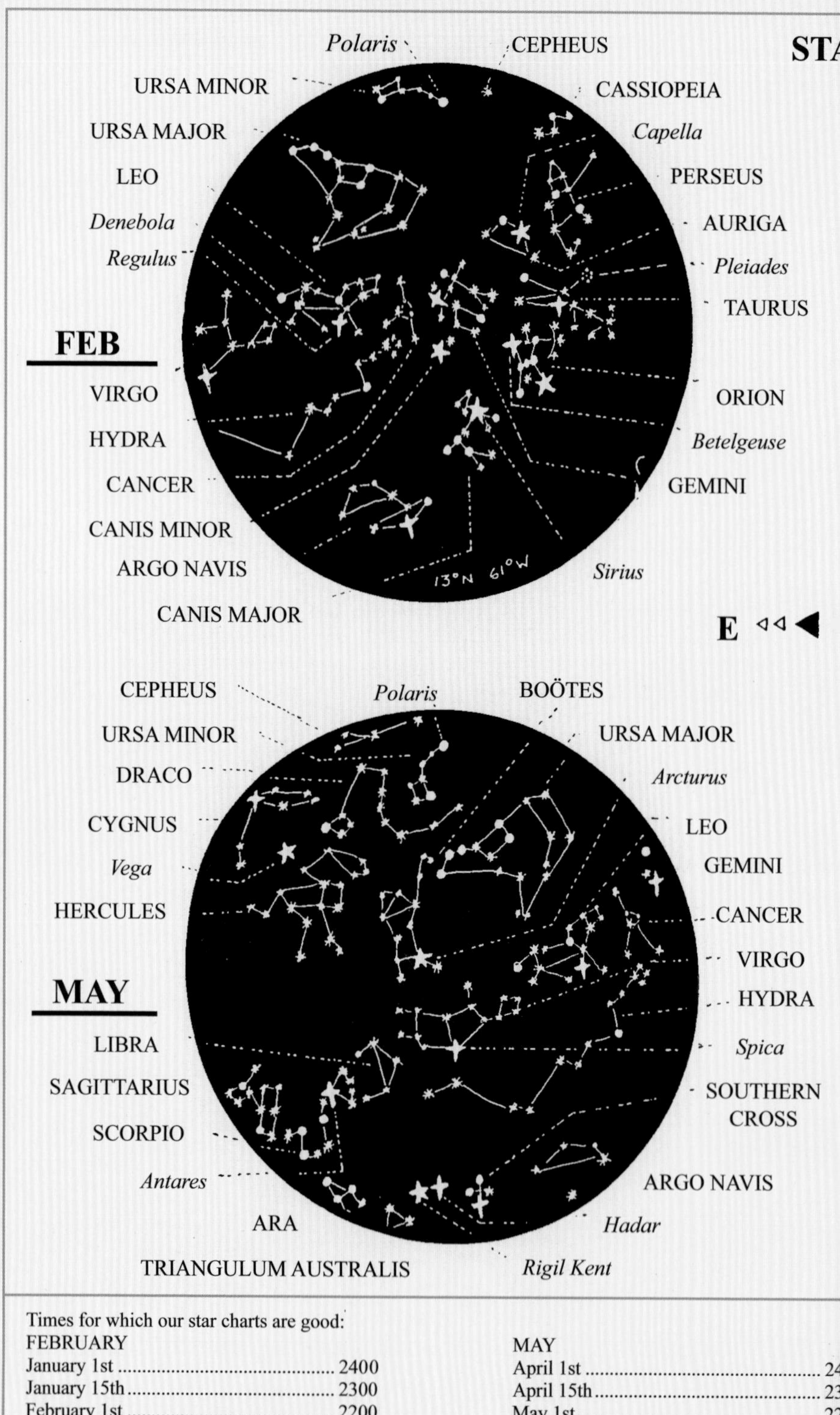

Times for which our star charts are good:

FEBRUARY		MAY	
January 1st	2400	April 1st	24
January 15th	2300	April 15th	23
February 1st	2200	May 1st	22
February 15th	2100	May 15th	21
March 1st	2000	June 1st	20
March 15th	1900	June 15th	19

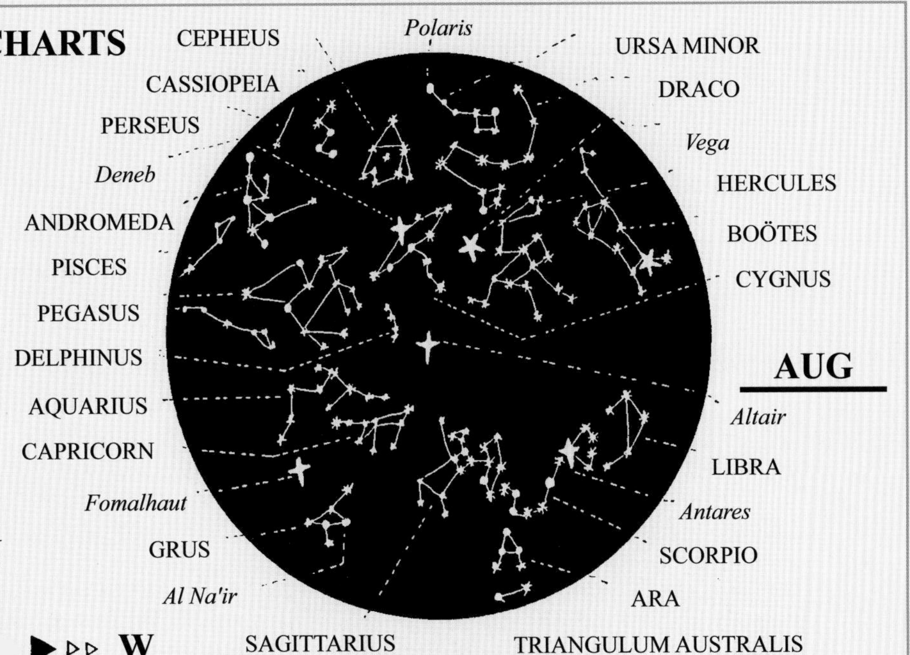

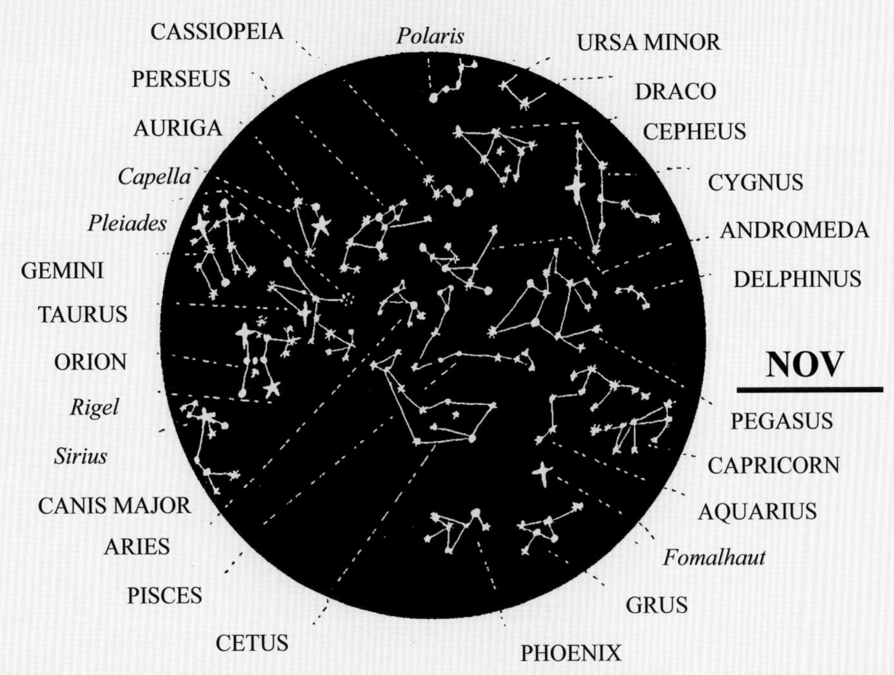

Note: Hold this book over your head with the east arrow pointing to the east (normally your bow).

AUGUST		NOVEMBER	
July 1st	2400	October 1st	2400
July 15th	2300	October 15th	2300
August 1st	2200	November 1st	2200
August 15th	2100	November 15th	2100
September 1st	2000	December 1st	2000
September 15th	1900	December 15th	1900

Sailing off Sandy Island

Introduction

The islands of the Caribbean sweep southward in a huge arc, like a string of giant-sized stepping stones from Florida to Venezuela. On the eastern, or windward, side, the Atlantic Ocean pounds the shore. On the leeward side, the calmer Caribbean Sea lies tranquil, sparkling in the sun.

The Windward Islands are at the southern end of this chain, the last links before Trinidad and South America. The British called them the Windwards, because you had to beat to windward to get there from many of their other possessions.

They lie almost across the easterly trade winds, which makes for easy passages north or south, and they are just far enough apart to allow for some wild romps in the open ocean before tucking into the calm of the next lee shore.

The four main Windward Islands ~ Martinique, St. Lucia, St. Vincent, and Grenada ~ are lush and richly tropical, with high mountains that trap the clouds and produce dense green vegetation. Here you can find excellent examples of tropical rainforest, easily accessible to those who hike.

Between St. Vincent and Grenada lie the Grenadines ~ a host of smaller islands, some with hills of a thousand feet, others no more than a reef-enclosed sand cay sprouting a few palms. Drier than the large islands, they all have perfect white beaches, crystal clear waters, and colorful reefs.

Over 2,000 years ago, the islands were colonized by the Arawaks, an oriental-looking people who were great navigators, artists, and sportsmen. They were somewhat peaceful. Those in residence when Columbus arrived were a more warlike tribe called the Kalinargo, renamed Caribs by Columbus. The Kalinargo resisted the Europeans and refused to be slaves. In Grenada, the northern town of Sauteurs marks the spot where the last of the Grenada Kalinargo leapt to their deaths rather than be taken captive. They held out the longest in St. Vincent, where the steep terrain made colonization harder. Even here the European colonists eventually

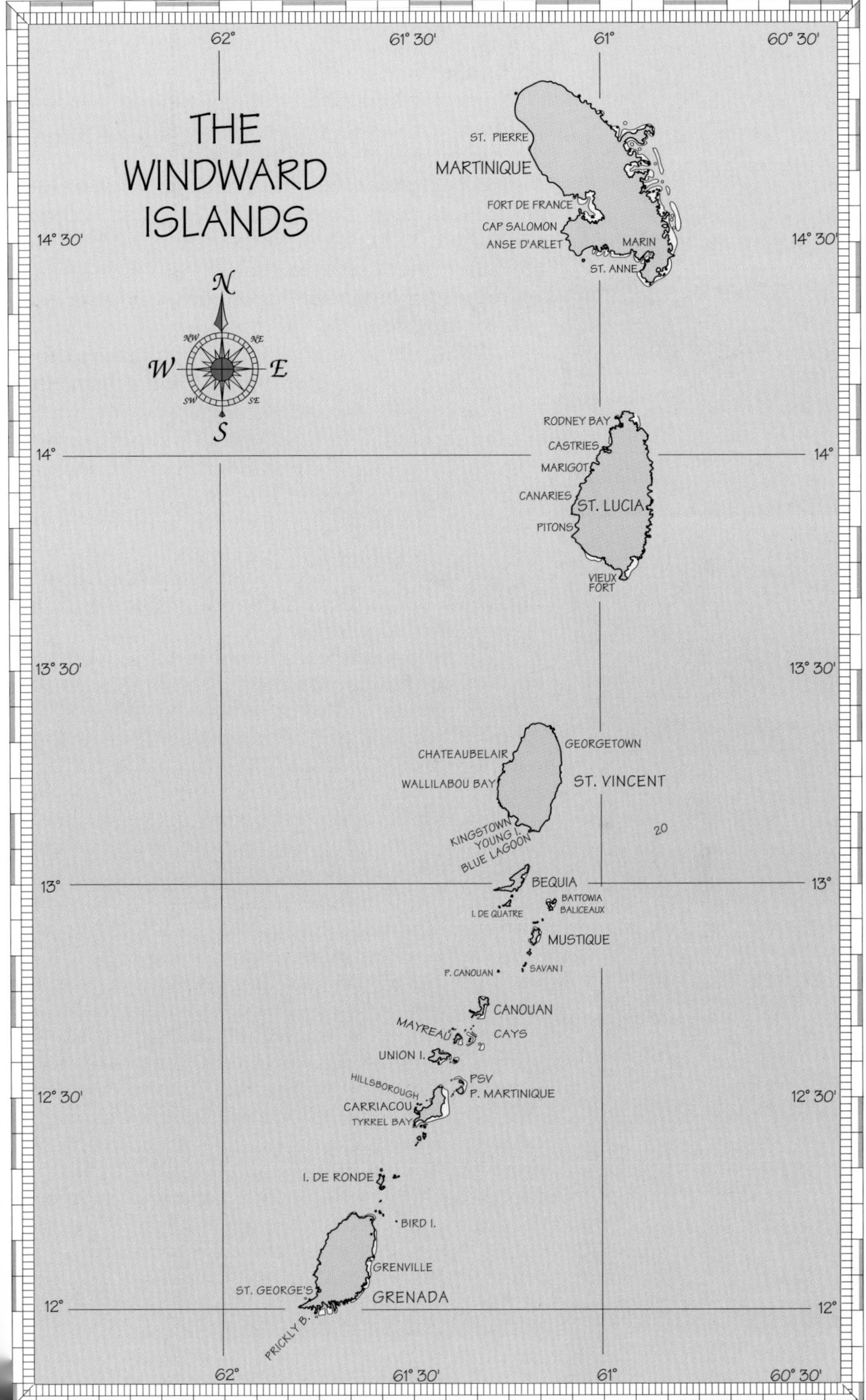

Planning & Cruising

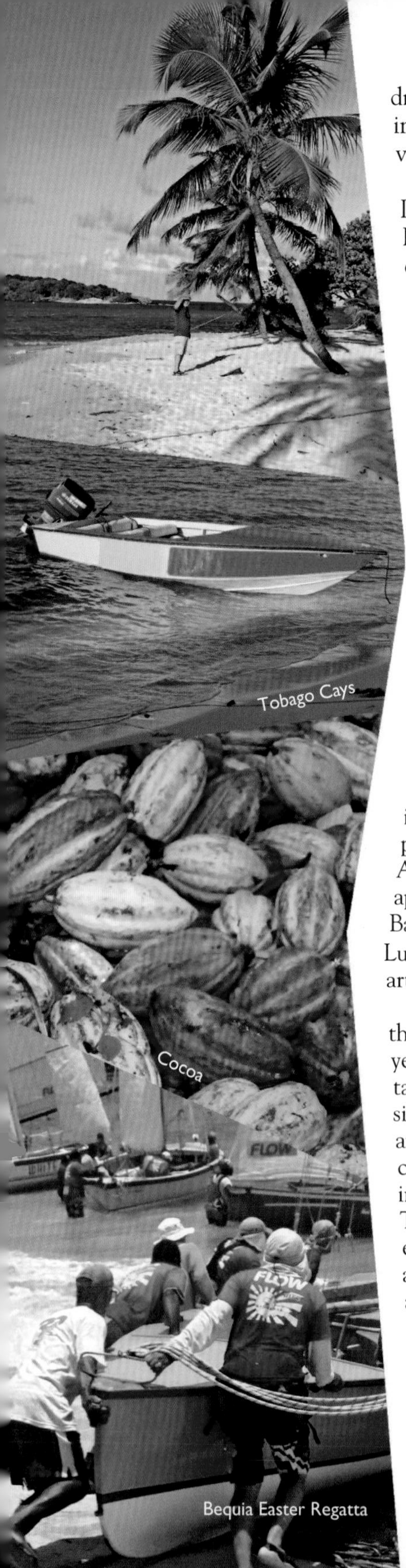
Tobago Cays
Cocoa
Bequia Easter Regatta

drove them out. Today, just a handful of Kalinargo remain in the Windwards, on the north end of St. Vincent in a village called Fancy.

Years of colonization followed, and the Windward Islands were fought over by the British and French. Plantation owners became rich from the production of sugar, and slaves were brought from Africa to work in the fields. After slavery was abolished, many former slaves showed a healthy disinclination to work for their previous masters, preferring to eke out a living fishing and farming. The planters imported East Indian laborers to take over the fieldwork.

Today, the intermingling of the races has produced an interesting blend of people who live in harmony.

During its colonial history, Martinique, the northernmost Windward Island, was nearly always in French hands. Today, it is still part of France and therefore a member of the European Union. The language and ambience are French, and while not essential, it certainly helps to speak the language.

St. Lucia, St. Vincent, and Grenada are now all independent nations with a British tradition. Each has its own laws and customs.

The main industries throughout this area are tourism, farming, fishing, and, more recently, international company services and yacht registration. While all the islands produce some rum, Martinique has a large industry producing their own specially flavored product, "Rhum Agricole." Farmers in Martinique also grow excellent pineapples. Grenada has traditionally grown nutmeg and cocoa. Bananas have been an important part of the economy in St. Lucia and St. Vincent. Both Grenada and St. Lucia have artisan chocolate factories that make delicious chocolate.

Tourism is probably responsible for much of the rise in the standard of living that has been visible over the last 30 years. There was a boom in selling land to visitors which tapered off with the last recession. Yachting tourism is a significant factor in the economy of many of these islands, and has encouraged the growth of restaurants, shops, handicraft artisans, and support services. The dollars you spend in the islands really do help the local people.

The Windwards are a joy for any sailor. Good trade winds ensure exhilarating passages, and delightful anchorages abound. The weather is pleasant year round, the people are friendly, and there are not too many annoying regulations. You are free to sail and enjoy some of the most beautiful islands on earth.

Welcome to the Windwards!

We, the authors of this book, are against the capture and containment of dolphins, and any forced interactions with humans.

This, and the cover photo, were taken off the west coast of Grenada during a wild encounter between a bottle-nose dolphin and Lexi Fisher, who was freediving. Such encounters are amazing when they happen.

Both photos were taken by Nicolas Winkler.

Local Lore

Currency

In Martinique the currency is the Euro, currently worth more than the US dollar. Change bureaus give better rates than banks.

In the other islands, the currency is the Eastern Caribbean (EC) dollar, at a fixed bank rate of 2.67 to one US dollar. This is usually a slightly better rate than that offered by shops or taxi drivers, though most people are willing to take US dollars. You get a lot of EC dollars for the US ones, but they are much more quickly spent. Oh well, "EC come, EC go," or, as Jimmy Buffet said, "It's much more fun to spend money with pictures of flowers and palm trees on it than money with pictures of green old men." Spend it all or change it back locally. Bankers will laugh if you try to change it back home.

Credit cards, especially the Visa/MasterCard group, are widely accepted and they are much safer and more convenient than sporting big wads of cash. Let your credit card company know you are traveling so they do not block your card.

Language

In Martinique the language is French, and though an increasing number of people speak English, it is by no means a bilingual society. Some knowledge of French is helpful. *French for Cruisers*, by Kathy Parsons, is a good aid and, unlike most phrase books, it includes boat and engine parts.

In the other Windwards, the official language is English, though the dialect can be hard to understand when locals talk fast among themselves. In St. Lucia, nearly everyone is bilingual. When you sit on a bus or hear people talking in the streets they are usually speaking in Patois, a dialect of French, influenced by English and African languages, which is the most commonly spoken language. However, English is used when writing or talking to visitors.

Tourist season

Charter and hotel rates vary with the time of year. Most people want to visit when it is cold up north, so the winter

months (November to April) are the high (expensive) season; the rest of the year is low season. Restaurant and bar prices are generally the same year round. During the quietest months (September and October), some small hotels close down and the staff go on holiday.

What to bring

Nearly all visitors bring too much luggage and do not realize that it is almost impossible to stow hard cases on a yacht. Only soft bags should be used. One of my charterers once arrived without luggage, the airline having spirited it away. Rather than wait, he bought a bathing suit, two pairs of shorts, and a shirt and wondered why he had ever bothered packing anything else.

If you need prescription drugs, bring an ample supply and make sure they stay in your carry-on bag.

Life is very informal here, and even in the best of eating places men can get by with a pair of slacks and a sports shirt, women with a simple dress.

Drugs

Marijuana grows in the Windwards and is part of the local Rasta religion. Despite

OVERSEAS CALLS

From local private, public, and GSM phones.

This is what you dial from the following islands:

Martinique: 00 + country & area code + number for Zone A & B*
St. Lucia/Grenada/St, Vincent: country & area code + number for Zone A
St. Lucia/Grenada: 011 + country & area code + number for Zone B
St. Vincent: 0 + country & area code + number for Zone B

** Except within French territories, where you just dial the area code and number.*
When dialing overseas, if the first digit of an area code is 0, leave it off.
When dialing Martinique from overseas, the number is +596 596 + 6 digits (regular phones) or +596 696 + 6 digits (mobile phones)

SATELLITE PHONES

For each phone we give the same example for calling Grenada, 444-4266

GLOBALSTAR
If you use a Globalstar phone set up for the Americas, it works just like a USA phone: For USA and NANP countries, dial 1 + the country & area code, + 7 digits. To call overseas dial 011 + country & area code + number. Example: dial 1-473-444-4266

IRIDIUM
Dial 00 + the country & area code - e.g. for the USA dial 001 then the area code + 7 digits. Example: dial 00-1-473-444-4266.

INMARSAT
Dial 00 + the country & area code - e.g. for the USA dial 001 then area code + 7 digits + #. The # key is used after all numbers are entered to initiate the call. Example: dial 00-1-473-444-4266-#

Country Codes
Zone A NANP
(North American Numbering Plan)
USA 1-(area code)
Anguilla 1-(264)
Antigua 1-(268)
Barbados 1-(246)
Dominica 1-(767)
Grenada 1-(473)
Montserrat 1-(664)
St. Lucia 1-(758)
St. Vincent 1-(784)
St. Kitts 1-(869)
Trinidad 1-(868)

Zone B
UK 44
Australia 61
New Zealand 64
Austria 43
Germany 49
Guadeloupe 590
Martinique 596
Denmark 45
France 33
Italy 39
Sweden 46
Switzerland 41

changing attitudes in our northern neighbors, it is still illegal here, as are most other mind-bending substances, except alcohol and tobacco. Laws are very strict, and those caught can expect yacht confiscation and up to life imprisonment (a longer vacation than you may have intended).

Communications

The Windwards have excellent communications, and even in quite small islands you will find internet cafes and WiFi. For both general calls and emergencies, it is best to have a phone on the boat. Most convenient are the phones that use prepaid cards, so there is no billing. You can buy a GSM phone locally, or bring your own and get a local SIM card ($25-50 EC). In either case take ID.

Both Digicel and Flow (Lime) are fairly seamless through all the islands from Grenada to St. Lucia (Barbados included). Take your phone with you when you want to top up or buy a new SIM. They work well for local and regional calls. Calls outside the region from an island other than the one where you bought your SIM are prohibitive, so it is best to buy another SIM. If you use your phone a lot, then Flow's "anywhere minutes" are a good deal; ask for details. Martinique is on a different system: Digicel will work in Martinique, but for more than a few calls it may be worth getting a Martinique SIM. To make a call in Martinique on a SIM from the other islands, you have to enter a + in front of the phone number. Orange Martinique has a worthwhile deal: for a few Euros you can buy a three-week Caribbean pass, which makes calls to the USA and the Caribbean the same price as the local calls.

All the GSM companies now offer data packages. So, many people hardly use the phone in the traditional way, instead they use web-based platforms, such as WhatsApp, and Skype for making phone calls and messaging. Some data packages even include free use of these apps.

Once you buy data you can also do emails and browse the web and, if you prefer to use a computer, you can set your phone as a hotspot, whereupon the whole crew can connect their computers to the internet. (Make sure they all turn off automatic updating.)

WiFi, which is now widely available, is also a communicaton option; many businesses offer it free to patrons, and people take their gadgets ashore and use it.

Those who want to stream or download movies on board, and need unlimited WiFi, sometimes buy available packages transmitted from shore. For this a booster WiFi aerial is essential to strengthen any weak signals. These come in a variety of configurations, and the tech-minded can use them to set up a private wireless network for everyone on board. If you can pick up a public pre-paid network such as Cruiser's WiFi or Hothothot spot, just turn on your computer and connect to it. Once you are connected, open a browser page and a registration and payment form should pop up (if you've made sure that pop-ups are enabled).

Satellite phones work everywhere and some can handle email. Some cruisers use an SSB-based service.

Local etiquette

Clothing. Unlike many other western seaside towns, people in the Caribbean will look somewhat askance at you if you wander away from the beach in a bathing suit or, perish the thought, a bikini. Away from the beach, even in that tiny waterfront village, people generally wear at least a shirt and pair of shorts or skirt. In the major towns, people dress much as you would if you were going to your local town.

For women, toplessness, for a while fashionable in Martinique, seems to have died owing to increasing awareness of skin cancer. It is illegal in most other islands. Complete nudity is best confined to anchorages where you can be sure of not being seen.

Greetings. Great store is set on greetings: "good morning" or "good afternoon" (or in Martinique "bonjour" or "bonne nuit"). It is considered rude to approach people with a question or to transact business without beginning with the appropriate greeting.

Tipping. Everyone likes to be tipped, but it is not always expected. In restaurants where no service charge is added, a 10% tip is normal. If service has already been included (as it is by law in Martinique), a little extra is appreciated, but not essential. Taxi drivers do not normally expect to be tipped, but if they go out of their way to help you, you can add a few dollars to the fare to show your appreciation. If you get help from kids carrying your suitcases, they will expect an EC dollar or two.

LGBTQ. Huge strides have been made in the acceptance of LGBTQ rights in many northern countries, where there is growing tolerance of diversity. Unfortunately, this is not always true in the Caribbean where homosexuality is often still illegal. So take care, change may take a while.

Water skiing, jet-skis

Local laws require that a water-ski vessel have at least two people on board. Water skiing or jet-skiing within 100 yards of a beach or in harbors where yachts are anchored is strictly forbidden. St. Vincent and the Grenadines have some enlightened environmental laws, and jet-skiing is completely forbidden throughout the country. Jet-skis are also forbidden in the Soufriere Marine Management Area in St. Lucia.

Suntanning

Whatever the season, the sun is intense and adequate protection is essential. It is advisable to bring down plenty of sunscreen (30+) and use it from the start, building up exposure slowly. The tops of your feet are vulnerable and light cotton socks can help. Loose, long-sleeved, cotton clothing, hats, and sunglasses are essential. Heavy burning can take place even on cloudy days and in shade.

Oxybenzone, aka benzophenone-3 or BP-3, an ingredient in many sunsreens, is harmful to reef organisms; use eco-friendly products. (See *Save our reefs*, page 38.)

Local food products

Many local products, some unavailable anywhere else, are sold in the islands. Some make great presents. Locally bottled peanuts and cashews taste fresher and better than imported ones. Grenada has four chocolate factories and St. Lucia two. Most islands have local rums, and on many islands you will find a variety of hot sauces. Local cocoa sticks can be grated into hot milk to make a rich cocoa. (Commercial cocoa has had most of the fat removed.)

Coconut water is sold in bottles in some islands and is delicious. Unfortunately, it has a short shelf life, so is not good to take back home. In many islands locally smoked fishis for sale

All the main islands have great fruit and

vegetable markets. These are always colorful, but Saturday morning is the best and busiest time, with the greatest selection (Friday in St. Lucia). Never be afraid to ask about things you do not recognize. The market ladies are helpful and will tell you how to cook different vegetables. Some things are not what they appear to be. For example, many fruits that look like bananas have to be cooked.

Transport

If you don't like to hoof it, you have a choice between taxis, buses, communal taxis, and rental cars.

Taxis are plentiful and come in all shapes and sizes. For long trips, some bargaining is usually possible. In any case, always ask for the fare in EC dollars (or, in Martinique, Euros) before you start. If you think you are being quoted too high a figure, try another driver.

Colorful, noisy, and cheerful, the buses in the English speaking islands are the mainstay of the transport system. They often bear such names as "Trust No Man," "De Bad Ride," "In God We Trust," and similar reflections. Not only is this an inexpensive way to travel, but you get to experience some local life. Most nowadays are minibuses. They are not for the claustrophobic, for there is always room for one more on a local bus. Just when you think the whole thing is packed to bursting, the conductor manages to create a tiny square of spare air and, like a conjuror, he whips out yet another seat ~ a pullout piece of wood that is jammed in to take the extra person. Most buses have stereo systems and the drivers like to run them, like their buses, at full bore. The buses are a wonderful example of the kind of service you can get with free enterprise. If you are carrying heavy shopping and wish to go off the normal route, this can be negotiated. In some islands, buses will stop to pick you up anywhere, in others (including St. Lucia), they are only allowed to pick up at designated stops. Buses do get rather few and far between after dark, and may be very limited when going to a distant spot. Before taking off to the other end of an island, make sure there will be a bus coming back.

If you arrive by air at a reasonable hour, without too much luggage, and can make it to the nearest main road, St. Lucia's Hewanorra Airport is on a bus route, and Martinique's airport is on a communal taxi route.

IATA (FAA) Airport Codes

IATA (FAA) Airport Codes

For on-line booking, or finding out if your travel agent has booked you the right airport

Martinique
FDF - Fort de France

Grenada
GND - Point Saline
CRU - Carriacou

Barbados
BGI - Bridgetown

St. Lucia
SLU - Vigie, Castries
UVF - Vieux Fort, Hewanorra

Trinidad
POS - Port of Spain (Piarco)

St. Vincent Grenadines
UNI - Union Island
MQS - Mustique
CIW - Canouan
BQU - Bequia
SVD - Arnos Vale (Kingstown)

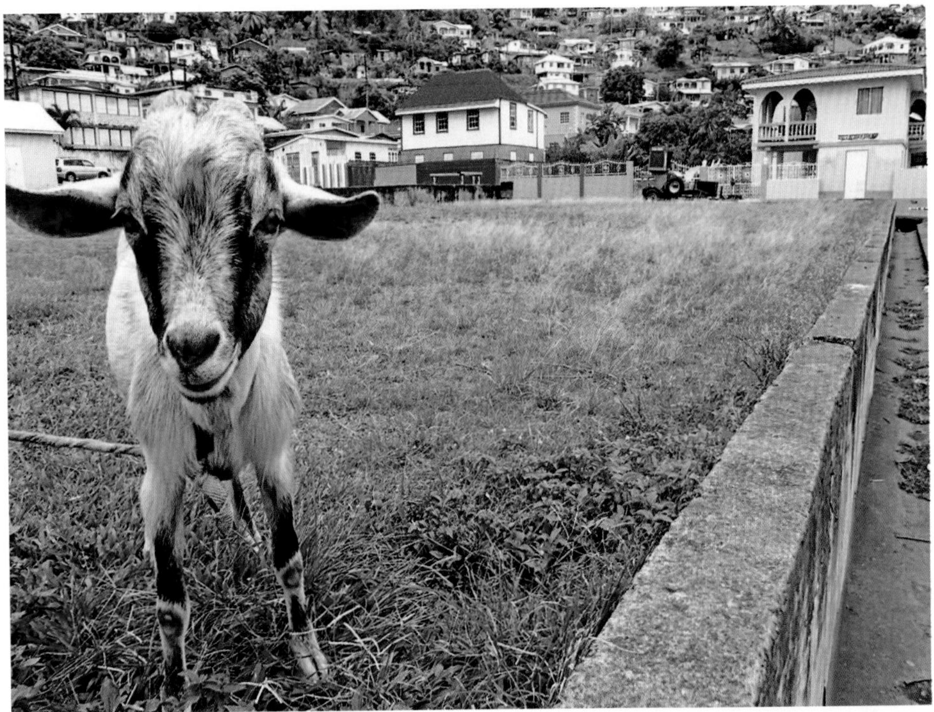

Bugs, Beasts, Plants, and People

Don't let the cockroaches bug you

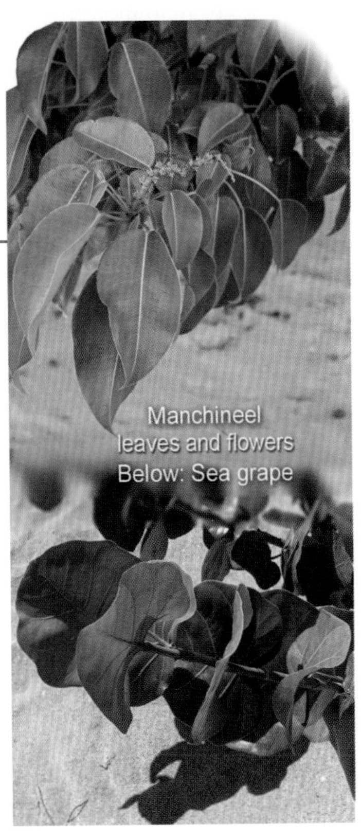

Manchineel leaves and flowers
Below: Sea grape

The unmentionable, indomitable cockroach thrives. If you are on a yacht, the odds are that eventually you will find yourself face to face with one of these miniature, armor-plated monstrosities. No need to panic. Despite their off-putting appearance, they are quite harmless, make good pets, and in reasonable quantities are not a reflection of the cleanliness of the boat. A good dose of spray will keep them out of sight for a couple of days. (This will be done automatically on a skippered yacht.) If you are on a boat with a bad infestation, the permanent cure is as follows: First, give a good spray to reduce the numbers (not necessary if you only have one or two). Then, using a mortar and pestle, grind equal quantities of boric acid and white sugar together and distribute freely under drawers, in bottoms of lockers, etc. This will normally give at least six months of cockroach-free living. Some people prefer to mix the boric acid into a gooey mess with condensed milk because they can then stick it on walls and ceilings. I also find some large versions of the "Sticky Box" (usually found in Martinique) to be very

Ma Peggy hike Bequia

effective. Cockroaches generally arrive on board as stowaways in cardboard cartons or among fruits and vegetables. It helps to keep "cockroach free" crates and boxes on board and transfer all incoming supplies into them. Examine fruits and vegetables before you stow them. So much for the bad news. The good news is that the boat variety, known as the German cockroach, is relatively small, quite unlike the huge shoreside monsters that grow up to two inches long and are aptly called "mahogany birds."

Aedes aegypti, a mosquito that thrives in the Caribbean, has stripy legs, most often bites by day, and can carry dengue, zika, and chikungunya viruses. Boating people are less often affected than dirt dwellers, and mosquitoes breed more in the rainy summer months than in the winter. A little repellent spray now and again will help keep you safe.

Mosquitoes are not usually a problem on board because of the breeze, but jungly anchorages or enclosed lagoons on the lee of the large islands are occasionally buggy. If you find yourself in such a bay, you can always resort to the mosquito coil. This is not a contraceptive device for mosquitoes, but a spiral of incense-like material that burns slowly and puts the mosquitoes to sleep. It is effective, but you should be warned that it does not usually kill the bugs and, should the coil go out before you awake, they will be up first and you will be breakfast.

In the evening, beaches can be buggy, especially on a still night in the rainy season, July to November. Worse than mosquitoes are the minute sand flies known as no-see-ums. Any brand of bug repellent will help prevent your sunset barbecue from becoming a free-for-all slapping match.

Dangers

Perhaps we should start with the rum punch. This delicious concoction, a mixture of rum and fruit juice, is available in any waterside bar. It can be positively euphoric in small doses and lethal in large. Strongly recommended at sunset, but be warned that the potency is often stronger than the flavor would suggest.

There are poisonous scorpions and centipedes on the islands, but luckily they are rare and not generally deadly. Still, take a good look at that old pile of twigs and leaves before you sit and take care when picking up coconut husks to burn for your barbecue.

A real danger is the manchineel tree (*Hippomane mancinella*), which grows abundantly along some beaches. This pretty tree with yellow-green apples is toxic. The leaves can produce a rash like poison ivy. It is all right to take shade under the tree, but never stand under a manchineel in the rain, and avoid using the branches for firewood, or that song "Smoke Gets in Your Eyes" may take on new meaning. If you eat the apples, they will cause blisters from stem to stern.

Martinique and St. Lucia are home to a deadly snake, the fer de lance, which is thankfully quite rare. Various parasites can live in fresh water. They usually need entry via a break in the skin. It is safest to stick to clear, fast-flowing streams. Swimming in murky, swollen rivers in the rainy season increases the risk.

The main dangers in swimming and snorkeling are negligent and speeding fishermen, yacht-tender drivers, and water taxis.

There have been some serious accidents over the years, so swimmers and snorkelers should be aware of small craft movement at all times. Lesser dangers include sea urchins. These are spiny creatures whose prickles penetrate the skin and break off on contact. This is quite painful, especially for the first few hours. They are virtually impossible to pull out once embedded, as they break into little pieces. It is best to leave them in and treat them with hot lime juice, as the acid helps dissolve them.

There are sharks and barracudas, but unlike their cousins in the movies, they have yet to attack anyone in these waters unless harassed and are not considered dangerous here. There is no question that spearfishing can excite these fish. I have dived and snorkeled at night with no problem, but since so few people swim at night, it is impossible to assess how safe it is. Despite their reputation, moray eels are short-sighted and timid, but it would be pushing your luck to stick your hand into holes in rock or coral.

Corals eat by stinging their prey, and many can sting you, so look and do not touch. This is also better for the coral. Coral scratches can become infected. If you get one, clean it well with soap and fresh water. Stinging jellyfish are not frequent but do exist, and occasionally the swimmer may feel a mild tingling from minute animals known as sea ants. If you do get a jellyfish sting, soaking with vinegar can help

A good book on dangerous marine animals would certainly list some more horrors, but the truth is that harm from any of these is rare and, provided you watch where you put your hands and feet and keep an eye on the sea conditions and current, snorkeling is safer than doing the weekly ironing and a lot more fun.

Taxi drivers

Taxi drivers are often colorful characters, owners of highly individualized cars, and they have a fund of local knowledge. The ambitious ones, who used to act as commission agents as well by shopping for customers, tracing lost luggage, and obtaining hard to find parts, have morphed into yacht agents. In Martinique, only a few of the drivers speak English, though they will bear with your French.

Unfortunately, among the good ones there are an overenthusiastic few who will bully or confuse the unwary passenger into going on a tour he or she really does not want. There are two basic rules: always discuss and agree on a price before you embark on a taxi ride and make sure you are both talking the same kind of dollars (EC or US) or, in Martinique, Euros.

Boat vendors

At some point, there will be a thump on your topsides and a voice shouting "Hey skip, want some limes? How about a nice T-shirt? Or a coconut boat? It sails very good." You are in islands with a great spirit of free enterprise ~ better get used to it. From the skipper's point of view, the most harrowing thing is that these vendor's boats are often built of several hundred pounds of rough wood and exposed nail heads, which bang your topsides as they hawk their wares. Their cheerful cry of "no problem, skip" does nothing to remove the scratch.

The problem is exacerbated in some areas where the competition is so keen that you may be approached two miles from port. This most often occurs with line handlers in the Soufriere/Pitons area in St. Lucia and the Cumberland/Wallilabou area in St. Vincent. In these places, line handlers offer a useful service, because the water is so deep it is necessary to drop an anchor and tie stern to a palm tree, and they help you tie up. However, some vendors you meet way out will want you to tow them in. It is unwise to tow these heavy boats and there are always line handlers close to the shore, so you can tell them "no" you can only tow boats in an emergency. When you get closer to shore, come to a standstill and negotiate the price before handing over any lines. (I offer a set fee of $10-20 EC on a "take it or leave it" basis.) When finally at anchor, put out at least two big fenders and make sure any local boats coming alongside stay on them.

You will probably be offered, at various times, t-shirts, jewelry, fruit, scrimshaw, model boats, ice, and bread. It is often worthwhile to consider what is offered.

Vendors are part of the local scene and endemic to undeveloped countries with struggling economies. Some visitors enjoy the interactions and the opportunity to do business in this way; most vendors are friendly and helpful. However, those who have no prior experience with vendors can find them irritating, and I have had letters from people saying they would not revisit some anchorages because of their experiences with vendors.

Dealing with vendors is easier once you know to expect them. Be straightforward, look them in the eye, always demand professional behavior, and keep your sense of humor and you will be okay. If you imagine yourself in their position, it is not hard to figure out how they operate and why.

You will find vendors in the Grenadines, St. Vincent, and St. Lucia. In the Grenadines, most are very professional. If you say no, they will leave you in peace. On the other hand, the situation on the west coast of St. Vincent reminds me of the airport in Grenada back in the early '70s, when it was very amusing to watch the hapless and unsuspecting passenger stagger forth into the daylight with his three or four suitcases.

Tobago Cays

Within seconds, three or four taxi drivers would rush up and each grab a bag and head in a different direction, entreating the passenger to follow as loudly as they could. He would stand confused and sweating in his traveling suit, wondering if this was the start of a trip to hell. Clearly, things could not go on that way, and a taxi-driver union was formed to prevent the chaos of competition. Such an organization would be helpful for boat vendors in Wallilabou, St. Vincent, where people sometimes find themselves surrounded by vendors all shouting at once.

People sometimes complain that while vendors are fine, there are just too many of them. If I were a charterer (prime customers for vendors; cruising folk don't have as many problems), I would make a couple of clearly visible signs I could hang from the lifelines near the cockpit saying "I am not buying now, leave me in peace ~ visit again when this sign is down."

You may also get vendors you should clearly not do business with. Sometimes someone will come out to your boat touting a local restaurant. This is fair enough, but when he or she tells you not to visit the other restaurant because the food is bad and the cockroaches in the kitchen are the size of small rats, common sense should tell you this is not an unbiased judgment. Some visitors are naive enough to heed such advice, and end up with the worst meal in the harbor as a result. (There is logic to this: restaurateurs who encourage such unscrupulous behavior are likely to be equally dastardly in the kitchen and in dealing with customers.) People have sometimes paid youths to watch their dinghy, which has resulted in the creation of an unnecessary service by dinghy watchers who are often rude. Lock your dinghy on with a cable and refuse such service, unless you really want it. Make sure your locking line is at least 16 feet long so that you do not block others approaching the dock. Never leave your outboard raised, as it is likely to damage other boats.

Some kids beg. "It's my birthday, what are you going to give me?" is a favorite line. It is important to bear in mind that wages for an unskilled adult may only be $50-100 EC a day. If young kids end up getting twice

PROTECT YOURSELF AGAINST PETTY THEFT

If you take the following precautions, you are unlikely to have a problem

- ✔ Lock up when you leave the boat and leave someone on board at night in main towns like St. George's, Castries, and Kingstown.
- ✔ Lock your outboard onto your boat at night.
- ✔ Lock your dinghy to the dock by day and onto your yacht by night.
- ✔ Be cautious about inviting strangers on board.

- ✔ Do not bring big wads of cash; use credit cards instead. Do not leave cash on the boat. Insure valuables such as cameras.
- ✔ Don't leave things unattended on the beach or in the dinghy in public places.
- ✔ Bring copies of CDs rather than your orginals.

that much liming around the docks, begging from tourists, or getting grossly overpaid for watching dinghies, they skip school and it is hard for them to adjust later when they need to go out to work. By all means, employ kids and find something useful for them to do; that helps the economy. But just throwing money around can be harmful. For those who like to give away money, there are a few beggars who have handicaps. Local associations for the handicapped are also happy to accept donations.

"Tiefs"

Most islanders and yachtspeople are very honest, but obviously there are shady characters, too: thieves, con men, and extortionists. Dinghies and outboards are sometimes stolen at night. It is hard to say how many, because no one wants to admit that his dinghy disappeared after that final rum punch because the "rabbit" lost its way while going through the "hole" to make the bowline. There have been cases where a dinghy was returned the next day and the finders demanded huge sums for the "rescue."

Boats occasionally get robbed when people are ashore. The thieves are mainly looking for cash and easily saleable items. Instead of cash, use credit cards (Visa and MasterCard are most widely accepted). Insure valuables such as cameras and binoculars. This way, if you do get a break in, the results will not be as bad.

There are a few locals who will provide a service and then demand outrageous sums, so always ask the price before accepting any service, including taxis, unless you are dealing with someone you know and trust. Make sure you are both referring to EC dollars.

Violent crimes, like armed robbery, assault, and rape, are rare but not unknown on yachts. Cruisers tend to be more worried than charterers, as they stay a lot longer. If you sleep with all hatches open, a portable chime alarm will help wake you if someone boards. An air fog horn and very bright light are my second line of defence. After 40 years of cruising I have not yet had to deploy them.

If you are planning to walk or hike into remote places, it doesn't hurt to ask around first, especially if you are alone or with just one other person. Daytime is generally safer than night. Keep in mind that while the islands are generally safe, there are isolated incidents, as there are anywhere in the world. For current information on where there are problems, ask in any charter company office and check my website (www.doyleguides.com), read the updates, and go to the security links on the advisories page. Also, read the free waterfront newspaper, *Caribbean Compass*, which often highlights areas where there are problems.

La Pagerie, Carriacou

Photography, Medical & Fishing

Photography

These days we are all using digital cameras, which makes photography much easier: instant results and no more running around looking for film.

The light in the Windwards is so bright that colors often photograph better in the early morning or late afternoon. This changes radically when you venture into the rainforest, where light levels are so low that a tripod is useful for long exposures.

Learn enough about the setup of your camera that when you venture into the forest you can take pictures with the camera set at an equivalent of 400 ASA.

A polarizing filter can enhance sea shots, giving dramatic results. You can watch the colors change as you twist the filter. Keep an eye on the sky as well as the sea, as it will turn gray at some angles.

It is polite to ask when you want to photograph someone. Local attitudes can be a little strange. People with cameras sometimes become a focal point for frustrations and feelings of being exploited. If you try to take a crowd scene, someone will often object, and funnily enough, that person might not even be in the picture. Vendors who deal with tourists are usually happy to say "yes," especially if you are buying something. Digital cameras help, as you can show the subject their image on the screen after you have taken it.

People also bring drone cameras to the the Caribbean. This is new, so try to find out about the lastest regulations.

St. Vincent has the best drone legislation. You need to apply for a license from Mr. Lyda Ollivierre at catcsvg@gmail.com and ask him to send you an application. You fill it out on your computer and email it back. When granted, you can pick up your license at the nearest airport. At the moment there is no charge. You are required to alert the nearest airport when flying to make sure there will be no problem.

In Grenada you should seek permission to fly a drone from the nearest police station.

Martinique has an 18 km drone exclusion zone around the airport unless you get a permit. This leaves just a bit of the north of Martinique and bit of the south where you can fly your drone with an altitude limit of 400 feet. Fines run up to 75,000 Eu.

In St. Lucia you may not fly within 2.2 miles of an airport or heliport, and no more than 400 feet high. In all islands stay outside of the no fly zones of airports, avoid flying over private property without permission, and fly thoughtfully; drones, like jet skis, can annoy others.

Medical care

There is adequate medical care for most ailments in all the larger islands, and any hotel or charter company will help you get in touch with a doctor. In emergencies, remember that all cruise ships stand by on VHF: 16 and have doctors on board. If you have a life-threatening situation or a serious head injury, plan on immediate transport to Martinique or Barbados. SVG Air (784-457-5124) does medical flights and the big hospitals may be able to organize a helicopter ambulance.

For diving accidents hyperbaric chambers are available in Martinique's Hôpital Pierre Zobda-Quimann (596) 55 20 00, Tapion in St. Lucia (758-459-2000, Saint Augustine Medical Center in Grenada (473-440-6173-5), and in Barbados (246 436-5483).

Martinique: For advice on facilities and to help with arrangements, call Douglas Yacht Services: 0696 45 89 75. The main hospital is Hôpital Pierre Zobda-Quimann (0596) 55 20 00. For lesser ailments, try the doctor in Marin Marina, or Dr. Jean Louis Deloge and Dr. Veronique Claisse (office 0596 74 98 24) in Marin.

St. Lucia: For most problems, the Rodney Bay Medical Center, (758) 452-8621, or the M-Care Medical Clinic, (758) 453-2552/452-9032, both within walking distace of the JQ supermaket dinghy dock in Rodney Bay, will suffice.

Tapion Hospital, (758) 459-2000, is a kind of medical mall with several doctors. Dr. Andrew Richardson, the general surgeon (also a sailing man), is good, and may also be consulted as a regular doctor. Tapion has a hyperbaric chamber for divers.

For dental care, Dr. Glace, in Rodney Bay, can handle everything from fillings to implants, (758) 458-0167.

St. Vincent: Maryfield Hospital, Kingstown: (784) 457-8991 (highly recommended by some of our readers).

In the **Grenadines**, Mustique is a good place to get sick. There is an excellent small clinic, (784) 458-4621 (ask for the clinic), situated next to the airport, in case you need to be flown out for further treatment. Bequia (784) 458-3294, VHF: 74 (24 hours), has a doctor and a little clinic in Port Elizabeth that responds to emergency calls. For dental care, Profamdental: (784) 529-2480/ 529-0745, run by Johanna Osborne, a dental and maxillofacial surgeon, has a surgery in St. Vincent weekdays and one in Bequia on Saturday mornings.

Grenada: If you need hospitalization, try the St. Augustine's Medical Services, (SAMS), (473) 440-6173/5. It is quite complete, with a lot of modern equipment.

For a doctor, Dr. Michael Radix, (473) 444-4850/440-4379 surgery or (473) 443-5330 home, is a good old-school doctor, who is pleasant to visit and makes house calls. If you need surgery, Dr. Yearwood is a general surgeon and urologist (also a competitive yachtsman): Ocean House, Grand Anse, (473) 444-1178. Dr. Jenny Isaacs is a good dermatogolist, (473) 440-3963

Good dentists include Dr. Roxanne Nedd, (473) 444-2273, in the Excel Mall in Grand Anse, and Island Dental Care (Dr. Tara Baksh and Dr. Victor Samaan), Wall Street, Grand Anse, (473) 437-4000.

Fishing

In some islands, dive shops organize hunts for the invasive lionfish, which are excellent eating. They use special three prong spears. Otherwise, forget spearfishing, Hawaiian slings, pots, nets, and diving down to pick up conch or sea urchins; it is illegal for visitors to engage in these activities. Fishing regulations are strict. Even though trolling and handlining may not be strictly legal unless you have a license, most islands have agreed to turn a blind eye to these activities, unless you are in a marine park or protected area. This courtesy does not extend to sports-fishing boats, which usually need a license. So, leave the rest, but get out

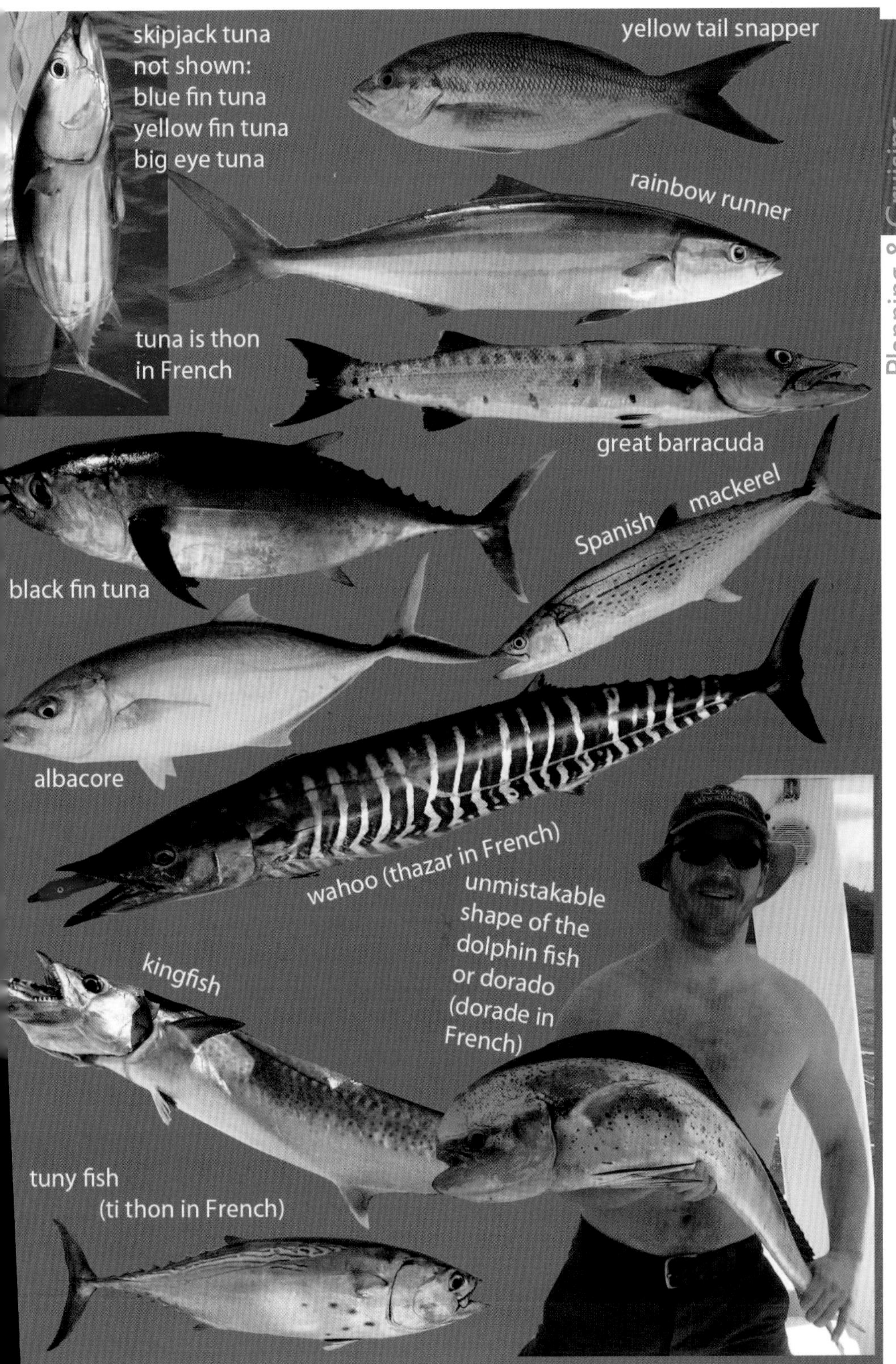
skipjack tuna
not shown:
blue fin tuna
yellow fin tuna
big eye tuna
yellow tail snapper
rainbow runner
tuna is thon
in French
great barracuda
black fin tuna
Spanish mackerel
albacore
wahoo (thazar in French)
unmistakable
shape of the
dolphin fish
or dorado
(dorade in
French)
kingfish
tuny fish
(ti thon in French)

your rod and enjoy.

Trolling for fish is fun and fish you catch yourself taste better. Be conscious of the environmental effects of overfishing, and throw back anything that is obviously juvenile or undersized. If you are on a short holiday, you can walk into any fishing-tackle shop and buy a couple of ready-to-go lines, complete with lures. Shell out extra for (or create) a good device that will let you know you have caught a fish. If you do not know a fish is there, it will likely break the line and you will lose both lure and fish. Setting two lines, one from each side of the boat doubles your chance of catching a fish. Set the lee long (about 50 yards) and keep the other short (about 25 yards); a little skipping does not hurt). Haul in for a weed check every 40 minutes or so. Remove any weeds.

When you catch a fish, you may need to slow the boat. If you have two lines out, have someone reel in the empty one so it doesn't get tangled. One easy way to slow down is to furl the jib. Luff also, if necessary, but not until the spare line is in. Gloves are a big plus when you heave your catch out of the water and into the cockpit, or at least on deck where someone can hold it. I put mine in a cooler, as this cuts down on the mess.

Proper reels are best. Not only will you instantly know when you have a fish, but the give of the reel will stop you losing the occasional fish when it strikes.

If you are making your own rig, you need a swivel on the end of your line, and a wire leader helps. Have the wire leader at about 10 lb lower breaking strain than the line so that a monster does not break the line. A test line of around 80 lb should bring in most of the fish you will catch. The lighter the line and gear, the more strikes you will get, but the more fish you will lose.

Any fish you catch in open water will almost certainly be good to eat. Ciguatera fish poisoning, common farther north, is a rarity here. One might be suspicious of a really large barracuda that could be down from up north visiting relatives, but smaller barracuda (around 5 lb) are delicious. Dorado, the tuna family (including tuny fish), albacore, and wahoo are not considered risky even in bad areas up north.

The photos of the most common catches are to help with identification. They were taken after the fish had been caught, so most of the subjects have lost a lot of color. The dorado (or dolphin fish; no relation to flipper) is the most dramatic at this ~ it gives a brilliant display of bright color, then fades to nothing. Most fish will change color significantly before your eyes, so shape and markings need to be taken even more seriously than color when making an identification. If you get a fish with a really large eye, it is probably a horse-eye jack. They are not choice, and are very bony, but some people eat them.

Fish can have worm-like parasites. Both cooking and deep-freezing will kill them. However, if you do the sushi thing, observe the flesh closely; the worst parasites are visible to the eye.

Lobster season is usually from the first of October to the end of April. During this time, lobsters can be bought from local fishermen, and the most likely places to find them are Mustique, Union, the Tobago Cays, and P.S.V.

It is against the law to buy lobster out of season, lobsters less than 9 inches long, or lobsters bearing eggs at any time, and the fines are steep. You may be offered one, but please refuse.

Entertainment & Special Events

Green flash

In the evenings, sunset brings an opportunity to look for the elusive "green flash." This happens as the sun disappears below the horizon. For about a second (blink and you've missed it), the very last bit of the sun to disappear turns bright green. To see this you need a clear horizon and the right atmospheric conditions. Some say rum punch helps. Binoculars make it a lot clearer. Photographers will need a telephoto lens and an auto drive.

Entertainment

The most popular form of evening entertainment is the "jump up." This usually happens in a bar or hotel and takes the form of a dance, most often to a live band. If enough rum flows, everyone does indeed "jump up." Both Martinique and St. Vincent have casinos, but these are low-key. Most of the larger hotels offer evening dancing with a floorshow. Some hotels serve Sunday lunch to the accompaniment of a steel band. You can dance, swim, or just enjoy the music.

Special events

There are a variety of local festivals and events for entertainment and partying. If you happen to be here at the right time, they are worth investigating; some are worth a special trip.

Carnival started as a riotous bacchanal before Lent. Carnivals feature costumed parades, calypso contests, steel bands, and days of dancing in the street. Martinique still has their carnival before Lent, but St. Vincent, St. Lucia, and Grenada have switched. Check our information on holidays at the beginning of each island section.

St. Lucia has a jazz festival that lasts about a week in early May. Some of the events are on Pigeon Island, and you can anchor your yacht below. Basil, in Mustique, runs a small but good blues festival in both Mustique and Bequia sometime during late January or early February. Carriacou has a Maroon and String Band Festival around the end of April/beginning of May. Carriacou has a Parang Festival before Christmas.

You can join in sailing events. In early June in Martinique there is a week with races from port to port around the island and plenty of good food and entertainment. If you are here on July 14th, the French national holiday, you may see yole (pirogue) races around Fort de France. Yole races also feature in each coastal village during celebrations for the village's patron saint. Anyone interested can get a list from the local tourist office. Martinique has a series of races that tour the island over several days in January and a sailing week at Schoelcher in February.

St. Lucia has many events, including the Mango Bowl Regatta, usually held in late November or early December.

Bequia's Easter Regatta is well worth attending. It includes yacht races, local "two-bow" fishing boat races, model boat races, and cultural shows.

The Grenada Sailing Festival is held in January. It is a program of race events backed by a well-organized social program. All entrants are welcome, from serious racing boats to live-aboards. The Round Grenada race, a two-day event with a stop in Carriacou, is arranged by the Petit Calivigny Yacht Club (PCYC) and normally takes place in August. The Carriacou Regatta, in late July or early August, is a local event featuring races for small fishing boats and the larger, cargo-carrying sloops. These are some of the finest sailing vessels made in the islands. Ashore there is plenty of fun.

People lose more dinghies in regattas and big parties than at any other time. Some drunks take the wrong dinghy and then fail to secure it. Other drunks untie your dinghy while trying to untie their own and let it go adrift. Many dinghies tied together tempt theives. Lock it up for security, especially during regatta time!

Tobago Cays

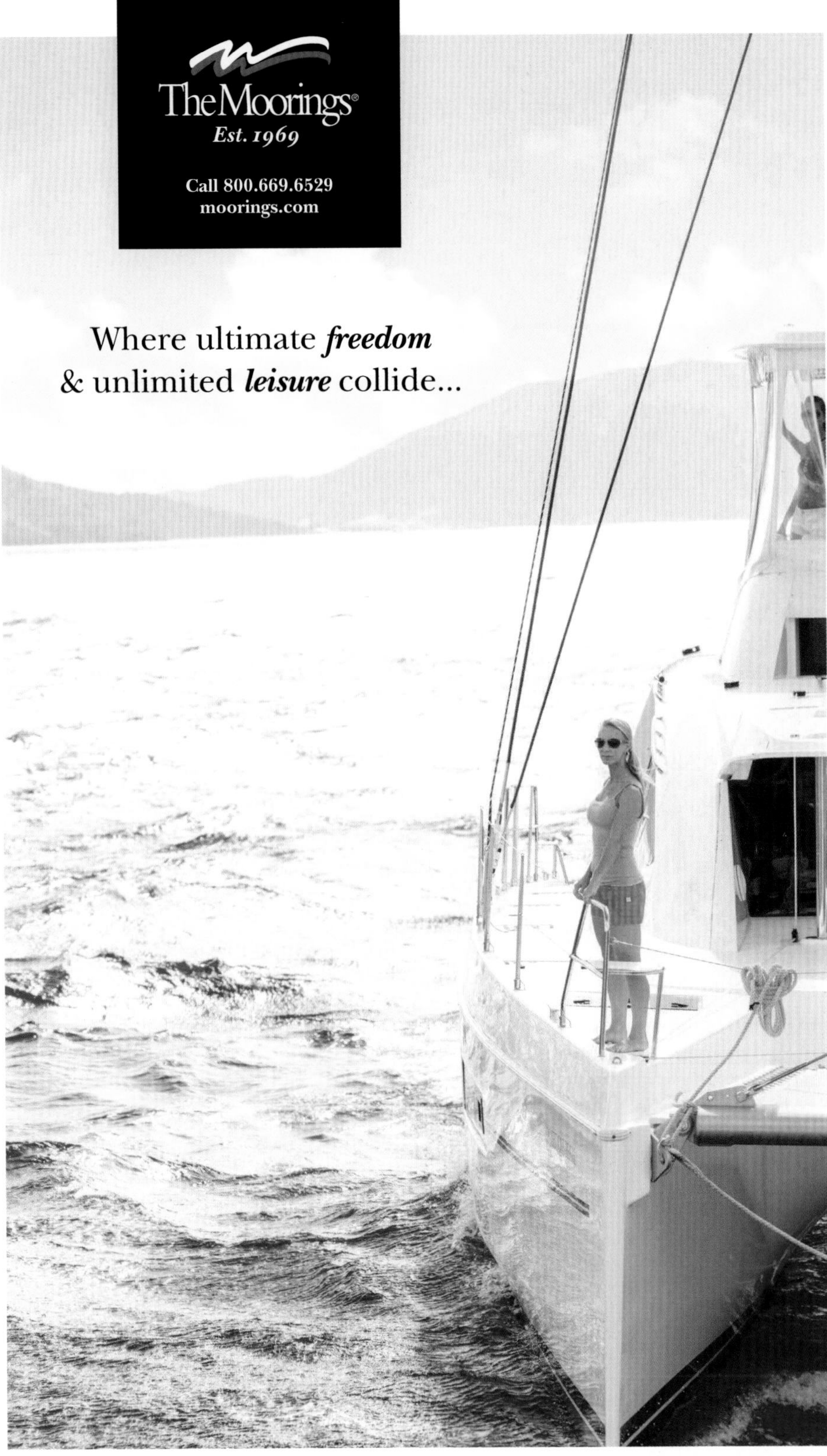

Planning & Cruising

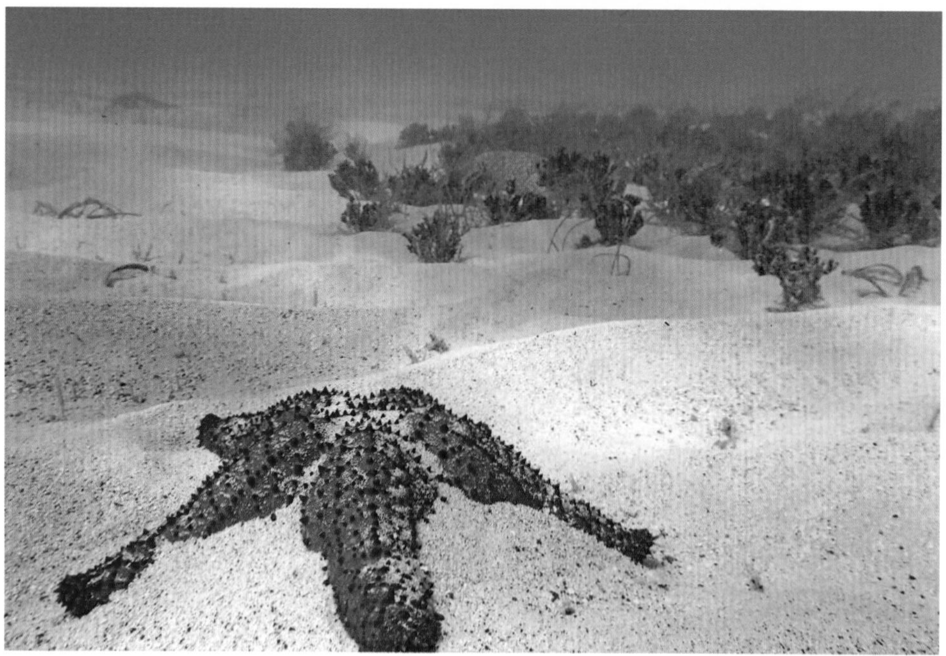

Protecting the Environment

Most visitors are courteous and well behaved. With the increasing volume of yachts in the area, it definitely helps to be considerate. Anchorages here have been reasonably free of loud noises, including drunken raucous laughter, stereo equipment, endlessly running generators, and loudly clanking halyards. Luckily, there is plenty of room in most anchorages, so those who want to make noise or need to run generators for much of the time can stay well away from everyone else. Most of us have to run our engines at some time during the day, but let us at least leave the hour around sunset free, so everyone can enjoy it in peace.

Happily, obnoxious windmills are now a rarity. Most are quiet and unobtrusive. A noisy one can destroy the natural peace of many a quiet anchorage and it does not have to be so, quiet blades are available for most brands.. If you have not yet bought a windmill, make sure the one you buy is quiet or, if you want to be sure, use solar panels. If you already own a noisy one, and cannot be bothered to get the quiet blades, try to anchor to the back of the fleet and, when your batteries are charged up, stop the blades.

Every boat needs an anchor light, a fixed light that shows all around. The use of strobe light for this is wrong. Strobe lights are suitable as an emergency light (alerting to a break in or needing help) and for navigation buoys; they are not anchor lights. To others they are annoying and confusing. If you see one, feel free to knock on the boat and ask what the problem is, especially in the early hours.

Right now you can don a mask and snorkel and dive in the water anywhere in the Windwards and find the seabed pretty clean. Let's keep it that way.

Fishing and hunting

The days have gone when we could jump over the side, bristling with knives and festooned with spearguns long enough to be sold by the yard, to decimate the local fish population. Spearfishing has proved too damaging and new laws have been passed to control it. It is now illegal for visitors to spearfish (or Hawaiian sling) anywhere from St. Lucia to Grenada. It should be mentioned that spearfishing, apart from being completely illegal, is harmful to the environment; spears that miss their target can damage coral and allow infection to take hold. Gloved hands grabbing coral, can also stress the reef. Most speared fish are reef cleaners, so removing them can affect the whole ecosystem. Lobsters, when speared, cannot be sized and checked for eggs. For this reason, even locals are not allowed to spearfish lobsters; they must use a snare. Try not to give moral support to other cruisers who boast about their spearfishing exploits. It is a bad thing to do, especially now, when reefs are already degraded, at least in part because of us.

Hunters should note that all cows, goats, and sheep, even on remote uninhabited islands, are privately owned. They are often put out to graze and left for months on end. They should not be harmed.

Garbage

Yacht garbage can be a problem in the Grenadine Islands, where it can totally overwhelm the available facilities. We need to cut down on what we bring ashore, and we have to be careful what we bring ashore. Food waste of all kinds should be stored in a separate container and dumped, far from reefs, when you are out at sea in deep water. Carrying organic matter from one island to another as garbage is a dangerous practice. Island agriculture is very sensitive, as we saw some years ago when an introduced pink mealy bug spread rapidly through some of the Windward Islands, costing millions of dollars in lost produce. More recently, a mango worm was introduced to Grenada, causing great harm. Organic matter may contain fruit flies, cockroaches, fungi, and other potentially dangerous pests, so take care when transporting and disposing of fresh fruit and vegetable matter. In addition, it is unwise to transport things like woven palm hats and baskets between islands.

Most harbors are open to the west, and if you are stuck in such a harbor too long, dinghy the food waste as far out of the harbor as you can and dump it there, preferably at dusk. Never do this in places like the Tobago Cays, where there are islands and reef downwind. Rinse all your empty cans and containers in seawater before putting them in the trash.

It is best to buy things with as little packing as possible and use returnable bottles. Take along your own shopping bags and avoid those plastic ones.

In addition, yachtspeople have caused considerable degradation by letting locals dispose of their garbage for a fee. Never give garbage to vendors. Some will offer to take your garbage for a couple of dollars. However, these people have no proper means of disposing of it. The good ones try to burn it, but combustion is never complete and the remains are left strewn around. Others dump your garbage in holes in the bushes, and the worst take it to the nearest beach, rummage through for items of interest, and abandon it. You are responsible for your own garbage. If you give it to someone else for a fee, they are considered your employee, and if they litter with your garbage, you are responsible.

Never throw plastics, including bags and bottled water containers, away at sea. Leatherback turtles eat jellyfish, and many have been found dead, their stomachs filled with plastic bags. Smelly bags can be rinsed in the ocean before storing. Other items that should never be thrown out at sea include string and fishing line, which might form a tangle trap somewhere or be eaten, or plastic-lined cardboard cartons (juice cartons, etc.) and tin foil. These can be rinsed in seawater before stowing. Similarly, anything that could be the least bit toxic, including aerosol sprays and chemicals, should not be dumped at sea.

Most garbage consists of paper, cardboard, cans, and bottles. Should we throw these at sea? Ideally, no. The ocean is not a dumping ground, and if we are not very careful where we dump such garbage, we can damage reef structures. On the other hand, we should not take these items ashore and dump them in the Grenadines, where the facilities are totally inadequate. So what to do? As far as possible, keep such garbage for an adequate refuse facility in one of the larger islands. Martinique has plenty of places to put garbage, and you will find adequate facilities in Rodney Bay and Marigot Bay in St. Lucia, and in Port Louis, The Yacht Club, and Spice Island Marine in Grenada.

If you are unable to do this, then it is probably marginally better to dump non-returnable bottles, cans, shredded paper, and cardboard far from land, with no islands or reefs in the lee, in water over 600 feet deep, than it is to pile them in a heap on land where they are not being collected. Paper and cardboard will eventually dissolve (though we do not know about the toxicity of the inks printed on them). Cans and bottles will sink and sit on the seabed, which, in deep water, is mainly sand or mud; they may provide homes for baby fish. Nothing should ever be dumped near a reef or in an anchorage.

Holding tanks

I have not yet seen a convincing study showing that pumping toilets into our anchorages has a measurable ecological impact. However, it can have an aesthetic one, and it is reassuring to know you are swimming in water that someone has not just dumped in. Some marine parks are now asking people to use holding tanks. If you do not have one, you can make a temporary one using a bucket (and a lid for when not in use), and carrying a bag of sawdust. Sprinkle the sawdust before and after each use. Empty and rinse the bucket after you have left the anchorage. Use the regular head for pee.

Save our reefs

In minutes, anchors can destroy what nature has taken generations to build. A coral structure is a colony of millions of minute animals called polyps. They are fragile, and reefs grow very slowly. Always anchor on sand, never on coral. If there is any doubt, have someone snorkeling when you drop your anchor. Dinghy anchors also do harm, so use a sand anchor for your dinghy and anchor on the sand beside the coral, rather than on the coral itself.

When snorkeling or diving, be careful of coral structures. Avoid standing, bumping into, getting swept onto, or grabbing coral. Even a small amount of damage can open a coral to being taken over by sponges and algae. Don't wear gloves when diving and snorkeling, and never take anything from the reef.

Unforunately, we now need to check out what is in our sunscreen. Some sunscreen chemicals kill reef organisms and have been implicated in coral bleaching. The worst is oxybenzone, (aka benzophenone-3 or BP-3). One drop of oxybenzone in six olympic-sized swimming pools results in a concentration that can damage reef organisms. Octinoxate (aka; escalol 557, heliopan new, octylmethoxycinnamate, OMC cinnamate, Parsol MCX) is also implicated in harming corals. Eco-friendly ingredients include non-nano zink oxide or titanium dioxide.

Marine Parks and Protected Areas

In an effort to preserve the natural beauty that draws us to the Caribbean, a growing number of designated marine protected areas (MPAs) have been created. Many MPAs restrict or forbid fishing, anchoring, and waste discharge, among other potentially detrimental activities. Some MPAs are multi-use and have designated areas for specific activities such as fishing, swimming,and scuba diving. The numerous stakeholders involved (including local businesses, fishermen, tourists, yachtspeople, and goverment) means that managment and enforcent can be complicated. Avoid fines and giving yachting a bad name by being aware and respectful of park boundaries and regulations, following the rules, and informing the relevant authorities or oganisations if you see someone violating regulations.

Eco-purchasing

Often, people don't realize how powerfully their dollars speak, and one of the very best things you can do for the environment is to spend wisely.

Dollars spent on wood carvings, jewelry made from decorative local seeds, banana crafts, straw goods, woven grasses, art, and anything made from coconut shells will help the economy and the environment. Jewelry

House of Chocolate, Grenada; lots of local products

made from conch shells is also okay, as these are caught for their meat and the shell is otherwise thrown away. (However, check importation regulations in your home country.) T-shirts and other locally manufactured items are fine, too.

Avoid buying coral and turtleshell products. Considerable damage to reef structures is done by youths who take corals to sell to jewelry makers. The hawksbill turtle, most often killed for its shell, is an endangered species, as are all Caribbean sea turtles, and importation of turtle shell is forbidden in most countries. These items are sold mainly to people on yachts, so let us say "no" to these vendors and support the turtles and reefs. If you visit during the lobster season and are buying lobsters, always turn them over to see if they have eggs underneath (easily seen as red caviar). If they do, refuse to buy them.

I am happy to say that in the years since I included this paragraph, the amount of coral and turtle shell products offered to yachtspeople has diminished significantly. Thank you!

One purchase that might significantly affect the environment is your choice of antifouling. TBT paints have been banned nearly everywhere in the world for their damage to the environment. In the Caribbean they are still legal. New eco-freindly paints using Econea instead of heavy metals are proving to be excellent. Make sure you know what your paint has in it, and choose wisely.

Your choice of fish while eating out or buying from local fishermen makes a difference. You can feel righteous eating the delicious but invasive lion fish. Small, fast recovering species like dorado (mahi-mahi), wahoo, and lobster, will have both lower mercury levels and less negative effect on the reef ecosystem than swordfish, grouper, marlin, and tuna, most of which are threatened by worldwide fishing. Blue fin and big eye tuna are threatened and yellow fin is overfished. The black fin and skipjack tuna (which you are most likely to catch) are more abundant. Both conch and urchin are critical to reef ecosystems. There is probably enough conch for local consumption, but large scale exports could be a threat. Once white sea urchins were extirpated thoughout much of the Caribbean, but they were reintroduced and current stocks are good, and collecting is carefully regulated.

Cruising Information

Weather

Continuous sunshine and balmy trade breezes, right? Well, not too far wrong.

There are two seasons, the dry and the wet, but they are not always well differentiated. During the dry season (February to June), there will often be weeks of clear, sunny weather broken only by an occasional small rain shower. In the wet season (July until January), there will still be plenty of sunshine, but with more frequent showers and occasional rainy days with no sun. There is very little temperature difference between the seasons; you can expect 78° to 87°F (25° to 31°C) year round.

The winds nearly always blow from between northeast and southeast at 10 to 25 knots; calms are rare. The wind tends to strengthen around the northern ends of islands. Rain usually arrives in intense squalls that can be seen coming from afar. Sometimes these squalls have a lot of wind in them (40 knots or more); often they do not. There is no way to tell before they arrive. Infrequently, a squall or cold front produces westerly winds, making the usual anchorages uncomfortable to untenable.

During the winter months, storms and cold fronts farther north sometimes produce swells that reach the Windwards. These northerly swells can make anchorages that are open to the north or west rolly and occasionally untenable. Few swells are really bad, but when they are, you have to be prepared to move to a calmer spot, even in the middle of the night. Swells have caused the demise of quite a few unattended yachts. Hurricanes also cause swells during the hurricane season. These swells may come from any direction, depending on the position of the storm.

In the winter a big high-pressure area to the northeast is a dominant feature. When the isobars get tight, the wind increases and is sometimes very fresh (25-30 knots). We call these Christmas winds. This high pressure is offset by cold fronts that come down from the northwest. They almost never make it as far as the Windwards, but as they approach, the weather is often calm and sunny, followed by wind and rain, as the tail ends affect this area.

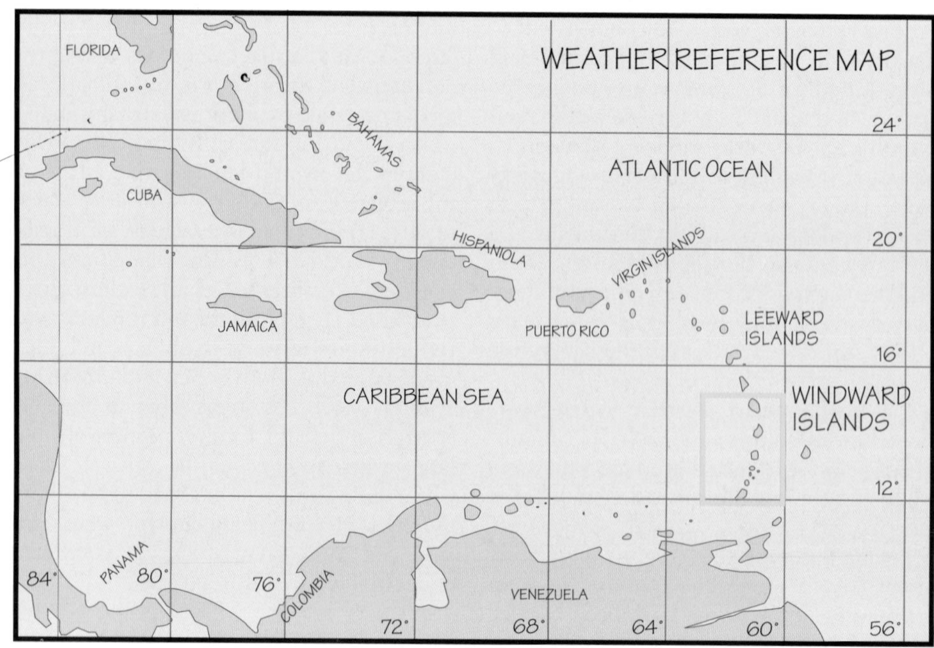

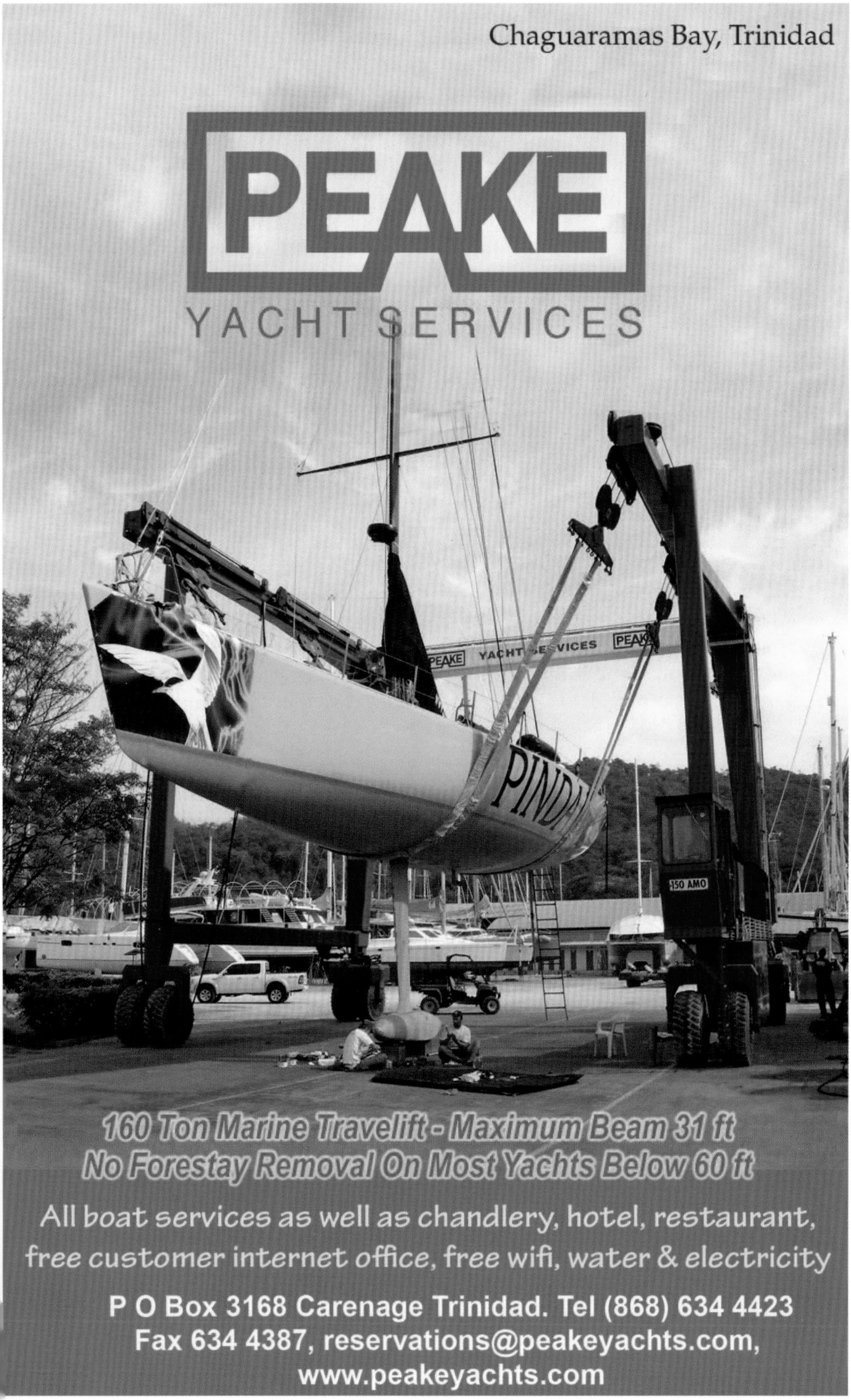

LOCAL RADIO

For news, views, and weather

FM

Grenada Broadcasting Network, Hott FM 98.5, 1055,
also 540 AM
St. Vincent Radio ------------------705
Waves (St. Lucia) -----------------94.5, 93.7
weather daily at 0730 & 1630
Sound of the Nation
(St. Vincent)------------------------90.7, 107.5
weather at 0700 after news and ads
St. Vincent -------------------------100.5,
weather 0745
Radio Caraibes (French)---------89.9

HAM & SSB (local times)

East Caribbean weather, 4045 and 8137 kHz USB @0600
Trinidad Emergency Net, 3855 kHz LSB/Ham @0630
Caribbean emergency /weather net, 3815 kHz LSB @ 0630
Caribbean Cocktail and weather net 7086 LSB @ 1730
0700 Caribbean Net 7250 LSB/Ham 0700
FOD E. Caribbean Weather 4420 USB @ 0745
For information on weather fax check:
http://tgftp.nws.noaa.gov/fax/marine.shtml
For more updated info on HAM and SSB

VHF

Cruisers nets (not Sunday)
Grenada, Channel 66 at 0730,
Bequia, Channel 68 at 0800
St. Lucia, Channel 68 at 0830 (usually only during big events)
In Martinique, COSMA gives forecasts in French at 0730 and 1830 on VHF: 11.

Visibility varies from an unusual low of 5 miles to a high of over 50 miles. Extremely hazy days are caused by dust from Africa. Sometimes, reddish traces may be found on the cabin and decks. On hazy days, avoid dust stains when doing the laundry by wiping off the lifelines before hanging out the washing.

The hurricane season is from June to October. People now talk of "named storms," only about half of which will reach hurricane strength. Hurricane frequency for the months of June, July, and October is about one hurricane every three years for the whole western Atlantic, including the Caribbean Sea and the Gulf of Mexico. During August and September, the number is around five each per year. Hurricanes frequently start well out in the Atlantic Ocean, often at the latitude of the Windwards, but then they usually swing north and pass through the Caribbean farther north. Very few hit the Windwards and sometimes years go by without one in this area, but it is essential to check the forecasts, especially in these days of rather active hurricane seasons. You can get weather on the radio, but it is hard to find consistently good forecasts.

It is probably easiest to get the weather on the web. (We give links to several forecasts on doyleguides.com.) Cruisers nets are good for weather. Local cruisers nets are Monday to Saturday. Grenada is on VHF: 66 international at 0730, Bequia is on VHF: 68 at 0800, St. Lucia (Rodney Bay) occasionally has one on VHF: 68 at 0830.

Here are some terms you will hear on the radio and what they mean: "Intertropical convergence zone" affecting the area: this is not any kind of low, but you may get some rain squalls or cloudy weather. "Tropical disturbance," "tropical wave," and "upper-level trough": poorly organized weather systems associated with rain squalls of varying intensity. A "tropical depression" is an organized weather system with sustained winds of up to 35 knots and rain. Sometimes these can be very nasty and other times they turn out to be nothing. A "tropical storm," on the other hand, is definitely something to be avoided, as it has lots of rain and sustained winds of 35-63 knots. When the sustained

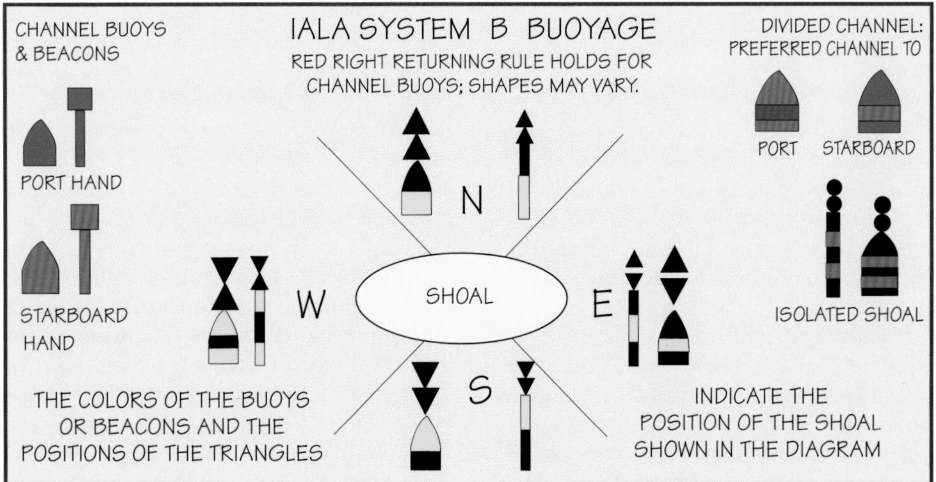

winds become more than 64 knots, it is called a hurricane.

Hurricane winds can come from any direction, so be prepared to get out of the way or run for one of the hurricane holes: Trois Ilets, or, better still, Cul de Sac Marin in Martinique; Rodney Bay Lagoon or Marigot Bay in St. Lucia; the mangrove swamp in Tyrrel Bay, Carriacou; and in Grenada, Port Egmont. Drive your boat aground bow first into the mangroves. Tie off to the biggest mangrove trees with all available lines (use at least ten). Put out two anchors astern, turn off all seacocks, remove all sails, awnings, and biminis, leave the boat, and find somewhere safe ashore.

During one of the few hurricanes that we did get, a charter party was advised by their company to make at once for a safe harbor to ride it out. "Oh no," they said "we have confirmed flights out and don't want to miss them. We will make it in time." They sailed north from St. Vincent to St. Lucia, but by the time they reached Soufriere, it was raining cats and dogs, and the wind was howling, so they anchored and went ashore. The boat soon began to drag and the skipper, aided by a local fisherman, tried to re-anchor. They managed to get their anchor line caught in the prop so they could not use power, and it was blowing too hard to make sail. In the end they drifted all night through the hurricane, and were rescued, after the winds fell, by a French coastguard boat off Martinique. I suppose the moral of the tale is that it is amazing what you can get away with, but better not to try.

Buoyage

All the islands now use the IALA B buoyage system. Main channels are marked with red and green buoys or beacons with red to starboard when entering: in other words "Red Right Returning." Other shoals and channels are indicated by black and yellow buoys or beacons coded with respect to both color and triangulation (using cones), as shown in the diagram. Lights and buoys in the Windwards are unreliable. Lights do not always work, buoys go adrift, and beacons lose color and cones. Treat navigational aids with great caution.

Tides and currents

The tidal range is around two feet, not enough to be critical except in a few places. The lowest tides are in the summer. An equatorial current sets to the west-northwest. This current is affected by the tide when you are within a few miles of land. A counter-current begins about one hour before low water, offsets the equatorial current, and can run up to one knot to the east. This continues for about five hours, until about four hours after low water. Skippers of boats that are very slow to windward can make use of this to help them when sailing between islands. However, it is a mixed blessing because the counter-current usually sets up much rougher seas.

Sargasso weed

When you fail at trolling, Sargasso weed is often the culprit. A strand catches on your hook and fish don't strike. A little of this weed has been around the Caribbean as long as we can remember. However, there is now far more of this weed, possibly due to global warming and it comes and goes. So far, except for fishing, it has not proved a problem at sea. Neither will it bother you aboard your boat under sail or at anchor, unless you anchor in some pretty strange places. In fact, it is not a problem until it aggregates ashore and begins to rot, which normally only happens on beaches, bays and harbors on the windward shores where it gets driven by the trade winds. You will hardly see these unless you take an island tour, though it can happen along the shore in windward harbors, of which Clifton Harbour in Union Island, is the most likely one you might visit. Except for a rather unpleasant smell of rotting eggs (hydrogen sulphide) right in town, which can sometimes last a few days, it is not a big problem. But it is worth noting that hydrogen sulphide is toxic and causes symptoms varying from headaches for long exposure at low concentrations to death at extreme concentrations. I visit on weedy days, but if I had young kids I would not leave them playing for hours in the weed along the shore.

Charts

You have a choice between British Admiralty (B.A.), U.S. Defense Mapping Agency (D.M.A), and yachting charts. U.K. charts are much more expensive in the U.S. and vice versa. New charts should be based on WG 84 data so they can be used with GPS.

Nautical Publications supply their charts in kits, each kit covering several islands. They are in color, and the format is relatively small (23.5 by 16.5 inches), so you never need to fold them. Each kit comes in a handy plastic see-through envelope that you can take into the cockpit with the current chart on top. This also ensures that rather than losing one chart over the side, the whole kit will blow over, so make a little hole in the plastic and tie the envelope down. Hasko Scheidt of Nautical Publication has done several surveys in the Caribbean, and in those areas he has surveyed, including the east coast of Antigua and the south coast of Barbuda, their charts are particularly good. His charts include very detailed land information as well as nautical information; the kit includes both paper and a DVD.

Imray Iolaire also does yachting charts, and these are printed on plastic so they almost last forever and you can get them wet. However, vigorous rubbing will take the color right off them, so experiment a little before you cover them with temporary pencil lines. These charts are sold individually, so you can tailor your collection to your needs, and while they are large-format, like the hydrographic charts, you need fewer of them, as most include detailed harbor plans. They also come in digital format, but these are sold separately.

Many people use cheap digital charts, which are better than a school atlas, but can be deadly if you rely on them, instead of using your eyes. Isle Forchue has a dangerous rock just as you enter. I could not see it on any of my digital charts. Eventually I found it - so small it was easily mistaken for a speck of dirt. In Laborie in St. Lucia one boat was wrecked and many others have gone aground using such charts. Take care!

GPS

GPS is the biggest leap in navigational science since the invention of the chronometer. Accurate though this system is, there are limitations. I have noticed occasional errors, up to a tenth of a mile, even when the GPS suggested better accuracy. Therefore, I would not advise using a GPS to navigate reef-strewn passages at night or in poor visibility. Older charts were created on unspecified formats, and inaccuracies of up to half a mile may occur. Newer charts are based on WG 84 data and work with GPS. The charts in this book are on GPS grids created by using a Garmin on WG 84 data, using much interpolation. No guarantee is offered about their accuracy. We include a table of

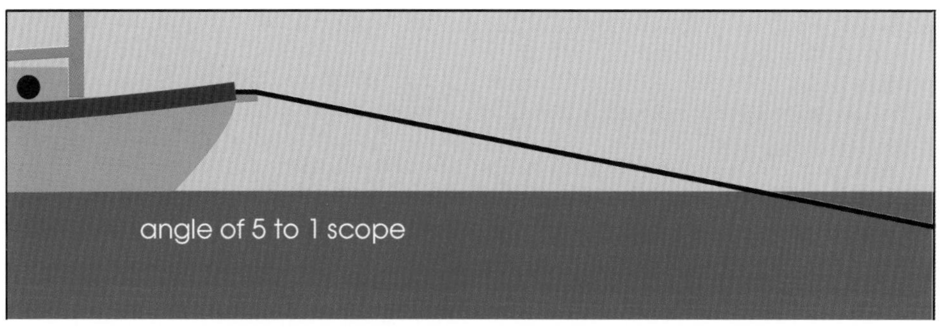

GPS positions for route planning. You can download them from www.doyleguides.com. Remember, land and shoals may be on your line of approach, depending on your route.

Customs and immigration

The Windwards contain four separate countries: Martinique, St. Lucia, St. Vincent (including the Grenadines to Petit St. Vincent), and Grenada (which includes Carriacou and Petite Martinique). Each has its own customs regulations, and it is necessary to clear in and out of each country. On arrival, you should hoist a yellow flag and anchor in a port of entry. As soon as possible, and definitely by first thing the next morning you must go ashore in search of customs and immigration officers. Take passports, ship's papers, and the clearance from your last port with you. All the Windwards now have simple one-page forms except St. Lucia, where immigration demands each person fills an extra form. (See page 137.)

In Martinique, you do your own entry on a customs computer. Elsewhere, a preclearance system called sailclear (www.sailclear.com) can ease formalities. You can preclear from any internet connection, and it saves you filling in all the forms. All your data are stored on the site, making it easy the next time. It currently works in most ports in St. Lucia and Grenada. With luck, it will soon work everywhere.

Customs and immigration officers will refuse to deal with anyone not wearing a shirt and looking reasonably presentable. Charges and other details are given under island and harbor headings.

Officers are often late to the office, so if you need to get going, clear the night before.

Dogs

So you've brought your pet all the way over the ocean and now you want to take it for a walk. Well, here is what you can expect from the local authorities. In Martinique and Grenada, if you have a rabies vaccination certificate handy when you clear in, you can walk your dog ashore. St. Vincent and St. Lucia are both rabies-free, and animals are not allowed ashore without significant paper work and a vet visit.

Dogs in the Caribbean are subject to a deadly heartworm. Check with a vet for appropriate counter-measures before leaving, or as soon as you get here.

Anchoring

It amazes me that you can safely keep a yacht in place with an anchor. Many yachts weigh from six to twenty tons and provide a stack of windage, yet we hold them in place with a tiny (35-60 lb) anchor. And it works, most of the time. Anchoring can be simple or fraught with dangers to your yacht and your relationship with your crew.

The first critical decision is where to drop the anchor. Check your chart for no-anchoring channels and for depths, then look at the boats and harbor for possible anchoring spots, and for places best avoided (like fish pots and moorings). Clear the foredeck for action, and shorten the dinghy painter so it does not end up in the prop.

In normal conditions, the wind in the Windwards will be blowing somewhere from the east, and you can expect to end up as the other anchored yachts are lying. It is safest to anchor behind the other yachts so there is no one for you to drag into. You can drop anchor as close as 50 feet behind another boat in most conditions. If you go in front of another yacht, you need to drop the anchor at least a hundred yards in front of them, or you will end up on top of them.

The wind often shifts 20 or 30 degrees: Will that put your boat over someone's anchor, or you over theirs? In rare calm conditions with boats facing all directions, you have no idea which way chains are laid out. All you can do is anchor well clear of other boats. Even if the wind is constant, boats swing from side to side, and each does it differently, so you do not want to end up close beside anyone.

It is best to anchor when the sun is high, so you can choose a light-colored sandy patch where the holding will be good, rather than a dark-colored weedy patch where you may drag. Always approach your spot into the wind.

To give the anchor a chance to hold, you need to let out at least five times as much chain or rope as the depth of water you anchor in, plus the height of your bow. (Let out more if bad weather is expected.) If you are anchoring on chain, the chain needs to be marked so you know how much you are letting out. This is imperative. Chandleries sell clever plastic chain markers in different colors, which sit inside the chain and do not interfere with the windlass. Cruisers can use these or paint their chain. Charterers should ask the company how they have marked the chain (and they should have). If they have not, you will need to flake it out on deck while you are still on the dock and mark it yourself. Good temporary markers are plastic electrical ties in different colors; use two or three for each mark, in case one breaks. Put the bulky bit inside the chain where it will not get crunched by the windlass. If these are not available, you could try whipping twine. You are never going to use less than 50 feet of chain, so this can be your first mark, then mark every 20 feet up to about 150 feet.

If you have a chain/rope combination, it is much easier to estimate how much you are letting out and also to see whether you have let out enough by the angle of the rode after it is set (see diagram below). While rope alone, or rope and 12 feet of chain, will work in sand and some other seabeds, you will need at least 50 feet of chain for beds of dead coral. If you use mostly rope, you will wander around more should the wind drop, and you need to allow for this.

To look good while anchoring, always bring the boat to a complete stop before dropping the anchor. Let out enough chain for the anchor to reach the bottom; then, as the boat swings back with the wind, keep letting out more, bit by bit, till you have let out the right amount. Never dump the chain or rope all at once. When the boat has settled down, facing the same way as all the others, nudge the engine into reverse at low revs till the rode becomes tight. If the boat does not drag, keep increasing the revs (take bearings ashore), and make sure you are holding. If the anchor holds at high revs in reverse, you are probably okay, but it is always good to dive on your anchor and make sure it is well dug in. If you do drag, the spot you are in is poor holding, so move to a different place and try again. Do not try the hard reverse if you are anchoring on soft mud; in that case, the anchor may need a very long time to settle.

The crew on the bow cannot hear the helmsman with the engine running, and the helmsman certainly cannot hear the crew. Hand signals look more professional and work better than screaming, but only if you figure out a signal system in advance.

If you do end up a little too close to someone else, you can often solve this by putting out a second anchor, at about 30 degrees to your first, which will pull you clear and restrict your swinging room.

Make sure the rope is cleated properly or the chain secure (the windlass does not secure it). Leave the foredeck clear of clutter, so that if you have to move in the middle of the night, you are not fighting surf boards and hammocks. Check your bearings periodically to make sure you have not dragged.

Mooring

Moorings are rapidly becoming much more widespread in the islands, which is a mixed blessing. Moorings do sometimes help protect the seagrass, which encourages turtles, echinoderms, and many kinds of fish.

	Ft. de France	Anse Mitan	G. Anse D'Arlet	Ste. Anne	Rodney Bay	Castries	Marigot	Pitons	Vieux Fort	Wallilabou	Kingstown	Young Island	Admiralty B.	Friendship B.	Mustique	Canouan	Mayreau	Tobago Cays	Union I.	P.S.V.	Hillsborough	Tyrrel Bay	St. George's	Prickly Bay	Mt. Hartman B.
St. Pierre	12	14	16	30	42	45	47	56	67	90	97	99	105	109	115	122	127	127	130	133	136	139	166	172	173
Fort de France		3	7	21	33	37	39	47	57	83	90	92	98	102	108	115	120	120	123	126	130	132	159	165	166
Anse Mitan			6	20	32	36	38	46	57	82	89	91	97	101	107	114	119	119	122	125	129	131	158	164	165
Gd Anse D'Arlet				15	26	30	32	41	52	77	84	86	92	96	102	109	114	114	117	120	123	126	152	158	159
St. Anne					21	26	30	39	50	76	83	85	91	95	101	108	113	113	116	119	123	126	156	161	162
Rodney Bay						5	8	18	29	55	62	64	70	74	80	87	92	92	95	98	102	105	135	140	141
Castries							4	13	24	50	57	59	65	69	75	82	87	87	90	93	97	100	130	135	136
Marigot								10	21	46	53	55	61	65	71	78	83	83	86	89	93	96	126	131	132
Pitons									11	36	43	45	51	55	61	68	73	73	76	79	83	86	116	121	122
Vieux Fort										34	41	43	49	53	59	66	71	71	74	77	81	84	114	119	120
Wallilabou											7	9	15	19	25	32	37	37	40	43	47	50	80	85	85
Kingstown												2	9	11	16	27	32	32	35	38	42	45	75	80	81
Young Island													8	10	15	27	32	32	35	38	42	45	75	80	81
Admiralty Bay														7	12	20	26	26	29	33	35	38	68	73	74
Friendship Bay															7	18	24	24	27	31	33	36	66	71	72
Mustique																14	19	19	25	26	28	31	61	66	67
Canouan																	7	6	10	14	16	19	49	54	55
Mayreau Saline Bay																		4	3	7	9	12	42	47	48
Tobago Cays																			4	7	11	14	44	49	50
Union (Clifton)																				4	7	10	40	45	46
P.S.V.																					7	9	39	44	45
Hillsborough																						4	34	39	40
Tyrrel Bay																							30	35	36
St. George's																								7	8
Prickly Bay																									2

MILEAGE CHART

This table is approximate and offered as a guide to planning. Distances sailed are often in excess of those shown due to wind and current.

GPS WAYPOINTS

For planning purposes only. These waypoints may be downloaded from www.doyleguides.com along with links to help you put them on your GPS.

All miles are nautical miles.

ID	Latitude	Longitude	Comment
	MARTINIQUE		
WMTQ01	N14°26.00'	W061°05.00'	Approach to Martinique's SW coast
WMTQ02	N14°44.50'	W061°10.70'	Off main dock St. Pierre
WMTQ03	N14°38.40'	W061°08.50'	0.1 miles W of harbor wall, Case Pilote
WMTQ04	N14°37.80'	W061°09.20'	Approach to Case Pilote
WMTQ05	N14°36.80'	W061°06.40'	Schoelcher
WMTQ06	N14°35.00'	W061°05.00'	Approach to Fort de France
WMTQ07	N14°35.70'	W061°04.50'	Approach Fort de France anchorage
WMTQ08	N14°32.90'	W061°02.10'	Approach to Trois Ilets
WMTQ09	N14°33.60'	W061°02.80'	Approach to Trou Etienne
WMTQ10	N14°33.70'	W061°03.40'	Pointe du Bout
WMTQ11	N14°33.00'	W061°04.00'	Approach for Anse A L'Ane
WMTQ12	N14°31.80'	W061°05.40'	Anse Noir
WMTQ13	N14°30.00'	W061°06.00'	Grand Anse D'Arlet
WMTQ14	N14°29.20'	W061°05.20'	Anses D'Arlet (middle of bay)
WMTQ15	N14°27.70'	W061°00.50'	Approach for Baie du Marigot
WMTQ16	N14°25.00'	W060°55.00'	Approach to St. Anne & Marin
WMTQ17	N14°26.70'	W060°54.00'	Cul de Sac Marin (entrance)
WMTQ18	N14°26.20'	W060°53.20'	Ste. Anne (western part of anchorage)
WMTQ19	N14°24.90'	W060°49.80'	Baie des Anglais (entrance)
WMTQ20	N14°24.00'	W060°53.80'	Approach to Grande Anse des Saline
	ST. LUCIA		
WSLU01	N14°05.50'	W060°58.20'	0.1 miles west of Pigeon Island
WSLU02	N14°04.73'	W060°57.40'	Rodney Bay Lagoon (entrance)
WSLU03	N14°04.10'	W060°58.70'	Southern approach, inside Barrel of Beef
WSLU04	N14°01.20'	W061°00.50'	Castries (entrance)
WSLU05	N13°58.05'	W061°01.90'	Marigot (entrance)
WSLU06	N13°56.40'	W061°03.20'	Anse La Raye (entrance)
WSLU07	N13°55.60'	W061°03.70'	Anse Cochon
WSLU08	N13°54.70'	W061°04.30'	Anse de Canaries
WSLU09	N13°51.50'	W061°05.20'	0.4 miles SW of Anse Chastanet reef
WSLU10	N13°51.20'	W061°03.80'	Soufriere
WSLU11	N13°48.50'	W061°05.00'	0.2 miles west of Gros Piton
WSLU12	N13°43.00'	W060°58.00'	0.75 miles WSW of dock Vieux Fort
WSLU13	N13°46.00'	W061°05.00'	2.3 miles south of Gros Piton
WSLU14	N13°44.50'	W061°00.00'	Entrance to Laborie
	ST. VINCENT		
WSTV01	N13°20.00'	W061°15.00'	2 miles northwest of Chateaubelair
WSTV02	N13°16.00'	W061°15.80'	Cumberland Bay (center of entrance)
WSTV03	N13°14.90'	W061°16.50'	Wallilabou (center of entrance)
WSTV04	N13°14.40'	W061°16.90'	0.1 miles W of Bottle & Glass
WSTV05	N13°11.40'	W061°16.20'	Buccament Bay (center)
WSTV06	N13°10.90'	W061°16.20'	Petit Byahaut

ST VINCENT (cont.)

WSTV07	N13°09.50'	W061°14.90'	Ottley Hall (entrance)
WSTV08	N13°09.00'	W061°14.00'	Kingstown (center of bay)
WSTV09	N13°07.60'	W061°12.40'	0.1 miles SW of Fort Duvernette
WSTV10	N13°07.50'	W061°11.90'	Approach to Blue Lagoon
	GRENADINES		
WGNS01	N13°00.70'	W061°15.10'	0.1 miles west of Devil's Table, Bequia
WGNS02	N12°59.50'	W061°17.60'	Bequia, West Cay (just off W end)
WGNS03	N12°59.10'	W061°14.00'	Bequia, Friendship Bay
WGNS04	N12°53.50'	W061°12.00'	Mustique approach, north of Montezuma
WGNS05	N12°52.50'	W061°12.00'	Mustique approach, south of Montezuma
WGNS06	N12°52.80'	W061°11.50'	Mustique, Britannia Bay
WGNS07	N12°44.40'	W061°20.00'	Canouan, northwest point
WGNS08	N12°42.70'	W061°20.20'	Canouan, Charlestown Bay (center of)
WGNS09	N12°42.40'	W061°21.40'	Just northwest of Glossy Hill, Canouan
WGNS10	N12°39.50'	W061°23.00'	0.5 miles west of Baline Rocks
WGNS11	N12°38.20'	W061°21.80'	0.1 miles W of Petit Rameau, Tobago Cays
WGNS12	N12°39.00'	W061°23.70'	Mayreau, Salt Whistle Bay
WGNS13	N12°38.00'	W061°24.50'	Mayreau, Saline Bay
WGNS14	N12°36.00'	W061°28.00'	0.25 miles W of Chatham Bay, Union
WGNS15	N12°36.00'	W061°24.20'	Union, northen approach to Union/Palm
WGNS16	N12°35.00'	W061°25.00'	0.25 miles W of Grand de Coi, Union
WGNS17	N12°32.90'	W061°24.10'	0.2 miles N of Mopion Channel, PSV
WGNS18	N12°32.00'	W061°23.50'	0.5 miles west of PSV dock
WGNS19	N12°32.00'	W061°27.00'	0.7 miles WNW of north end of Carriacou
WGNS20	N12°30.00'	W061°30.80'	2.8 miles west of Jack a Dan, Carriacou
WGNS21	N12°29.70'	W061°28.20'	Just west of Jack a Dan, Carriacou
WGNS22	N12°27.00'	W061°30.00'	Tyrrel Bay (entrance)
WGNS23	N12°19.00'	W061°36.00'	Isle de Ronde
	GRENADA		
WGDA01	N12°15.00'	W061°40.00'	1 mile N of David Point
WGDA02	N12°06.70'	W061°45.00'	Halifax Harbour (entrance)
WGDA03	N12°05.20'	W061°45.90'	Dragon Bay (entrance)
WGDA3A	N12°05.50'	W061°45.90'	Happy Hill (approach)
WGDA3B	N12°04.40'	W061°45.70'	Grand Mal Bay (approach)
WGDA04	N12°02.70'	W061°45.50'	0.25 miles W of entrance to St. George's
WGDA05	N12°00.20'	W061°48.40'	Point Saline (just off tip of land)
WGDA06	N11°59.60'	W061°46.20'	True Blue (entrance)
WGDA07	N11°59.30'	W061°46.00'	Prickly Bay (entrance)
WGDA08	N11°58.60'	W061°45.90'	0.25 miles W of Porpoises rocks
WGDA09	N11°59.00'	W061°45.10'	Approach for Mt. Hartman Bay
WGDA10	N11°59.00'	W061°44.20'	Approach for Hog Island
WGDA11	N11°59.10'	W061°43.50'	Approach for Clarkes Court Bay
WGDAPB	N11°59.30'	W061°42.90'	Approach for Phare Bleu Marina
WGDA12	N11°59.30'	W061°42.70'	Approach for Port Egmont
WGDA13	N12°00.00'	W061°42.10'	Approach for Calivigny harbour
WGDA14	N12°00.60'	W061°41.30'	Approach P. Bacaye/Bacelot Bay
WGDA15	N12°00.60'	W061°40.70'	St. David's Harbour (entrance)

Owners of rentable moorings include towns (especially Martinique), marinas, marine parks, charter companies (St. Vincent), and private individuals. The technology to properly design, place, and maintain moorings at a level where they will not fail has existed for years. Where I grew up in the UK, hundreds of boats were on town moorings. These were hauled and inspected annually, and they had to withstand major storms; I do not remember a single failure.

Unfortunately, moorings in the Caribbean are not well maintained, and because nearly every bad consequence of failure (and there have been many), has landed on the yacht owner, not the mooring owner, there has been no incentive for improvement. Official moorings are generally correctly put down, but there is often little or no maintenance. In some places, mooring use is compulsory. I avoid using moorings where possible, and snorkel on them if there is no alternative. Never run a line from one side of your boat through the mooring to the other, because as the boat swings the rope will chafe through. Use a separate line on each side.

In the Grenadines, outside official marine park moorings, locals view moorings as a personal parking meter to gather income. Most of these are poorly designed and constructed, and the guiding philosophy for most mooring owners is to rent it till it breaks, and then fix it. I would not trust any of them without a very close underwater inspection. They are almost never properly installed, and often not a single shackle has been wired, so they can fall apart. Lines can often catch on the concrete block and chafe right through, and the size of the block or the means of attachment is frequently inadequate. They have no legal status; there is even a warning about them in the Bequia customs office. You can anchor right beside one; the owner has absolutely no rights over the seabed and cannot make you move, though he is quite likely to act like a jerk. If you take one, and it is too close to a boat that is already anchored, you must move; such moorings carry no rights. If you decide to take one of these moorings, you are taking substantial risk, so make sure your insurance covers it.

If we think moorings are okay, we will mention that in the text.

Saltwhistle Bay, Mayreau

Chartering

Whether you want to go bareboat, fully crewed, one way, multihull, or monohull, you can find something to suit in the Windwards. I give a list of charter companies in the directory, and links to them on doyleguides.com.

For bareboaters without much experience, the easiest sail is from St. Vincent to Union or Grenada. Most charter companies will be happy to arrange one-way charters for an extra fee, and most skippered yachts will pick up and drop off at ports of your choice for no extra charge.

The sail from St. Lucia to St. Vincent is a long, hard day's sail. The return trip is often worse. If you are starting a charter in St. Lucia or Martinique, it makes a lot of sense to sail one way and finish in Union Island or Grenada. This is especially true if you only have a week or so.

Bareboating

I had the pleasure of running one of the first Caribbean bareboats ~ a little 31-footer called Rustler. When we said "bareboat," we meant it. Rustler came with a hand-start diesel that would barely push her out of the anchorage, a small icebox full of ice, and 40 gallons of water, which were pumped up by hand. Mechanical complexities consisted of a massive British marine toilet, with endless valves and pumps. This antiquity was almost impossible to clog, but at the same time, however much you worked on the packing gland, within a couple of days it tended to squirt you in the eye. The outboard was a close relative ~ all chrome and stainless, with no cover. You had to wind the cord round the flywheel for every start and go through an elaborate system of switching valves and vents and bleeding for exactly the right number of seconds. The only thing to be said in its favor was that even the roughest of mechanics could do a major overhaul with a screwdriver, a big hammer, and a pair of pliers.

When I look at some of the bareboat ads these days, it seems that people want to take it all with them when they get away from it all. Freezers, fridges, hair dryers, microwave

Tobago Cays

ovens, TV, telephones, and DVD players are all available.

One thing that years of sailing has taught me is that anything mechanical, electrical, or electronic, when installed on a well-used yacht, will eventually go wrong. Bareboats are particularly susceptible because of all the different people using the gear. In practical terms, this means that breakdowns are part and parcel of a modern sophisticated yacht, and not necessarily a reflection on the efficiency and ability of the charter company. The charter people realize this, so they all help each other's yachts and do their best to have a breakdown and backup service, despite the problems posed by the Windwards, which are well spread out. But it is important that bareboaters appreciate the essentially adventurous nature of a bareboat holiday and not let it be ruined by a malfunctioning hair dryer.

I still have the log book from Rustler, and there is an entry I am especially fond of. At the beginning, it is written in the hand of the group's self-appointed leader, Dr. Smith, who was not the least bit happy. Each day was another disaster. He couldn't make the outboard start, he couldn't find the boat hook, one of the navigation lights malfunctioned, he was "very disappointed" in the condition of the boat. Then the handwriting changed and the new entry said: "Dr. Smith had to return home for pressing personal reasons. Rustler is now a fine yacht, the weather is perfect, the sailing fantastic. We are having a marvelous time."

A good thing about chartering is that those occasions that are terrible at the time make great stories later. Some years ago, a bareboat was on a reef in the middle of nowhere and the skipper was on the radio to the company's local representative, who was trying to assess the situation.

"We are hard aground, the rudder is broken, and we cannot steer," lamented the charterer.

"Ok. I've got that," said the rep. "Now tell me, are you taking on water?"

There was a pause of a few seconds, then back came a very definite answer, "Oh no, we did that yesterday in St. Vincent."

Crewed charters

Having spent years both running bareboats and skippering charters, I can attest without question that skippered charters produce more glowing praise. A crewed charter is also a real holiday for everyone, with no galley and cleaning chores.

Many agents talk a lot about matching charterers to crew. In fact, most charterers are happy, easy to please, and good company, and good professional skippers can adapt themselves to all kinds of people. Cooks develop a sensitivity to produce the right kind of food.

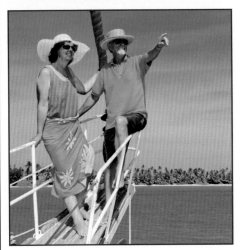

The modern large charter yachts that now make up the bulk of the fleet have enough crew, and guests are separated from the crew, so it is a bit like having your own mini-cruiseship, but with much better food and service.

Tipping is a big item for most crews, as this makes up a large part of their income. Unless otherwise stated, 10 percent of the total charter fee is the norm and an appropriate figure for good service.

On smaller yachts, with only a captain and cook, it is worth keeping in mind that although yacht crews enjoy what they are doing and genuinely like their guests, there is some strain to always being on one's best behavior and there are a few things that can make life a lot easier. It is a huge help if all the charterers go ashore for a couple of hours each day, either to shop, walk, or go to the beach. At this point, the crew can put on their favorite music full blast and clean the boat with much banging and gay abandon. The charterers will return to a clean boat and a much-refreshed crew.

Cooks hate to be watched while they work. It makes them nervous and upsets their concentration. There is no way you would know this, because they are trained to smile and answer a string of questions; much better to leave them alone in the galley, and give them the attention they deserve when they produce that final work of art.

The cook usually works much harder than the skipper, so it is a great break if the guests decide to eat out, even if it is just a matter of having a sandwich ashore instead of returning for lunch. Unfairly, the best cooks get the fewest breaks, as no one can bear to miss a single meal.

It is a tradition on smaller yachts that at some point, the guests take their crew out for dinner. For the crew, the break is more important than the dinner, and if you are on a budget, they don't mind if it is somewhere quite simple.

We list charter companies in the directory and on doyleguides.com.

Marigot, St. Lucia

Professional Yachts

Most cruisers quickly adjust to island time. If it doesn't get done today, tomorrow will suffice. This does not work for professional charter and superyachts on strict timetables, with guests arriving, chores to get done, and breakdowns to be coped with. I remember once many years ago arriving in Grenada with a charter turnaround on the eve of some holiday and not being able to get laundry done at any price.

Happily, things are much better today. There are a number of good businesses that cater to professional yachts, and they will do what it takes to make things happen. I list these below.

Many of these agents have reasonable standard fees for things like clearing customs, and it would pay bareboaters or cruisers with short stops (one day to clear in and out and tour the island, for example) to take advantage of these services.

AGENTS

Martinique

Note: when dialing Martinique from overseas, dial + 596 596 + 6 digits, unless it is a mobile phone, in which case it is, + 596 696 + 6 digits

You can base a superyacht in Martinique. It has all necessary support services, and you will find Douglas Rapier (he is available 24/7) of Douglas Yacht Services to offer the very highest standard of professional service in everything a superyacht may want, from full provisioning and technical help to overseeing travel, private plane arrivals, restaurant reservations, and personal arrangements. English is his native tongue, so you will have no communications problems. His office is in Marin Marina, but he keeps his mobile with him.

Douglas Yacht Services, (0696) 45 89 75, (0596) 52 14 28, F: (0596) 52 07 36, VHF: 09, douglas@yachtservices.fr

St. Lucia

St. Lucia has dedicated agents to work with the large yachts. They can deal with customs, clear parts, and arrange fuel, local provisions, and anything else. They all will work in any of St. Lucia's ports.

With the IGY Rodney Bay Marina, and the Cappella Marina and Resort in Marigot Bay, St. Lucia has become a good place to base a superyacht.

Ben Saltibus in Soufriere has been at it forever and is very professional. You will be in good hands with him. He works quite closely with Sam Taxi Service in St. Vincent and Henry Safari Tours in Grenada.

Benny Adjouda is the other accredited yacht agent.

CJ Taxi Service in Rodney Bay Marina will also help with most things locally.

Ben's Taxi Service, (758) 459-5457, F:(758) 459-5719, Cell: (758) 484-0708

Harmony Yacht Services (Benny), (758) 518-0081, cell: (758) 287 4261, F: (758) 458-5033, VHF: 16, harmonyiii@hotmail.com

CJ Taxi, (758) 584-3530, F: (758) 452-0185, VHF: 16

See also Rodney Bay Marina and Capella Marina & Resort under *Marinas and fueling*. Both can arrange most things.

St. Vincent & the Grenadines

This archipelago offers ample support for a visiting superyacht. Sam, of Sam Taxi Tours, is an official ship agent and works with large yachts and some cruise ships. He has sub-agencies in Bequia and Union Island. He can clear your yacht in or out from most anchorages and handle all other needs. He has an office up on a hill where he and his team keep an eye on arriving yachts.

Erika's Marine Services can handle yachts anywhere in St. Vincent and the Grenadines. They have agents in Union Island, their main base, and St. Vincent, Bequia, and Canouan. They are efficient and friendly and have a plane.

Sam Taxi Tours, (784) 456-4338, F: (784) 456-4233, cell: (784) 528-3340, VHF:68/16, sam-taxi-tours@vincysurf.com.

Erika's Marine Services, (784) 458-8335, Cell: (784) 533-2847, VHF: 68, VIP@erikamarine.com

Grenada

Grenada makes a good superyacht base and has superyacht agents. They will handle anything you need, from checking in through customs to finding dock space, provisioning, and dealing with problems, and they will visit all Grenada's ports.

Roger and Claire Spronk run Spronk Ltd., a company based in True Blue. In addition to helping superyachts, they own both a gourmet store and a wholesale provisioning business, which handles a considerable quantity of the island's seafood, so they are particularly good at provisioning. Their base is at their restaurant, Bananas, in True Blue. They have started work on a waterfront base in Benji Bay.

Dennis Henry, of Henry's Safari Tours, has been at it the longest and he is professional, imaginative, and reliable, with a good back-up team. He owns four laundries, a large fleet of taxis and a cooking gas depot. Henry rather likes to be challenged on the odd occasion when he is thrown a problem he has not had to cope with before.

Henry's Safari Tours, (473) 444-5313, Cell: (473) 405 6313/407 0522, F: (473) 444-4460, VHF: 68, info@henrysafari.com,

Spronk Mega Yacht Services, (473) 407-3688/435-6342/534-6342 Fax: (473) 444-4677, office@spronkmegayacht.com

MARINAS AND FUELING

In Martinique, large yachts can fuel and dock in Marin Marina.

Marin Marina, (0596) 74 83 83, F: (0596) 74 92 20, VHF: 09, port.marin@wanadoo.fr

In St. Lucia, IGY Rodney Bay Marina has fueling, but check the current depth into the lagoon.

IGY Rodney Bay Marina, (758) 458-4892, F: (758) 452-0185, VHF: 16, rbm@igymarinas.com

Capella Marigot Resort & Marina has fueling on their large yacht docks.

Capella Marigot Resort and Marina, (758) 451-4275/1, 728-9900, VHF: 16/12, marigotbay@capellahotels.com, manager@marigotbaymarina.com

Other fueling options include St. Lucia Yacht Services in Vigie and Cool Breeze fuel station by the main town dock in Soufriere. Contact the agents to arrange tanker truck fueling in the main dock in Castries or Vieux Fort.

Cool Breeze Gas Station, (758) 459-7729/459-7831, F: 459-5309

St. Lucia Yacht Services (758) 452-5057/484-7641, VHF: 16

In St. Vincent, call Sam Taxi Tours. He will usually arrange for a tanker truck alongside the main docks in Kingstown.

Sam Taxi Tours, (784) 456-4338/528-3340, F: (784) 456-4233, VHF: 68/16, sam-taxi-tours@vincysurf.com

An easy and good fuel dock in the Grenadines is B & C Fuels in Petit Martinique.

B&C Fuels, (473) 443-9110, F: (473) 443-9075, BabdCfuels@gmail.com

Carriacou Marine sells fuel, including duty-free, but draft is limited to about 8 feet. You can arrange fueling on the main dock in Tyrrel Bay through Bullens in Hillsborough.

Bullen's, (473) 443-7468/7469, F: (473) 443 8194, vbs@spiceisle.com

In St. George's, Grenada you can arrange fuel at the Grenada Yacht Club in St. George's. They can take boats about 160 feet long on their dock. You can also get fuel at the new Port Louis Marina, taking it from one of the superyacht berths, or you can arrange fuel on the main St. George's wharf through an agent.

Grenada Yacht Club, (473) 440-3050/440-6826, F: (473) 440-6826, VHF: 16, gycdockinfo@gmail.com

Port Louis Marina, (473) 435-7431/2, dockmaster: (473) 415-0820, VHF: 14, reservations@cnportlouismarina. com

Docking and fuel can be found at Prickly Bay Marina in Prickly Bay and Secret Harbour Marina in Mt. Hartman Bay. Take care to choose a channel suitable to your depth. Either marina can take almost any size of yacht that can make it into the bay.

Secret Harbour Marina, (473) 444-4449, F: (473) 444-2090, VHF: 16 &71, secretharbour@spiceisle.com

Prickly Bay Marina, (473) 439-5265, VHF: 16, info@pricklybaymarina.com

Tuglett at Whirlpool, Carriacou

Scuba Diving

"It's fantastic. I could breathe underwater just like a fish, and fish swam up and looked at me. What an incredible feeling."

"It's the greatest sensation I've ever felt. When we swam back with the current it was just like gliding through a beautiful garden!"

These are typical comments from first-time divers who find that scuba diving is the most exciting thing they have ever done. No wonder ~ it is the closest most of us will ever come to visiting an alien planet. Not only that, underwater we are weightless and seem to fly. Like birds, we can soar, hover, and dive down to see anything of interest.

The underwater world is full of wonders: tall, soft, waving "plants" that are really colonies of tiny animals, sponges that look like ancient urns in colors ranging from yellow to a psychedelic luminous blue. Huge schools of fish swim by, unconcerned by our presence. Little squids move by jet propulsion, turtles and giant rays glide with elegant ease.

Yet many people are put off by diving because they are under the impression that it is complicated and difficult. But, with modern equipment, diving is very simple, and with the popular Resort Course (also known as Discover Scuba Diving courses or Try Dives), you can be diving in half a day. In fact, the problem most divers have is boring their non-diving friends to distraction with tales of undersea adventure. The minimum age for most courses is ten.

Equipment

Experienced divers will want to bring their own masks, fins, and regulators. Your own comfortable BCD (buoyancy control device) is worth bringing, too. As for the rest, forget it. There is no point in humping tanks and weight belts; far better to rent them here. Those without any equipment

Ornate Elysia, Polly Philipson photo

Stoplight parrotfish

Secretary Blenny, Polly Philipson photo

Flying Gunard

don't need to worry. Dive shops will supply everything, and it is usually excellent, up-to-date gear. In many parts of the world, you have to wear a protective wet suit against the cold, but in the Windwards the water is warm enough that, for most people, this isn't necessary.

Courses for beginners

Anyone who just wants to give diving a go can do so very quickly with a "Discover Scuba Diving" course. It will take one whole morning or afternoon. First you get a short briefing that explains in simple language what diving is all about. Then you try out the equipment in shallow water, and lastly, you go for your first dive. It is not a certification, and only qualifies you to dive under the close supervision of an instructor at the same dive shop.

First dive

Wherever you take a resort course, the instructors will choose a site that is easy, but interesting enough to attract aficionados. A typical example is Devil's Table in Bequia. The rocks and coral start at 12 feet and slope down to about 35 feet deep. You enter the water and may feel a bit nervous, but you breathe out and gently sink. Soon your attention turns outwards. Large pillar corals rise from among the rocks. They look fuzzy, but if you swish your hand really close to them, the tentacles withdraw, leaving them looking like rocks. You stop to examine some pretty shells clinging to a waving sea fan, and to your surprise a tiny damsel fish shoots up and tries to chase you away. He's protecting his patch, and you don't scare him; it's then you learn that you can even laugh through your regulator. There is a great deal more to see: brightly colored parrotfish and angelfish, moray eels staring from their holes, strange-looking arrow crabs, and brightly banded coral shrimp. You enjoyed it? Good! Time to go to the next level.

Certification

If you've ever thought about getting certified, or if you try a dive and like it, then it makes sense to get certified on your holiday. You can start the certification process at home, doing all the theory work and initial confined water dives in a swimming pool, and then bring your referral paperwork to a dive shop in the Windwards, where you will complete your course with open water dives on dramatic reef landscapes, rather than in some frigid, grey lake. In the Caribbean, you can train at a cost not much greater than the dives alone. The course includes all equipment, you do everything in open water, the dives are fantastic, and you can take home a diving certificate as well as your memories. There are several diving associations that have accredited diving instructors who can train you and give you a certificate. These include PADI and NAUI, which are equally good. The next step from the resort course is the PADI Scuba Diver. This two-and-a-half-day course certifies you to dive with any divemaster at any shop to a depth of 40 feet. It is a good introduction and, being short, it is easy to do on holiday. You can complete your training on your next holiday, as this course counts as credit towards being an independent open water diver.

The full Open Water diving course takes four to five days and includes a couple of hours of instruction each day, followed by a dive, during which you master important practical and safety skills.

For qualified divers

Some people, especially those chartering yachts, prefer to rent gear and go off diving by themselves. Others prefer to join a dive with professionals. At least for your first dives, I recommend going with an accredited shop. They know all the good sites: the hidden caves, the special ledge where angelfish live, and maybe where there is a tame octopus, seahorse, or frogfish. A good dive professional is a good guide and can point out many things that would otherwise be missed. Perhaps the most important reason is that many good dive sites are in places that can only be reached with a powerful dive boat rather than a dinghy. I have worked with many charterers who have tried it both ways and noticed that those who went with dive professionals had a much better time than those who went on their own. Diving in the Windwards varies from island to island and from one dive site to the next, so enthusiasts will want to try diving in several different spots. Since the introduction of the predatory and invasive lionfish, many dive shops organize occasional lionfish hunts, to keep at least some reefs clear of them. They teach you how to avoid the poisonous spines.

We will mention the good sites and their accessibility in the text under each anchorage section. Dive shops are listed in our directory.

Look for easy-to-visit dive and snorkel sites on our sketch charts. They are marked by flags.

Diving ▬ Snorkeling ▬

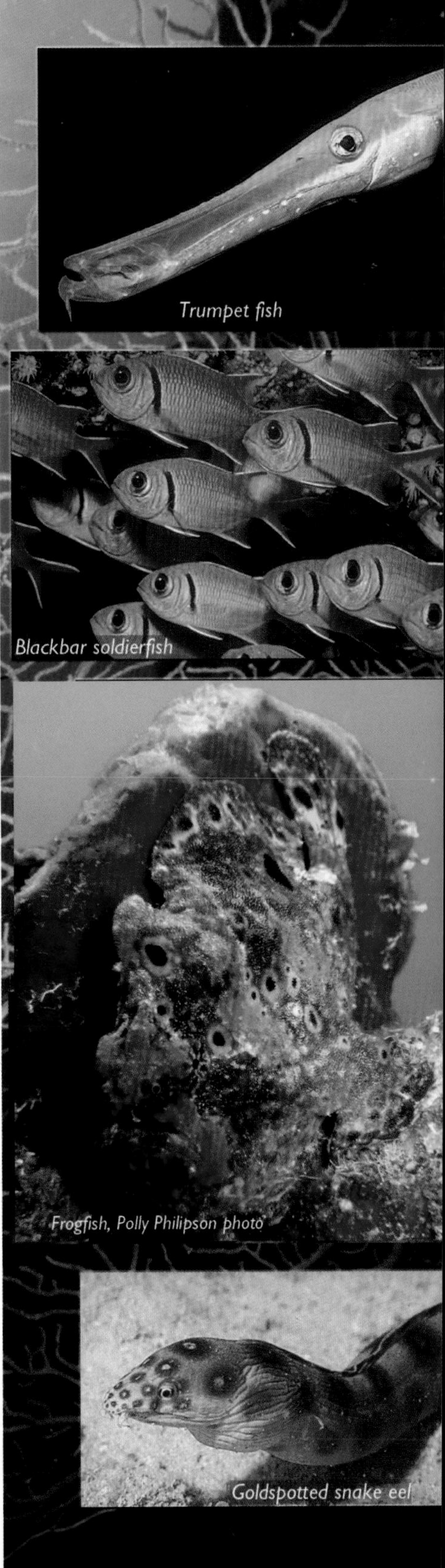

Trumpet fish

Blackbar soldierfish

Frogfish, Polly Philipson photo

Goldspotted snake eel

Anchorages in the WINDWARD

Martinique, St. Lucia, St. Vincent & the Grenadines, Grenada, Carriacou, & Petite Martinique

ISLANDS

The Pinnacle, Union I, Jeremie Tronet Photo

Martinique

La Dunette, St. Anne

Martinique at a glance

Regulations

Clear customs in Fort de France, Marin, Anse Mitan, Les Anses D'Arlet, Ste. Anne, or St. Pierre. Yachts in Martinique waters over six months in one year are liable to import duty, with exemptions for storing your yacht while you fly abroad. Visas are not necessary for EU or US citizens. Other nationals should check. For places and time to clear, see our anchorage sections. Yachts pay no overtime fees or charges. Foreign yachts over 5 tons need national registration. (US state registration is not accepted.)

A 5-knot speed limit is in effect within 300 meters of all coastline.

Shopping hours

Shops often open 0800-1200 and 1500-1730, Monday through Saturday. Many offices close on Saturday. Supermarkets often stay open till 1900 and open on Sunday mornings.

Holidays

Jan 1 & 2, New Year's Day & Recovery
Carnival Monday to Wednesday, 40 days before Easter, March 4-5, 2019, Feb, 24-25, 2020
Feb 22, Independence Day
Easter Friday, Sunday & Monday, April 19, 21-22, 2019, and April 10, 12-13, 2020
May 1, Labor Day
May 8, Victory Day (1945)
Ascension Day, May 30 2019 May 21 2020
Whit Monday, June 10, 2019, June 1, 2020
May 22, Abolition of Slavery
Corpus Christi, June 20, 2019; June 11, 2020
July 14, Bastille Day
August 15, Virgin Mary Day
Nov 1, All Saints Day
Nov 11, Victory Day (1918)
Dec 25, Christmas Day

Telephones

The simplest thing is to use a mobile phone and get a local sim; Carte Orange or Digicel. They cost around 15 Eu with 5 Eu credit. If you are calling the USA on Orange dial #141# to buy a pass Caraibes which will give you calls to the US and other Caribbean islands at the same rate as local calls.

Dial + or 00 to get out of the country and then the country code and number you want. Martinique numbers are 10 digits, starting 0596, except cell phones, which are 0696. To call from the US, dial 011 596 then the whole number, excluding the first 0. It will start:

011 596 596... or 011 596 696....

If you are roaming on a mobile phone, you will have to add + to the beginning of the number. Local sims are available from Cart Orange and Digicel, as are prepaid USB ports for internet.

Transport

Martinique has a good system of buses or communal taxis (TC). These are reasonably priced, are found on most town squares, and run on fixed routes, mainly to and from Fort de France. There are also taxis. Typical taxi rates in Euros for up to 4 are:

Airport to Fort de France 25
Airport to Anse Mitan/Marin ...60
Anse Mitan to golf course 10
Fort de France to Carrefour 10
St. Pierre to Fort de France........55
St. Pierre to Airport...................75
Short ride 10
Shopping/tours per hour for 4....40
Over 4, pp, per hour 10

Rental cars are available. You can use your own license. Drive on the right.

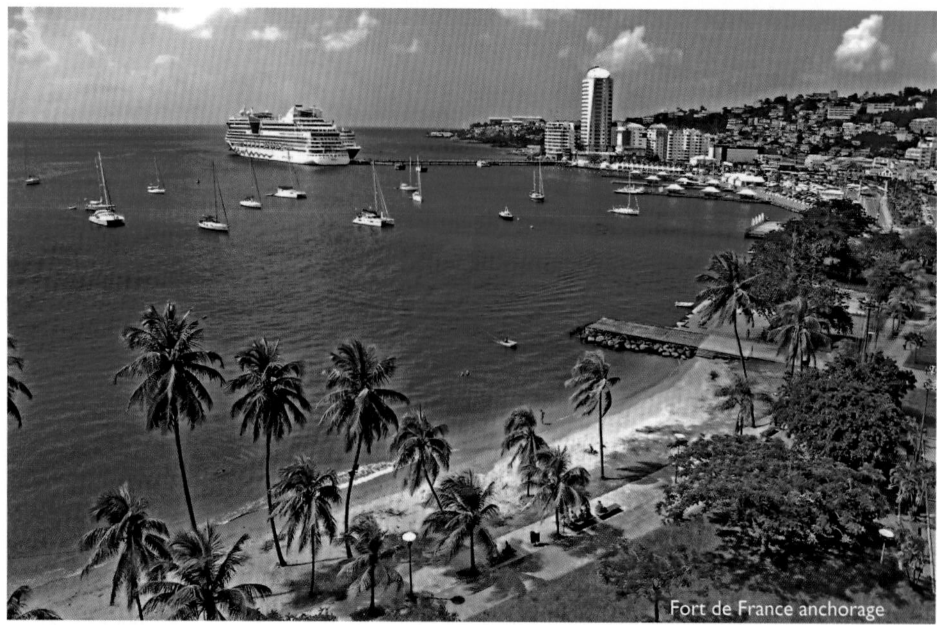
Fort de France anchorage

The Caribs called Martinique *Madinina* ~ Island of Flowers. It is the largest of the Windwards and, apart from a few short spells under the British, has been French since it was colonized. It is a part of France and feels it, with excellent roads and a thriving economy. Nearly every bay has a wonderful government-built dock, ideal for leaving your dinghy. Fort de France is a busy city, bustling with shoppers and cars. The smaller towns are quieter and some look so clean they could have just been scrubbed. You will notice the smells of wonderful coffee and delicious cooking.

You can get almost anything done in Martinique ~ from galvanizing your boat to having stainless steel tanks made. The sailmakers are first rate, the chandleries magnificently stocked, and restaurants and boutiques abound. In short, when you have had enough deserted beaches and raw nature, Martinique is the place for a breath of civilization. And the island has enough excellent and varied anchorages for a week or two of exploring. Choose bays with fashionable resorts, sleepy waterfront villages, or visit deserted bays with excellent snorkeling. Well-marked trails make hiking a delight.

The Martinique Yachting Association aims to ensure you will have a wonderful visit. They are the voice of yachting in Martinique and they try to keep officialdom yacht friendly and see that there are adequate facilities. They speak good English, so call them if you have any questions about Martinique. If you need to get something done, or need help in dealings with authorities, they will put you in touch with a good professional service. They cannot help in trade disputes, as this is the realm of the tourist office, which you can visit in Marin Marina. They want your input as to what is good and bad and have a survey for this purpose on their web page. Let your feelings be known at: martiniqueyachtingassociation.fr

Empress Josephine grew up in Martinique on a 200-acre, 150-slave estate near Trois Ilets. A strange quirk of fate links Josephine and Martinique to the Battle of Trafalgar. In 1804, Napoleon was master of Europe, but the British still had naval supremacy and largely controlled Caribbean waters. However, ships were always scarce and some bright spark noticed that Diamond Rock on the south coast of Martinique was just about where the British would station another ves-

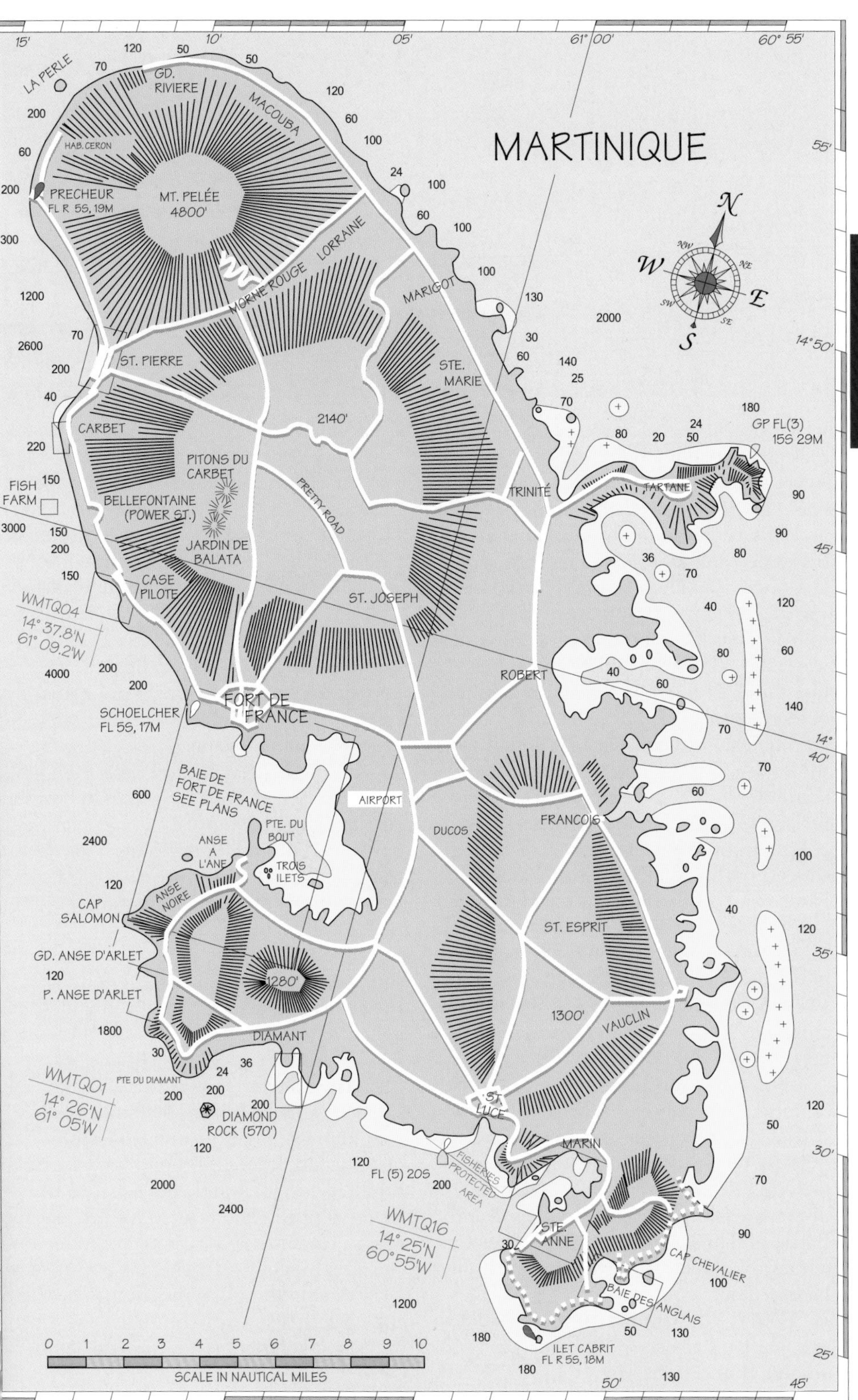
MARTINIQUE
MT. PELÉE
4800'
PRECHEUR
FL R 5S, 19M
HAB. CERON
GD. RIVIERE
MACOUBA
LA PERLE
MORNE ROUGE
LORRAINE
MARIGOT
ST. PIERRE
STE. MARIE
CARBET
2140'
PITONS DU CARBET
BELLEFONTAINE (POWER ST.)
JARDIN DE BALATA
PRETTY ROAD
TRINITÉ
TARTANE
GP FL(3) 15S 29M
FISH FARM
CASE PILOTE
ST. JOSEPH
WMTQ04
14° 37.8'N
61° 09.2'W
ROBERT
FORT DE FRANCE
SCHOELCHER
FL 5S, 17M
BAIE DE FORT DE FRANCE SEE PLANS
AIRPORT
PTE. DU BOUT
TROIS ILETS
ANSE A L'ANE
ANSE NOIRE
CAP SALOMON
DUCOS
FRANCOIS
ST. ESPRIT
GD. ANSE D'ARLET
P. ANSE D'ARLET
1280'
1300'
VAUCLIN
DIAMANT
PTE DU DIAMANT
WMTQ01
14° 26'N
61° 05'W
DIAMOND ROCK (570')
ST. LUCE
FL (5) 20S
FISHERIES PROTECTED AREA
MARIN
WMTQ16
14° 25'N
60° 55'W
STE. ANNE
CAP CHEVALIER
BAIE DES ANGLAIS
ILET CABRIT
FL R 5S, 18M
0 1 2 3 4 5 6 7 8 9 10
SCALE IN NAUTICAL MILES
N
S
E
W
NW
NE
SW
SE
15'
10'
05'
61° 00'
60° 55'
55'
14° 50'
45'
14° 40'
35'
30'
25'
50'
45'

Part of the estate where Josephine grew up.

sel if they had one, so they commissioned the rock as a ship. It was quite a feat to climb this steep, barren, snake-infested pinnacle and to equip it with cannons and enough supplies and water for a full crew of men. But they succeeded and for some 18 months H.M.S. Diamond Rock was a highly unpleasant surprise for unsuspecting ships sailing into Martinique. Napoleon was incensed; this was, after all, the birthplace of his beloved Josephine. Brilliant as he was on land, Napoleon never really understood his navy or its problems and considered his men to be shirkers. Consequently, he ordered them to sea under Admiral Villeneuve, to free the rock and destroy the British admiral Horatio Nelson while they were about it. Villeneuve slipped out under the British blockade of France and headed straight for Martinique. Lord Nelson smelled blood and bounty and hurtled off from England in hot pursuit. Poor information sent him on a wild goose chase to Trinidad, so Villeneuve was able to liberate the rock and return to France, prudently keeping well clear of Nelson.

Napoleon was none too pleased with Villeneuve because the British fleet was still in control of the high seas, so he was ordered to report in disgrace. Villeneuve preferred death to dishonor, so he put his ill-prepared fleet to sea to fight Nelson at the Battle of Trafalgar. Ironically, Villeneuve, who wished to die, survived the battle, and Nelson died.

Today Martinique is very civilized, and while it helps to speak French, it is not absolutely necessary. Many more locals now speak English.

Numerous ATM machines will keep you in cash, and most restaurants and businesses accept Visa and MasterCard. However, one or two only accept French cards. Ask before that seven-course meal or you may spend many hours washing dishes.

Navigation

The west coast (excluding the Bay of Fort de France) up to St. Pierre is mainly steep-to, and a quarter of a mile offshore clears any natural dangers.

Fish farms pop up off the coast from time to time. These are not dangerous by day but can be at night. They usually have flashing lights marking the outer limits. Currently, there is one off Bellefontaine with a clear passage inside or outside, approximate position 14° 40.2, 61° 10.2

The Bay of Fort de France has many shoals, especially at its eastern end. Check the charts and instructions given under the appropriate section.

The south coast of Martinique between Ste. Anne and Diamond Rock has several shoals extending up to a half mile offshore. Fish traps are plentiful and two or three are often tied together. It is best to stay in several hundred feet of water, outside the heavily fished area. The beat to Marin, usually against the current, is in protected water and can be exhilarating. It generally pays to tack fairly close to shore. On the rising tide, when the current sets east, the south coast can occasionally resemble a washing machine.

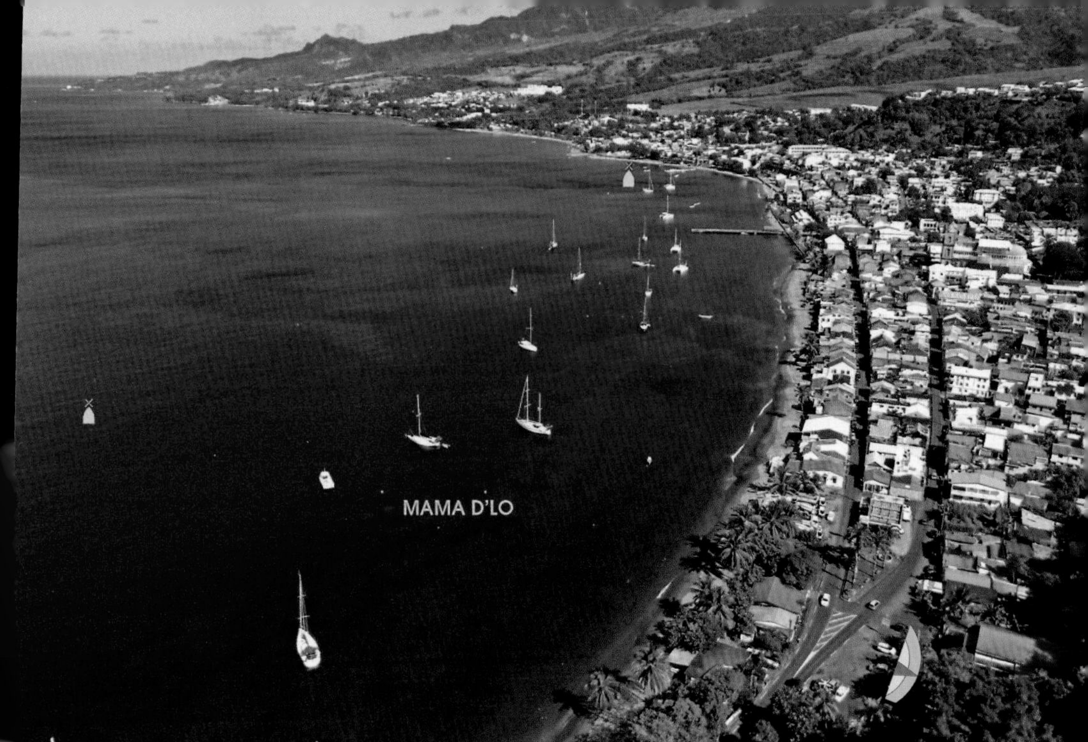

St. Pierre with visible anchorage zone buoys overlaid

ST. PIERRE

St. Pierre lies at the foot of the Mt. Pelée volcano, not far from where European settlers wiped out the last of the Carib residents in 1658. It is said that before the last ones died they uttered horrible curses, invoking the mountain to take its revenge. Mt. Pelée, in true Caribbean fashion, took its own sweet time, until Ascension Day, the 8th of May, in 1902.

At that time, St. Pierre, with a population of 30,000, was known as the Paris of the Caribbean and was the commercial, cultural, and social center of Martinique. The wealth of the island lay in the plantations and the richest of these surrounded St. Pierre. Ships would take on rum, sugar, coffee, and cocoa, and enough was sold to make several of the plantation owners multi-millionaires. There were also enough cheap bars, brothels, and dancing girls to satisfy the sailors.

The volcano gave some warning. Minor rumblings began early in April, and on April 23 a sizeable eruption covered the town in ash. Refugees from outlying villages started pouring in. On the 2nd of May a major eruption covered the city with enough ash to kill some birds and animals. Later the same day, Pierre Laveniere, a planter with an estate to the south of St. Pierre, went to inspect his crops with a party of workers and they were swept away by a vast avalanche of boiling volcanic mud. On the 5th of May, it was the turn of the Guerin Estate, just a couple of miles north of St. Pierre and one of the richest in the area. A torrent of volcanic effluent, including mud, lava, boiling gasses, and rocks, estimated to be a quarter of a mile wide and 100 feet high, completely buried the estate, much of the family and many workers.

Even before Ascension Day, many people had been killed in and around St. Pierre. So why did people stay? Evacuation posed huge problems, the roads were primitive and rough, and the ferries, the main form of transport, did not have the capacity.

Governor Mouttet, on the island for less than a year, desperately wanted the problem to go away and was encouraged to sit tight by most of the planters and business leaders who would have suffered financial losses if St. Pierre were evacuated. If he had gone against them, and the volcano had not gone off, his career would have been over. He formed a

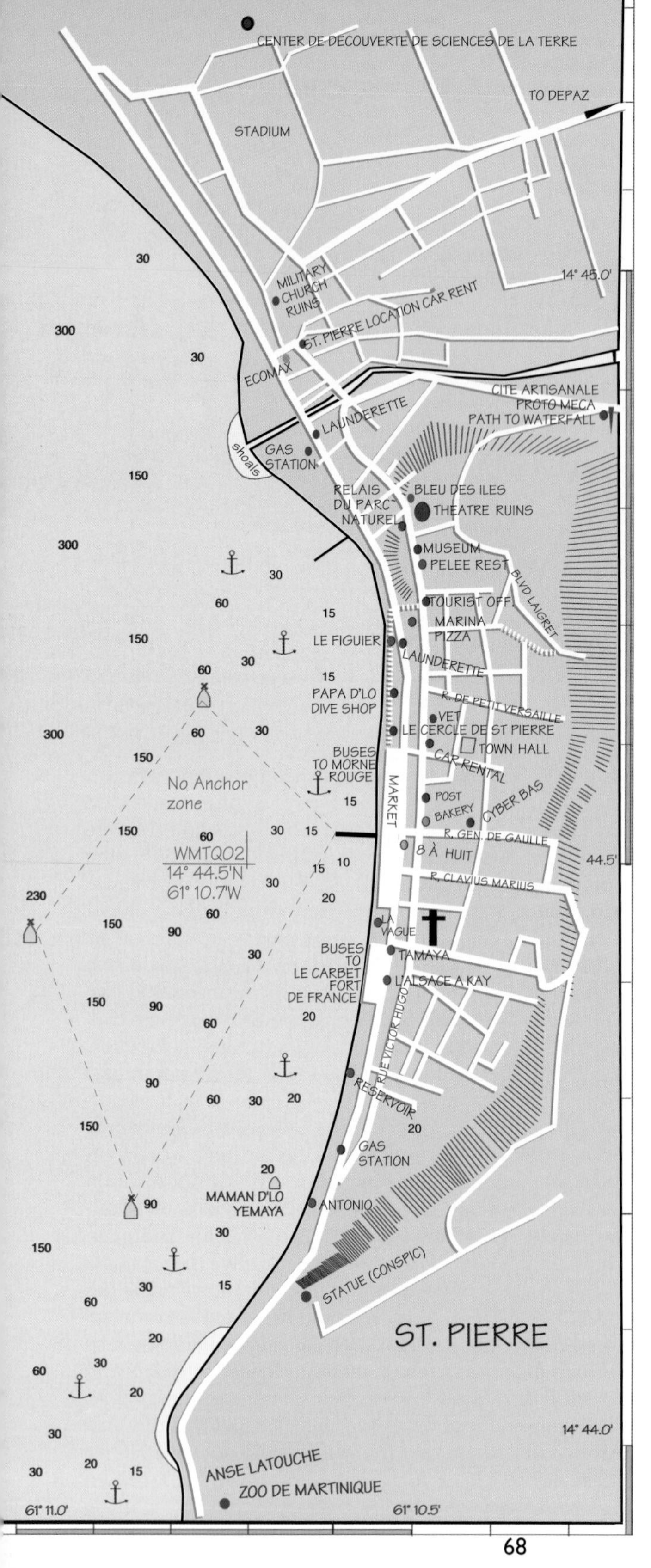

committee to assess the risk, led by the science teacher at the school, Professor Landes, and they concluded there was no danger, a premature conclusion, given the scant knowledge of volcanoes at the time.

Evacuation would also have affected the coming elections, in which black voters were seriously challenging the status quo for the first time. The local paper, *Les Colonies*, also did its best to persuade people that there was no danger, despite the deaths. Several hundred individuals had the sense to leave, but for the rest the destruction of such an important city was unimaginable.

Many were eyewitnesses to the disaster. People were approaching from Fort de France for the Ascension Day church service when they saw heavy, red smoke from the volcano descend on St. Pierre. Rather than continue, they climbed the surrounding hills to see what would happen next. The end came at two minutes past eight in the morning. The side of the volcano facing St. Pierre glowed red and burst open, releasing a giant fireball of superheated gas that flowed down over the city, releasing more energy than an atomic bomb. All that remained were smoking ruins. An estimated 29,933 people burned to death, leaving only two survivors in the center of town: Leon Compere-Leandre, a cobbler, and the famous Louis-Auguste Cyparis, imprisoned for murder in a stone cell. Twelve ships in the bay were destroyed at anchor. One managed to limp away with a few survivors.

Looking over the theater ruins (left) and the police station ruin where Cyparis jail stands (right).

Many ruins still remain. Post-disaster buildings have been built onto old structures, so many new buildings share at least one wall with the past. Ruins also form garden walls, and some have been tidied up as historical icons. A museum in a modern building depicts that era and the tragedy. It stands on top of old walls that are artistically lit up at night, making an enchanting backdrop for those anchored below. (You can read a more detailed history on doyleguides.com.)

Navigation

St. Pierre makes a good overnight anchorage except when there are heavy northerly swells. There is an adequate shelf on which to anchor, about 25 feet deep, the drop-off is steep, so make sure you are well hooked. Occasionally, you have to move for local fishermen.

A series of yellow buoys, each with a cross on top, designate a no-anchoring area to protect the dive-site wrecks. The wrecks are also buoyed. The anchoring shelf gets wider round at Anse Latouche, so there is plenty of room.

A conspicuous statue on the hill at the southern end of town is lit at night.

Regulations/communication

St. Pierre is a port of entry. L'Alsace a Kay is the closest place to clear with a customs computer. Closed Thursday they otherwise open at 1030 till 1700 except Mondays, Tuesdays, Fridays and Saturdays when they are open till 2200. Most restaurants have WiFi, but L'Alsace a Kay is choice with a fabulous upstairs dining room overlooking the harbor. Go mid-morning or afternoon between meals. They are also a restaurant and shop (see *Provisioning and Restaurants*).

You can check in at the tourist office, on the east side of the road just south of the museum. They open weekdays 0800-1200, 1400-1600.

Cyber Base (closed Mondays) is a big internet station, open 0900-1300.

General yacht services

Tie your dinghy towards the inner end of the main dock. Do not use the outer end. Charter yachts come alongside the outer end during the day, and a giant ferry comes once a week to the north side. Do your wash at one

of two laundromats, the smaller waterfront one or the larger one near the river mouth.

Restaurant LE TAMAYA
0596 78 29 09
MENU
RESTAURANT
LE TAMAYA
WiFi
Saint Pierre
When you reach the road from the dinghy dock, turn right, we are on your left three blocks away
Open for lunch every day. except Wednesday
Open for dinner from 1830 every day except in low season closed Tuesday.
Peggy and Jean-Luc welcome you! We speak French, English, German and Italian.
Phone: 0596 78 29 09
+ 596-596 78 29 09

Technical yacht services

Proto Meca is in the Cité Artisanale on the edge of town. Proto Meca is owned and run by Jean-Michel Trébeau, who trained as an aviation machinist in France and now has a first-rate shop. Anything you can break, he can fix, be it in stainless, aluminum, or bronze. He welds these metals and does all kinds of machining. He can rebuild your engine and resurface the block.

If you are having a really bad day, a coffin maker is in the same area.

Provisioning/shopping

The waterfront area has been renovated and includes an elegant replica of the old financial center. There are a couple of banks, several ATMs (the one at the post office is reliable), pharmacies, and a convenient 8 à Huit supermarket that closes for lunch and half an hour earlier than its name suggests. It also opens Sunday mornings. This is a good and quite large supermarket, but half of it is upstairs, so make sure you visit both floors. Most other businesses and shops close Saturday afternoon.

The morning market offers a variety of reasonably priced produce and is best on Saturdays. You sometimes get a couple of vendors on Sunday mornings. The fish market is just below and sometimes open. Good bread and pâtisseries can be found at three bakeries on the back street. L'Alsace a Kay, a gourmet store, has lots of specialty foods mainly from Alsace, including St. Pierre beer, which comes from St. Pierre in Alsace in man-sized bottles. It is also a restaurant.

Ecomax supermarket is inexpensive with a limited range. Clothing boutiques, souvenir shops, and places selling local fabrics abound.

Restaurants

St. Pierre has lots of restaurants, several open for both lunch and dinner. Le Tamaya [$$] is an excellent little French restaurant, smart and clean, with nautical decor, and both the food and presentation rank considerably higher than the very reasonable prices charged (a good two-course menu starts at about 15 Eu), making it one of the best restaurants to visit in Martinique. It opens daily for lunch and dinner except Wednesday when it closes for dinner. It is owned by Peggy and Jean-Luc who are welcoming and who sailed the Atlantic and cruised the Caribbean. Seafood is always available, as are delicious desserts. Peggy speaks excellent English as well as German, French and some Italian. They open for lunch and reopen for dinner at 1830. They have WiFi, but this is not an internet cafe (see *Communications*).

Philippe Mehn's L'Alsace a Kay [$$$$] has a lovely upstairs dining room overlooking the bay. When you enter, you sit in lounging chairs while you can take an apéritif and order. They call you to the table when it is ready. They specialize in cuisine from Alsace, which has a strong German influence. The meals are hearty and delicious. (My only regret is I had no room for dessert.) They are closed Thursdays but otherwise open daily for lunch, when in addition to the regular menu, they often have an in-

St. Pierre, with Mt. Pelee free of clouds

expensive special. They open for dinner on Mondays, Tuesdays, Fridays, and Saturdays. You often need a reservation.

Gerard's Bleu des Iles [$$] is right next to the old theater ruins; you climb a few steps to get to the door, which is above the road. They have a terrace with a good view of Mt. Pelée and a glimpse of the sea. This is a simple, but very nice French-Créole restaurant that offers a tasty local lunch menu every day except Thursday, when they close. Their fish and christophene au gratin is very good. They stay open for dinner on Monday, Tuesday, Friday and Saturday.

Two restaurants opened in 2016 on the new waterfront promenade. Le Cercle de Sainte-Pierre [$$] is an authentic Breton crêperie and glacier, friendly and good. It opens 1130-1430 and 1800-2100, Tuesday to Saturday. Le Figuier [$] is a pizzeria that also serves Créole food.

Caraibes is popular come sunset, with its tables right out on the street. They serve meals and sometimes have entertainment. Next door is Tai Loong, a Chinese snack bar. On the west side of the road, La Vague [$$] has an impressive waterfront location and you can enjoy an inexpensive Créole meal here.

Heading south are two restaurants with doors on the road and dining rooms on the beach; both offer a perfect view. Le Reservoir [$$] is a little grill and crêperie. The owners are welcoming and they open at about 1130 and stay open in the evening. They work hard and serve good food from a little kitchen. Antonio Restaurant is farther down, near the gas station. They close Thursdays but are otherwise open every day 1130-1530. On Monday, Wednesday, Friday, and Saturday they open for dinner 1900-2130. They are reasonably priced and serve traditional Créole food.

Marina Pizza [$] is a pizza/pasta place and an ice cream parlor, open in the evening. Be guided by the aroma as the sign has gone. Delice Pierrotin serves fast food during the day including takeaway.

More restaurants open just for lunch. Chez Marie-Claire [$$] and Le Guerin [$] are upstairs in the restored market and both serve inexpensive local Créole food. Up on the hill by the museum at Pelée [$] you can eat out under awnings overlooking the harbor.

Ashore

Pet lovers can find a recommended vet, Dr. Patrick Arien, at 159 Rue Bouille (not far from the dock) (0596) 78 10 03.

St. Pierre sits amid the most magnificent scenery in Martinique, so if you are thinking of sightseeing, this is an excellent place to begin. Rental cars are available from St. Pierre Location and Bethel-Loc, but you need to book long in advance. The tourist office may be able to help.

Visit the tourist office, ask for maps of St. Pierre that show most of the historical monuments and you will be able to make your own walking tour. Get a hiking map for

Martinique and ask for details of particular hikes. The tourist map will get you to the start of the hiking trails, and more detailed maps of the trails are posted by the trail parking areas.

The museum on the hill is dedicated to the 1902 eruption. It opens daily 0900-1200 and 1500-1700. There is an admission charge. It was started by Le Clerk, who escaped St. Pierre just before the eruption, and is now somewhat dated. The much newer Centre de Decouverte des Sciences de la Terre gives a clearer view of the events of 1902 and is about a 20-minute walk. Go to Economax and take a curious lane that runs from its north side. A big rock overhangs the lane at the top. Follow this past the old military church ruins until it turns to dirt, and keep going till you get to a major road. Turn right and the Museum is right ahead, just past the Stadium. It is closed Monday but otherwise opens at 0930. The entry fee is about 5 Eu. Pick up an English speaking player which will describe everything to you. Upstairs, ask them to add English subtitles to the next movie, and take a seat, you will feel you experienced the deadly eruption. You are now half-way to Distillerie Depaz (see below), so you can keep going.

Two of the most interesting places to visit in town are the theater ruins beyond the museum and the prison where Cyparis was jailed, which is just below the theater (no charge).

For the energetic, there is a great walk (about an hour round trip) up to the statue of the Virgin Mary, which has the best view of St. Pierre. Our map shows the way.

It is a 45-minute walk to Distillerie Depaz, and those used to hiking can make it. As an incentive, visiting is free and they give you rum to taste. The distillery is in lovely grounds set against Mt. Pelée as a backdrop and is open weekdays 1000 to 1700, Saturdays 0900-1600. (You can visit on Sundays but no rum shop for tasting.) The machinery is run by a steam engine and this is a perfect place to learn why that French white rum makes such distinctive petit punch. You can spend a long time wandering around and stay for lunch [$$$] at the restaurant, perfectly situated on a hill overlooking cane fields to the sea beyond. Make sure to visit the magnificent old plantation house. You can go inside (5 Eu fee) Tuesday to Friday 1000-1600, Saturday 0900-1530. They close for lunch for half an hour at 1300.

Zoo de Martinique in Habitation Latouche started as a garden among the ruins of a big estate that was built in 1650 and destroyed by the volcano in 1902. They added a zoo (and pirate house) to increase the appeal. It is very close, about a 10-minute walk on a busy road. As you leave the town heading south, the road follows one headland then comes to a beach. The garden is behind this beach. You could dinghy there. It is a wonderful excursion, designed by Jean Philippe Those, who created Jardin de Balata. You walk one-way, mainly on a raised wooden path, that takes you through lovely gardens amid ruins. They have a variety of animals, though the huge walk-in aviaries are best, with some great rosy flamingos and scarlet ibis in one and the other is a giant aviary of very tame Australian lorikeets that will likely land on your hat. It takes an hour or two, so you will be happy to end at a good, inexpensive snack bar. They open every day 0900-1700, entry fee is about 15 Eu.

St. Pierre has a lovely little waterfall, with a small pool just deep enough to sit in and cool off. Take the dirt road to the right just after the Cite Artisanale and follow it till it turns into a path and a gate. Go through the gate and continue. The Relais du Parc Naturel have a plan for a park and garden here. In the meantime, although it is not an official attraction, nothing stops you from visiting.

Relais du Parc Regional Naturel de la Martinique, just north of the museum, is the place to visit for information on parks and trails for St. Pierre and the rest of the island. You can pick up maps, ask questions, and buy locally made goodies like jams, honey, woven articles, and souvenirs. They show a movie (free) about the history of St. Pierre and you can book from a variety of guided tours in the town and surrounding countryside. They open Tuesday to Saturday 0930-1400. Visit before you try the attractions below and ask about conditions as the Canal and northern route were closed early 2018.

In the mountains to the south of St. Pierre, there is an extraordinary walk along the Canal de Beauregard. Built by slaves in 1760, this canal brought water around a steep mountain to supply the distilleries of St. Pierre. It is most interesting to start at the bottom end of the canal and walk towards the source. The canal is fairly level, often shady and easy, but you must have a head for heights, for you walk along the outer canal wall, which is about 18 inches wide, and the panoramic views are often dizzyingly precipitous.

If you drive past Precheur till the road ends, a footpath continues to Grand Rivière on the north coast.

If the weather is clear, ambitious hikers can head up Mt. Pelée. A road takes you within a mile and a half of the summit. Turn right just at the entrance to Precheur on the Chameuse Road. Non-hikers can enjoy the view from the top of the road.

For a scenic drive, the rainforest starts behind St. Pierre and the road up to the conspicuous volcanic observatory is impressive.

Gorges de la Falaise are dramatic waterfalls in a narrow canyon on the east side of Mt. Pelée. The hike takes about an hour and a half from the entrance and it is closed in heavy rains.

Water sports

Snorkeling is surprisingly interesting on the grass in the anchorage and off the pier. Baby reef fish hang out in the grass, as do snake eels and trumpet fish.

Snorkel, too, on Maman d'Lo, an underwater sculpture in about 15 feet of water, about 50 yards off the beach in front of Antionio Beach restaurant, and marked by a big yellow buoy inside the smaller ones around (clearly seen in our aerial photo). It is a Siren lying in the sand, partly submerged, made by Laurent Valere in 2004. A little sister called Yemaya (several tons, in 3 parts; head, buttocks and tail), belted, with a conch crown, just joined her in 2015 in her mission to protect the sanctuary of the Bay of Saint-Pierre.

Twelve wrecks of ships that sank in the tragedy of 1902 are nearby, most within dinghy range of the anchorage, and at depths

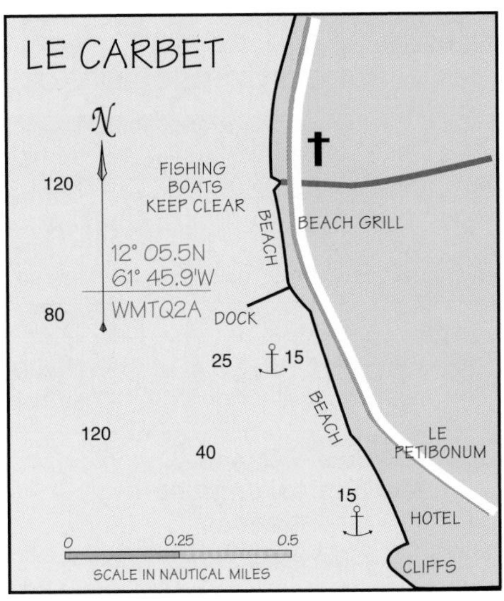

from 30 to 150 feet. The best way to find them is to dive with a local dive shop. Otherwise, watch the local dive boats, which visit them frequently (most of the wrecks are now buoyed). In addition, the north coast has the best diving in Martinique, with dramatic walls, canyons, and reefs, and many more fish than you find farther south.

If you are diving on your own, there is an easy dive right off the beach in front of the big wall under the museum. It is a good reef, dropping from 40 to 90 feet, decorated with old anchors, a huge old chain draped over the coral, and plenty of fish.

Papa D'Lo is a good dive shop, on the front street north of the main dock. Owner Serge Rueff will take you on a good wreck dive. Surcouf, is another dive shop at the south end of town, just past the gas station. They will fill tanks.

Amphitrite, 0696 80 38 62, is a business that will find you dolphins and does fishing tours.

LE CARBET

Carbet is a small town on the headland just south of the bay of St. Pierre. You do not want to be here in northerly swells, but otherwise it makes a reasonable lunch stop, and in suitable conditions you could overnight. Edge quite close to the beach south of the dock. Some people like to anchor all the way down off the hotel in the south. Use the dock for your dinghy with a stern anchor to keep you clear, or beach it.

The attraction is a lovely beach on which there are several restaurants. Two of these are worth special mention.

Just north of the dock, Beach Grill [$$$] is right on the beach (the floor is sand) and open to the sea. The food is good, and the generous portions are artistically presented. They open for lunch Tuesday to Sunday and for dinner Wednesday to Saturday.

At the south end, Le Petibonum [$$$$] is famous for excellent food, more gourmet style, served right on the beach, and they open every day for lunch and dinner. Either can be crowded, so reservations are a good idea.

Art lovers should see the museum about Gauguin on the road towards St. Pierre. It includes letters, documents, artifacts, and reproductions of Gauguin paintings.

CASE-PILOTE

Case-Pilote is a picturesque fishing port, both charming and unspoiled, with Martinique's oldest church. With new restaurants and a ferry it has become a happening place, popular for lunch on the weekends, but not yet a tourist hot spot. The ferry to Fort de France is frequent and inexpensive (about Eu 5 return), so if you prefer to hang out in a peaceful place and take the ferry to town it is perfect.

You can anchor outside the port but leave room for the ferry. Fishermen occasionally put out seine nets at about 0600 hours, and may wake you to ask them you to move. It is not every day, but do move willingly and right away, if asked. If that worries you, stop for lunch on your way up or down.

Regulations/Services

The ferry runs to and from Fort de France on the hour from 0600-0900, 1030, 1200, 1430, 1630, 1730 and 1900. They leave half an hour earlier from Fort de France.

There are no customs in Case-Pilote; clear elsewhere. You can leave your dinghy in the port. You will find garbage bins around the port or the village. A small Maxi Peche

Case-Pilote

in the marina sells fishing gear and ice, but they cannot supply yachts with fuel. For that and for diesel, you will have to jug it from the gas station. You can call for a renatl car: 0696 27-40-51/ 34-52-33

People come here to visit Frank Ågren's Inboard Diesel Service, which is right at the entrance to the port. Frank is the regional headquarters for Volvo Penta for much of the Eastern Caribbean and does Volvo surveys and diagnostics up and down the islands. He also does warranty work. His big shop has a whole floor devoted to spares and he has the largest stock in the Windwards. He can supply spares at somewhat lower prices than you might pay elsewhere and shipping parts to other Caribbean islands is no problem. Beatrice, in his office, takes care of this. Frank has a hotline to the factory and, being Swedish, he speaks the same language as the engine, so anyone having Volvo Penta problems should give him a call. Frank and his team are o a fully qualified sales and service agency for Northern Lights Generators and MTU engines, which should help the large yachts. Those visiting Frank can come inside the port, where he has about three reserved spaces with free WiFi. Frank speaks perfect English. A large supply of new and secondhand spares is kept in stock, as are new engines and generators. Inboard Diesel Service has fast service boats and can, if necessary, visit other ports and islands. Frank has a shop in Marin and

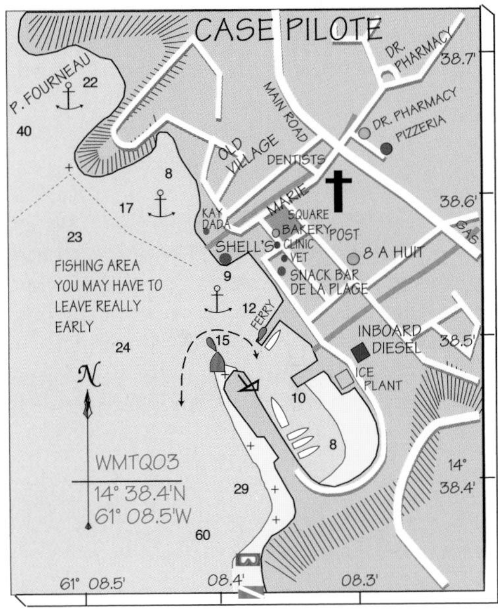

Volvo associates in most other islands, he can take care of you anywhere from Grenada to Antigua.

Restaurants

Snack Bar de La Plage [$] is a lovely authentic Creole restaurant on the waterfront. Owner Max specializes in seafood, and his fish can be excellent and the prices are great. It is open Monday to Saturday for lunch and sometimes in season for dinner. Recently it has become very popular so go early.

Shell's [$$$$] is flashy and new, with beach day beds, a high up platform and other intriguing hideaway spots, with cooling misters outside. It is designed to entice you to hang out in comfort all day. Their menu is upmarket. They open 1200-1400, 1900-2200, closed Sunday evening.

Kay DADA [$] is a fisherman's bar and occasional hot spot a few steps further north. It is sometimes open.

A new seafood restaurant is nearing completion opposite the fishing dock

Ashore

Case-Pilote is one of the oldest villages in Martinique, founded around 1640 when the church was built. Now a historical monument, the exterior of the building is particularly beautiful, with its brand new tiled roof and the newly renovated Presbytery beside it. Inside, you will notice that the architecture of the church leaves you no doubt that Case-Pilote has always been turned toward the sea. In the cemetery behind the old church is the final resting place of Victor Severe, born in Case-Pilote in 1867 and the deputy for Martinique who led the cause for liberation in the French Assembly. He participated in the French resistance and died in 1957 at the age of 90.

Although fishing is the major economic activity, market gardening takes place on level areas. Lettuce, tomatoes and herbs as well as cabbages and local root vegetables thrive, and everyone owns chickens. (There is even a memorial to a favorite cock in one of the tombs.)

The fruit and vegetable market opens on Fridays from 1600. They also sell local liquors and syrups like coco punch. Sometimes an accras truck will be selling hot, fresh accras and doughnuts. The Town Hall Cultural attaché sometimes organizes an art exposition and fairs for local artists.

For topping up provisions, visit 8 à Huit, open Monday to Saturday 0700-2000. They also open Sundays and holidays in the morning.

Across the main road from the church is a small shopping center. Here you will

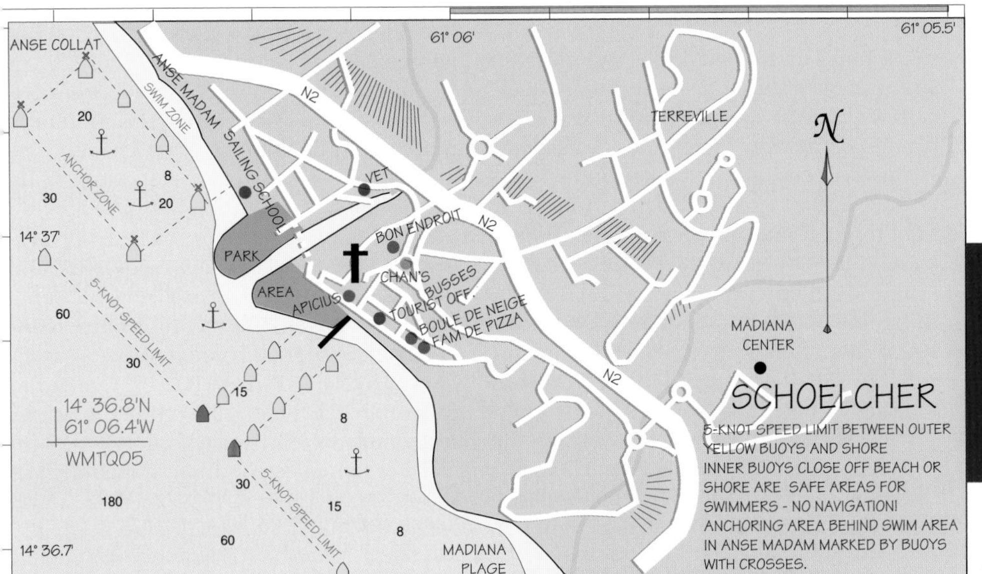

find a pharmacy, a doctor upstairs from the pharmacy (no appointment necessary: just wait your turn), and Remy Pizza. Enjoy the bakery. It has a splendid little Parisian-style terrace for that morning coffee and croissant

Opposite the shopping center is another small collection of buildings in which a second doctor is located. Fletchons, a more modern pharmacy, is on a side road to the left just after the N2 takes a curve when heading towards Fort de France.

This is a convenient place for pet owners to come for a vet. You will find Dr. Fournier at 2, Rue Schoelcher, (0596) 69 38 91, emergency: (0696) 01 84 48. A new health services building opposite the veterinarian is occupied by a physical therapist, and a nurse who can take blood tests. Three dentists work out of the same building on Rue Allegre, up from the Town Hall

Water sports

Diving and snorkeling off the headland just south of the marina are good. Huge rocks rise from 70 feet and the whole area is filled with brightly colored sponges, corals, and fish. If you don't have your own gear, contact the Case-Pilote Diving Club. For those interested in wildlife, there is a bat cave in the cliffs behind the snorkeling area.

If you want to see dolphins check out Amphitrite on the dock (0696 80 38 62).

SCHOELCHER

Originally Case Navire, this town was famous for the water provided by its two rivers, making it a vital rest stop for ships of old. It was renamed after Victor Schoelcher, the anti-slavery advocate, and now covers a large area, bisected by the west coast highway N2. The waterfront part is easily accessible to yachts and has the atmosphere of a tiny town on its own. It is a less urban anchorage than Fort de France, with pleasant beaches. Buses run to Fort de France frequently; it takes 15 minutes. It is easier here than in Fort de France to rent a car and organize shopping runs or trips to the mountains. The tourist office will help you.

The official anchoring area off Anse Madam is marked on our chart. All buoys were missing in 2018 except for the channel into the dock. People still anchor off the renovated waterfront and beach south of the dock. If you do that, be prepared to move if fishermen or officials ask you to. You can tie your dinghy to the town dock, though you will need a dinghy anchor. The waterfront adjoining the dock is a park area. Anse Madam has a long beach and is home to one of the largest and best sailing schools in the area. You can also pull your dinghy up here and tie it to a tree.

Ashore

Chan's is a good little supermarket within easy walking distance of the dock. O Bon Endroit, evenings only is a tapas bar and restaurant. The beachside Boule de Neige [$] opens early for coffee and sells ice creams, crepes and sandwiches from 0900 right through into the evening. Fan de Pizza [$] next door opens in the evening for good pizza and grilled foods. Apicius [$$] is an entertaining Italian restaurant, evenings only. It gets full, so book: 0596 78 44 73.

The Madiana Center is also within walking distance for the reasonably energetic. This entertainment center has the best cinema in Martinique. (On Thursdays they show movies in their original language.) One of the restaurants here will delight pub aficionados, as it has a microbrewery on site with good beer.

For a major provisioning, you will need a cab or a car to visit the huge malls on the road to Fort de France. Or try Leader Price at Terreville. Go out of town and straight up the hill on the road to L'Enclos.

L'Ajoupa Deux Gros lies in a bay halfway between the town of Shoelcher and Case-Pilote. There is no problem anchoring there, but forget landing on the little concrete wall or the beach if there are any swells. However, if you do make it (a big tender can do so from either port), it is one of the fancier restaurants in Martinique.

Pet owners can find a recommended vet shown on our chart (0596) 61 05 08, emergency (0696) 27 17 47 called Veto-Dom.

Fort de France from Fort St. Louis

FORT DE FRANCE

Fort de France, the capital of Martinique, is the largest and liveliest city in the Windwards. It is a great place for shops, restaurants, and people-watching. It has a pleasant city anchorage under Fort St. Louis, opposite the park and close by the public beach, which is well used most days. The new waterfront has a huge boardwalk where bouncing waves whistle below. This is also the dinghy dock and it leads onto a great kids' playground. In the late afternoon kids come to play, people hang out, and vendors set up on the roadside with snack foods and drinks. If you are puzzled by the turnstiles on the way out, they are to keep obnoxious kids from zooming up and down the boardwalk on scooters.

Occasionally, kids play in dinghies and damage them. If worried, the higher dock to the west of the dinghy dock, and first part of the dock beyond that are probably safer.

In town, the central Rue de la République has been converted into a delightful pedestrian street and the large Cours Perrinon Mall is right in town. Those wanting to explore Martinique can take advantage of the many buses that use the capital as their hub. You are close to chandleries and many yacht services.

Navigation

When approaching Fort de France from Cap Salomon, it is hard to see at a glance exactly where the harbor is, as the surrounding area is built up, including a huge hotel and some apartment blocks at Schoelcher, a couple of miles west of Fort de France. As you approach, you can identify the main yacht anchorage by the prominent slab-sided fort wall, the big new turquoise circular office tower, and the yachts at anchor.

The yacht anchorage is on the east side of the bay, between Fort St. Louis and a line between the red and yellow buoys in the center of the bay. Leave the red buoy to starboard to avoid the isolated rocky shoal

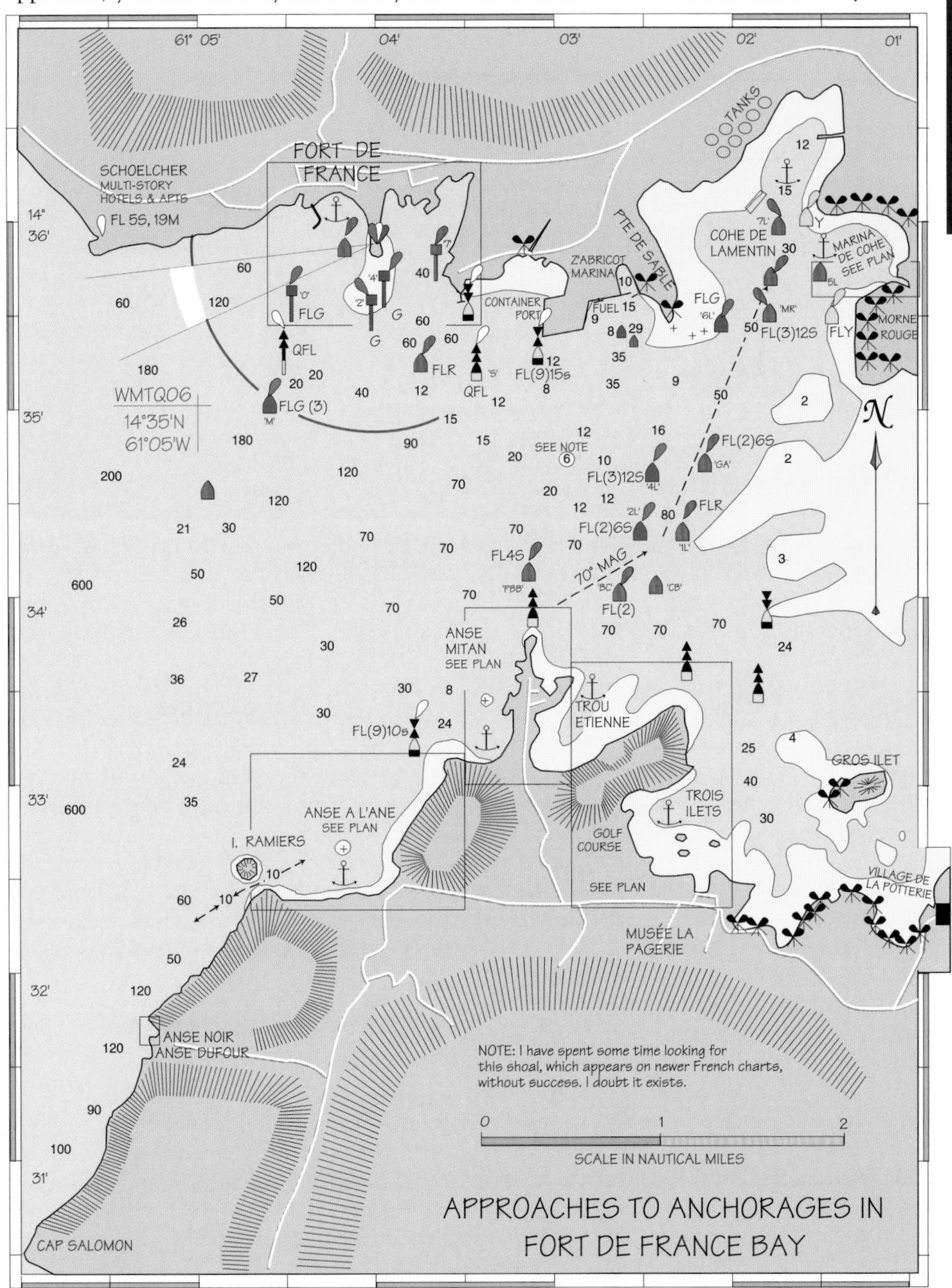

to its southeast. Charts show only about 5 feet on this shoal. I could not find any depths much less than 7 feet, but there may be shallower rocks (see chart page 83).

The water is shallow and rocky if you get close to Fort St. Louis, but level in many areas once the depth reaches about 9 feet. The anchorage is deeper (25-40 feet) towards the center of the bay for deep-draft yachts. Holding in the bay is good when you hit clay-like sand, variable in soft mud. Fort de France is connected to Case-Pilote, Anse Mitan, Anse à L'Ane, and Trois Ilets by frequent ferries, which make the anchorage rolly from time to time.

If you need work done, you can find a work berth in the Baie des Tourelles. (Make arrangements in advance and give cruise ships wide clearance.) If you are heading east to get there or southeast toward Anse Mitan, keep well clear of the shoals off the fort. It is possible to cut somewhat inside the green buoys, but to be on the safe side, go around them.

Marina Z'Abricots is a good new marina serving Fort de France and is by Pte. du Sable. See our section on *The Industrial Zones*. If you visit Fort de France by car, the easiest pay parking is one of the many Vinci-parking lots. There is one in the block next to Sea Services.

Regulations

Clearing in and out is easy in Sea Services. Fill the form out on the customs computer, print your clearance, and have one of the staff stamp it. You can peruse the chandlery at the same time (open weekdays 0830-1715; Saturdays 0830-1230). Or you can dinghy to the DCML fuel dock, open 0800-1800, Sundays and holidays 0900-1500.

Communications

The Marie has a Cyber Base in the lovely old Pavillon Bougenot building on Rue Victor Severe. Closed Monday, they open 0900-1600 on Tuesday and Wednesday, 1300-1600 on Thursday, and 0900-1200 on Friday and Saturday. Turn left at the Schoelcher Library and look opposite the

police station. It can be crowded. You can call 0596 55 68 48 for reservations. Another called SAAPE is not far away on Rue Felix Eboue, open 0830-1200, 1330-1730

Lina's cafe has comfy seating, air-conditioning, great coffee, and is perfect for WiFi.

General yacht services

A good dinghy dock lies all along La Savanne. Small litter bins line the dock. Bigger tips are on Rue Déproge, but since they have wheels, check out the location before carting in garbage.

DCML is a good fuel dock in Baie des Tourelles. It is a low floating dock so you may need to deploy a ladder to get down. They offer fuel, water, oils, beer, coffee, cube and chipped ice, lunch sandwiches, and sundry items. This is the easiest place to get ice in Fort de France. They open 0800-1800 daily except Sundays and holidays 0900-1500. They may close earlier in the summer. Charter yachts qualify for duty-free when they have cleared out. Take the boat down or, for small things, dinghy down.

Marina Z'Abricots has a fuel dock on the outer marina wall. It is a low floating dock, substantially built with 9 feet of water alongside. They sell diesel, gasoline and ice, but no duty free.

La Laverie de la Pointe, is open from 0645 to 2200 seven days a week. Washers for 7, 11 or 14 kilos of laundry and dryers vary in price from 7 to 10 euros.

You cannot get gas tanks filled in Martinique. In an emergency, buy a small new French butane tank at a snack store beside the fire station on Blvd Admiral Gueydon. Continue along the canal to see Fontaine Gueydon, once part of the water

system and now a monument.

Barnacles bugging you? Need a new stainless fuel tank? The yacht services compound in Baie des Tourelles should solve your problems. You can dinghy there, bring the yacht, or check it out on foot. The walk to Quai des Tourelles is about 15 minutes from town. Head past Quai Ouest on the main road out of town heading east. Turn right immediately after the big, new buildings on the right side of the road. Follow the road and turn left when you come to a junction. This leads you to the new basin. At the heart of this compound is a haul-out run by Carenantilles, who have a larger facility in Marin. If you need to come alongside ask about depth. The haul-out has a 35-ton marine hoist that can haul boats about 1.9 meters deep. Artisans and engineers can do everything you need. Small boats can be stored on racks. Language is not a problem, as most people speak some English.

If you are too long, wide, heavy, or ugly to haul elsewhere, you can arrange to be slipped alongside a ship in the huge Martinique dry dock, which will take anything up to a cruise ship (see also *Marin Services*).

Chandlery

Sea Services, on Rue Déproge, is one of Martinique's largest chandleries. It is owned by Christophe Sirodot who worked for some years in the US. Valerie, the manager, has been here the longest and speaks English, as do most of the other staff, and all are attentive.

Sea Services is really two adjoining stores. The western store sells yacht gear, including International Paints, 3-M products, 316 stainless fasteners, tenders, liferafts, stoves, anchors, barbecues, charts, and guides. Their rope stock includes the new ropes that replace wire for rigging. They stock a good range of electrical equipment, from wire and connectors to solar panels, windlasses, and Aerogen wind generators, as well as a good stock of yacht electronics. They are big on Matt Chem cleaners in both yacht and commercial sizes, also Aquasale biodegradable products, including soaps. They have a full rigging service from a dinghy locking line upwards. Their on-the-spot swaging works for up to 12mm wire and they do larger diameters by order. They sell and service inflatable life jackets. Sea Services regularly delivers antifouling paint to all Martinique haul-out facilities, and can arrange haul-out quantities duty-free for visiting yachts for use in Martinique or to take away.

The eastern part of Sea Services features decorative nautical objets d'art, tableware, and linens, but most of all a wide selection of good nautical casual and sportswear, including St. James, and TBS. Many superyachts come here to outfit the crew with shorts and shirts. They also have goodies for kids, microfiber products, elegant soft towels, non-skid molded shoes with removable soles, and all kinds of carriers, from backpacks to wallets.

You will find other chandleries in the Baie de Tourelles Carenantilles, an easy dinghy ride away. Max and Cedric's Polymar is a big chandlery, and very strong on construction materials. It has a stock of ropes, fittings, lots of fishing gear, including commercial equipment, yacht hardware,

and general accessories. Polymar sells many products for projects, including marine and teak ply, which can be bought cut to size (they often have a box of off cuts for sale that may be perfect for a project), resins, gel coat, cores, foams, cloths, and paints (including the International line).They sell and service Lecomble Schmitt hydraulics. They have a good selection of hinges and other fittings, also steering seats and pedestals. This is a good place to look at electrics and electronics, sound systems, speakers, gauges, and bilge pumps. Polymar is also the place to get your scuba tanks filled. You can talk to them about glass repair. They have stores in Marin and Robert.

Maxipeche near Polymar, is a giant fishing store, both sports and commercial with some yacht gear, mainly ropes, lights and electrical bits.

Back in town, Anniepeche on Boulevard Allegre is a small fishing store.

Technical yacht services

Most yacht services are to be found at the Carenantilles compound in Baie des Tourelles.

Marc Eugene at Renovboat has a mobile workshop and can work anywhere, but does much of his work in the haul out yards in

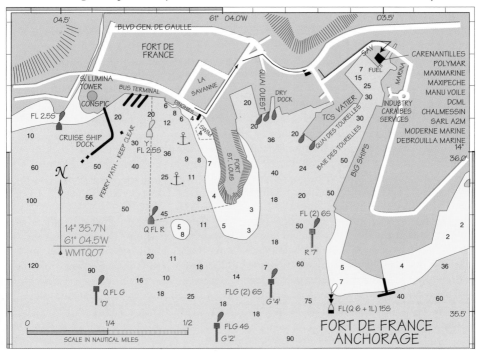

FORT DE FRANCE ANCHORAGE

both Fort de France and Marin. He speaks English and has trained in both the US and France.

He does marine electric and electronics repairs, including battery charge systems, inverters, windlasses, bow thrusters, GPS, and autopilots. If you are going on a dock he can rent you marine isolation transformers to cope with 110 Volts/ 60 Cycles. Marc can bring in parts from the USA and Europe fast and he understands the problems of crossing electrical systems. He is an agent for Ocean Volts motors and can also fix fridges

Marc is a marine surveyor and ABYC member. It is easiest to contact him by phone (0696-25-01-92).

Jean Pierre and François Chalmessin can work wonders with titanium (one of the few places that can weld it), stainless, and aluminum, including welding, bending, building, and machining. Whether you have a broken winch or want a new pulpit or water tank, they can do it. They can fix most marine cooking stoves.

Emanuel Plisson's Sarl A2M is another large metal shop a few doors down with TIG and MIG welders, and they can fabricate anything in aluminum and stainless.

Manu Voile is a sailmaking shop owned by Emmanuel Resin, who has sewn sails as long as I have written guides. He has help and can tackle anything from new sails (any size) to repairs, biminis, and cushions. Their location, right on the waterfront, is convenient for unloading sails. They also make lazy bags for the mainsail and are open weekdays 0800-1300 and 1430-1800 and can collect and deliver.

Bellance at Debrouilla Marine specializes in household and marine electronic and electric work They also fix Mercury outboards, They have a small retail shop, which includes killer speakers and LED lights. They also sell and maintain boat lifts.

Maxi Marine has a magnificent showroom and workshop. They are agents for Mercury outboards and Mercruiser inboards, which they sell, install, and repair. They are also sales and repair agents for Nanni Diesel. They own MaxiPeche, described under chandlery.

Moderne Marine on the canal side of the buildings service Mercruiser inboard diesels, and being close to the water can hoist them in and out of the boat. These services are all in Carenantilles. Just outside are two more.

Jerome Solinga's Industry Caraibes Services is a full propeller and shaft shop. He can reshape and balance big boat propellers, and can rebush your outboard propeller, replacing those rubber seals that give out over time, or in response to hitting things. As you sail south, the next prop shop is in Trinidad, so this is an excellent alternative for the islands in between. Give him a call or, to find his shop, turn right out of Carenantilles, follow the road hard right and continue to the roundabout. Turn right here and bear left when the road divides, and when you come to a guarded gate, ask for his shop. He will visit the Marin yards where he can fix your prop and straighten your shaft.

S.A.V. des Moteurs, run by Joseph Féré, is on the road just west of Carenantilles. He services PLP (Evinrude and Johnson) outboards.

Injectors or injection pumps need servicing? Check out our section on the *Industrial Zones*.

Provisioning

(See plans pages 87 and 90-91)

If you need cash ATM machines are everywhere, most intimidatingly public. Just beyond Sea Services, outside the car park, is an enclosed room where you can get cash without being right on the street. The bank in the Cours Perrinon is also somewhat discreet.

Change Caraibes, which is at the Savanne end of Rue Ernest Déproge will probably give you the best rates for changing currencies. They opens weekdays 0800-1730, Saturdays 0800-1230.

Provisioning in Fort de France is a pleasure, but when shopping remember to take bags. The Carrefour Market in the Cours Perrinon is large and good, the best in town. Leader Price, opposite Sea Services, is a popular market, with bargain prices on canned and dry goods, beer, and more. They have reasonable frozen and produce sections. It can be crowded and slow. Neither of these stores delivers.

The place for fresh produce and spices is the main market, best in the mornings, especially on Saturday.

Friandises des Isles are great little bakeries with a variety of bread, including whole wheat, and baked delights. You can buy some food and a coffee too. A large one is on Rue de la Republique, and a small one right next The Crew Restaurant close to the sea.

For the fun of shopping in a really big supermarket, visit the out-of-town malls, where small shops surround gargantuan modern supermarkets, called hyper-marchés. Buses go to all these places from the big bus and TC station in Point Simon, right beside the dinghy dock. Two of the best supermarkets, Carrefour and La Galleria, are described in *The Industrial Zones.*

The others are towards Schoelcher and the closest is HyperU at Le Rond Point. It can be reached via the Schoelcher communal taxi, which leaves from the big taxi stand in front of the anchorage. The energetic may prefer to walk. It is rather uphill, but half an hour will get you there at an easy pace. En route, you may want to check out Weldom, a really giant hardware store with a vast range of household and project-related stock. Villa Verde is a garden store with lots of hose fittings and Christmas lights, and Sport 2000 is a giant sports store that includes kayaks and water sports. Farther along (next roundabout, we are no longer walking) is a Casino Géant, which has good frozen fish and many Chinese fixings.

For duty-free supplies, Martinique customs deem that you must be a charter boat. The definition of a charter boat is rather left up to the business. You must mark charter yacht on your customs form, and a brochure helps. But even if you do not qualify, the duty-free purveyors offer good wholesale prices on cases of beer and wine. Go to Quai de Tourelles and check TCS, a drinks wholesaler, who also has a retail jewelry store, or

Approaches to Baie des Tourelles

call Vatier, who mainly stocks drinks.

Fun shopping

Visit the tourist office in La Savanne or the one on Rue Lazare Carnot. They will give you a good Fort de France map as well as a Martinique one, and they will answer your questions. Ask for their dining guide.

Cours Perrinon is a big mall right in the middle of town, open 0800-1900. With two floors, it has glass-fronted elevators, escalators, and lots of shops, restaurants, and a large bookshop (opposite the supermarket) with computers, stationery, and more.

If you need printer inks or special paper, check Encre Pour Tous on Rue Perrinon.

Right opposite Sea Services, Diamond Distribution is a good hardware shop with lots of tools and household stuff. Upstairs in Cours Perrinon La Foire Fouille is a giant household store, generally cheap and junky, but it nearly always has something you need. Another, even cheaper, place is Bazar Pas Cher on Rue de la République.

Fort de France is the place for both fashionable shopping and souvenir hunting. The biggest handicraft market is on Boulevard Alfassa and another is near the fish market. You will find everything from jewelry to handbags, paintings, and varnished palm fruits. Half the artists and carvers in Haiti must be kept busy whipping out an overwhelming number of coconut trees, banana plants, fruits, and models in balsa wood. These are available all over town, with quite a few on La Savanne.

Fort de France is the only place in the Windwards for Paris fashions and stylish clothing shops. Make a beeline for Cours Perrinon, which has lots of shops, and enjoy Rue de La République, which is mainly pedestrian. Otherwise just wander around all the town's little streets and enjoy. When you need a break, you can have a coffee at Lina's. Don't forget to check out the St. James line of clothing at Sea Services (see *Chandlery*) or visit the local market.

Levalois Racing sold personal protection, such as gas guns. This year their store was boarded up. I have been shown a new location on Rue Xavier Orville, but have not visited.

Restaurants

Restaurants are plentiful, geared to the local market, and for the most part, prices are moderate and the food is straightforward and correctly prepared. Lunch is the best value for money, as restaurants compete to attract the workers. Fort de France has a pleasant atmosphere in the evening, with outside seating in several places, not many people are around, and it is quiet.

For a continental breakfast or coffee, try L'Impeatrice [$]. They have wicker chairs and outside seating and it is inexpensive.

If you want to sit out on the street in the shade and watch the world go by, try Instant Food for a beer and Creole food, Hasta La Pizza (below La Baie) for pizza, crepes and ice cream, or La Savanne, which has several snack bars, with outside seating.

A pleasant place to take lunch is in the main market, between Rue Victor Hugo and Rue Antoine Siger, amid the bustle of people selling fruits, tropical flowers, exotic alcoholic drinks, souvenirs of all kinds, and straw goods. Tables are set out both at one end of the market and upstairs. About half a dozen small restaurateurs [$] offer typical Créole meals at bargain prices. There is a fresh fruit juice stand where you choose your fruits and watch them being juiced.

Hotel Simon beside the conspicuous Sophie Lumina tower will sweep you into a world of black and white floor tiles, perfectly coordinated cushions and gold painted bamboo. If you climb the steps from the cruise ship area you come to 4 Senses [$$$], a restaurant with a gourmet shop and wine cellar. Modern and clean they close Sundays but otherwise open from 1100 into the evening. Both the food and service are first rate. For more, go west outside the hotel, down the next steps and turn sharp right into the hotel entrance. Take the lift to the main floor. At the end of a long corridor you come to a series of restaurants, which are rooms rather than separate entities. The biggest at the end is the Boli Bar [$$$], a comfortable lounging area with WiFi. You can get an excellent lunch here. Just a few steps back are two of the most gourmet restaurants in town, both small and intimate. Le Bistrot des Flamandes [$$$$] and La Table de Marcel [$$$$$]. Le

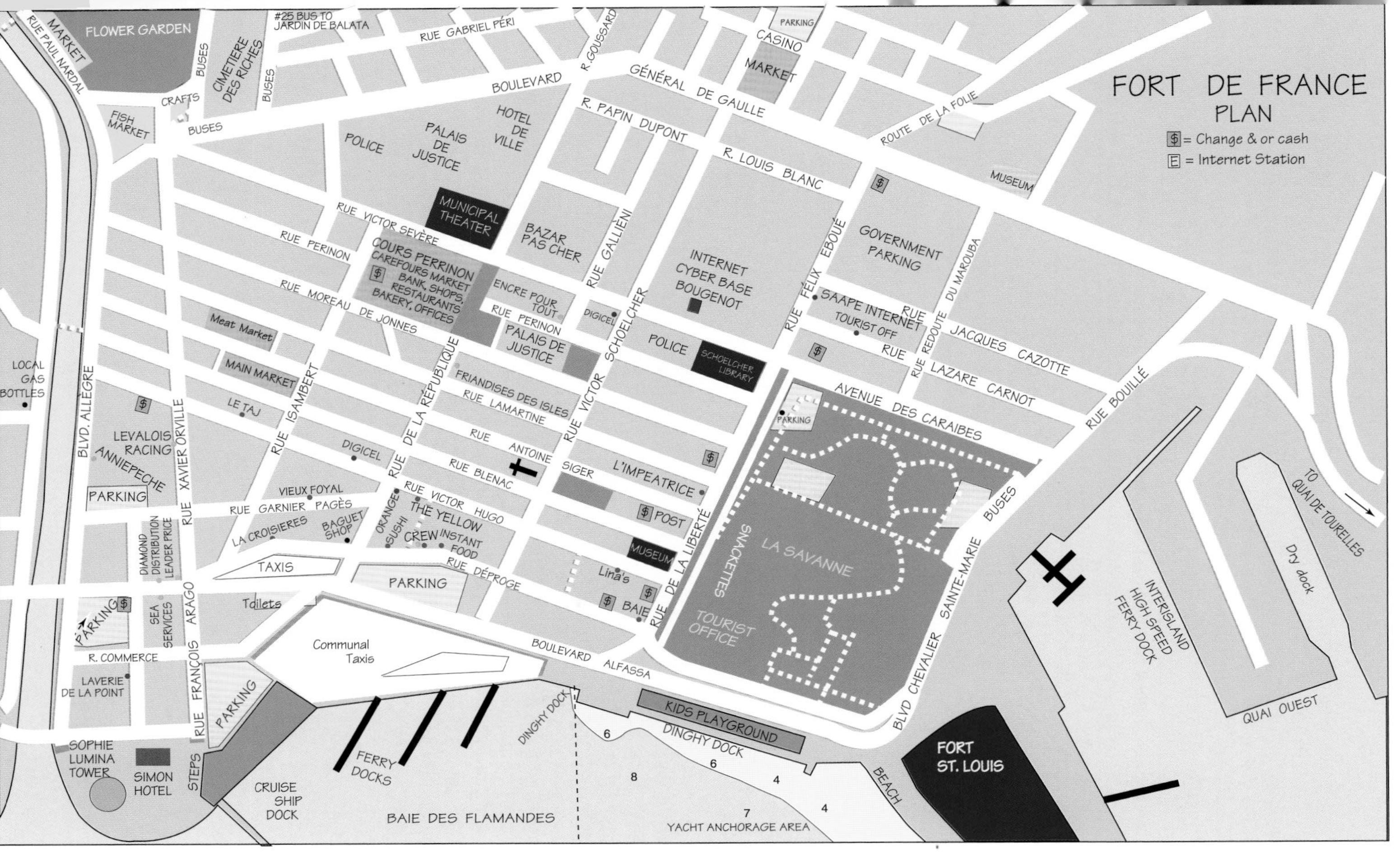
FORT DE FRANCE
PLAN
$ = Change & or cash
E = Internet Station
TO QUAI DE TOURELLES
Dry dock
QUAI OUEST
INTERISLAND HIGH SPEED FERRY DOCK
FORT ST. LOUIS
BEACH
YACHT ANCHORAGE AREA
KIDS PLAYGROUND
DINGHY DOCK
BAIE DES FLAMANDES
FERRY DOCKS
CRUISE SHIP DOCK
Communal Taxis
TAXIS
Toilets
PARKING
STEPS
SIMON HOTEL
SOPHIE LUMINA TOWER
LAVERIE DE LA POINT
R. COMMERCE
SEA SERVICES
DIAMOND DISTRIBUTION LEADER PRICE
RUE FRANÇOIS ARAGO
RUE XAVIER ORVILLE
LEVALOIS RACING
ANNIEPECHE
BLVD. ALLÈGRE
LOCAL GAS BOTTLES
FLOWER GARDEN
MARKET
RUE PAUL NARDAL
FISH MARKET
CRAFTS
BUSES
CIMETIERE DES RICHES
#25 BUS TO JARDIN DE BALATA
RUE GABRIEL PÉRI
R. GOUSSARD
BOULEVARD GÉNÉRAL DE GAULLE
CASINO
MARKET
POLICE
PALAIS DE JUSTICE
HOTEL DE VILLE
MUNICIPAL THEATER
R. PAPIN DUPONT
R. LOUIS BLANC
ROUTE DE LA FOLIE
MUSEUM
GOVERNMENT PARKING
RUE REDOUTE DU MAROUBA
RUE JACQUES CAZOTTE
RUE LAZARE CARNOT
AVENUE DES CARAIBES
RUE BOUILLÉ
BUSES
BLVD CHEVALIER SAINTE-MARIE
LA SAVANNE
SNACKETTES
TOURIST OFFICE
RUE DE LA LIBERTÉ
BOULEVARD ALFASSA
RUE FÉLIX EBOUÉ
SAAPE INTERNET
TOURIST OFF
INTERNET CYBER BASE BOUGENOT
SCHOELCHER LIBRARY
POLICE
RUE VICTOR SCHOELCHER
RUE GALLIÉNI
DIGICEL
BAZAR PAS CHER
ENCRE POUR TOUT
RUE PERINON
PALAIS DE JUSTICE
FRIANDISES DES ISLES
RUE LAMARTINE
RUE ANTOINE SIGER
L'IMPEATRICE
POST
MUSEUM
Lina's
BAIE
RUE BLENAC
RUE VICTOR HUGO
THE YELLOW CREW INSTANT FOOD
RUE DÉPROGE
COURS PERRINON
CAREFOURS MARKET
BANK, SHOPS, RESTAURANTS, BAKERY, OFFICES
RUE DE LA RÉPUBLIQUE
SUSHI
ORANGE
RUE VICTOR SEVÈRE
RUE PERINON
RUE MOREAU DE JONNES
DIGICEL
VIEUX FOYAL
RUE GARNIER PAGÈS
BAGUET SHOP
LA CROISIERES
RUE ISAMBERT
Meat Market
MAIN MARKET
LE TAJ

Bistrot is a little bigger, and Le Table de Marcel more exclusive and upmarket. You would be wise to reserve.

Back in town, The Crew [$$$], closed Saturday and Sunday evenings] is reliable and moderately priced. They serve good French food. It is easy to find room at dinner, though it can be packed for lunch.

The Yellow [$$$$], upstairs on Rue Victor Hugo, opens Monday to Friday from 1200-1500 and Monday to Saturday in the evening from 1900-2300. It is a comfortable and relaxing place to dine. While their selection is not huge, they change their menu every few days. The food is artistically presented and their sauces are tasty. At lunchtime they include daily specials which are about half the normal price, so this is a bargain. On full moon nights they do something special in the evening: anything from a wine tasting to a visiting chef.

La Croisière [$$$], closed Sunday, is a pleasant upstairs restaurant with a great balcony for watching life on the street below. It is informal, relatively inexpensive, and serves both French and Créole dishes for lunch or dinner. Owner Alex Zizi has good local jazz groups on Friday and Saturday nights.

The interior of Fuji Sushi [$$], is simple with wooden tables. If you stop in for lunch you just choose your dishes and drinks from the shelves, pay and sit down. The sushi and side dishes are good, and this may be the only restaurant in Martinique to offer free carafes of tap water. Asking them to give you elegant square plates, instead of eating out of the plastic containers makes it more enjoyable. In the evening it is a regular restaurant.

Le Vieux Foyal [$$$] is an atmospheric jazz bar and restaurant with seating on the street, inside the bar, or in the interior garden. They open Monday to Saturday 1100-1500 and Tuesday to Saturday, 1900-2400. Live music on Thursdays.

La Baie [$$$], is a pleasant upstairs restaurant overlooking the anchorage and park. You can sit inside in air conditioning or outside on the balcony. They serve Créole dishes, and the food is generally good.

Fancy a smoked salmon sandwich? Then Lina's [$] on Rue Victor Hugo is just the ticket, with elegant sandwiches and salads and wine by the glass, all in a pleasant air-conditioned building with seating on two floors. Leave some room for dessert and excellent coffee. Lina's is open till 2200.

For Indian food, Taj, an upmarket Indian restaurant, looks promising. If you want Indian ingredients, ask about their Ganesh store. Open for lunch 1130-1400, dinner from 1900.

Le Grand Bleu is the restaurant in Carenantilles. They have a sports fishing operation and a fancy boat, so the fish should be fresh.

Wherever you eat, beware of little green peppers. They are often put beside the food as decoration, and they are the hottest of hot.

Transport

Fort de France is a convenient starting point to see the island, as there are buses and communal taxis that go to all major towns and villages. Currently, many of them start right outside the new ferry docks. If you are going to the airport, take the "Ducos" car. The charge is just a few euros. Most of the Buses to Dillon, Balata, and Didier go from the west end of Blvd. Général de Gaulle. Buses to Schoelcher go from a bus point towards the west of the Communal taxi area. Communal taxis to Lamentin will take you to the big supermarkets to the east.

A trip to Jardin de Balata is easy from Fort de France. The gardens are set in the rain forest, beautifully maintained, and include a canopy walk, a pond, and lots of flowers and hummingbirds. It is best when there are not too many cruise ships in port. Entrance is around 13 Eu. Take bus no. 25 from the east side of the cemetery (just a little north of where we show it on our plan), which takes you right there and costs about 3 euros for a round trip.

Taxis are available. Tours and shopping trips work out at about 40 Eu an hour for up to 4 people, 10 Eu per person per hour for more than 4. Some drivers speak good English. Vincent Thomas has three sizes of car and works with his wife Elodie. He is easy to contact by mobile phone 0696-07-54-37 and he speaks excellent English. He is based in Rivière Salée, and he knows the

industrial area well. For all day tours he will pick up in Marin.

Marc Pharose is also a good English-speaking taxi driver who knows where everything is (0696 45 09 56). He does not work on Sundays.

Ashore

For years I have wistfully looked up at Fort Saint Louis wishing I could explore it. That is not possible, as it is still an active navy base, but at least now we can now take a guided tour and stand high on the ramparts. The tour takes an hour and a quarter, and gives you a detailed history of the fort. To join, go to the tourist kiosk in La Savanne and ask. It costs about 8 Eu and you can get English or French tours.

History buffs should visit the little pre-Columbian museum on Rue de la Liberté [closed Sunday] and the Ethnic History Museum on Blvd. Général de Gaule. Architecture buffs should see the Schoelcher Library, a very elaborate metal building designed by Gustav Eiffel, made in France and shipped here. La Cimetière des Riches is also of interest as, until recently, only the rich and famous could be buried there.

THE INDUSTRIAL ZONES

With coastal regions collecting top dollar for rentals, it is not surprising that more and more businesses are now found in the industrial zones, which run from Fort de France, past the airport, to Rivière Salée. If you are renting a car, drive to Carrefour

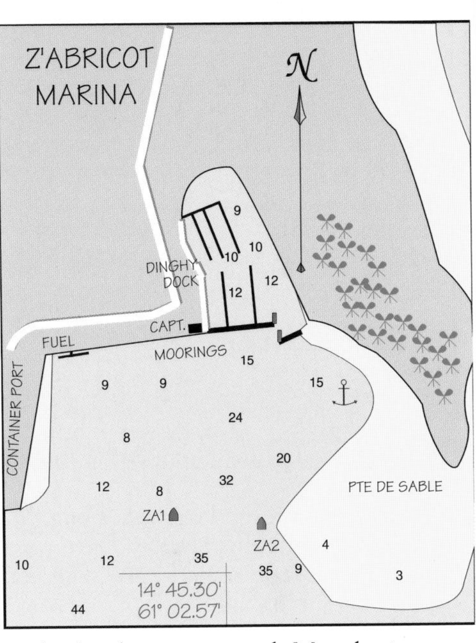

and take the airport road. Most businesses are reached from one of the following major exits: the first is Rivière Roche, the second Jambette, the third Californie, and the fourth, which is easily identifiable by La Galleria, is Les Mangles. Note also the turnoff to Le Lamentin or La Lezarde. Lareinty is a zone right opposite the airport. Continue on for Rivière Salée, using the same exit as for Trois Ilets. Taxis can be of help. Buses go to Carrefour from the western end of Blvd. Général de Gaulle, by the cemetery.

Marina Z'Abricots

Port de Plaisance de L'Etang Z'Abricots (Marina Z'Abricots) is an excellent new community-owned marina. It is peaceful, quiet, and clean, with mangroves to the east

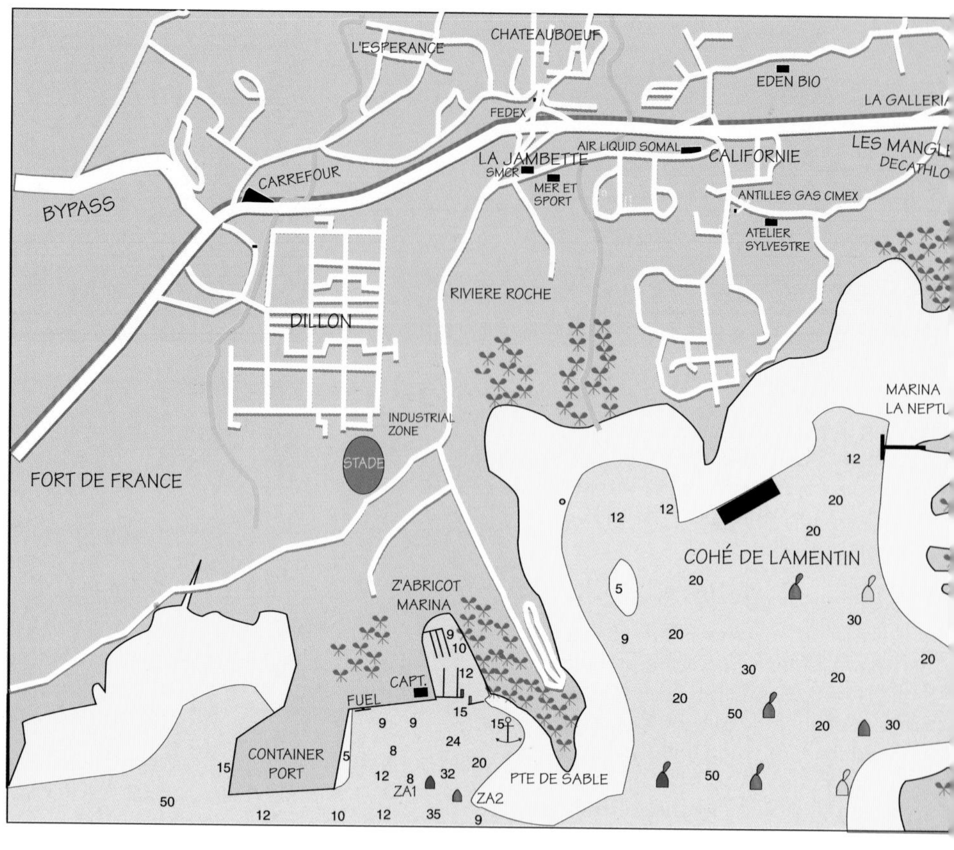

and coral and fish on the stones along the wall. It is an excellent place to leave your boat safely while you rent a car to shop or explore, but it is not hurricane proof, so not suitable for hurricane storage.

For the deepest approach, come from the south and pass between the red and green buoys. The entrance between the outer floating docks is marked with red and green beacons. You can ask for assistance coming in (0596 75 11 57). On the larger yacht docks (the ones nearest the bay) each berth has a mooring line attached to a cleat. You have to pull it up and take it to the bow (a dinghy could help).

The marina has a few large white moorings outside the wall which they rent for 16 Eu day or 200 Eu a month. There is also anchoring room outside.

The Marina [VHF:09] has a customs computer and you can clear here. It offers security, free WiFi, water and electricity, with showers and toilets, and a bill-operated laundry. Various garbage bins allow you to recycle. They have a separate fuel dock outside to the west where you can buy diesel, water, gasoline and ice. The dock is very low, so you may need ladders to get down. There is 9 feet of water on the dock. There is a dry storage area for boats with trailers. Office hours are 0700-1200, 1300-1700, except on weekends when they start at 0900. A restaurant is planned soon.

Provisioning

Carrefour at Dillon is the first large and well-laid-out supermarket you come to on the airport road and it is excellent for a major provisioning. Some prefer to go a little farther, to the giant La Galleria, with over a hundred shops, lots of restaurants, and glass-fronted lifts and escalators, making it a favorite hangout for the young. Their Hyper U supermarket has everything. Price differences exist between this market and Carrefour, but neither is consistently higher.

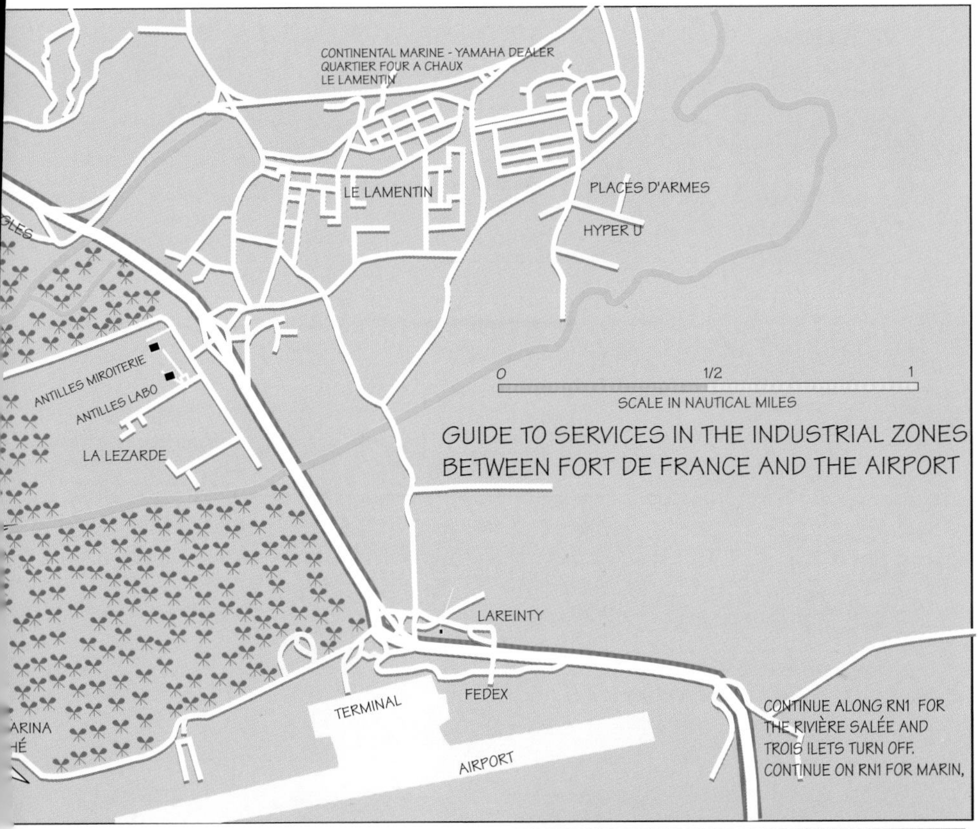

GUIDE TO SERVICES IN THE INDUSTRIAL ZONES BETWEEN FORT DE FRANCE AND THE AIRPORT

CONTINENTAL MARINE - YAMAHA DEALER
QUARTIER FOUR A CHAUX
LE LAMENTIN
LE LAMENTIN
PLACES D'ARMES
HYPER U
ANTILLES MIROITERIE
ANTILLES LABO
LA LEZARDE
0 1/2 1
SCALE IN NAUTICAL MILES
LAREINTY
FEDEX
TERMINAL
AIRPORT
CONTINUE ALONG RN1 FOR THE RIVIÈRE SALÉE AND TROIS ILETS TURN OFF. CONTINUE ON RN1 FOR MARIN,

If you are coming from Marin, Euromarché at Genipa is the market of choice, between Rivière Salée and the airport, or there is the Hyper U at Place D'Arms; both of these will keep you out of the heavy traffic nearer town.

Eden Bio is a good and reasonably priced organic food store with many interesting products.

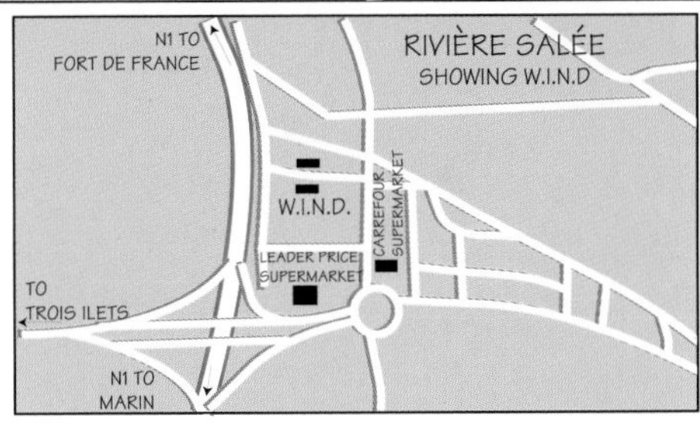

Chandleries and services

Intersport is across the major highway from Carrefour. It is a vast general sports shop that includes fishing, boating, kayaking, windsurfing, and surf-kiting gear. You might not find what you are looking for, but you will certainly find something you want. Decathlon is a large super sports store not too far from Galleria, they cover all sports, and the prices are reasonable.

Turn off at Californie for Atelier Sylvestre, the hydraulic hose specialists. They can remake any hose. They also stock many special hoses and you can buy fuel-resistant hoses or very heavy-duty hoses. Fittings are available in stainless or aluminum, and the owners speak English.

Of interest at La Lezarde is Antilles Miroiterie. They stock glass, mirrors, acrylic sheet in various thicknesses and quality, and PVC. They will cut all materials to shape.

The Fedex office is near the airport, in the original airport block. Continental Marine in Lamentin is the Yamaha agent. It has spares and can sort out Yamaha problems.

Rivière Salée is the home of West Indies Nautic Distribution (WIND), a big

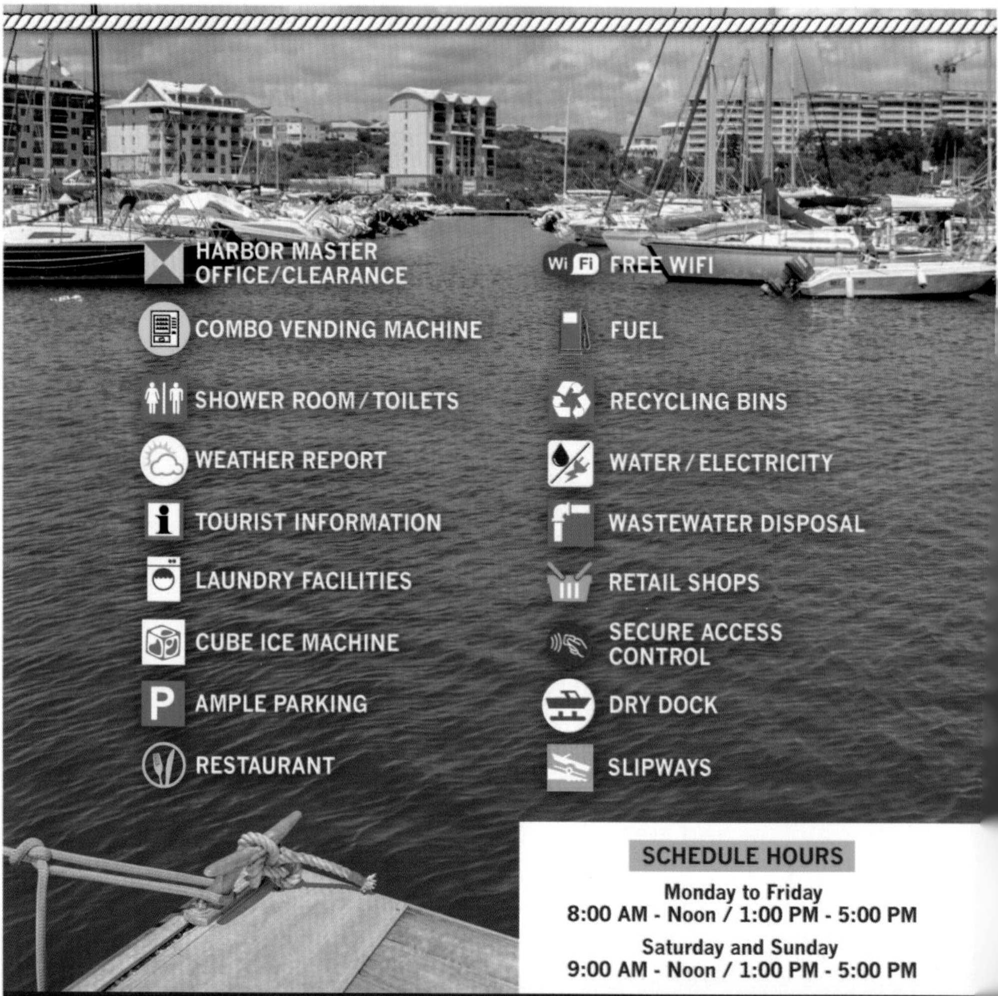

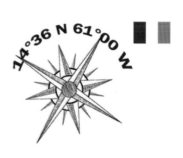

store with a good showroom. They have everything you need for any kind of boat job, as well as selling marine batteries, and they sell wholesale and retail. They sell epoxy and polyester resins, fiberglass materials, and the latest cores. They have high-quality ply, including teak and holly flooring ply. They sell sandpaper, masks, gloves, brushes, and all the application tools. On big jobs you can negotiate wholesale prices. Their Seajet 038 Taisho, antifouling is very effective, free of heavy metals, biodegradable and eco-friendly. WIND is the best flag outlet in the Eastern Caribbean. They have or can quickly get any kind of courtesy flag or ensign. They also wholesale flags. You can check out flags of all nations on their web page (www.wind-flag.com). It is worth visiting the store, but if you cannot make it personally, email or call they will happily deliver to your boat.

Madinina Diesel is also here, near Leader Price. This is the place to service injectors and pumps

While here and with a car, and if you are in too much of a hurry to make the giant stores, you can shop at Leader Price, which has easy parking.

TROIS ILETS

Trois Ilets is a photogenic town, not overrun with visitors. Most of the old houses are built of wood or stone and capped with fish-scale tile roofs. A handsome square lies between the church and the town hall. This pleasant area offers several scenic, quiet, and secure places to anchor, some of which are protected enough to ride out a hurricane. Tie your dinghy to the inner end of the ferry dock, walk along the waterfront walkway and head towards the church.

Approach from Anse Mitan by leaving the black and yellow buoys off Pte. du Bout, Pte. de la Rose, and Pte. Angboeuf to starboard. The easiest anchorage is found by following the coast in from Pte. Angboeuf and anchoring off the golf course. There is one 4-foot shoal, but otherwise the approach is easy. The approach to town is between the

islands. Steer for the eastern island till you see the green buoy and leave it to port. After rounding the buoy, turn a little east again to avoid the shoals off the island to the west. Do not anchor in the main channel marked by yellow buoys. Holding is variable.

Communications

For internet, visit Cyber Base des Trois Ilets above the library. Open weekdays 08001400, Wednesday and Friday 0830-1300 and 1430-1700, Saturday and Sunday 0800-1300.

Restaurants

Il Gallo Rosso is Italian and opens for dinner. A few steps farther along Green [$$] has Créole food and occasional entertainment. Beyond that is an inexpensive snack bar that serves Créole lunch and farther down on the other side of the road a pizzeria and a grill. On the waterfront, some small snack bars offer a great location for a drink.

Ashore

A ferry to Fort de France runs about every half hour. Garbage bins are at either end of the waterfront.

In town you will find a local market

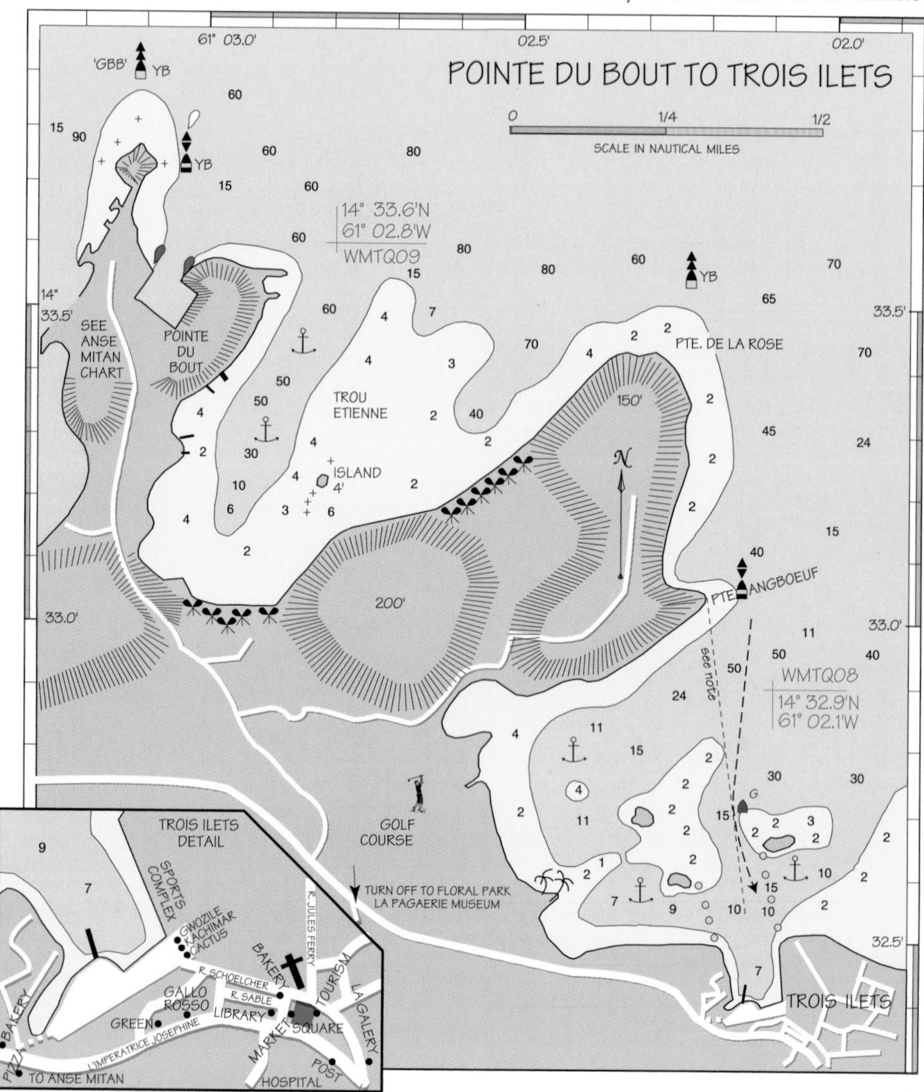

Anse Mitan

(open every day), a post office, a butcher, a wonderful boulangerie/patisserie/ice creamery, a pharmacy, a couple of general stores, and a hospital. A tourist office is stationed in the market square, and should you wish to rent a car, they will help.

Plenty of attractions are a fair walk away. You can play golf overlooking your yacht in the bay below. Opposite the 18-hole golf course is La Pagerie Museum, the original home of Empress Josephine. Our guide explained that most of the old estate house burned down when Josephine was three years old, and her father was such a gambler and womanizer that he could not afford to rebuild. They lived in part of the factory, where she stayed until she left for France for an arranged marriage at the age of 16. Her first husband was killed in the French revolution, but she escaped thanks to a lover (of which our guide emphasized she had plenty). When she married Napoleon he was 27 and she was 33. Since this was an unthinkable age difference, it was published that they were both 28.

About one and a half nautical miles to the east are some potteries, one of which produces the lovely fish-scale roof tiles used both in Trois Ilets and in St. George's, Grenada. Around these is the Village de la Potterie, a visitor attraction with numerous boutiques, restaurants, and a place to rent kayaks for mucking in the mangroves. The adventurous can dinghy there, tide permitting. It is opposite Gros Ilet and obvious because of the big industrial-looking brick warehouse and red roofs. Head east from Trois Ilets, follow the coast till you get past the first shoal on your port, then head towards Gros Ilet about half way before heading into the pottery. Tie up amid the bricks before you come to the tiny kayak dock. You might be able to make use of a couple of makeshift wooden landing platforms. Take care in the shallows.

TROU ETIENNE

Swells have occasionally driven me to anchor in Trou Etienne when I had things to do in Pointe du Bout, though without a pressing need to be there, Trois Ilets is a better option. As you come from the west, leave both the yellow and black buoys to starboard and as you enter the bay, do not go too close to shore. There are many private moorings and the water is either rather deep or too shallow for easy anchoring. Docks and roads are private, but there is a small public access path overgrown and hard to find.

ANSE MITAN

Anse Mitan is part of the Trois Ilets district, and the head of the peninsula is called Pte. du Bout. It is attractive and popular, and there is always space to anchor.

Anse Mitan has a lot to offer, including beaches, boutiques, and restaurants, and it is fun for people-watching. Two ferry services run to Fort de France and Anse à L'Ane: one out of the marina at Pte. du Bout, the other

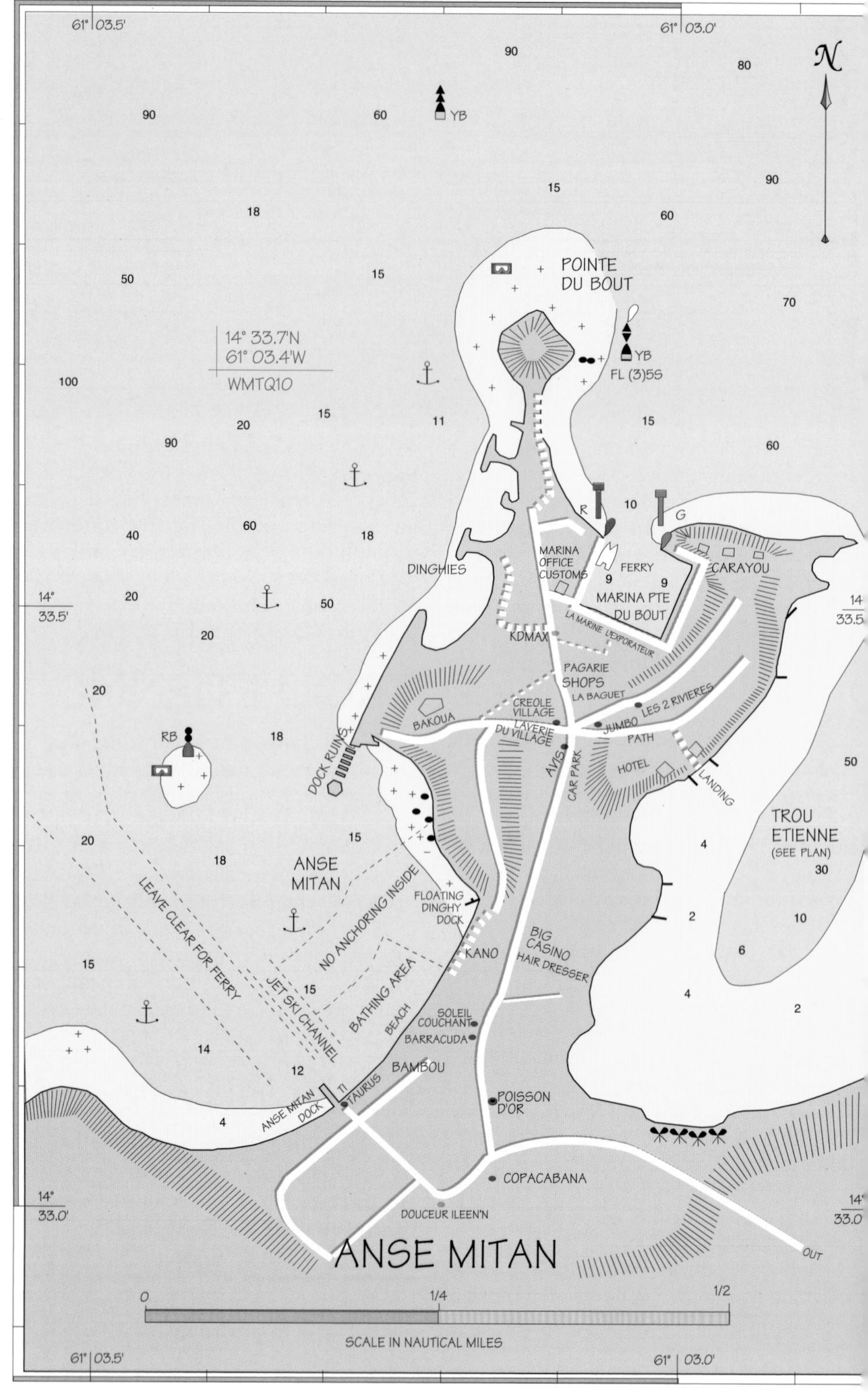
POINTE DU BOUT
14° 33.7'N
61° 03.4'W
WMTQ10
YB
FL (3)5S
DINGHIES
MARINA OFFICE CUSTOMS
FERRY
MARINA PTE DU BOUT
CARAYOU
KDMAX
LA MARINE L'EXPORATEUR
PAGARIE SHOPS
LA BAGUET
CREOLE VILLAGE
LAVERIE DU VILLAGE
BAKOUA
LES 2 RIVIERES
JUMBO
PATH
HOTEL
LANDING
AVIS
CAR PARK
DOCK RUINS
RB
TROU ETIENNE
(SEE PLAN)
ANSE MITAN
FLOATING DINGHY DOCK
NO ANCHORING INSIDE
LEAVE CLEAR FOR FERRY
JET SKI CHANNEL
BATHING AREA
BEACH
KANO
BIG CASINO
HAIR DRESSER
SOLEIL COUCHANT
BARRACUDA
BAMBOU
TAURUS
TI
ANSE MITAN DOCK
POISSON D'OR
COPACABANA
DOUCEUR ILEEN'N
OUT
ANSE MITAN
SCALE IN NAUTICAL MILES
61° 03.5'
61° 03.0'
14° 33.5'
14° 33.0'

from the Anse Mitan Dock. Ferries start at around 0600 and finish at about 2300. Check times on the notice boards on the docks.

When approaching Anse Mitan, the main danger is the reef lying 200 yards west of Le Bakoua, which is marked by a red and black buoy. Anchor anywhere among the other yachts. Holding is good in sand, but poor on patches of dead coral. Leave a couple of hundred feet in front of the beach clear for swimmers and leave the channel clear for the ferry. The various areas are often marked by yellow buoys.

On those very rare occasions when there is a bad northwesterly swell, go to Trou Etienne, on the other side of Pte. du Bout, or better, to Trois Ilets.

Regulations

You can clear customs via a computer in Marina Pointe du Bout office. Opening hours are 0800-1800 weekdays, 0800-1400 Saturday, and 0800-1100 Sunday.

Communications

Most bars and restaurants offer free WiFi.

General yacht services

You can tie your dinghy on the inside of the ferry dock. A tiny floating dinghy dock has been added at the north end of the beach and is still half afloat. It is convenient for everything. Many people use the rocks and palm trees in the bay just north of Bakoua. You can find garbage dumpsters all through town.

Marina Pte. du Bout [VHF: 9] is a small marina offering stern-to berthing with water and electricity (no fuel yet). Short- and long-term berths are occasionally available for yachts up to 50 feet and with less than 9-foot draft. Three docks are reserved for transients.

La Laverie du Village by Village Créole is a fast laundry, open from 0830. Get your laundry in as early as possible and Sonia, the owner, will get it done the same day. She will iron if you wish.

Provisioning

Kdmax is a compact supermarket with most things. They open 0830-1930 Monday to Saturday, 0830-1230 Sundays and holidays. Stock up on baked goodies in La Baguet. Vegetable sellers sometimes set up on the roadside.

For more provisions, rent a car and drive to the giant Carrefour at Genipa. Turn left towards Fort de France, pass two roundabouts, and then take the tiny turnoff with a very small Genipa sign. Go under the highway and it is on the left.

Fun shopping

Like ice-cream? Well, you will find lots of it here, and all of it good. Italian Cocco Bello is on the outer part of Créole Village; more glaceries are inside, and Ice'n Coffee is on the road to the marina.

Pointe du Bout is a shopper's dream of trendy little boutiques. Try starting at the Créole Village, beside the entrance to the Bakoua. It is built in Caribbean style, just Disneyfied enough to make it theatrically enticing. It is chock-a-block with shops that sell elegant clothing, kid's clothes, jewelry, handicrafts, and objets d'art. Continue down the street towards the marina for more of the same, plus more casual clothing, souvenirs, magazines, and books. There are several hairdressers, a pharmacy, and a massage parlor/beauty salon.

Restaurants

One of the delights of Anse Mitan is to stroll over to La Baguet and have a breakfast of French coffee, fresh croissants, and pain au chocolat. Dozens of restaurants line the streets. I mention a few.

Cristophe Luon's Kano [$$$] is open daily 1230-1500 for lunch and then 1700 for drinks and starters, serving main meals about 1930. It is in a pleasant Créole house that rambles seaward from the road until it opens right out onto the sea. It has several rooms and garden areas. A little floating dinghy dock is a few steps away. There are some lounging areas and nice old pieces of furniture. The walls are covered in good art, which is for sale, with a revolving exhibit that changes every couple of months. The food is traditional Créole and nicely presented. The coconut flan with mango sauce is wonderful. They have typical Créole music such as Zouk at least once a week. They have a dj most days and they stay open quite late should you be out on the town. Reservations may be necessary for both lunch and dinner. Arrive in time for happy hour, 1700-1800 except Monday when it is 1700-2000.

For something cheap and cheerful, Al Dente is an Italian take-away, next to Kano, but they do have a few seats.

For the pleasure of sitting on the beach and watching scantily clad beautiful people, check out Au Soleil Couchant or Barracuda [$$]. If you prefer to watch people clad in designer clothes, try one of the restaurants by the marina. The most reliable is La Marine [$$$]. Here you sit out in the open, facing the marina, the surroundings are pleasant, and the food fair value. For a simple sandwich or salad, Vit' et Frais, just behind La Marine is good.

There are seven restaurants in La Village Créole. Havana Café is the place to sip a drink and watch people pass. Le Bistrot d'en Face [$$$] has a nice pub-like atmosphere and their food is good. La Pause has pleasant outside seating in a garden under a tent roof.

Copacabana [$$$$] is both a Brazilian restaurant and a pizzeria. Go when you feel in need of stoking up on some really good meat, prepared the Brazilian way.

Ti Taurus right by the Anse Mitan dock, is cheerful and has a great location.

In the marina block behind La Marine New Dragon de Chine serves good Chinese food in portions generous enough to satisfy the famished sailor.

Ashore

Anse Mitan has car rentals and it is a good place from which to explore the island. The taxi stand is on the main road opposite Somatras Marina.

Water sports

If you want to go diving, check out Espace Plongée in Marina Pointe du Bout.

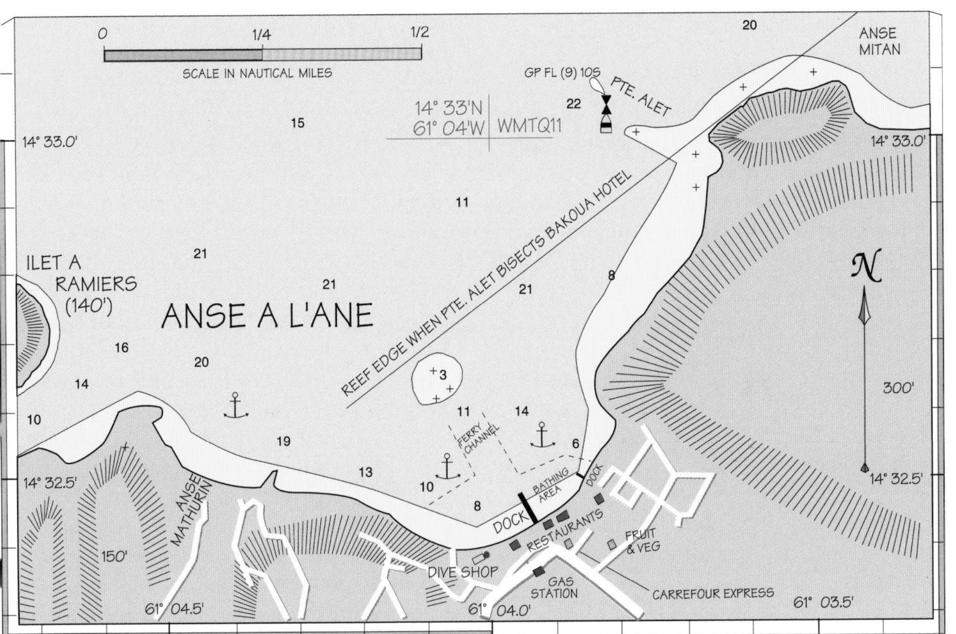

ANSE A L'ANE

Just around the corner from Anse Mitan is Anse à l'Ane, a sweet little bay with a charming beach. Water sports and the regular Fort de France ferry can make it choppy; heading down towards Anse Mathurin can be calmer

Right in the middle of the bay, about one-third of a mile offshore, is a hard-to-spot reef about four feet deep. You can pass on either side to anchor in about 12 feet on a sand bottom. Make sure your anchor is well dug in and leave the ferry channel clear (it is sometimes buoyed). Anse à l'Ane is open to the northwest and should be avoided in times of heavy ground swells. When approaching from Anse Mitan, give the first headland a wide clearance as it is all rocky and shoals stick out 270 yards at Pte. Alet (see chart). When heading toward Cap Salomon from Anse à L'Ane, you have about 9 feet of water between Ilet à Ramiers and the mainland, enough for many yachts to pass.

Services/shopping

Anse à l'Ane is a holiday area, though much less built up than Anse Mitan. The beach has some shade, provided by sea grapes and palm trees. Leave your dinghy on the dinghy dock (swells permitting) or on the very inner end of the ferry dock.

Garbage bins are at either end of the car park and a gas station that sells ice can be found on the main road. A good Carrefour Express supermarket is open 0800-2000 except Sunday when it closes at 1300. Rental

Anse a L'Ane

cars and boutiques are in the same place.

Restaurants

Restaurants line the beach. Right off the dinghy dock on the east side of the bridge, are Ti Tresure Gourmand beach bar and a beach shack. Over the bridge La Case a Glace [$$] is big and open, and Kreol K Fe [$$$] is a pleasant little restaurant for French and Creole food.

If you want to eat really well, Pignon Nouvelle Vague [$$$$ closed Monday] is the fanciest restaurant, and serves excellent food with good service. The same family's Pignon sur Mer is also quite good. Les 3 V is an inexpensive snack bar restaurant and ice cream shop near the main dock.

The hotel at the west end of the beach is abandoned for the time being but may rise again.

Water sports

Dive with the dive shop Corail Club Caraibes. David Dauphin takes people dolphin watching. Jump In offers water sports.

ANSE NOIRE & ANSE DUFOUR

Anse Noire and Anse Dufour lie about halfway between Ilet à Ramiers and Cap Salomon; two bays, one white sand, the other black, both with good snorkeling. They should be avoided in northerly swells but are otherwise well protected. Anse Noire is a lovely hideaway and there is an excellent dinghy dock. Small, colorful cliffs rise on the southern headland and there is a steep hill on the northern one. Palms line the black sand beach at the head of the bay and a large fancy dock juts out from the beach. Behind the beach, a steep jungly valley rises into the mountains. Popular as a daytime anchorage, Anse Noire is usually deserted and peaceful at night. The wind swings in all directions.

Anse Dufour is a picturesque small fishing village with a white sand beach, and lots of bougainvillea. Visitors love it because of the beach and snorkeling. You will find good anchorage in 20 feet off the beach or on the south side behind moored fishing boats. Be prepared to move for the fishermen if they ask.

Ashore

It is pleasant just to sit in Anse Noire and watch the kingfishers and other birds on the cliffs. An interesting trail follows the shady strip of riverine forest up the seasonal river behind the beach to the main road or right over to Anse A L'Ane. Domaine de

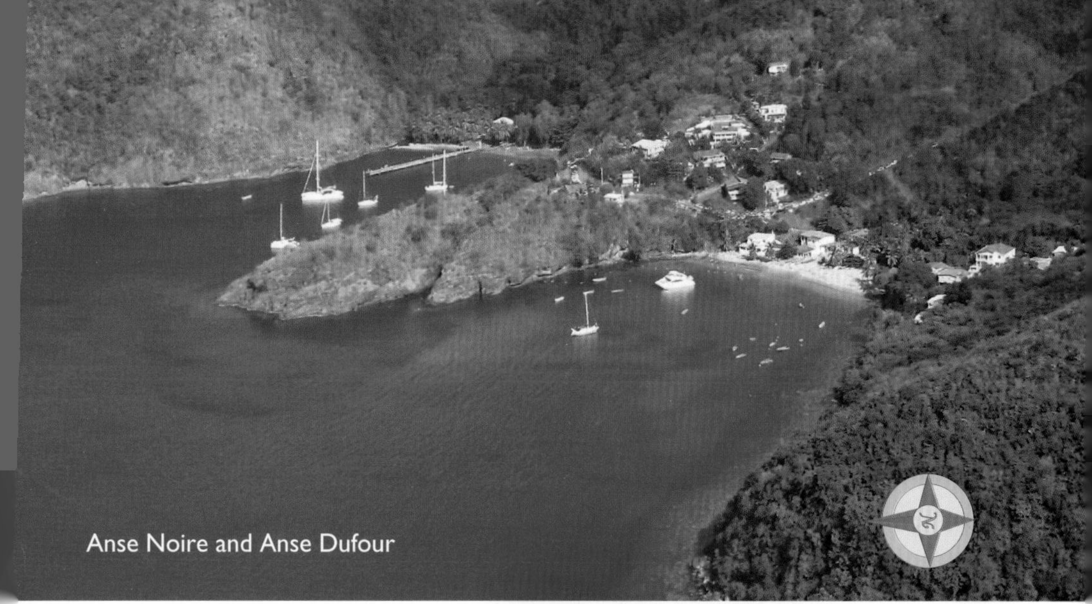

Anse Noire and Anse Dufour

Robinson, behind the beach, sometimes has rooms to rent.

For lunch, climb the steps to Sable D'Or [$$$, closed Tuesday], which specializes in fresh seafood and Créole meat dishes at reasonable prices.

Or, in Anse Dufour, you can choose between Chez Marie Jo [$$], closed Sunday], Maga Most [$], and Snack Chez Nini [$], on the beach.

Barrel Sponge at Anse Dufour

Water sports

The snorkeling around the headland into Anse Dufour is superb: walls, crevices, and rocks decorated with sponges, tubeworms, and anemones, which attract a large variety of small fish. A particularly lovely deep grotto is halfway in Anse Dufour. (You can see it in the aerial photo.) The snorkeling is even better on the south side of Anse Dufour, with rocks and lots of fish. It is worth trying a dive

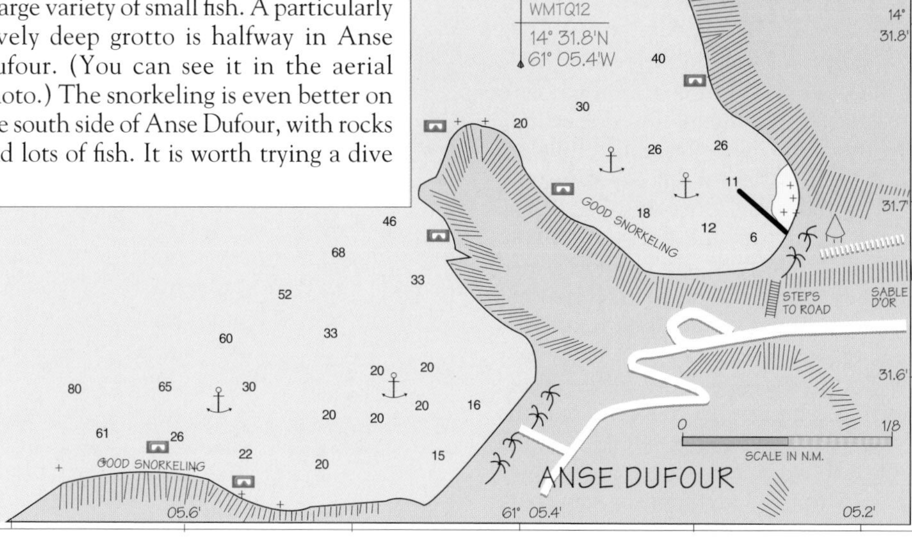

Grand Anse D'Arlet

AROUND A HUNDRED MOORINGS WERE PLACED IN THESE TWO BAYS. MAINTANENCE WAS INADEQUATE, NO FEES WERE COLLECTED, MOORINGS WENT ADRFIT EVENTUALLY THE REST WERE REMOVED FROM THE SANDSCREW UP. THE SANDSCREWS REMAIN IN PLACE. ROPES AND ANCHORS COULD GET SNAGGED ON THEM BUT IT DOES NOT SEEM TO HAPPEN OFTEN.

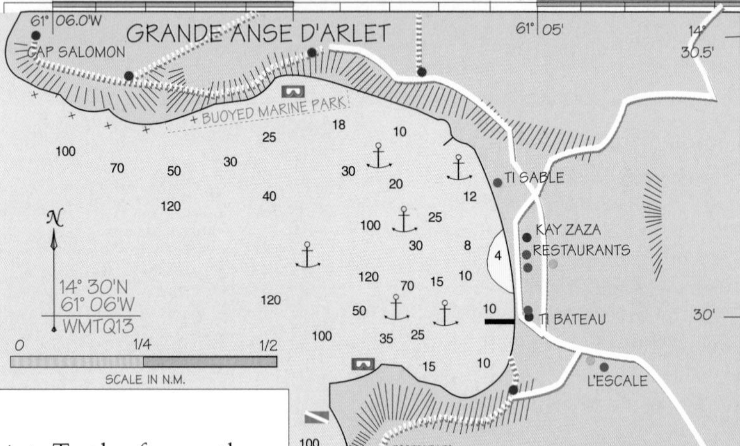

here, off the point. Turtles frequently visit the bays.

GRANDE ANSE D'ARLET

Grande Anse d'Arlet is a little village set on a white sand beach with magnificent mountains towering behind. In the right light, when the hills are lush green, it has the feel of some exotic Pacific hideaway. Once a fishing village, a few dugout fishing pirogues remain, though for the most part it is now geared to tourism and the northern corner has a touch of the Riviera, with brightly colored beach umbrellas. A fancy new walkway runs behind the beach. Avoid sailing too close to the center of the village, as a shoal area extends seaward several hundred feet. The holding is variable, with weed and some broken coral,

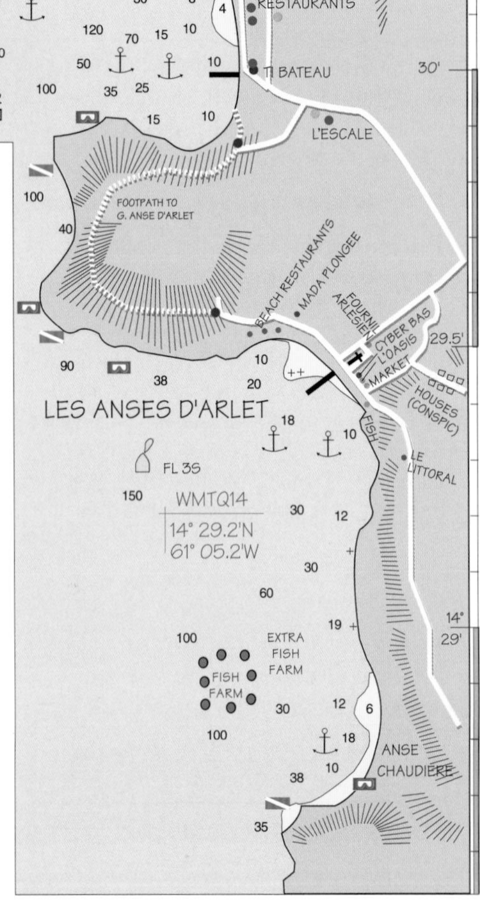

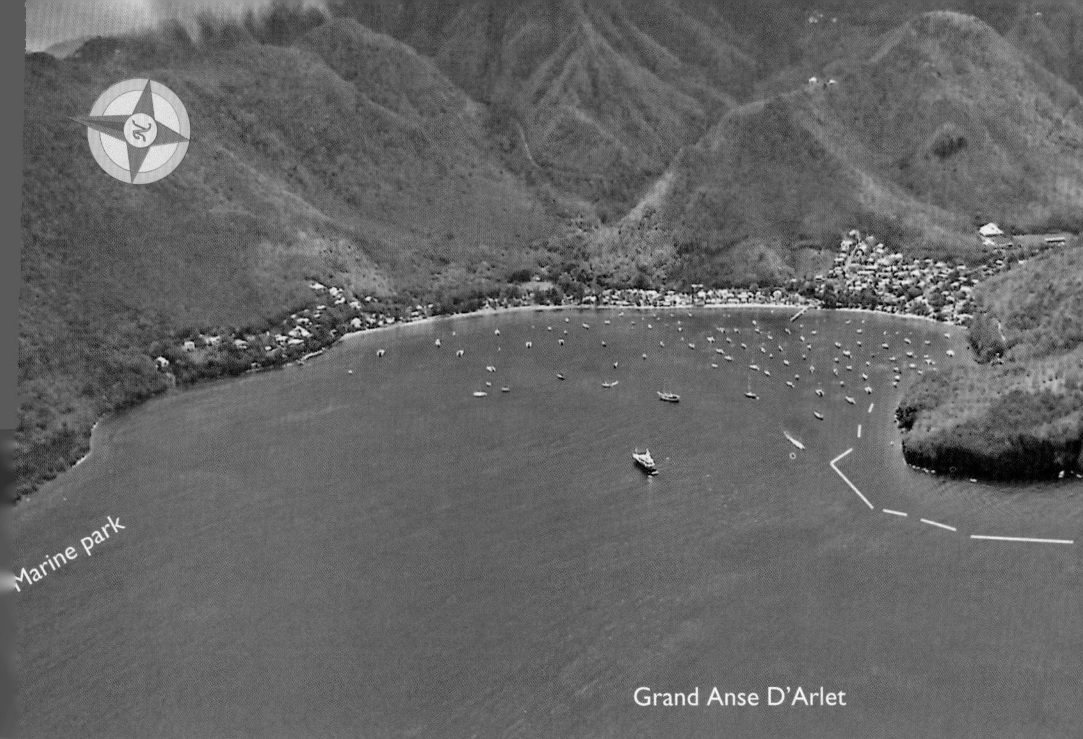

as well as good sand. Approach with care as snorkelers swim all over the bay looking for turtles.

Regulations

You can walk 20 minutes to customs in Les Anses D'Arlet.

General yacht services

From 1000-1200, Le P'Ti Bateau can provide water on the dock. Most bars and restaurants have WiFi.

Isabel's Kay Zaza is a boutique and laundry. Isabel will wash, or wash, dry, and fold by the 5 kg load, normally ready the next day. Kay Zaza is an artistic shop with gifts, ornaments, casual clothing, hats, art, and jewelry. They sell stamps and postcards and will mail them for you.

Ashore

Grand Anse d'Arlet wakes late and is ready for the day by about 1100. Earlier risers wander down to L'Abre Pain for coffee at their beach bar in the form of a boat, which can be quite a gathering place from 0900.

Two small food stores sell groceries and ice. When you get to the dock, go to the main road, and whichever direction you turn, you will come to one. These open at 0800. For more, you will have to visit Les Anses D'Arlet.

Le P'Ti Bateau [$$$], right at the head of the dock, is a pleasant, reasonably priced restaurant, open only for lunch. You sit at tables right on the beach.

At the northern end of the beach, behind all the fancy Mediterranean-style sunshades, is Ti Sable [$$$$]. It is beach chic, with a sand floor but sturdy wooden tables on little wooden islands. They serve good Créole food. You occasionally need to book for lunch, though not for dinner.

Otherwise, Bidjoul [$$$], Les Arcades [$$$], L'Abre Pain [$$$], and Ti Payot [$$$] are all Créole restaurants along the pathway behind the beach. They set tables and chairs on the beach to create an enchanting spot for a waterfront meal. The location is lovely, food and service varies.

Just beyond Ti Payot is a restaurant owned by Plongée Passion. They do a good local lunch on the beach. Chez Evelyne and Chez Nita are also open for lunch only at the southern end of the beach.

For a really good meal, leave the tourists on the beach and walk back to L'Ecale [$$$$]. It opens Tuesday to Sunday for din-

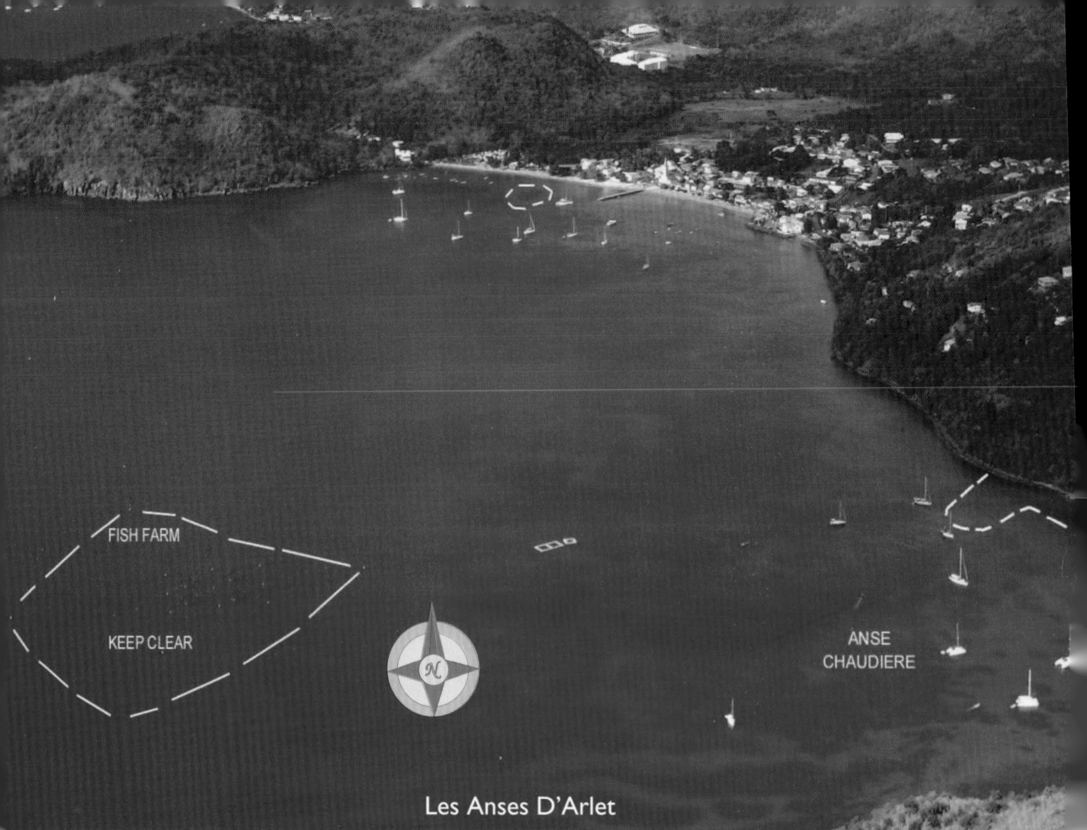

Les Anses D'Arlet

ner and Friday to Sunday for lunch. Owners Chef Mattius and his brother Jonathan, the maitre d, and their team of young enthusiasts dress informally and have fun, creating a relaxed and friendly atmosphere. But they are serious about the food and service. The food is excellent and this a great place to come for a fine meal. If you want a sampler they do a four-tapas special, but leave room for dessert. It is popular, so reserve.

The coast road from Anse d'Arlet, which winds over the hills to Diamant, offers spectacular views, and cars can be rented from the beach area. Anse d'Arlet is within easy walking distance.

An excellent trail follows the headland to Anse d'Arlet. From the dinghy dock, turn right on the road and look for the sign on your righthand side, or head south along the beach and look for a red arrow on the left. Another trail at the north end of the bay takes you to Cap Solomon and includes a mangrove walkway. You can also hike from here to Anse Dufours. We show the trails on our sketch chartandmore details are available at doyleguides.com.

Water sports

Snorkeling is excellent when the water is clear. The main grassy anchorage is often full of turtles and starfish. A marine park on the south shore has lovely snorkeling, and the north shore and all round to Anses D'Arlet is also good. Divers can join Plongée Passion, Deep Turtle, Alpha Dive, or Bubbles.

LES ANSES D'ARLET

The photogenic small town of Les Anses D'Arlet has some lovely old houses and a picturesque church. Everything is well painted and maintained. A handsome promenade follows the waterfront. Les Anses D'Arlet makes a good overnight anchorage unless the wind is too far in the south.

When approaching town, look out for the rocks to the west of the dock. Some are visible, but others extend some yards seaward. Watch also for snorkelers who go all over the anchorage looking for turtles. An unmarked fish farm is in the southern part of the bay. Avoid this area at night and keep a good lookout by day.

Anchorage may also be found at Anse Chaudière in the southeastern corner of the bay, which is a great hideaway with good snorkeling. Approach with caution, as isolated rocks extend about 100 feet offshore. Anchor on the sand bottom in 10 to 12 feet.

Regulations

The Customs computer is in Cyber Base, a short walk towards the market from the church and just before L'Oasis boutique; the sign is small and easy to miss. They open 0800-1300 and 1400-1730, except Tuesday 0800-1300, Saturday 0800-1100, and Sunday they are closed. This is also a major internet station.

Services/ashore

The market has crafts, some produce, and an ATM by the entrance. Fresh fish is sold opposite. Fournil Arlesien has good bread, pain au chocolat, and more, a few steps farther on. Alain's L'Oasis boutique is connected to Zaza's in Grand Anse d'Arlet, and Alain should be able to arrange to take laundry there for you. He also sells casual clothing, hammocks, pareos, and many colorful gifts.

For lunch, gravitate to the plastic chairs set out on the beach northwest of the river. Sandwiches and local meals are available from many small restaurants. This area has been carefully renovated, with a pleasant walkway along the waterfront. Some of these restaurants also open in the evening. Le Table du Boulanger is a new pizzeria, which also sells baked goodies from the bakery, and is open for breakfast and lunch daily, also Friday and Saturday nights. Le Littoral [$$$] is a pleasant little Créole restaurant a short walk away on the road leading south out of town. They have a great view overlooking the bay and open every day 1100-1500 and 1900-2200.

You can hike from here over the headland to Grand Anse d'Arlet and return by the road, which is shorter.

Les Anses D'Arlet

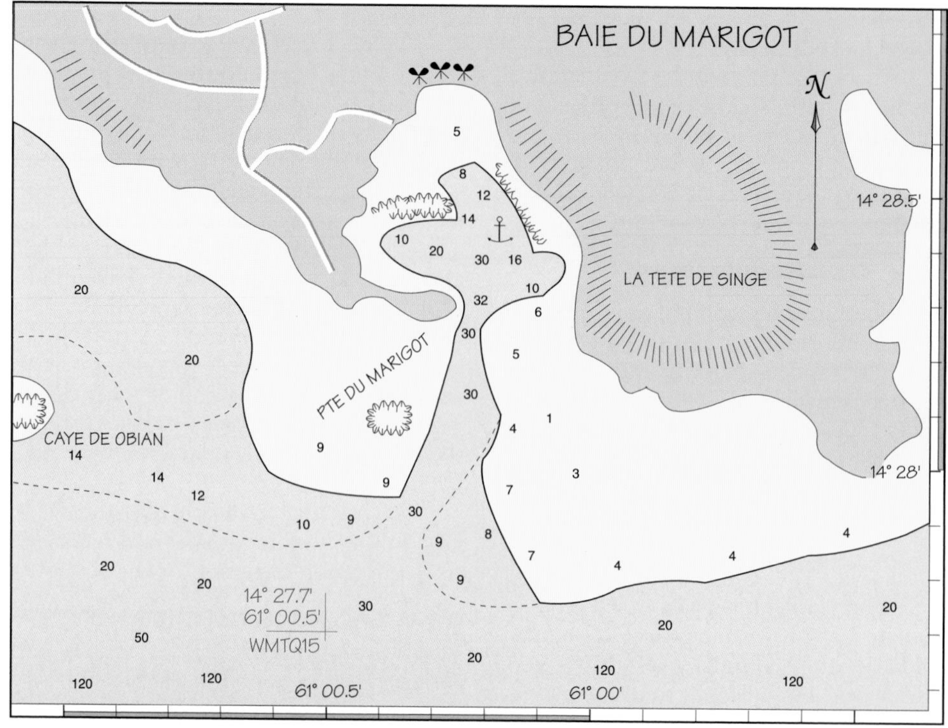

Water sports

Mada Plongée will be happy to take you diving, and David, the owner, speaks English. Snorkeling is good in Anse Chaudière. It may be worth giving scuba a go here as well. If you are anchored in town, try the rocks off the dock - everyone else does.

THE SOUTH COAST OF MARTINIQUE

There are no good anchorages along Martinique's south coast until you get to the eastern end. Several shoals along this coast extend up to half a mile offshore. There is deep water (over 100 feet) outside these shoals. It is best to stay in this deep water to avoid the many fish traps at lesser depths.

As long as you don't get too far offshore, the sail east to Ste. Anne is usually a brisk beat to windward in protected water, and can be a great sail. Sometimes on a rising tide, when the current reverses to the east, it can become a bit like being in a washing machine. If it gets really rough, head well offshore till you are away from the tidal influence.

BAIE DU MARIGOT

Having said there are no good anchorages along this coast, there *is* an anchorage. It is not good, in that it often rolls (though this should be no problem for multihulls), and entry is extremely tricky and should only be attempted by those with years of Caribbean and reef navigation experience. The reefs are not at all easy to see and they are dangerous, with swells often building as you go in. Once inside, it is a delightful bay now that the large Novotel has been demolished.

Navigation

Baie du Marigot lies to the east of the town of Diamant. When coming from the

west, you see a conspicuous peaky hill behind. A reef, Caye de Obian, lies almost on a direct line between Pte. du Diamant and the entrance. It is about a mile offshore.

The approach is down a very narrow channel, 30 feet deep, with shallow banks and reefs on either side, up to half a mile offshore. While there is just enough water to stray onto the banks in some places, you want to stay in the deep water. Swells usually roll into the shore, making the approach dangerous if you make a mistake. The channel includes a curve. The approach should only be made in calm, sunny conditions, with good light for spotting the shallows, which are often hard to pick out. It is strictly a matter of eyeball navigation.

Once inside, there is ample room for anchoring. The prettiest area is towards the eastern headland. If you are on a monohull,

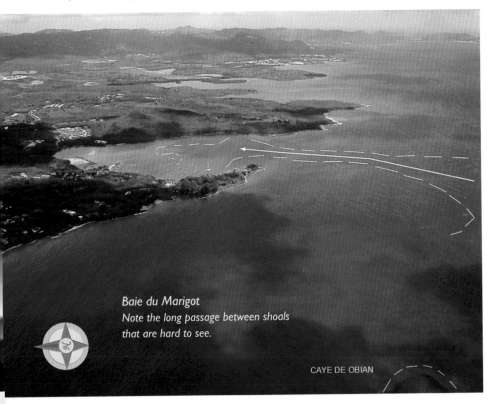

Baie du Marigot
Note the long passage between shoals that are hard to see.

CAYE DE OBIAN

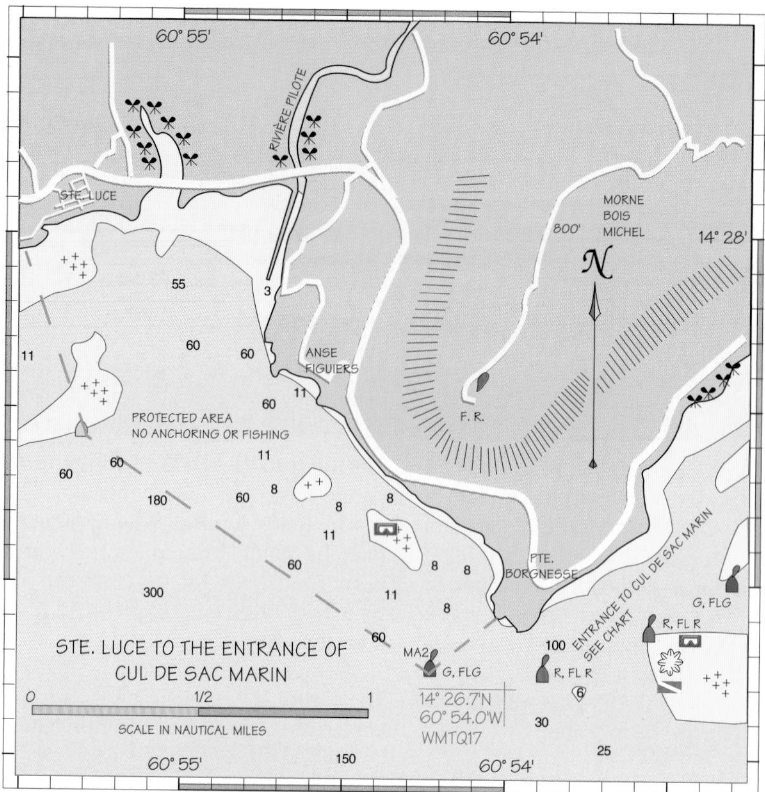

you will probably need to use a stern anchor to make life bearable.

PTE. BORGNESSE TO ANSE FIGUIERS

Pte. Borgnesse is the western headland as you enter Cul de Sac Marin. A couple of pleasant areas for dinghy exploration and snorkeling lie between this headland and Anse Figuiers, with some quiet hidden beaches. This is a protected area and fishing and anchoring are prohibited.

Navigation

A wide shelf, about 9-14 feet deep, follows this coast. Off the shelf, the depth drops rapidly to 200 feet. There are some large shallow areas on the shelf that must be avoided. A mile to the northwest, Anse Figuiers is a delightful bay and a popular holiday beach, behind which you can see the eco-museum building with its conspicuous chimney.

There is ample water to dinghy up the Rivière Pilote for a couple miles to the town of Rivière Pilote. This is an entertaining exercise and the scenery is quite pretty. Along the eastern shore is an area with a number of junked railway cars from the days when sugar cane was moved by rail. Entry to the river is close to shore between the coast and a manmade causeway. You will see many fishing boats and even a mini-marina along the first part of the trip.

Martinque Cruisers Net with local info in English Monday, Wednesday and Friday 0830 VHF ch 08. Check the Martinique cruisers facebook page for updates

St. Anne

STE. ANNE

The white buildings of Ste. Anne stand out clearly against the surrounding green hills. Above the lovely historic church, a walled path zigzags up a small hill to a shrine. At each turn of the path an agony of Christ is depicted. This is a lovely short walk with rewarding views.

Ste. Anne is a delightful seaside town, with a relaxing holiday atmosphere. The town is tiny, but it has an adjoining beach that is magnificent and popular. The surrounding countryside is attractive, with short walks to even better beaches.

Navigation

Yellow buoys delineate a no-anchoring area off the beach and town. Some years they drift away, so yachts anchor back in town. The anchoring area in any case is huge. You can also eyeball your way south and anchor off the Caritan Hotel. The water is 10 to 20 feet deep, sand bottom. Most is good holding, though there are patches where the sand is too hard to get the anchor down, and there are some boulders. Shoals lie close to shore between Ste. Anne and Anse Caritan and off the southern part of Anse Caritan.

Weather permitting, you can visit pretty daytime anchorages south of Ste. Anne off Anse Meunier and Grande Anse des Salines. Approach Anse Meunier with caution, as the bay is quite shallow. Avoid the rocky shallows between Pointe Catherine and Pointe Pie. Grande Anse des Salines is spectacular and popular. (See chart page 111).

Regulations/communications

You can clear customs at Snack Boubou (closed Wednesdays and for occasional holidays). It is next to Les Tamariniers. The customs computer is open 0800-1900 and the bar is open longer. Call them at 0596 76 28 46 for details. They have WiFi.

An active English language cruisers net is on VHF: 08 at 0830 on Mondays, Wednesdays, and Fridays. Updated times are on the Martinique cruisers Facebook page.

Cyber Base is a government-run internet center upstairs at the back of a big building (take the side street). It opens Monday to Friday 0730-1330, also 1500-1700 on Monday and Thursday, subject to change.

La Dunette and Paille Coco, among others, have WiFi. Take your computer in and have a coffee to get the password. It might work from anchor.

Supermarket 8 a Huit sells time on Digicel and Orange phones.

Services

The town dock is good for dinghies, though often crowded. Garbage bins are just beyond the dock. Other bins are towards the market.

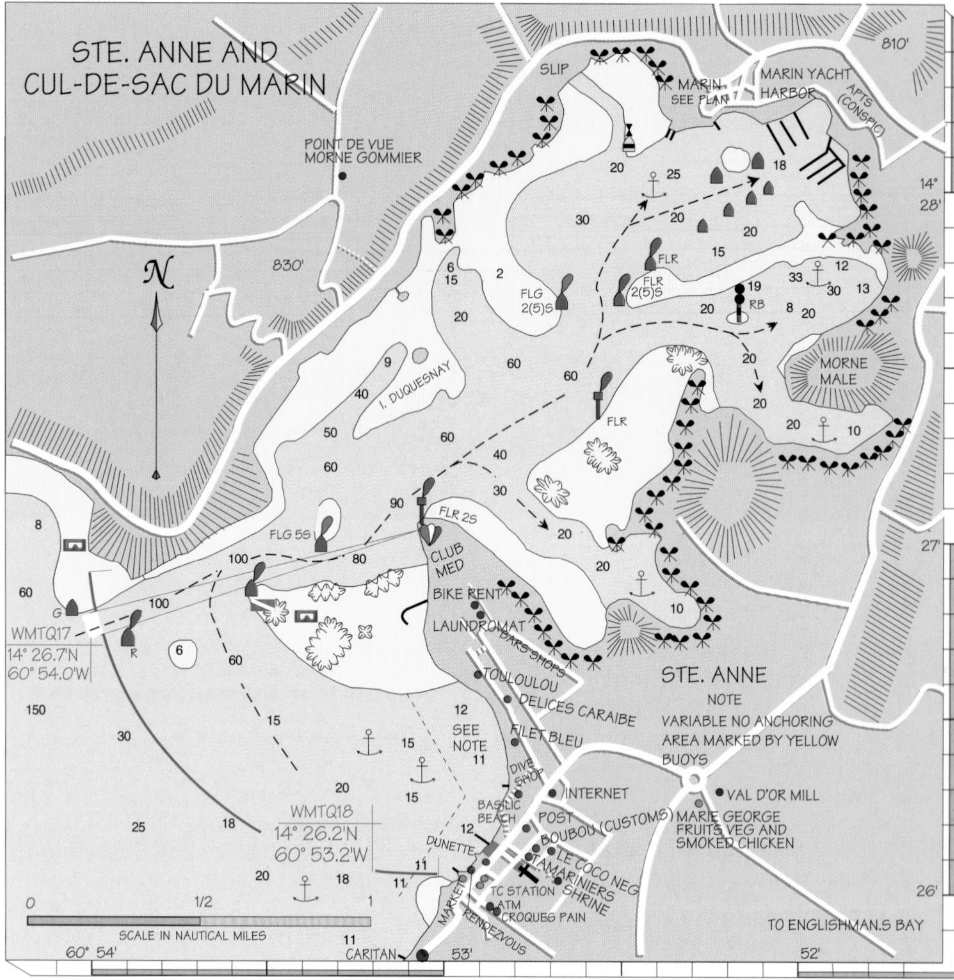

Chris (0696) 97 90 15, VHF: 10 at Little Ship, Caritan, is your one-stop service station, and he speaks good English. His office/workshop is next to the laundromat at Anse Caritan. (Tie your dinghy to the Pirate restaurant dock.) His micro-tanker will deliver water and ice alongside in St. Anne or Marin and the sound of old bike horns lets you know he is around. He takes laundry and does it overnight at the laundromat. Chris and his team are mechanics and can fix both outboard and inboard motors, and arrange any other repairs. Chris has a friend who seems to be able to replace the screens on old electronics. He is agent for some compact GPS trackers for safeguarding your dinghy or boat, and can source any yacht hardware. They should be carrying Tohatsu outboards by 2019. They have cars and are willing to help out if you need a drop at the airport or, if you order from a supermarket, they can deliver to your boat. Chris is planning a yacht club where you can get all these services at a better rate.

By day you can dinghy down to the Caritan, tie to the dinghy dock and walk uphill a few hundred feet to the laundromat.

Abrilav laundromat is close to the Club Med behind all the beach restaurants (see the sketch chart).

Provisioning/shopping

Get cash at one of the two ATMs: one is at the post office. Step off the dock and turn right, walk down the street, and you will find two small supermarkets adequate for topping up your stores. Chez Mireille opens 0630- 2000 Monday to Saturday, 0630-1930 Sundays and holidays, Just beyond is an 8 à Huit, which is larger and has more produce.

Cherie Doudou, the boulangerie/patisserie, has room on the beach side for coffee, pain au chocolat, or sandwiches. The market is farther down the street on the right, fish market first, then the general market, with fresh meat, fruits, vegetables, and handicrafts. You will find a pharmacy in the main square

If you are willing to walk the best part of a mile to the roundabout on the main road, Marie George has a great fruit and veg stand and also sells smoked chicken. Opposite you can visit Moulin Val d'Or (see *Ashore*).

Casual shoppers will enjoy the little craft stores and boutiques on every street. Ozar, by the market, is the most interesting, with work of many local artists and craftsmen.

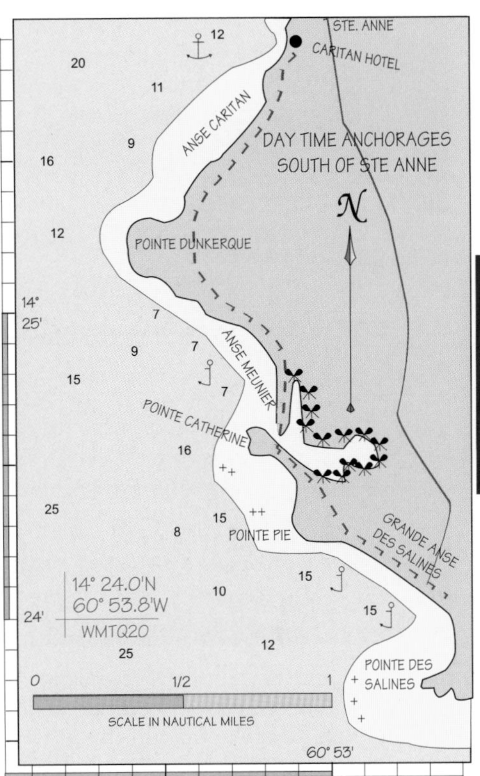

Restaurants

Restaurants abound, both in town and on the beach that stretches from Ste. Anne to the Club Med.

Gerard's hotel La Dunette [$$$] has a perfect location and a dinghy dock. A long dock offers tables with a sea view, day beds, loungers, swinging chairs, and the sea to cool off in. The restaurant is open all day and if you need a night ashore, this is the place.

Their restaurant serves seafood, including fresh fish tatare, and the portions are generous. Lunch starts around midday, dinner at 1930.

They also have a snack bar where you can get a perfectly cooked tuna frites for 10 Eu. Come for a sunset rum punch and take your choice. This is a happening place, with live music from time to time.

Chez La Martine, a shop on the little street opposite La Dunette, is the place to be at 1800. They put tables on the street and serve accras, beer, and other drinks at bargain prices.

One of the cheapest eateries is Snack Boubou, where you clear customs. They are famous for their lunch Bokits - bakes stuffed with a filling of your choice. If you come for breakfast, Snack Boubou, La Dunette, and the boulangerie are the places to try.

Le Coco Neg is a tiny back street restaurant with a pleasant atmosphere that serves traditional Créole meals. Otantic, on the hill by the cemetery has a great sunset view, and La Daurade, opposite the market, is inexpensive. Les Tamariniers [$$$] has a cute exterior, and Le Rendezvous has a good waterfront location. Paille Coco, in front of Cherie Doudou, the boulangerie, has an even better one with good fresh seafood. The town also has a couple of pizza/snack bars, another boulangerie on the back street, and in the bus station a creperie opens for dinner.

The whole of the long beach is lined with restaurants mostly open only at lunch. Basilic Beach is inexpensive and does tasty fresh seafood. Farther down the beach, Madi's Delices Caraibe is excellent value, with good seafood and daily specials. To

St. Anne waterfront

impress a friend, pay a little more and get the giant mixed-seafood plate. The service is first rate and they all spoke English this year. It has an adjoining snack bar called Ti Kano.

Le Filet Bleu has been around forever and is quite popular. This is the only beach restaurant that might be open for dinner.

Ashore

The church square leads to two main streets, one along the waterfront and a parallel one at the back. From the dock, turn left along the front street to climb over the hill, past the cemetery, and down to the popular beach that stretches all the way to Club Med.

The coastal area from Ste. Anne right round the south and back up the east coast to Anse Trabaud is a park with a trail. Hikers and bikers should take the road toward Anse Caritan and then follow the trail that goes all the way along, or just behind, the shore to Anse des Salines. Anse des Salines is one of Martinique's finest palm-backed beaches, and very popular, ideal for people watching. Those who prefer a more private setting will pass several smaller beaches along the way. Bikers can continue on to Anse Trabaud and back over the middle. (The trail is such that you will push a lot.) It takes about three and a half hours at a leisurely pace. You can rent bikes from Herve at Velo Club Aosa Cap 110 [closed Monday]. He also organizes cycling tours around the island. He is near Club Med, next to the laundromat. Give him a call: (0696) 25 34 18. Busses run to Marin. Communal taxis run to Fort de France.

Moulin Val d'Or, a recently rebuilt 18th century donkey-powered sugar cane mill, is about a mile away at the roundabout. It is open Thursday to Sunday 0900-1200, 1400-1700. Guided tours in English are available.

Water sports

A good place to start snorkeling or diving is at the second red buoy in the channel toward Marin. Snorkelers can follow the shallow part of the reef and divers can head south into deeper water, where they will find a large collection of sponges, including some unusual shapes. This is a good place to see corallimorphs, pencil urchins, and small, colorful reef fish.

Kalinargo, the local dive shop, is at the Ste. Anne end of the beach that leads to Club Med. They dive twice daily, at 0830 and 1330. They fill tanks.

Another dive shop, Natiyabel, is at the fishing port and rents kayaks.

Small sailing catamarans and sailboards are available for rent on the beach.

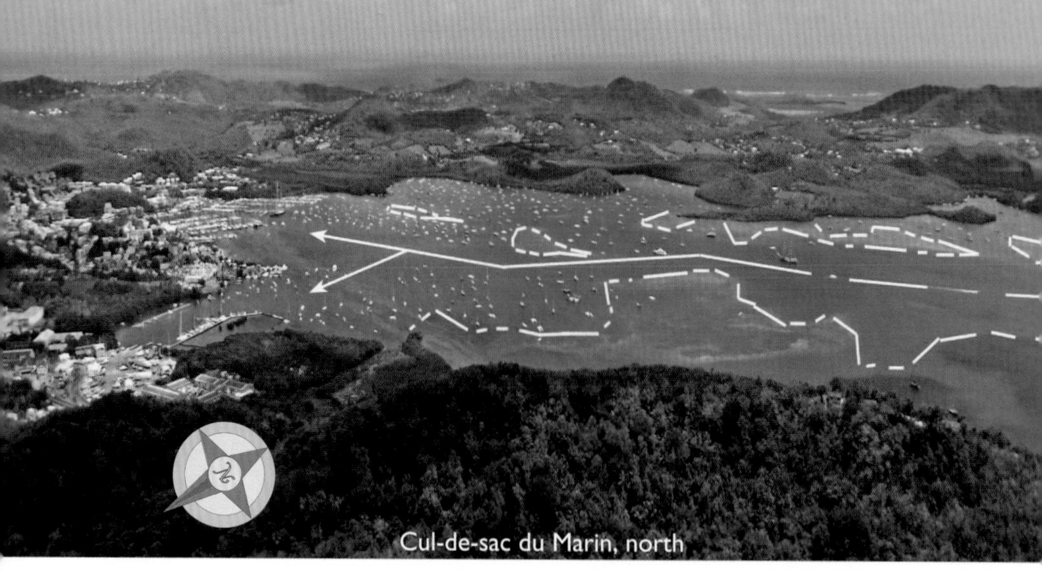
Cul-de-sac du Marin, north

MARIN

Marin, a pleasant small town, is one of the Caribbean's largest yacht centers, with the huge Marin Marina, a big haul-out facility, and a large array of yacht services and technicians. Where else in the Windwards can you walk into a mechanic's shop and view a row of marine engines on show and ready to install? You can find technicians of all stripes and they are generally helpful and good at what they do ~ and there is not much that cannot be done. This is the main base for the Martinique charter industry: Star Voyage, Outremer Concept, Dream Yacht Caribbean, Punch Croisieres, Azur Spirit, VPM Dufour, and Corail Caraibes, all have bases here.

June 21 is the French national music day, a good day to visit when you can be sure of some free concerts in town. Ask the marina for details. Marin and St. Anne combined often have up to 2,500 yachts at any one time. As a result, this area pulls in about 30% of all tourist dollars spent in Martinique.

Navigation

Cul-de-Sac du Marin is a big, deeply indented bay, surrounded by hills and lined with mangroves. It is full of shoals that are visible in good light. It is a gunkholer's dream and the best place to be in Martinique during a hurricane. The entrance channel is well marked by buoys and beacons. After you pass Club Med, head for the apartment buildings behind the forest of masts until you see the big red and green buoys in the middle of the bay. Pass between them, leaving the red one

Cul-de-sac du Marin, south

to starboard and the green one to port. Follow the channel in, leaving the red buoys to starboard. Shoals lie in the "no anchoring" area off Marin Beach, so avoid it.

Small yachts going between Marin and Ste. Anne can take a short cut between the outer two red buoys. Avoid the 6-foot shoal that lies east of the outer red buoy (see our sketch chart, page 110).

Regulations

Marin is a port of entry. Do-it-yourself customs computers are in the capitainerie in the Marina Mall. Clear 0800-1730 Monday to Saturday and 0800-1230 Sundays. There is a charge of 5 Eu. Add half an hour, and these are also the marina office hours.

It is possible for non-European yachts to bring things in VAT-Free; Douglas Rapier can handle clearance for you. He can also pre-clear large yachts via the internet.

European-registered yachts that have been exported tax-free will likely be charged tax on entry.

Anchoring is forbidden except where shown.

Communications

An English language cruisers net is on VHF: 08, at 0830 on Mondays, Wednesday sand Fridays. You can find updated times on the Martinique cruisers Facebook page.

You can access the web through a smart phone with either an Orange or Digicel SIM. There is an Orange/Digicel store in Artimer, a main Digicel one in the Annette Mall, and one of each in the Marin Bay Commercial Center (a short walk from Leader Price). The mini mart next to the market sells Orange time.

Many people take their computers into Mango Bay, which has free WiFi for customers. Those on the hard can use the computer in the Carenantilles main office.

Captain has a good bay-wide WiFi system which also works in St. Anne. Marin Marina has WiFi covering their docks and moorings.

General yacht services

Services, shops, and restaurants in Marin are in several locations, easy to reach by dinghy. Some are close around the marina; others are over by Carenantilles, the large slipway, or at Artimer. All have dinghy docks, and Zanzibar has a nice new one.

Artimer is a big development, designed to include the boating trade. It has been cleverly designed to use the river and you can dinghy right up; the dinghy ride is novel. You pass the anchored yachts off Carenantilles, staying quite well inshore until you see the marked channel. Pass down the channel, leaving red right returning, then enter the river. For a short while you get a river ride among the mangroves in the middle of nowhere with herons and egrets. Suddenly, you arrive in a giant shopping mall where dinghies tie up in a little basin. You need to be able to climb one of the ladders, which are very large and secure. Carenantilles and Artimer are close to each other for easy walking.

You will find garbage disposal at both the marina and the haul-out, with glass, paper and plastic, and oil and battery recycling. You can get water and fuel at the Marina.

Marin Marina [VHF: 09] (Marina du Marin) is the only giant marina in Martinique. Owned by the Jean-Joseph family and managed by Eric, it is good, friendly, and inexpensive, and all the staff you deal with speak English. They have won top awards (5 rings) from the French marina rating system and are one of only two marinas in France to score that high, including the blue flag award as an environmentally friendly marina.

Dinghy docks are in front of the nautical block (by Mango Bay) and at the Marina Mall (Capitainerie). With 830 berths, there is normally plenty of room for visitors who are placed on the most accessible berths; Docks 4 and 5 (see sketch chart). The fuel dock takes three or four yachts (or one superyacht) and you can get diesel, gasoline, and water daily: 0730-1730. Superyacht fueling is at 12,000 liters an hour. Dockage is available with 220-volt/50-cycle electricity; 110-volt transformers are also available. (The 220-volt does not work with two lines of 110.) Four hundred volts is available for superyachts. They have 140 moorings and it is best to call and book one in advance. Call on VHF: 09 to get help coming in. Docks 3 and 4 have holding-tank pump out. C and H docks have finger piers rather than stern-to berthing. The marina is huge, but most of it is connected with a waterfront walkway. The marina facilities are in two blocks. The original Marina nautical block has chandleries and many services. The Capitainerie (Port Office) is in the huge Marina Mall at the head of the bay. This big block has restaurants, charter companies, shops, and nautical services. The Capitainerie can change $US/EC/pounds.

Some berths are suitable for mega yachts of any length and up to 4.5 meters draft. At Douglas Yacht Services, Douglas Rapier and his team, including Eugenie, Karen, and Hoelenn, will help you in every way. Douglas is perfect for those who want utterly dependable, top quality service and are willing to pay for it. Douglas has some berths with dedicated WiFi service for his customers.

Douglas and his team are there to ensure that big yachts have everything they need. They can pre-clear yachts before arrival and do full provisioning and refueling, as well as providing technical support, and arranging travel, private jet arrival, medical, and other personal arrangements. Douglas is available 24/7 and keeps his phone at his side. For smaller yachts, he does project management (see *Technical yacht services*).

If you are doing a large maintenance project, it is now possible to get all the hauling and work VAT free and all parts shipped in duty and VAT-free. You do need to set this up in advance, and Douglas is the man to speak to about this.

He is agent for Axxess Marine, a high-end internet service for the Caribbean. It starts at $390 US for 50 gigabytes per month but you can get much more. You only pay for months you want to use it. To have it working properly, giving you WiFi throughout your boat, you will need to buy the right gear, not only to ensure sufficient bandwidth, but to allow Axxess to help you if you have any problems. For a heavy user this turns out to be less expensive per gigabyte than the Eu 15 that I pay Digicel for one.

Douglas also represents Sevenstar Yacht Transport, and you can make all arrangements with him for shipping your yacht most places in the world.

Carenantilles [VHF: 16/73] is a large haul-out facility, newly renovated. We show their location on our sketch chart. You can easily visit by dinghy, but it is gated, so it is not as easy to access the land as it once was. However, if you are a customer of Carene Shop, which has doors on both sides, you can probably get someone to give you the code number for the gate. The new dinghy dock at the head of the long dock is big, but fills right up. The Bichic fuel facility is leaving, I am not sure just what will be in their spot, but fuel will not be available.

Carenantilles is for hauling and working on boats. They have plenty of docks for going stern-to with moorings and some alongside. They have two for superyachts, with side pillars. They have one dock with no shore access.

Carenantilles holds about 230 boats ashore, and they have two marine hoists. The small one is 80 tons and takes about 28 foot beam, the larger is 440 tons and takes about 43 foot beam.

For the most part, there is plenty of water in the bay for the approach. If you start at the outer buoy and head towards the dock, you should have 14 feet. The shallowest part is out by the buoy. While Carenantilles are happy to store boats, they concentrate on boats undergoing work. Rates depend on how long you need to be ashore and the current exchange rate for the euro. Fax them for a rate sheet. You can do your own work on the slip, or many good workshops can do it for you (see *Technical yacht services*). Facilities include toilets, showers, and a restaurant. The yard is run by Arthur De Lucey; Jocelyne, who speaks good English, manages the reception with Maggir and Karynne.

Dock Cleaner Ecologique is an ecologically friendly floating dry dock run by Dream Yachts. It can take anything up to 55 tons, 13 meters wide, and 1.8 meters deep. Call Alain Rollet: 0696 92-62-47.

Blanc Marine is a convenient modern launderette in the Marina Mall. It has a central computerized system that takes both coins and notes. If you have a big load they have a 14 kilo machine, as well as several at 7 kilos, and the driers are large. Soap is available, and for those big party nights, there is a dishwasher. It is open daily 0600-2200. They are also the only laundry in the marina that will collect and deliver your laundry, ironed if you want. E-mail them for a quote.

Otherwise, there is Lav@net in the Annette Mall.

Martinique has boat brokers in every corner. Caribbean Yachts, managed by Stephanie, is part of a larger company, with offices in Guadeloupe, St. Martin, the Dominican Republic, and Panama. They are in the Marina Mall and they sell a lot of boats of all types. They offer full brokerage and also offer a web based boat for sale by owner site.

Azur Spirit in the nautical block is run by Jimy, who has a big listing. He also charters yachts and looks after and repairs boats (see *Technical yacht services: Project management*).

Net Boat sells new and second hand Lagoons and Beneteaus, and provides service for those that own them.

Eric Vasse's Neo Marine are the Caribbean agents for Nautitech cats offering sales and service. They are also a general sales broker, look after boats when owners go away, and do project management.

A&C brokers sell new and used Fontaine Pajots, and other brands, and offer customer service for them. Other charter companies also sometimes sell used yachts.

If you need a survey, Jacques Scharwatt is a surveyor and his office is upstairs, next to Diginav.

Medical problems can be fixed according to severity and need. There is a kind of medical Mall upstairs in the marina with doctors, a nurse, physiotherapists (Kino) and more. Or, walk up the hill from the market, and you will find Dr. Jean Louis Deloge and Dr. Veronique Claisse. Dr. Claisse specializes in sports medicine, perfect for tortured muscles and joints. Behind Leader Price is the big Alizes Medical Center. You can walk in, but will probably have to wait quite a while.

If you need serious and immediate attention, get Douglas at Douglas Yacht Services to help you. Otherwise, the emergency number is 115.

For eyeglasses, La Lunetterie is modern, big and in the Artimer Mall.

Chandlery

Marin has wonderful chandleries; the best collection in the Windwards. They are packed with good equipment and each one is different. In the marina nautical block Le Ship is a great chandlery with a big stock. You will find stoves, heads, anchors, including the new Rocna, very high grade chain, rope, charts, pumps, stoves, a great collection of LED bulbs, electronics, cruising guides, charts, Lofrans winches, and all kinds of yacht hardware. They have some good buys on Trois D Tenders, aluminum-hulled PVC inflatable dinghies. This is also the place for good acrylic wine glasses, linens, and some fun and fancy nautical decorations.

Caraibe Marine, which is combined with a number of technical services, is the largest chandlery not only in Martinique but also in the Windwards, with many departments. Owner Philippe Leconte started as a rigger and then expanded into electrics and built a chandlery. He now has workshops that cover rigging (Caraibes Gréement), electrics, and watermakers (Caraibes Energie), electronics, (Caraibes Electronique), refrigeration (Caraibes Refrigeration), woodworking (Caraibes Menuiserie) and metal work (Caraibes Metal). For details see *Technical yacht services*. This expansion is reflected in the chandlery, which is a super store with many departments. It also means if you buy something that needs installation,

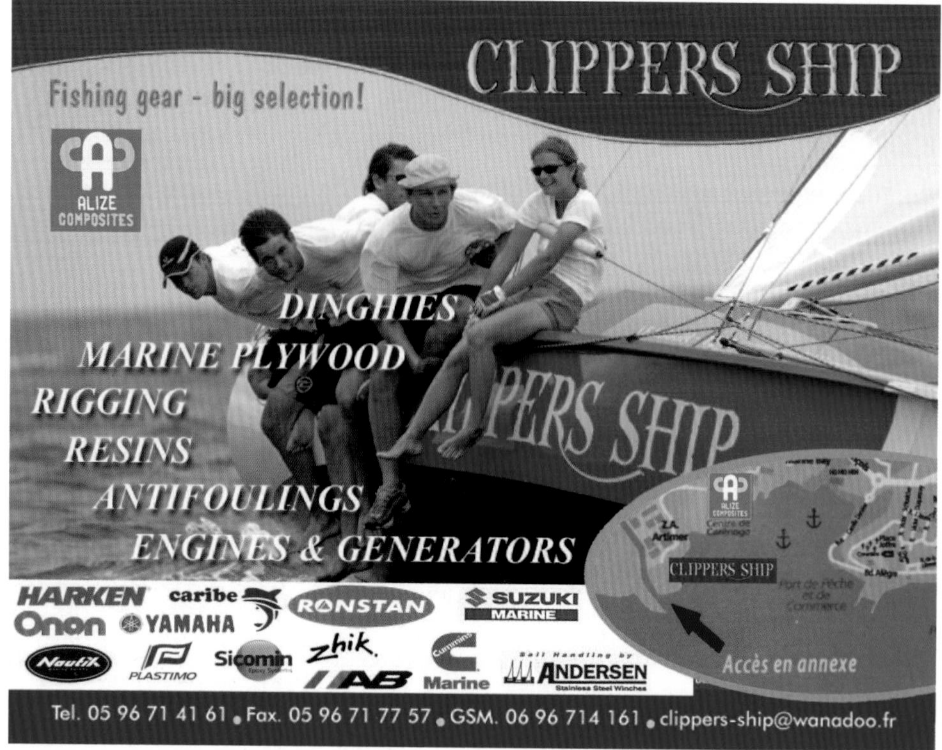

they can do it for you, and if it later needs service, they can do that, too. Need some new hatches? Caraibe Marine will have them in all shapes and sizes, as well as all the seals when you need a replacement. I am impressed because they stock things like the little plastic inserts for track cars that wear out, and are hard to come by. They sell lots of Highfield aluminum ribs, both neoprene and PVC. You will find a wide range of general chandlery, including safety gear and general hardware, as well as cooking stoves, charts, ropes, paints, and electronics ~ everything down to a kettle.

MARIN MARINA MALL
UPSTAIRS DOWNSTAIRS
B = BOUTIQUE
DREAM YACHT
DOUCEURS MARINOISES
LAWYERS OFFICE
VISUELLE PRINTING
TOURIST OFFICE
MEDICAL OFFICES
TILIKUM
PONCHON,
CARAIBES YACHTS
AMEL
LAVERIE
OXALIS
TOILETS
INFOGEEK
ATM
AKWABA
R&M
NAUTIQUE
MEDICAL OFFICES
DREAM YACHTS
GD LOC
AZUR SPIRIT
MADE FOR MARIN B
CAP DECO B
CARGOT B
FDF
KOCOARUM
LE TOUCAN
SUSHI O JADE
L'ANNEX
LES COMPTOIR DE COTONS B
MAXI MARINE
NORTH SAILS
POST OFFICE
AUTREMER CONCEPT
CAPITAINERIE (CUSTOMS)
PIZZA AMIS
MARKET PLACE
NUMERO 20
DINGHY DOCK
MARINA DOCKS

Caraibe Marine also has a large electrical showroom. Ask Philippe about solar panels. He advises 24-volt panels for a 12-volt system with a converter, because this gives a higher input over a longer time. Upstairs is a complete nautical boutique with elegant casual, sailing, and beachwear with labels from Musto, Sebaco, Sun Valley, and many more. They have bathing costumes in all sizes. Caraibe Marine is the Caribbean service center for Fountaine Pajot, Jeanneau, CBN (the larger Lagoons) and Catana.

Dinghy over to Artimer to visit Clippers Ship, another giant chandlery that takes up two floors. It is owned by Jocelyne and her son Emmanuel, helped by Lurent. They are all helpful and speak good English. They have a wide selection of materials and fittings, including sheets of marine ply, resins, cloth, Awlgrip and coppercoat paints, An-

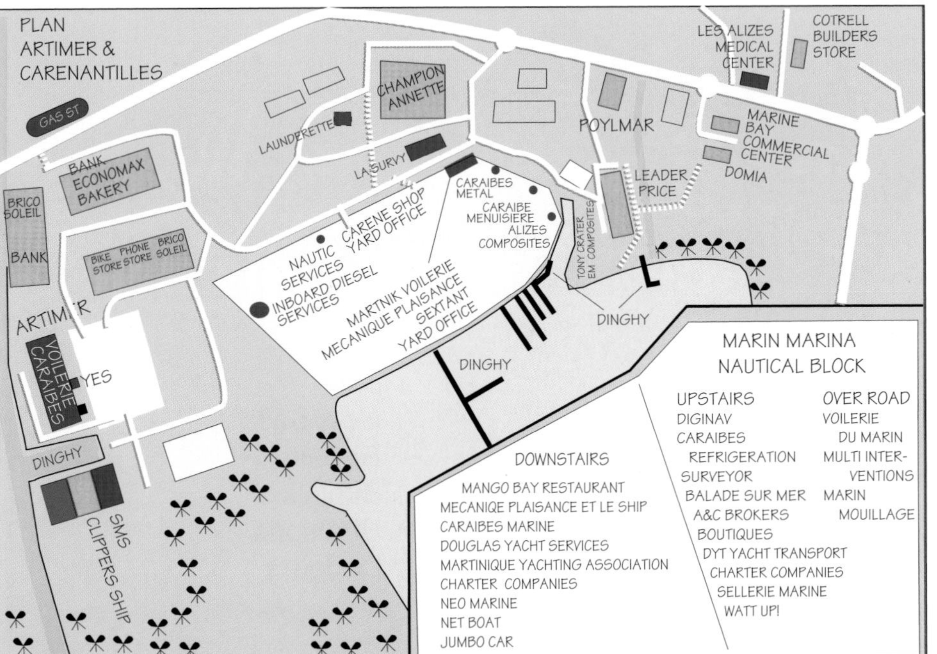

PLAN
ARTIMER &
CARENANTILLES
GAS ST
LAUNDERETTE
CHAMPION ANNETTE
LES ALIZES MEDICAL CENTER
COTRELL BUILDERS STORE
POYLMAR
MARINE BAY COMMERCIAL CENTER
DOMIA
LEADER PRICE
BANK ECONOMAX BAKERY
LA SURVY
BRICO SOLEIL
BANK
CARAIBES METAL
CARAIBE MENUISIERE
ALIZES COMPOSITES
TONY CRATER EM COMPOSITES
NAUTIC SERVICES
CARENE SHOP YARD OFFICE
INBOARD DIESEL SERVICES
BIKE STORE
PHONE STORE
BRICO SOLEIL
MARTNIK VOILERIE
MECANIQUE PLAISANCE
SEXTANT YARD OFFICE
DINGHY
ARTIMER
VOILERIE CARAIBES
YES
DINGHY
DINGHY
SMS CLIPPERS SHIP
MARIN MARINA NAUTICAL BLOCK
UPSTAIRS
DIGINAV
CARAIBES REFRIGERATION
SURVEYOR
BALADE SUR MER
A&C BROKERS
BOUTIQUES
DYT YACHT TRANSPORT
CHARTER COMPANIES
SELLERIE MARINE
WATT UP!
OVER ROAD
VOILERIE DU MARIN
MULTI INTERVENTIONS
MARIN MOUILLAGE
DOWNSTAIRS
MANGO BAY RESTAURANT
MECANIQE PLAISANCE ET LE SHIP
CARAIBES MARINE
DOUGLAS YACHT SERVICES
MARTINIQUE YACHTING ASSOCIATION
CHARTER COMPANIES
NEO MARINE
NET BOAT
JUMBO CAR

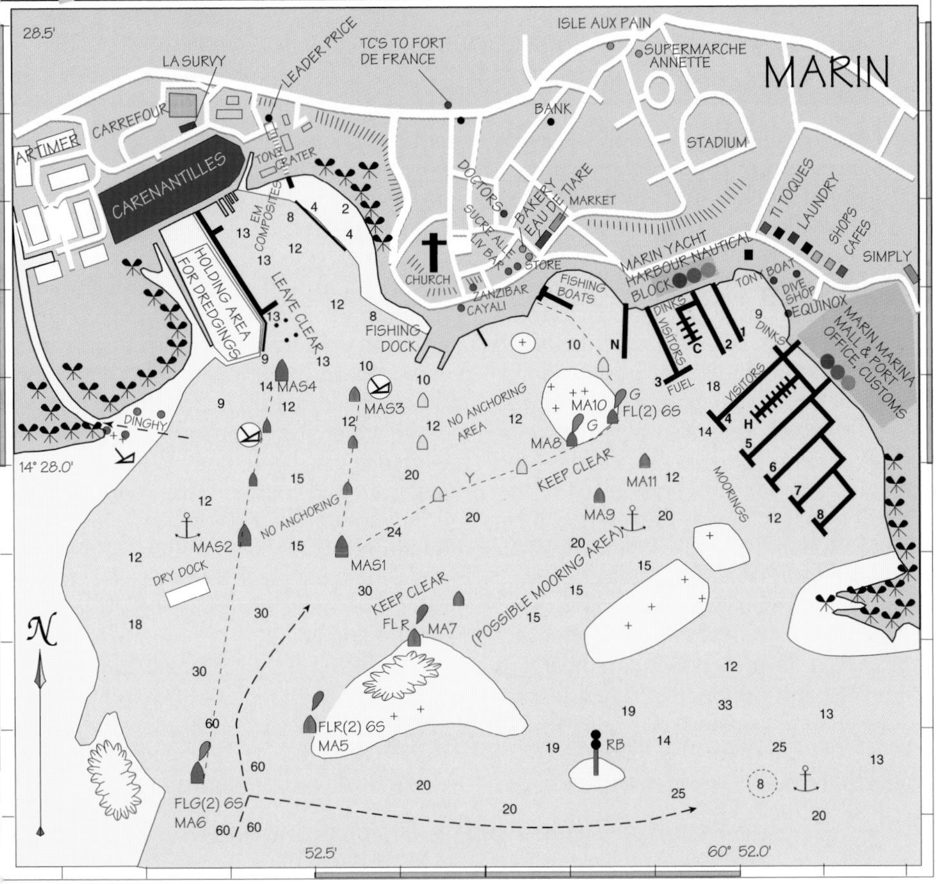

MARIN
28.5'
LA SURVY
LEADER PRICE
TC'S TO FORT DE FRANCE
ISLE AUX PAIN
SUPERMARCHE ANNETTE
BANK
STADIUM
CARREFOUR
ARTIMER
CARENANTILLES
TONY CRATER
EM COMPOSITES
HOLDING AREA FOR DREDGINGS
LEAVE CLEAR
DOCTORS
SUCRE ALLE LIV BAR
BAKERY
EAU DE TIARE
MARKET
CHURCH
STORE
ZANZIBAR
CAYALI
FISHING BOATS
FISHING DOCK
MARIN YACHT HARBOUR NAUTICAL BLOCK
DINKS
VISITORS
FUEL
TONY BOAT
DIVE SHOP
EQUINOX
TI TOQUES
LAUNDRY
SHOPS
CAFES
SIMPLY
MARIN MARINA MALL & PORT OFFICE, CUSTOMS
DINKS
VISITORS
MOORINGS
N
C
H
MAS4
MAS3
MAS2
MAS1
MA10
MA8
MA11
MA9
MA7
MA5
MA6
FL(2) 6S
FLR
FLR(2) 6S
FLG(2) 6S
RB
G
Y
DINGHY
NO ANCHORING AREA
NO ANCHORING
KEEP CLEAR
KEEP CLEAR
(POSSIBLE MOORING AREA)
DRY DOCK
14° 28.0'
52.5'
60° 52.0'
N

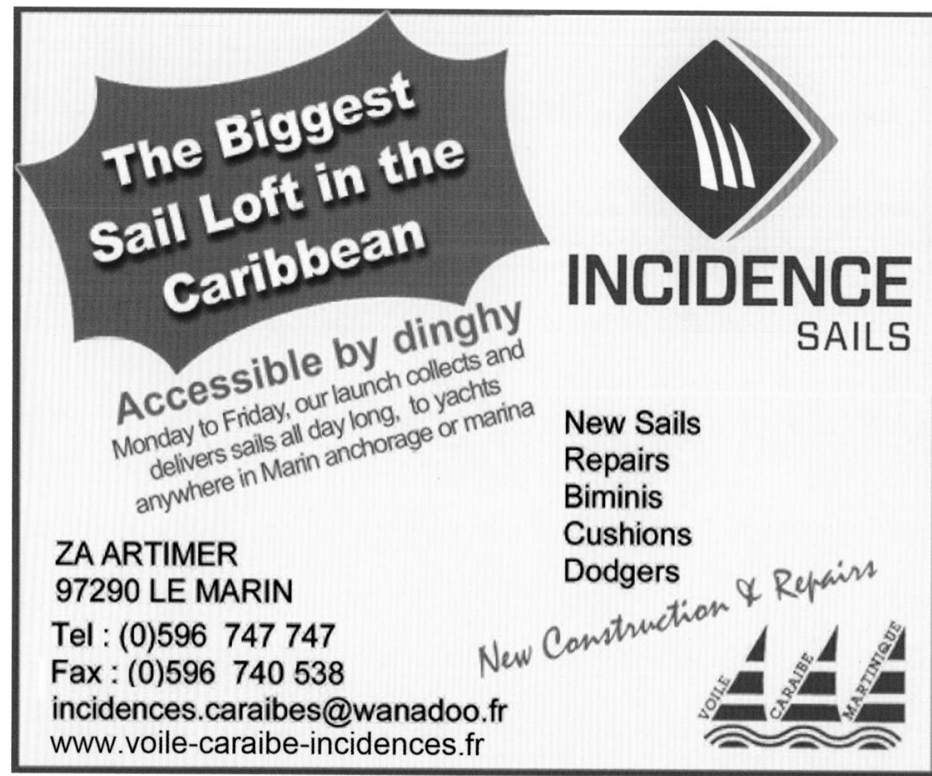

dersen winches and spares, electrical panels, solar panels, electronics, anchor winches, Morse cables, hatches, and portlights. They have an excellent selection of pumps and light fittings, with all the latest LED bulbs. They stock stainless and aluminum pipe, icemakers, windmills, Lewmar and Harken hardware. Upstairs has a big selection of AB and Caribe inflatable dinghies. They stock Onan generators, and Suzuki and Yamaha outboards, which they also repair and service. They carry Zhik racing clothes and nautical shoes. This is a good place to buy snorkeling gear. Clippers Ship carries a big range of fasteners, sold in convenient packages, which makes building a collection easy. They also sell rivets, which can be hard to find. Emmanuel also owns Alizes Composites with Nicolas. They do all kinds of fiberglass repairs and construction. See *Technical yacht services: Glass and paintwork.*

Over in Carenantilles, Carene Shop, owned by Hervé Ferrari, is in the Carenantilles compound. It has two floors with two names. Downstairs, Carene Shop is a good technical chandlery for everything you might need on the slip or for a job. Paints, antifoulings, epoxies, polyesters, and cloths are carried, as well as zincs, through-hulls, plumbing, cleaning and polishing products, and a huge stock of marine batteries. You can buy marine ply, acrylic sheet, PVC and Starboard cut to size, and sometimes offcuts.

Upstairs (Le Grenier du Marin) is a fascinating place with both new and second-hand gear, and you can bring your treasures of the bilge to sell. It has general chandlery, including inflatables, fasteners, and safety gear, with some great bargains. One time I visited they had a selection of good second-hand folding bikes.

At the top of the car park behind Leader Price there is a branch of Max and Cedric's Polymar, who also have branches in Baie de Tourelles and Robert. It is a big shop geared to practical, rather than fancy, stock, at

See Polymar Ad in Fort de France page 80

good prices. You will find lots of fishing gear, including commercial equipment, safety gear, electronics, LED lights and electrical components, ropes, paints and construction materials, tools, yacht fittings, deck gear, and more. They sell and service Lacomble Schmitt hydraulics. Closed Sunday, they open 0830-1300 on Wednesdays 0830-1200 on Saturdays and 0830-1300, 1400-1700 the other days.

YES is not a chandlery but they keep a big stock of solar panels and a collection of led bulbs and lights at good prices, along with other electrical accessories and watermakers. Thierry, the owner, also does electrical and watermaker repairs (see *Technical yacht services*).

Maxi Marine in the Marina Mall has a general chandlery with some useful items, including lots of safety gear, fastenings, anchors, and a big well-laid-out rope section. They are somewhat geared toward power yachts and so have plenty of rollers. They sell and service Mercury and Mercruiser motors.

For general hardware, Brico Soliel is a good small hardware store in Artimer, and for more than that, Cotrell is a building supplier.

Technical yacht services
Sailmakers/Canvas/Cushions

Technical yacht services are found in Marin Marina, in Carenantilles, and in Artimer.

In Artimer, the Incidences (Voilerie Caraibes) sail loft, some 6000 square feet of state-of-the-art design, is the largest and most capable in the Caribbean, a giant by international standards. Hervé Lepault, the owner, speaks perfect English and he and his team can tackle any job, from windsurfer to superyacht. Sails may be brought in by launch or truck and hoisted straight up into the loft on a giant traveler system. Their launch collects and delivers sails on board anywhere in the Marin anchorage or Marin Marina at any time during working hours from Monday to Friday, with no extra charge. Call 0596 74 77 47.

This is a huge, efficient loft that does excellent work, and turn-around time on repairs is fast. They do canvas work, including dinghy chaps, awnings, and biminis. Hervé has an upholstery department for boat cushions and will bring in any color fabric to suit your job. New sails are by Incidence, the well-known French sailmaker, and carry their guarantee. They are computer-designed in France and sewn here. If you want a better sail at about 40% higher cost, they make many cruising sails in woven Spectra, which has a life and weight similar to Dacron but is more resistant to abrasion and will hold its shape significantly better. With this giant loft there is plenty of capacity for making new sails fast.

North Sails has a loft in the Marina Mall. This excellent, small, personal, and friendly operation is run by Gavin Dove. Gavin is the son of Andrew Dove, who started the big North Sails Caribbean, now based in Antigua, and being half-English, he is bilingual. Some of the staff speak Spanish. They can get you an instant quote for a new sail and repair your old one, however technically sophisticated. They also do straightforward canvas work, but not cushions or biminis. They have long hours in season; weekdays 0700-1800, Saturday 0800-1200, 1400- 1700. Out of season it is Monday to Saturday, 0800-1200, 1400-1700. This small loft is part of a group with representatives in nearly every country in the Eastern Caribbean. They can arrange collection of your sail and delivery. If you need a little Dacron, tape, or other sewing supplies for your own project, Gavin will be happy to sell them to you if he has enough.

Voilerie du Marin, run by Daniel Karner, is opposite the nautical block. Dan is the agent for Doyle Sails. He can measure your boat for a new set and get a quote. He also repairs lots of sails, whatever the make, and he does all kinds of canvas work.

Upstairs in the nautical block Iain's Sellerie Marine has a small but well-organized space to do any kind of canvas work, including biminis, awnings and covers, and dinghy chaps, or interior cushions, curtains ,and blinds.

Jean Luke's Martnik Voilerie is upstairs in Carenantilles, though the access is outside round the back of the building. This

is a small friendly shop. Jean Luke repairs sails, does all kinds of canvas work, including biminis and lazy bags, and he makes cushions.

Technical yacht services
Electrics, Electronics & Watermakers

Upstairs in the marina nautical block is Jacques Fauquet's Diginav electronics showroom and workshop. Jacques has been in this business for over 30 years. He knows more about marine electronics than anyone else in Martinique and is one of the few who is willing to pull electronics apart and change components on a board, so if you want something fixed, ask him. He works on all makes and knows what goes wrong with many of them, so when a repair becomes due, he can work efficiently, repairing if possible, only replacing when necessary. Jacques speaks English and is pleasant to deal with.

Diginav's showroom has a good display of Raymarine, Furuno, Brookes and Gatehouse, Simrad, and Garmin electronics in stock, as well as many spares.

Marin, Artimer and Carenantilles

He can set you up with a satellite communication system or a WiFi bullet, as well as safety gear like EPIRBs. He does a lot of sales and installation work for American and European yachts, and is agent for the well-built Silentwind generators.

Jacques is technically excellent, and can handle the most complex systems, including superyacht electronics. It is helpful if you contact him in advance (email is fine).

Caraibe Energie, part of Caraibe Marine, sells, installs, and repairs electrics and watermakers. They are agents for Sea Recovery, HRO, and Aquabase watermakers, for Kohler, Fischer-Panda, and Onan generators. They stock batteries, solar panels, and wind generators, including the cost-effective LE300, and you will find all kinds of electrical components, including Link and Blue Sea, as well as electrical parts and water filters.

Caraibe Electronique, also in the Caraibe Marine stable, sell, install, and service Raymarine, NKE, Furuno, Icom, MC technologies, and Nexus. Since they are together with Caraibe Gréement, it is convenient when you are getting a new mast or taking the old one out for service, that they can install most of the electronics at the same time without having to deal with a third party. (See them at Caraibe Marine; see *Chandlery*.)

Frank Vadi speaks good English, is welcoming and you will enjoy having him on your boat. His company is called Multi Interventions and he is a marine electrics specialist, can sort out any of your electrical problems, and he can help design new systems and install them. Much of Frank's work is looking after boats when owners are away. He can organize any work or projects that need doing in the owner's absence, even have the boat hauled and painted, launched and ready to go. He has some small yacht lockers if you want to store anything ashore.

Renovboat is owned by Marc Eugene, who has had a good reputation in the yachting industry for as long as I have been writing guides. He does electric and electronic repair and works out of his van so he can visit you anywhere in Martinique. He has trained in both the US and Europe, speaks excellent English, and is an ABYC member. He is the right man to help US yachts work on Martinique electricity and knows the cross compliances. He repairs pretty much anything electrical: battery charging systems, solar panels, converters, lighting, windlasses, bow thrusters, fridges, GPSes, and autopilots. He rents marine isolation transformers for foreign boats plugging into 110 Volts/ 60 Cycles. He is an agent for Ocean Volts electric motors and can order any electrical part, whatever the brand, for quick delivery from both the USA and Europe.

Frederic, of Tilikum, in the Marina Mall is an experienced electrical man and Mr. Victron Energy for the Caribbean, where he is their main station. You can buy all their equipment here and get any warranty work done. Fred is good at all charging systems, inverters, and problem solving

Pochon Marine, in the Marina Mall, is a branch of a large French electronics company. They sell Furuno, Icom, Garmin, Lowrance, Simrad, Magellen, B&G, MC Technologies, Raymarine, Cobra, NKE, Sharp, and Hummingbird, and they are agents for Kannad and other EPIRBs. They have Thrane and Thrane Sailor communications, and Schenker watermakers. They also carry televisions for yachts, windmills, and hydro-generators and are agents for torqueedo electric outboards.

Artimer is the home base of Thierry's Yachting Engineering Services (YES). They fix all electrical problems and install any kind of electrical equipment. They sell, service, and install solar panels and watermakers, and fix all makes. They have a van and can make visits to other harbors. YES also keeps a big stock of solar panels, electrical accessories, and watermakers (see *Chandlery*).

Technical yacht services
Rigging

In the marina, Caraibe Gréement (part of Caraibe Marine) is a full rigging service run by Philippe Leconte. Philippe can handle any rigging problem you may have, from replacing stays to a complete re-rig of your yacht, even including a new mast. This is probably the best rigging shop in the Windwards. They can swage up to 26 mm and have equipment for some rod rigging and hydraulic hoses. Difficult splices, including rope to wire, are a breeze. Caraibe Gréement are agents for Profurl, Facnor, Lewmar, Navtec, Gioit, Z-spar, Spectra, Selden Harken, Reckman, and many other brands. They keep spare booms, poles, and all kinds of battens in stock. Anything they do not have can be shipped in on short order by Carole, the special-order specialist. They are happy to work on your yacht and make repairs aloft. They fix and sell hydraulics, including Lecomble. They will also reglaze and seal your worn-out, leaky hatches.

Their new website allows you to estimate the cost and order rigging and other items online. Visit them at Caraibe Marine (see *Chandlery*).

Technical yacht services
Refrigeration

Patrice Fougerouse, at Caraibes Refrigeration is part of the Caraibe Marine group. Patrice is a first-rate refrigeration man, the shop is agent for Webasto, Danfoss, Cruisair, Climma, and Frigoboat, Dometic,

Frigonautica, Vitrifrigo, and Air Marine air conditioning. He will fix any make of refrigeration and air-conditioning and can sell you a new unit and do full installation. You will find him upstairs in the marina nautical block near Diginav.

Nautic Froid is a small refrigeration shop. The owner works out of his boat in the marina, so it is easiest to call.

Technical yacht services

Mechanics/Welding/Fabrication

Mecanique Plaisance is in the marina. Their shop stocks a good range of Perkins, Volvo, Westerbeke, and Yanmar engines and generators, as well as Honda and Tohatsu outboards at competitive prices. The diesel engines can be sold to overseas yachts tax-free. The shop sells a full range of spares for most things mechanical, including filters for fuel and oil. They have inverters, batteries, fasteners, and isotherm fridge units (no service on these). They have a big repair shop over in Carenantilles and are the main repair shop for all the brands of motors they sell. They help out with other makes of engine when they have time. They guarantee their work. There is easy access to come alongside to remove an engine.

Frank Agren's Inboard Diesel Service, is a great place to go for all Volvos, MTUs and Northern Lights generators. They have two big workshops. A new one in Marin at Carenantilles, the other in Case Pilote. Ludovic is the head mechanic in Marin and takes care of all problem from small cruisers to superyachts. They have a team that takes care of these engines in many other islands. They keep a big stock of spares and have work boats that enable them to visit yachts when necessary and Carenantilles has a long dock if you need to be stern to or alongside for work.

Caraibes Metal is in a big building in the corner of Carenantilles, ahead and to the right as you come off the dock. Part of Philippe Leconte's Caraibes Marine Group, this is a giant machine and fabrication shop, with a huge amount of modern equipment for any kind of fabrication or repair. If your project is too big for the others, this is the place to come, though they handle small jobs as well and, since it is the Caraibes Marine group, you know they will be good and efficient. It is run by Anthony Icard, and he speaks enough English to fix your problem.

Laurent Dubois (Kashmir) has Equinox, a metal shop to the north of the Marina Mall at the head of the bay. This is a first class shop for welding, machining, and mechanical work. They are on the waterfront just north of the Marina Mall and they have two docks for yachts needing work. They have a launch and mobile welding unit with a generator for working on board in St. Anne or at anchor. They speak excellent English. Kashmir, the owner, started as an artist in France, but when the market ran dry for giant interactive mobile installations he turned to fixing and fabrication in Martinique. He has a machine shop run by Chris, a German who can make parts, fix broken winches and other mechanical bits. He has a mechanical shop run by Simon from Finland who can repair any kind of inboard or outboard motor.

Maxi Marine, the chandlery in the Marina Mall, offers full sales and support for Mercury and Mercruiser.

Meca Bats is in the nautical block of the marina. It is run by Rubin Martial who used to be a BMW mechanic, and he fixes both inboards and outboards. He is very good, but he is a one-man show, so try to give him a little notice, especially for a big job.

Crater Tony works in a container in back of EM Composites outside Carenantilles. He does TIG and plasma welding and fabricates, welds, and polishes stainless and aluminum and makes many bimini frames.

See Clippers Ship for sales and service of Suzuki outboards.

Technical yacht services
Glass and Paintwork

Alizes Composites is owned and run by Gillet and Emmanuel. They have a big paint shed in Carenantilles and a young and energetic team. They speak good English and do all kinds of fiberglass repairs and construction, including composites. They match gel coat, spray topsides, and treat osmosis. They also construct and repair wood-epoxy. They can check out work and do some jobs onboard at anchor using their work rib. You can ask at Clippers Ship, with which they are closely associated. (See *Chandlery*.)

Talba Gaston's Nautic Services in the Carenantilles compound is a good place to get your boat's antifouling, epoxy, or coal tar priming done. He is an authorized antifouling applicator for International, Sea Hawk, and many other brands, and he works with brush, roller, or spray. Gaston has a giant sandblaster, and one of his specialties is removing old antifouling by judicious and careful wet sandblasting. If you prefer to do things yourself, he rents some equipment, including a high-pressure washer. Gaston makes cradles for shipping yachts long-distance.

EM Composites is on the other side of the river from Carenantilles; just walk out of the gate and keep turning right. Etienne Maran does fiberglass construction: fishing boats, dinghies, tanks, and two-part polyurethane spray painting. He has waterside access for large runabouts or very small yachts.

Technical yacht services
Woodwork

Serge Pivan runs a woodworking shop in Carenantilles called Caraibe Menuiserie, which is part of Caraibe Marine. He is a good man to see for all your woodwork, from planks to joinery.

Technical yacht services
Liferafts & Inflatables

La Survy (outside the Carenantilles gates) is run by the Phillias family who have been working with inflatables forever. They will fix any kind of inflatable and are warranty agents for Zodiac, Avon, Bombard, BFA, and Plastimo. They stock inflatables, liferafts, and safety gear.

Technical yacht services
Project Management and Other Services

If you are going to leave your boat in Martinique and have work done while you are away, it makes a lot of sense to have a project manager. Several people can do this; they are all pleasant to deal with, and work well.

Frank Vadi at Multi Interventions (see *Electrics*) speaks good English, has storage lockers for rent, and looks after boats when people go away. He can arrange and supervise work; his specialty is marine electrics.

Douglas Rapier of Douglas Yacht Services will act for you in this capacity. English is his first language, he has all the right contacts, and will make sure you get a top class job on time, with great attention to detail. He has an excellent team and is the person to go to when you want the best and don't mind paying a little extra for it.

If you have a big project in mind he can arrange the hauling and work to be VAT-free and any imported parts to be duty-free, but paper work is involved and this needs to be set up in advance. If you are in a hurry and need some work done quickly, he can organize it for you.

Azur Spirit in the Marina Mall is run by Jimy. Jimy looks after boats when the owners are away and does any repairs and maintenance that might be needed. He also sells boats and has some for charter.

Roberto Maxera at RM, is half Italian and half Argentinian, and he once lived in England, so is fluent in English, Spanish, Portugese, Italian, and French. He is an excellent generalist who can take care of maintenance and most boat problems.

Frank has a computer shop called Infologeek in the Marina Mall. He can fix your laptop and sort out computer problems. He works on integrated marine computer systems of the kind found on fancy yachts. He does much of this work in association with Douglas Yacht Services.

If you need a new name on your boat, check out Jean Luc Neugnat at SMS in Artimer next to Clippers Ship. He designs all kinds of graphics, numbers, and names, and then makes the transfers to put on your boat or he can do that for you. He can also make t-shirts, so if you want your favorite photo on a t-shirt, go talk to him.

If you have a Lagoon that needs help, Corail Caraibes Charter is the Caribbean agent (unless it is a big one, in which case it is Caraibe Marine). If you have a Jeanneau, Catana, or Fountaine Pajot, contact Caraibe Gréement. If you have an Amel that needs help, Jean Collin is the agent in the Marina Mall.

Transport

We give the location of the TC stop on our map, and it is easy to get to Fort de France. Your bike can get you a lot of places. Car rental agencies include Jumbo, in the nautical block, and GD location, in the Marina Mall.

Watt Up! is a new company in its own building in the Nautical Block. Carolyne Geny and Stephane Beguet, are very welcoming, speak English, and rent and sell all electric vehicles and boats. Their vehicles, include E-mokes, scooters, and electric bikes. Maximum range on the e-mokes is 100 km. They have a variety of boats for exploring the mangroves or having a party. They can even supply a pannier of food to go with it. For shopping or fun the E-mokes are the simplest, most economical, and environmentally friendly rental. They are working on insalling Watt Up! recharging stations

in many locations.

Taxis stand by just outside the marina on the town side. If you need a cab, try Thierry Belon. He is personable and reliable and he speaks a little English (0696 25 88 52). If you need someone more fluent in English, call Max Lamon (0696 26 03 94). If you are going on a long jaunt, consider Vincent Thomas (0696 07 54 37) from Rivière Salée, who is highly recommended. Don't want to sail home? Check Douglas Yacht Services or Dockwise Yacht Transport.

Provisioning

Douglas Yacht Services does full provisioning for superyachts. This is a fully professional service, and items not available in Martinique are flown in from France.

Appro Zagaya is a good provisioning service. Contact them by phone, fax, or email, or go onto their web site (www.appro-zagaya.fr) and shop or download their lists. They deliver right to your dock, or if you are chartering a bareboat, they load it on board. They need three days' notice, and your order needs to be over 200 Eu.

Market Marina in the Marina Mall has both a store and does full provisioning.

If you prefer to shop yourself, remember to take your own shopping bags. You have a choice of supermarkets and shops.

Leader Price has the best location, with its own dinghy dock. This is a reasonably priced market that is popular with locals and often has good fresh produce, frozen meats, fish, and shrimp. Many things they sell, like Real Cola, are their own brand. Mix it with enough rum and lime and no one will ever know.

The Carrefour Supermarket in the Centre Commercial Annette, just behind Carenantilles, is in a mall that includes a mobile store, beauty shops, gift shops, a boulangerie/patisserie, and launderette. It is not too far from the Leader Price or Artimer dinghy docks.

Simply is the most spacious market, very modern with big, wide aisles. You will not feel claustrophobic here. They have a pretty good selection and are just behind the Marina Mall, within easy walking distance through the car park. They open 0800-1930 except Sunday, when they close at 1230.

Economax, at Artimer, is inexpensive but very limited.

In the marina nautical block, Le Millesime is a fancy wine, liquor, and tobacco store. You can sit down with them and sort out your wine collection.

The local supermarkets are okay, but not the best. For a giant, modern, really good supermarket, Carrefour at Genipa is the closest and avoids the heavy traffic near Fort de France. Drive past the Rivière Salée exit, pass two roundabouts, and look for a tiny right turn with a small Genipa sign (blink and you've missed it). Pass under the highway; it is right ahead. You can make it with a Watt Up! E-moke.

The local market is good for produce, spices, local drinks, and souvenirs, especially on Saturday mornings.

Douceurs Mainoises is a great boulangerie/patisserie in the Marina Mall, and there is another just across the road. You can find a health food store in the Annette Mall.

Marin Marina

Fun shopping

The Marina Mall has lots of levels, corners, steps, and even a spiral staircase. It is a natural for kids, and in the afternoon parents let their kids explore while they check out all the boutiques. These include Made for Marin, Cargot, Madras design, and Les Comptois du Cotton. One Sunday morning every two months the whole marina turns into a big open air market.

Fishing enthusiasts can get their hooks into shopping at Akwaba, in the Marina Mall. This is a giant fishing store, with rows of rods and hooks, lines, and sinkers. They have nautical clothing, snorkeling gear, lots of good tackle boxes, and any kind of fishing gadget you might want.

The giant Domia household store is fun to visit in the Marine Bay Commercial Center, where you will also find a fair stationery store. If all this coincides with lunch, check out Le Midi du Marin. If they serve you the best meal you have ever had, you clearly need to get out more. But it is cheap, quiet, not bad, and, being cafeteria style, instant. They also sell good bread.

Bizar Chinois is on the road below Annette Mall and sells a mass of very inexpensive bits and pieces, everything from alarm clocks and luggage to pens and mugs.

Oye Oye is a mixed-bag store near Leader Price ~ from power tools to household and exercise machines. If you need a bike or music store, Artimer has both.

Restaurants

There are many restaurants to choose from. I mention a few. Mango Bay [$$$] is right in the marina nautical block, hanging out over the water with a great view of the boats. It is casual enough that you will be welcome in shorts. This is an excellent place to come for breakfast, lunch, or dinner. They have a deli with good sandwiches, croissants, pain au chocolat, and ice cream. Their bar is a gathering place in the evenings for many yacht crews. They have free WiFi and there is a section where you see people busy on their computers. But don't be fooled by all this casual bustle. Mango Bay is also a restaurant that serves good food, and one of the most reliable restaurants in Marin for a meal on the water's edge. Daily specials, pizza and pasta, and a menu that changes every few months are available for both lunch and dinner. They cook French and Italian food and their daily special is usually a bargain.

In Marin behind the beach, Zanzibar [$$$$] is fancy, on two floors, and open to the breeze with a pleasing atmosphere. I prefer the upstairs balcony, and if you want that, then reservations are a good idea. They have an excellent dinghy dock right outside. Their food is good, and some desserts and starters are excellent.

A few steps away, Sucre Ale [$] is a

cute little cafe to hang out at after being on the beach. They offer coffee, drinks, salads, crepes, and ice creams. It is pretty enough to make a selfie background, and cheap enough to visit for a crepe anytime you do not feel like cooking dinner.

The Marina Mall has become a popular restaurant area. From breakfast to dinner, people congregate to hang out or eat and it is enlivened many times a week by live music.

Sushi O Jade [$$$] is upstairs and open in the evenings only. Their shrimp tempura is excellent as are all their sushi dishes.

Kokoarum [$$$] is cheerful, open to the view, and serves burgers, barbecued foods, and a good lunch special. They offer a variety of tasty ice creams and sorbets. They often have live music.

Numero20 [$$$] sprawls across the top floor and you pretty much bump into it on your way to the Capitainerie. They sometimes have live music.

On hot days L'Annexe [$$$] has an interesting cooling system; cold water is shot out as a vapor. This is helpful when you select their "pierrades". You choose your meat or fish and they bring it to you raw, accompanied by an incredibly hot stone. They also have generous pasta dishes, wraps, and salads. Occasional they have music.

Pizza Amis [$$] is a popular pizza place where many come to hang out when work is over. Across the road is a whole row of even cheaper little bistros.

Marin Mouillage [$$] is cute and upstairs right behind the marina. They do a brisk lunch trade, with tasty local specials, and are open Friday and Saturday evenings for a barbecue. The food is good and reasonably priced.

Ti Toques [$$$] is a smart, modern, street-side establishment open to the breeze, with fast, snappy service. Their food is generally good. They post old favorites and daily specials on a blackboard. While they serve mainly French cuisine, they also do pizza and ice cream. Eat there or take away.

Indigo [$$$] is the floating restaurant, just outside the Marina Mall. It serves Créole food.

Le Sextant (closed Sunday and Monday) is the Carenantilles restaurant in the new block at the back. They serve generous daily lunch specials, which are great value and geared to hungry workers. In the evening it is a bar and hangout with live music, usually a couple of times a week.

Restaurant La Paillote Cayali [$$] is for those who want to eat right on the beach. Sit out next to the waves and eat a variety of local specialties at reasonable prices. Open all day every day.

Ashore

One of the better shore treats is to visit Eau de Tiaré, a complete beauty and health spa run by Kathy. Kathy is a Vincentian who grew up in Mustique, so English is her first language. She is full of fun and will make you feel immediately at home. She has created a lovely spa in top floor of the historic building next to the market that houses the big pharmacy. The door is on the road leading up the hill. You have to climb to the top, but the view is great when you get here, and she has a sauna, massage, treatment rooms, and showers. Kathy offers all kinds of beauty treatments, including manicure, pedicure, facials, waxing, and more, as well as a variety of massages. Prices vary from about 40 to 80 Eu.

Marin is a good area to shake the rust off your old bike and give it a run. The road up to Le Cap and over to Macouba is pleasant, and from here, trails lead south along the coast. If you like parasailing, you will find a lot of it in the area of Cap Chevalier.

If you rent a car or hike, make an effort to climb the hill on the west side of Marin for the spectacular view over the bay and all the way to Baie des Anglais. As you leave Marin and head for Fort de France there is a roundabout just opposite Ilet Dupres. Follow the signposts for Morne Glommier and enjoy the ridge. Point de Vue du Morne Gommnier is on a small hill top, gardened, and you pay 4EU for the view; I found it worth it.

Water sports

If you want to go diving, check out Christophe at Immersion Caraibe. He speaks English and will make it easy. You will find him near Equinox.

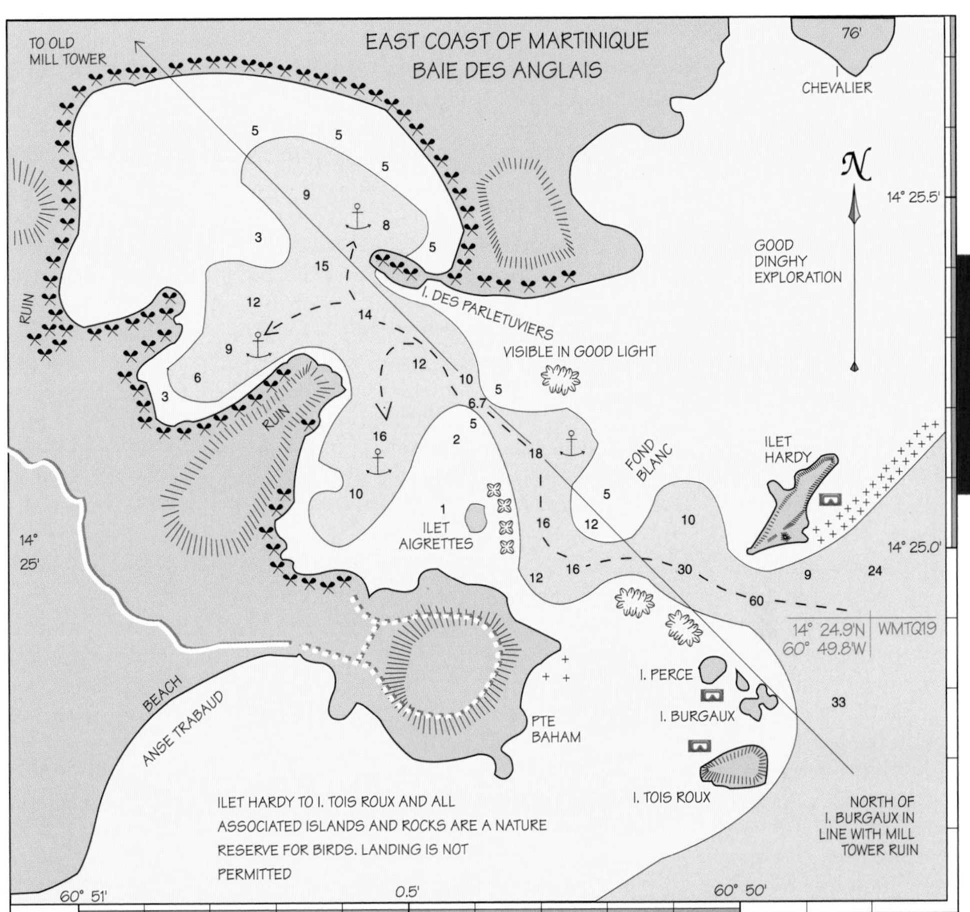

THE EAST COAST OF MARTINIQUE

This guide covers all the most frequently used anchorages, but does not include most of Martinique's east coast. This area is pleasant and interesting, but it is also tricky, with many reefs and shoals in water that is often difficult to read. The charts that are available are short on details where it matters, and over the years it has claimed more than its fair share of hulls. Adventurous cruisers who wish to visit should buy the Trois Rivières guide to Martinique by Jerome Nouel. It is now only in French but it has color photographs, and is the only guide that covers this area well. We do include Baie des Anglais, the closest east coast anchorage.

BAIE DES ANGLAIS

The wine locker is full, you are stuffed on restaurant meals, you have seen enough elegant boutiques to last a lifetime. What next? Consider a few days of quiet recovery in Baie des Anglais. Baie des Anglais is less than three miles up Martinique's east coast. It is a large mangrove-lined bay, with some small beaches and several little islands for dinghy exploration. There are no restaurants, no shops, and while there may be another boat or two, you are likely to have it to yourself.

Regulations

The islands at the entrance to Baie des Anglais, including Ilet Hardy, Ilet Perce, Ilet Burgaux, and Ilet Tois Roux, are bird sanctuaries, and going ashore is not permitted.

Navigation

The navigation is tricky and Baie des Anglais should only be visited in relatively light trade winds (<15 knots). The entrance is downwind and down sea. Enter between Ilet Hardy and the group of islands that include Ilet Perce, Ilet Burgaux, and Ilet Tois Roux. Ilet Hardy has a distinctive rock knoll on its southeastern shore. Once past Ilet Hardy, look for the two reefs to the northwest of Ilet Perce and pass fairly close to them. (You will see Fond Blanc to starboard.) Note that there are quite a few isolated rocks just to the east of Ilet Aigrettes. By now the seas should be relatively calm, and you will find a large daytime anchoring area about 20 feet deep to the west of Fond Blanc, between Ilet Aigrettes and the visible reef on the other side of the channel.

Your strategy from here on in depends on your draft, the size of your engine, the strength of the wind, and whether your insurance premium is up to date. You have to cross a bar of soft mud in unreadable water with the wind right behind you. For boats of less than 6-foot draft, there will probably be little problem. For boats of 6.5-foot or 7-foot draft, the width of the deepest channel is very narrow, and at low tide sounds out at about 7 feet. The seamanlike thing to do is to anchor in the deep water and sound out the channel with a lead line in your dinghy. As you look at Ilet des Parletuviers, you will see an old mill tower just behind it, a little to its left. A range I found helpful is to be on a line between the northern edge of Ilet Burgaux and this old mill tower. The deepest water is probably a hair to the southwest of this line. Once over the bar, you have plenty of water and many perfectly protected anchoring spots. Inside, Ilet des Parletuviers is the most popular. If you dinghy to the shore near Ilet Aigrettes, you can find a way through to Anse Trabaud, a lovely but fairly popular beach. Dinghy exploration is good up to Ilet Chevalier.

Go to Baie des Anglais well provisioned, because should the wind and sea get up while you are there, seas break across the entrance and you may have to wait a while to get out.

For an adventure, dinghy up behind Ilet Chevalier, carry on to the beach with the kite-surfing, and land the dinghy.

A coastal footpath takes you round to Ste. Anne in the south and Anses Macabou in the north.

PASSAGE BETWEEN MARTINIQUE AND ST. LUCIA

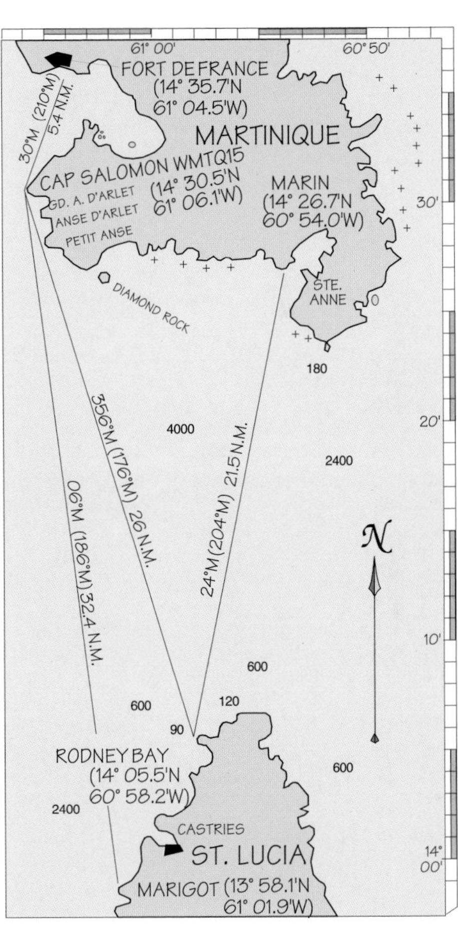

Northbound

The passage from St. Lucia to Fort de France is usually a fast reach. A course of due north from Rodney Bay gets you close to the lee coast. It doesn't hurt to be a little offshore when you arrive, as the wind tends to follow along the coast and is fluky close in. If Martinique is visible at the outset, it will appear as two islands, because the low-lying land in the center is not visible from St. Lucia. As you approach Martinique, Diamond Rock stands out as a clear landmark. If you are heading for Les Anse D'Arlet, be aware that Petit Anse is a small fishing village in one bay south of them, and occasionally mistaken for Les Anses D'Arlet.

If you are heading for Ste. Anne, you can often make it in one tack, but be sure to head up a bit to allow for current as you cross.

Southbound

The southerly passage from Grande Anse d'Arlet is sometimes a pleasant reach. At other times it can be hard on the wind. As the wind flows round the land, you will be pointing high as you follow the coast. It often pays to motor sail to stay reasonably close to shore before setting off across the channel. If sailing, it may pay to sail fast on the southerly tack and hope to play lifts later. When you see St. Lucia, head for the highest (rather rounded) mountain in the north end of the island until you make out the distinctive shape of Pigeon Island, a clear double peak joined by a slope. The higher twin mounds of Mt. Pimard and Mt. Flambeau (see Rodney Bay chart) also sometimes stand out.

The sail from Ste. Anne to St. Lucia is usually an easy reach.

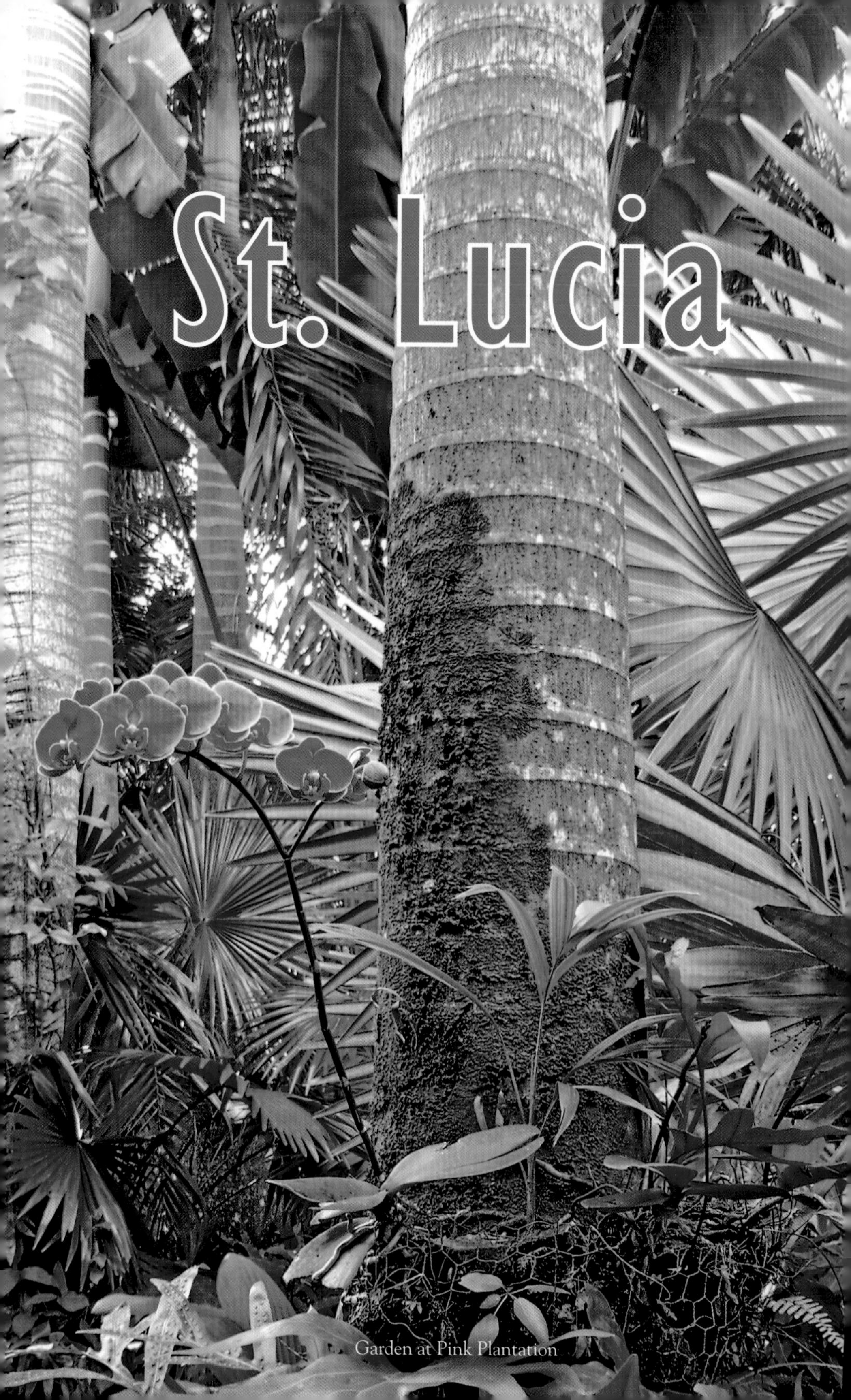

Garden at Pink Plantation

St. Lucia at a glance

Regulations

Ports of entry are Rodney Bay, Castries, Marigot Bay, Soufriere, and Vieux Fort. Entry charges in $EC are: $15 navigational aids, $10 practique (up to 100 tons), and clearance fees of $5 under 40 feet and $15 over 40 feet. In addition, charter yachts less than 40 feet pay $20; between 40 and 70 feet, $30; and over 70 feet, $40. Charter yachts also pay $15 per passenger. Three day in-and-out clearance is available with the same crew and you can save paperwork and pre-clear on sailclear.com. Immigration insists everyone fill in an immigration form (download from Doyleguides.com). They usually give six months on entry.

Normal office hours are weekdays 0800-1200 and 1330-1615. Those clearing outside these hours pay $100 overtime fee. One or two customs officers may ask you where you want to visit. If you list Rodney Bay, Marigot, Soufriere, and Vieux Fort, and go where you want, you should be okay. If you list anywhere else, a few officers may charge you a permit fee.

Spearfishing, damaging corals, and buying coral, turtle shell, or out-of-season lobsters (lobster season changes annually; it is usually August to February or later) are forbidden. Sailing yachts are generally allowed to troll a single line or handline for pleasure, others need a fishing license. No scuba diving (except for underwater work on your yacht) may be done without a qualified guide. Taking a pet ashore involves considerable advance planning and paperwork . Personal watercraft need a license from the ministry of tourism.

Holidays

Jan 1 and 2
Easter Friday, Sunday & Monday, April 19, 21-22, 2019, and April 10, 12-13, 2020
Feb 22, Independence Day
May 1, Labor Day
Whit Monday, June 10, 2019, June 1, 2020
Corpus Christi, June 20, 2019; June 11, 2020
Carnival (varies) – Monday and Tuesday, around the middle of July
First Friday in August, Emancipation Day
Thanksgiving, October (variable)
All Saints' Day, 1-2 November
St. Cecilia Day, 22 November
December 13, National Day
December 25 and 26, Christmas

Shopping hours

Most shops open 0830-1230, then 1330-1600. Saturday is a half-day. Banks close by 1500 except Fridays, when they are open till 1700. Supermarkets open longer.

Telephones

Flow or Digicel cell phones are the easiest way to go. For the USA & NANP countries, dial 1 + 10 digits (see page 19). For other overseas calls, dial 011 + country code + number. When dialing from overseas, the area code is 758 followed by a 7-digit number.

Transport

Buses ($1.50-$7 EC) run to most towns and villages. If you are going a long way, check on the time of the last returning bus. Taxis are plentiful. The sample taxi rates below (for 1-3 people):

	$EC
Rodney Bay to Vigie	66
Rodney Bay to Castries	66
Rodney Bay to Hewanorra	220
Castries to Hewanorra	180
Rodney Bay to Marigot	130
Short ride	20
Day tour	500

Extra charges after 2200, before 0600, and for more than three people.

There are plenty of rental cars. You need to get a temporary local license for $54 EC.

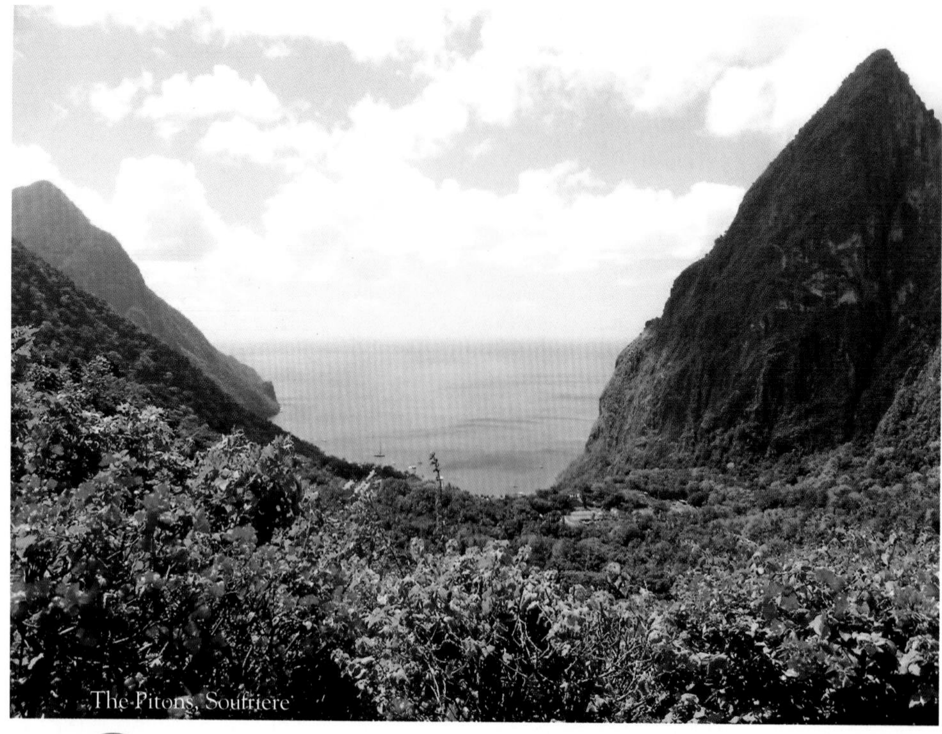
The Pitons, Soufriere

St. Lucia, the largest of the English speaking Windwards, is mountainous and lush, with many beautiful white sand beaches. Tropical rainforest covers the steep slopes of the center and gives way to cultivated agricultural land around the more moderately sloping coastal fringe. Bananas are still a major crop. For sheer physical beauty, the area around Soufriere and the Pitons is outstanding.

St. Lucia offers excellent sightseeing and hiking. You can see most of it by taxi, bus, or rental car. Adventurous travelers willing to combine driving with hiking will want to rent a four-wheel drive vehicle and explore some faraway corners such as Grand Anse or Anse Louvet on the windward shore. Any taxi driver will be delighted to take you on a tour. St. Lucia has several ziplines on which you can fly through the countryside. If that is too energetic, you can take an aerial rainforest canopy tram.

Those interested in nature should contact the National Trust, which runs tours to Frigate Island and the Maria Islands as well as turtle-watching tours. It is worth calling the forestry department about rainforest tours. They can supply knowledgeable guides.

There are many marked trails in St. Lucia that you can follow on your own, including rainforest hikes at the height of land as you drive across the island on the main road to the airport.

Cocoa Sainte Lucie is a new, small (one woman for now), organic chocolate factory based in Canaries. It is run by Maria Jackson, and her chocolate is excellent; her "spice" chocolate is special. If you want more details, call her at 459-4401. Otherwise, look for her chocolate in Zaka in Soufriere or Drop Anchor in Rodney Bay.

St. Lucia has an excellent, full-service marina with a haul-out in Rodney Bay, and a smaller marina in Marigot. The choice of restaurants is the best in the Windwards. St. Lucia is a charter center, with several charter companies in Rodney Bay including The Moorings, Sunsail and DSL.

IGY: RODNEY BAY MARINA

ST. LUCIA

Arriving is Just the Beginning

Located in a well-protected lagoon with a full- service boatyard and excellent facilities for yachts up to 285', the 5 Anchor Award Rodney Bay Marina is a premier yachting destination in the Eastern Caribbean. Rodney Bay Marina is the regional home of the Atlantic Rally for Cruisers and St. Lucia's leading center for yachting, sporting and cruising.

253 BERTHS | WATERFRONT DINING | FULL-SERVICE BOATYARD

- 253 Berths / 32 Megayacht Slips
- Duty Free High-Speed Fueling
- Onsite Customs & Immigration Clearance
- Full-Service Boatyard with Caretaking Packages
- Waterfront Dining, Nightlife & Taxi Services
- Concierge, Provisioning & Ship's Chandlery
- Laundry Services, Showers, Pool & Spa
- Security, Free Wi-Fi and Local Amenities

t: + 1 758 458 7200 | f: +1 758 452 0185
e: rbm@igymarinas.com | w: www.igy-rodneybay.com

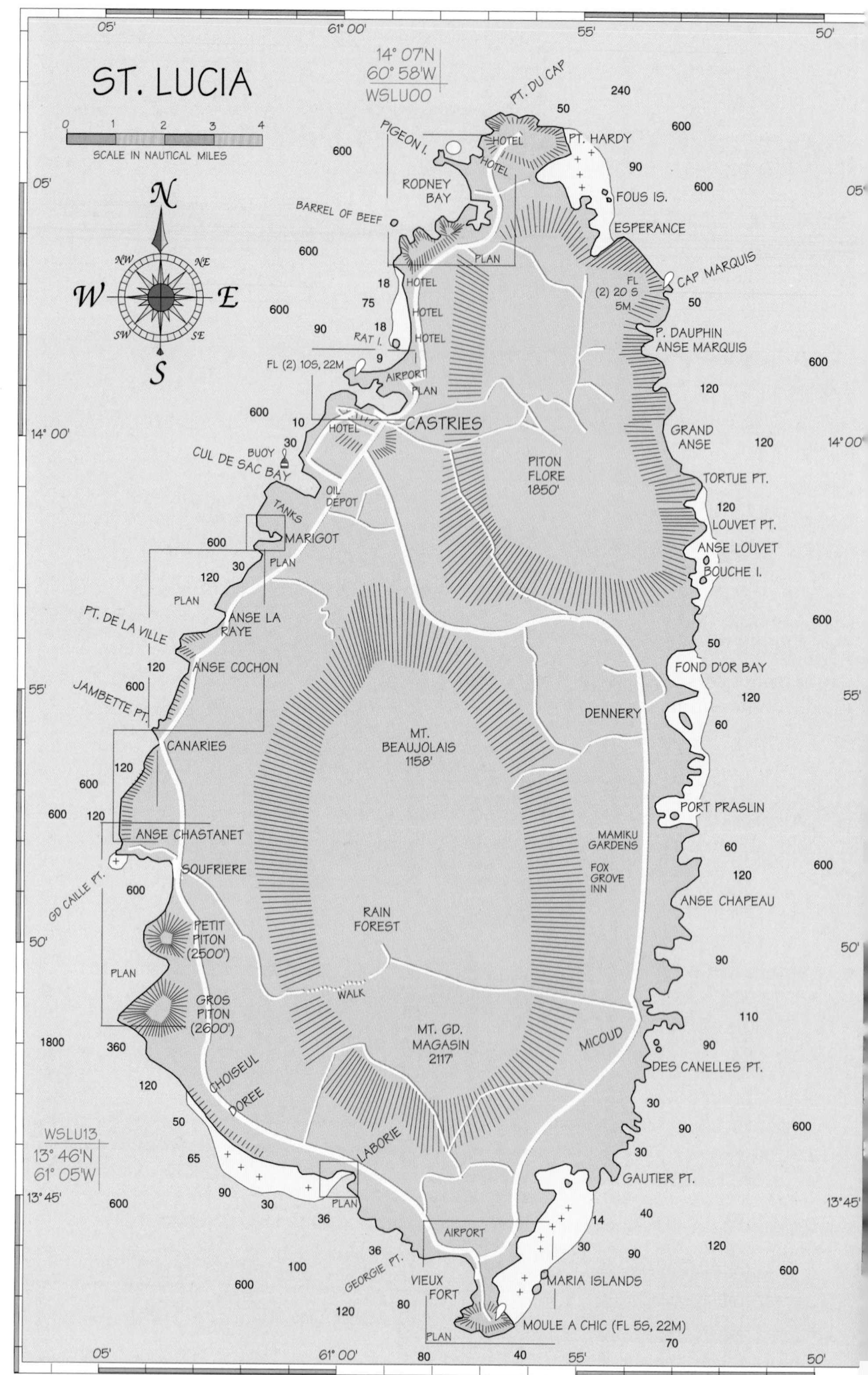

ST. LUCIA
SCALE IN NAUTICAL MILES
14° 07'N
60° 58'W
WSLU00
13° 46'N
61° 05'W
WSLU13
PIGEON I.
PT. DU CAP
PT. HARDY
FOUS IS.
ESPERANCE
RODNEY BAY
BARREL OF BEEF
CAP MARQUIS
FL (2) 20 S 5M
P. DAUPHIN
ANSE MARQUIS
RAT I.
FL (2) 10S, 22M
AIRPORT
CASTRIES
GRAND ANSE
PITON FLORE 1850'
TORTUE PT.
LOUVET PT.
ANSE LOUVET
BOUCHE I.
CUL DE SAC BAY
BUOY
OIL DEPOT
TANKS
MARIGOT
PT. DE LA VILLE
ANSE LA RAYE
ANSE COCHON
JAMBETTE PT.
CANARIES
FOND D'OR BAY
DENNERY
MT. BEAUJOLAIS 1158'
PORT PRASLIN
MAMIKU GARDENS
FOX GROVE INN
ANSE CHASTANET
SOUFRIERE
GD CAILLE PT.
ANSE CHAPEAU
RAIN FOREST
PETIT PITON (2500')
GROS PITON (2600')
WALK
MT. GD. MAGASIN 2117'
MICOUD
DES CANELLES PT.
CHOISEUL
DOREE
LABORIE
GAUTIER PT.
GEORGIE PT.
VIEUX FORT
MARIA ISLANDS
MOULE A CHIC (FL 5S, 22M)
HOTEL
PLAN

Navigation, west coast

There are several shoals and no anchorages between the northern tip of St. Lucia and Rodney Bay, so it is best to keep clear.

Rodney Bay offers several anchorages that are dealt with in detail below.

Barrel of Beef is a low-lying rock about a quarter of a mile off the southern side of the entrance to Rodney Bay. It is marked by a white light that flashes every five seconds. The water is deep enough (about 18 feet) for most yachts to pass inside it.

Between Barrel of Beef and Castries, the coast sweeps back in a large bay containing Rat Island. The northern part of this bay is full of reefs and is best avoided. On heading south from Rodney Bay, the normal route is to pass either side of Barrel of Beef and head directly toward Castries Harbor.

Tapion Rock forms the southern entrance to Castries Harbor. There are some rocks close by, so give it a reasonable clearance. Two miles south of Castries, Cul de Sac Bay is a huge depot for Hess Oil. It is well lit and makes an obvious landmark by day or night. There is a flashing buoy in the middle of the entrance to this bay.

From Cul de Sac Bay to the Pitons, St. Lucia is mainly steep-to, and keeping a quarter of a mile offshore clears all dangers. There are a few rock hazards lying up to 100 yards or more offshore. The worst is a sizable rock patch off the southern end of Anse Chastanet that should be given wide clearance.

RODNEY BAY

Rodney Bay is over a mile long. On the northern shore, a causeway, built in 1972, connects Pigeon Island, which was once but is no more an island, to the mainland, providing the bay with protection. In the old days, when Europeans entertained themselves by sailing around in wooden boats taking potshots at each other, Pigeon Island was the main base for the British navy in this area. It was ideally situated, being in sight (on most days) of Martinique, the main French base. There used to be a fort, hospital buildings, barracks, and storerooms. Now the St. Lucia National Trust conserves it as a delightful park. There are shady gardens, and the fort has been partly restored. The climb to the top of both peaks is well rewarded by the views. Strategically placed signboards tell you about the history.

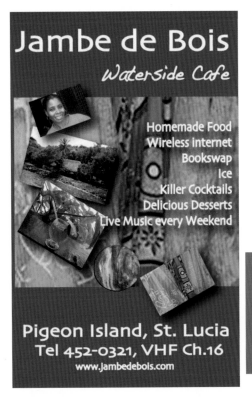

An entry charge to the park (about $8 US) helps finance the National Trust, which works to preserve the environment as well as the historic sites. This is particularly important now as the government has withdrawn its funding because the National Trust is refusing to turn the park into a dolphin interaction center, which would ruin the park, the anchorage, and the environment. The anchorage off Pigeon Island is scenic and breezy. If you are staying here a long time and wish to use the park often, consider becoming a member of the National Trust, as the entry fees can add up.

Near the Pigeon Island Park dinghy dock, you will find Jambe de Bois [$], a delightful restaurant/bar and art gallery run by Barbara Tipson, an active member of the local animal-welfare organization, which often helps place unwanted animals. Jambe de Bois is slightly offbeat, with an arty atmosphere.

St. Lucia

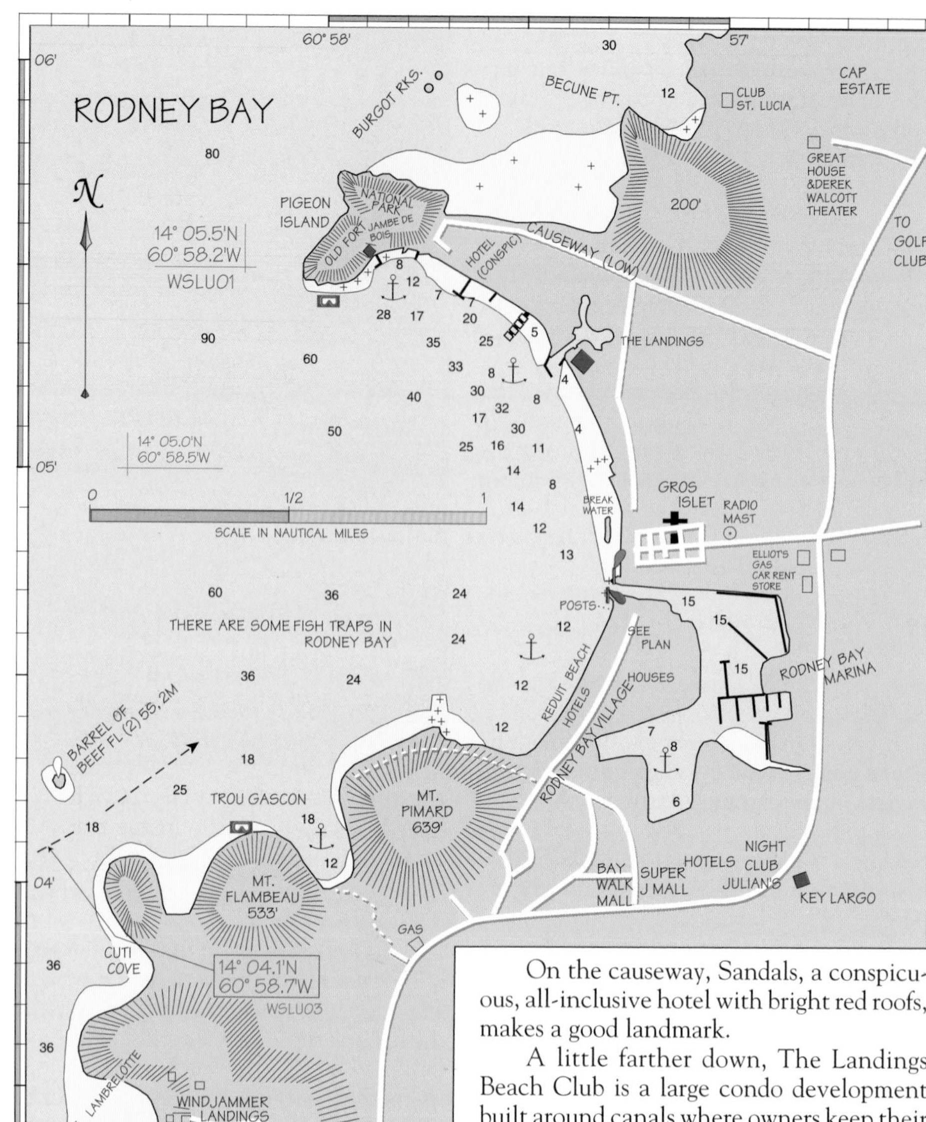

You can relax in an easy chair, catch up on email on their WiFi, check the bookswap, and enjoy local art. It makes a great hangout, with comfy corners inside and breezy spots on the Hobbit furniture outside. Jambe de Bois opens daily 1000-2200, except Mondays, when they close at 1700. They feature jazz Friday to Sunday You have to pay the park entry fee until 1700. The restaurant does a late breakfast, as well as lunch and dinner. Fresh fruit juice is available, along with many daily specials and snacks.

On the causeway, Sandals, a conspicuous, all-inclusive hotel with bright red roofs, makes a good landmark.

A little farther down, The Landings Beach Club is a large condo development built around canals where owners keep their yachts. You can dinghy up to their Beach Club [$$$], an informal restaurant set between the beach and the canal. It is open all day, offering everything from sandwiches and burgers to full meals and daily specials. A fancier dinner is to be had at Palms [$$$$$], a gourmet restaurant near reception, and they also have a beach bar open for lunch called the Callaloo [$$$].

Outside the lagoon, on the north side is Gros Islet Village, which has seen some robberies. Marine patrols have kept things under some control, but dinghy thefts have been a problems recently, so take care.

To the south of the channel entrance is Reduit Beach, one of St. Lucia's finest beaches and the home of many hotels and the St. Lucia Yacht Club. This is a popular anchorage. Trou Gascon is a nice little lunch hide out.

Navigation

Rodney Bay Lagoon is a large and completely protected inner lagoon that is entered via a dredged channel between Reduit Beach and Gros Islet village. This is lit by port and starboard lights at the entrance and at the inner end of the channel. Approach the channel in the center. IGY Rodney Bay Marina has dredged the entrance and marina area, so there is sufficient depth for yachts of 13 feet draft to come in. Yachts of 15 feet draft have made it with care and attention to tides. The shallowest water is just outside the entrance, so if you can make it into the channel, you should be good to the big boat dock.

Many yachts tie up at the marina. It is also possible to take an IGY marina mooring in the inner lagoon, where depths are 7-9 feet. You may anchor in the outer bay to the southeast of Pigeon Island, anywhere off the causeway to Gros Islet, and off Reduit Beach. Holding is variable with a lot of dead coral rubble and some softer sand.

The outside beach anchorages occasionally become untenable in unusually extreme northerly swells. Anywhere within acoustic range of Gros Islet beach can be noisy; (more so out in Rodney Bay than in the lagoon).

Rodney Bay is a major hub of tourist activities, with hotels, malls, restaurants, and an 18-hole golf course nearby.

IGY Marina has 24-hour security with many cameras. If you have a problem, call them at 720-4139 or VHF: 16. They will come directly if you are in the marina, or pass it on to marine police and coastguard if you are at anchor.

Regulations

IGY Rodney Bay Marina is a good place to clear in. If you plan to stay in the marina, go into a berth (see below) and walk to the customs office, or anchor and dinghy in.

Customs open daily 0800-1200 and 1330-1630. On Fridays they often stay open till 1800. Overtime charges ($100 EC) apply on weekends, holidays, during lunch, or after

Pigeon Island, view from the fort

1615. Entry charges are $30-40 EC, depending on the size of the boat, with extra fees if you are on charter. Details of fees are given at the beginning of this chapter. Only the skipper should come ashore to clear; other crew should stay on the yacht till clearance is complete. If you have internet access, you can save time and effort by pre-clearing the entry on sailclear.com. St. Lucia has more paperwork than other islands as they insist everyone fills in an immigration form. To save time, download it at doyleguides.com

If you need clearance when everything is closed, ask Ben's Yacht Services to help, or try the customs guardroom in Castries, (758) 468-4859.

Do not exceed the 4-knot speed limit in Rodney Bay Lagoon or close by other anchored yachts in the bay. This applies to all vessels, including inflatables and dinghies. Anchoring is not allowed in the lagoon, but IGY moorings are available.

Shipping in parts? Invoices and shipping papers must be marked "for transshipment." Many items are duty-free. There are charges for documentation, and you need to use one

Jus' Sail taking a tour of Rodney Bay

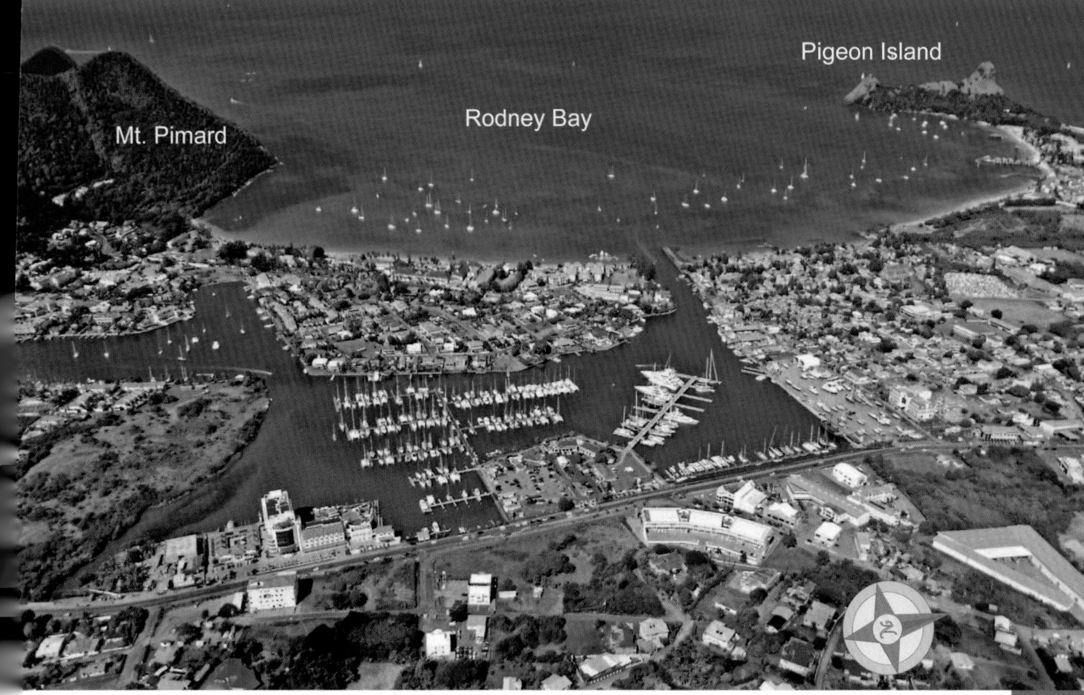

of the two excellent agents. Ian Duzauzay (Reliant Brokerage) will clear your package in and can also rent you a car. Lisa Kessel, the wife of Chris, the surveyor, does a lot of shipments for yachts.

Communications

A cruisers net on VHF: 68 at 0830, Monday to Saturday works intermittently, mainly during big events. You can use Rodney Bay Marina as a postal drop and for sending faxes. If you have a marina berth or mooring, the marina WiFi should cover you.

Other internet and office services can be found behind Harmony apartments and in Rodney Bay Village near Home Services. Digicel and Flow have sales outlets in the Baywalk Mall. Nearly all restaurants and bars have free WiFi.

General yacht services

IGY Rodney Bay Marina [VHF: 16] is an attractive marina with a large, solid dock that can take 32 superyachts up to 285 feet long. Fancy floating docks accommodate 221 regular yachts. They have 30 convenient and well-maintained moorings in the inner lagoon (daily rate $0.50 US per foot, decreasing the longer you stay).

Rodney Bay Marina is a pleasant place to stay, well protected from the elements amid lawns and coconut palms, dockside restaurants, and cafes. It is home to a business community that includes a bank, marine services, a food store, boutiques, massage therapists, and many taxi drivers, as well as a well-stocked, duty-free chandlery. A few charter companies are based here. The businesses are friendly, and for many yachting folk, Rodney Bay Marina has become a home-away-from-home in the Caribbean, creating a sense of community.

The manager, Sean Devaux, is open, accessible, helpful, and popular with his customers. You will usually get a spot in the marina, though it can be packed when the A.R.C. arrives in mid-December. Call for a dock space and the staff will help you in.

Dock I, the big concrete dock, is available for yachts up to 250 feet long and has 110, 220, and limited 380 volts up to three phase and both 50- and 60-cycle electricity. This dock also has high-speed fueling.

All docks have 220-volt, 50-cycle electricity. Docks F and G also have 110-volt, 60-cycle electricity. All docks have water and WiFi and, if you have a suitable aerial, WiFi is available on the moorings.

Hot showers are a pleasant feature, and they use Greening the Caribbean for garbage

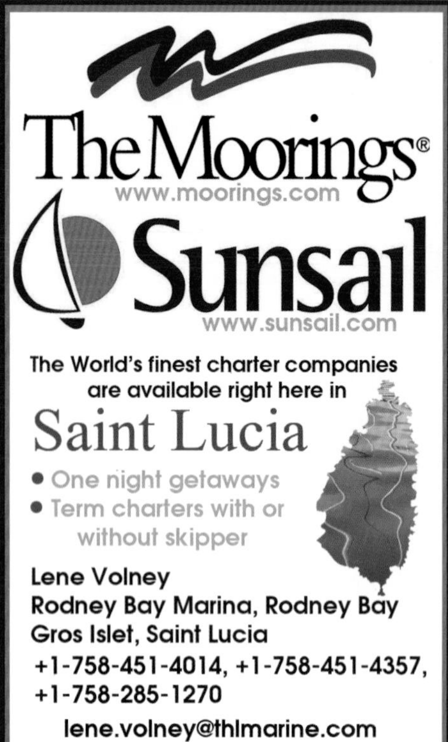

disposal so you can recycle by separating cardboard and paper, tins and glass, tech stuff (computers/batteries/etc.), oil and general rubbish. There is a place for used engine oil.

If you need a technician, or help with varnishing, the main desk will have a list of registered independent contractors and day workers. You can get your laundry done and fill all kinds of LPG gas tanks at Suds Laundry, which is fast and efficient under Pat's hand. If you need to get boat parts cleared in, ask at the front desk.

A convenient bus runs from outside the marina to town, and some of the best restaurants in the Windwards and a golf course are close by. Within the marina, day trips to Martinique or along the coast are available.

Rodney Bay Marina Boatyard [VHF: 16] is part of the marina and is St. Lucia's only haul-out facility. It is well organized. Yard supervisor Milton McKenzie or Juliatta will answer your questions in the yard. The travel lift is 75 tons and can take up to a 28-foot beam. For most boats it will not be necessary to remove a stay. They have room for about 120 yachts in long-term storage and another 20 undergoing work. You may live aboard. The yard has cradles and tie-downs if you are leaving your yacht here in the summer months.

You can work yourself or the marina boatyard can organize subcontractors to get your work done. A gelcoat stripper is available for osmosis work, and they have two big under-cover paint sheds.

The fuel and work dock (open weekdays 0800-1700, weekends 0800-1600, Sundays and holidays 0800-1300) is alongside, to the east of the travel lift, making lifting and working on engines and masts easy. High-speed fueling is also available on Dock I. Anyone who has cleared out can buy fuel duty-free. The fuel dock also sells water, ice, soft drinks, and lubricants. If there is a problem getting water on the fuel dock you can ask the dockmaster about the possibility of a space on a regular dock for buying water. They often go for lunch from 1200-1300 .

A little fuel dock stands on the northern side of the Rodney Bay entrance canal,

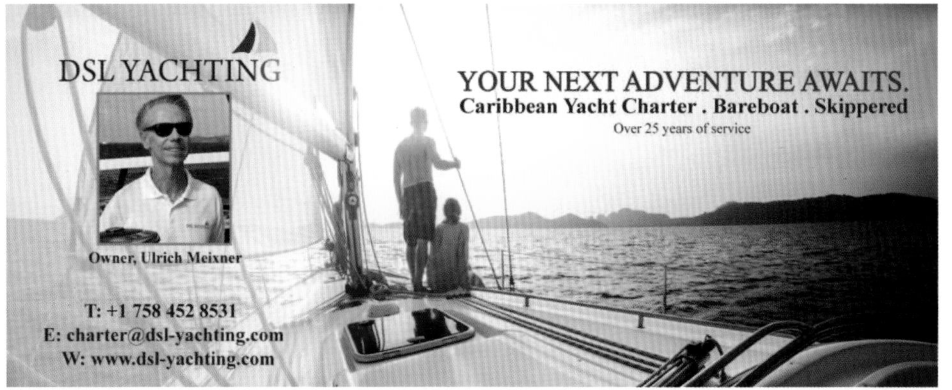

where the fishing boats tie up; they sell diesel, gasoline, and engine oils. You can tie your dinghy there, but the dock is not suitable for most yachts. It has often saved my bacon when the marina is closed.

Island-wide superyacht services are offered by Ben Taxi, who has self-contained rooms to rent overlooking Rodney Bay and offers jeep rentals. He lives in Soufriere but has people in Rodney Bay.

Superyachts can also find help from Tracy at Cox and Co, which offers full yacht services; customs, immigration issues, provisioning, and full concierge services.

Rodney Bay Marina provides some concierge services.

Rodney Bay Is home to three charter companies; The Moorings, Sunsail, and DSL. If you are chartering with these companies you will find Lene Volney at Moorings/ Sunsail and Uli at DSL very helpful. If you are in a boring hotel talk to one of them about an overnight charter and escape to a quiet little cove.

When boats come out of charter at Sunsail and Moorings, they are often offered for sale, so if you are looking for a second hand boat this is a good place to check.

DSL is a much more comprehensive general broker. People come to Uli when they want to sell or buy boats, and he can fix them up for owners to get them perfect before they are sold; he usually has a big selection on offer. Uli can also sometimes put suitable boats in his charter fleet. DSL is also an agent for Doyle Sails, and can measure your boat up for a new set.

Medical services

You won't find a better place for dental work in the Caribbean (and beyond) than Kent Glace and Associates, just a few steps from the dinghy dock by Baywalk Mall. Pass the Baywalk Mall towards the main road and look on your right behind Caribbean Smiles. Kent Glace is excellent, and, in addition to regular dentistry, he does all the surgical work: implants, complex extractions, crowns, cosmetics, root canals, and fixing root canals that have gone bad. He is aided by two other dentists, Dr. Barnard and Dr. Michel, and two qualified hygienists, a rarity in the Caribbean. You will get top-quality care here, with all the latest equipment, including laser whitening, at less expense than in the USA.

Kent Glace and Associates is open weekdays 0800-1700 and Saturdays 0900-1200. Kent himself works in town on Thursdays, but the other staff members are still there. If you have kids, Desma, at Caribbean Smiles next door, is an orthodontist. Doctors abound, including specialists. I have been getting excellent reports about M-Care walk-in Medical Clinic, open Monday to Saturday 0800-1800, with two good GPs, both women. It is a few hundred yards beyond the Rodney Bay Medical Center, which is a block east of the JQ Mall.

On the top floor of JQ Mall, is Dr. Marlina Joseph a dermatologist. She is very convenient as she is often available at short notice (walk up and ask).

Rodney Bay Medical Center is also good to walk in, and they have several GPs, as well as a visiting dermatologist, an ear,

nose and throat specialist, a pediatrician, and testing services. Nearer the dinghy dock is a pain clinic with an orthopedic surgeon and physiotherapist. Prices vary, so ask. Tapion Hospital in Castries has many medical services, including a heart specialist, surgeons, and lab facilities. Marie Grandison Didier is an excellent dermatologist, but you need an appointment Call for details and appointments.

Chandlery

Island Water World is a large, duty-free chandlery managed by Ian Cowan, one of St. Lucia's most knowledgeable yachtsmen, and his wife, Rosemary. They have an excellent team, including Sophie, who has been answering questions from those on yachts for many years. This store is part of the Caribbean-wide chain, which has been in operation for over 50 years. You can get just about anything here, from electronics to toilets and fridge units, plus cores, ply, and Burma teak. If you don't see what you want, ask Ian. If it cannot be had in St. Lucia, he

can order, ship, clear, and deliver anything from a main engine to a small part directly to your boat. Island Water World stocks Nissan outboards., and sells Caribe and Walker Bay inflatables. Ian is the person to source your Yanmar parts.

Johnsons Hardware is a large marine and general hardware store on two floors opposite Rodney Bay Marina. They keep a good stock of basic marine equipment at reasonable prices. This includes deck gear, rope, chain, anchors, fenders, fastenings, electrical fittings, lights, wiring and fuses, paint and sandpaper, fishing and snorkeling gear, fuel and oil filters, and outboard accessories. They are agents for Sea Hawk antifouling. They can special-order any marine hardware, duty-free. In addition, they keep a big selection of plumbing, and electrical supplies, gardening supplies, household goods, and hardware, including power tools. In the building over the road they have wood and appliances.

See also Liferaft and International Inflatable under *Technical yacht services*.

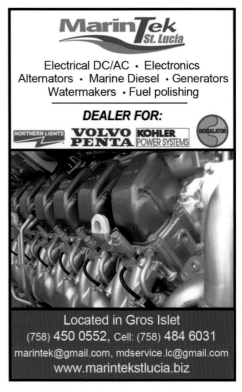

Technical yacht services

Sails/Rigging/Cushions

Rodney Bay Sails is the sail loft and rigging shop in the marina. Kenny Abernaty is the man to see. He has worked as a sailmaker for over 30 years, is very good, and owns the loft. Rodney Bay Sails does any form of sail or canvas repair and will create new biminis, awnings, and covers. They build many bimini and awning frames and are set up to work and bend 1-inch stainless tube. You can order new sails from Doyle Sails in Barbados.

When Kenny has time, Rodney Bay Sails also do rigging and can handle anything from replacing a shroud to ordering and installing a complete new rig. (They do not do swaging, however.) In this, they work closely with Ian Cowan, who is the agent for Selden masts, Furlex, and Profurl.

Technical yacht services

Electrics/Electronics/Watermakers

You will be in good hands at MarinTek, run by Egbert Charles, who speaks French and Spanish as well as English and has many

years of experience working with yachts. Egbert is the Volvo dealer, and this is a good place to buy an engine as he keeps a stock of engines and sail drives from 30 hp to 55 hp, including those in the Volvo Compact Collection. He also custom orders. He does Volvo warranty work and is factory-qualified for all Volvo engines, including electronic diagnosis.

Marin Tek is the dealer for Northern Lights and Kohler generators. They may be able to help with other generators if they have time. They are excellent at electrical installations or fixing electrical problems, and they have a department for rewiring starters and alternators.

MarinTek is the agent for Dessalator watermakers, and the company sells, repairs and services this brand. In addition they polish fuel and clean tanks. It is easiest to call them, but if you want to visit the shop, it is north of the boatyard on our map of Rodney Bay Lagoon.

Regis Electronics is the St. Lucian branch of the UK Greenham Regis chain. Jon White, the owner, offers sales, installation, and service for all marine electronics, air conditioning, charging systems, refrigeration, and watermakers. He is the agent for most brands of electronics and keeps both new equipment and many spare parts in stock, which makes Regis the best place for your electronic requirements, whether you are buying a whole new system or upgrading or repairing your present one.

Regis is a factory-authorized dealer for all the major manufacturers, including Amptech, Balmar, B&G, Cruisair, Furuno, Fischer Panda, Garmin, HRO, Icom, Marine Air, Mastervolt, Onan, Raymarine, Spectra Watermakers, Seafresh, Simrad, Schenker, Victron, Waeco, and Westerbeke. You can

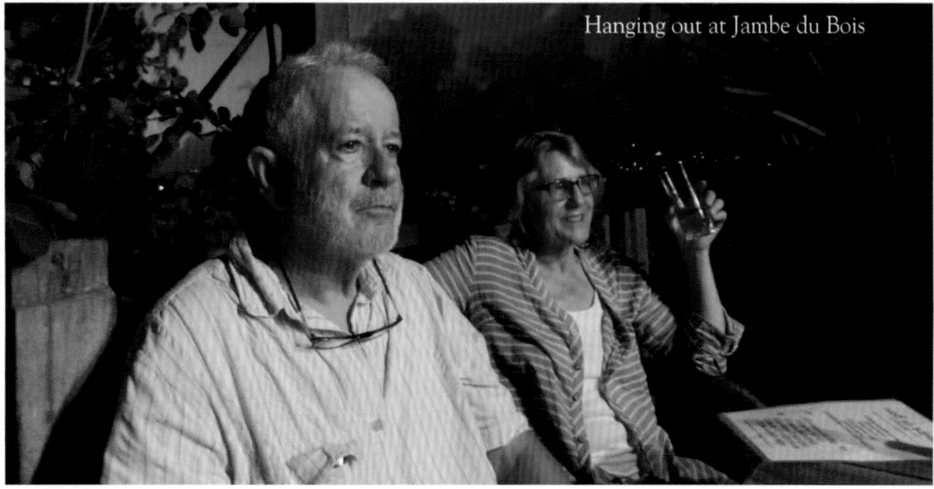
Hanging out at Jambe du Bois

start from scratch here and order new gear from the catalog. Jon and his team will have some good ideas on what to buy, have it shipped duty-free, and install it on your boat.

Technical yacht services
Project Management & Maintenance

Ulrich, at Destination St. Lucia (DSL), is very helpful, straightforward, and knowledgeable about boats and local technicians. His crew can get your boat repaired, your refrigeration cooling, and your engine back working. If there is something they cannot handle, they will recommend the right technician. DSL will look after your yacht while you go away and will undertake all kinds of yacht management, repair, and refit. This is a long-established company you can rely on.

Technical yacht services
Mechanical/Metalwork

Quick and Reliable Mechanical Services is run by Alwin Augustin, who lives up to the company's name. He works on all diesel engines, from Caterpillars on super-yachts to Yanmars on cruisers. He does mechanical work on generators, including Onan, Fischer Panda, and Northern Lights, and he has an excellent reputation for efficiency, service, and skill. It is easiest to contact him via his mobile, (758) 520-5544/584-6544. For parts, he works with Ian Cowan at Island Water World, who can bring in all parts fast and is hooked into the Yanmar computerized system.

Tony's Engineering is run by Tony George, a good, careful general mechanic who can weld and repair diesel engines of all makes including Caterpillar, Detroit, and Perkins. He can come to the yard to sort out your alignment and shaft problems. It is easiest to call him (715-8719) If you cannot get him there, try 712-1109 and ask Geraine where he is.

Gregoire Louis's KP Marine shares a big dock with Liferaft and Inflatable Center in the canal into the lagoon. KP Marine is the Yamaha agent, and they sell and service all Yamaha outboards and keep parts for them, They can import and service any Yamaha product including pumps and generators. They do not work on other brands. The big dock makes it easy to bring in motors for repair.

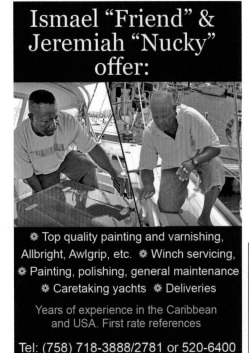

Caribbean Yacht Services is owned and run by George Bevan, who is excellent at fixing anything on boats. He can weld and machine, and fix inboards and outboards whatever their make. He is also a refrigeration man, and can get your beer cold, and keep your frozen foods frozen.

In the boatyard compound, Lawrence (Chinaman) runs the metalworking shop. He can weld and fabricate in any metal.

Heading down the channel, Rory MacNamara's Mac's Marine sells Evinrude Ecotech and the smaller Mapi outboards (which seem very similar to Yamaha), and fixes all brands. They have a dock where you can unload your engine for repair.

Island Marine Supplies, run by Pinkley, is next to Mac's Marine. It is the sales and service agent for Mariner, Mercury, and Mercruiser. They keep a good range of engines in stock for all sizes of boats, and fix all makes of outboard.

Roger is a mechanic who often works in the marina. He can get your outboard up and running again and he works on inboards. Call him at (284-6050).

For Volvo diesels, Northern Lights, and Kohler, see MarineTek under *Electrics*.

Technical yacht services
Glass/woodwork/paint

On the marina docks, Ismael "Friend" and Jeremiah "Nucky" (718-3888, 520-6400) often work together to do first-rate brush and roller painting, both two-part polyurethane and regular, cleaning, polishing, servicing winches, and general care and maintenance. They take care of yachts when the owners go away. They have had years of experience here and in the US, with owners who have flown them up to help in the summer. They also work in Marigot Bay.

In the boatyard compound, Elvis (Mermaid Repair) does a good job on all glass repairs, painting, and general on-the-slip work.

Fiber (721-0272) is another contractor who does fiberglass repairs of all types, gel-coat matching, spray painting, and anti-fouling. Kelly Charles is another good paint-and-glass man, as well as a varnisher (715-3369).

Richard Cox of Cox Enterprises has years of fiberglass, woodworking, and other maintenance experience. He can sometimes be found around Mac's Marine, where he helps build boats.

Robin Unwin (485-1101) does both glasswork (including composites) and all kinds of woodwork.

A couple of good guys who can handle your carpentry, including decking, joinery, and planking are Pride (284-7948), and Simon Edwards (458-0213. You generally have to call them, as their shops are not close to the marina.

Sean Kessel is kept busy by Regis Electronics most of the winter months, where he works on watermakers and climbs up masts. In the summer, if things are slow, he works independently on general boat maintenance, including plumbing, electrics, simple rigging, and just about anything a first-rate yacht maintenance man can do (720-3394).

Technical yacht services
Inflatable Repair

Debra and Francis's Liferaft and Inflatable Center is on the left side of the channel as you enter the lagoon. They have an 80-foot customer dock with about 10 feet alongside, making it easy to drop off and collect dinghies. They have been in business 22 years and are IRSA approved.

The business has two sides, the Liferaft and Inflatable Center for repair and International Inflatable Ltd. for duty-free sales of dinghies, outboards, and other gear.

The Liferaft and Inflatable Center tests, fixes, and vacuum-bags all makes of liferafts; are certified for Zodiac, Avon, Bombard, and Ocean Safety, and are approved for SOLAS. You are invited to watch them unpack and examine the contents and decide what gear should go back in. They have one of the few Caribbean stations that can test and fill liferaft cylinders. Apart from liferafts, you can bring your fire extinguishers, lifejackets, and M.O.B modules for testing and servicing.

They repair all makes of inflatables,

do some of the best work in the islands, and guarantee their work on hypalon for a year. They have a 24-hour turn around. If you have an expensive aging RIB, they can re-tube it. They can apply dinghy names along the fabric on both sides. They also offer repair and renovation for solid fiberglass and RIB boats up to 30 feet. They are an approved repair station for AB and Zodiac. You can alk to them if you have outboard problems.

When you take an inflatable in for repair, be there when they give it a good check over, so you can decide if it is better to replace it; International Inflatables takes old dinghies and dinghy/outboards in trade. This makes buying the new one more affordable and means they often have guaranteed, beautifully restored secondhand inflatables for sale. International Inflatables (same office) has a nice showroom for inflatables and outboards and stock duty-free AB and Zodiac dinghies, and Tohatsu outboards. They also keep a stock of inflatable accessories, and are agents for Budget Marine. Order anything you need out of the catalogue and they will bring it in fast by DHL duty-free.

Technical yacht services
Refrigeration

Regis Electronics, Caribbean Yacht Services, Prudent Repairs and Wayne's Quick Fix refrigeration, can all help you get things cool again.

Technical yacht services
Other Services

Chris Kessell (Kessel Marine) is the local yacht surveyor; his prices are reasonable, and you can arrange for him to come and visit anywhere in St. Lucia, or beyond. If you need a yacht brochure, yacht video or just a cool aerial of your yacht, Chris is a master drone pilot for photography.

John and Verniel Leo can give a helping hand. They have a modern, air-conditioned mini-bus taxi, and are happy to run you around. Verniel does laundry (she collects and delivers, it is done well and at a good price), as well as interior boat cleaning. John does detailed cleaning or polishing inside or out and can generally lend a hand. Call 520 5747/486 7872/721 0817. You might also see Sparkle, another laundry.

Jo Boxall has Scribble, a design studio in her home. She will design boat names and signs and arrange for the transfers to be cut and placed. She can design fancy yacht brochures, and she has a contact for helicopter photos.

If you need a new yacht mattress or sheets to fit your triangular bunk, try Lubeco bedding factory, which has an outlet in American Dry Wall on the road to Castries. They supply both fitted and flat sheets for any size bunk (take a pattern) and have nice fabrics, including cotton and organic cotton. Regular sheet sizes are kept in stock. They also produce good-quality, high-density foam mattresses, properly finished with a quilted cover. You need to make sure they understand the size and shape.

Windward Island Gases, just beyond

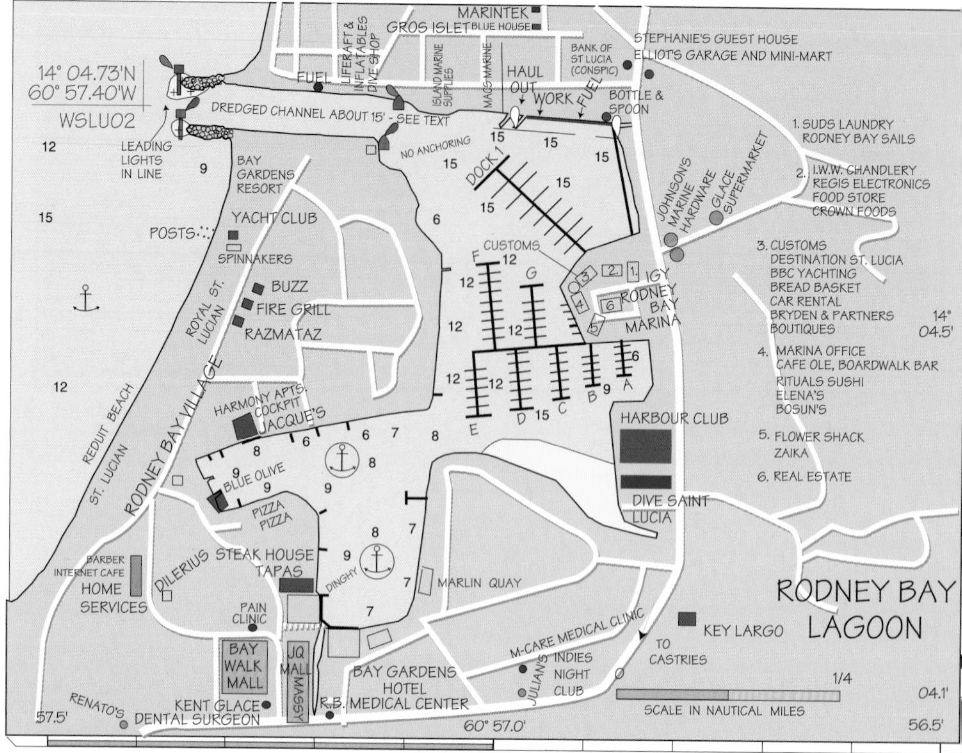

Glace Motors, tests scuba tanks and can fill most kinds of gas bottles, including CO_2, argon, helium, and nitrogen.

Ask Uli, MarinTek, or Tony George about hydraulics. Some hydraulics can be fixed, but if the job is complex and requires high pressure, Martinique is probably the nearest place to get difficult problems solved.

Provisioning

Flower Shack, a great little flower shop, is in the marina, close by the dinghy dock. Deirdre, the owner, cuts flowers either the day they sell or the day before, so they are fresh and long lasting. Her business has its own greenhouses for anthuriums and orchids, and she also sells potted plants. Deirdre does flower arrangements and can handle all the demands of the superyachts. She sells little herb plants like basil, dill, and parsley hat you can keep and grow on your boat; with just a little water you can have a few fresh leaves to liven up your salad or flavor your fish. She will deliver anywhere in St. Lucia. Deirdre also has an apartment to rent on Airbnb.

Market Place is the marina's great new food and liquor store owned by Ben and Charlie of Cafe Ole. Service and convenience are hallmarks of this store, which opens every day from 0730-2000. The friendly staff are happy to help you.

The wine and liquor section takes up a good part of the store and includes wines you will not find in the supermarkets. They offer foods and staples, with a variety of cheese and deli items, including mozzarella strips wrapped in Prosciutto. Organic fresh produce, including fresh herbs to liven up cooking, and the best locally baked breads are in stock. They can provision for you, whether you are on a superyacht in a rush, or a charter customer who would rather meet a provisioned yacht than spend time in the local supermarkets. Just call up and ask.

A local farmer's market sets up on the marina lawn early on Wednesdays and Saturdays. They have lots of produce, coconut water by the bottle, and locally processed coconut oil. Morning is best time to go.

The Bread Basket (BB's) sells fresh bread, croissants, cakes, Danishes, and other baked goods. For really large quantities, contact them in advance.

Kevin White's Crown Foods is a fancy delicatessen and provisioner in Rodney Bay Marina. The prices of their meats, seafoods, and cheeses are listed on the blackboard.

For large supermarkets and more shopping, dinghy over to the malls in the southern part of Rodney Bay, in the general area known as Rodney Bay Village. There is a dinghy dock close by. Massy is in the JQ Mall, and Food Market is in the Baywalk Mall. Both are owned by Massy. Neither has a big variety of local produce but both are otherwise excellent. Food Market is fancier, more spacious, with more upmarket items. Both open 0700-2200 Monday to Saturday, 0700-1800 Sundays and holidays.

Massy stores have a big grip on St. Lucia supermakets. Glace supermarkets are some of the only independent supermarkets left. There is one down the road beyond Johnson's Hardware. Their prices can be very good and this is the place to take in your empty case of Pitons and get a new one.

Fun shopping

Island Mix, art emporium and cafe, has its own dingy dock right next to Tapas. Nadia Jabour has created a hub of artistry - part shop, part school, part gathering place, and part restaurant. Eighty local artists are represented in the informal gallery which spans several rooms and includes crafts as well as Nadia's jewelry. For those on yachts who like to paint, they have lessons in both arts and crafts. They open Monday to Saturday 1000 to 1800 staying open later on Thursday nights when they serve fish and chips. They serve lunch, and have music nights every third Thursday. It is like walking into someone's house and studio.

Right in the marina, Drop Anchor is a branch of the famous Sea Island Cotton Shop, with a wide range of casual wear and attractive handicrafts.

Rodney Bay has giant malls with cash machines, pharmacies, clothing shops, household goods, computers, and more. The JQ Mall has 60 stores and businesses, including a stationery store. The inside shops in JQ are generally small and adjoining, making for easy browsing. The even bigger Baywalk

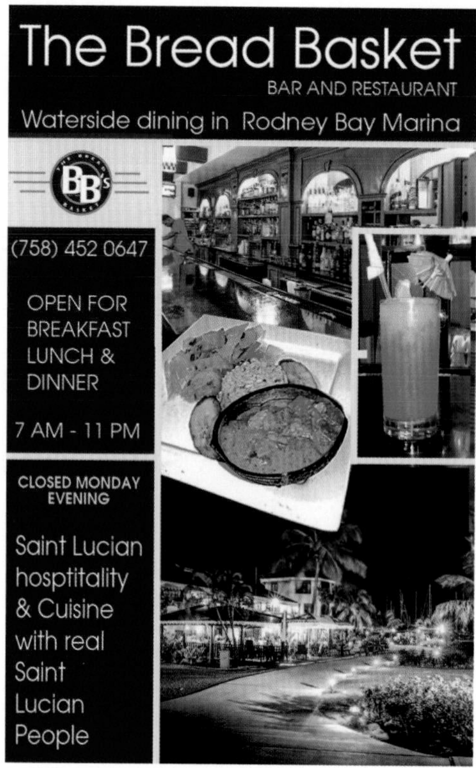

restaurants in the Windwards, with many of St. Lucia's top chefs in attendance. Restaurants are excellent, with five in the marina alone. Nowhere else has such a choice of really fine places to eat out.

One place to start the day in the marina is the Taylor family's Bread Basket (BB) [$] any time after 0730 for coffee with a full cooked breakfast or a plate of fresh croissants. Nick, Carmen, and family run this delightful marina restaurant specializing in local food. The inexpensive lunch specials are as good a bargain as you will find, and locals come here to eat or take away. Their snack menu, which includes rotis and sandwiches, is available morning to evening.

In the evening, the Bread Basket changes character; the bar comes alive, the decorative lights turn on, and it becomes a pleasant place for a reasonably priced dinner [$$] in an informal atmosphere; come in shorts if you want. The food is local both in origin and style, straightforward, carefully cooked the local way, and very tasty. The menu includes fish and shrimp

Mall has endless shops, banks, restaurants, and vendors' stands. The shops here tend to be larger, with lots of clothing.

Walk out of the JQ Mall and turn left and you will find a big new pharmacy that sells a lot of household things. If you cannot find the perfect gift in the marina or Rodney Bay Village, check out the boutiques in the big beach hotels.

Transport

When you want to get out and about, you will find a taxi stand by the gate of the marina and buses on the main road. All the registered Marina taxi drivers (452-9957) wear uniforms and are reliable. They are used to dealing with yachtspeople, and if, when you return to your yacht and find that you forgot your camera or handbag on their seat, you know where to find them. JQ Mall has another stand.

If you want to join a tour, check out Tropical Discoveries by Flower Shack.

Restaurants

Rodney Bay has the best collection of

at about 1230, has a popular happy hour from 1700 to 1800, and keeps going till midnight. You can get food from Café Olé.

For excellent pizzas, visit the family run Key Largo [$], a short walk from the marina. Key Largo is the only place that consistently bakes thin crust pizzas to perfection, a skill they acquired way back in the days when Rodney Bay Marina was first built. They bake in a giant wood-fired oven with meticulous temperature control. The family includes a colorful mix of influences from south London and St. Lucia to Italy and Sweden. Marie and her brother Val have been in from the start and the team now includes by Palo, Marie's son, and Linda, Val's wife. They are closed Monday, otherwise open every evening from 1700. They have plenty of room for special occasions or functions. They also make great calamari, salads, pasta and more. This is the best pizza in the Windwards!

Walk into Big Chef Steak House [$$$$] on any night of the week and you'll find the appetizing aroma of steaks and seafood dishes, steak and ribs, and best of all the curry that is served in a coconut. All the sides are local. Arrive in time for happy hour, 1600-1900, with two-for-one beers, wines, and rum punches; sit at the long bar or in the outside seats. They barbecue chicken pork and fish on Wednesday and Friday evenings, as well as for lunch on Sunday when they have music from 1200-1400. They also have music (often steel pan) most Wednesday, Friday and Saturday nights. A big TV shows important games.

Café Olé is charming, with a delightful eating space outside facing the marina. They serve good coffee and always have a selection of delicious baked goodies to choose from. This is a great place for lunchtime sandwiches and salads. To ensure a seat for lunch, go early. Charlotte (Charlie) and Ben, who own it, are welcoming and helpful. Café Olé opens at 0700 for breakfast and stays open through the evening. Meals and snacks are always available. Ben and Charlie also have the adjoining Boardwalk Bar, which is the marina's most popular meeting spot. It opens

on the grill and the cheerful buzz of happy patrons, many of them regulars. The piano bar provides piano, jazz, and vocals. On Mondays and Thursdays Kenson Hippolyte plays rhythm and blues from the 1930s, on Saturday nights Ronald Boo Hinkson and Semi Francis play jazz, classical guitar, and vocals.

Owners Rosie and Marc serve excellent steak and seafood and this is among St. Lucia's finest restaurants. Rosie has been a teacher at the English Cordon Bleu and she completed the Sydney-Hobart Race. They run a super operation, with first-rate service, top-quality ingredients, and the finest cuisine and presentation. You will not get a better steaks. They start with certified Angus beef, cook it the way you want, and present it artistically. If you order one of their largest [32 oz.] steaks, you can return for a free steak another night. But leave room for dessert because their crème brulée is divine. The Big Chef Steak House opens every night at 1800. They have WiFi.

Rosie and Marc from Big Chef own the adjoining Tapas on the Bay set on a breezy deck overlooking the lagoon right next to the dinghy dock for the JQ Mall. Tapas on the Bay opens from noon to 2300 Monday to Friday, except Tuesdays when it closed. Every Friday live music starts at 1900 featuring Rob Zi Taylor and Phyness (Sax and vocals), among others.

On Saturdays and Sundays Tapas on the Bay is open from 1000 to 2300, serving breakfast from 1000-1300.

The food is Mediterranean, both plates and the lighter Tapas, which are ideal for mixing and sharing. Save room for homemade desert: artisan gelato- salted caramel, tiramisu, mango sorbet, and more.

They serve first-rate coffee and this is a good place to catch up using their WiFi. The JQ Mall dinghy dock makes for easy access from Rodney Bay Marina for Tapas on the Bay and Big Chef. Adjoining Big Chef and Tapas they have six self-contained modern rooms/apartments (one with handicap access) for long- or short-term stays.

When shopping, look for the excellent

If you would like to meet some of the local yachting community, the best place to do so is at the St. Lucia Yacht Club [$]. They have an upstairs bar right on the beach, which opens in the season Monday to Friday from 1500. Weekends and holidays are special, when they open from 1000 and serve inexpensive, simple, and good lunches. Although it is a members' club, visiting yachtspeople are always very welcome, and the atmosphere is pleasant and friendly. The club has an interesting book swap, a TV for sports events, WiFi, and world-class squash courts. You can pull your dinghy up on the beach outside or walk from one of the dinghy docks. This is the place to find out about local sailing events and they run a first-rate program to teach children how to sail. Consider becoming a member. Overseas membership is very reasonable, supports local youth sailing, and gives you discounts in the club.

At some point you may dinghy over to the Mall and need a bite to eat. Easy, small snack bars line both sides of the street. Try Cream n Bean on the JQ side, look for the Big Chef bakery breads.

Another of St. Lucia's top restaurants for fine dining and simple elegance is Jacques Waterfront Dining [$$$$$], open for lunch and dinner. They close Sunday night and Monday lunch in season and close all day Sunday in low season.

You can dinghy over and tie up on the eating deck railing, which runs along the water with just inches of freeboard; it is a superb location in the peaceful inner lagoon. I first ate at Jacques about 20 years ago when they opened in Vigie, I still love it, and find the owners, Jacques and his wife Kathy, warmly welcoming.

Jacques brings his training and experience as a skilled chef from the Loire Valley and has adapted this to local ingredients to produce what Kathy calls "an exciting blend of flavors, herbs, and spices of France and the Caribbean." Jacques provides many different flavors that will delight and surprise. His cooking is inventive and he is very much into seafood. You will eat well here and enjoy the ambience. Come relax on Sundays when they offer a jazz brunch from 1130 to 1500.

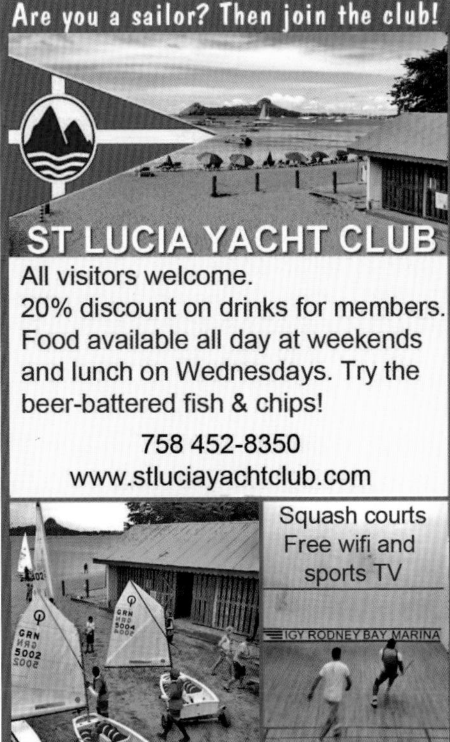

magenta tables. This cafe and ice cream shop opens daily 0800-2130, Sundays 1100-1900. They serve the best croissants and baguettes; fresh, warm and righteously stuffed with your choice of filling. Their Ferrons ice cream is dessert, (Ferrons opened in 1948 as a dairy) all the ice creams and sorbets are made locally, and flavors change depending on the fruits that are in season.

The Cockpit [$$], open all day every day, is a simple quiet restaurant for the Harmony apartments, and you can tie to their dinghy dock. The food is good, with fresh salads and local fish in a dining room that is open to the garden.

In the marina, Rituals Sushi (closed Mondays) opens at 1100, serves lunch till 1600 and stays open for dinner. They have excellent sushi, served as individual dishes or platters, and lots of other dishes like beef and chicken teriyaki, and some great appetizers, including a big plate of spicy calamari. It is a good place to visit and popular, especially in the evenings, and they offer takeout.

Close by is Elena's [$$], open from breakfast (cooked or continental) through dinner. They make fresh fruit juices, crepes, sandwiches, and salads that are available any time during the day. Their ice cream is good and they have a pizza oven.

Upstairs, Bosuns [$$] has a comfy, pub-like atmosphere where tables are set out on a balcony with a view of the marina. They open every day till late at night and have good food.

Zaika [$$$] is owned by Sachin Nahari and Ashok Vaswani, who have created an authentic Indian interior full of intricate detail. It is near the dinghy dock and adjoining the marina swimming pool. Zaika is open daily for lunch and dinner.

Razmataz, a first-rate traditional Indian restaurant, has been around much longer than the others. The old wooden building and decor could have been dreamed up by Somerset Maugham. Owner Sue is in the process of putting it up for sale, so it may or may not still be there.

Harbor Club [$$$$] is the new hotel beside Dive Saint Lucia. It has a big perimeter deck/dock with plenty of room to tie your dinghy at either end. When you want expensive elegance, come relax by their infinity pool, waterfalls and numerous little waterways. On the deck are a pool bar and a pizza hut, which also serves snacks. Julia's restaurant adjoins the pool with inside and outside seating. Their finest restaurant is Positano Santa Lucia, open for dinner on the top floor with views over the northern coast, including Pigeon Island and Martinique. Check out the Sky Lounge bar on the roof, the Crew Bar on the first floor Sushi Deck and the 7th Heaven Artisanal Pastry Shop.

Spice of India [$$, closed Mondays] is

Shrimps, Big Chef

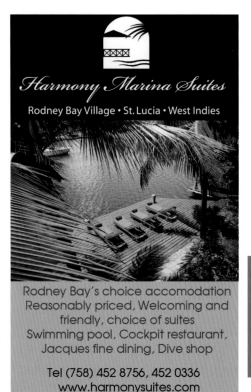

in Baywalk Mall. Owner Adil Pervez Shwerwani is from Delhi and keeps people happy. Cool out for lunch in their air-conditioned dining room. Dinner starts at 1800.

Bay Gardens Beach Resort [$$$] is open and friendly with WiFi, a swimming pool, jacuzzi, and a first-rate restaurant. They sometimes host get-together women's lunch on Wednesdays (listen to the morning net VHF: 68, 0830 for details). They have an excellent beach buffet with live music and other entertainment on Saturday nights.

Ashore

Extra crew flying in and need somewhere ashore for a night or two? The best, reasonably-priced, and most personal place to stay is in Harmony Suites right in Rodney Bay Lagoon with its own dinghy dock. It is small, and friendly with a lovely flower garden and swimming pool. All the rooms are nicely furnished with marine paintings on the wall. Some rooms have more cooking facilities than others. It is home to Cockpit Restaurant and Jacques (see *Restaurants*). It is a handy place to leave your dinghy. Book early though, as it is often full.

Face to Face spa takes up two upstairs floors near the marine office, with balconies and comfortable places to relax while waiting for treatments. Owner Tracy Farrin has been in the business 30 years and her parlor is up to top international standards, with several employees. They have a big shower, so yachties can get really cleaned up. They offer all kinds of massage and cosmetic work, including waxing, pedicure, and manicure. They are happy to make boat visits.

Cas-en-bas is a lovely beach on the east coast, a couple of miles from Rodney Bay (main road north, turn right at the Gros

Seafood Salad, Jacques

Islet turn-off). The road is rough but walkable, with good hiking north or south from Cas-en-bas. Marjorie's offers a reasonable local lunch on the beach. Marjorie recently retired, but the restaurant keeps going. You will also find Aquaholics kite surfing here (726-0600). If horse riding is more your style, call Trimm's (758-8273).

If you have a mountain bike, this east coast area, from Cap Estate to Esperance Harbour, is perfect.

Thinking about property in St. Lucia? If having your boat close to your house is important, then look at some of the available properties in Rodney Bay lagoon with docking facilities. Enough units were built that some are usually on the market.

An agent who handles these and properties all over the island is fellow yachtsman Jonathan Everett. He is very straightforward and will give you the honest low-down on local ownership. He may retire but till then you will find him at Home Services, an office in Rodney Bay Village.

The small town of Gros Islet is pic-esque, with lots of small restaurants. On Friday night the village is closed to traffic and everyone dances in the streets or wanders from bar to bar. All along the street, stalls sell such goodies as barbecued conch on a skewer and barbecued fish and chicken. Security was a problem here for a while. It seems better now, but to be safe, go in a group or by cab or bus and return the same way. Stay in well-lit areas.

Water sports

There is passable snorkeling around Pigeon Island. New scuba sites are being found in the north. If there is not too much surge, you often see eagle rays at Burgot Rocks. Barrel of Beef has boulders, sponges, and colorful reef fish, including sergeant majors. Fisheries regulations require that visiting scuba divers go with an approved dive shop.

Dive Saint Lucia is ahead of most Caribbean dive shops with its own on-site purpose-built pool and state-of-the-art classroom facilities. Couple this with great retail facilities and top-class staff.

Their dive boats match the shop: spacious cabin cruisers that take up to 30 divers, with fully stocked fridges for refreshments before and after dives.

Dive Saint Lucia is a Scubapro dealer offering new gear and servicing older equipment. Their retail shop has a stack of accessories from cameras to Lycra diving shirts, along with towing toys popular with the big yachts.

Dive Saint Lucia is a PADI 5 star IDC center offering all PADI courses from beginner to instructor together with guided dives and snorkel tours of all the best dive sites in St. Lucia. It is run by Marcel Buechler and Dawn Shewan who, with a team of highly trained St. Lucian instructors, also participate in education, community involvement and environmental projects.

Dive Saint Lucia generally dives every day, often starting about 0900 and returning about 1500 for a two-dive excursion. They are open to locals and tourists alike. For diving, snorkeling or learning, give them a call. They are available for private dive charters, and in this case will pick up from your yacht as far away as Soufriere.

Scuba Steve's Diving is a PADI 5-star Golden Palm Resort owned by Stephen. They are highly qualified and can do nitrox, as Steve is a gas blender and EFR instructor. They will be happy to teach you or take you on a dive in their fast boats with bimini protection. You will find them behind Jacque's restaurant in the Harmony Suites car park.

Flying Gunard

FROM CAP ESTATE TO VIGIE

Outside Rodney Bay, from Cap Estate to Vigie, are more attractions just a walk, bus ride, or taxi-hop away.

Ashore

S&S Plaza is on the right as you head towards Castries, but farther than most would want to walk. Their store sells a vast array of household items, along with inexpensive clothes, stationary, watches, and much more. It They have a Cream 'n Bean here with sandwiches and ice cream.

Sunbilt is a big hardware store about a mile and a half towards Castries. A little farther is Computer World, a giant computer store where you can buy computers or get yours fixed. Another mile or so brings you to the first roundabout and Mega J, a giant store selling everything from foods (bulk or retail) to plumbing, with auto accessories, electrical, household, and pharmacy items thrown in.

The Gablewoods Shopping Center is about halfway between Rodney Bay Marina and Castries. As you approach Vigie, American Drywall is on your left (includes a bike shop and Lubeco bedding factory), and opposite is Home Depot, a good household store. At the next roundabout is Fedex.

Cap Estate, a luxury development, is set in green, rolling hills to the north of Gros Islet. Golfers will be happy to know that this is the place to play golf. The National Trust has a nice little park at Pt. du Cap (Morne Pavillon), which makes a good walk from Rodney Bay (see doyleguides.com).

Windjammer Landings is an upmarket villa development just south of Rodney Bay. The anchorage is tricky, so those who want to go there by boat should contact the managers and they will provide a guide. They have restaurants and boutiques.

Travel World is owned by Jocelyn and run out of her home. If you have ticketing problems, she is a good person to call. She is also good at finding rental cars and booking hotels.

Pottery, Pink Plantation

CASTRIES AND VIGIE

Castries is a reasonable anchorage, so when you are ready to visit town, by yacht is a fine way to do it. Half a mile away from Castries is the quiet Vigie Cove, also a good, if small, anchorage. When cruise ships are in town, these two anchorages are linked by numerous little ferries that tour around the harbor, stopping at the Coal Pot, Pointe Seraphine, and the craft market.

CASTRIES TOWN

Castries lacks a unifying architectural style but has plenty of variety. Some effort has been made to retain the Caribbean character of the buildings that face Derek Walcott Square along Brazil Street. The area between Peynier Street and Chaussee Road, along Brazil, Micoud, Chisel, and Coral Streets has a Creole atmosphere, with balconies, gingerbread, and old and new buildings. Happily, many smaller new buildings are now being designed in keeping with the old architectural character.

The new buildings on the north side of the waterfront are of a more recent style, and these, plus other new blocks in town, look modern and clean. The big market, with food, handicrafts, and clothes, is fascinating. For fresh food, Fridays and Saturdays are better than earlier in the week.

Regulations

Castries is a port of entry, though it is much easier to clear

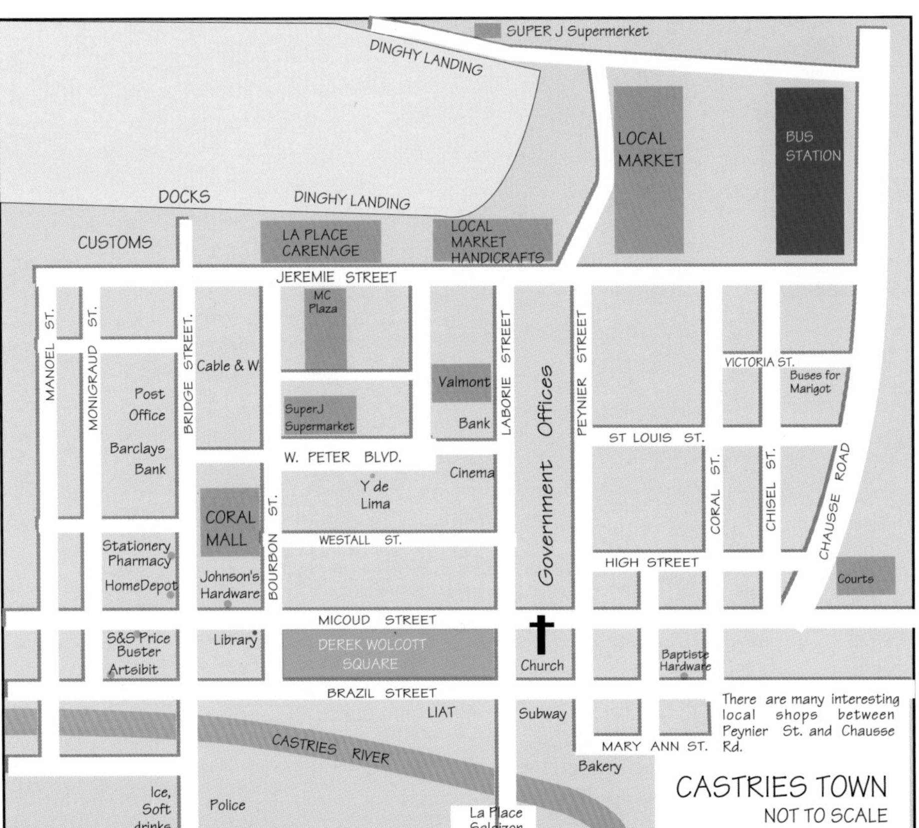

in Rodney Bay or Marigot. The officials insist that entering yachts come straight to the customs dock, or if there is no room, to the anchorage right beside it.

Give the cruise ships a wide berth when entering and leaving so you don't make the port police anxious.

Communications

Restaurants and bars have WiFi.

Transport/Services

The big bus station is behind the local produce market. All routes are numbered: 1A is Gros Islet, 2H is Vieux Fort, 3D is Soufriere. The Marigot and Canaries buses go from Victoria Street.

You can find a place to leave your dinghy between the craft market and La Place Carenage, but make sure your dinghy does not interfere with the ferries. Entry is through La Place Carenage, which makes it pretty safe, but it closes at night, so ask what time. You can leave the dinghy on the north shore, which is always open and unguarded. You can find a sign or tree to lock to.

Provisioning

The easiest supermarket is Massy, close to the market. You can tie your dinghy close by. Pharmacy and stationery stores are on Bridge Street.

You will find general and household hardware at Home Depot or Valmont. If you need acrylic sheet or synthetic canvas, then J. N. Baptiste is the specialist. For auto, electrical, and other household items, try Johnson's. Bandag sells auto parts.

La Place Carenage has duty-free liquor stores, well situated for stocking up on small or large quantities of wine, liquor, and Cuban cigars. It is right on the main wharf in town, so you can load up your dinghy.

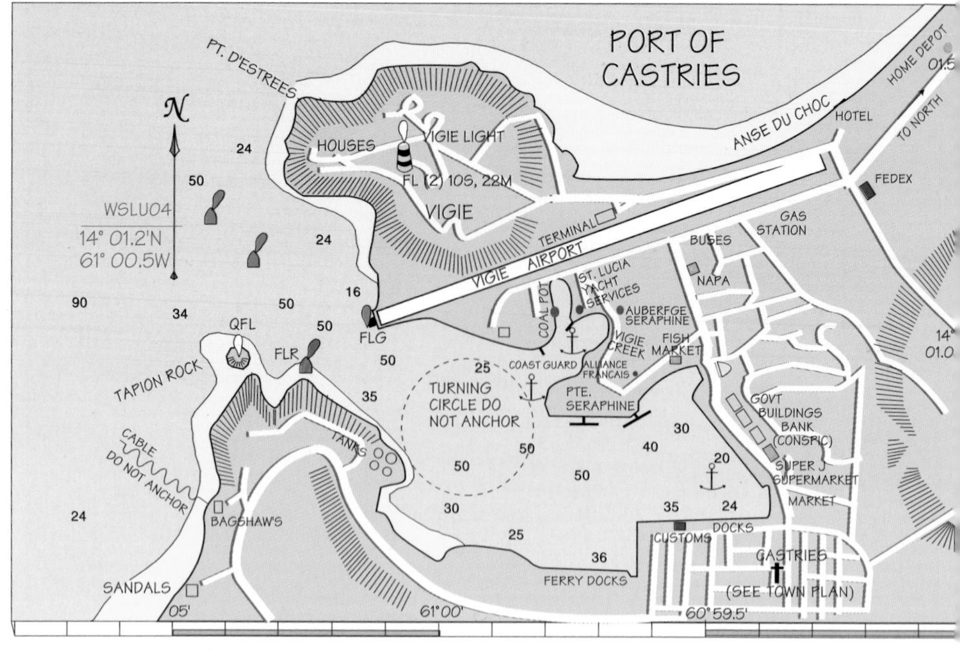

Fun shopping

St. Lucia's local market ranks among the best in the islands. It occupies several buildings, as well as outdoor areas, and spreads to both sides of the road. It is a riot of color and excitement as many dozens of local vendors sell their wares. Spend an hour or two here enjoying the scene and take the opportunity to stock up on local foods, t-shirts, coal pots, straw work, and handicrafts. The market includes a street of tiny food stalls, each owning a single outside table. Here you will find cheap and tasty local food. A ferry links the market with Pointe Seraphine, the duty-free shopping mall that has about 50 pleasantly laid out tourist shops. Take your passport for the duty free.

Just down the road, La Place Carenage is another place for tourist shops ~ lots of them, all pleasantly laid out with everything from international jewelry to handicrafts in a cool air-conditioned atmosphere. They have a theater where they run Our Planet, an interactive light and sound production.

Coral Mall has a good selection of local shops.

Restaurants

The Pink Plantation House [$$$$] is a special restaurant, one of the best in St. Lucia for lunch. It is on Chef Harry Drive, just outside Castries (a short taxi ride), set high on the Morne with a spectacular view over Castries. It belongs to Michelle, one of St. Lucia's best local artists and potters. She has shops in Pointe Seraphine, JQ Mall, and she also owns the Coal Pot (see Vigie). Michelle has taken this historic estate house with beautiful gardens and created a gorgeous restaurant on the generous balcony. The food is traditional Caribbean and excellent. You can wander in the garden, which has an extensive collection of orchids, and you can see Michelle's work in the house, both pottery and paintings. While doing so you will soak in the atmosphere of the lovely old Caribbean estate house, which will give you a feeling of the Caribbean from years ago. The Plantation house opens for lunch, call and make a reservation. They will do special functions at night and open for dinner occasionally. Well worth a visit from Rodney Bay.

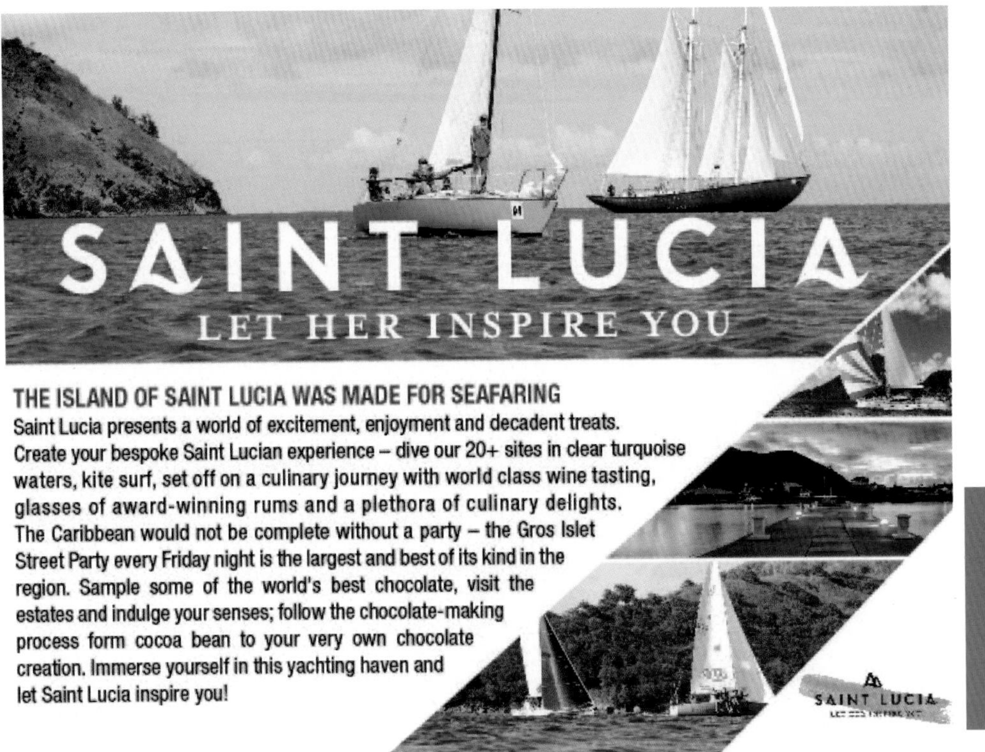

SAINT LUCIA
LET HER INSPIRE YOU
THE ISLAND OF SAINT LUCIA WAS MADE FOR SEAFARING
Saint Lucia presents a world of excitement, enjoyment and decadent treats. Create your bespoke Saint Lucian experience – dive our 20+ sites in clear turquoise waters, kite surf, set off on a culinary journey with world class wine tasting, glasses of award-winning rums and a plethora of culinary delights. The Caribbean would not be complete without a party – the Gros Islet Street Party every Friday night is the largest and best of its kind in the region. Sample some of the world's best chocolate, visit the estates and indulge your senses; follow the chocolate-making process form cocoa bean to your very own chocolate creation. Immerse yourself in this yachting haven and let Saint Lucia inspire you!
SAINT LUCIA

VIGIE

A light on Vigie Hill (flashing twice every 10 seconds) is helpful in identifying Castries Harbor at night.

Vigie is a good overnight stop on your way north or south; take dinner at the Coal Pot and maybe a quick trip to town. It is handy for Vigie Airport as well. You can anchor either inside or outside Vigie Creek. Although generally well protected, Vigie Cove does suffer from a surge in a really bad northwesterly swell.

Anchoring in the creek can be tight but there is more room outside. Carnival Cruises have several moorings; the outer two are white and used for their catamarans when swells come in. If there are no swells, ask the crew on the catamarans if you can use one for a small fee. On cruise ship days Vigie bustles with ferries and day-charter boats. There is easy access to Pointe Seraphine.

Services/provisioning

St. Lucia Yacht Services (SLYS) has a fuel dock and they sell water and fuel weekdays 0800-1600, weekends 0800-1400.

There is no public dinghy dock but you can use the SLYS dock after hours, and some of the surrounding waterfront at other times. If you are visiting the Coal Pot, tie your dinghy up by their waterfront shed, or dock your yacht on their big dock just beyond the restaurant. Pointe Seraphine has its own dock, but you must stay clear of the ferries and be off when day-charter cats come in.

A short walk on the road to town gets you to a big NAPA agency, which stocks filters, parts, sprays, seals, polishes, and tools. They are agents for OMC outboards, with full sales and service. In addition, they stock inflatables, ropes, and some marine hardware.

If you need a taxi, give Theresa a call. She is good and reliable and stationed at Vigie Airport (384-9197/458-4444). The main Fedex office is a mile away, opposite the bottom of the runway.

Also in Vigie (in the white pyramid opposite the Pointe Seraphine entrance)

Heron, Auberge Seraphine

is the Alliance Francais. They offer French lessons and an internet cafe, and it is worth checking out their coming cultural events.

Restaurants

A good reason to come to Vigie is to eat at the Coal Pot [$$$$, closed Saturday lunch and all Sunday]. It has a romantic setting on the waterfront. Many years ago, Bob Elliot sailed across the Atlantic and into this cove. He fell in love and married Sonia, whose family owned the land, and they built this as their house. Michelle, their daughter, spent her first few years growing up here. Later, Bob converted the house to a storehouse for his beloved day-charter brig, Unicorn, and then into a restaurant, keeping the nautical decor. Michelle now runs the restaurant, and the food is good. Mango Moon, a gym, is on the Coal Pot grounds.

While in Vigie, check out the colony of egrets and other birds around the colorful lily pond in front of Auberge Seraphine. Auberge Seraphine is also a fine place for coffee or a meal and they have WiFi and an internet station.

Navigation
Castries to Marigot Bay

As you leave Castries, give a reasonable clearance to Tapion Rock.

Marigot lies about a mile south of Hess Oil's huge tanker depot at Cul de Sac Bay. In the old days, it was so well tucked away that a British admiral is reputed to have hidden his fleet here, disguising the masts by tying coconut fronds in the rigging. Today you cannot miss it, with the prominent buildings of the Marina Village and all the yachts inside. Once you pass the Hess Oil depot the wind tends to become light and contrary, not a bad place to start powering.

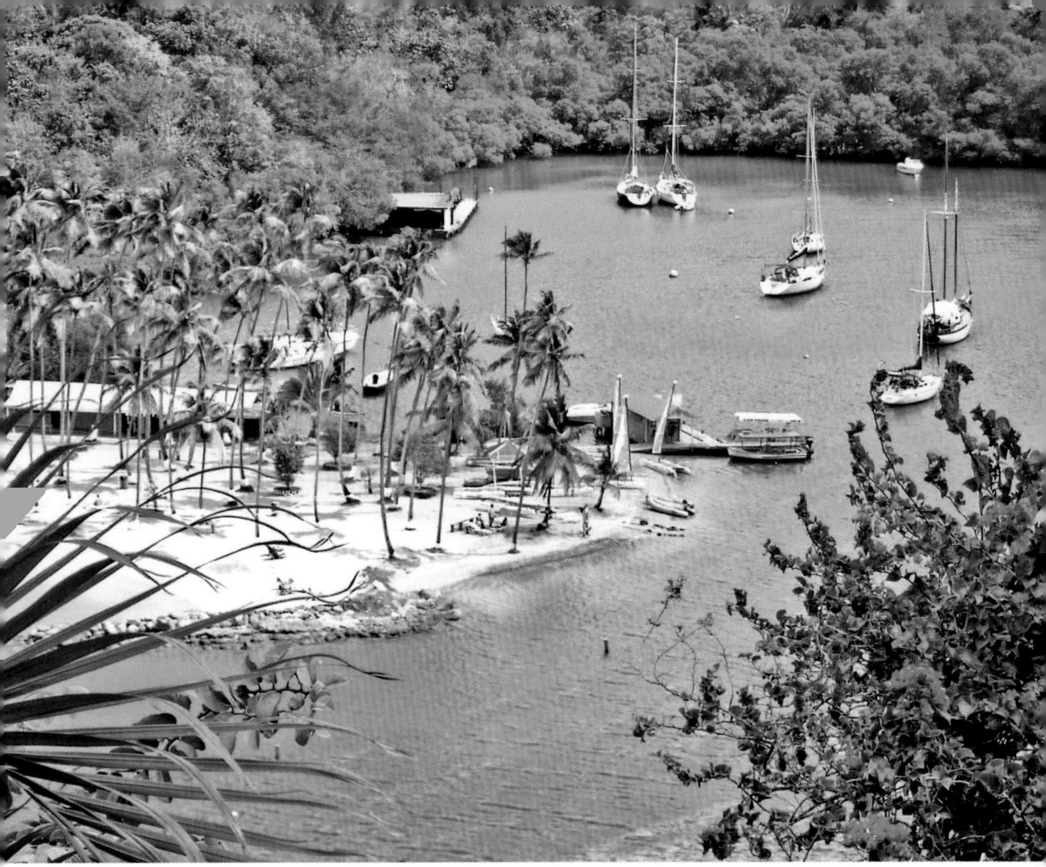

MARIGOT BAY

Marigot Bay is a completely sheltered, mangrove-lined bay, famous as a hurricane harbor. From inside, as you look across the beach spit with its lacy palms, it affords a perfect backdrop for a sunset photo and rum punch. Over the years it has grown from a sleepy backwater, where nothing happened, to being a pleasant place to shop, eat out, take a stroll, or hike, and see what super-yachts may be in.

Navigation

Enter down the channel, which favors the southern shore and avoids a shoal that extends out from Marigot Beach Resort. The channel buoys were missing in 2018. The minimum depth in the channel and inner bay is 5 meters (16.5 feet). Costly and delicate underwater electric cables and water pipes cross right at the entrance to the inner harbor. Do not anchor!

You can anchor on either side of the channel where there is adequate depth, or inside if you can find room among the moorings, where the holding is passable in soft mud. Capella Marigot Bay Marina and resort has 20 reliable moorings in the inner harbor, which are white with a blue stripe. They cost $30 US a night ($20 in the summer). If you call the marina they will send a dinghy to help you tie up. Otherwise, many locals will be happy to tie you up for a tip. Do not pay them for the mooring, go into the marina office and pay.

Many will greet you, offering unofficial moorings (all the outside ones, and one or two inside) that look just like the official moorings. Some of these moorings are poor and go adrift, so you are taking a chance. Just say "no" to anyone who becomes persistent, pushy, or in any way objectionable. Check doyleguides.com for any updates. Outside is a lovely anchorage, but you get more vendors and speeding dinghies than in the lagoon, as wekk as more thefts. If you are eating at Chateau Mygo you can tie to their dock at no charge if they have room.

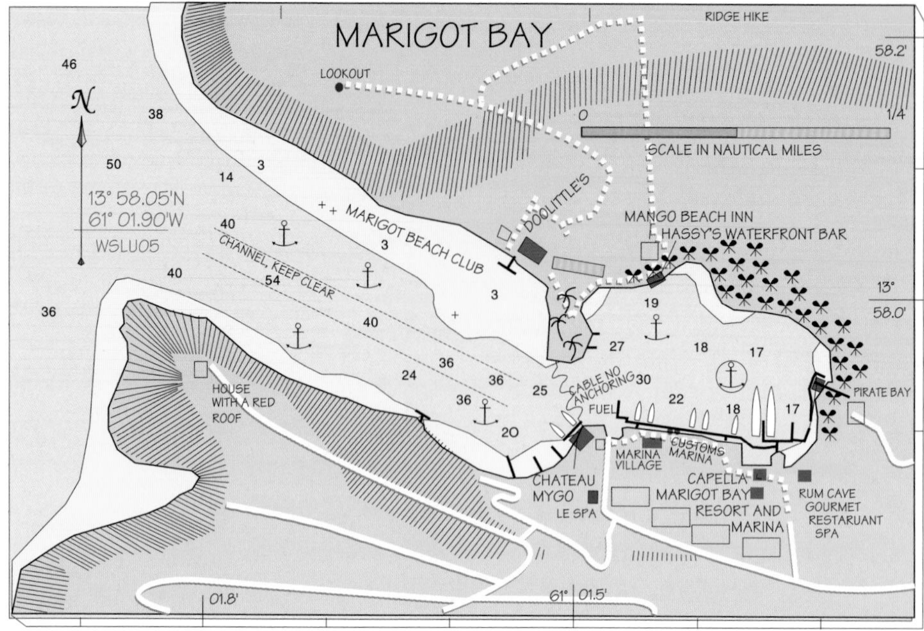

Regulations

There is a 4-knot speed limit in the harbor. Marigot Bay is an official port of entry, with customs, immigration and SLASPA (port authority), which collects the entry fees. They are usually open 0800-1200 and 1330-1615. The offices adjoin the marina office on the dock. Sailclear works well. If you know you will arrive after closing, and someone is leaving early the next morning, contact one of the agents for help.

Yachts in Capella Marina should ask about garbage (they often collect from the dock). Others should take garbage to the public dump in the car park straight back down the road.

Communications

Capella has variable WiFi for their customers. Doolittle's has an IT bar with WiFi and power outlets. Chateau Mygo also has WiFi.

General yacht services

Dinghy docks are at Chateau Mygo, in the Marina Village, by the Rum Cave, at Doolittle's Restaurant, or at JJ's. Dinghies must not be tied to the yacht docks.

Capella Marigot Bay Resort and Marina has moorings and both alongside and stern-to berths for yachts up to 250 feet. Contact manager Troy and the marina team (451-4275/728-9948, VHF: 16/12). The marina and the hotel are integrated, and if you use the docks you can get room service on board. Their lower pool, above the Rum Cave, is open to marina visitors. You can put meals on your marina tab. The emphasis is on exceptional customer service, and you can expect the marina staff to make sure you have everything you need.

Agents, such as Ben Yacht Services, come on a regular basis (see *Soufriere*), and you are welcome to use them. They will take care of you in all St. Lucia's ports. The marina can also assign you a personal assistant.

The superyacht berths have high-speed, sealed fueling, and smaller yachts can get diesel at their berth. For visitors, diesel and gasoline are available on the fuel dock next to the ferry dock. Duty free is available. Electricity, 110- and 220-volt, 50- and 60-cycle, is available, as is 410-volt, 3-phase for superyachts. They provide a holding-tank pump-out. Ask the marina about rates on hotel nights ashore; they can also arrange laundry (9 kg is about $20 US).

The marina can help organize day labor, and Saltwater in the marina village sells phone cards, has local information,

Chateau Mygo
MARIGOT BAY
SAINT LUCIA
• Free docking for groups of 5 or more
• Open everyday: Breakfast, Lunch & Dinner
• Ice & Water • Free Water Taxi Pick Up
• Express Laundry Service (wash - dry - fold)
Marigot Bay
HURRICANE HOLE
• Happy Hour 5-6PM
• Dinghy Dock
• Free WIFI
Chateau Mygo Villas
MARIGOT BAY SAINT LUCIA
(758) 451 4772 | VHF 16
info@chateaumygo.com
www.chateaumygo.com

Ismael "Friend" and Jeremiah "Nucky" see ad Page 151

arranges taxis or reservations, and provides all manner of tours.

Chateau Mygo [VHF: 16] offers laundry services ($50-$150 EC depending on the load); ironing is extra. They have berths and moorings for their charter company. They do not rent these, but if you are having dinner, they will be happy to give you a free berth, or mooring, when there is room.

Technical yacht services

Shaid has a team to repair and fix his charter fleet and he offers this service to visiting yachts. If anything goes wrong, from the motor to the mast, this is a good place to start. For larger yachts, the Marina staff will organize what is needed.

Ismael "Friend" and "Nucky" (718-3888, 520-6400) are great varnishers. They also clean, polish, service winches, and do general maintenance. They take care of yachts when the owners go away. They live nearby and are happy to work here or in Rodney Bay.

On the other side of the bay Complete Marine Services has a work barge with a crane. Their main line of work is marine construction. They also do yacht surveys, and excellent underwater and salvage work. They watch boats when owners are away, undertake project management, install new

Marigot Bay,
Shaid Rambally Chateau Mygo photo

equipment, and fix things. If it is not something they like to do, they will point you in the right direction.

Provisioning/fun shopping

Mari Gourmet, behind the Marina Village, is a good, small supermarket. They are open 0800-1900, except Sundays and holidays, 0800-1300. They can sell duty-free cigarettes and liquor. Next door is an ATM.

Chateau Mygo has many suppliers for their restaurant and are happy to provision for yachts, either a full provisioning, or getting some things you cannot source in Marigot.

A local market sometimes takes place in the Village Marina square, 0800-1400.

The village has some boutiques, Doolittle's has one and vendors sell souvenirs on the beach.

Transport

Ferries and water taxis are available to go anywhere in the bay or to and from your yacht. Chateau Mygo [VHF: 16] has several water taxis and land taxis and offers all kinds of tours, or will run you where you need to go.

Taxi Service Marigot [451-4406, VHF: 16] are the local taxi drivers who wait near the public dock at the end of the road.

Restaurants/ashore

Chateau Mygo [$$$, VHF: 16] is a large enterprise run by the Rambally family. Years ago Mama Sheila started it as a no-frills food shack. Now, a waterfront restaurant, guest houses, Le Spa, and boutiques are set in tropical gardens that go from the road to the beach.

The Ramballys are a Caribbean/East Indian family with many ties to yachting. Doreen runs the restaurant with her son Shaid, and they both like cruising, so whichever one is not off sailing runs the restaurant. Shaid speaks English like a Californian and Spanish like a Costa Rican, which is where Andrea, his wife, is from. Among them, the family speaks English, Spanish, Italian, French, Norwegian, Patois, and Hindu. Chateau Mygo restaurant stands on legs out over the water and has a main menu and a variety of thin-crust Italian pizzas.

Their food is essentially Caribbean from fresh local sources, spiced with ideas garnered from around the world. Local seafood is their specialty, including lobster, shrimp, lambi, scallops, and a variety of fish. Their grilled fish in mango and passion fruit sauce is delicious. Baby-back ribs and USDA black angus steaks are popular with many sailors.

In season they have live music on Tuesday and Thursday nights. For lunch try their fish taco with local salsa, or their wonderful shrimp burrito.

Shaid hosts a local TV cooking show (Stir it Up) that includes sailing, surfing, and cooking; he is known as the Adventure Chef. Once a fortnight or so he hosts a fun and reasonably priced cooking program. He takes the group to the market, and then you return and learn to cook the dishes before enjoying them.

Their little "Hurricane Hole" beach bar, named after the first hotel in the bay, is fun in the evening, and sometimes the liveliest spot in the harbor. It is also a great spot for an open air breakfast. On the road they have a gelato ice cream shop. Chateau Mygo opens for breakfast and is a great place to start the day.

Gloria, another Rambally, runs Le Spa Marigot here. She has you covered head to toe with the best barber in St. Lucia, a good hair stylist, manicures, pedicures, nails, massages, and even make up. She is popular locally for doing complete make-overs for brides, and will even arrange the wedding. Her team will do treatments onboard and her prices are reasonable.

Shaid runs a charter company (Bateau Mygo) with both day- and term-charters available from his dock as well as reasonably priced bare-boat charters to qualified people. He uses locally trained crew. In addition, the Ramballys have villas to rent and a small real-estate office.

In the marina village square, open to the water, the Hurricane Hole Cafe [$$$$] (to separate it from Chateau Mygo's Hurricane Hole Bar) opens early for breakfast and keeps going into the night with good coffee, baked goodies, hamburgers, and meals. People use it as a general meeting place, a hang out, and a rest stop. Two big TV screens provide any important sports action.

Across the water Hassy's Waterfront Bar [$$] stands on a wooden platform that intermingles with the mangroves, which makes for a lovely atmosphere late at night. Hassy (another Rambally) is a lovely barman, friendly, smiling, and welcoming as soon as he gets there, which is usually 1700, but sometimes 1800. Hassy's is a bar with a barbecue. Limited choices often include crispy barbecued pizza, wings, ribs, occasionally fish and lobster, usually served with garlic bread or fries and a dash of cole slaw. Prices are reasonable and the food tasty, nicely served, and no frills. Book if you want lobster.

Above, and connected, is the bright and sunny Marigot Beach Inn, with a lovely bay view, and perfect for shore time. It is run by Judith Verity.

Cappella has three restaurants amid beautifully gardened walkways. Service in all three is excellent. You dinghy to the Rum Cave [$$$] dock, which is under the bridge. It is casual, with a big selection of rums and offers finger foods, salads, sandwiches and both a lunch and dinner menu. Up one level is the Grill 14°61 [$$$$$], which opens for breakfast and dinner. The dinner is fine and fancy French cuisine on a lovely deck overlooking the bay, good for a special night out. Another level up at the upper pool is Brut [$$$$], a lovely pool bar that serves light and healthy food: sushi, sashimi, seafood, and some meat. They have lunch specials, but are not open at night. To reserve, call the Capella (458-5300).

On the north shore, by the entrance, is Marigot Beach Club, owned by Dave from England. This is a delightful area, magnificently gardened and leading onto the beach. His Doolittle's restaurant [VHF: 16, $$$] is comfortable and right on the waterfront. Nightly happy hour, two-for-one, is 1700-1900. Live entertainment is frequent in season, and it is a great hangout. They offer a wide variety of food and have specials every night. Marigot Beach Club has rooms for nights ashore.

Ulrich Augustin has Pirate Bay, a French-style Bistro, built on the dock. It opens every day for lunch and dinner, and specializes in a wide variety of seafood, including the big "Seafood Feast". The food is good, fresh, and served with flair, which has made them popular with visitors and locals. They do hibachi grills so you can cook food yourself right at the table. They have their own special ales on tap: Pale Mutiny and Golden Buccaneer. If a hoard of day charter people from Martinique are visiting, you might want to come back another time.

Upstairs in the marina village, Massala Bay ($$$) is a very pleasant Indian restaurant run by Chef Govind Joshi. The service is wonderful and they serve both Indian and Hakka (from the Chinese/Indian border) cuisine.

If you walk up the hill behind JJ's, you come to Marigot village, which is local, friendly, and enjoyed by locals and visitors. At the top of the hill you can enjoy the view, buy souvenirs, and get a drink. Julietta's Restaurant [$$$] is high on stilts with a magnificent view of Marigot. Do not come when you are rushed, but do come and enjoy; the food is good. Opening hours vary.

At the top of the hill on the north side of Marigot Bay is a national park with a wonderful short hike (about an hour and a quarter). Dock at Mango Bay Inn, walk up to their building, and ask them to show you the trail. It is a very steep straight climb to the ridge. Hike down along the ridge till you come to the crossroads to either the Lookout or Oasis. Go to the Lookout, then back a short way and take the trail down to Oasis, and thus to Doolittles. From here a path runs behind the mangroves back to Mango Bay Inn dock. This whole area is a favorite with birders.

Walk about a mile to the main road to catch a bus to Castries. On the return journey most bus drivers are willing to bring you all the way to the customs dock for a little extra.

Water sports

Dive Fair Helen's office is in Doolittle's. They will be delighted to take you on one of several excellent dives just south of Marigot in the area of Anse Cochon, or down to Soufriere.

Marigot to Soufriere regulations

The Soufriere Marine Management Association (SMMA) manages two multi-use areas, from Marigot to Choiseul. The northern part is the Canaries and Anse la Raye Marine Management Area (CAMMA), and the southern part is the Soufriere Marine Management Association SMMA [VHF: 16]. They regulate all anchoring, snorkeling, diving, and fishing. They have placed many yacht moorings, which are white (some with a blue stripe) for yachts up to 70 feet. Red or orange moorings are for dive boats or snorkeling dinghies. Five moorings are available for yachts up to 120 feet. In some places you may also anchor (see section descriptions). For details see Soufriere and the Pitons.

MARIGOT TO ANSE LA RAYE

Trou l'Oranger is a small white sand beach occasionally used by day-charter boats. Anchoring off this beach is only permissible 0900-1700. In calm, pleasant weather, it can be worth a stop for a swim and a snorkel.

Anse La Raye is a picturesque fishing village and a fair overnight anchorage. It is good in settled conditions with no northerly swells. Currently no fees are collected. There is plenty of swinging room off the town in 15 to 20 feet. The northern part of the bay shoals quite rapidly. The night to go is Friday, when they have a fish fest. Tables and chairs are put right down the center of the front street, and vendors set up stalls on both sides of the road and cook seafood: fish, lobster, lambi, and floats to go with them. It is very popular with locals and has an atmosphere of peace, good will, and good food. You can use the big new dock or pull your dinghy up on the beach, swells permitting.

River Rock Falls is a good 2-mile hike up a pretty road that starts on the northern edge of the village. It is well signposted. Robberies on the way up are not unknown, though once there you should be okay, as workers are often around. Do not expect a wild, tropical falls; this is a gardened area where the fall and rock pool have been augmented with concrete. What you lose in immediate visual satisfaction you gain by the convenience of seats, tables, changing rooms, and a generous balcony overlooking the falls. Currently there is no fee because of the lack of security. You may have it to yourself.

The much wilder and more beautiful Bois de Nave fall is in the hills to the southeast of the village. You will probably need to hire a guide to show you the way. The hiking in this area is excellent, with trails

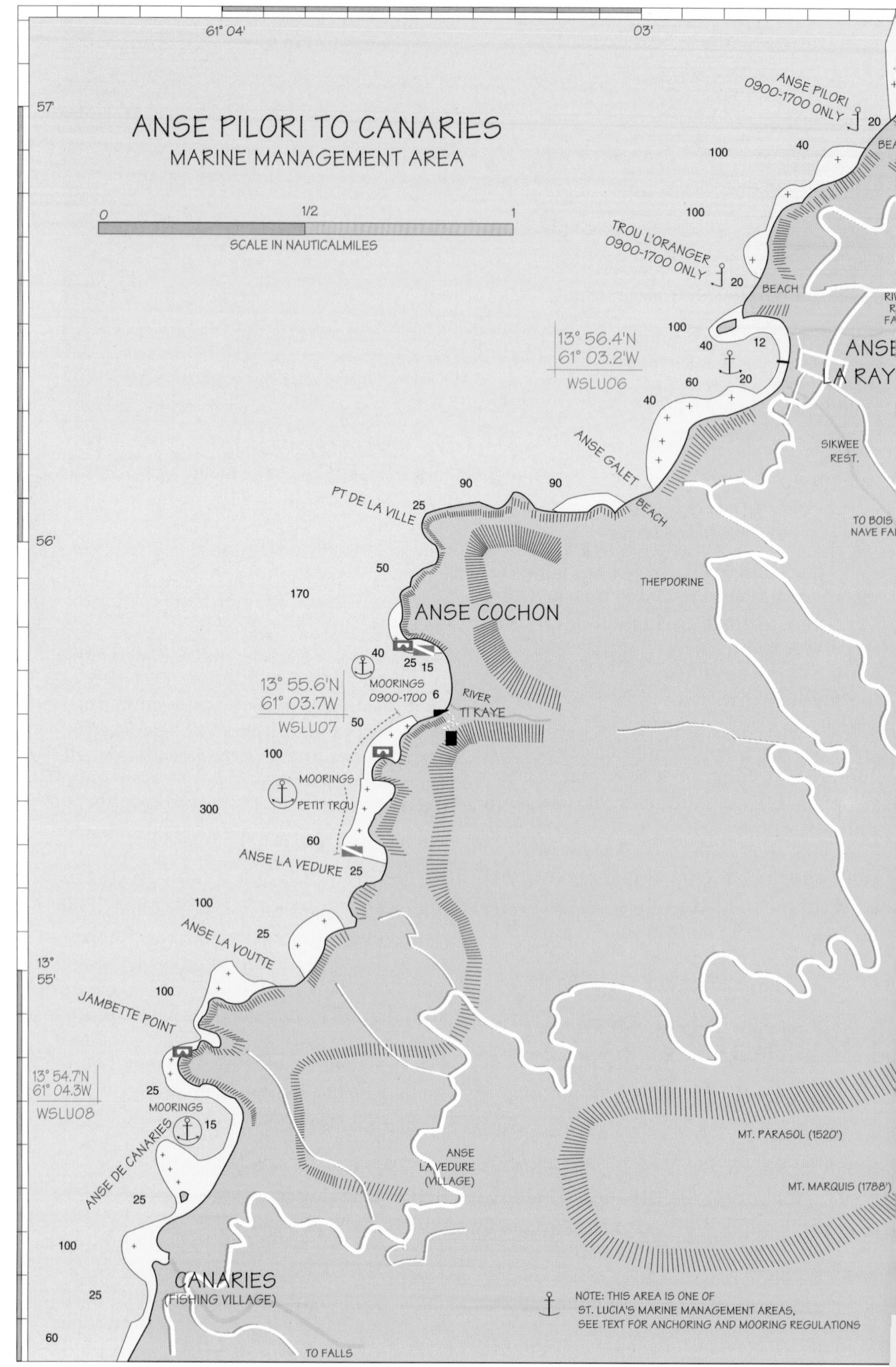
ANSE PILORI TO CANARIES
MARINE MANAGEMENT AREA
SCALE IN NAUTICALMILES
0
1/2
1
61° 04'
03'
57'
56'
13° 55'
ANSE PILORI 0900-1700 ONLY
TROU L'ORANGER 0900-1700 ONLY
BEACH
13° 56.4'N 61° 03.2'W
WSLU06
ANSE LA RAY
SIKWEE REST.
ANSE GALET
BEACH
TO BOIS NAVE FA
PT DE LA VILLE
THEPDORINE
ANSE COCHON
MOORINGS 0900-1700
13° 55.6'N 61° 03.7W
WSLU07
RIVER TI KAYE
MOORINGS
PETIT TROU
ANSE LA VEDURE
ANSE LA VOUTTE
JAMBETTE POINT
13° 54.7N 61° 04.3W
WSLU08
MOORINGS
ANSE DE CANARIES
ANSE LA VEDURE (VILLAGE)
MT. PARASOL (1520')
MT. MARQUIS (1788')
CANARIES (FISHING VILLAGE)
TO FALLS
NOTE: THIS AREA IS ONE OF ST. LUCIA'S MARINE MANAGEMENT AREAS, SEE TEXT FOR ANCHORING AND MOORING REGULATIONS

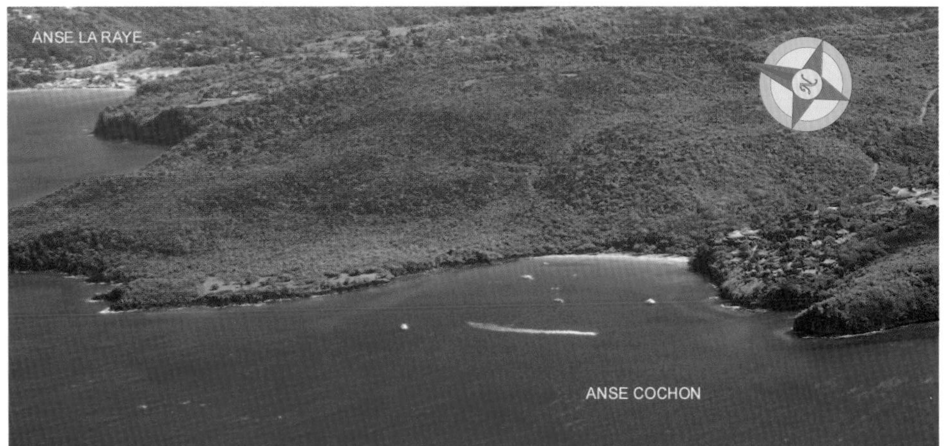

laid out by Jungle Tours. However, swimming in the falls is not encouraged, as it is a drinking-water source. After hiking you can cool off in the big pool to the left of the road on your way back to the village. This large pool, by a cleft in the rocks, is the most popular bathing place for locals.

Anse La Ray has a few bars and Albi's looks like it would serve you a good and reasonably priced meal.

ANSE COCHON TO ANSE LA VEDURE

Anse Cochon is a beautiful little bay with an attractive beach and Ti Kaye, an enchanting little hotel on one headland. It lies about 3 miles south of Marigot. You pass Anse La Raye, after which is a rocky headland. Anse Cochon is tucked up in the corner just past this headland. SMMA has Moorings in Anse Cochon. They are white with a blue stripe. There are also specific moorings for local tourism charter boats, but they are easily distinguishable from the rest. Moorings continue about half a mile south to Anse La Vedure. There may also be moorings at the northern end of Canaries in a picturesque bay just before the village. The coastline is attractive all the way along and usually comfortable enough for overnighting. If no moorings are available, anchor on sand.

Ti Kaye has a small dock, which is used by the dive boat. If the dive boat leaves for the night you can use the dock for your dinghy. You may need a stern anchor. Other times, beach the dinghy; taking great care in swells. Ti Kaye has WiFi, which you can probably get from your yacht.

Ashore

Ti Kaye [VHF: 16] is a charming cottage hotel perched on the southern headland of Anse Cochon. The gardens, the view, and the exceptionally friendly staff make you feel like you have arrived in a little Garden of Eden. Whatever you decide to do here, you do need to make reservations as they have a lot of their own guests and want to be sure you are not disappointed. On the beach, Ti Manje [$$$], set on a big deck over the rocks, makes a perfect lunch stop; the view is perfect, the food good and reasonably priced.

Climb the scenic staircase up to the top of the hill and into a world with lovely gardens, a pool, and fabulous views over the bay. Plan a trip to Kai Koko Spa, which is spectacularly beautiful, perched on the edge of the cliff, the precipitous view of the bay filling one side of each room. Allow some relaxing time in the welcome room, with a hot tub right by the open view (bring a bathing costume). Enjoy many kinds of massage and beauty treatments. If you arrange it for late afternoon it will allow time for a relaxing drink after, followed by dinner, which starts at 1830.

Kai Manje [$$$$], with its panoramic

view, is the main restaurant. You can get a photo of your yacht below and this is the best platform for viewing the green flash. Dinner is an imaginative blend of local, oriental, and other dishes, artistically presented with a daily changing menu that usually includes lots of fresh seafood and meat. Vegetarians are catered to and the food is excellent. They serve lunch if you want a break from the beach. For your pre-dinner drink, Kai Manje's bar (open from 1500) is air-conditioned and built on the edge of the cliff, with the whole of the west wall in glass looking over the bay. A happy hour with two-for-one on selected drinks is 1800-1900 every day except Wednesday, when they have the manager's cocktail party and a band in the restaurant. Ti Cave is their famous wine cellar under the main restaurant. They have a huge collection, including some at the very top of the line, and they sell these by the bottle. Managers Chris and Sarah usually organize a wine tasting three times a week at about 1600. The Cellar can also be booked for private wine dinners. Call for details.

Water sports

Island Divers make diving here really easy and the diving is in small groups. They are a full PADI shop. Talk with Curtis, 456-8110. They keep their fast, comfortable dive boat in Castries, so can easily pick up dive groups from yachts in Marigot and meet up with yachts in Soufriere. Snorkeling and land/sea trips are available.

The diving is excellent. The water is 25-60 feet deep, with a coral and rock slope descending onto sand. Isolated rock outcroppings on the sand are covered in corals and sponges. These underwater fairy castles teem with small fish. Though there are not many large fish, the abundance and variety of small fish and reef creatures more than compensates. The wreck of the Lesleen-M is in the middle of the bay. It is a 165-foot freighter and lies in 67 feet of water. It was deliberately sunk in 1986 to make a dive site. The wreck has attracted an exceptional collection of invertebrates, many of which are uncommon elsewhere. Rosamond's Trench is another delightful dive in this area. It starts between two small canyon walls and there are many sponges, invertebrates, and colorful reef fish.

The snorkeling on the south side ranges from interesting to excellent, especially for more experienced snorkelers. Snorkeling off the rocky headland at the north end of Anse Cochon is fair, with brightly colored sponges, corals, and parrotfish.

ANSE DE CANARIES

Anse de Canaries is supposed to have several moorings about a third of a mile north of the village. They keep getting stolen, but you can anchor in the same spot in about 20 feet of water. Cliffs surround this pleasant, quiet area, and overnighting is permitted. The snorkeling is good, but move for fishermen if asked.

Canaries has great hiking, interesting

bars, restaurants, a night club, and a street party. Unfortunately, the dock is pretty useless for a dinghy. You can beach the dinghy if swells permit.

Margaret Edwards (459-4402/4701) has the beautiful La Maison Estate with lovely gardens, high in the town on your way towards Castries. She has another establishment called Moon River, which is on the road along the river (turn left after the bridge). Moon River often has events on a Friday night open to the public, and both places are open for private functions.

Enjoy excellent hiking to two waterfalls in the area. To find them, go to the main road and head south across the bridge. Take the road on your left just over the bridge. This soon leaves civilization as it winds back into the forest. After a couple of miles you look at an amazingly verdant and broad valley surrounded by hills. Follow the well-marked road till it becomes a path and continue for another half-hour till you come to an old bridge crossing the river. Keep straight (do not cross the bridge) and you come to the first falls, small and dramatically set in a grotto, with the water pouring through a hole in the rock. The lighting can be spectacular mid- to late morning, when the sun shines through the hole. A good pool for swimming lies below. If you have the energy, return to the bridge and continue another hour for the second, even prettier falls. Take $5 EC each to pay the owners of the land. You can get a trained guide who knows the history and the plants. Ask anyone for Dave Julien.

Cocoa Sainte Lucie, an excellent one-woman chocolate factory, is up the hill heading for Soufriere. If you want to visit, call Maria Jackson, the chocolatier: 459-4401.

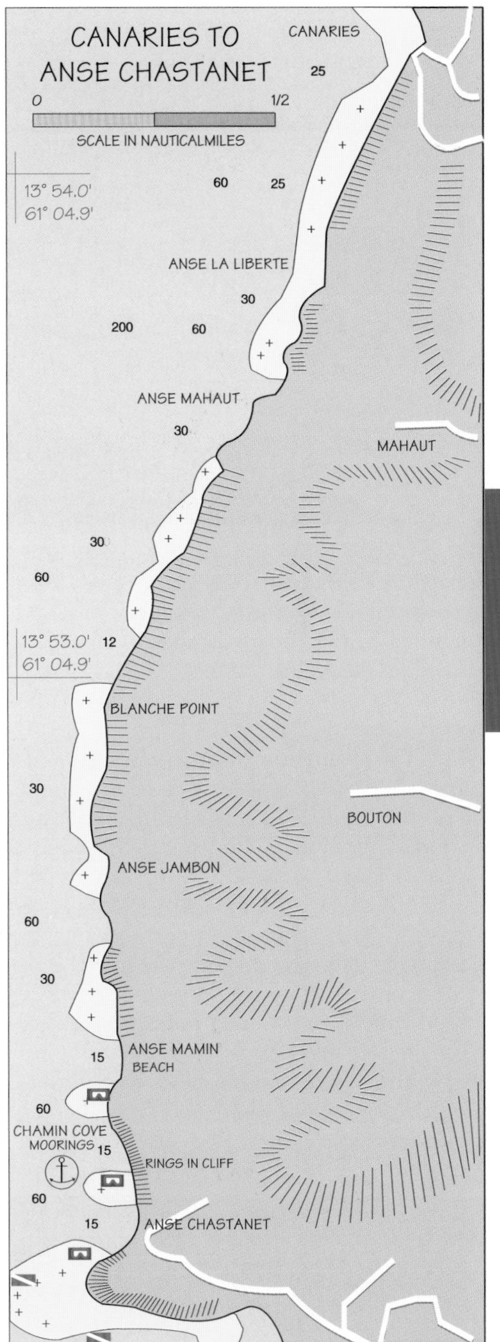

SOUFRIERE AND THE PITONS

Soufriere is a small, picturesque town set amidst a scenic wonderland dominated by the towering twin Pitons. Its exceptional beauty will enthrall hikers and photographers. The surrounding water is a magnificent marine park. There are many great things to see and do, the coastline is wonderful, there are lots of small restaurants, and those who like snorkeling, hiking, and diving could easily spend a week in the area.

When approaching Soufriere from the

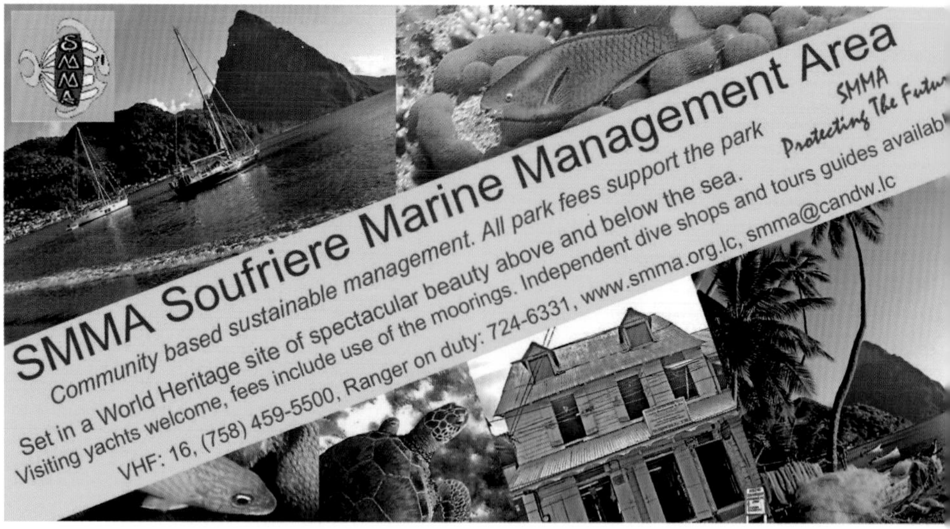

north beware of the shoal that extends from the south side of Anse Chastanet, off Grand Caille Point. If you run aground, you will be fined for damaging the reef.

SMMA
SMMA Soufriere Marine Management Area
SMMA
Protecting The Future
Community based sustainable management. All park fees support the park
Set in a World Heritage site of spectacular beauty above and below the sea.
Visiting yachts welcome, fees include use of the moorings. Independent dive shops and tours guides availab
VHF: 16, (758) 459-5500, Ranger on duty: 724-6331, www.smma.org.lc, smma@candw.lc

Regulations

The Soufriere Marine Management Association (SMMA) [VHF: 16] manages this area. They regulate all anchoring, snorkeling, diving, and fishing. They have placed many yacht moorings, which are white (some with a blue stripe) for yachts up to 70 feet. (Red or orange moorings are for dive boats or snorkeling dinghies.) Five moorings are available for yachts up to 120 feet. Anchoring is not permitted unless directed by a ranger.

The SMMA has an office in Soufriere on the waterfront where you can check up on the latest weather. The current manager is Michael Bobb. The rangers stand by on VHF:16. The ranger on duty carries a cell: 724-6331. If for any reason you cannot get through, call Peter Butcher, the head ranger, 718-1196, or Jackie, another ranger 724-6333. Unless it is an emergency do not call Peter and Jackie after hours.

You may call rangers in advance and book a mooring. Booked moorings have a reserved sign on them. Do not pick up a mooring with a reserved sign unless it is booked for you.

The charges for taking a yacht into the Marine Management Areas, which includes use of the moorings, are as follows:

Boats up to 70 ft. Half day= $15 US
1 Night = $20 US. 1 week = $120 US
Boats 70-120 ft 1 Night = $100 US
Boats over 120 ft, 1 Night = $200 US

Personal watercraft (Jet skis) are not

Solomon and crew

Priscus Joseph (John)

allowed in the park. As in the rest of St. Lucia, spearfishing and damaging, taking, or buying coral or sponges are strictly forbidden, as is dumping garbage, oil, etc. Fishing is forbidden in the marine reserves. You can pick up any available mooring. Always put your mooring line through the loop on the mooring rope. Do not put the loop on the mooring rope on your cleat. An SMMA ranger will come by to collect the fees, or fees can be paid at the SMMA office in Soufriere if you clear customs, as they are in the same building. SMMA rangers carry identification and give official receipts. The SMMA staff are very helpful with finding taxis, giving weather alerts, and making yachters feel welcome.

Soufriere has some rough edges, and while serious harassment is a thing of the past, a few waterfront youths pester visitors, do not seem to know what they are doing, and are best avoided.

Here are the waterfront people who I consider to be reliable: Solomon's Water Taxi and Tours (Justice) (384-4087/725 8681/460-4516), Livity (488-7820/717-2019), Johnson, (721 0229), Priscus Joseph (John), 722-4585, and Malcolm's Water taxi (722-5048/286-2277). Call one of them to arrange for him to meet you, tie you up if you want, and take care of anything you need.

They all do tours and they would love to organize one for you. Solomon is the most organized in as much as he has three employees, two boats, and a taxi. You can check his tours at solomon-saintlucia.com. I had a great hike up to Tete Paul with Livity, (see the Between the Pitons section). He can also organize lobster, and any of them can organize a great beach barbecue. They will take you to the most popular places including Jerusalem hot baths, the Pitons hot falls, the sulphur springs, and Tete Paul. Some of these have quite steep entry fees, which are normally included in the price which may be $50 or $60 US per person (four minimum) for half a day.

You can also use Ben's Yacht Services. Ben started running a taxi and renting cars and has since become St. Lucia's main yacht agent. Most large yachts work with him, as do many smaller ones. He is not on the water himself but sends out his water taxi.

These guys will look after you and help with whatever you need; if you want to go into

Ben, Ben's Yacht Services

Livity

Johnson

Malcome

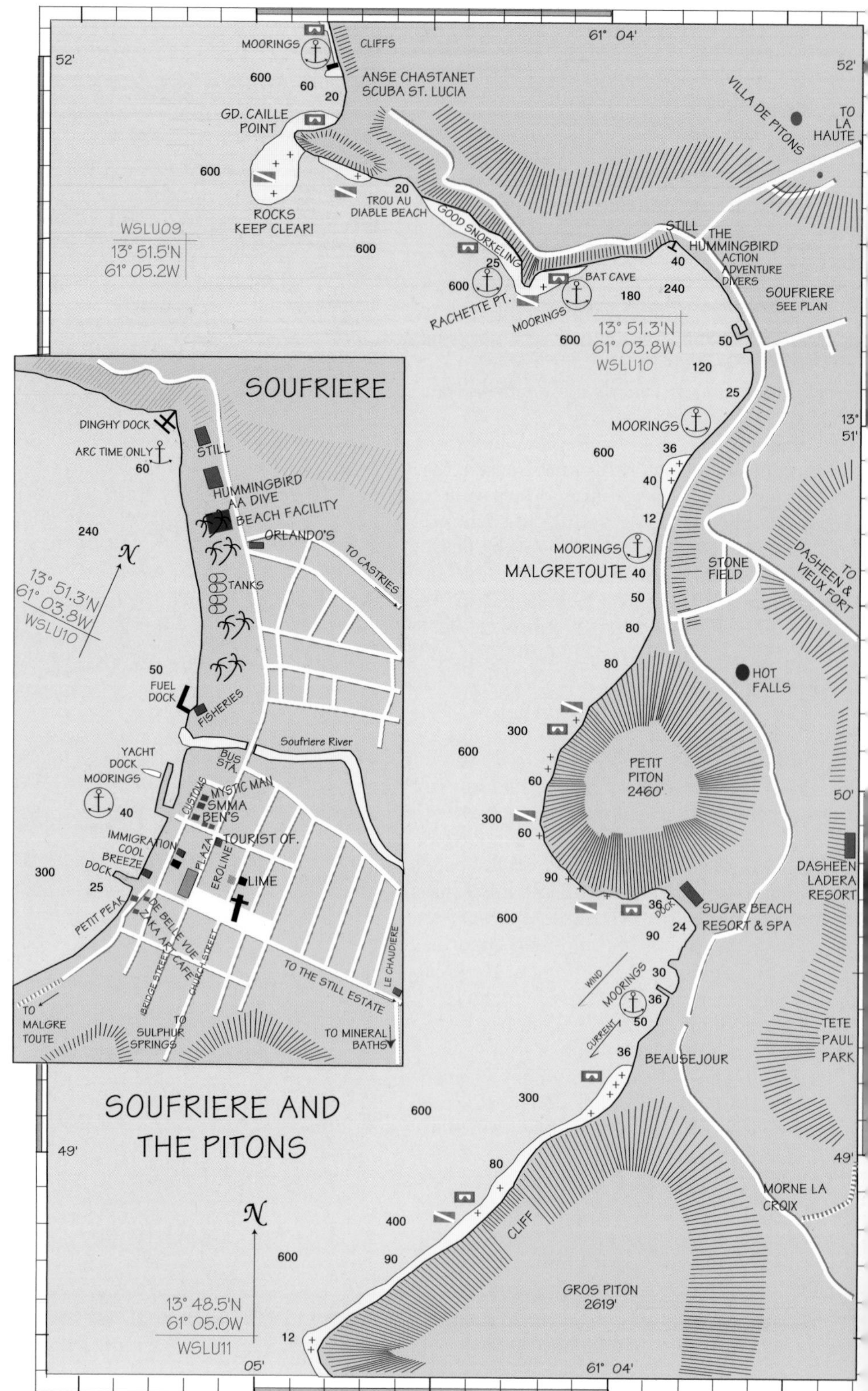
SOUFRIERE AND THE PITONS
MOORINGS
CLIFFS
ANSE CHASTANET
SCUBA ST. LUCIA
GD. CAILLE POINT
ROCKS KEEP CLEAR!
TROU AU DIABLE BEACH
GOOD SNORKELING
VILLA DE PITONS
TO LA HAUTE
RACHETTE PT.
BAT CAVE
STILL
THE HUMMINGBIRD
ACTION ADVENTURE DIVERS
SOUFRIERE SEE PLAN
WSLU09
13° 51.5'N
61° 05.2W
13° 51.3'N
61° 03.8W
WSLU10
MALGRETOUTE
STONE FIELD
TO DASHEEN & VIEUX FORT
HOT FALLS
PETIT PITON 2460'
SUGAR BEACH RESORT & SPA
DASHEEN LADERA RESORT
WIND
CURRENT
BEAUSEJOUR
TETE PAUL PARK
MORNE LA CROIX
CLIFF
GROS PITON 2619'
13° 48.5'N
61° 05.0W
WSLU11
SOUFRIERE
DINGHY DOCK
ARC TIME ONLY
HUMMINGBIRD AA DIVE
BEACH FACILITY
ORLANDO'S
TO CASTRIES
TANKS
FUEL DOCK
FISHERIES
Soufriere River
BUS STA.
YACHT DOCK
CUSTOMS
MYSTIC MAN
SMMA
BEN'S
TOURIST OF.
IMMIGRATION
COOL BREEZE
DOCK
PLAZA
EROLINE
LIME
PETIT PEAK
DE BELLE VUE
ZAKA ART CAFE
BRIDGE STREET
CHURCH STREET
TO THE STILL ESTATE
LE CHAUDIERE
TO MALGRE TOUTE
TO SULPHUR SPRINGS
TO MINERAL BATHS

town they will take you, which saves all the hassle of the youths on the dock. From Malgretout or Rachette Point a drop in and back later would be about $60 EC for up to four people. If you want to go out to dinner they will also keep an eye on your boat, and then the rate would be a minimum of $100 EC for up to four, more if you are gone for a long time. Malcom and Solomon both do laundry.

Once you have selected someone to help you, if anyone else approaches as you come in, I suggest saying "I am being looked after by (whichever one you choose)" and they will leave you alone.

If you are doing a tour I doubt you would be charged for a tie up. If not, and if they come out to meet you, then probably $20 EC is fair.

If you don't contact anyone and some kid gets between you and the mooring and insists on tying you up, then $15 EC is reasonable.

Security in the park is good. Both the park rangers and the marine police make patrols both day and night. At the time of writing there had been no incidents since this patrols were implemented.

In the past the area around Rachette Point has been problematic, with many thefts. Since the patrols there has not been a problem, but if you moor here and are go out to dinner, I recommend the use of a vendor as a water taxi and to keep an eye on the boat.

The biggest danger is speeding pirogues and other craft. Stay alert, especially when swimming and snorkeling.

If you need any assistance the SMMA staff are very friendly and welcoming.

ANSE CHASTANET courtesy SMMA

Soufriere is a port of clearance for pleasure yachts. Customs is in the SMMA building and immigration is at the end of the police station block. Customs hours are Monday-Thursday 0800-1630, Friday 0800-1800, Saturday and Sunday 0800-1630. You will pay $10-$15 EC overtime after 1630 on Fridays and on weekends. Sailclear sometimes works. Port fees are due, but not currently collected in Soufriere, they will charge you when you clear out. (For fees see *St. Lucia at a glance*, page 137.)

Don't give garbage to kids on surf boards, as they will dump it in the sea. Take smallish bags into town and ask the SMMA where to put it. If you are using Ben's yacht services, he collects it by water taxi.

Scuba divers must be accompanied by an official dive guide. An SMMA diving fee applies to all dives within the SMMA and CAMMA. It is $5.00 US/ $13.00 EC for one day, or $15 US for the season. Pay an SMMA ranger or the dive shop. If you are an accredited diver and have your own equipment, the SMMA may be able to put you in contact with an official guide, or visit one of the yacht-friendly dive shops. Action Adventure Divers provides all levels of service, including guides and yacht pick-ups (see *Hummingbird Anchorage*). Island Divers do rendezvous pickups (See *Anse Cochon*).

If you have diving accident, Tapion Hospital has a hyperbaric chamber.

Services

Above we have mentioned good water taxis who can run you to town or arrange a land tour. If you need to go a distance, say to Marigot or Castries, which are reached faster by boat than car, then you need a bigger boat Solomon has one, as do members of the Soufriere Taxi Association, or the Watercraft Association [VHF: 16], which are professional groups of properly equipped water taxis. Try also Ben's Yacht Services or Mystic Man Tours.

ANSE CHASTANET

Anse Chastanet is an attractive cottage hotel built on a hill that slopes to the sea. Several yacht moorings are usually available off the cliffs north of the beach in Chamin Cove. Underwater rocks lie just south and north of the moorings, so approach with caution. While often reasonably peaceful, this area can be untenable in times of a northerly swell. The snorkeling right from your boat is superb.

The Anse Chastanet beach bar is a

congenial lunch spot, with two boutiques in the same area. For dinner they have a very fancy restaurant called Jade up the hill.

Water sports

Scuba St. Lucia at Anse Chastanet [VHF: 16] is one of the largest dive operations in the Windwards, with two resort courses and four dives daily. They do not fill tanks. Scuba St. Lucia takes divers on the Anse Chastanet Reef for their first dive at 1100. It is best to turn up half an hour early and remember to bring your diving certification card. If you are not certified, resort courses are available, and these usually start at around 0900.

Anse Chastanet reef extends seaward from the beach and is still in reasonably good condition. The shallower parts are fair for snorkeling, but avoid cruise ship days. Diving is excellent along the length of the reef, which slopes from about 30 to 80 feet. Sheet corals, solitary corals, and brain corals are abundant, as are a delightful variety of sponges, from the azure vase sponge to large barrel sponges. The water is clear and reef fish abound, with clouds of brown and blue chromis, along with sergeant majors, brilliantly colored parrotfish, and goatfish. All kinds of jacks and snappers cruise just off the reef. Currents are fierce on the outer part of the reef.

Snorkeling is excellent along much of this coast.

Navigation

When you go from Anse Chastanet toward Soufriere be very careful of the reef off Grand Caille Point. Not only might you damage your boat, but you will also be liable for hefty fines (up to $5,000 US) for damaging the reef.

TROU AU DIABLE

This beach lies between Gd. Caille Point and Rachette Point. Sand covers the middle of the bay, but there are lovely coral gardens, ideal for snorkeling and diving, to both the east and west. The snorkeling is better to the east, the diving to the west. It is a reasonable dinghy ride from Soufriere or the Hummingbird, and you can tie to an orange dive buoy, if available, or to one of the SMMA marker buoys if not. Two overnight buoys have now been added close to Rachette Point.

HUMMINGBIRD ANCHORAGE

During rush times, like the ARC, rangers sometimes allow anchoring stern-to at the Hummingbird Restaurant. Usually they will have worked something out with the fishermen, but this is a fishing priority area so you must move promptly if asked to do so by fishermen.

Otherwise, use one of the seven yacht

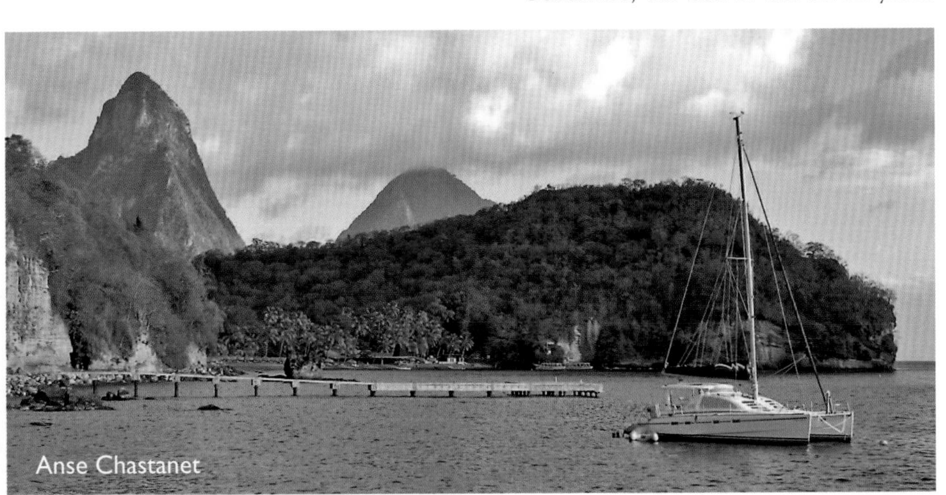

Anse Chastanet

moorings in the area of the bat cave, or the two on the other side of Rachette Point. It has an attractive, remote feel, and the snorkeling is good right off your boat. Security can be a problem here, so if you are dining out, use one of the vendors to take you ashore and keep an eye on your boat. A dinghy dock in the corner of the bay makes getting ashore easy by day. Use a stern anchor for swells, or tie bow and stern between docks. Be prepared to deal with unneeded dinghy watchers. I would not use this dinghy dock at night, as at least one robbery has been reported here. It is safer to use the beach right outside the Hummingbird. If you are eating at the Hummingbird, ask them to watch it for you.

Communications/services

The Hummingbird offers free customer WiFi and the staff will help customers with telephone calls or faxes during normal office hours. You can check your email here. WiFi from other sources may reach the moorings.

Owner Joyce has run the Hummingbird for over 30 years, now with her son David as chef. Joyce was awarded an M.B.E. for her services to St. Lucia's tourism, and gets much of her business from yachts and welcomes them warmly. Dinner guests from yachts are welcome to a free shower, 12 gallons of fresh water if they bring containers, and a bag or two of free ice to take back on board.

Ashore

The Hummingbird Restaurant [VHF: 16, $$$$] is the most elegant and charming of Soufriere's waterfront restaurants, featuring wonderful hand carvings and an exquisite view across the pool to the Pitons beyond. The food is excellent ~ a blend of French and Creole cuisine, with seafood a specialty and generous portions.

A skipper bringing in a party of five or more gets a meal selected by the house for free. Meal guests are welcome to use the pool. They have live music most Wednesday nights in season. If you are leaving your dinghy on the dock by day, tell one of the security guys and they will keep an eye on it for you (a tip after is appreciated).

Joyce also has the Hummingbird's Rum Shack Beach Bar, which is popular for sunset or moonlight cocktails. Happy hour is 1700-1800 and the bar keeps going till the last person leaves. If there is no one there you may have to ask for a barman to come down.

Hummingbird is a great daytime hangout with soups, salads, and sandwiches or full meals for lunch.

The office is helpful with advice, will answer any questions, and arrange taxis and tours at a local rate. Colorful batiks, handmade by David on the premises, are featured in their boutique, and Joyce offers people on yachts a 10% discount on batiks (but not other items). Rooms are available, with discounts to yachts.

Orlando's [$$$$$] is close to Hummingbird on the road to Soufriere. Orlando is one of St. Lucia's most famous chefs. Like some good chefs, he is part showman and is at home giving cooking demonstrations and teaching. He was one of the first to create an exciting new artfully presented Caribbean cuisine from all fresh local ingredients. His restaurant has attracted some famous chefs and other celebrities, including John Major (former British Prime Minister). You can see pictures of Orlando with other celebrities he has cooked for including David Bowie and Davy Jones.

The restaurant has a pleasant courtyard atmosphere and includes a bar with WiFi where you can hang out and eat "Ti Manje" (little eats). Orlando's food ranks among the best in St. Lucia, is elegantly served, and will please the most demanding gourmet. Orlando has a knack for mixing local fruits into many dishes, providing a light and delicious touch, and his desserts are excellent. For a real feast, try his five-course taster menu. He is open Tuesday to Sunday for dinner and Wednesday to Sunday for lunch. I would make a reservation as he may adjust the lunch opening days. Lunches are lighter and less expensive, but very good. Orlando is available as an on-board guest chef or for demonstrations. He likes the challenge of a small galley.

The Still Beach Restaurant [$$] is next to the Hummingbird and, with the associated Ruby Estate, which lies just out of town, is run by David Dubolais. This restaurant has

a big balcony overlooking the anchorage and serves good local food. The staff is welcoming and friendly, and you can ask them about Ruby Estate and the tours that are available.

Construction is nearing completion on a big beach facility next to the Hummingbird. It is called the Hummingbird Beach Project and will include shops and restaurants.

Water sports

Snorkeling is good all the way between the anchorage and Trou au Diable Beach. If you snorkel in shallow water off the beach in front of the Still Beach Restaurant you are likely to see streams of bubbles rising to the surface. They are from a minor underwater volcanic vent.

Action Adventure Divers, in the Hummingbird, work with yachts people wanting to dive in the SMMA. It is run by two brothers from a fishing family in the area: Chester (an advanced PADI instructor) and Vincent (a dive master). They know all the good spots. You can contact them by phone or on VHF: 16. They will come by your yacht and pick you up and they offer a variety of services, from resort courses to full certification, and, if you have your own gear and boat, their charges can be as low as $25 US per person, the standard rate for a guide. They use a pirogue with a bimini for sun cover, are flexible and helpful, and are delighted to work with those on yachts, who they see as their main customer base. You can ask them about underwater hull cleaning.

SOUFRIERE TOWN

(See also *Soufriere and the Pitons* page 179)

The town of Soufriere was the set of the movie *Water*, starring Michael Caine, and it has many charming old Creole buildings with balconies and gingerbread. Much has been done recently to upgrade the town and waterfront. Unfortunately, two of the loveliest and most historic buildings were recently lost to fire.

There is a yacht and general-purpose dock just off the SMMA that you can use for your dinghy. Guards on duty (0800-1600) do not seem to try to prevent would-be dinghy watchers, but if you tell the watchers that the guards are going to watch it for you, they lose interest and disappear. You take your dinghy inside and will need a stern anchor to keep it from going under the dock.

Moorings start to the south of town and continue right round into Malgretout. Security in the SMMA is now good. Rachette Point used to have problems, so if you go there, use a water taxi if you go out to dinner and have them watch your boat.

Communications

Ben's Yacht Services and Pier 28 Bistro and Lounge have the big building next to the SMMA office. Both have WiFi and Ben has a computer for his customers. Many other places have WiFi. You might pick up a WiFi signal on a mooring.

Peter Butcher, head SMMA ranger

Services

Water, fuel (gas and diesel), and chipped ice are available alongside the fishing port dock, open 0630-1800 every day. You can also buy fish here.

Ben's Yacht Services has been in business for a long time and has an excellent reputation. They offer yacht services all over the island. You will find them in the big building next to the SMMA right opposite the dinghy dock. Enter through his niece's Pier 28 Bistro downstairs; his office is upstairs. Ben offers fueling, provisioning, taxis, car rentals, customs clearance, and laundry. He can book and save a mooring for you. In addition, they will source parts, find technicians, and organize crew visas. Pier 28 has WiFi, and Ben keeps a computer for customers who need to get on the internet. If you have a problem or need a water taxi, call Ben. (See also *Transport*)

If you are contacting Ben by VHF, there can be confusion, as Benny [VHF: 16: Harmony Yacht Services] may pick up, as might his son, who has Ben Taxi and Tours, as may other taxi drivers called Ben. Phone is more reliable.

Charles Richards (Mystic Man Tours) can organize water for you on the town dock outside the SMMA. He is easy to reach, with an office next to the SMMA. The dock is in constant use, so make arrangements with him in advance. He also operates a professional water taxi service, has a good success rate if you want to go sports fishing, runs great whale-watching tours, and is good for longer trips (getting to Castries, for example). In addition, he fixes most of the local outboards in the area (his workshop is in the fishing complex) and he can get yours running again if you have a problem.

Transport

Ben's Yacht Services stands by on VHF: 16 and has an office right opposite the dinghy dock. Ben has a fleet of taxis and will take you on a tour of the area, help you provision, find fresh flowers or fruits, get your guests to the airport, make restaurant reservations, take you there, and be your general helper in Soufriere. He has a fleet of taxis and good drivers, and rents cars and jeeps. Call him on the phone. For a half day tour Ben generally charges $20 US per person, minimum four. For a whole day it is likely to be around $70 US depending on what is involved. His one way rates (for four) to La Haut or Morne Coubaril are about $10 US, for Dasheen, $20 US. Ben also offers full superyacht services (see *Services*).

Unfortunately, there are no set rates for short one way taxi trips so everything is negotiable, and taxi drivers are more interested in tours than rides.

However, it is also easy to take a bus, and most things that you want to see are on a bus route.

Right now the buses all line up on the main square., but a big bus station is under construction by the bridge a few steps from the SMMA, so I expect they will soon start

At Ladera Resort

from there. Most buses either go north to Castries or south towards Vieux Fort. Everything is uphill from Soufriere, so riding one way then walking back downhill is a good option. La Haut is to the north, Morne Coubaril, the drive-in volcano and Ladera Resort are to the south.

Provisioning/fun shopping

In town, Eroline's Foods is a fair little supermarket, with a reasonable array of foods. It is connected to Fond Doux Estate, which supplies much of their produce. It opens 0800-2000 Monday to Saturday, and 0900-2100 on Sundays and holidays. If you buy more than you can carry, ask them about delivery to your nearest dock. Soufriere has a couple of banks and pharmacies.

A couple of good guys may come by in boats to sell fruits and vegetables; Distant Thunder is most often around and you can call him, 718-8592. He will work as a water taxi.

Zaka Art Cafe, on Bridge Street, is a wonderful cacophony of bright colors and interesting characters. The walls are covered in Zaka masks found throughout the Caribbean decorating restaurants and homes. They pick their own coffee in the surrounding hills and process it in-house. It has a wonderful flavor while being non-acidic. You will want to buy a bag to take with you. Fresh fruit smoothies are made on the spot. Breakfast is from 0900, and, if you give Leah a little notice, she will produce a fine local lunch or dinner. This is a good place to buy the Cocoa Sainte Lucie organic chocolate. Stop by for a drink and take a look at the masks, maybe see some being created. Zaka may move, but probably not too far.

Restaurants

There is lots of tasty, inexpensive food available in town, probably cheaper than cooking for yourself. Lisa William's Pier 28 [$] is air-conditioned and opposite the main dinghy dock, along with Ben's Yacht Services. If you prefer to be outside, she also has the two beach bars with outside tables across the road. All have WiFi. She makes good coffee, has local lunch specials that are generous and delicious and a general menu. I am told that, when available, the hamburgers are top class.

Skipper's and Archie's [$], side by side next door, are also excellent cheap-and-cheerful joints. The cooking is local and good, and they serve food all day long. Archie's has a big TV and shows the latest sports events. Skipper's is open to the street and has some outside tables.

De Belle Vue Restaurant [$$] is in a cute room upstairs looking out over the water, and they cook good local food. Opposite, Petit Peak [$$] is in the building that served as the town courthouse back in 1898.

The more exciting and memorable restaurants are outside town (see also Hummingbird Anchorage, just a short walk away). Some you can hike to, others are a short taxi or bus ride away (see *Transport*) The Dasheen Restaurant at Ladera Resort [$$$$$] has the most awesome view of any bar in the Caribbean; just to walk in is unforgettable. The original owner/designer made the most of the location, keeping the buildings small and interesting and completely open to the view. He was called back as architect when they expanded, and under his hand, the restaurant and bar are exotically designed as a series of three completely open rooms climbing the ridge line. They are perched on the edge of a giant precipice looking straight down the valley between the Pitons. It is hard not to exclaim "Wow!" when you first see it. From the top room you look down through both the second room and the bar to the bright blue swimming pool set in a flower garden below. It gives a spectacular 3-D effect within the hotel and beyond to a dramatic Pitons view. Ladera Resort is managed by Daly Mariatte. The staff will welcome you for lunch or dinner and are attentive and friendly.

Lunch is, of course, a great time for the view, though if you arrive for an early cocktail, dinnertime offers you both a day and night perspective, with the chance of a dramatic sunset. Nights are spectacular when the moon is full. Gourmets will prefer evenings, when the gold-medal-winning chef creates a dinner that is a fitting accompaniment to the view. In addition to the restaurant, ample snacks and sandwiches are available in the bar for lunch (make sure you try the chocolate mousse). Sunday buffet brunch is an excellent choice, but come reasonably early. Do use the bar, because if you just want to walk in to look at the view there is a charge of $25 US per person. While there, do not miss their new boutique, which stocks local crafts, pottery, books, and essentials.

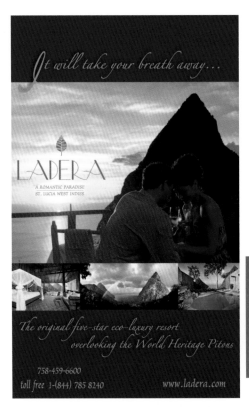

By day, the energetic can walk up to Dasheen from Malgretoute. Walk up the Jalousie road away from Petit Piton, turn right on the main road, and keep going; it is a fair hike.

Opposite Dasheen is Hotel Chocolat, originally Rabot Estate, owned by the English chocolate maker. They cultivate cocoa for their chocolate (made in England), have pricey plantation tours and rooms for rent, along with a tall spidery restaurant [$$$$$]. Happily, over the last few years, vegetation has covered much of the lackluster architecture. The restaurant is pleasant inside, and the food is good. They have a gorgeous old estate house on the grounds in contrast to

St. Lucia

their more modern architecture.

More pleasing in appearance is Morne Fond Doux, another old estate with a nice restaurant. It has some lovely, authentic Caribbean buildings. They have added rooms by buying pretty traditional buildings from various parts of the island and rebuilding them on the estate. Their restaurant is open for both lunch and dinner [$$$], and you can take a half-hour estate tour on delightful trails.

In the other direction, the road from Soufriere to Castries climbs a steep hill, and several restaurants lie along this road. All have great views over Soufriere.

La Haut Resort [$$] has good food and a spectacular panoramic view of the Pitons, which is greatly enhanced by a brilliant display of bougainvillea planted in the foreground, making a perfect photograph. The grounds have been artfully gardened and include little fishponds, and many people find them rewarding for bird-watching. Owner Stephanie Allain, from Canada, offers a variety of dishes using local ingredients enhanced by ideas from the outside. Come for lunch or dinner. If you come for dinner, arrive before sunset, and in any case bring your swim suit and plan to spend some time hanging out in the pool with its spectacular Pitons view. La Haut is a mile and a half uphill from Soufriere. Get a bus or taxi up (see *Transport*). Walk back down: just keep sticking one foot in front of the other and gravity takes care of the rest.

Villa de Pitons [$$] has a rather quaint atmosphere, with lots of rooms linked by many steps around a central swimming pool with a fountain, and murals and batiks covering the walls. They open from breakfast to dinner, with a lighter lunch menu.

The Beacon is even farther uphill than La Haut. They have a big open platform restaurant with a good view over Soufriere, and they host special functions.

Water sports

Snorkeling and diving are good throughout the area. Action Adventure Divers will arrange whatever kind of dives you want (see *Hummingbird Anchorage*).

Ashore

The naturally hot Diamond Baths and tropical gardens are scenic and pleasant, built by Louis the 16th. They are a 20 minute walk out the back of town. Take the road to Soufriere Estate (look at our chart), pass the Estate and look for a road on your right. It is posted to the Daimond gardens, but you may have to pass the sign and look back to read it.

Take a few dollars and your towel and you can luxuriate in baths set amid a well-tended tropical garden. My favorite are the big private baths at the top, where piping hot water comes straight from the volcano into two huge tubs. Pay the person in charge as you go in: $10 EC per person to enter the gardens, or $15 EC per person for the private baths, or $10 EC for the tepid outdoor pools. They have a snack bar and shop on the river.

As you head uphill to the south from Soufriere, Morne Coubaril is opposite the road that goes to Jalousie (about a mile). It is a delightful old estate with a restaurant, and they have half-hour estate tours, ziplining and horse riding. Their zipline trail is pleasant and scenic. Many of the lines start on platforms up big old banyan and mango trees. The guides are entertaining and knowledgeable, as well as very safety conscious.

The turnoff to the Drive-in Volcano (Sulphur springs) is a little farther down the road. When you take the turn it is less than a mile from the main road and looks like a scene straight from hell, with barren, brightly colored earth, bubbling pools, and huge spurts of steam. They have an area here where you can take a mud bath.

In this area, the lovely little Sapphire water falls is set amid lush tropical vegetation. The river comes from the volcano, tepid and a little gray. It reaches a high rock promontory and falls in two streams. Just below the falls is an area of volcanic mud, perfect to use for a face or body pack. There is no swimming hole, but standing under the falls is wonderfully refreshing and delivers a whole body massage. Come late morning or early afternoon when the falls are in full sun, stand in them, look down, and a beautiful rainbow forms right round you. It is a blissful place, on the land of Jahrod, who will charge $15 US per person for a visit.

Petit Piton view

It is easy to find, you take the main road from Soufriere to the turn off for the sulphur spring (a short bus ride, or $10 US taxi if you use Ben). Right where the road to the Sulphur springs starts, you will see a small road ahead. Take this and follow the signs. It is a very pretty walk that takes about half an hour. If you prefer a guide, call Jahrod (716-8396), and arrange to meet him at the beginning of the road to the Sulphur Springs. For $20 US per person he will hike in with you (about 20 minutes), give you as much time as you need to enjoy the falls and then walk you down to the road that takes you to Diamond baths and gardens and back to Soufriere. Jahrod is the hiking and waterfall man, and he can hike with you to many beautiful falls in the area.

The rainforest area near Morne Fond St. Jacques has exquisite views for walking. You are required to have a guide and pay a fee when hiking in the rainforest reserve ($10 US per person), but walking on the road leading to it, amid the lush vegetation with hidden glimpses of the Pitons below, is also beautiful. For hikes in the rainforest, ask the Soufriere Foundation to call the forestry department. They have knowledgeable guides in the Soufriere area who can arrange to take you on a rainforest tour. One of the most interesting is a 2.5-hour loop tour to the Maho waterfalls. Take your bathing things for a shower in the falls, and a swim in the pool above it.

On the road to Fond St. Jacques New Jerusalem and Toraille (in a lovely little garden), are pleasant little waterfalls; take your swim things.

See also *Between the Pitons*.

MALGRETOUT

This is a lovely place to moor, along a beautiful beach. The Marine Park has put in moorings, including at least two that take yachts up to 120 feet.

A pretty old road (now a trail) runs from the waterfront in Soufriere to the far end of Malgretoute beach, which makes walking to town easy. A big new hotel started and stalled here. Since this road is on their property, I am not sure of its future, though

SOUFRIERE AND THE PITONS

it has been a right of way for generations, so should stay.

Restaurants/Ashore

This is an area in transition, as a big hotel group has bought most of the shore and many locals were pressured to sell out to them. But, having emptied out the old people's home and put up a fence, the project seems to have stopped.

Just above the anchorage you can see Stonefield Estate [$$$]. This elegant family hotel has a lovely restaurant with a swimming pool and a view over the yachts. Trails lead to some excellent examples of Carib petroglyphs.

If you walk up the rough road behind the beach towards its southern end you will join the big concrete Jalousie road. Turn left (away from the Pitons) and follow it uphill. Stonefield Estate is to the left and is marked. They serve elegant Creole food. (See also the section on Humming bird and Soufriere town, all a dinghy ride away).

If you pass Stonefield Estate and keep walking, you come to the main road. Hikers can turn right on the main road and walk to the sulfur springs and Ladera.

If you turn right on the lower concrete road towards Sugar Beach, there is a trail to a cute little gardened hot water fall you can visit for a small fee.

Diving and snorkeling are excellent around Petit Piton, though there is current. Drift-snorkel with your dinghy from Malgretoute.

BETWEEN THE PITONS

Moorings are available in the area shown from Sugar Beach Resort south along the shore. Local boat vendors will probably reach your mooring before you, to help with your lines. The wind and current can be strong in this area, and the current is sometimes against the wind. This area is sometimes calm, sometimes rolly, and it can change with the tides. It is also popular, and sometimes full. The three outer moorings are suitable for yachts up to 120 feet.

The beach between the Pitons is part of Sugar Beach, a Viceroy Resort, which has a spectacular setting, though they rather spoilt it by overbuilding. To access the beach and restaurants, tie your dinghy to the end of the jetty off the beach, but do not lock it, and leave the sides clear. If you are hiking leave it onshore south of the other huge white sand beach on the south side of the bay.

Ashore

Sugar Beach Resort [$$$$$] is open to the public, with two restaurants and the Cane Bar, which opens around 1800 and serves sushi and light dishes.

The Bayside Bar and Restaurant is on the beach and serves both lunch and dinner, and at other times you can get snacks and sandwiches from the bar next door. The Great Room, for fine dining, is in the main building. Walk into Bayside for lunch, book for dinner in either restaurant. They have an excellent spa, with a massage center, facials, hairdressers, saunas, and hot tubs.

There is a lovely hike from this anchorage up to Tete Paul which has a really spectacular precipice view of Petit Piton and the anchorage (2-3 hours). You go through the villages of Morne La Croix and Chateaubelair. The easiest way to do this is to contact Anthony (488-7820/717-2019), who runs the water-taxi Livity. He is a great guide and will collect you from your boat, drive you up to Morne La Croix, hike with you, and bring you back through farmland and a beautiful private estate for about $30 US a head (minimum four people or $120 US). There is also a Tete Morne trail fee of about $5 US per person. You can ask him about climbing Gros Piton and any other hikes. He is good at arranging beach barbecues or picnics.

Lesser mortals might want to at least walk from the anchorage up to the village of Morne La Croix; it has to be one of the steepest roads in the world.

Water sports

You can talk to the dive shop here, or call Action Divers. The dive around the base of Petit Piton is excellent. Start from close to the beach and explore at whatever depth

Laborie

you feel comfortable. There are wonderful sponges, good coral formations, and an extraordinary variety of fish. Sometimes huge schools of fish make magical patterns in the sunlight. Apart from reef fish, such as angelfish, blue chromis, parrotfish, scorpionfish, and damselfish, there are lots of hunters out there: jacks and snappers swim in fair-sized schools, and occasionally one sees a monster fish. Another good site for both snorkeling and scuba is under Gros Piton, just below the prominent cliff. A sloping dropoff with plenty of fish and coral goes down to great depths. There are sometimes currents in this area.

Navigation South coast: Pitons to Vieux Fort

The trip from the Pitons to Vieux Fort is against both wind and current, but it is only about 11 miles and is usually somewhat protected. Keep clear of the reefs that extend about half a mile offshore between Choiseul and Laborie. Laborie, about three miles before Vieux Fort, is a delightful little harbor.

LABORIE

Laborie is an authentic small fishing village on the south coast, about three miles west of Vieux Fort. It is easily identified by the big quarry just to its west. If you are tired of tourist spots, visit Laborie: The locals are friendly and not intrusive, the pace of life is easy-going and it is easy to feel right at home. You are a short tax/ bus ride from Vieux Fort. If you visit on the last Friday of the month, you can enjoy their Fish Fete.

Navigation

Some charts and map readers show a big reef north of Petit Trou extending west, and no reef west of the dock. If yours looks like that, ignore it and use our chart or your eyes.

Approach from the south or southeast to avoid Laborie Reef, which lies up to half a mile offshore on the west side of the bay. The entrance was fully buoyed, I have put the few buoys that remain on my chart, but do not rely on them.

The approach is easy in good light, and if the sun is in your eyes, you can anchor in Petit Trou. The best anchorage is right off the town dock in about 15 feet of water.

Or you can find your way in towards the beach on the other side of the center reef, and you might even explore the broken reef farther up the beach for an anchoring spot. (Best to do this with a dinghy first, as it is tricky.)

Laborie is exposed to the south, reasonably well protected in most conditions, and often a little rolly.

Services

You may be able to pick up WiFi from your yacht. A fuel station is at the head of the dock. Rene (488-5433) is the local taxi

driver. Or you can call Winson (584-1183) in Vieux Fort. Caroline at Salt Rush Cafe has a couple of moorings for her customers (call VHF:16).

Ashore

Turn left on high Street. A big community center and post office are conspicuous, and then comes a small local market, a basic supermarket, and an active fish market. Listen for the conch shell horn as the boats arrive. Bars abound.

The restaurants in town are inexpensive, locally owned, and good. Take a few steps along the beach from dock and have coffee, a snack, lunch or dinner in the Salt Rush Cafe [VHF: 16] right on the beach open 0900-2100. This is the gathering place for enthusiastic kayakers and you can ask them about trips. They serve fresh bread, sandwiches, baked goodies, meals and more. Caroline will be happy to tell you about the town.

Mama Rose (Market Place) Restaurant [$$] was one of the first Laborie restaurants, opened by Mama Rose and now run by grandchildren Adon, Quill, and Minel. They open Monday to Saturday 0900-2300, serve good local food, as well as tasty fish 'n chips, and always offer an inexpensive local lunch plate.

Across the road Feter's Bar and Grill [$$] is new and looks fancy from the outside. Next door, Big Bamboo Cafe [$$] is under new management. It is cheap and cheerful with the big bamboo bar open to the street. Check them out; neither was open when I visited.

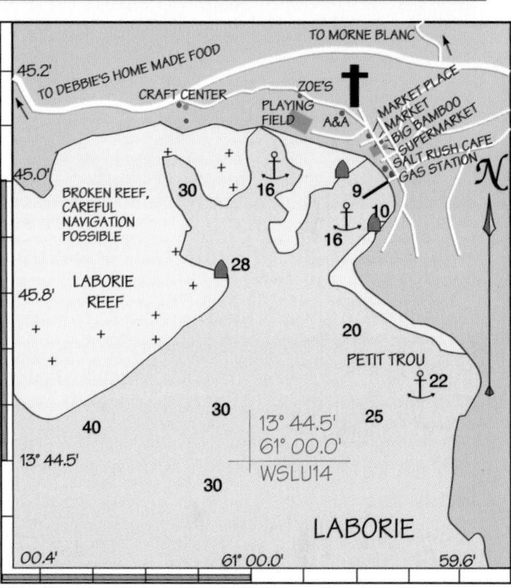

You will probably have to ask to find the little hole in the wall called Anna's Place. Here you can get a good local lunch plate for $10-12 EC. She opens every day for lunch only, and you sit on the beach.

Farther west, over the bridge, you can get a great roti at Ann Marie's A & A. It is a tiny building marked only by a Piton sign. Farther down the road is the Craft Center with a spa, shops, and Miranda's little cafe [$$]. She opens daily 1100-2000, and serves good and inexpensive local food, with seats out in the open.

Moonlight Bay is a bar on the beach below. They generally open Wednesday to Sunday.

If you take any bus heading to Soufriere, you can get off a mile or two down the road at Debbie's Home Cooking [$$]. But

call in advance, Debbie now only cooks by reservation.

Walk the spectacular long beach. Way up in the hills behind Laborie is Morne le Blanc (aka The Top of the South). The GSM aerials on the hill will show you where it is. They have a picnic spot and a viewing platform with a panoramic view towards Vieux Fort.

VIEUX FORT

Vieux Fort is convenient for Hewanorra airport. It does not have a tourist bone in its body and is a thriving local town with some great old wooden houses and two active ports: commercial and fishing. The people are generally friendly and welcoming, and you will find supermarkets and hardware stores in shopping malls. The fishing port makes it amenable for visiting yachts, though if you are used to the tourist scene, you may suffer from culture shock. There are some rough edges and, with a brief intermission when the marine police patrolled, there were a string of thefts and even one murder over some years. It is best to leave someone onboard. Laborie is an alternative, more secure, and only a few miles down the coast on a bus route.

The anchorage is well protected and a long walk (or short ride) away is one of the Caribbean's most magnificent windward beaches, a beach so long that you are guaranteed half a mile or so to yourself.

I have seen plans for a Chinese super city to the north of town, complete with marinas, cruise ship berths, and skyscrapers. I don't think it will happen, but if you see what looks like Hong Kong, you will know I was wrong.

Navigation

The sail to Vieux Fort from the Pitons is 11 miles, usually to windward. It is somewhat protected, but if the current is running to the west, it can be rough. Keep well clear of the reef that extends about half a mile offshore between Choiseul and Laborie.

The most convenient anchorage for getting ashore is west of the new fishing port. Leave the green marker to port as you approach. Anchor between the marker and the western wall in 10-20 feet of water, or outside the green marker in 25 feet of water. Avoid the shoal along the northern wall of the fishing harbor that extends both north and west. Here you are close to town and can leave your dinghy in the fishing port. The holding varies between good and poor,

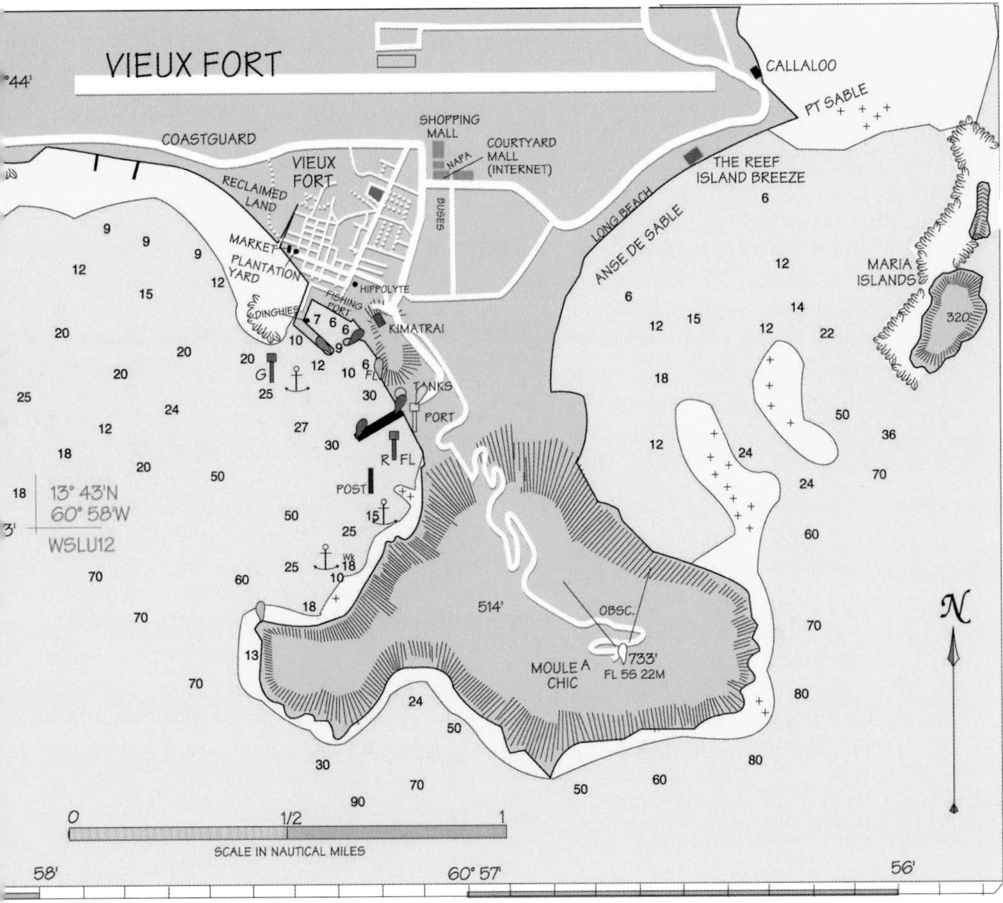

so make sure you are well dug in before going ashore.

You can also anchor in either of the bays southwest of the large ship harbor marked on our chart. Anchor south of all the beacons. Shoals extend from the shore, so approach cautiously. To enter the first bay, pass to the west of the big, rusty post just outside the bay, as there is a shoal inside this post toward the shore. The second bay is far more scenic, with some passable snorkeling. A shoal comes out from the middle of the bay but you can anchor either side of it, or outside it. Several wrecks in both bays manage to snag anchors. If you are worried, have someone snorkel to help pick the spot.

The large ship port is run by St. Lucia Marine Terminals. They are not geared for yachts but have been quite helpful. You can often leave your dinghy alongside the roll-on dock to the north of the main pier. You cannot leave it here when the dock is in use. For town, use the fishing port.

Regulations

Vieux Fort is a port of entry, and customs and immigration are at the head of the large ship dock (not the fishing port). If they are closed, try the airport. Sailclear does not work here yet.

Yachts may not anchor by the Maria Islands, as it is a protected area.

Communications

The Document Center, an office store with internet and Fedex, is in the big building where Clarke St. joins the highway. Most bars have WiFi.

Services

Ice and outboard fuel are available in the fishing port on the eastern dock. You could stay overnight in the fishing port stern-to on the northwest wall if there is room. You may be charged $20 EC. There are no dockside services; ask first. Depths in the fishing port are about 6 feet close to the eastern dock, and about 7-8 feet farther out, where you can stay the night.

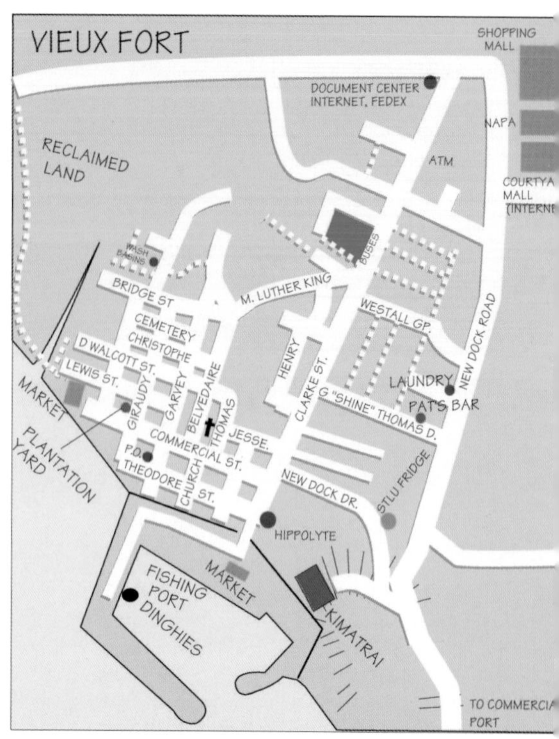

Winson Edward (584-1183, 520-5231) is an excellent taxi driver. He is knowledgeable, reliable, and likes to hike. Bayne (720-8425) has another taxi.

Filling with water is possible alongside the roll-on dock in the commercial port (when free). Talk to someone in the operations department, as you will have to arrange it with the water department. Big yachts can have fuel trucked to the commercial port. There is no water for filling a yacht in the fishing port, but you can probably arrange to fill a couple of jerry jugs in the port for a small fee if you ask security. Cooking gas is available at the gas depot just outside the commercial port.

Fletcher's Laundry and Dry Cleaning is on New Dock Road. Virginia Fletcher charges $30 EC for a load to wash and dry and can turn it round in a day if you get it in early enough, otherwiseit takes 24 hours. She opens approximately 0900 to 1700.

The fishing port is the obvious place to leave your dinghy. Put it in the northwest corner on the dock. Lock it up and, if leaving it at night, ask the security guard to keep an eye on it for you and tip him when you come back. On holidays and weekends, school kids can be pestiferous. Bribing one to guard the dinghy works, but it would still be smart to take the red kill switch with you. If you have a problem, there is a good chance you can leave it on the roll-on dock at the secure Commercial Port, where they are very helpful, though ingenuity is necessary for tying up, as there are no rings.

KP Marine are in the fishing port for all Yamaha sales and service.

Hippolyte, right outside the dock area, is the DHL agent and can clear parts through customs. Francis Raymond, of St. Lucia Refrigeration on New Dock Drive, has lots of refrigeration and stove parts, but he does not make repairs.

Lubeco bedding factory is owned by Stephanie Allain, who also has La Haut in Soufriere. They supply both fitted and flat sheets for any size bunk (take a pattern) and have really nice fabrics in many designs, including cotton and organic cotton. They also sell towels and they produce good-quality, high-density foam mattresses cut to any shape. You get a mattress properly finished with a quilted cover, which adds comfort. Lubeco is in the industrial estate, just off the road to Laborie. They also have a store in American Dry Wall near Castries.

Provisioning

Shopping is good, and most banks have ATMs. One large supermarket is in the mall by the roundabout. The even bigger Gablewoods South is a few miles down the main road heading towards Laborie. Fruits and vegetables in town are good and are less expensive than in Castries. The fish market in the fishing port has great buys on fresh fish.

Napa has batteries and tools, and there

are other hardware stores.

Restaurants

You need to know about The Reef [$$, closed Monday evenings], whether visiting by boat or car. It is ideal when you have to make airport runs, and it is more fun to hang out there than at the airport after you have checked in.

It is on the eastern shore on the long beach, about a mile from Vieux Fort (a very short taxi ride). The owner, Cecile Wiltshire, is a software engineer (yes they have WiFi) and kitesurfing instructor. The Reef has a kite surfing school, and the flying kites make a colorful display off the beach.

The Reef is open for breakfast, lunch, and dinner, serving local dishes. Seamoss and coconut water, saltfish bakes, lambi, and squid are on the menu, as are pizzas. The Reef collects interesting people, makes a great hangout, and is an excellent place to spend a few hours. It has four simple rooms for an overnight.

Their Kite 'n Surf Center next door has international instructors and all the latest kitesurfing and sailboard gear. It normally opens from November to June. Secondhand gear is often for sale.

Nest door, Island Breeze [$$] bar/restaurant on the beach, open every day for lunch and dinner, serving beach bites, burgers and grilled food.

East of Vieux Fort, the Maria Islands are a nature reserve and home to a species of lizard and a snake unknown anywhere else in the world. The National Trust building is right beside The Reef, and you can arrange for a guided trip. (You are not allowed to anchor there.) The energetic should hike up to the Moule a Chique lighthouse for the view.

You will find some local restaurants in town. Kimatrai [$$] stands on the hill overlooking the yacht anchorage. It is an old-fashioned hotel, cool and breezy, with a marvelous view of the harbor. It is open all day and is a great place to hang out, relax, write postcards, play pool, use the WiFi, catch up on your diary, or watch cable TV. It has a perfect location for sunset, and they serve food.

Maria Islands from The Reef

PASSAGES BETWEEN ST. LUCIA & ST. VINCENT

Northbound

The northbound passage between St. Vincent and St. Lucia can be hard on the wind and hard on the body. The north end of St. Vincent is unbelievably gusty on occasion and more than a little bumpy. It is not unusual to have gusts of 30 to 40 knots for a few miles, so it pays to be prepared. I often do this trip single-handed and am not overly fond of it, but find the easiest way to do it is as follows: motor-sail close to the coast under reefed main and engine and wait until the full force of the wind hits before deciding what to do. If you are comfortable under main and engine, keep going that way until the wind steadies down. Otherwise, if you have roller furling, just unroll a little of the jib until it gets calmer. The main thing is not to arrive at the north end with too much canvas, where reducing sail can degenerate into hanging onto flailing Dacron as the boat bucks about and tries to throw you over. Once you get about five miles north of St. Vincent, wind and seas generally become more constant and you can adjust sail accordingly. The current will set you to the west, so head up if possible. It is going to be a long day, so plan to leave early from Cumberland Bay or Wallilabou, as that will make it seem shorter.

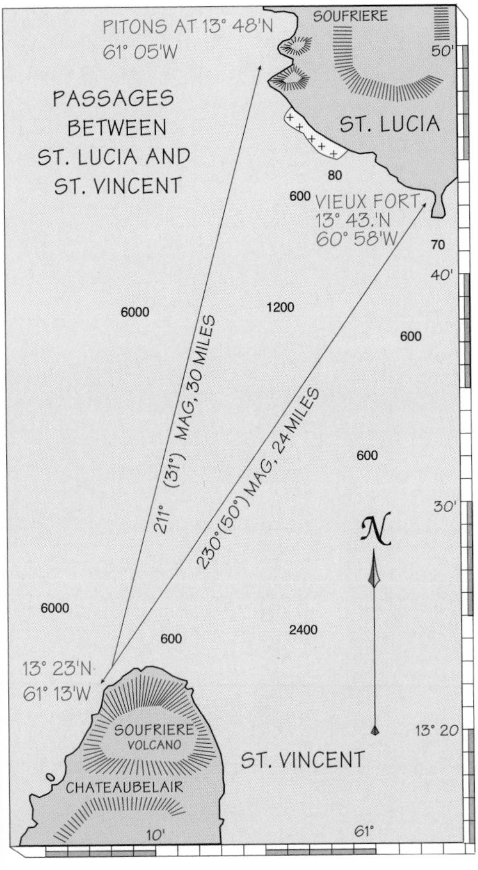

You may be able to avoid some wind and sea by heading offshore from Wallilabou, but in that case you are likely to have a hard beat to St. Lucia.

If heading north from Blue Lagoon in reasonable weather, the passage up the windward side of St. Vincent is shorter and you get the windward part over early, leaving a good sail to the Pitons. The trick is to tack about 4 miles to the east of St. Vincent to stay well off any bad seas close to shore. If the wind is in the north you may have to make more than one tack. There is a windward lee under the Soufriere volcano (back pressure). When you reach this, if you tack out a few miles, you will get better wind and a better angle for crossing the channel.

Southbound

The southbound trip is usually a lovely broad reach. If you cannot see St. Vincent from St. Lucia, a course of 208° magnetic should start you in the right direction. If you plan to stop in St. Vincent, nature lovers will favor Cumberland or Wallilabou (you can clear in Chateaubelair) and those who like waterfront bars can clear customs in Blue Lagoon. If you plan to go all the way to Bequia make sure you allow plenty of time.

In reasonable conditions you may prefer to go to windward of St. Vincent when sailing from Vieux Fort to Bequia or Blue Lagoon.

Blue Lagoon

St. Vincent & the Grenadines

St. Vincent at a glance

Regulations

St. Vincent and the Grenadines together make up one country. The customs stations are in Chateaubelair, Wallilabou, Kingstown, Blue Lagoon, Bequia, Union Island, Mustique, and Canouan.

The entry charge is $35 EC per person per month, unless you leave within that month, in which case you pay again when you reenter. In addition, charter yachts based outside St. Vincent are charged $5 EC per foot per month, with a $125 temporary license fee. You can cruise here as long as you wish. You will normally be stamped in for a month and then return for extensions, which are in the same office and easy to obtain. Those clearing outside normal office hours (weekdays 0800-1200, 1300-1600) will pay overtime.

Overtime fees on Sundays/holidays are: customs $63 EC, immigration $50 EC. Regular fees are: customs $45 EC, immigration $35 EC.

No jet skis or similar craft are allowed anywhere in St. Vincent and the Grenadines. Spearfishing is strictly forbidden to all visitors. Drone operators need a license.

You are welcome to fish, but only for your own consumption. You can troll when sailing, or hand-line at anchor or from the shore, except in any marine park or protected area, where no fishing is allowed. Buying lobster out of season (the lobstering season is October 1 to April 30) is illegal, as is buying a female lobster with eggs (easily seen as red "caviar" under the tail), or any lobster less than 9" in length. Corals must not be damaged. Fines run at around $5,000 EC.

Holidays

Jan. 1, New Year's Day
Jan. 2, Recovery Day
Jan. 22, Discovery Day
Easter Friday, Sunday & Monday, April 19-21, 2019; April 10-13, 2020
First Monday in May, Labor Day
Whit Monday, June 10, 2019; June 1, 2020
Carnival, 2nd Monday and Tuesday in July
August bank holiday; 1st Monday in August
October 27, Independence Day
Dec. 25, Christmas
Dec. 26, Boxing Day

Shopping hours

Most shops open 0800-1200 and 1300-1600. Saturday is a half day and most places are closed by noon. Banks normally open Monday through Thursday 0800-1200 and 1300-1500; Fridays 0800-1200 and 1500-1700.

Telephones

It is simplest to get a cell phone and use a local SIM card. For calls to USA and other NANP countries, dial 1 plus the full number. For other overseas calls, dial 0 + country code + number. When dialing from overseas the area code is 784, followed by a 7-digit number.

Transport

There are inexpensive ($1.50-$6 EC) buses running to most villages. If you are going a long way, check on the time of the last returning bus. Taxis are plentiful. Sample taxi rates for up to four people are:

	$EC
Blue Lagoon to Airport	60
Kingstown to Young Island	40
Airport to Young Island	70
Kingstown to Blue Lagoon	50
Short ride	25
By the hour	80
Arnos Vale shopping run	80

Rental cars and motorbikes are available (see our directory). You will need to buy a local license, which costs $65 EC. Drive on the left.

Montreal Gardens

St. Vincent

St. Vincent is an island of towering mountains, craggy peaks, and dramatic precipices. Everything is dressed in a tangle of dense green forest. St. Vincent's steep and wild terrain was among the last to be settled by Europeans. At the time Columbus sailed through the islands St. Vincent was inhabited by the Kalinargo, who had migrated from South America and had a more poetic name for the island, Hairoun, which means "home of the blessed." They were a fierce tribe and had wrested the land from the Arawak people who preceded them. Columbus called them Caribs.

While the newly arrived Europeans exploited nearby islands, a slave ship was wrecked off Bequia and the Caribs took the slaves as their own. However, these slaves were also fierce and warlike and proved to be a problem. To combat this, the Caribs decided to kill all the young male black children. This caused a revolt among the slaves, who killed all the Caribs they could, stole their women, and ran into the hills. They kept the names the Caribs had given them, followed some Carib customs, and became known as the Black Caribs. Over the years they took control of much of the land from the original Caribs and put up intense resistance to British settlement. Finally, in the late 18th century, the Black Caribs were defeated by a superior British force and shipped en masse to Honduras.

The northern end of the island is dominated by Soufriere, a 3,000-foot volcano. A friend of mine was anchored under the volcano in April 1979 with an amateur geologist on board. Together they scaled the volcano and peered into the depths. The geologist declared it safely dormant. That night, which happened to be both Friday the 13th and Good Friday,

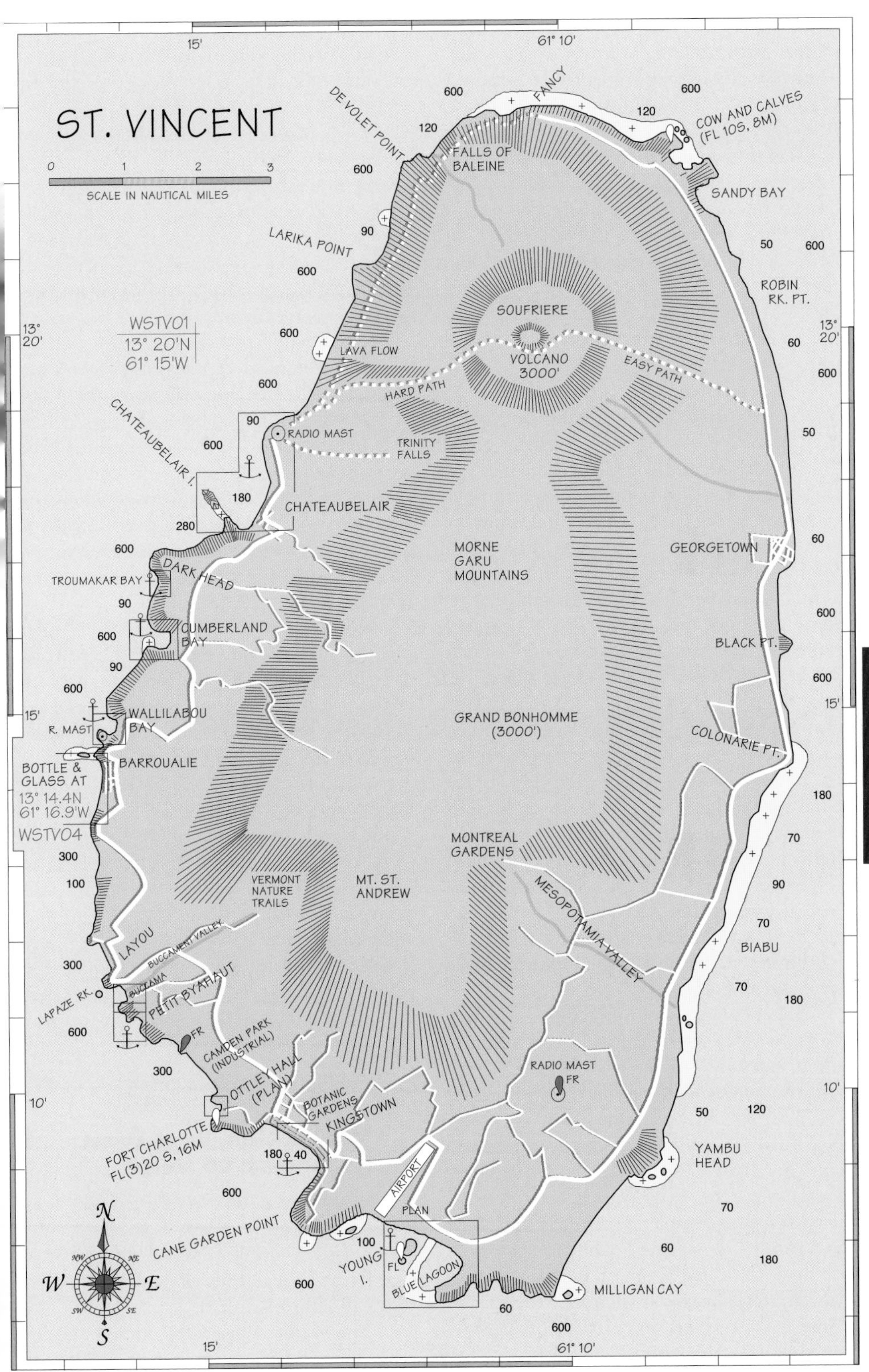

ST. VINCENT
SCALE IN NAUTICAL MILES
0 1 2 3
DE VOLET POINT
FANCY
COW AND CALVES (FL 10S, 8M)
FALLS OF BALEINE
SANDY BAY
LARIKA POINT
ROBIN RK. PT.
SOUFRIERE VOLCANO 3000'
LAVA FLOW
HARD PATH
EASY PATH
WSTV01 13° 20'N 61° 15'W
CHATEAUBELAIR I.
RADIO MAST
TRINITY FALLS
CHATEAUBELAIR
MORNE GARU MOUNTAINS
GEORGETOWN
TROUMAKAR BAY
DARK HEAD
CUMBERLAND BAY
BLACK PT.
WALLILABOU BAY
R. MAST
BARROUALIE
BOTTLE & GLASS AT 13° 14.4N 61° 16.9'W
WSTV04
GRAND BONHOMME (3000')
COLONARIE PT.
MONTREAL GARDENS
VERMONT NATURE TRAILS
MT. ST. ANDREW
MESOPOTAMIA VALLEY
BIABU
LAYOU
BUCCAMENT VALLEY
BUCCAMA
LAPAZE RK.
PETIT BYAHAUT
CAMDEN PARK (INDUSTRIAL)
OTTLEY HALL (PLAN)
BOTANIC GARDENS
KINGSTOWN
RADIO MAST FR
FORT CHARLOTTE FL(3)20 S, 16M
YAMBU HEAD
AIRPORT
PLAN
CANE GARDEN POINT
YOUNG I.
BLUE LAGOON
MILLIGAN CAY
15'
61° 10'
13° 20'
10'

there was a rumbling from the very bowels of the earth and the volcano erupted with a massive cloud that landed dust hundreds of miles away. It created murk in the area so thick they couldn't see to the bow of the boat and had to leave completely blind, steering by compass to get away. The eruptions, which lasted for some days, were Soufriere's second since 1902. The other was in 1973. As you sail by you can see some rivers of dark volcanic matter that flowed down from the summit. Despite the absence of any warning, everyone left soon after the first eruption and there were no casualties.

The enthusiastic should hike up Soufriere, as it is unquestionably one of the Windwards' best and most exciting hikes. Starting on the windward side there is a clear trail that begins in farmland and goes through rainforest, montane forest, and then into an area where only tiny plants can survive. The mountain top is often in cloud, and you need a little luck to see down into the crater or get the views over the island. The wind often blows hard, and it is cool and damp, so take a rain jacket. Be careful not to get blown into the crater, which is a sheer 1,000-foot drop with no guardrail. Take lunch with you and eat it near the top; the longer you spend there, the more likely you are to get windows in the clouds and be able to see into the crater. The crater is an impressive cone with a huge, growing, smoking volcanic dome in the middle. The crater rim is at 3,000 feet; the mountains to the north attain 3,800 feet. The volcano can be approached from the leeward side, but it is a much longer hike (about four hours each way) and a reliable guide is essential.

It seems that neither nature nor man was sure they wanted tourism in St. Vincent, for it lacks the acres of white sand beach and the convenient, easy anchorages of the Grenadines. In compensation, this very beautiful island remains unspoiled, and you can drive or hike amid exotic, almost theatrical, scenery. Its rugged terrain is the perfect scenic complement to the appealing and gentle Grenadines farther south. Those doing a round trip from St. Lucia who only wish to stop one way are better off visiting St. Vincent on the way north, as this makes the northbound trip shorter.

Try to see some of St. Vincent's interior, which is totally wild. Roads run up both of St. Vincent's coasts, but none goes all the way around or crosses the middle.

I love Montreal Gardens in the Mesopotamia Valley. Perched upon the very threshold of the mountains, they are at the end of the road. Tim Vaughn and his team maintain these gardens as a work of art. Little paths, dense vegetation, a river, and broad views make the gardens a perfect place to spend an hour or two away from it all.

Those who like things closer to town can tour the Botanical Gardens and Fort Charlotte. The Botanical Gardens are the oldest in the western hemisphere, and it was here that Captain Bligh brought the breadfruit tree after the mutiny on the Bounty fiasco. A direct descendant from his original tree is on display. You will find many youths to guide you through the gardens. One or two are good and entertaining, but negotiate fees in advance.

While many places are good for wandering off on your own, a guide is essential for some hikes, especially the western approach to the volcano. Bad robberies have occurred in this area, which has also become the smoke basket of the ganja generation.

Good guides who will cover everything mentioned above are available. Clint and Millie Hazel, who run HazECO Tours, come from Vincentian families dating back to the 1700s, and they have an exceptional and intimate view of the island's history, politics, and society. They are willing to arrange tours from Cumberland and Wallilabou, but you will need to contact them in advance, as their radio does not reach these little bays: call 457-8631. Many people contact them from Bequia and get met on the ferry. We mention other guides under various anchorages.

Navigation, west coast: north to south

Navigation along this section of the coast is straightforward: the land is steep-to except for the clearly visible Bottle and Glass rocks near Barrouallie. A quarter of a mile offshore clears all other dangers.

One yachtsman was murdered and another injured in a robbery in Wallilabou in

Chateaubelair: Chateaubelair Island is in the foreground

March 2016. The assailants came by boat and the murder is not yet solved. This has led some to avoid the west coast. Others, including us, continue to visit, and so far the assailants have not struck again.

CHATEAUBELAIR

Chateaubelair lies at the southern foot of Soufriere, St. Vincent's volcano. The coast here is rugged and photogenic, with dramatic hill and mountain outlines, cliffs, and beach. In settled weather it can be a dream. However, in times of really bad northerly swells Chateaubelair can be untenable, so use caution during the winter months. A steep cliffy slope covered in palm trees lies along the eastern half of the bay. This is the calmest and most scenic place to anchor. There is an ample anchoring shelf, 20-40 feet deep. Don't anchor too close to shore, as rocky patches extend in places. The bottom is sand, but some of the boulders you see tumbling into the sea along the water's edge have made it onto the sand, so if you anchor on rope, snorkel on your anchor. There is also a good sandy anchoring shelf with excellent holding in front of the Beach Front Restaurant, though just to the northeast of the restaurant is a deep hole. Anchoring south of the dock along the shore is the closest for just clearing customs.

Richmond Vale Academy (RVA) is a climate change and sustainability training center. In 2017 they were in the process of installing moorings around the bay, which will be available for yachts up to 60 feet, from October to June each year ($50 EC per day.) One of their moorings is just off the point to allow easy access to their dive shop, which offers guided dives, gear rental,

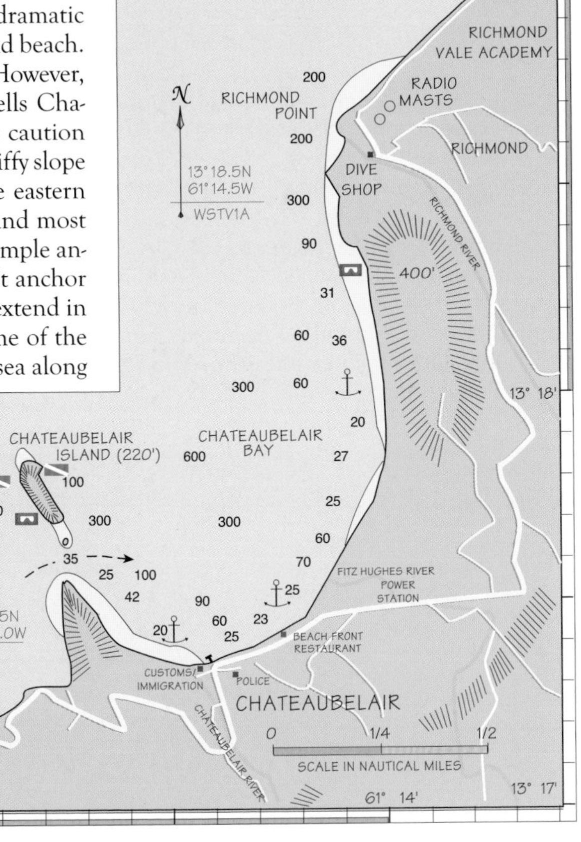

St. Vincent & the Grenadines

and tank filling. Two are in front of the main dock, close to the customs and immigration offices, and the remaining four are along the northeast coast. They offer security for yachts on their moorings, but call ahead to make sure it is in place (491-9761.) If you take one, check it carefully.

A rock lies in the middle of the channel between Chateaubelair Island and the mainland. A navigable passage, some 35 feet deep, runs just south of this rock (between the rock and the mainland). There are rocks around, so only attempt this in good light.

Be prepared to move for fishermen if they ask. Getting ashore may be hard to impossible in any swell. The best place is the stub of the old dock remains.

Serious security concerns come and go in this area. It is generally safe as a daytime anchorage, and people do overnight here, but Cumberland Bay has a better track record. The local police number is 458-2229.

Regulations

Chateaubelair is a port of clearance. To get to the Customs and Immigrations office, turn right from the dock remains and walk along the beach a couple of hundred feet from the dock. Look for a path leading to the left beside a house. When we were there in 2018 it was sign-posted. Customs (Cesar, 491-1849) and Immigration (Phillip, 527-6398) are both in this house. Whenever I have cleared in here it has been a friendly experience. Immigration is open from Monday to Friday from 0800 until 1600, and every other Saturday from 0800 until 1400. If you are there on the off Saturday, go to the police station and they may arrange it for you. Customs shares the same hours, except all day Monday and Tuesday morning when the officer is in town to file paperwork. When leaving it may be wise to clear out before you sail here, in case customs are away.

Ashore

Most people in the north of St. Vincent are naturally friendly in the nicest way. Try to keep it that way by treating people with friendly respect. It is good to buy produce if vendors come out and offer it to you, but beware of giving anyone money to go buy fruits or run errands in the village. We don't give to beggars unless they have real handicaps.

Esron Thompson's Beach Front Restaurant [$] is a conspicuous building on the beach. He and his wife Gail will cook you the most wonderful fresh fish at very reasonable prices that are geared to the local market. If you are not overnighting, this makes a great lunch spot when heading south; anchor right off the restaurant. They do sometimes have very loud, late-night music on weekends.

Chateaubelair lies in the heart of some of St. Vincent's best hiking. The volcano is a full day's hike. Darkview Falls are a pleasant 40-minute hike, with a second falls higher up. Take your bathing things, for you can take a good shower here. Ask about the ancient carved stones. Taxi tours and walking guides are available through the Beach Front Restaurant (Felix, a cook there, is an eager candidate) and Richmond Vale Academy, which will organize guided hikes that include water and a packed lunch. Contact Jesper Friis (491-9761.)

Chateaubelair

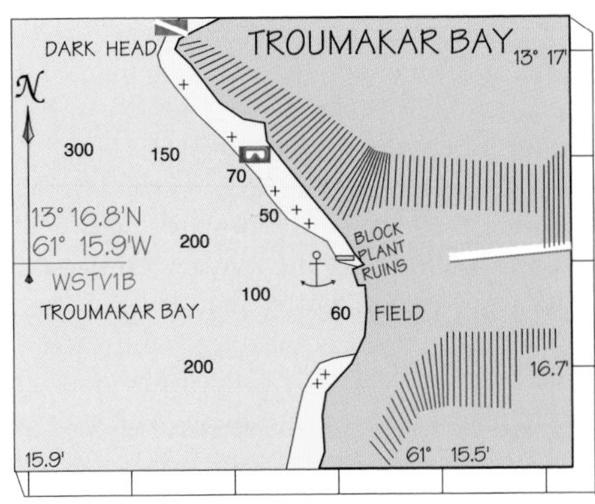

Water sports

Richmond Vale Academy has a dive shop on the northern headland and will take you diving, rent you gear, or fill your tanks.

The whole of Chateaubelair Bay is an invitation to snorkel. Interesting boulders and rocks abound. For divers, Chateaubelair Island is magnificent and you can find a good dive almost anywhere around it. On the west side, a steep wall has been sculpted by the sea into ravines, hollows, and tiny caves that are home to eels, soapfish, and other creatures. It is decorated by a variety of black corals, including wire coral. Giant gray angelfish often gather over the sand at about 90 feet. You will find a reef 40 feet deep where huge structures covered with a colorful mixture of corals rise from the sand like fairy castles. Pufferfish swim by with what look like broad smiles on their faces. Huge schools of tiny silver fish catch the sun in a brilliant display. You will see a good variety of brightly colored reef fish and creatures such as Christmas tree worms, snake eels, and maybe an octopus. On the north end of the eastern side a dramatic wall plunges to about 130 feet, with elegant soft coral formations. Farther south, diving is not as deep but is equally pretty. You might be lucky and find the dive mooring just off-island, in the passage between the island and the mainland.

TROUMAKAR BAY

This small, isolated bay has room for only a handful of yachts. It is well protected, except in bad northerly swells. Steep hills ashore afford panoramic views for energetic walkers. There is good snorkeling all along the northern shore. The water here is deep; you begin to think the bottom does not exist as you approach the beach. Anchor bow or stern to the old block plant ruins at the northern end of the beach, or tie to a palm tree.

CUMBERLAND BAY

This deep and enchanting bay is part of an estate in the heart of St. Vincent's wildest and richest land. A forest of coconut trees and bananas flows down the valley to the beach. At dusk, cattle egrets roost together in nearby trees and at night the tree frogs set up a rich chorus. Sometimes the bay becomes a boiling mass of jumping tuna and fishermen can often be seen with their seine nets, waiting patiently.

Cumberland is unspoiled by tourism. There are many here happy to take you on a tour or feed you, but it is all so unsophisticated that it has the charm of an untouched settlement. This is a very friendly little bay. The land around is steep and dramatic, with excellent hiking. Enter toward the north of the bay to avoid the large rocky shoal that extends from the southwestern headland. Cumberland is very deep and you will need to anchor bow or stern to a palm tree. Many will be eager to help. Do not tow anyone into

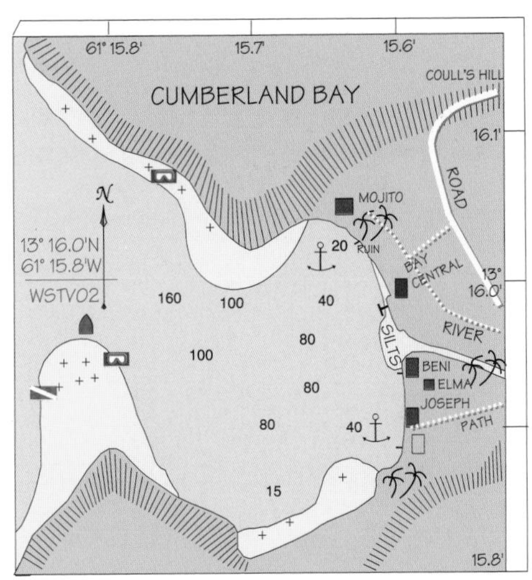

the bay; wait until you get right in and choose one of the people inside the bay itself. You can anchor to the north or south of Bay Central. The water on the north side is shallower.

Regulations/services

Cumberland Bay has no customs; clear in or out at Wallilabou or Chateaubelair.

Bay Central (Cumberland Beach and Recreation Park) is a government-built facility with WiFi ($5 for 24 hours) that has a good signal for most of the bay (though it is sometimes out of commission), a dock selling water ($50 EC up to 200 gallons), ice, a launderette ($35 EC wash and dry), showers (for $5 EC), bar and restaurant, and a welcome center. The dock was severely damaged in hurricane Maria, but repairs are planned. They have surveillance cameras that take in their dock and much of the bay. Once repaired, you will be able to come alongside for water (up to about 2 meters draft), and deeper boats can come stern-to; the depth drops off fast. The staff, including Matthew, Cheryl, and Althea, are very helpful. Some of the people who have businesses sleep on the beach, so there are generally people about.

Restaurants

Four local restaurants line the bay. All depend on visiting yachts and all are reasonably priced and fun, so plan to eat out for lunch or dinner.

Two cousins, Julian and Lloyd, started Mojito [$$] at the north end of the beach. It has a great view over the rest of the bay. No need to get your feet wet; dinghy to Bay Central and walk. Someone may well dinghy or swim you a menu, which includes pineapple and lemon grass seafood curry and rack of lamb with coffee mint sauce. The captain eats free with five or more guests. Venetia and Dean, who serve you, are both lovely, and the food is good.

Bay Central [$] has a little restaurant that open from 0800 until the last customer leaves. This is the cheapest place to eat, you get good local Creole fish or chicken, and they have a dinghy dock. They have karaoke on alternative Saturday nights.

Joseph is a fisherman who has been here for as long as I can remember. He has a restaurant right on the beach, DJ-20 or Joseph's Place [$$], now run by his son Gregory and his wife. They cook local-style barbecue of fresh fish or chicken and are into music, so entertainment can be arranged. Joseph is often out and about in the bay fishing, taking yacht lines, selling a little handicraft, and helping however he can.

Bennett [$] has a bar/restaurant called Beni in the middle of the beach. He has been

Houses looking down on Cumberland Bay

here for a long time. It is an amusing place to hang out, and he sometimes has a steel band on Wednesday nights. Beni can cook a good local meal, especially seafood, and serves fresh local juice. But he needs advance notice, so give him a call (593-9143). Bennett is also a good man to talk to about hiking. The new Cumberland Nature Trail (about three hours) is in the rainforest high above Spring Village, near the water source for the hydro-electric piping which carries water to a series of several small generators. You need a taxi to take you there. Beni can also take you on other hikes, including Darkview Falls. Beni has a great package, which includes a tour and full dinner with a drink afterwards. If you are eating in his restaurant he will give you free water and ice.

Mama Elma [$] is near Joseph and open for lunch and dinner every day. You can get everything from goat water to lobster, with plenty of fish and chicken. She sometimes has local provisions for sale.

Ashore

Although some of the locals look like the bad guys in a spaghetti western, for the most part they couldn't be nicer and more helpful. Joseph will sell you fish, and Ricky, Billy, or Charles will bring round a crate of fruits. Wesley Roy Mason sells produce out of his boat.

Carlos and Brother have water taxis and arrange coastal trips. Suzanne Stapleton often hangs out in Bay Central and sells her crochet handicrafts, occasionally acting as a guide. Kenny takes lines and guides. Rasta Joseph helps with lines and takes around Juniel who makes her own handicrafts. James and Joseph sell handicrafts. Others will take your lines and be generally helpful. You will have to be the judge. Try not to do business with anyone you find aggressive or objectionable in any way. A young man called William sometimes comes out in a borrowed inflatable to take lines. If you use him, agree on price in advance. He seems to get angry and cuss rather easily; not the most desirable traits for someone in tourism.

Walking here is fun. An easy walk is up Coull's Hill to the north, which rewards you with a great view of the anchorage. Walk back to the road, turn left and keep going. (If you land on the south side of the bay you must ford a small river, but that is part of the fun.) There is a rum shop on Coull's Hill, just at the point when you are dying for a drink.

Better yet, arrange for someone to take you on the Cumberland Nature Trail in the rainforest. You need transport to get you to the start, which is up above Spring Village.

The Black Baron, at the south end of the beach, was a tavern run by a couple from France that has now gone out of business. The building itself has lots of character, with a pirate's den complete with replica artifacts. It's worth taking a peek in, even if no one is around.

WALLILABOU

Wallilabou, a picturesque bay surrounded by dramatic hills, is about a mile south of Cumberland. Here you are in the heart of St. Vincent, among charming and delightful people. A picturesque waterfall lies just a mile down the road. In 2003 Wallilabou became famous as the main location for the movie "Pirates of the Caribbean," starring Johnny Depp. Wallilabou Anchorage, a pleasant restaurant/hotel, makes part of the waterfront. They maintain a room full of artifacts from the movie and have some of the props for you to see. It is occasionally inundated with cruise ship passengers from Kingstown.

Enter in the middle of the bay and pick up the moorings put down by the Wallilabou Anchorage Restaurant, or anchor where there are no moorings and tie bow or stern to the wall, or to a tree. In times of northerly swells the northern corner of the bay is more protected. The bay has long had a reputation for occasional thievery. I was told there were video cameras monitored by the coast guard and security guards with flashlights at the Wallilabou Anchorage Hotel; this did not seem to help, as there was a murder here in 2016 that is currently unsolved. It seems likely that the assailants arrived by boat.

Men in rowing boats occasionally approach you from as far as three miles away asking to take your stern line ashore. Refuse all such offers; there are always plenty of line helpers in Wallilabou itself. The good guys tried to organize themselves as an association, although their success is questionable. They include Yellowman (Moorings agent), Donald, Speed, and Ron Jordan (one of two twin brothers known as 'the twins').

The going rate for someone to help you with your lines is $20 EC.

You may enjoy buying fruits and vegetables on display by vendors, but beware of the offer to "go fetch you nice produce." The quality of the product rarely matches the description, and if you give them money in advance you may never see the vendor again.

You can also stop in Keartons Bay, one bay south. Rock Side Cafe has five well-maintained bow and stern moorings, which they keep for lunch or dinner guests. Call them before you come in and they will arrange for someone reliable to help you (see *Restaurants*.)

Regulations

Customs clearance is available during the week between 1700 and 1800. Overtime is charged. It is only customs clearance, and if you are entering you will need to check with immigration at the next port. If you are leaving you will probably get away with customs only. Rock Side Cafe often keeps tabs on them, so it is a good idea to call ahead to confirm that customs will be around.

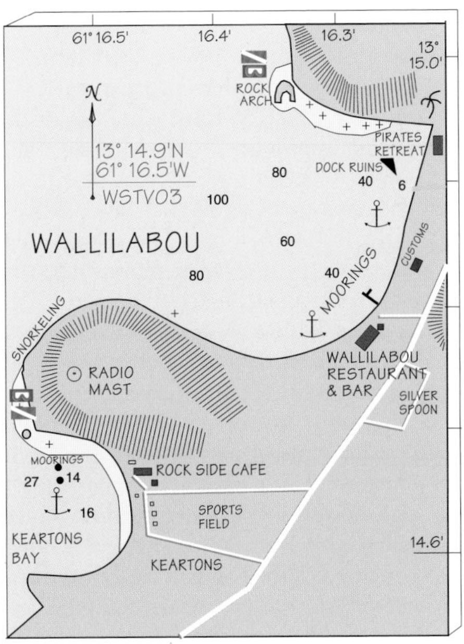

Communications

Wallilabou Anchorage Restaurant has WiFi, for which you need a password. You can get it in the bar, and it may reach your yacht.

Services

Steve and Jane Russell, who run the Wallilabou Anchorage Restaurant [VHF: 68], are keen to attract yachting customers. They have a good dinghy dock and offer moorings ($20 EC, refundable when you have a meal ashore), free showers, and inexpensive water via a long hose from the dock. Phone, fax, and WiFi are available, as is cube ice, and they may be able to provide overnight accommodation. Do not give garbage to the boat vendors; most stick it in the rocks. Wrap it well and take it ashore to the restaurant and they will show you where to put it (no charge).

In Keartons, Rock Side Cafe has internet, WiFi, laundry, showers, and can provide water to the moorings via a long hose. These are mainly provided for their dinner guests.

If you need a mechanic, Yellowman is your best bet and can fix most things. If you want to go hiking, talk to Association members Donald, Speed, Cedric, or Ron, or set it up with Rock Side Cafe. Local hikes of interest include the Soufriere volcano, Darkview Falls, and Vermont Nature Trails. If you have

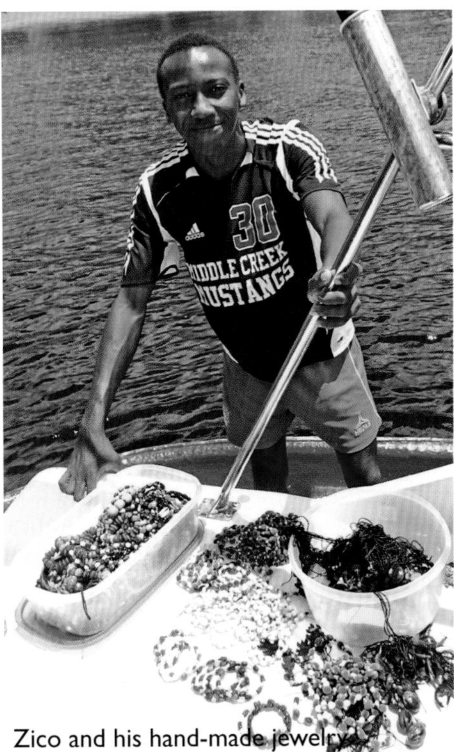

Zico and his hand-made jewelry

any problem with any vendor, call the coast guard: 457-5445.

Zico is young, friendly, and eager, and may approach you in his small red boat to sell his jewelry made from local seeds and handmade beads. His mother, Francine, bakes coconut, banana, and wheat bread, which he will happily deliver.

Restaurants

Rock Side Cafe [VHF: 16/68, $$$$] in Keartons, away from the bustle of Wallilabou, is a magical tiny garden oasis overlooking the bay. Orlando, from St. Vincent, and Rosi from Germany, are the owners. They are the Trans-Ocean Support base, and if you need to clear customs they can tell you the way or take you there. They keep moorings for their dinner guests; call and book so they can arrange for someone reliable to help you tie up. You can also walk over from Wallilabou or ask them to arrange a taxi. The small size of this place is part of its charm: you eat outside under a thatched roof. You need to call them to get ashore (they will bring you in or show you the way), as a reef lies along much of the beach. Rosi and Orlando are wonderfully welcoming and treat you as friends. They can also provide water, internet, WiFi, showers, fresh produce, and laundry. The food is usually fresh fish and really excellent; visiting is a special experience. Give them at least a couple of hours' notice, if possible.

Orlando can arrange hiking, driving, and boat tours, and for German guests, Rosi often guides.

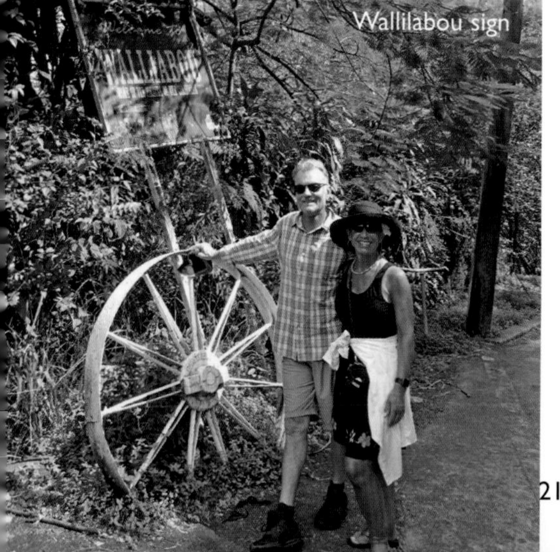
Wallilabou sign

The Wallilabou Anchorage Hotel, Restaurant and Boutique [VHF: 68, $$$] has a delightful location where you can eat looking out over your yacht, in a "Pirates of the Caribbean" ambience. Owners Steve, who is from St. Vincent, and his wife Jane, from England, are very pleasant and sometimes are in the bar in the evenings. The restaurant is great for seafood. It serves generous portions of well-prepared local food, particularly fish, shrimp, and lobster in season. They have a small museum with some magnificent Carib stone head carvings, plus ancient telephones, whalebones, a room of "Pirates" movie artifacts, and lots of pet tortoises. They will provide a lively little band by special request.

Behind the ruins of the big dock in the north of the bay is the Pirates Retreat. Known affectionately as "the bar with the bras", this is a rough-and-ready establishment. Come here and have a good rum punch hand-made by the owner Anthony (The Shadow) Edwards, aka Captain Jack Spanner. Anthony is probably the most entertaining character in the bay, and he likes music.

Ashore

A little waterfall garden with a perfect swimming hole lies about a mile up the road from Wallilabou. It is a mini park with a bar, changing rooms, and toilets. Gardens with pretty walkways surround the falls and show the old dam ruins at their best. Bring a towel for a beautiful and refreshing swim; you will feel far from the sea, and it is worth going just to see the magnificent old fig tree that has become part of the wall on the far side of the old dam. Entry is $5 EC per person, and while the park officially closes at 1700, the guard will usually let you in later. The walk here, through lush countryside, is delightful. Go to the main road and turn left; look for the falls on your right. Along the road you will pass Morna's Craft Shop. Here, Berthold "Junior" does impressive machinery sculptures and weaves great baskets and bowls. He also sells brightly colored t-shirts and his own guava liqueur made from the guava tree outside.

Wallilabou makes a good base for exploring St. Vincent. The Soufriere volcano, the rainforest, Trinity Falls, and the Vermont Nature Trails are not too far away. The ap-

proach to the volcano from this side passes rather close to the center of the Marijuana Growers Association land. This is not a smart place to venture on your own. Arrange for a guide and stay with them.

Water sports

The diving in this area is excellent. For those who like to go on their own, a fair dive can be made right off the rock arch on the northern side of the bay (the snorkeling is good here also). You will find a pleasant reef at 30-40 feet, with lots of colorful sponges and soft corals inhabited by many reef fish, including angelfish.

For other dives you will need a seaworthy dinghy or local pirogue and guide. Castle Cove is off the headland just north of Troumakar Bay. This dive has a fabulous terrain of steep slopes and cliffs full of crevices, holes, and tunnels. The sponges are brightly colored and plenty of hiding places usually harbor lots of fish. The return trip along the top of the cliff makes for some great views, with schools of brown chromis hovering on the edge. We saw spotted drums, angelfish, and slipper lobsters. Seahorses and frogfish are not uncommon here.

Rock Pile is off Mount Wayne (the second long black sand beach south of Barrouallie). This unusual dive is along a massive pile of rocks about 20-30 feet deep. The outer edge of the rocks is shaped much like the bow of a boat, and the presence of an old anchor here makes one wonder whether there may be a wreck buried among the rocks. Rock Pile is very colorful, with many sponges

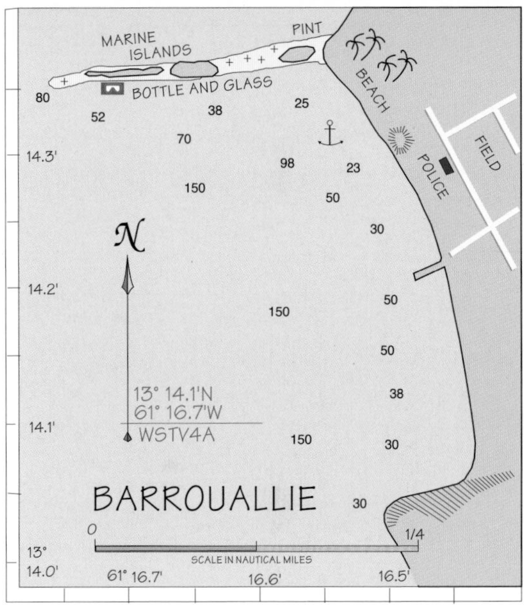

and soft corals. Schools of barracuda are the norm, and lots of moray eels live here. You have a good chance of seeing frogfish.

Peter's Hope is off the old factory south of Barrouallie. This is a colorful shallow reef, from 20 to 60 feet, where you find a lot of king crabs and have a good chance of seeing turtles.

BARROUALLIE

You can easily identify Barrouallie by the conspicuous Bottle and Glass rocks. It is a picturesque local town with a few quaint buildings. People used to stop here to clear customs. That no longer happens, but if you want to experience a laid-back local village, this is it.

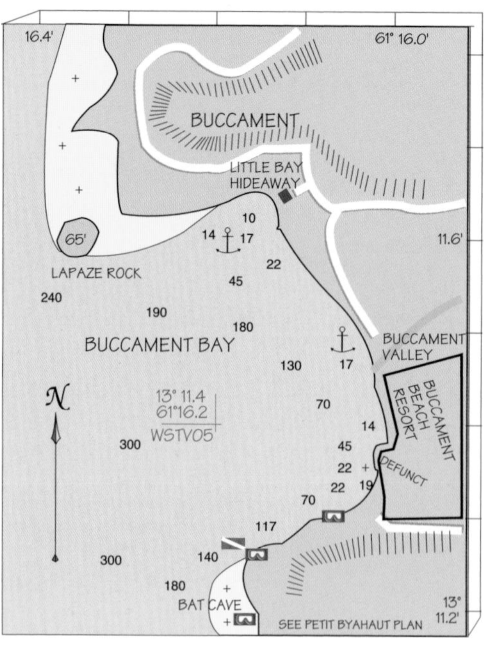

BUCCAMENT BAY

Buccament Bay lies at the base of the Buccament Valley, one of the longest, deepest, and most scenic valleys on the leeward coast. The hills attract showers that often hang there without reaching the coast; in the afternoon, it is not unusual to see an ever-changing rainbow over the valley for up to half an hour at a time.

The bay is well-protected and very calm, though like any west coast anchorage, it is susceptible to exceptionally bad northerly swells. It is well protected from the southerly surge that can affect other south coast anchorages farther east. The easiest place to anchor is close to the beach from the north corner to the river. The water is very deep off the shelf, so make sure you are well hooked.

Navigation

If you are coming from the north give a reasonable clearance to the last visible rock in Bottle and Glass, as there is an underwater rock that extends seaward a few hundred feet. Anchor between the town dock and Pint Rock. There is an adequate anchoring shelf for a quick stop in about 25 feet of water. For overnighting, it is advisable to get one anchor hooked in the shallow water, drop back, and set another in the deeper water, holding the boat bow to the beach. You can tie your dinghy to the town dock. You do not need any line handlers here.

Ashore

Buccament Bay Beach Resort is a high-density waterfront resort. As you sail by it sticks out like a badly fitting toupee: a glowing white beach of imported sand for tourists along a coast of black sand beaches. This does not stop it being a very pleasant place to stop ashore for a day on the beach. The resort went bankrupt and closed in 2016 and has remained so until 2018 when we visited. We are told that it will reopen "soon." It is possible, but not very likely.

Some big yachts use the town dock at Layou to the north to drop off paperwork. It is not tender friendly.

Water sports

The snorkeling from this bay round to Petit Byahaut is exceptionally good, with lots of brightly colored sponges, small healthy corals, many reef fish, octopuses, and more. Tow your dinghy; anchor it here and there in spots you like, and use it to return when you are tired.

PETIT BYAHAUT

This small and beautiful bay has a little beach backed by hills, with several conspicuous peaky outcroppings of rock. It is a perfect hideaway anchorage with excellent snorkeling. Usually a good overnight anchorage, it is occasionally uncomfortable in southerly swells, when a stern anchor will help cut the roll. Be prepared to move for fishermen if they ask.

If you are coming from the north you pass the village of Layou, then Buccament Bay with the big new development. The next major bay is Petit Byahaut. Byahaut Point is a distinctive rounded headland. Pass the headland, head into the bay, and anchor. The seabed is mainly weed, so make sure you are holding. If you are coming from Kingstown, Byahaut Point is the farthest headland you see after you leave Kingstown Bay, after Camden Park, Questelles, and Clare Valley. Ashore, Petit Byahaut looks private; you may see a small green roof poking out of the vegetation.

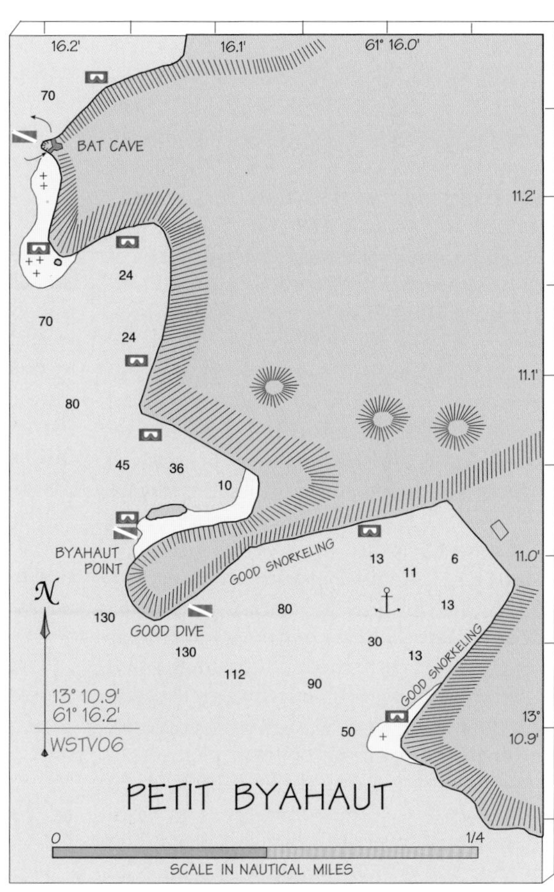

Ashore

Petit Byahaut, approachable only by sea, is a charming, edge-of-the-world spot. It used to be a mini tent hotel, which is now ruins, and the bay is for sale.

Water sports

Snorkeling is super in Petit Byahaut Bay and there is excellent snorkeling and diving easily accessible by dinghy right along the coast to Buccament Bay. However, currents can be strong. The bat cave is a short dinghy ride away and can be done as a dive or a snorkel in calm conditions. There is about three feet of water at the cave entrance. You can find somewhere to anchor your dinghy outside, and there is good snorkeling in the general area. Inside the cave it is quite dark but you can see the bats, which cling by the hundreds to the cave walls and roof. Crabs climb up among the bats. You can just glimpse a tunnel that leads off to the left by the hint of light at the end of it. This tunnel is about 30 feet long and about 4 feet wide. You rise and fall on the swells, and if the swells are large it can be dangerous. The tunnel leads out into a fissure about 30 feet high and 40 feet deep. Below, the water is a brilliant blue. You swim out through the fissure, and divers can dive to two huge rocks at 80 and 130 feet that are covered in sponges and corals and teeming with all kinds of fish. The ascent is up a wall textured with nooks and crannies. If you swim through the bat cave it is most important not to disturb the bats. Two species live here: fishing bats (*Noctilio leporinus*), which eat fish and insects, and the St. Vincent fruit-eating bat (*Brachyphylia cavernarum*), which was thought to be extirpated, and is in any case endangered. So swim quietly through the cave, without talking or splashing, and don't use flashlights or take flash photographs.

Dinosaur Head is the face of Byahaut Point that faces the anchorage. Below is a 120-foot wall covered in coral, sponges, and sea fans. You swim through large schools of tangs and see queen angelfish, eels, snappers, and spotted drums.

OTTLEY HALL

Ottley Hall yachting facility lies just to the west of Kingstown, on the far side of Fort Charlotte.

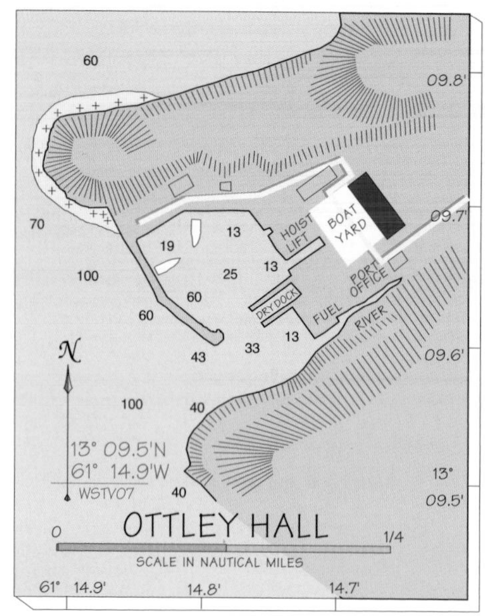

Services

This yard has a 35-ton travel lift, a 200-ton ship lift, and a dry-dock for anything up to 65 meters long, 15 meters wide, and 6 meters deep. Special covered sheds on rails can be rolled over yachts on the hard or in the dry-dock so that re-spraying and repainting can be done out of the rain. There is a fuel dock and long-term storage for smaller yachts. A marina area in front of the work space is passable under many conditions, but when swells come in it can be untenable.

Ashore

Ottley Hall has been taken over by a private company, part Vincentian, part Venezuelan. Check it out for yourself and see if it suits.

KINGSTOWN

Kingstown, St. Vincent's capital, is an interesting local town for those who want to see the authentic, rough edges and all. It has some charming corners with old stone buildings, cobblestone sidewalks, and handsome arches. The older buildings date back to the late 1700s. An unusual feature of the architecture is that many buildings have pillars on the outside of the pavement supporting floors above, leaving a covered walkway underneath. The new market is a fascinating place to shop, despite the building being architecturally challenged with a gloomy interior. (Designed by a foreigner, it seems to me a strong argument for governments to have more faith in their own people.) It has several floors of stalls and small shops, with excellent fresh fruits and vegetables on the ground floor and clothing and handicrafts upstairs.

Attractions in Kingstown include the botanical gardens (you can walk there) and Fort Charlotte for the great views (take a taxi). Check out the lovely old National Trust building, which has a permanent exhibit of Kalinargo pottery.

The new cruise ship facility has a yacht dock at its inner end where superyachts can tie up to clear customs and provision. Facilities for smaller yachts are poor. You can anchor west of the bus station and may find a space to tie up your dinghy at the cruise ship facility. Keep yacht and dinghy guarded. Most yachtspeople currently visit Kingstown by road or ferry. Taxis and buses are readily available from both Young Island Cut and Blue Lagoon, and ferries connect Kingstown with Bequia.

Regulations

Entry here can be long-winded. Customs are in the baggage hall and are normally fast, but immigration, down the road at the police station, often has long lines of passport applicants. The system is not designed for yachts. It is much better to clear in Blue Lagoon. Sam Taxi Service can do it all for you from any anchorage.

Communications

Internet stations are fast, air-conditioned, and inexpensive. Try Computec on Egmont Street.

Chandlery

For yacht chandlery, look at our section on Young Island Cut and Blue Lagoon. Of interest in Kingstown is St. Vincent Sales and Services, a modern shop conveniently placed opposite the ferry dock. They are a NAPA jobber, have excellent buys on filters, and carry a few other retail items.

For more general hardware visit Ace or

Kingstown Harbour, with the cruise ship dock on the right

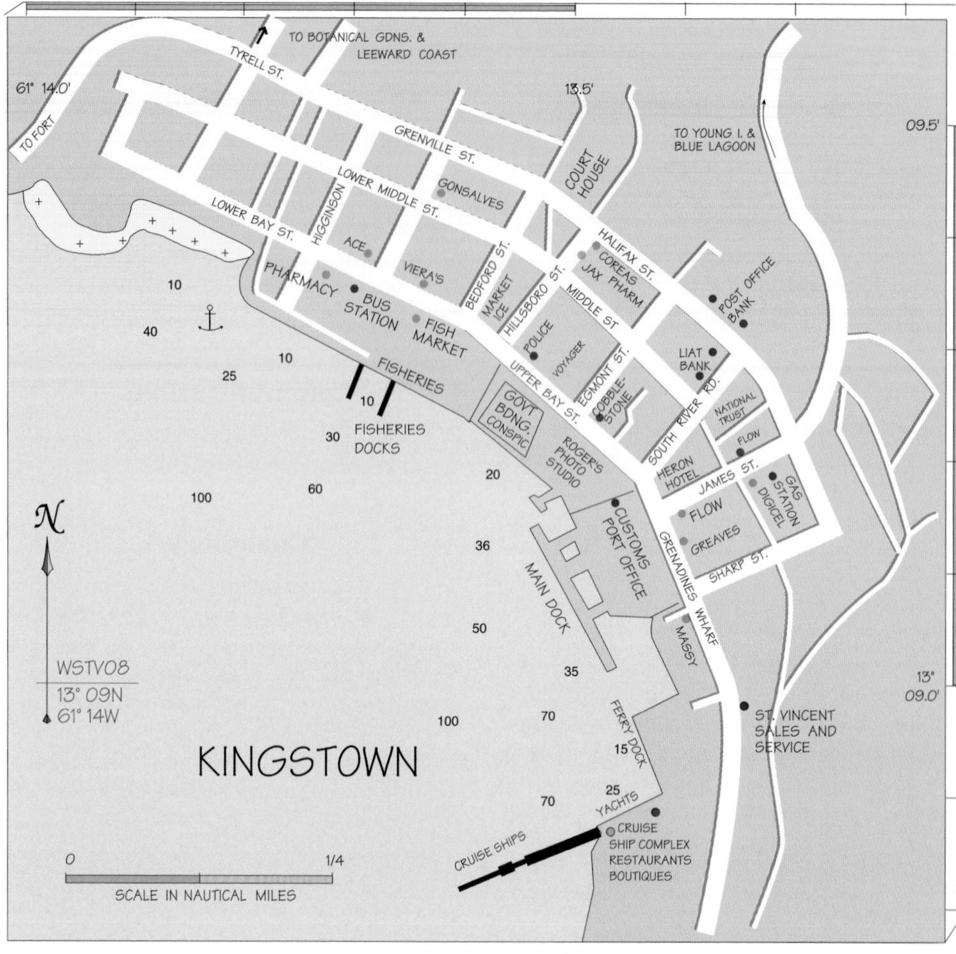

Viera, opposite the bus station. They have good buys on silicone seal, 5200, sandpaper, and tools. Trottman's has a good range of electrical supplies, and you can find several lumber yards, as well as plumbing and hardware stores.

Provisioning

The biggest and best downtown supermarket is C.K. Greaves, which is open 0800-1700 Monday to Thursday, 0800-1900 on Fridays, and 0700-1300 on Saturdays. Its subsidiary by the airport is open till 2000 nightly except Thursdays and Fridays when it opens till 2100, and Sundays when it opens 0800-1100. The Greaves in town gives a charter yacht discount (just tell the cashier), and delivery to Young Island Cut is negotiable (talk to a supervisor). Products include delicatessen meats, smoked fish, French cheeses, whipping cream, and a good selection of wines and liquors. You can contact them in advance for a full provisioning service, and if you need anything they do not have, they will find it for you.

Opposite Greaves is Massy's, another big supermarket with excellent buys on some items.

The local market and surrounding area is overflowing with fresh produce at prices generally much more reasonable than in the other Windward Islands.

Gonsalves is a state-of-the-art wine and liquor shop set in a historic building. They have a climate-controlled wine cellar in a lovely old brick room, it is one of the nicest wine stores of its type in the Windwards. It is a pleasure to visit. They sell wholesale as well as retail and have a huge selection from all over the world. You can contact them in advance for a list of products. They will deliver to the nearest dock, and their staff can give good advice on their wines. They are open Monday to Friday 0800-1700, and Saturday 0800-1300.

Fun shopping

Shopping in Kingstown can be fun ~ the stores are all interesting and local. You sometimes find car batteries rubbing shoulders with fabrics. Department stores include Laynes, and Jax. Middle Street is quaint and like a local clothing market, with stalls down much of one side.

Wander down to the cruise ship complex for boutiques geared to tourists.

Restaurants

Andrew and Jolene's Flow wine bar is a good choice. It opens weekdays at 1100 and Saturdays at 1800. The entrance, which is poorly sign posted, is upstairs over Subway. Walk up a flight of stairs away from the bustle of town into Flow's casually elegant ambience. They offer a good selection of wines as well as Krew beers that they brew themselves, including an American pale ale, an IPA, and an amber ale. For food, they offer many delightful tapas-sized dishes, sandwiches, salads, and pizzas. It is all freshly made and artistically served. Andrew and Jolene also own Bungalow, a restaurant across from Young Island, which is also very good.

You can climb up the stairs to Flyt where a couple of tables are amid the rooftops. Pleasant at night, it has views over Kingstown and the hills around and is popular with smokers.

Basil's, in the Cobblestone Inn [$$], is cool, spacious, and sociable. Here you can get a first-rate lunch buffet, and this is where everyone meets. Or, head round the back and upstairs to the Cobblestone Inn's roof garden, where you can get breakfast or lunch with a good view.

Several small lunch places [$] are on the cruise ship pier area. You can sit outside overlooking the bay and take your choice. Mona's is usually open and good for local food.

Grenadine House [$$$$] is a really nice upmarket restaurant with excellent food. It is in a hotel and part of the same group as

Bequia Beach Hotel in Bequia. Take a short taxi ride there. You can walk back.

THE SOUTH COAST OF ST. VINCENT

Navigation

The current along this coast is predominantly westward, up to two knots. It reverses weakly to the east for a few hours on the rising tide, which can create choppy seas.

When leaving Kingstown for Young Island give the headland good clearance as there is a submerged rock about 200 feet south of its eastern end.

Two good anchorages, Young Island Cut and Blue Lagoon, lie close together. Both are well served by buses to Kingstown and are well placed for exploring St. Vincent. These anchorages are within dinghy reach of each other and we treat them as one area.

Several bareboat companies have bases here, including Barefoot Yacht Charters,

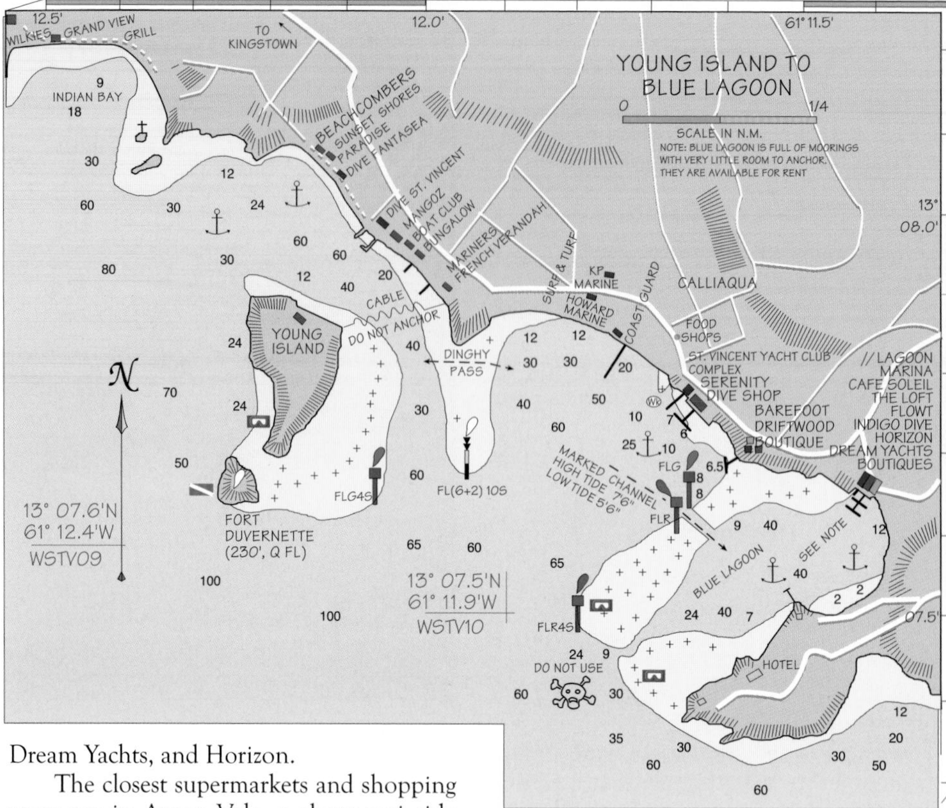

Dream Yachts, and Horizon.

The closest supermarkets and shopping areas are in Arnos Vale, a short taxi ride away. A cooking gas filling station is in the same area.

YOUNG ISLAND CUT & BLUE LAGOON

The coast from Young Island to Blue Lagoon is St. Vincent's main yachting center, with several charter companies and plenty of services. It is a lovely area, with the first-rate Blue Lagoon Marina and Hotel and some places to anchor, as well as a big choice of restaurants and bars. This is a marine park area; the water is clear, with plenty of reefs and good snorkeling. You can climb the historic Fort Duvernette. This is an excellent spot to use as a base to explore St. Vincent and hike the volcano.

Blue Lagoon is a pleasant reef-enclosed bay with a beach backed by palm trees. You can lie comfortably, protected by land and reef. Large beacons mark the main shoals between Blue Lagoon and Young Island (see sketch chart above.) These are in fairly shallow water, so do not cut them too fine.

Two large beacons (red and green) mark the entrance channel. Pass between them. The water is deeper a shade north of the center. After that, head straight across the cut into deep water. Depths in the channel vary with the tide, from about five feet nine inches to about seven-and-a-half feet. Call Blue Lagoon Marina on VHF: 68, or Desmond the dock master (528-2416) for the state of the tide. Kelly Glass, who owns Blue Lagoon Marina, plans to deepen this channel and mark the deeper entrance on the south. Until that happens, do not use the south one, as it is dangerous and has gotten many a yacht in trouble. If you are really in a hurry, or have a draft between 6 and 12 feet, the marina or one of the charter companies can have Ras Mike pilot you in for $20 US.

Once inside, you can tie up at the marina or pick up one of the many moorings, which have a good record for reliability. Fourteen of the most comfortable ones belong to the marina, and the fee of $27 US per night includes free WiFi. About 20 belong to Barefoot Yacht Charters and are $15 US (some are a little rolly). Three belong to Ras Mike who charges $20 US a night, and the price is negotiable for stays of several days. You can try to call him to arrange one: 496-7783, but cell phone number management is not his strong suit. There is very little room to anchor, though you might manage stern to the beach.

Young Island Cut lies in clear water between Young Island and the mainland. Young Island Cut is open and easily entered from the west. The channel to the east of Young Island curves, is narrow, and is best given a miss, even with the beacons.

You have to anchor with care. The current sweeps through both ways and the center of the cut is as deep as 60 feet. There is good holding in the northern or western parts of the anchorage, but it occasionally rolls. Anchoring bow and stern is essential or your boat will swing with the change of current and bang into someone else. Holding is poor close to Young Island. Young Island's electrical cable carries 11,000 volts, enough to make your whole boat glow, so anchor well clear or use a mooring.

Moorings are available in Young Island Cut and are a great help as anchoring is not easy. The present system of unauthorized moorings is managed by Sam Taxi Tours and Charlie Tango, who both feel that if you rent one of their moorings you should also take their taxi. To avoid two boats competing for your business when you arrive, call on the VHF and book a mooring in advance. Mooring rates for boats up to 80 feet are $20 US. Charlie charges the same for bigger boats. Sam charges $28 for larger boats. As with all private moorings, do your best to check them for yourself. Charlie is a diver and does check his.

You can also anchor outside the lagoon off the St. Vincent Yacht Club dock and Barefoot. This tends to be more rolly than tucked well up in the Lagoon.

Regulations

Blue Lagoon Marina has customs open daily from about 0900 to 1800. The office is just to the west of the main building, in the same area as Flowt. Clearance here is simple, fast, and good.

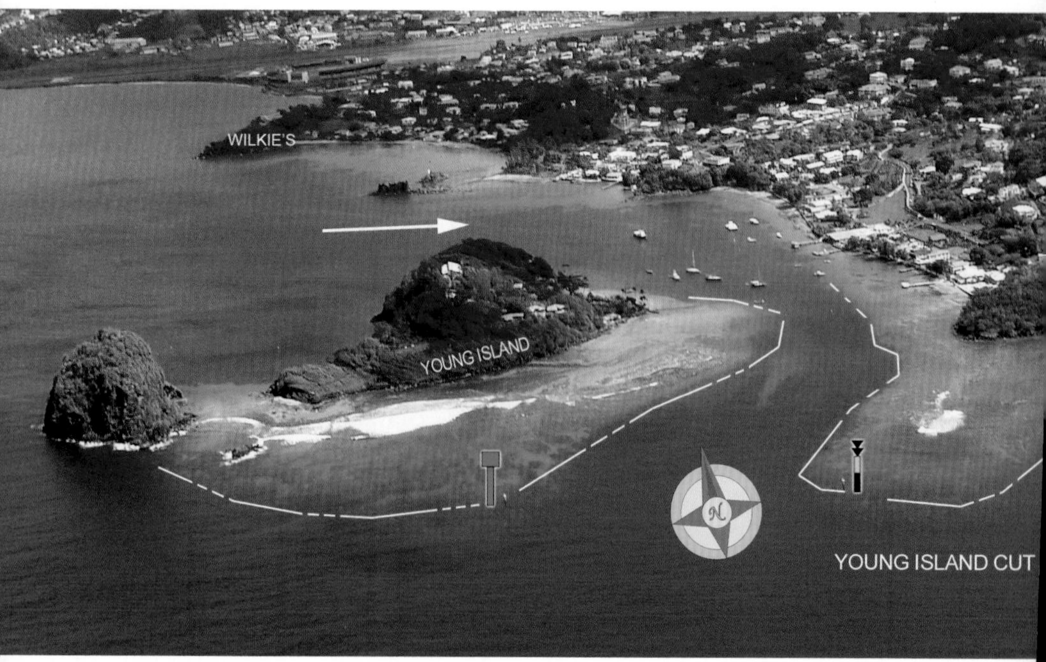

YOUNG ISLAND
COASTGUARD
TMM
SVG YACHT CLUB
BAREFOOT
DRIFTWOOD
LAGOON
MARINA
BLUE LAGOON

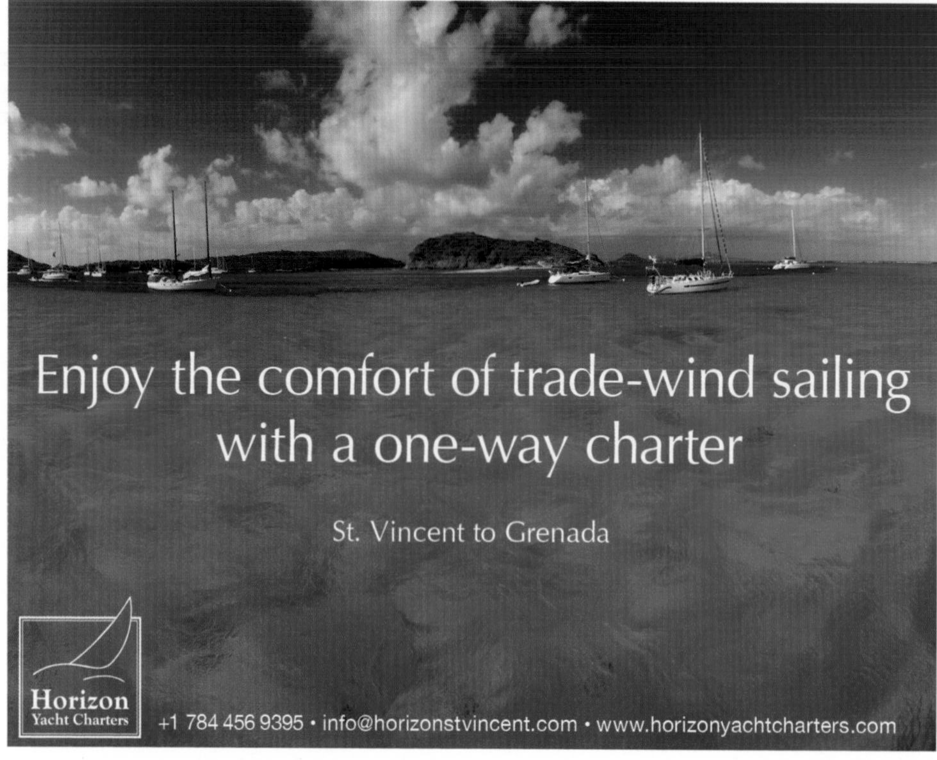

Communications

Blue Lagoon Marina has good WiFi, as does nearly every bar and restaurant. Sam Taxi Tours has a WiFi system that works in Young Island Cut. Beachcombers has an internet computer available during normal business hours.

General yacht services

The Blue Lagoon Marina and Hotel [VHF: 68] is a pleasant marina with wide floating docks. Electricity (110/220-volt, 50 cycles) can be arranged at the dock. If you prefer, you can take one of their orange moorings ($27 US per night). Top up on water, fuel (both diesel and gasoline), and ice. Other services include showers, a laundry ($82 EC for a big machine load), and free WiFi. They can take yachts up to 80 feet. Desmond the dock master (VHF: 16, 532-8347) will help you in, and the main desk will find you anything you need, like taxis and rental cars. Kelly and Janke Glass, who own the marina, have done a wonderful job of converting a very basic boatel into a lovely and elegant little boutique hotel and marina, which is a real pleasure to visit.

A wide board-walk carries you round the marina and to the beach. The cafe, beach bar, and a restaurant are all delightful. Should you want a night ashore, they have lovely rooms with balconies looking out over the lagoon. Several charter companies including Horizon and Dream Yachts use this as a base. It is home to Indigo Dive shop.

Phillip Barnard, his mother Mary, and Mark run Barefoot Charters and Marine Center [VHF: 68]. They are the only charter company here that has an ASA-accredited sailing school. Their dock is on the outside of the reef, with about 6.5 feet at the end at low tide. They have a few moorings outside and 20 moorings inside. They offer diesel, laundry, water, ice, full communications, a travel agency, and air charter service (SVG Air). Their moorings are reliable and cost $15 US a night. Barefoot has five lovely balconied rooms with views available for nights ashore, and their center includes a restaurant, sail loft, and other services. They can often fill cooking gas bottles.

The St. Vincent Yacht Club is a yacht dock outside the reef. Reg and Reggie Adams built a basic docking facility along the foreshore to the east of Barefoot. At the time of this writing it was severely damaged and not operational, but the restaurant is open. They have seven rooms for a night ashore, each with a big balcony overlooking the bay.

Sam, of Sam Taxi Tours [VHF: 68], is one of those who rents moorings in Young Island Cut. Sam is an agent for large yachts and even cruise ships. With agents in Mustique, Bequia, Canouan, and Union, Sam can handle big yacht needs right through the islands. His customs clearance is very popular and he can arrange it anywhere, even the Tobago Cays, through his agent in Union. Sam charges $80 US for yachts up 80 feet, and up to $400 US for really large yachts with many people. (Extra transportation charges are applicable in some anchorages.)

His crew does laundry and fills gas bottles. Sam Taxi Service handles communications (including email), and many skippers get their spares sent here, which Sam will clear through customs. Sam Taxi Tours also rents cars and has a fleet of taxis for scenic or shopping trips, and he arranges duty-free fuel bunkering for larger yachts. He will collect and dispose of well-wrapped garbage in Young Island ($5 EC a bag.)

Charlie Tango [VHF: 68] is the other moorings man; Charlie runs a full taxi and tour service, has apartments for rent, does laundry, and will help in any way he can. He is also a diver and works on his own moorings.

Erika's Marine Services is another superyacht agency based in Union Island. They, too, have agents in St. Vincent, Bequia, Mustique, and Canouan. (See *Union Island* for a full description.)

Chandlery

Barefoot Charters and Marine Center keep a good stock of spares for their boats and will help cruisers if they need a part, or can order parts from the catalogs. They work with Budget Marine and Lewis Marine and will bring in anything at catalog price plus freight; they are good and efficient, and can often get parts not in the catalogs.

KP Marine, in Calliaqua, owned by Keith Howard, is the sales and service agent for Yamaha outboards, which in St. Vincent are duty-free. His prices are among the best. Between KP and Howard Marine (same owner) across the street, you can buy Yamaha and Johnson outboards and Yanmar inboards. KP Marine also stocks general chandlery, with chain, anchors, rope, antifouling paint, resins, West system epoxy, some electronics, and more. Two-stroke outboard oils are available wholesale for those with large engines. They sell to both local fishermen and powerboat enthusiasts.

Technical yacht services

Barefoot Charters and Marine Center is your best bet for sorting out any boat problems; they have an excellent services center. This includes a large new sail loft managed by Phillip Barnard, a top racing sailor who knows about racing sails as well as cruising ones. They sell and service both Doyle and North Sails and will take care of the measurement and fitting. They repair sails, do cushions and canvas, and can make bimini frames. They weld Weblon and True Tarp, so you can get a stitch-free top that does not leak. They can do small onboard weld repairs. They are agents for Harken and can help out with rigging.

Barefoot repairs and maintains all kinds of diesel engines; they run diesel engine repair courses, and can help you with your engine. They do good gel-coat matching and cosmetic repairs. In addition, they sell Raymarine and can help with installation. You can also talk to them if you have an electronics problem.

Horizon Yachts is a charter company that has found that the team that keeps their boats running can also help maintain and fix yours. They offer help with all repairs and maintenance, and if you wish to leave your boat in their care or have a full refit, you can

Parrot at Young Island

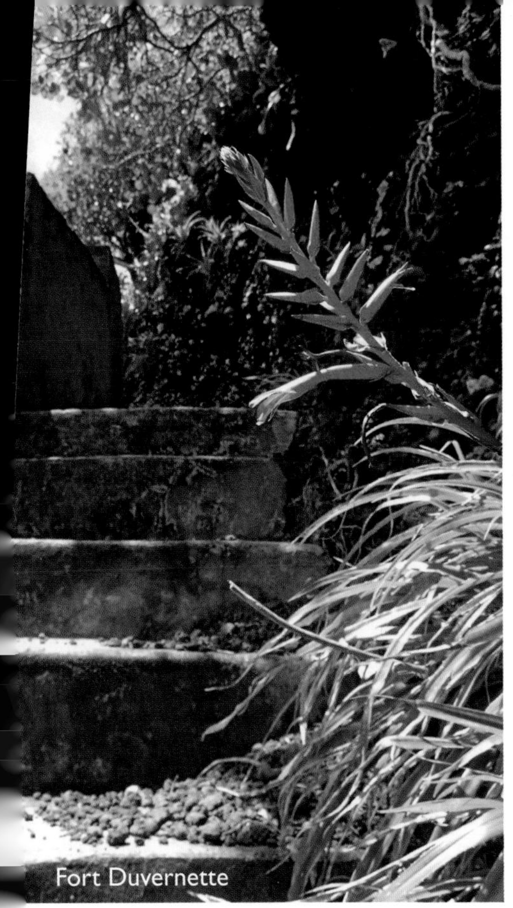
Fort Duvernette

arrange it here, though they will want to do most work in Grenada.

Howard Marine [VHF: 68] fixes all makes of outboard and they are agents for Johnson. They are happy to fix all diesels, and are agents for Yanmar.

Verrol, at Nichols Marine, has an efficient mechanized workshop where he repairs and reconditions alternators and starter motors in a few hours. They come back looking and working like new. Call him on the telephone and he will come and sort out your problem, wherever you are in St. Vincent (in Bequia, call and ask where to leave your broken items.) Verrol's workshop is in Belaire, just behind the airport, which is closer to the south coast than to town. Oscar's Machine Center is a few houses down from Verrol. Oscar is good and can do all manner of jobs on all kinds of metals, resurface engine blocks, or fix your old winches.

Provisioning

The Lagoon Marketplace in Blue Lagoon Marina is a food store, open every day from 0730-2230. It is convenient for picking up heavy items like bottled water as you can bring your dinghy very close. They have a good selection of liquor, some frozen foods, and a few cleaning and boat maintenance products.

You can sometimes buy fish from the fish market in Calliaqua in the afternoon when the boats come in ~ try around 1600.

About half way to Kingstown the road makes a giant U as it skirts Arnos Vale, St. Vincent's original airport (now defunct). Many shops lie along this road. Sunrise Supermarket, opposite the original airport's terminal, is one of the biggest and best markets, and is part of C.K. Greaves.

From Greaves, Massy's supermarket is on the left heading toward Calliaqua. Nearby is a large Ace hardware store.

Trottman's has a branch of their electrical store a little farther down on the left side of the road.

Where the road hangs a sharp left you will find several more supermarkets. Delco has not only food but quite a selection of hardware. Another new supermarket lies just round the corner.

It is easy and cheap, though occasionally terrifying, to catch a bus to this area or to town. Bus drivers usually have music at full blast and handle their vehicles like racing cars. There are plenty of buses, but in the mornings quite a few are full.

Fun Shopping

Caribbean Lifestyles in Blue Lagoon Marina sells nice jewelry, hand bags, and beach wear.

Restaurants

There are many restaurants. Some are on a boardwalk that runs from The French Verandah to the beach. Along the beach are more, and others are in Blue Lagoon Marina and Barefoot Yachts.

Some of the most pleasant restaurants here are up a few steps, on broad verandas overlooking the sea. One of them is Barefoot's Driftwood Restaurant and Lounge [VHF: 68, $$$]. It is comfortable, with a touch of elegance and a great open view south to Bequia. They have nightly specials and a big

Young Island and Fort Duvernette

choice of good food, including fresh seafood, burgers, ribs, pastas, pizzas, and salads, and brunch on Sundays. It is sometimes packed in the evening, so make a reservation to be sure of a table. If you blow it, you can always eat at the bar.

The Loft [$$$$$], upstairs in Lagoon Marina, has a sweeping panoramic view of the marina, the bay, and the beach. The bar is a great hangout and the restaurant is open from breakfast through dinner. The service is attentive and friendly. It is a tad more upmarket than the other marina restaurants. You will enjoy the food, which is elaborate and artistically served, with well thought out combinations of flavors using fresh local ingredients.

Downstairs, the popular Cafe Soleil [$$$] adds a touch of continental elegance with its outside shaded seating on two sides of the marina boardwalk. Open to the bay and beach, it is a perfect setting, as long as it is not raining (they have a few seats inside in case it is.) It is a great place to start the day with breakfast, and it stays open all day, with a variety of tasty food. This includes starters and snacks, fresh salads, soups and sandwiches, seafood and meat dishes, and ice creams and desserts.

Also in Blue Lagoon, Flowt Beach Bar [$] is an ideal cruiser's bar; a shack on the beach with seats on a deck. They open at 1400 and keep going till the last person leaves. You can get inexpensive local grilled fish, burgers, and chicken, along with chips or vegetables. The food is simple but beautifully cooked, making it a prime choice when you cannot be bothered to cook for yourself. If you see a sailing yacht enter the lagoon (under sail or power), call it out to the barman and you will get your next drink half-price.

Back in Young Island Cut is Beachcombers [VHF: 68, $$$], at the western end of the beach. You can leave your dinghy at one of the docks in Young Island Cut and walk down the boardwalk to the beach. Depending on the tide, you may need to time waves or risk getting your feet wet. Steps lead up from the beach to their large wooden sunning/pool deck with the adjoining restaurant open to the view. It is airy and pleasant, with a view of the sea framed by almond trees. Delightful flower gardens are out back. Seafood, local specialties, snacks, burgers, and more are available. They are open all day every day. Beachcombers has rooms for rent and a popular spa.

The Mariners Hotel and its French Verandah restaurant [$$$$] is owned and run by Vidal Browne, who also has a big share in Young Island Hotel and has been in the hospitality industry for years. They have their own dinghy dock, although it is in need of repair. They serve fine French food and, on the lighter side, milk shakes and ice cream.

Next door, Bungalow [$$, closed Tuesday] is another lovely waterfront restaurant and has a good dinghy dock. Owned by the same people as Flow in Kingstown and Flowt at Blue Lagoon, Bungalow's crisp, modern atmosphere is refreshing. Friendly service and a reasonably priced menu make it more than worthwhile for dinner. The menu includes pizzas, pastas, and burgers, with Krew beers on tap. They open from 1600 until 2300 during the week, and from 1200 on weekends. The dock has power and water and space for a single boat, but this must be arranged at least a day in advance. Desiree, the manager, will put you in touch with the right people.

A little farther down is Mangoz, open for lunch and dinner. The open-air dining room is chic and relaxing, with a great view of Young Island. They serve a bit of everything, including sushi, pizza, and Mexican dishes. In season they have a live lobster tank, and put together a Sunday buffet every week that starts at 1100. When we visited in 2018 they were building a dock, which should be well finished by the time this book is published.

On the beach, Paradise Beach Hotel [$$$] is run by Earl and Kim Halbich, who also own the Fantasea tour operation. It is large and open, serving good local food, and is a very pleasant place to eat. They have a popular captain's barbecue on Fridays from 1900. They have rooms for a night or two ashore.

Sunset Shores is a slightly formal hotel with a pool, just behind the beach. The cooking is international.

Boat Club [$$] is an informal local hangout and disco. They open daily from about 0800 till late at night and serve local food. Their pool table is often in use.

Across the water, with a good dinghy dock, Young Island Resort [VHF: 68, $$$$] is a wonderful place of tropical flowers and trees, and well worth a visit for a sundowner. They have a steel band and other entertainment on a weekly basis (call for details). If you wish to dine at Young Island Resort, make reservations in advance.

Sue's Surfside Restaurant [$$] is in Calliaqua. She runs a good restaurant that serves pizzas and snacks, along with grilled fish and chicken.

The Yacht Club have their own (Mrs. Seappy's) bar and restaurant, good for beers and local snacks.

If you look west from Young island Cut you will see a large building at the end of the beach, to the west of Young Island Cut, in Indian Bay. This is the Grand View Beach Hotel, opened in 1964 and owned by the Sardine family.

Old-style and gracious, Wilkie's Restaurant ($$$$) is in the hotel, and a few steps outside is one of St. Vincent's most panoramic views from atop a cactus knoll. On the beach, their Grand View Grill ($$) is more casual and opens mid-afternoon through dinner.

Ashore

Fort Duvernette stands behind Young Island, a monument to the ingenuity of the soldiers of a bygone age who managed to get cannons up to the top. Fort Duvernette was used in the late 18th century, when the settlers were fighting off the Black Caribs inland and the French at sea. Cannons face in both directions. There is a small place to tie a dinghy. About 250 concrete steps take you up. After being abandoned for some years, these were rebuilt in 2011 with the help of a grant from Finland to the National Trust. The views from the top are splendid, and if you take lunch up you can enjoy it at a shaded table.

Blue Lagoon and Young Island are ideally situated to visit St. Vincent's interior. Make every effort to spend a few hours at Montreal Gardens in the Mesopotamia Valley. The drive through this rich agricultural valley is reward enough in itself, with spectacular views in every direction. Montreal Gardens, tucked in right at the head of the valley against the steep mountains, is the most spectacular garden in the Eastern Caribbean. Owner Tim Vaughn and his team have taken seven acres and created a totally crazy and beautiful space. Their art has been planning and planting and then letting nature run riot with the plants, so rather than being well ordered and neat, it is wild and jungly and brilliantly colorful. There are winding paths, bridges, steps, and a river, all among brilliant tropical flowers. The only sounds are running water and bird song. You feel like you are in a fantasy world. He charges a very nominal fee for entry. You can see the gardens in an hour, but it is much better to spend several and really soak up the atmosphere. Bring lunch and enjoy it in one of the garden shelters. (Montreal Gardens is open December to August, Monday to Friday, 0900-1600 only.) You can sometimes get Tim on his cell: 432-6840. The taxi fare is high enough that you might want to have four to share. You can also take buses. First, take one to the roundabout at Arnos Vale at the top of what used to be the airport. Take the next bus to Richland Park Junction. Get the driver to show you the road; it is a two-mile walk from there. You can ask if he would take you there for an extra fee. (If you start in Kingstown, just get the bus to Richland Park Junction.)

Another world-class hike that is easy to do from here is the St. Vincent volcano. It takes a whole day, but it is a day you will remember.

Transport

Blue Lagoon is a good place to leave your boat while you explore ashore. The marina can arrange a car rental or call you one of their taxi drivers: Ivan Oliver (529-1222) or Harold (493-3779).

If you are in Young Island, Sam Taxi Tours and Charlie Tango are the main taxi drivers.

Water sports

Diving in St. Vincent is really wonderful. The rugged shoreline is equally dramatic below the surface. Walls and reefs that drop far deeper than any sane person can dive are common, and fish are everywhere ~ feeding in schools, tucked under rocks, and hiding in sponges. The long coastline and the presence of only a few divers has kept this environment pristine.

Right in the Marina is Indigo Dive, run by Jo and Leyla Chapalay, from the French side of Switzerland. They are pleasant, enthusiastic, and informal, running the technical

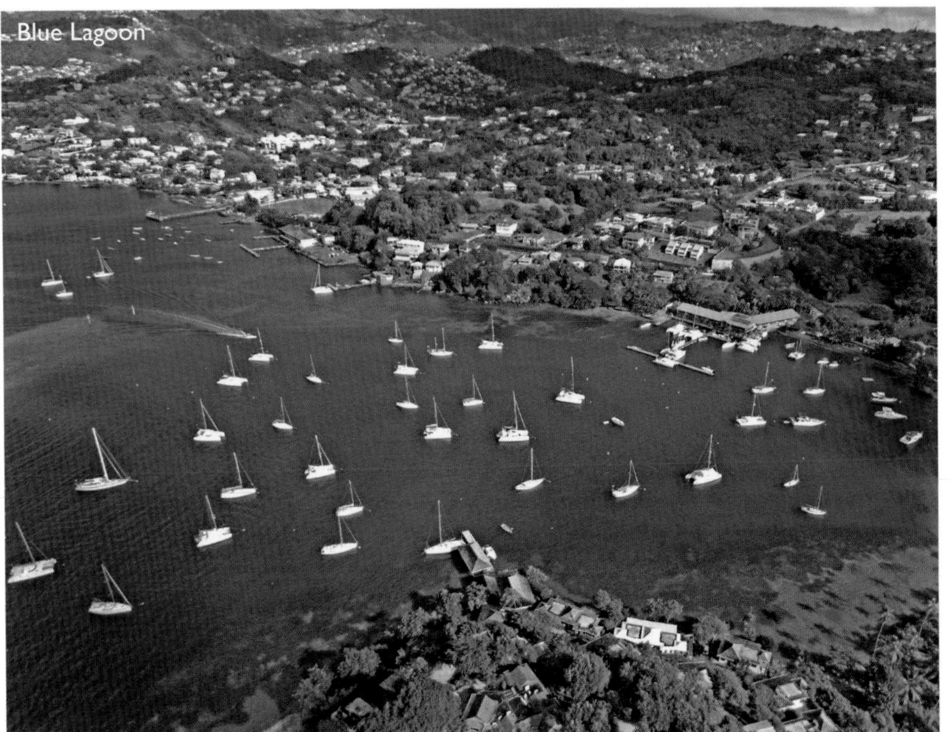

side like the Swiss and then relaxing like the French. This is a PADI 5-star shop, and they offer SSI and TDI tech diving. They normally go out in the morning and afternoon, and they teach all the usual courses in English, French, and German. They are happy to pick up divers from their yachts in most St. Vincent anchorages. They have a big boat with shade and private dives can be arranged. The shop has a small retail space where they sell snorkel gear.

You will also enjoy diving or snorkeling with Vaughn Martin at Serenity Dive. He used to run the Canouan dive shop and has now opened his own. You will find him helpful, friendly, and enthusiastic. They are avid lionfish hunters and do a fish fry on the last Friday of every month at the Yacht Club restaurant beside the shop.

Dive St. Vincent [VHF: 68], facing the main Young Island dock, is owned by PADI/NAUI instructor Bill Tewes and run by Jackie, DJ, and Cally. They usually head out for a one- or two-tank dive around 0900 in the morning. They rent both diving and snorkeling gear to yachts heading out on charter.

Barefoot Yachts has a snorkeling shop where you can rent snorkeling gear when going on charter.

Fantasea Tours has four excellent boats for tours and a water taxi service, and is run by Earl and Kim Halbich. They do coastal and whale-watching trips and often take charter guests to and from their boats in other islands. They are based in Young Island Cut, at the Paradise Beach Hotel, where Fantasea also has a cute boutique.

Those diving on their own will find the base of Fort Duvernette easily accessible, though you do have to be mindful of the current that tries to sweep you out to sea. Anchor your dinghy to the west of the Fort Duvernette dinghy dock. Follow the base of Fort Duvernette down. Almost as soon as you begin you will be surrounded by large schools of brown chromis. At 40 feet you find yourself in a pleasant area of house-sized boulders, with nooks and crannies where eels, shrimps, and angelfish hide out. Large schools of sergeant majors hug the rocks while jacks, mackerels, and schools of margates patrol a little farther out.

Other, even better dives are best done with a local dive shop as the anchorages are dangerous for yachts, and local knowledge about the currents is essential. Bottle Reef, under Fort Charlotte, starts at 25 feet. You descend along the foot of an underwater rock headland. On your right is a gentle slope of coral, decorated by sponges and many smaller soft corals. On the left, the headland turns into a sheer wall adorned by deep-water sea fans. There are small bushes of black coral in several colors. At the bottom we found several cherub fish. These little critters, the smallest of the angelfish, are only a couple of inches long. You round the bottom of the headland at 100 feet and ascend through huge schools of grunts and even larger schools of brown chromis that seem to explode into a variety of patterns all around. There is always a chance of finding ancient bottles. A curious current pattern here makes it possible to have the current with you the whole way.

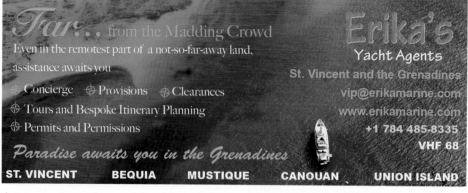

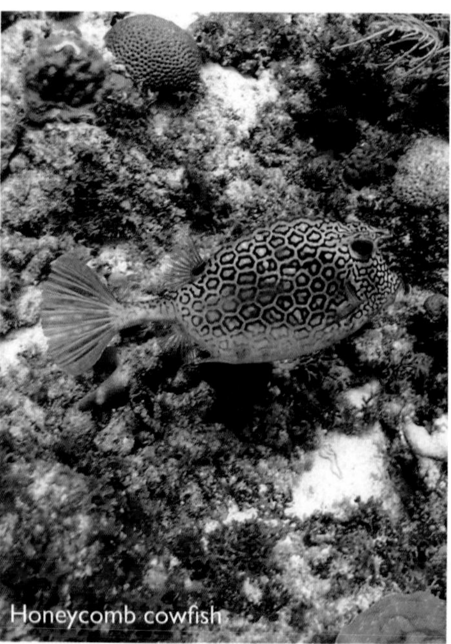
Honeycomb cowfish

Kingstown South is on the south side of Kingstown Harbor. You can see by looking at the sheer cliffs above and the schooling chromis below that this will be an interesting dive. The descent is down a steep slope, and this is the place to look for the unusual red-banded lobster. This colorful little crustacean is clearly marked in bands and spots of red, white, and gold. Unlike other Caribbean lobsters it has claws, though they are tiny. We saw one as we finished our descent and three more later, as well as a slipper lobster and the more common spiny lobster. We circled slowly counter-clockwise up the slope, looking at sponges, corals, and big rocks. You often see large pelagic fish swimming out toward the sea. Among the many reef fish you will meet are spotted drums and filefish. There are also three wreck dives in the harbor. One is an ancient French sailing frigate. There is not much left but you might get lucky and find a bottle.

There is a good advanced wreck dive in Camden Park. The Romark, a 160-foot freighter, sits upright on the bottom in excellent condition. It is deep (mast at 55 feet, bottom at 135 feet).

New Guinea Reef is on the east side of Petit Byahaut. This spectacular dive takes you down a wall to 90 feet, where large black corals occur in bushes of white, pink, dark green, light green, brown, and red. Fish include black jacks, parrotfish, French angelfish, and occasional sightings of the rather rare frilled goby, frogfish, and seahorses. An overhang near the bottom makes this dive visually spectacular.

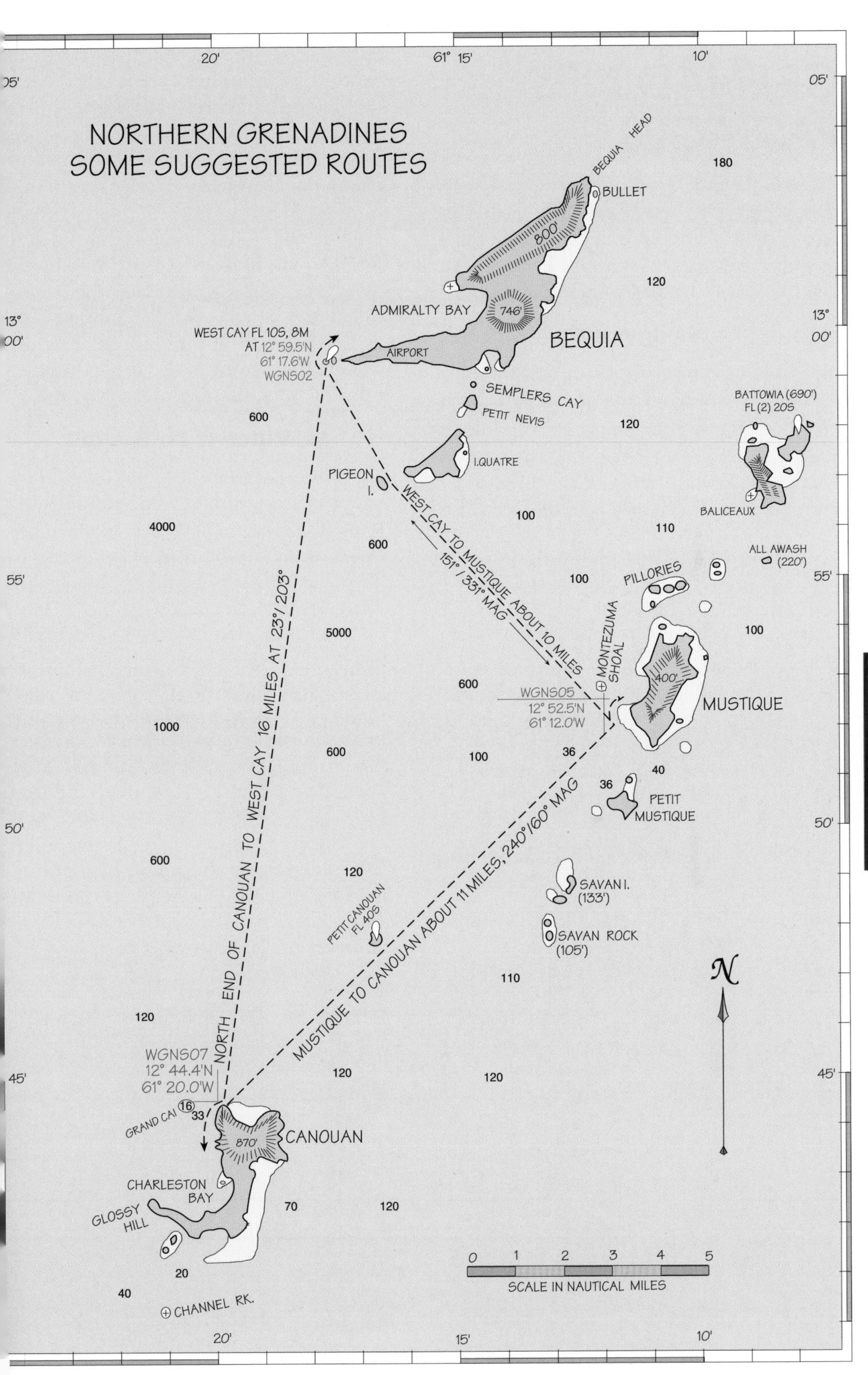

St. Vincent & the Grenadines

NORTHERN GRENADINES PASSAGES

Bequia and Mustique, in the northern Grenadines, are both frequently visited by yachtspeople. Although only about eight miles apart (geographically) at their closest points, they are very different from each other.

Navigation

A strong current sets to the west throughout the Grenadines. Its effect is particularly noticeable in the Bequia and Canouan channels, so whether you head north or south it is advisable to point east of your destination and check your bearings periodically to see how much you are being set. There is least set when the tidal stream runs counter to the regular current, but this is a mixed blessing, since the seas become rougher and sometimes positively uncomfortable. The roughest seas are to be found just north of Canouan and off the Bequia side of the Bequia Channel, especially up by Bequia Head. It is not unusual for the current to be going in two different directions on opposite sides of the channel.

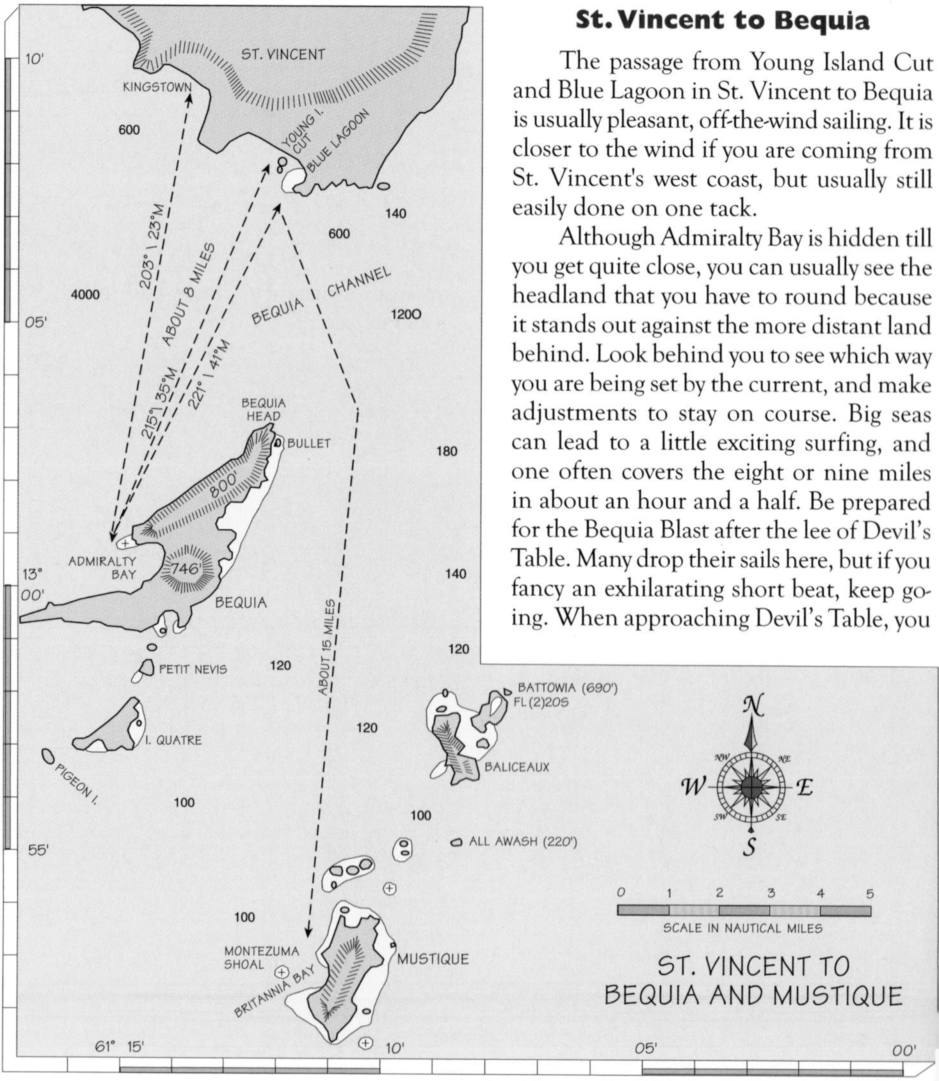

St. Vincent to Bequia

The passage from Young Island Cut and Blue Lagoon in St. Vincent to Bequia is usually pleasant, off-the-wind sailing. It is closer to the wind if you are coming from St. Vincent's west coast, but usually still easily done on one tack.

Although Admiralty Bay is hidden till you get quite close, you can usually see the headland that you have to round because it stands out against the more distant land behind. Look behind you to see which way you are being set by the current, and make adjustments to stay on course. Big seas can lead to a little exciting surfing, and one often covers the eight or nine miles in about an hour and a half. Be prepared for the Bequia Blast after the lee of Devil's Table. Many drop their sails here, but if you fancy an exhilarating short beat, keep going. When approaching Devil's Table, you

ST. VINCENT TO BEQUIA AND MUSTIQUE

might notice what appears to be a madman zooming around your yacht, standing up in a tiny inflatable and being badly bounced by the waves. Fear not ~ it is just Kenmore Henville, who makes his living taking photographs of arriving yachts. If he takes your yacht's picture he will bring a proof for you to see. There is no obligation to buy. If you want to be sure of a picture, call him in advance.

Sailing the other way is a different matter. To make Young Island or Blue Lagoon from Admiralty Bay you normally have to tack against a foul current. It usually takes two hours, and can take three or more. It is generally quicker to tack or motor sail up the Bequia coast and then shoot across from Anse Chemin, the bay just southwest of Bequia Head. This is fine in calm weather, but on rough days you can sail straight into a range of liquid mountains near Bequia Head. If the seas are rough, head straight over to St. Vincent and then work back up the coast.

Sailing to the west coast of St. Vincent is usually a fine reach.

St. Vincent to Mustique

The trip between Blue Lagoon and Mustique is about 15 miles, and in good conditions it takes two-and-a-half to three hours. The seas around the north end of Bequia can be rough, but one often gets an exhilarating reach. Whether you are sailing north or south, keep well off Bequia Head and the Bullet, as the current pulls you down that way. Otherwise, just strap everything down, hang on tight, and ride 'em!

Bequia to Mustique

Most people approach Mustique from Admiralty Bay. The easiest way is to round West Cay and sail out between Pigeon Island and Isle de Quatre. As you approach Mustique, Montezuma Shoal is a real danger, more so now since the big beacon washed away and has been replaced by a buoy. Keep well clear.

There are passages between Semplers Cay and Petit Nevis, and between Petit Nevis and Isle de Quatre, but they can be rough and the current extremely strong. Furthermore, a reef extends well south of Petit Nevis, so serious thought should be given to prevailing conditions before choosing either of these routes. It is an easy seven-mile reach from Friendship Bay to Mustique or back.

Bequia to Canouan

As you round West Cay (Bequia) and head south it will be possible to see Petit Canouan. If the visibility is good, Canouan itself will be in sight. Glossy (Glass) Hill, the southwestern point of Canouan, is joined to the rest of the land by a low isthmus that stays below the horizon till you get quite close, so from a distance Glossy Hill looks like a separate island.

Mustique to Canouan

This trip can be a rolly run, with the wind right behind. I often tack downwind to make it a reach.

Canouan

Deep draft vessels (over 12 feet) should avoid Grand Cai, a small, isolated 16-foot shoal about 0.75 miles west of Jupiter Point at 12° 44.490'N, 61° 20.645'W. Seas in this area are often 6-8 feet high.

Approaching Bequia from St. Vincent

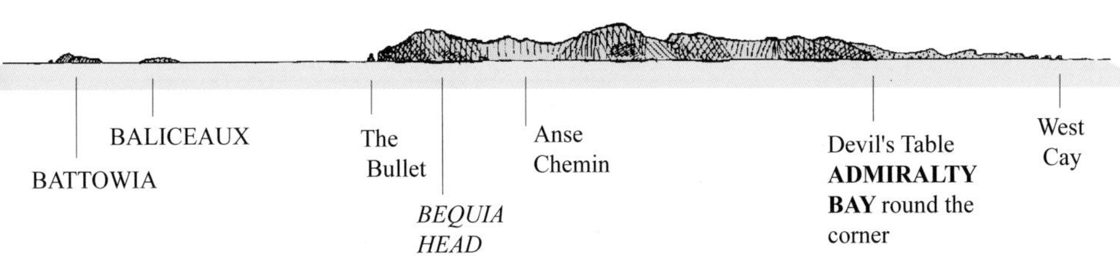

Bequia at a glance

Regulations

Port Elizabeth is a port of entry for St. Vincent and the Grenadines. The procedure is simple.

The entry charge is $35 EC per person per month, unless you leave within that month, in which case you pay again when you re-enter. In addition, charter yachts based outside St. Vincent are charged $5 EC per foot per month. You can cruise here as long as you wish. You will normally be stamped in for a month, and then return for extensions, which are in the same office and easy to obtain. Forms may cost a few dollars.

There is an occasional license fee that applies to any boat that doesn't have the owner on board (this includes bareboat charter yachts). It is $60 EC for boats less than 30 feet, $125 EC for boats less than 50 feet, and $140 EC for boats 51 feet and over.

Customs is open weekdays 0830-1800 (overtime after 1600). On Saturdays, they open 0830-1200 and (overtime) 1500-1800. Sundays and holidays, they open (overtime) 0900-1200 and 1500-1800. They close for lunch between 1200 and 1300.

Overtime fees apply on Sundays and holidays, and they are an additional: $63 EC (customs) and $50 EC (immigration).

Jet skis and the like are strictly forbidden throughout the Grenadines, as is spearfishing by visitors (see also *St. Vincent*).

Garbage must be taken to the facility by the market, or you can pay Daffodil to take it. Do not give it to other vendors.

Shopping Hours

Office and bank hours are as for St.Vincent. Most stores open 0800-1200 and 1400-1700.

Telephones

Card and coin phones may be found near the tourist office. You can buy cell phone cards in many stores. See also *St. Vincent*.

Holidays

See *St. Vincent*.

Transport

Inexpensive buses run to many parts of the island. Ask in the tourist office on the quay. Taxis are plentiful and reasonable. Only use those approved by the SVG Tourism Association, and these will have a badge. Sample taxi rates for up to four people are:

	$EC
Most rides	25
Longer rides	35-55
Airport	50
Tours	95 per hour

(for 5+ $8 US per person per hour)

Rental jeeps and motorbikes are available. You need to buy a local license, which costs $65 EC. Drive on the left.

Admiralty Bay coastline

Nail-biting action aboard Zemi, Bequia Regatta

Bequia

Bequia has long been a favorite of yachtspeople. Isolated enough to remain relatively unspoiled, yet lively enough to be stimulating and entertaining, it provides a blend of the old and new that many find perfect. It is well connected with St. Vincent and the other Grenadines, both by a small airport and by the cheaper and more traditional ferries. Some yachtspeople leave their boats anchored in Bequia and take a ferry to visit St. Vincent.

Bequia is an island of sailors and boats, linked to the outside world mainly by the sea, and the old traditions continue. Boats are built on the beach in the shade of palm trees, though these days the building methods are a lot more high tech and the traditional fishing boats have morphed into sports boats capable of speeds well over 10 knots. Bequians travel all over the world on cargo vessels, quite a few have ended up owning their own, and some are intrepid fishermen who venture all over the Grenadines in little open boats.

The island has an active whaling station in a low-key and traditional way. By International Whaling Commission agreement local whalers can take four whales a year, but in some years they do not get any. The whaling season is from February to April. At this time of year humpback whales leave their northern feeding grounds and head south to mate and bear young. Few people are left in Bequia with the skills necessary to hunt them ~ a daring feat in an open sailing boat, using hand-thrown harpoons. On the rare occasions that they make a kill, the hunters tow the whale to Semplers Cay for butchering.

Much of Bequia's tourist industry is based on visiting yachts, so you will find good yacht services, restaurants, shops, and handicrafts, many made only here. Best of all, Bequians understand yachting.

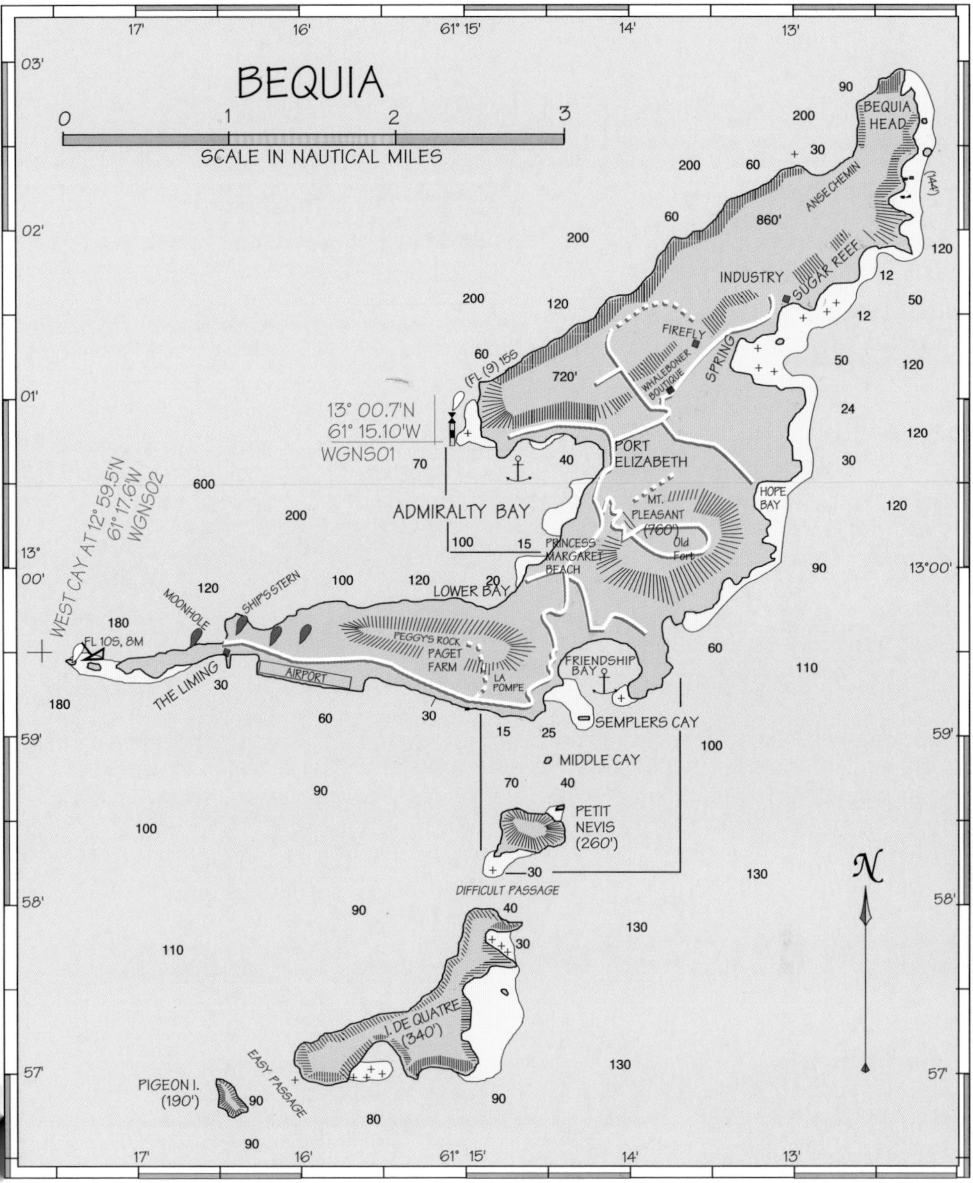

Bequians are a proud people, descendants of settlers who came from North America on whaling boats from farms in Scotland, from France as freebooters, and as slaves from Africa.

Bequia's main harbor is Admiralty Bay. Friendship Bay is a harbor on the south coast, and there is a daytime anchorage at Petit Nevis.

Morphing into sports boats...

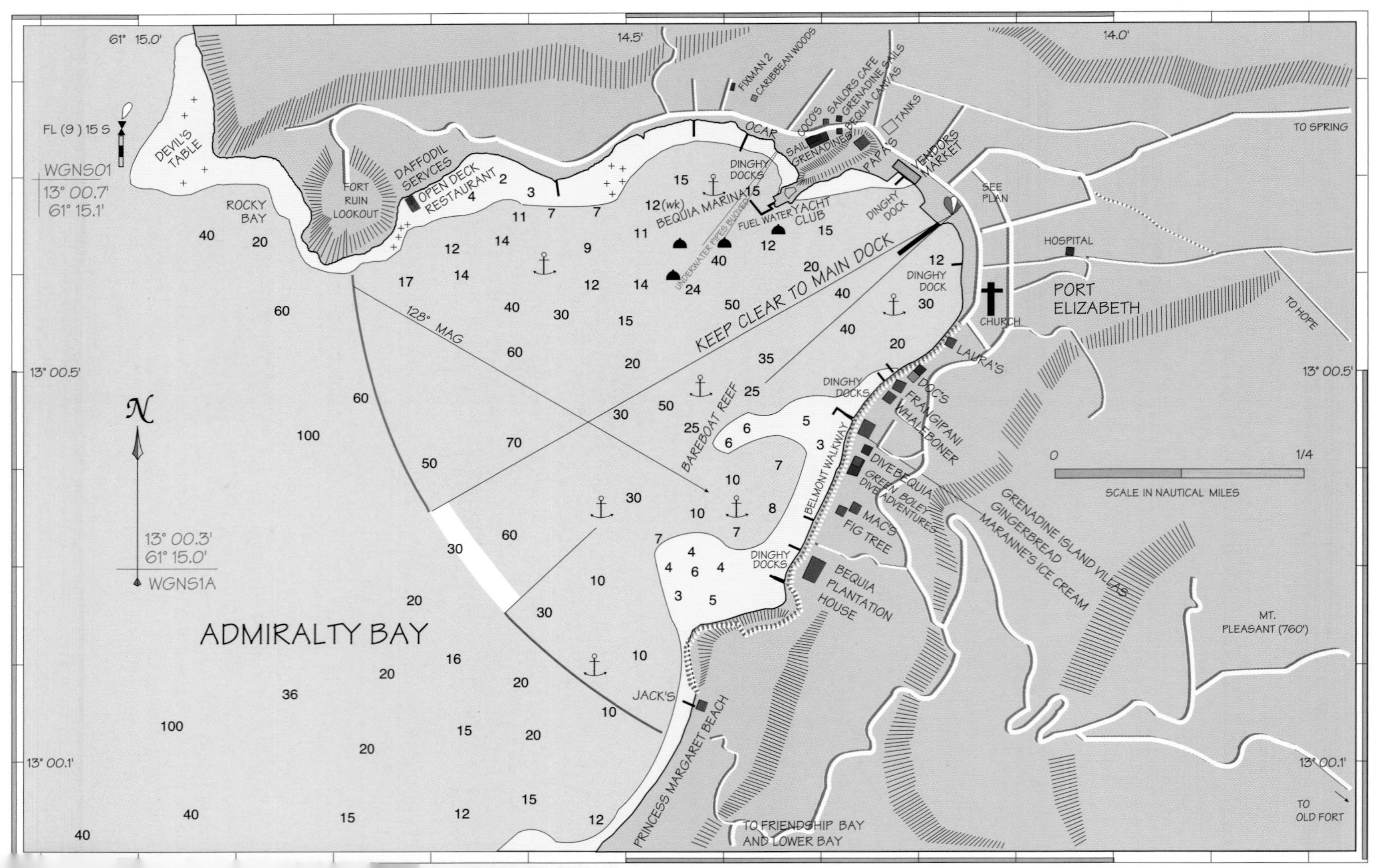
ADMIRALTY BAY
PORT ELIZABETH
KEEP CLEAR TO MAIN DOCK
BAREBOAT REEF
BELMONT WALKWAY
PRINCESS MARGARET BEACH
JACK'S
BEQUIA PLANTATION HOUSE
MAC'S
FIG TREE
DIVE BEQUIA
GREEN BOLEY
DIVE ADVENTURES
WHALEBONER
FRANGIPANI
DOC'S
LAURA'S
CHURCH
HOSPITAL
SEE PLAN
MARKET
VENDORS
TANKS
PAPA'S
DINGHY DOCK
DINGHY DOCKS
GRENADINE SAILS
BEQUIA CANVAS
SAILORS CAFE
COCOS
CARIBBEAN WOODS
FIXMAN 2
OCAR
SAIL GRENADINES
YACHT CLUB
FUEL WATER
BEQUIA MARINA
UNDERWATER PIPES BUOYED
DAFFODIL SERVICES
OPEN DECK RESTAURANT
FORT RUIN LOOKOUT
ROCKY BAY
DEVIL'S TABLE
FL (9) 15 S
WGNS01
13° 00.7'
61° 15.1'
13° 00.3'
61° 15.0'
WGNS1A
128° MAG
GRENADINE ISLAND VILLAS
GINGERBREAD
MARANNE'S ICE CREAM
SCALE IN NAUTICAL MILES
0
1/4
MT. PLEASANT (760')
TO SPRING
TO HOPE
TO OLD FORT
TO FRIENDSHIP BAY AND LOWER BAY
13° 00.5'
13° 00.1'
14.0'
14.5'
61° 15.0'

ADMIRALTY BAY

Admiralty Bay is a huge, well-protected bay with Bequia's only town, Port Elizabeth, at its head. Small hotels, bars, restaurants, and shops spread from town along both shores, strung together in the south by the popular Belmont walkway. This delightful coastal path, renovated and extended by Action Bequia, meanders along the shore, skirting a few trees to Plantation House. Here it climbs the hill before bringing you back to the sea via a lovely wooden staircase. It then turns into a causeway that takes you to Princess Margaret beach.

Several yacht services are grouped together in Ocar on the northern shore. Others are in Port Elizabeth. Good dinghy docks are spaced around the bay.

Navigation

The entrance to Admiralty Bay is straightforward. As you approach from the north, the bay begins to open up, and you can see two fine beaches, Lower Bay and Princess Margaret, separated by a distinct headland. East of Princess Margaret Beach, from the Plantation House to town, the waterfront becomes more built up.

When approaching, allow plenty of room for Devil's Table, which extends a good way from shore; it is marked by a yellow and black beacon. Once in the harbor take care not to hit the shoals that lie offshore between the eastern end of Princess Margaret Beach and the Green Boley. Yachts anchor inside some of these shoals, so it looks like tempting empty space. If entering at night, avoid the unlit, heavy metal buoys near Ocar. These are used for big ship tie-ups. A line of smaller yellow cone buoys are lit and mark hoses running underwater to the shore. Keep clear.

Anchor well clear of the local ferry channel to the main dock. The ferries are large and need plenty of turning room. Keep out of their way at all times. Yachts may not tie up to the ferry dock or the dinghy dock.

There are many places to anchor. Some choose a spot in town, off the Frangipani Hotel. The water is deep, and it takes lots of anchor line and sometimes a couple of tries to get hooked in the muddy sand.

The area by Ocar is calm. Avoid anchoring on the wreck that is at 13° 00.67'N, 61°

14.47'W and another (Tail Wagger) a few hundred feet farther east. They both have at least 12 feet of water over them, but have tied up many an anchor. Some yachts anchor off the Fig Tree and the Plantation House. This area is mainly 8 to 10 feet deep, shoaling toward the shore, shoaling outwards from the western headland, and from the Gingerbread. Shallow draft boats can go practically anywhere here, but those with deeper draft need to use caution.

Sometimes this is a beautiful spot, calm as a lake, the water decorated with floating pink blossoms from the white cedar trees that line the shore. Yet, in times of bad northerly swells it is untenable. The banks on both sides of the harbor (8-20 feet) contain patches of hard sand and dead coral, which make for poor holding. You need to let out ample chain and make sure you are well hooked.

Princess Margaret Beach is one of the easiest and prettiest anchorages and is within a reasonable dinghy ride to town. Holding is good in sand, close to the beach. It occasionally becomes rolly in northerly swells, when landing a dinghy on the beach can be hazardous. The new dinghy dock at Jack's helps. Lower Bay is also easy and picturesque, though a little farther away and more subject to swells.

Moorings are available and the usual charge is $60 EC per night. They are uncontrolled and (except Daffodil's) without legal standing. The customs office posts a warning about them, and some are better than others. Some people know Bequia well and trust a particular mooring owner. For a stranger, it is a problem. I have dived on many of them and have found most to be poorly designed and executed, and they break free quite often. In general, I do not trust them. On the other hand, they sometimes hold better than the way some bareboats anchor. If you take one, snorkel on it to make sure it is okay. Ask for a receipt, or at least know to whom you are paying money. The moorings on the south side, on the bank off the Fig Tree, are occasionally untenable in bad northerly swells, which usually arrive in the middle of the night. If you anchor close to an empty illegal mooring, you cannot be made to move. Similarly, if you take a mooring and an anchored boat swings too close, you must move if they were there first. Rely on your judgment: the vendors are *only* interested in collecting the fee. Keep this in mind when they give you advice about shore services. Daffodil, Phat Shag, and African probably check their moorings more often than most.

Regulations

Port Elizabeth is a port of entry. Customs and immigration, along with the post office, are in a comfortable office right behind the ferry dock. Formalities are simple ~ just one single-sheet form, or better still, check sailclear.com to see if they have joined the SailClear system yet. If they have, you can pre-clear online (not in 2018). Customs opens weekdays 0830-1800 (overtime after 1600). On Saturdays they open 0830-1200 and (overtime) 1500-1800. Sundays and holidays (all overtime) they open 0900-1200 and 1500-1800. Fees are given in *Bequia at a Glance* (page 240).

There is a 5-knot speed limit in the harbor. This applies to dinghies, tenders, and water taxis, as well as to yachts and ships. If you need to speed into town, do so only in the main shipping channel in the center of the harbor. Currently, small, fast boats are the most serious danger to life and limb in this harbor. There has already been one death, and several bad accidents. Is five minutes worth it?

Communications

In many cases you can connect to WiFi from your yacht. But if you go to an internet place, most are air-conditioned, and many will help you with overseas calls. This includes either net-to-phone or via the operator, at rates that are better than the public phones.

Most restaurants have WiFi. If you are anchored close enough you can probably pick one up. Hothothot spot usually has a signal throughout the bay.

When you need a computer, RMS, run by Ros, is conveniently placed just opposite the market and very close to the market dinghy dock. Ros has several computers and a digital photo center where you can download and print digital pictures, as well as make posters and burn CDs. Ros does customs brokerage, photocopying, phone and fax, typing, laminating, and creates cards and flyers. She will rent Digicel phones and sells the cards to go with them.

Campbell's Bequia Technology Center (look for the Digicel sign), next to Andy's, has a savvy owner. They provide phone, fax, software engineering, CD creation, and photo work, and will top up your phone.

Antoinette runs the Hothothot spot WiFi system, but sometimes it is more off than on.

For computers, electronics, accessories, USB keys or SD cards, Andrew is the man to see at ACS Computer Services, above the old Grenadines Yacht Equipment (GYE). He is also the Bequia DHL agent.

General yacht services

Daffo at Daffodil's Marine Services has made a name for herself with a great alongside water, fuel, ice, and laundry delivery system. Nowhere in the Caribbean is this easier. Just give her a call [VHF: 67] and a service boat arrives right alongside. They will send a smaller boat for laundry and ice delivery or garbage pick-up. Daffodil usually carries block ice as

In case you loose your way at Keegan's

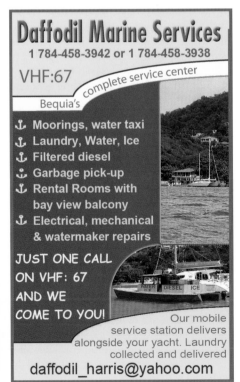

well as cubes. Her laundry is excellent: fast, efficient, and properly washed and dried.

Miranda also collects and delivers laundry. She does a good job and can be reached at Miranda's Laundry [VHF: 68]. She also has a boat for water, as does King. Be aware that water sold in Bequia often comes from storage tanks. It is drinkable, but the flavor can vary.

Sparkles Laundry [VHF: 68] is beside the bookstore and has a boat in the bay that will pick up and deliver. Andy, below Maria's Cafe, has machines where you can do laundry yourself.

Dockside Marine has a dinghy dock and fills cooking gas bottles. If you drop your cylinder off early enough, you can usually get it back the same day.

Max Gas, across from the main dinghy dock, fills cooking gas bottles. It takes overnight. Cube ice may be found at the Porthole, Gingerbread Cafe, and the Frangipani.

When it comes to garbage in Bequia, please continue to observe the following: put garbage in the big dumpsters near the head of the market dinghy dock (no charge). Or call

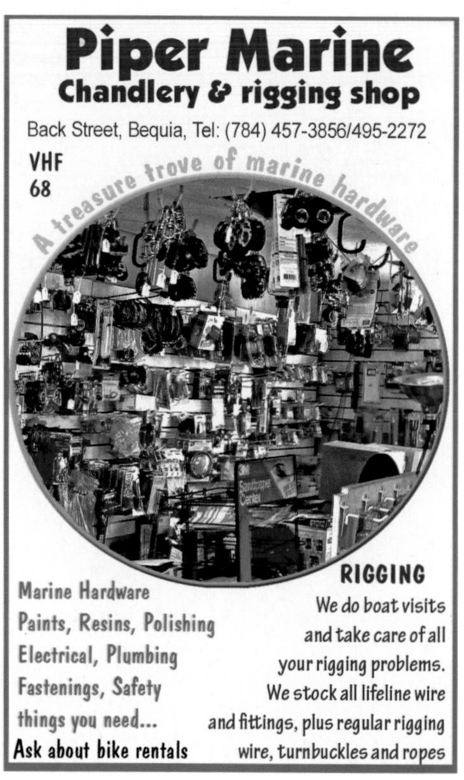

Daffodil Marine any time and they will collect it from you at a charge of $10 EC a bag. They take it to the main dump, not to town. Never accept offers from anyone else to "take your garbage!"

African (Winston Simmons) looks after boats when people go away and can organize work to be done on them. He will also help with provisioning or anything else. He does deliveries, has a 41-foot lagoon charter cat, and rents moorings (593-3986, VHF: 68).

The Yacht Club, aka Bequia Marina (VHF: 68), belongs to Tradewinds Yacht Charters. Gas and water may be available to the general public but, as of this writing, the restaurant and chandlery were defunct.

Local water taxis are painted brightly and bear such names as Outernet, African, McCarthy, and Radio. Their charges vary depending on the destination and time of day. Didi (455-5681), on Blessing, with her little sun awning, is very popular because she drives carefully and will take up to four people almost anywhere in the bay during the day for $20 EC (more than four and night trips are more). Others who drive carefully are African (593-3986) and McCarthy (495-3425). McCarthy provides an excellent service every morning by delivering bread in the anchorage from around 0700. He is a low-key salesman, so you will have to watch out for him and give him a shout, or call him on VHF: 68. In season, vendors sell lobster.

Superyachts requiring help can check with Sam Taxi Service (St. Vincent), or Erika's Marine Services (Union). Vernamay Ollivierre, Erika's Bequia representative, is very helpful and easy to deal with.

Bequia is the home of *Caribbean Compass*, the Caribbean's best waterfront paper. Pick up your free copy practically anywhere in town.

Chandlery

With two chandleries in town you will usually find what you need. They have completely different suppliers, so each stocks different things. Dockside Marine, right in town, is both a good marine hardware and a fishing store. They carry hand-held VHF radios, rope, blocks, shackles, stainless yacht hardware, stainless chain, Delta anchors, fenders, flags, West System epoxy, and first-rate safety gear. There is often new and interesting stock. This is an excellent fishing store, with many lures, rods, and both Penn and Shimano reels (sales and service). In addition, they stock snorkeling gear and some diving equipment.

Piper Marine, under Alick's sail loft, is another interesting chandlery. Piper has an excellent stock of cleaning products and consumables, plus lots of general chandlery, including cloth and West System epoxy, pumps, lights, and safety gear. He has some really good pulley blocks and other yacht hardware you won't find elsewhere. Piper is a rigger (see *Technical yacht services*) and he may have a bike to rent.

Lulley's Tackle Shop is upstairs in the big building that has Island Life Boutique. Wander up and take a look. This is the oldest fishing shop in Bequia and it is still used by many of the island's professional fishermen. It has a wide range of fishing gear, snorkeling gear, and knives. They carry heavy commercial gear, as well as sporting equipment. They have a vast variety of lures and you can get ready-made tackle that is easy to use, as well as rods.

Bequia Easter Regatta

Caribbean Woods sells South American hardwoods and has a good woodworking shop as well. They can put you in touch with someone who will cut that special bit of wood to size or make you a fancy book shelf. Upstairs is an excellent paint shop with paints, fillers, sandpaper, and resins, as well as good tools, including power sanders, bits, and cutting blades.

For general hardware, check out Bequia Venture, Knights (upstairs), and J's Outlet Tools, which also has household items.

Technical yacht services
Sails/Canvas/Cushions

Several places do sail and canvas work and all are good. Bequia Canvas does just about everything but sails: interior and exterior cushions, awnings, and sail covers. It is an efficient operation run by Chris Lochner from Germany and Norrell from Bequia. They keep a wide range of materials, including closed-cell foam. Wander by and you might find just the tote bag or ditty hanger you have been looking for. You can call them and arrange for Chris to come to your yacht to discuss a job.

Grenadines Sails is owned by Avell Davis, a Bequian who has spent years making sails in Bequia and Canada. His shop is close to Bequia Marina. Avell has the widest range of experience, from traditional, handmade sails to modern, high-tech ones. New awnings, covers, dinghy chaps, and alterations can easily be done in the loft. Avell does excellent biminis and bimini frames.

Alick [VHF: 68] is in Port Elizabeth, on a back street, not too far from the town dinghy dock. Alick is low key, personable, thorough, and reasonably priced. You can ask him about new sails, awnings, cushions, and covers. Alick (who trained under Lincoln Simmons) is an excellent man to tackle that devilish splice in one of those new ropes. He will even show you how to do it. At his store he keeps a stock of fabrics, foams, and webbing that you can buy for your own project.

Technical yacht services
Other Services

Don Lewis at the chandlery Piper Marine [VHF: 68] is the man to fix rigging problems. He carries rigging wire, a full range of life-line wire, and press fittings. He will be happy to come to your yacht, where he will get his nephew, Jason, to go up the mast to do whatever is needed. He lives on a sailboat himself. Give him a call or drop by the shop.

John Sharratt of SVG Yacht Services is a qualified surveyor and does general maintenance and engineering, project management, and consulting. He works closely with his partner Katie at Sail Grenadines and is a Budget Marine agent.

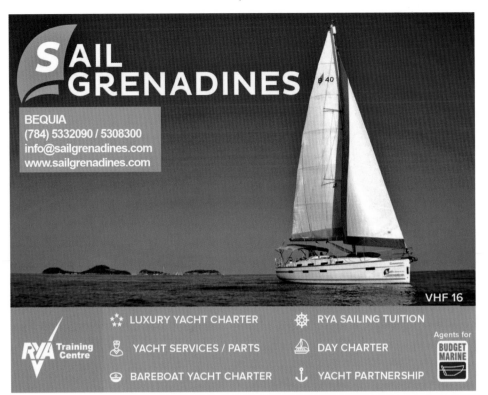

KMS Marine Services [VHF: 68] is run by Kerry Ollivierre from Mount Pleasant. Kerry worked for many years for various charter companies where he learned to fix everything that usually goes wrong: diesel engines, starters, alternators, outboards, refrigerators, water makers, electrical gadgets, and, of course, heads, macerator pumps, and plumbing. Kerry can weld and is often asked to install solar panels.

Tyrone Caesar, at Caribbean Diesel [VHF: 68], spent nine years as an engineer on cargo carriers and several more working for large organizations such as Cummins. He is a well-trained diesel mechanic, especially with Perkins, Northern Lights, Detroit Diesels, GMs, and Yanmars.

Tyrone has a complete mobile fuel polishing system (diesel or gas) for cleaning fuel tanks, and can handle any size of tank. It comes with bendable rods that can fit into tight spaces. He can sample your tank and assess the state of the fuel at the bottom. His shop is in the church yard, but it is probably easiest to call. If you cannot find him, ask in Piper Marine Chandlery.

Sam Saville of Knock Refrigeration provides excellent and quick service for both refrigeration and air-conditioning. You will find him two doors east from Sail Grenadines, or call him on his cell: 529-1682.

Oscar has an excellent machine shop in St. Vincent with full machining, milling, and turning gear. He can fix just about anything, and can weld stainless and aluminum.

Oscar is near Verrol Nichols of Nichols Marine, the starter and alternator magician. Verrol will fix anything and send it back looking like new. You can arrange to leave work for either of these specialists personally or get KMS Marine Services to come and deal with it for you.

Quality meats, smoked fish, shrimp, wines, cheeses, gourmet foods
Doris Fresh Food
yacht Provisioning
VHF:68, Phone:(784) 458-3625, Fax:(784) 457-3134
Now on Back Street, behind Customs
For yacht provisioning
The place to shop
French Bread (baguettes) daily Dieter's special whole wheat bread with yogurt (keeps wonderfully). Fresh croissants daily in season.
MasterCard and Visa welcome
wir sprechen Deutsch

Handy Andy is a good, two-part polyurethane spray painter who can still occasionally be persuaded to tackle a job. Bequia also has many shipwrights and carpenters.

Provisioning

Bequia is quite a good place to stock up on provisions. Doris Fresh Foods [VHF: 68/16] is almost legendary in Bequia. It is a great, air-conditioned supermarket on the back street where you will find excellent cheeses and deli foods, good wines, local chutney, gourmet items, and good, fresh produce. You will not find a better selection of frozen meats and gluten-free items. Baked goodies include 8-grain bread, which tastes good and keeps well, making it popular with those setting out to sea. Fresh French bread is baked daily in season, as are croissants and fancy pastries. So far, Doris has been unmatched for variety and availability of harder-to-find foods. When I have failed to find such things as unsweetened dried coconut and dried ginger in Grenada, I come to Doris, and there they are.

Another place for fancy pastries, including quiches, is from Stelton at the Plantation House. He cooks for their restaurant, so for provisioning quantities you need to order in advance.

Noeline Taylor's Shoreline Mini-Market is associated with her Porthole Restaurant, so you can shop from early in the morning to late at night. If you see it closed, just ask in the restaurant and Noeline will open. You can tie your dinghy to the Dockside Marine dock outside, making it convenient for carrying cases of beer. It is well stocked with most things including wine, French baguettes, and whole-wheat bread baked daily. Shoreline closes on Sundays in the off season.

Just down the boardwalk is Doc's Art Gallery where you will find a freezer full of his wife Virginie's homemade fresh frozen gourmet French soups, sauces, and patés. Pick them up any day between 1000 and 1300 or 1600 and 1900.

On the north side of the harbor, O. King, the beer wholesaler, has the best buys on cases of beer.

Knight's Trading is one of the older and larger of the Bequia supermarkets. They stock almost everything except fresh produce, and their prices are often good. They will deliver to the dinghy dock. You can do one-stop shopping here, as upstairs they have a lumber/hardware/electrical store. Knight's has a smaller outlet on Front Street.

Select Wines, next to De Bistro, has a well-organized and large selection of wine, soft drinks, beer, cheese, meat, French bread, and lots of specialty items, like chocolate-covered hazelnuts. In addition, they have a fair selection of regular canned and dried foods. They open from about 0800 to 2200, so it is almost never too late to shop.

Bequia Foodstore has a good selection of canned and dry goods. It is open daily 0800-2000, making it also convenient for late shopping.

In the Bayshore Mall, Lina's is a great little bakery/delicatessen. When they bake they have a large selection of good bread, both yeast and sourdough. They sell Danish, pain au chocolat, and more. Get a cup of excellent coffee here in the morning and sit outside under the umbrellas. Return for a lunchtime sandwich. Lina's also stocks specialty foods, including the Caribbean's widest selection of pepper (the spice).

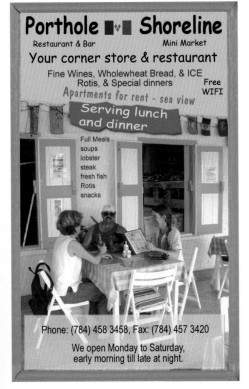

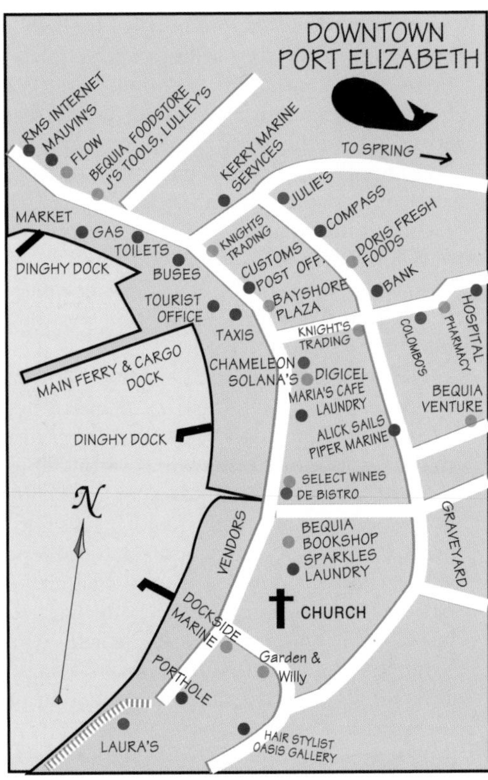

You can buy fruits and vegetables in the market. The selection is good, but high-pressure Rasta salesmanship has driven many locals and regulars to Doris, or to the quieter stalls dotted around the main street. (Check out the notice painted on the wall of the market.)

The Gingerbread Cafe has baked goods, coffee, and a few other items. Maranne's has yogurt and homemade ice cream.

In Lower Bay, Nature Zone is a one-room shop attached to a small organic garden run by Jacqueline McLean. You can find great fresh items here, straight from the garden. Jacqueline also bakes bread and banana bread, makes chutneys, pickles, fresh juices and all kinds of good things. If you need something special, give her a call at 432-7706.

Fun shopping

Bequia has long had boutiques, but as town rental rates rose beyond the means of most craftsmen, they took to the waterfront along the main street. Rent is free, but they have to cover up quickly for every rain shower.

As a result, the waterfront in Port Elizabeth is colorful, with vendors selling t-shirts, model boats, and handicrafts. Bequians produce excellent handicrafts, of very high quality, that are unique to the island. This, along with the boutiques, make Bequia a great place to shop.

The Chameleon Cafe's clothing department has the smartest and most elegant line of swim, beach, and casual wear, with brands like Hurley, Reef, and Nike at duty-free prices. It is hard to know it is there, but if you walk into the cafe you will see it.

Patrick 'Doc" Chevailler and his wife Virginie recently relocated to Bequia after 22 years on Palm Island. A well-known artist in the Caribbean, Doc's bold, colorful depictions of sea life, coral landscapes, and commissioned work are captivating. He sells both originals and high-quality prints in his gallery, along with some lovely coasters which make perfect gifts. Doc is always happy to chat and has a medical practice here. He sells his wife Virginie's homemade gourmet soups, sauces, and pates (see *Provisioning*) from a corner of the gallery.

The building of model boats has been a Bequia specialty for generations. Craftsmen will build any design to order, but all-time favorites are the model whaling boats, both full and half models. They are artfully built and beautifully painted. Check out Mauvin's, near the market, or Sargeant's, closer to Bequia Marina.

Kingsley has taken the coconut boat tradition to the level of real artistry with his glossy coconut boats. You can see some at the Oasis Art Gallery, which also features the wonderful art of L.D. Lucy.

Hand-painted calabashes and coconuts by Pinky, who is based in Bequia, are lovely and deservedly popular. You will find some in Solana's.

Scrimshaw is another Bequia tradition, you can find it in the Bequia Bookstore and along the waterfront.

Bequia has a wide range of small, pleasant boutiques. The market has its own dinghy dock. Many shops here sell t-shirts, souvenirs, and gifts. Others are scattered through town.

Solana's, run by Carmette and Solana,

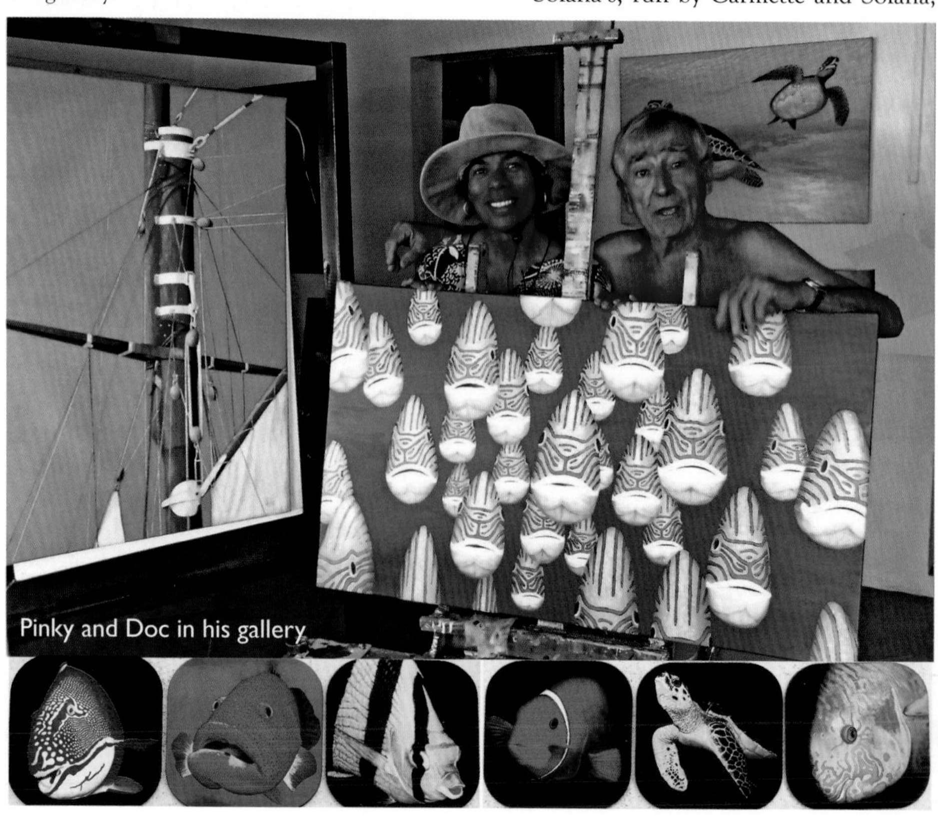

Pinky and Doc in his gallery

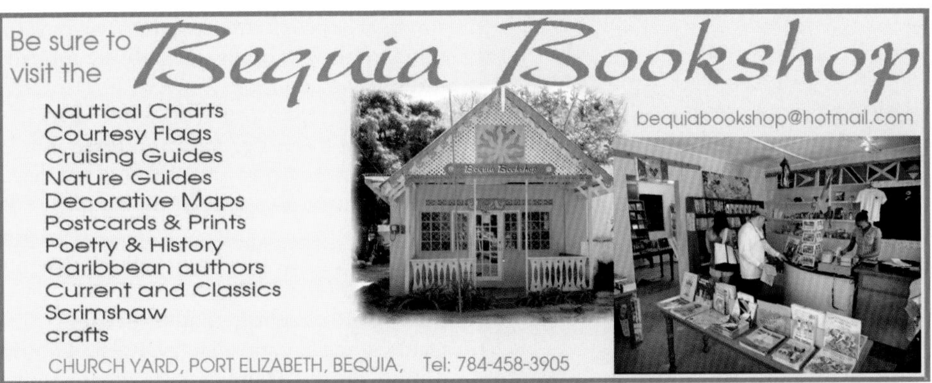

is packed with hand-painted t-shirts, shorts, and batik work, as well as handicrafts, jewelry, books, videos, flags, phone cards, and maps. Solana's is the FedEx agent, and they sell Digicel cards. They also have a lovely house for rent overlooking Princess Margaret Beach and can arrange car rentals.

The Bequia Bookshop, in the church compound, is spread through two rooms with an excellent range of nautical books, charts, local books, videos, and novels. They sell postcards, souvenirs, games, well-made courtesy flags, and art by local artists, including the popular Carol Nicholas. Scrimshaw, locally hand-crafted by Sam McDowell, is on display.

Manager Cheryl also runs Sweety Bird, a garden cafe down the road with elegant teas, coffee, fresh juices, and a great lunch at local prices. A good place to read the novel you have just bought or wait for the ferry. Cheryl also runs The Fig Tree and has a reading club for kids every Saturday and always needs volunteers to help out. If you are interested, ask her about it.

In the Bayshore Mall you can find boutiques, a barber, and a travel agent.

The Garden Boutique, behind Dockside Marine, sells hand painted batik clothing, scarves, pillow covers, and other souvenirs.

Restaurants

The waterfront has a wonderful mixture of bars and restaurants. Those on the south side of the harbour are linked together by the Bequia walkway, recently completed by Action Bequia and others, that runs from Port Elizabeth to Plantation House, then over the hill to Princess Margaret Beach.

I am delighted to see the Plantation House back in action. Built as a hotel, it was originally called the Sunny Caribbee. Many years ago it was bought by an Italian offshore banker who had aspirations and renamed it Plantation House, filled the garden with statues and the rooms with clients he wished to impress. He had to suddenly flee various authorities and the property declined and became derelict. Kelly Glass (who also has Blue Lagoon Marina and Hotel) has done a magnificent job of renovating and improving the property, creating an elegant but affordable boutique hotel.

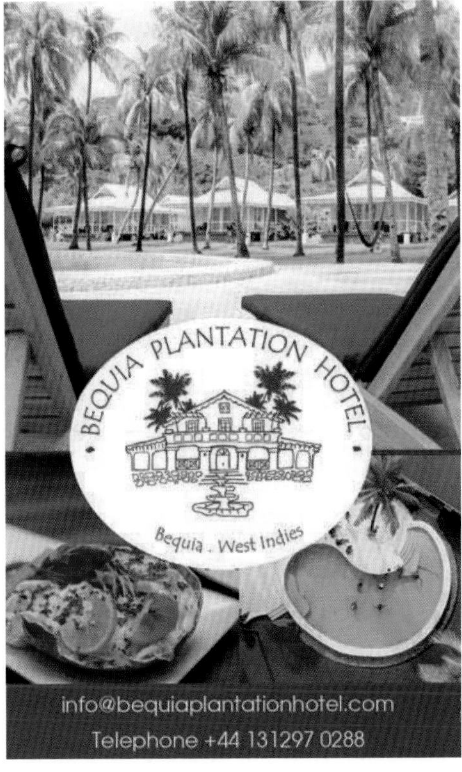

At the head of their dinghy dock is the beachfront bar and restaurant [$$$$]. This is open to the bay on one side and the pool on the other. People wander in for breakfast or mid-morning for coffee and some fine pâtisseries created by their pastry chef, Stelton Levy, who trained under Ali in Mustique, making fancy pastries for the rich and famous. (If there are leftovers at happy hour, sometimes they sell them at a discount.) They have a traditional pizza oven, which is fired up at noon and keeps going for lunch and dinner. They cook thin-crust pizzas with your choice of three toppings, generously applied, and you can add more if you wish. They also offer quiches and other dishes, and in the evenings you can opt for a full three-course meal. Happy hour is 1700-1900, and they have entertainment about three times a week. If you want a night ashore, elegant rooms are available both in the main building and in cottages. All have balconies.

A big new venture under the same management as Plantation House is The Liming Bequia. Several "Limings" are planned and the Bequia one is the first. It is on the south coast, west of the airport, and should be open by the time this guide comes out. It has very luxurious rooms and a spacious waterfront restaurant. A breakwater by the restaurant provides ample depth and shelter for small power boats, day sailors, and seaworthy tenders.

Papa's [$$], up on the hill above Bequia Marina, is owned and managed by Beth and Gert Ludicke. It overlooks the bay and is well worth the walk. It has an informal clubby atmosphere with comfy lounge seats, a giant covered deck looking over the harbor, and a backyard with a tent, bar, and barbecue area. This is the place to come for a big sports event like the Superbowl as they have four TVs and four large projection screens. They open every day for lunch and dinner, with a menu and daily specials. The food is good, straightforward in style, and includes burgers, chicken, lobster in season, and sandwiches. They have live music several days a week, and have recently added a scenic rooftop balcony.

Cheryl's Fig Tree [$$] is along the waterfront close to Mac's Pizza and Kitchen:

just follow the coastal path. This restaurant is right on the water. The food is local and delicious for lunch or dinner. You get a nice array of local vegetables and they do a chocolate samosa, which while not exactly Caribbean, is totally scrumptious. Lafayette, Cheryl's daughter, who is always around and welcoming, also organizes the cruisers' VHF net in the morning at 0800. She runs a children's reading group here every Saturday (cruisers' children welcome) and always needs volunteers from yachts to help children read. If anyone is looking for a place for a meeting, scrabble competition, or other event, it is likely they will come here. Every Friday in season is "Fish Friday", with seafood specials and live music. It is very popular, so book in advance. On Saturday mornings there is a salsa class at 0930, come back that night to show off your new moves. Tuesday is open mic, followed by Latin night on Wednesday, and there is often live music on Sundays.

The Chameleon Cafe and clothing store is on main street in Port Elizabeth. With a

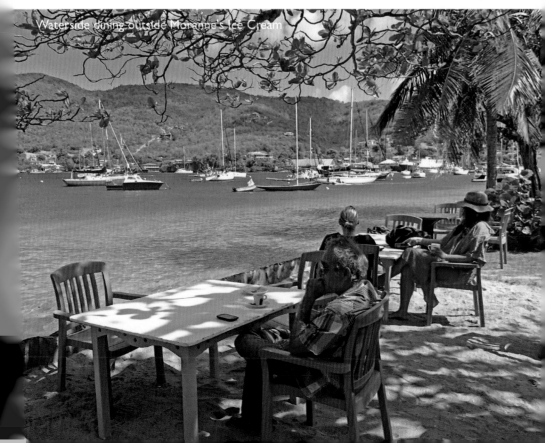

Waterside dining outside Moranne's Ice Cream

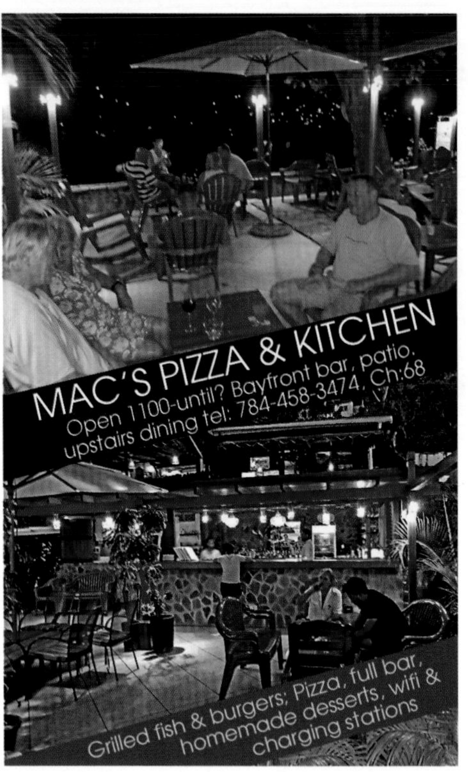

broad balcony, brightly colored cushions, and the wonderful aroma of freshly brewed coffee, it adds a touch of casual sophistication to town. They open at 0830 for breakfast, Continental or full, and stay open till the last person leaves, or till 1900 if no one is around. All day long you can get delightful salads (including fresh tuna), quiches, sandwiches, and starters, along with baked goodies and their famous lime cheese cake. They serve beer, wine, fruit smoothies (you can add a little rum), cocktails, and coconut water. The space is intimate, and sometimes quite a few people are there using the free WiFi, so if you want to be sure of a table for lunch come early or, if it is a big group, call. In the evening they serve tasty tapas; share a few and make a meal of it. While there, take a look in their clothing store (see *Fun shopping*).

MAC'S PIZZA & KITCHEN
Open 1100-until? Bayfront bar, patio.
upstairs dining tel: 784-458-3474, Ch:68
Grilled fish & burgers; Pizza, full bar,
homemade desserts, wifi &
charging stations

Kevin and Drasi have expanded both the menu and dining space at Mac's Pizza and Kitchen [$$$]. Their tasty pizzas are legendary among yachtspeople, with many choices, including lobster. They have turned the lower levels into inviting lounge spaces where you can enjoy cocktails and tapas under the stars. You can also get grilled lobster, Japanese-style seared tuna, and home made ice cream, along with daily specials. The atmosphere is congenial, and it is popular. In season it is essential to make a reservation. They are open for lunch and dinner, including take out, and will deliver to yachts in the bay.

Patrick from Sweden has been a chef in Bequia for many years, and has recently taken over The Open Deck [$$$$$] at Daffodil's. He creates daily set menus from fresh, local ingredients. Lunch is three courses, and dinner is five. The food is light and flavorful, wonderfully presented, and service is attentive; a great option for a special night out. As of this writing the restaurant was undergoing some repairs to the dinghy dock and canopy that should be completed by the time of publishing. They open for lunch from 1300 until 1600, and for dinner from 1900 until late. Reservations are appreciated (455-3962, VHF:68).

There are plenty of places to get good local food. Noeline Taylor's Porthole [$] is a popular meeting place for breakfast, morning

coffee, lunch rotis, an afternoon beer, or a relaxing dinner. Noeline has local fresh juices and a large menu, with everything from snacks to freshly caught fish. Check out the menu posted outside showing the daily specials. Entertainment is usually on Wednesdays and Sundays. Noeline has a book swap, so you often see people browsing through the shelves. There is a very nominal charge that enables Noeline to keep the books in good order. Let Noeline know before you do your swap.

Maria's Cafe is upstairs on Front Street.

This is a gathering place where people come and use the internet computers and WiFi, or to meet and chat while looking out from the magnificent balcony that overlooks life below and in the harbor. It brings in people of all nationalities and types, and the atmosphere is casual. Their menu has something for everyone, from burgers to lobster, with some good conch and other seafood. Everything is cooked from scratch, so it is fresh and tasty.

Andy, the owner, is often around. He runs the Bequia Youth Sailing Program and has an office which sells property downstairs.

Laura's [$$] is proud to be the only place in Bequia to get fresh, homemade pasta, which has been highly recommended. They serve both international and local food for lunch and dinner and occasionally have live music. Reservations are appreciated.

The Gingerbread Hotel [$$] is in an impressive Caribbean-style building with an adjoining hotel managed by Gretel Mitchell. It has delightful rooms with big balconies, looking over the harbor and the Gingerbread coffee shop under the trees at the head of their dinghy dock. This popular gathering place sells coffee, fresh local juice, and baked goodies. In the same compound, check out Maranne's to try her famous gourmet ice cream, frozen yogurt, or sorbet. Everything is homemade from fresh ingredients.

The Frangipani Hotel [$$$$, VHF: 68, closed September] is owned by Son Mitchell, former Prime minister of St. Vincent and the Grenadines, and has been in his family since the turn of the last century. The upper floor of the main building used to be the family home, and downstairs was the storehouse for the Gloria Colita, which, at 131 feet long, was the largest schooner ever built in Bequia. In 1940, she disappeared at sea and was later found drifting empty in the Bermuda Triangle. Today, Son's daughter Sabrina manages the Frangipani. By day, it is a good place to meet people and enjoy a great fresh tuna sandwich for lunch. By night, they offer romantic candlelit dinners of Caribbean specialties. Everyone comes by on Thursday nights when they have a barbecue and jump up to a steel band. They also have music on Mondays.

The Hinkson family owns and runs the Whaleboner [$$]. It is conveniently situated next to the Frangipani. Much of the food comes from their farm, so you know it is fresh. True to its name, the bar, stools, and entrance have all been built of whalebone from the old whaling days. Angie and her daughter Ruth cook good pizzas, chicken, fish and full evening meals at a reasonable price. The meat comes from their hand-raised animals. Chicken and fish are always available, as is lobster in season. Come for the daily happy hour (1700-1900) and enjoy entertainment on Monday and Tuesday nights, in season, and on other special occasions. The same family owns the silk-screen factory on the road to Spring. If you'd like to visit, make an appointment at the restaurant.

Coco's [VHF: 68, $$] is upstairs in the first building on the road behind Bequia Marina. They have an excellent view of the yachts at anchor and Caribbean décor. Coco is known for good, local cooking, especially seafood. In season they do a fabulous Sunday buffet lunch, and they generally have music on Tuesdays and Fridays.

De Bistro [$$] is open to the main street. They have hearty meals, pizzas, and hamburgers, as well as local fish, shrimp, and lobster. It is a great place to enjoy a few drinks or a cup of coffee and watch the world pass by.

For a cheap and cheerful lunch, consider Colombo's [$]. They cook excellent pizza and pasta, and their lasagna is great. (You can buy it by the tray for a party.)

Other local restaurants include Lyston Williams's Green Boley [$], a popular bar; Isola McIntosh's Julie's Guest House [VHF: 68, $$], where advance booking is necessary;

and the Pizza Hut, which is self-explanatory, but which also sells French bread.

Tantie Pearl's [VHF: 68, $$$] is an aerobic 7-minute walk up a steep hill behind the cemetery. The restaurant is perched on the edge of a steep slope with a bird's-eye view of the harbor. Tantie Pearl offers good local food, but book before you go.

Behind the slipway is the Sailor's Cafe [VHF: 68, $$]. Owner Elfic Grant, aka The Singing Chef, is entertaining and runs a good, clean establishment. You can drop in for soup and some good Chinese fried rice or chow mein. For more elaborate fare, you need to book in advance. The bar makes a pleasant hangout; ask about happy hour.

These are just the restaurants in Admiralty Bay. There are also good restaurants in other places, and taxi fares are reasonable ($15-25 EC). (See also *Restaurants in Friendship Bay*, later in this chapter; it is a long walk or short drive away.)

For a lovely get-away, go to Industry. Here you will you will find Sugar Reef set in a big stone building on the waterfront. It is a big, light open space, looking through palms

Bequia walkway

and seagrapes to the beach where the water is protected by a reef.

This is part of a big estate owned by Emmet and it is managed by Judith. The food is local and fresh; much of it is from the estate. You can feel good about drinking piña coladas here, as they make the coconut milk from fresh coconuts. They offer great salads and rotis (including lobster roti) as well as delights such as callaloo lasagna. They have a fine dinner menu, much of it seafood, but they also serve meat, vegetarian, and vegan meals. At their full-moon party they feature a special menu, often exploring a particular cuisine such as Thai, Indian, or Japanese, with a string band. For anyone who wants a real retreat, rooms are available.

Jack's Beach Bar [$$$], on Princess Margaret Beach is big and open, built of wood and canvas. The location is fabulous, right on the beach. You can dinghy over and tie up to their dock. They have fancy cocktails and serve lunch and dinner overlooking the garden and beach. The food is good, fresh, and hearty, and they will deliver (for a fee) to boats up to 3km away. Daily happy hour is from 1730 to 1900, and Tuesday night is live music from 1900. They open daily from 1100 to 2300 and have beach chairs and stand up paddle boards (SUPs) for rent.

Firefly Hotel [$$$] at Spring, a mile or so back towards town, is owned by Stan and Elizabeth who also own the Firefly in Mustique. It looks across a swimming pool over a field of palm trees towards the east coast, with the feel of being in the country. The manager, Rodney, and his staff are welcoming and friendly. Much of the food comes from the estate. Their Sunday curry lunch and Wednesday Creole lunch are both popular. They have a daily happy hour from 1730 to 1900. On Friday nights they have Caribbean night with Caribbean food and music, and on Saturday nights they continue the Caribbean theme with jerk food and reggae.

They offer an estate tour for $10 EC a person; Keith will show you around and tell you about the local plants and their uses.

If you're planning on being in this area make an appointment to visit the Whaleboner silk-screen factory (see *Restaurants*).

Lower Bay has one of Bequia's best

beaches, set in a low-key, rural atmosphere of fishing boats and drying nets. While here check out Nature Zone, a tiny fresh food store, (see *Provisioning*). Great for swimming by day and romantic on a full-moon night, it is a popular place to hang out, especially on Sundays. Recently, people have begun to gravitate here for an evening of inexpensive seafood dinners. Lower Bay makes an acceptable anchorage in settled conditions and is within dinghy reach of Admiralty Bay. However, there is usually enough swell to make landing on the beach a damp affair, so it is better to take a cab or water taxi ($15-25 EC). By day, it is interesting to follow the walkway to Princess Margaret Beach, and walk over to the next bluff to Lower Bay.

Once you arrive, there are several local restaurants to choose from. De Reef [VHF: 68, $$], right on the beach, is the most famous, popular for lunch, and is a major gathering place for locals on Sundays. You can get chicken, fish, conch, or sandwiches any day of the week. By night they serve dinners by reservation, and from time to time they throw a wild fete.

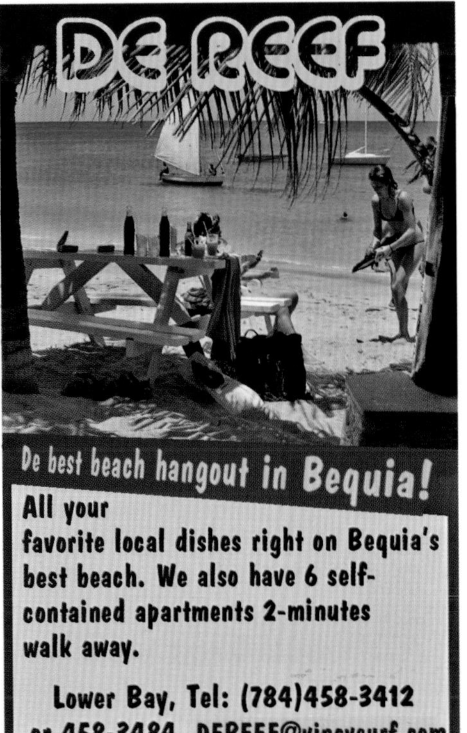

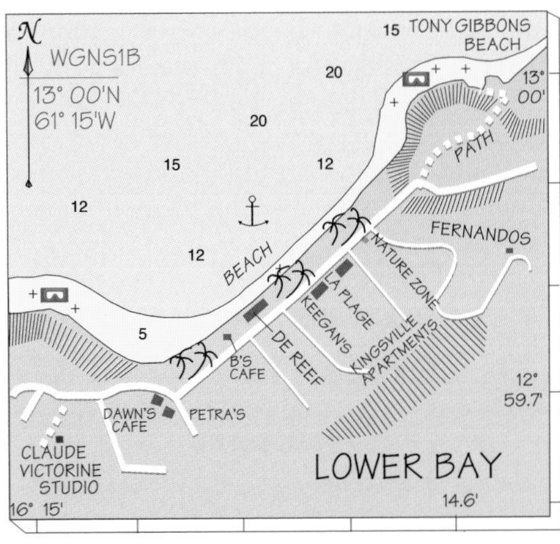

La Plage [$$] is a good restaurant with seating inside the building as well as on the other side of the road, hanging over the beach. It is run by Cecile, who is an excellent French cook. Her menu runs from burgers to steak and seafood. While she is open most days in season, as soon as the crowd dies it is weekends only.

Keegan's [$$], opposite the beach, with on-the-beach seating, offers inexpensive meals featuring chicken, shrimp, fish, or conch. By day they do fish or chicken 'n chips, snacks, and all day breakfast.

Farther down, Dawn's Cafe [$] is a real jewel. It is in a simple but attractive open building behind the beach in a pleasant garden. Dawn serves breakfast, soups, sandwiches, burgers, and often a daily special. Prices are very inexpensive; her food is delicious and she is open quite late, so you can also eat a simple evening meal here.

Right beside Dawn's is Petra's Mini Mart and Restaurant [$]. She is open for breakfast, lunch, and dinner from 0700 until late. Petra has daily specials and the lobster is especially good, and the most affordable on the island. She does a Sunday lobster brunch.

Fernando's Hideaway [$$], run by Fernando, is simple, low-key, and serves very good meals of local fish and meat. Fernando is a fisherman and catches the fish himself. Advance reservations are pretty much essential. It is down a back road, take a taxi so you can find it.

While you are in Lower Bay consider seeing if you can visit the home of French artist Claude Victorine (now in her nineties and going strong). Claude's main medium is painting on silk. She creates superb cushion covers, wall hangings, and fabrics that are guaranteed to add a touch of class to any boat or home. Paintings are also on show. Claude accepts the occasional visitor by appointment only (458-3150).

On Princess Margaret Beach you can find Willie among the jewelry salesmen. Willie does a beach barbecue to order, which was highly recommended.

Transport

Two different companies run ferries to St. Vincent: Admiral Ferry and Bequia Express. The Admiral makes two or three trips on weekdays and three on Saturday. The first ferry normally leaves Bequia at 0630, and the last returns at 1630. You can get the complete ferry schedule in the Bequia Tourist Office by the main dock.

Local buses can be useful for getting around the island, especially if you are going to La Pompe or Paget Farm, both of which can seem like a never-ending walk. Just watch for one and stick out your hand.

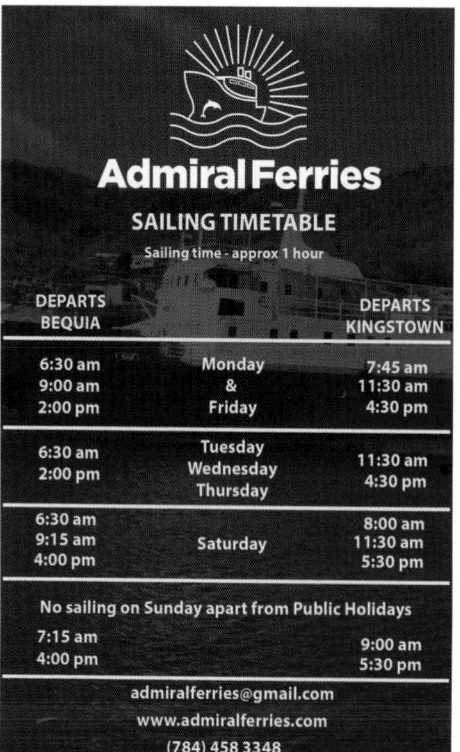

DEPARTS BEQUIA		DEPARTS KINGSTOWN
6:30 am 9:00 am 2:00 pm	Monday & Friday	7:45 am 11:30 am 4:30 pm
6:30 am 2:00 pm	Tuesday Wednesday Thursday	11:30 am 4:30 pm
6:30 am 9:15 am 4:00 pm	Saturday	8:00 am 11:30 am 5:30 pm
No sailing on Sunday apart from Public Holidays		
7:15 am 4:00 pm		9:00 am 5:30 pm

Taxis are fairly inexpensive in Bequia, and sightseeing is highly recommended. (Check out some of the attractions under *Ashore*.) If you call a taxi in advance they can meet you outside the Gingerbread or Frangipani. Most of the taxi drivers are good. There may be one or two who hustle a bit too much. Make sure to only use those who are approved by the SVG Tourism Association, they will have a badge. Those I mention are pleasant, punctual, reliable, and always straightforward and informative about the island and its people. Gideon has three taxis, works well with the yachts, and listens to VHF: 68. His rates are reasonable and he also has four-wheel-drive rentals.

The Ollivierre family has been involved in Bequia boatbuilding from way back, and were among the first taxi drivers. Lubin Ollivierre, De Best, will be happy to tell you about history or current events. Sandra and Curtis Ollivierre have a couple of bright yellow taxis and some four-wheel-drive cars for rent. They listen to VHF: 68.

Sightseeing cab fares are reasonable. You can see a lot in an hour, and the whole island in four hours. If you just want to visit Spring, Friendship, or Lower Bay, or want to try some different places for dinner, hop in a taxi.

Ashore

If the hair on your head is beginning to resemble the stringy weed growing under your hull, then both men and women can contact Gillian's Hair Salon (457-3600), well down the road and up the hill past Bequia Venture.

Johanna Osborne, a dentist and maxillofacial surgeon, now runs a clinic on Saturdays. Her office is on the road towards Spring, near the high school. Call for an appointment: 529-0745.

Patrick 'Doc' Chevailler's medical practice shares a building with his art gallery. Find him there daily from 1000 to 1300 and 1600 to 1900, or call to make an appointment (458-8829).

Bequia has good walks. If you follow the coastal path along the waterfront to Princess Margaret beach, you can walk from there along the beach and over the next headland to Lower Bay. If you laze on the beach and swim, keep an eye on your handbags and cameras.

Watch a sunset from Mount Pleasant, or walk to Friendship Bay, Spring, or Industry for lunch or dinner and enjoy the great variety of views along the way.

If you want to go on an adventurous hike, then Brent "Bushman" Gooding will be happy to guide you. He knows all the trails. Call him at 495-2524.

You will find that Bequia is far more than the waterfront. The hills of Mount Pleasant

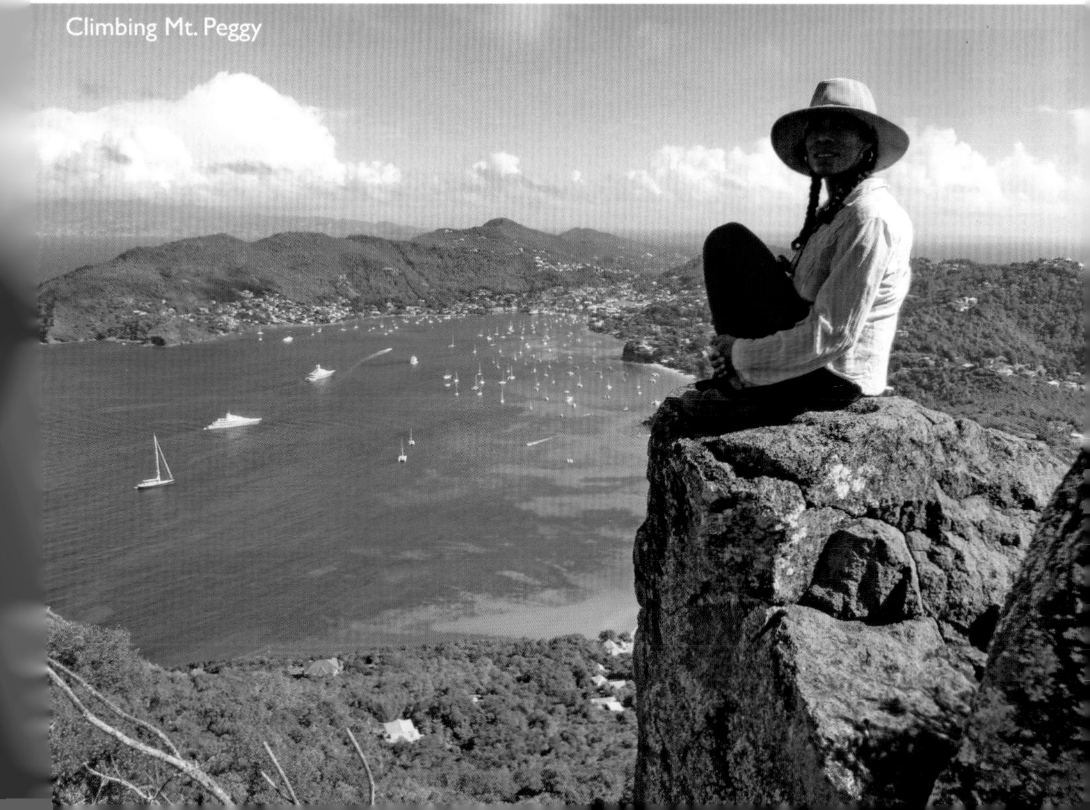

Climbing Mt. Peggy

are almost like another world. If you are not inclined to walk, take a cab one way or both. You can see all the best and most scenic spots in a leisurely three-hour tour. Each place you visit seems so different that sometimes Bequia feels like several islands in one. Highlights include an old fort looking over the harbor, Bequia's summit, Mount Pleasant, the beautiful windward beach of Spring, and the new Maritime Museum in Friendship Bay. The taxi drivers are proud of their island and are knowledgeable guides.

The Old Hegg Turtle Sanctuary at Industry is an interesting destination. Brother King takes turtle eggs and rears turtles till they are old enough to have a better chance of survival. The establishment of the sanctuary has done much to raise environmental consciousness in Bequia. There is a small charge ($5 US) to visit, which goes toward the cost of feeding and housing the turtles.

You can hike to Hope, a lovely, remote beach where the shallow water sets up long lines of breakers often suitable for bodysurfing (but watch the undertow).

There is an exceptionally pleasant hike (about 40 minutes each way) to Peggy's Rock, right on a ridge line, with a spectacular view of Admiralty Bay. You start by the Bequia Whaling and Maritime Museum. Take a taxi or bus there; it is on the road to the airport. Hike details may be found on doyleguides.com

You can visit the other Bequia Maritime Museum in town in exchange for a contribution ($5 US suggested). Lawson Sargeant, the original model boat builder, runs it. Inside are some awesome, historically correct, giant models of whaling boats and schooners, along with photos of historic Bequia boats and the harbor from about 50 years ago. It is best to call for an appointment (495-8559/457-3685). Tennis courts are available at Gingerbread.

If you come at Easter you can get involved in the Bequia Regatta, a four-day extravaganza of local boat races, yacht races, and lots of partying. This may be the best, friendliest, and most successful of the Caribbean's medium-sized regattas. Everyone is made to feel welcome.

Christmas is a popular time in Bequia, but "Nine Mornings," which starts some two weeks before Christmas, can make the town anchorage throb with disco music through the night.

You can also get off-island. Bequia has a special day-charter boat, the Friendship Rose, a sailing schooner, which for years was the island's only ferry. Given the price of mooring in Mustique, some yachties figure it is worth taking a day tour on the Rose instead. Friendship Rose does diving, waterfall, and other tours that are not as easy on your own boat. Their office is by the Frangipani and you can check out their itinerary. The same group runs Grenadine Island Villas, which rents and sells villas, so if the whole family comes to visit, you can house them ashore.

Bequia has a very active youth sailing program to get the youngsters learning. They have a fleet of small sailing boats, plus one or two J 24s. The boats are kept opposite De Bistro. If you feel like getting involved by contributing some time or money, Handy Andy is the man to talk to.

Serenity Day Spa is run by Darcel John in the Southerby's Building (a 5-minute walk up the hill from the Fig Tree). She does it all, from Swedish massage to waxing and nails. Her prices are quite reasonable. Drop by and pick up a flier.

Water sports

Katie Bingham runs Sail Grenadines out of Bequia Marina. Katie is very friendly and helpful and they offer fully crewed, semi-bareboat, and bareboat charters. They do short-term charters to pick you up in one island and drop you off in another. Those who want to advance their skills should ask about their full gamut of practical Royal Yachting Association courses, which one can join as an individual. Katie works closely with her partner John of SVG Yacht Services who does maintenance and engineering (see *Technical Yacht Services*).

Sail Grenadines rents kayaks and Jack's

http://www.bequiayouthsailors.org/

rents SUPs.

Diving in Bequia is excellent and not to be missed by scuba fans. For the uninitiated, it is an ideal place for a 'discover scuba diving' course. There are two dive shops in Admiralty Bay.

Dive Bequia is the dive shop near the Gingerbread, owned by Bob Sachs. Sachs is one of scuba's greatest enthusiasts and Bequia's most experienced diver. His wife, Cathy, is charming and an excellent teacher, especially for kids, or for those who are nervous (a view endorsed by quite a few reader emails). Call Dive Bequia [VHF: 68/16], and Bob or one of his staff will arrange to collect you from your yacht, conditions permitting. Return to the bar later to socialize with them and other divers. Their seaworthy dive boats make getting in and out easy and allow for occasional diving and exploring trips to St. Vincent or the other Grenadines.

Bequia Dive Adventures [VHF: 68] is on the waterfront next to Mac's Pizza and Kitchen. It is run by Ron, an instructor from Bequia. He is experienced and operates with small groups and does many levels of training, from discover scuba diving through rescue diver training. He is happy to do boat pickups and drop-offs.

Both dive shops have small retail sections with snorkeling and diving gear for sale. Both will help with equipment service or rental, and tank fills.

For those diving on their own, the most accessible good dives are around Devil's Table. A reef extends from the shore to the black and yellow beacon. There are moorings, so you can tie up your dinghy. (The moorings belong to the dive shops, so leave plenty of line so they can tie up alongside you.) From the shallow inshore end you can dive out along one side of the rocky shoal and back on the other. The depth at the outer end of the reef is about 65 feet. There are plenty of different corals and reef fish. Sergeant majors can often be seen guarding their eggs. An even prettier dive is along the stretch of coast from inside this reef northwards to Northwest Point. There is a sloping reef all along this shore. The maximum depth is about 60 feet at Northwest Point. Coral formations include lots of pillar corals, and there are usually large schools of blue chromis. Garden eels pop their heads out over the sand. On both dives you must mind the current.

More exciting dives are far from the anchorage, and a strong current makes them drift dives. Flat Rock drift dive is on Bequia's northwest coast, starting at the western end of Anse Chemin. This is a gentle, easy dive where you hardly have to use your fins and there is time to examine all the little creatures. You swim along a captivating reef that slopes gently into sand at 60 feet. You will see an excellent selection of soft and hard corals, lots of fish, arrow crabs, lobsters, tubeworms, and anemones. A couple of spotted snake eels hang out here, and you will often see a ray.

The Boulders is a pleasant drift dive about two-thirds of the way between Admiralty Bay and Moonhole. A gentle descent 60 feet down a coral slope takes you into an area where hundreds of fish, including huge schools of blue chromis and sennets, make ever-changing patterns as you drift with the current. Barracudas patrol up and down; moray eels, lobsters, crabs, and shrimps can be found. The reef gets deeper till you come to the boulders, which are tall rock formations, each about 20 feet high, starting from a bottom depth of 93 feet. There are tunnels to pass through and holes and caverns that provide hiding places for nurse sharks, groupers, angelfish, and jacks. As you return to the dive boat you may see a frogfish or seahorse.

Pigeon Island, to the west of Isle de Quatre, has beautiful dives. The island slopes off steeply to around 100 feet. There are walls, overhangs, rifts, and hollows decorated by deepwater lace coral. The visibility is generally excellent, and you will see huge schools of blue and brown chromis, big groupers, passing pelagic fish, and sometimes rays and turtles.

The Wall (West Cay, northern side) is an adventure dive down to 114 feet with dramatic vistas, the odd large pelagic, and lots of great stuff to examine along the wall on your way up. Moonhole (outside the Moonhole complex) offers temporary anchorage, though I would leave a crew member on board. Make sure you are anchored in sand and do not tie to the dive moorings. The easiest dive starts right in the bay and follows the reef around the point to the east, but watch for currents. This is a gentle dive to 60 feet, with hard and soft corals and a variety of smaller fish.

Snorkeling is good around Devil's Table and along the coast to Northwest Point. The dive shops also offer snorkeling trips.

House at Moonhole

Photo courtesy of Robert and Carroll Rooth

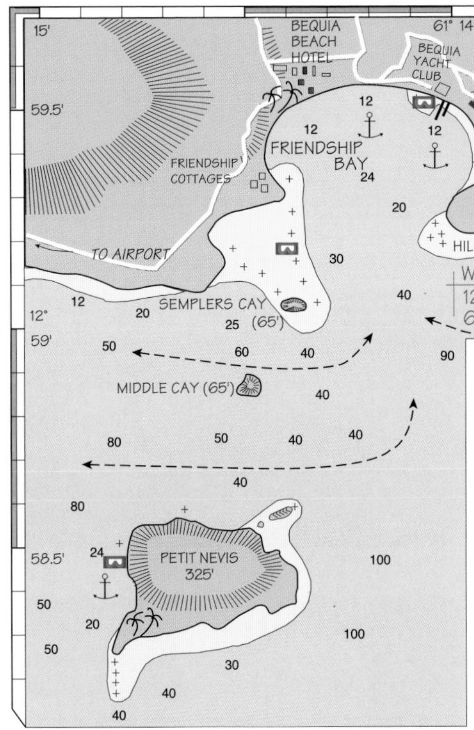

nature sanctuary and marine reserve. They ask that powerboats give the area a wide berth and that yachtspeople not anchor in the bay below to preserve the reef. If you must anchor, only do so in sand.

Bequia's airport is built along the south coast. There is a fishing dock about a third of a mile to its east, off Paget Farm, where in an emergency you can get ashore from a tenable, if rolly, anchorage. The Liming Bequia also has a dock with dinghy access.

MOONHOLE TO FRIENDSHIP BAY

If you are sailing from Admiralty Bay to West Cay you will undoubtedly catch sight of Moonhole. This rather isolated community, founded by the late American architect Tom Johnson, is not easily accessible by either land or sea, there being no road or good anchorage. Moonhole houses are certainly different; the original was built under a natural arch known as "Moonhole." It was abandoned when a huge boulder fell from the ceiling and crushed the empty bed below. The other houses grow out of the rocks without straight lines or right angles. They have huge arches, fantastic views, and lovely patios. There is seldom glass in the windows and the breeze is constant. Originally there was no electricity, but in recent years some have installed solar panels. Moonhole is a special kind of vacation home for the right people. The architecture is worth marveling at as you sail by.

The current managers, Robert and Carroll Rooth, are operating Moonhole as a

FRIENDSHIP BAY AND PETIT NEVIS

Friendship Bay, on the south side of Bequia, is gorgeous, with a lovely white beach. The anchorage is secure, with good holding, and in times of northerly swells it provides better protection than Admiralty Bay. A small swell often creeps in from the southeast, but you can cut the roll with a second anchor from the stern to keep yourself into the swells.

Navigation

A reef extends from the shore to Semplers Cay and beyond. Don't try to sail in or out that way, as some have. On the opposite side of the harbor a reef extends out a fair way from Hilaire Point (locally called "Hillary"). Keep in the center of the channel. Once inside, anchor in the east of the bay or off the Bequia Yacht Club dock. Note that a reef extends from the west side of the Bequia Yacht Club dock down to the beach.

Communications

Bequia Beach Hotel has WiFi at the bar, and you can carry your computer in.

Ashore

On the western half of the beach is the Bequia Beach Hotel, one of Bequia's largest, and run well. It starts on the beach and flows uphill to the road.

Their Bagatelle Restaurant [$$$$] is open and on the beach, with waves lapping just outside. The food is a fusion of local and European cuisine, beautifully cooked and served. This a very popular destination, not only for people anchored in Friendship Bay but also as a "getaway" from Admiralty Bay. Their Blue Tropic Restaurant is up the hill, open weekday evenings only, for fine Italian food. Reservations are essential.

If you are making a day of it over here, ask about the Bequia Beach Hotel's day passes and spa treatments.

For yachts, their Bequia Yacht Club at the east end of the bay is, at the moment, just one long refurbished dock. The club plans to rebuild the dinghy dock to its east and extend the main dock, then link the two to make suitable stern-to docking for superyachts up to 50 meters. Water and electricity should be available, and mansions are being built on the hillside behind the dock.

To the east of the Friendship Bay Hotel, progress has been made on the Bequia Heritage Foundation's Bequia Boat Museum. Some of Bequia's traditional whaling and fishing boats are here, along with a dug-out canoe.

Hibiscus

A walk-around platform, always open, will ensure that you can always see the exhibits. Take the road that goes around the back of Friendship Bay Hotel and the museum will be on your right.

Water sports

The best snorkeling in Friendship Bay is between Semplers Cay and the shore. Or try the reef along the shore to the west of the old Friendship Bay Resort dock.

PETIT NEVIS

Petit Nevis was the original whale-rendering island. It makes an interesting daytime anchorage with good exploring. The snorkeling along the shore is good, although the current can be strong out of the lee. If passing southward, note the long, southerly reef.

Mustique at a glance

Regulations

Mustique is a private island. Anchoring is only allowed in Britannia Bay, and there are fees. Access to shore is sometimes restricted. See Mustique text for details.

If you need clearance, customs and immigration are at the airport, normally 0800-1800, but the island is so small that they cannot be too far away out of hours. They charge an overtime fee outside of these hours, on Sundays, and holidays.

Jet skis and the like are strictly forbidden, as are spearfishing and anchoring without supervision. Water-skiing is not permitted in the yacht anchorage area.

Vessels carrying more than 25 passengers are not allowed in Mustique.

Shopping Hours

Corea's food store: Mon-Sat, 0800-1200, 1500-1800. Boutiques: 0900-1200 and 1400-1800. Some boutiques, Ali's, and Corea's are open Sunday mornings.

Holidays

See *St. Vincent*.

Telephones

Most Mustique numbers start (784) 488 + four digits. If you are using a private phone in Mustique, you just dial the last four digits of 488 numbers. The most used such phone is in Basil's Bar.

Basil's, 8350
Corea's, 8479
Firefly, 8414
Dive shop, 8486
Mustique Moorings, 8363
Security, 8848/8342
Horse riding, 8316
MMS (bike, mule rental), 8555
Mustique Company, 8424,
Airport, 8336
Customs, 8410
Immigration, 8368
Police, 8711
Medical clinic, 8353
Cotton House, 8125 or
(784) 456-4777

Transport

Ask Mustique Moorings or call:
Johnny P, (784) 530-6285
Pecky, (784) 433-8074
Eddie Boom, (784) 532-1834

The Cotton House Beach Bar

Mustique

Mustique was developed by Colin Tennant as a playground for the colorful, rich, and famous. The house owners bought the island from him and have restricted further development. House prices have soared from about a million to over ten times that much. Ownership has transitioned from the exotic to business people who value their privacy and don't want nautical yahoos with cameras hiding behind hedges, mistaking them for aging rock stars and models.

Mustique, although private and exclusive, has been kept as friendly and open to yachting visitors as possible. However, some restrictions apply (see *Regulations*). Please help keep it open. Use common courtesy: stick to the roads, do not walk up people's driveways or onto private property. Use the beach south of the anchorage for beach time, or the Cotton House beach if you are hanging out at the beach bar there. Take scenic photos for your own use, but do not photograph residents.

Mustique has about 90 large houses, one hotel, a guesthouse, a beach bar, a few boutiques, a small local village, and a fishing camp. About half the houses are available for rent when the owners are not in residence. As you would expect for an island of this type, prices are geared to the well-heeled. An excellent small medical clinic is run by Dr. Michael Bunbury, with good equipment for its size. Call 488-8353 for surgery hours.

What is wonderful about Mustique is that much of the island has been left wild, there are lovely trails and not much traffic. As other islands sprout buildings like some invasive weed, much of Mustique remains beautiful and unspoiled, an island where you can often hike or bike in peace on one of the best preserved Grenadine islands, with fabulous beaches and shady pathways.

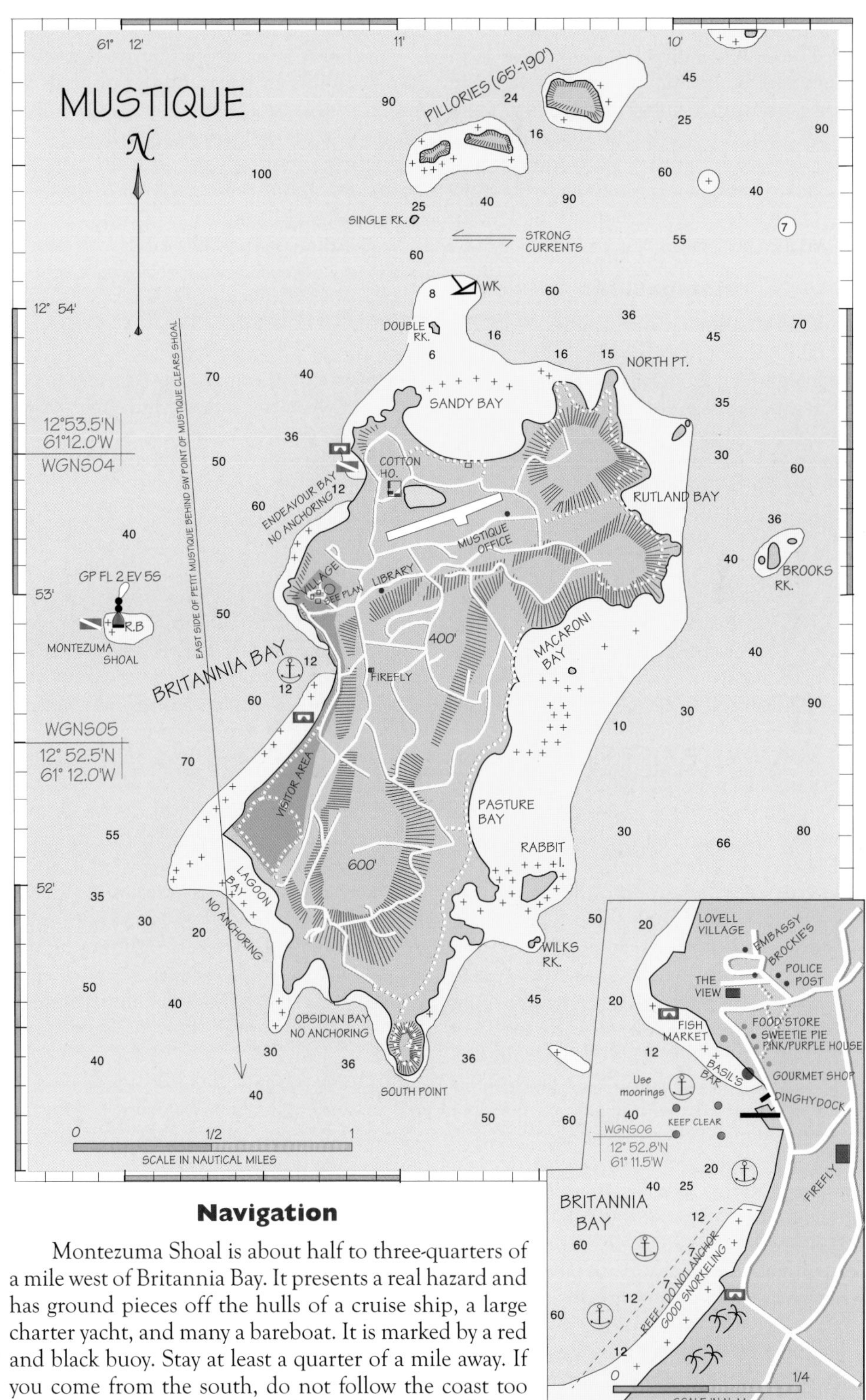

Navigation

Montezuma Shoal is about half to three-quarters of a mile west of Britannia Bay. It presents a real hazard and has ground pieces off the hulls of a cruise ship, a large charter yacht, and many a bareboat. It is marked by a red and black buoy. Stay at least a quarter of a mile away. If you come from the south, do not follow the coast too closely, as there is quite a reef extending seaward from the southern point of Britannia Bay.

The only permissible anchorage is in Britannia Bay. If you see a yacht moored in Endeavour Bay, it belongs to one of the house owners. Britannia Bay has sparkling clear water and is a lovely area for swimming and snorkeling, though it is generally rather rolly. The north side of the harbor has loud music on Wednesday nights.

Regulations

The Mustique Company controls the coastal waters of Mustique and provides 35 well-maintained moorings for yachts up to 60 feet; legally they cannot take yachts even one inch longer. Yachts over 60 feet must anchor outside the moorings under the direction of Berris Little, the harbormaster (Mustique Moorings, VHF: 16/68, (784) 488-8363/533-0216). The Mustique Moorings crew are around most of the day from 0800-1800, but sometimes away 1230-1430.

There is a conservation fee that entitles you to a three-consecutive-night stay. This fee in $EC is: up to 70 feet, $210; 71-100 feet, $450; 101-150 feet, $550; over 151 feet, $1000. Berris or Sean Snagg collect the fees and give you an official receipt. Their hut is at the end of the jetty. The moorings do not lift, so can be hard to reach. Call Berris or Sean and someone will come out and help. Otherwise, put a dinghy in the water or, if you have a stern platform, come stern-to so you are low enough to tie onto the mooring. There is no extra charge for the moorings.

Each buoy has a swivel on top. Attach your lines through the swivel. Use two lines, one to each side of your bow. Allow plenty of line to increase the scope (20 feet minimum, more if your bow is high off the water). Never use a single line from one side of the boat through the mooring to the other side. Yachts of up to 45 feet and 6- to 7-foot draft can use any mooring. Longer and deeper yachts should use the outer moorings which are more widely spaced over sand. If you are over 60 feet, or if all the moorings are taken, contact Berris for anchoring instructions.

Day-charter yachts visiting Mustique pay a landing fee of $40 EC per head or $300 EC per day. This is also charged to those on yachts taking day trips and tours; ask Berris for details.

Tenders should only be used to drop people ashore in Britannia Bay or go to the beach in the same bay. They should not be used to visit other parts of the island.

Drones and press photography are banned unless express permission has been given by The Mustique Company.

Mustique is a private island, with owners who are concerned about privacy and security. Unfortunately, a few guests from yachts have trespassed in private houses. Captains are responsible for their crew and guests, and The Mustique Company has the right to permanently ban any captain and yacht whose passengers or crew misbehave.

Regulations may be changed by The Mustique Company at any time. Here is how things stand:

The designated visitor area is open. This goes all the way from the local village past the anchorage, and south along the western shore as far as the salt pond, and you can walk the salt pond trail. If you wish to go outside this area, please talk to Berris or Sean at the moorings office and let them know what you wish to do. This way they will know who is wandering about the island and what they are doing.

Sometimes (normally three weeks over Christmas and the new year, two weeks in August, and two weeks over Easter), land access is restricted and you cannot go outside the visitors area unless you have a confirmed reservation for the Cotton House or Firefly, in which case you must ask them to send transport for you. If, at these times, you need to visit customs or the clinic, arrange it with Berris or Sean.

There is some flexibility, and during these times call Berris before you come to discuss what you want to do. You may be able to hike, though you may have to take a local guide.

Beach picnic tables have been set up for the use of residents. People on yachts may sometimes be able to use the ones in the visitor area at no charge; ask Berris for details.

Communications

Mustique has an excellent library where you can catch up on the internet (six computers) or read the latest magazines and peruse their books. You can send faxes or make photocopies. Contributions of good books are always welcome. They open Monday to Friday 0900-1300, 1500-1800, and Saturday 0900-1200.

There is WiFi around Basil's and Sweetie Pie, and you might be able to get it at anchor.

Services

Garbage disposal is at the head of the dock. Transport within the island is provided by taxis, and these can sometimes take you on an island tour. They can be found outside Mustique Moorings and Berris can help make arrangements.

When you realize the roll is so bad that you won't be able to sleep a wink, contact The View, Firefly House, or The Cotton House to see if they have rooms available. (Basil's Bar can put you in touch.)

Provisioning and shopping

Corea's supermarket has a good selection. Augment this with fresh fruit and vegetables from Stanley's photogenic little stall, where prices are reasonable and the service unbeatable. Go to Basil's Gourmet store for wines and specialty foods and for local/nature books and music CDs. For fish, try the fish market, where you can buy fresh fish and lobster in season. Glendina sometimes sells fresh produce at a stand on the road to the local village.

In the morning, head down to Sweetie Pie Bakery, Cafe, and Boulangerie between the pink and purple houses to stock up on fresh croissants, pain au chocolat, and Danish, along with many other pastries. French owner Ali bakes these, plus many kinds of excellent bread. Ali will be happy to discuss charter boat requirements. They also sell coffee, ice cream, and lunch-time sandwiches. They have comfortable outdoor seating and are open 0700-1800.

The Purple House is an excellent boutique run by Susie, who has a collection of swimwear, casual and not-so casual clothing, hand-crafted gifts and souvenirs, games, hats, pareos, hand-painted calabash art, costume jewelry, and more. The Pink House has a more complete range of elegant clothing, plus some casual clothing and kids' toys, and a big selection of jewelry.

Basil's boutique should be open by the time this book is published.

The Cotton House has a boutique on the left, just before Endeavour Bay, in the same building as the gym. If you need household hardware, get a taxi to take you to the Mustique Depot.

Restaurants

Basil's Bar [VHF: 68, $$$$] is now owned by The Mustique Company, which has done a good job of renovating the space while maintaining the original look and feel that everyone loves. Built of wood and bamboo, it is perched on stilts over the water, with waves lapping underneath. Informal and the most popular establishment with the yachting community, this is the Caribbean's most famous beach bar. It is the place to meet people, to contact other establishments on the island, to relax and look at the sunset, or just to get off your rolling boat for dinner. Seafood and lobster are specialties.

The Mustique Company is currently revamping the menu in addition to the space, but has promised to keep many of the old favorites, and should have a full menu by the time this is published. Many come for the popular Wednesday night barbecue buffet, which is followed by a jump-up. They usually have light jazz/blues music on Sundays, often featuring Jan and Louis. In addition, The Mustique Blues Festival is a superb two-week blues festival towards the end of January to early February, which also visits Bequia.

Basil's

Proceeds from the sale of CDs from this go to Basil Charles Education Foundation, supporting local students and schools throughout the country. If you are interested in helping, pick up a flyer at Basil's.

The local village is always open to yachts and here Lisa Lewis has a restaurant with an incredible view of Britannia Bay, naturally called The View [$$]. Take the short cut up the hill: take the little path at the side of the boutiques, bear left at the bird cage, turn right on the road, and then left up the steps shortly after. At the top, turn left, walk to the end, and you are there.

Lisa opens from breakfast to dinner every day. For lunch, Lisa does a big trade in takeout for both locals and visitors. You can walk in for lunch, but calling in advance is much better and will give you a choice of food. If you are coming to dinner you have to give her a little warning. She is personable, hardworking, and will cook you a delicious meal with good fresh vegetables for a reasonable price. Her fish is fresh and her sautéed conch delightful. You can also get beef, mutton, and chicken. Saturday night she does a popular barbecue. If you need a night ashore, Lisa has some rooms.

Other village restaurants include Brockie's, owned by Becky, and Selwyn's Embassy Bar [both $], both of which serve good lunch specials most days. Brockie's sometimes has chicken and chips in the evenings and both will cook a good dinner to order. If you want to just hang out for a drink, try Hill Top Bar.

Stan and Elizabeth, from England, own a guesthouse and bar/restaurant called Firefly [$$$$$]. It has a dramatic view over the floodlit swimming pool to Britannia Bay. The atmosphere is elegant and a touch formal, yet friendly, making it popular with those who spend time on the island. Regulars gather round the bar in the evening, and a piano occasionally inspires one of them to play for a while. Their food is an inventive blend of Caribbean and European cuisine, using fresh ingredients. You will love the desserts. Wander up for lunch or dinner. The short walk will whet your appetite, but for those who prefer to ride, a staff member will come and collect dinner guests from the dock. Reservations are advisable.

For superb cuisine in lavish elegance, don your best evening pants or a dress (it is somewhat formal) and call the Cotton House [$$$$$]. It is about a 15-minute walk, but if you make dinner reservations they are happy to come and get you. Cotton House, owned and run by The Mustique Company, is one of the fanciest hotels in the Caribbean. Originally an 18th century coral warehouse and sugar mill, it was artfully rebuilt by the late British designer Oliver Messel.

They usually have top chefs and, when on form, their dinner restaurant, The Veranda, produces the best cuisine on the island. The Beach Cafe, right on the beach in Endeavour Bay, is perfect for a morning coffee and pastry, ice cream, or lunch of fresh fish or lobster (1230-1500). It opens in the evening until 1900, and is sometimes available for private functions.

For a real treat, renovate your body with a visit to the Cotton House Spa, featuring ila treatments and a gym. Cotton House has a museum in the sugar mill with some good pre-Columbian pottery and stone work. It is usually open, just walk in and take look.

Ashore

For a quick view of the island you can see if a Mustique taxi can do a tour, although this is sometimes restricted. To really enjoy the beauty of this island, go hiking. Basil's Gourmet store has great books on the natural history of Mustique. If you turn right at the main dock and follow the road south, staying on the path that follows the shore, you will have a delightful walk. It joins a trail that goes around the salt pond, and brings you to a perfect beach at Lagoon Bay.

If you get more ambitious, (and if there are no restrictions) follow our map, taking the roads that lead to Obsidian Bay. Head south from the dock, staying on the road. After about 20 minutes you will pass a couple of roads on your right and see gate posts on the road; continue through the gate posts. Turn left at a junction where there is a concrete shed on the left corner and a grate across the road, and a sign saying "Penthouse" opposite. Go up the hill, and where you have a choice of concrete (left fork) and dirt track (right fork). Take the right fork. This brings you to Obsidian Bay, and from there you can follow wonderful trails around South Point and up the east coast to Pasture Bay. From here you can walk back to Britannia Bay (total hike 3-4 hours).

Another excellent hike is around North Point, from the north around to the east, till you can see Macaroni and Pasture Bays. For this one, you need to get a taxi to drop you off at the trail head right by L'Ansecou House. The trail starts down what looks like a nameless private drive, but just before the "private" sign, the trail leads off to the right. It follows the coast, sometimes along open cliffs, sometimes bounded by dry scrub trees. By the time you have walked back to Britannia Bay it will take about three hours, though you can bail out halfway at Rutland Bay. Keep your eye open on all hikes for the pretty land tortoises.

Horseback riding is done in the cool of the day, at 0800, 0900, 1500 or 1600. Mountain bikes are sometimes available through Mustique Mechanical Services or Mustique Moorings.

Water sports

You can go sailboarding or diving at Mustique Water Sports [VHF: 68]. Brian Richards, the dive instructor and manager, is very good and will pick divers up from their yachts when space is available. The water is generally very clear, and diving is pleasant.

Walk-in Reef is just off the dive shop dock and ideal for beginners. South Britannia is a drift dive. Let the current carry you through a delightful garden of soft corals as you watch large schools of Bermuda chubs and Creole wrasses. The occasional sight of an eagle ray makes it perfect. The wreck of the Jonas, a 90-foot dredge, lies in 40 feet of water on the east side of Montezuma Shoal. Beautiful coral formations are home to barracudas and nurse sharks. Southeast Pillory is another drift dive; the current sweeps you along a steep slope, which drops from 20 feet to 90 feet. The scenery is ever changing as you go along, with lots of reef fish and large soft corals. Dry Rock (on the south side of Petit Mustique) is the place for big fish: schools of barracudas, nurse sharks, and rays. You often see turtles.

Canouan (For information on holidays, customs, etc., see *St. Vincent*)

Canouan is a lovely island with spectacular beaches, pleasant walks, and great views almost anywhere. Walk up the hill to the east and see the fabulous windward lagoon, where an outer reef protects the island.

It is also an island of three parts. The local central part has moved from a sleepy backwater of small wooden houses and fields of pigeon peas to a prosperous settlement of big solid houses. This local part surrounds the main anchorage and is warm and welcoming; the people are friendly and provide a variety of services to yachtspeople.

The Canouan Resort Development Company (CRD) owns, has developed, and manages the north of the island. This, the largest part,

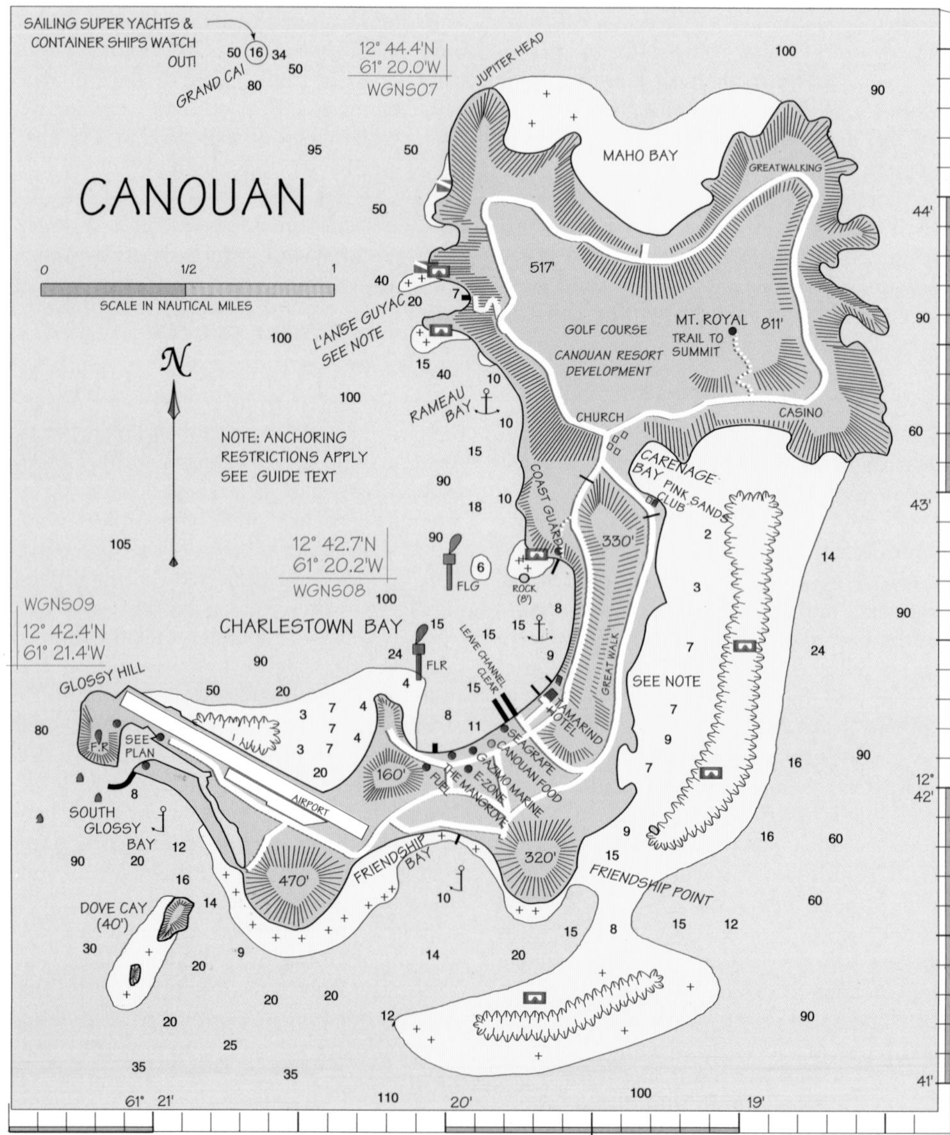

is gated, with guards at the entry points, and locals and visitors alike need permission to enter. CRD built a hotel of about 180 rooms with a giant beach restaurant and pool. Now they have torn it all down and built a boutique hotel of about 25 rooms farther down the shore.

To the southeast, Dermot Desmond has the big new Glossy Bay Marina project well under way. It will take boats up to 100 meters long with 5.3 meters draft. This too is gated with guards, but they have two restaurants which you will usually be able to get permission to visit. The gating of over 50 percent of Canouan, both in the north and in the south of the island, must annoy the 1,500 local residents who live in the middle.

The airport is excellent, with plenty of room for the largest private jet, and it may be the cutest thatched-roof airport building in the world.

Navigation

Deep-draft vessels should avoid Grand Cai, about 0.75 miles west of Jupiter Point. While this shoal is generally about 36 feet deep, it has a small isolated 16-foot shoal at 12° 44.490'N, 61° 20.645'W. Seas in this general area are often 6-8 feet high, further reducing the depth. It badly damaged the keel of a sailing super-yacht. It is too small to cause a noticeable difference in the sea state and is normally of no consequence to yachts with less than 10-foot draft.

Planes approaching the airport come in low over the sea, so give the western end of the runway good clearance.

Rameau Bay is a pleasant spot, far from the village. You may have to try a couple of times to get the anchor dug in, and the wind shifts around, so two anchors are advisable. Make sure you do not damage the coral. L'Anse Guyac (aka Corbay) is one of the most protected anchorages on the island. Mr. Pignataro, one of the developers, built a private eating house here, imported many tons of white sand and persuaded the government to ban anchoring in the bay. You can anchor just outside in about 20 feet of water. Watch out for the reefs off both headlands.

Whether you anchor here, in Rameau Bay, or in town, you should dinghy to this beach to enjoy it and the good snorkeling around the headlands. Guards may try to shoo you off, but all beaches 66 feet back from high tide are public; tell them you are on the Queen's chain.

Charlestown Bay is the main anchorage and the entrance is marked by a red and green beacon on either side. Pass between them. You can anchor anywhere in the bay except close to the Tamarind Beach Hotel, where you must anchor outside any moorings. The anchorage can be pleasant, but northeasterly winds with northerly swells will make it uncomfortable and, in extreme conditions, untenable. The holding is fairly good in sand, poor in weed. Leave a large, clear channel into the big dock for ferries.

On windy days the wind gets held up in the hills and then shoots down from the north

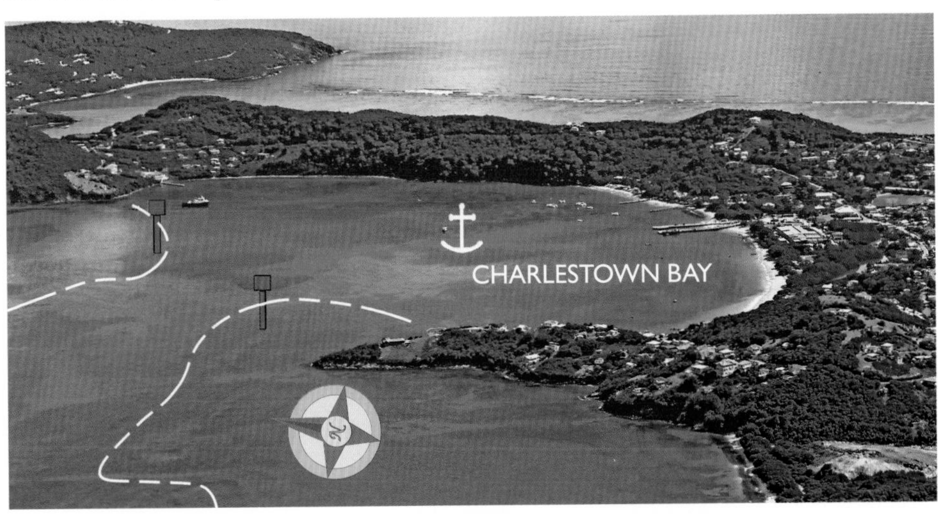

in intense gusts. Boats swing every which way.

Regulations

Customs and immigration are in the big government revenue office building in town, open 0800-1600 on weekdays. They are also at the airport almost any time of day, and on weekends.

Communications

The Tamarind Beach Hotel has WiFi, passwords are available from reception. Both Digicel and Flow have offices in town, which tend to open around 1000.

General yacht services

A large ferry dock and roll on platform is on the beach, and two docks are just south at the Tamarind Beach Hotel. In big swells they are all dangerous. The big ferry dock is high and difficult. You may use the Tamarind Beach Hotel dock as long as the swells are not too big. The other hotel dock is abandoned.

Two marine services, run by cousins Marcus and John, provide most things you need. They offer moorings at $50 EC a night (dive and check them). They sell ice and water (currently it is good desalinated town water delivered alongside, making Canouan the best place in the Grenadines to top up). They will also take your garbage for a small fee. Either can take you ashore, and help arrange any kind of tour or anything else you need.

Call Marcus Marine Services or John's Marine Services on VHF: 16. Many of their moorings are in front of the Tamarind Beach Hotel. (If you anchor inside these, you are too close to the hotel.) Marcus's son Mark normally runs his boat. John is sometimes on his boat, or his assistant Christopher, who is friendly and helpful. You will be happy with either service; both are professional.

Gazimo plans to bring in a fuel barge which will deliver diesel and gasoline alongside. In the meantime, John and Marcus can help you out with fuel.

The Tamarind Beach Hotel staff [VHF: 16] are helpful, friendly, and happy to help if they can. They sell freshly made bread at Italian delicatessen (see *Provisioning*) and the

Palapa Restaurant. Ice is also available. They have a massage and body-care center, and a taxi service. Hotel day pass rates are available; ask at reception.

There are garbage bins ashore: two are often close to the big government building, and a couple of others are on the main street. Try not to bring in too much.

The coast guard station and dock are in the north end of the bay. Diesel and gas are sold at the gas station behind the southern end of the beach, as well as from the Glossy Bay Marina.

Technical yacht services

Gazimo Marine Services [VHF:16] is owned and run by Gazimo (Earl) who worked for years as head mechanic in a Toronto marina repair shop. He is competent, easy to work with, and can deal with any problem you have, from a clogged head to a jammed winch. He is an excellent diesel mechanic and can fix outboards. He has tons of experience fixing broken charter yachts in Canada, and his ex-boss, Robert, who has a holiday house here, occasionally likes to help out. Gazimo is also the man to see if you have a torn sail - he does not sew himself, but there is a woman on the island with a big heavy machine and he can arrange it. Gazimo also rents golf-carts and mules. See *Transport*. He can bring in a fuel barge for alongside delivery of gas and diesel (see *General yacht services*)

Provisioning and shopping

Tamarind Beach Hotel's Italian deli, Buon Appetito, is a fancy delicatessen selling the finest Italian cold cuts and cheeses, preserves, pastas, cookies and sauces, along with a wide selection of Italian wines, French champagne, and liqueurs. They are open 1000-1400 and 1800-2000, closed Sundays.

Panini and freshly baked bread are available daily. You will find all kind of specialty food, such as pate, truffles, and buffalo mozzarella. They can prepare gift baskets. If you come for lunch you can use the seats in Pirate's Cove Bar.

Canouan Food Limited is on the main street and opens 0800-2000, except Sunday: 0800-1200. They have a good selection for a small market, including quite a few local and imported vegetables. If you are buying cases of beer or more than you can carry, they will deliver to the dock. Some other shops are okay; check out Rock Steady bakery next to Gazimo. The bank has an ATM.

Market stalls on the street leading to the ferry dock have local produce.

Restaurants

The Tamarind Beach Hotel [VHF: 16, $$$$] has an ideal beach location with a good dinghy dock and yachts are welcome. This elegant hotel has two waterfront restaurants under the picturesque thatched roofs that have been built in the traditional South American style.

La Palapa is the most formal restaurant and is open for breakfast, lunch and dinner (in season). You are asked to wear long trousers, shirts and closed shoes for dinner. It is advisable to make reservations in advance to be sure of seating.

The informal Pirate's Cove Restaurant and Bar opens at 1600. You are welcome in shorts and casual wear. Comfortable seating in a garden setting overlooking the bay makes this an ideal hangout. Meals are available and include seafood and meat dishes as well as pasta. They also prepare great pizzas in a wooden pizza oven. Live music is common for holidays and special events.

The hotel Beach Bar opens from 1000-1800. You can get lunch, a light snack, or a fancy cocktail.

Mangrove [$$] is a good local restaurant owned by Albert, who also owns Canouan Food Limited. It is quite far down the road, just where the airport road turns up the hill. The beach location is perfect, the prices and food are local, with very inexpensive lunches and moderately priced dinners, including fresh fish and lobster. They open for lunch and dinner every day.

The Pink Sands Club [$$$$$] has recently changed management and may be changing names. It is a very fancy boutique hotel in the gated northern part of the island, with tennis courts, villas, and a golf course. They offer day passes, golf passes, and you may be able to visit for a meal.

Andre's Sea Grape [$$] is just south of the main dock. He has done a great job renovating this building, which is on the beach. It is open 0900-2200 every day but Wednesday. You can get lunch and dinner, but you need to make reservations for dinner. They serve good local food, specializing in fresh seafood, but also have meat dishes.

Other restaurants include Pompy's Bar and Restaurant, Tip Toe Bar (opens at 1900; for a meal call Chester Deroche in advance, 458-8021), Honey Chrome, Frontline, and Glimpses Bar.

Transport

Gazimo and his partner Deborah at Gazimo Marine Services [VHF: 16], rent various sized mules and golf carts, which are ideal for anything you need to do on the island, be it a fun tour, leaving from the airport, or provisioning. These carts have a roof but are otherwise open to the breeze and view. The golf carts are easy to drive, can do a U-turn on any road, and are perfect for this small island. They are not expensive, there is no paperwork, and they will rent them by the half-day which is great for an island tour.

You can arrange a regular taxi with the Tamarind Beach Hotel.

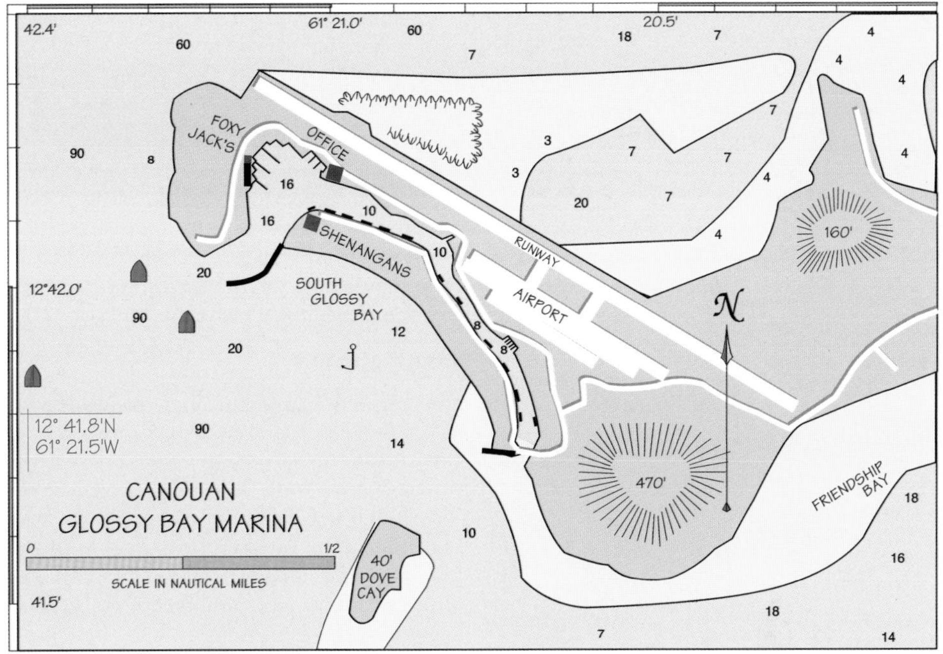

Ashore

Rent one of Gazimo's mules or golf carts and take a tour; there are many spectacular views. Or at least walk up to the ridge to see the wonderful, reef-protected lagoon.

Mount Royal is the highest hill in Canouan, with great views. It is in the gated part of the island so you will have to phone and arrange a guide to take you (about $20 US per head). The Tamarind Beach Hotel can do this for you, as well as arrange island tours or picnics on secluded beaches.

SOUTH GLOSSY BAY

You can anchor off this lovely beach. The water here is gorgeous, but it can be rolly.

Glossy Bay Marina is an upmarket, exclusive marina, attractively gardened and perfectly maintained, with water colors reminiscent of a swimming pool rather than a marina. Construction of buildings ashore will be ongoing but is not normally obtrusive. The marina is a joint project between Dermont Desmond and the government, and is managed by Mithat Can Alagoz from Turkey.

They have room for 120 yachts in a series of finger docks, with water, gas, diesel, and power (50 and 60 cycle) available along side. They can take yachts up to 100 meters in length and 5.3 meters in draft.

Swells occasionally affect the berths, and while they are barely visible, they have been known to strain docking lines.

Ashore, Shenanigans and Foxy Jacks are their two restaurants [$$$$$]. Both are good, but sometimes only one is open. Reservations are essential. Shenanigans has a pool which guests can use if they spend over $50 US on their meal.

Yachts anchoring outside can dinghy in and some services are available (transfer to the airport for about $300 US). If you dinghy in to use the restaurant ask if there is a minimum charge.

FRIENDSHIP BAY

Keen snorkelers might be interested in a daytime stop at Friendship Bay on Canouan's south coast. Approach past Glossy Bay, pass inside or outside Dove Cay and associated rocks, and follow the coast, keeping a lookout for coral heads. Friendship Bay is usually a bit rolly, but is the best anchorage in large

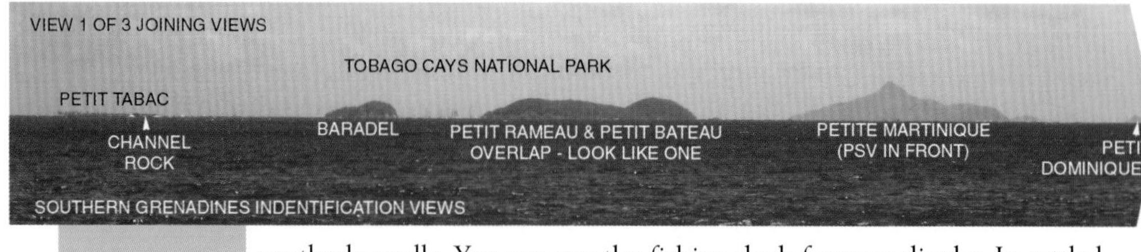

northerly swells. You can use the fishing dock for your dinghy. In settled conditions you can dinghy up the windward side of Canouan inside the reefs, where the snorkeling is good and some yachts anchor and kitesurf. The government has currently banned this, but a few yachts still go.

Water sports

At least 10 good dives can be found in Canouan. There are walls with giant boulders and sloping reefs, and sharks, turtles, and rays are often spotted. For those diving on their own, the easiest spot to anchor for a dive is in Corbay. Dive to seaward of the rocky headland on the northern side of the bay, or you can dinghy north up the coast and look for your own spot. Snorkeling is also good around the rocks in Rameau Bay.

SOUTHERN GRENADINES PASSAGES

From Canouan to Carriacou the Grenadines huddle together, each just a short hop from the next. The islands are generally small and quiet.

Any island with a few inhabitants will also have a rum shop where you can meet people and learn to drink Jack Iron ~ a powerful, rough white rum, sometimes distilled far from government inspectors. A small shot is poured into a glass, and the idea is to down it all in one gulp, preferably without tasting. Then you reach for a large glass of water to put out the fire.

Navigation

The current sets to the west most of the time, so head east of your destination until you have gotten the feel of its strength. The southern Grenadines

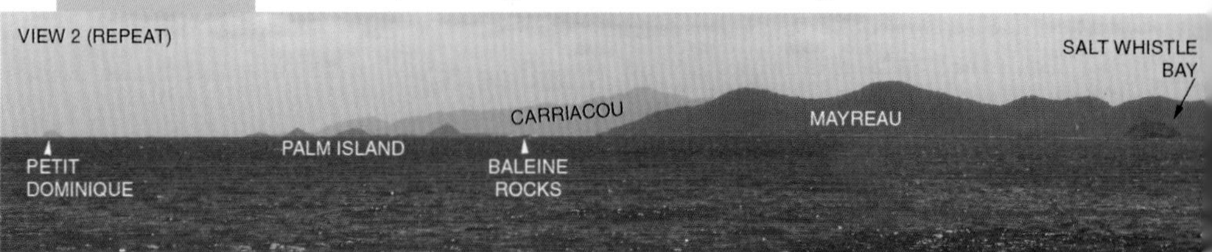

are strewn with keel-hungry reefs. This is the area where people make the most mistakes, and several yachts have been lost. Usually this is because people misidentify islands. If you approach this area with just a shade of apprehension and self-questioning, you should be okay.

Several navigational beacons help. Most of them are on the edges of shoals, so keep well clear.

Sailing south

When you round Glossy (Glass) Hill at Canouan, you must be sure you know which island is which. Mayreau lies in front of Union, and some people see the two as one island and then mistake the Tobago Cays for Mayreau. If you are heading for the lee of Mayreau, your compass heading should be around 225-230° magnetic. If you find yourself sailing between south and 200°, you are probably heading for the Tobago Cays ~ and trouble.

Tobago Cays. (See also sketch charts, page 292 and 296), If you approach the Tobago Cays from the north, the easiest and best route is as follows: after you round Glossy Hill, head for the middle of Mayreau (about 228° magnetic). As you approach Mayreau, you can see Baleine Rocks. Leave these to port, giving them reasonable clearance, and sail on until you are over halfway between them and Mayreau, before heading up into the Tobago Cays. Line up the day markers in the Cays if you can see them. (Note: Petit Rameau and Petit Bateau look like one island for much of the approach.)

An alternative, and much trickier approach is to head a bit to the east of Mayreau from Glossy Hill, and then sail 100 yards to the east of Baleine Rocks, between the rocks and the northwest end of Horseshoe Reef. This entrance channel is about a quarter-of-a-mile wide, and Horseshoe Reef is often not visible, so caution is advised. The current can be strong, so make

sure you are not being set down onto the rocks. Once past the rocks, hold course until the day markers line up, then head up into the islands.

Mayreau. When approaching Mayreau, you have to avoid Dry Shingle, which only has a stump of a marker. Pass close to Salt Whistle Bay. When sailing round the lee of Mayreau, watch out for the reef off Grand Col Point, which is sometimes marked by a red buoy. It is unreliable and was missing in 2018. Pass well outside this reef. When heading to Palm or Union, you need to head well up, at least to the middle of Palm Island, until you figure out how much you are being set down, as the current can be very strong. Watching the airport on Union against Carriacou gives an idea of current set. Union's deadly windward reef (Newlands Reef) extends halfway to Palm Island, so you have to sail almost to Palm before heading west into Clifton Harbour. Note that there are three red beacons on Newlands Reef. Leave these to starboard as you head into Clifton. Swing in a curve well outside them.

Grand de Coi, between Union and Palm, is a dangerous reef. It is not quite as bad as it used to be, as the center part of it is now usually above water and visible. There is a yellow and black beacon on its western side. You must always pass to the west (Union Island side) of this beacon, keeping well clear. A number of yachts have run aground here, and several have been destroyed, usually coming from Petit St. Vincent (PSV) to Palm or Union. The following pointers may also be helpful in gauging your position.

All directions: When there is a gap between PSV and Petite Martinique, you are too far south to hit Grand de Coi. When this gap is closed, keep clear of Grand de Coi by watching the western side of Mayreau against the Union Island airport. If you keep the west side of Mayreau behind the airport you will be west of Grand de Coi. A gap between the two stands you in danger.

For all directions heading south: Sail to the entrance of Clifton Harbor, then pass west of the Grand de Coi beacon.

To Carriacou: Head toward the northwest coast. When you approach Hillsborough, it is safest to pass to the west of Jack a Dan before rounding up into town.

To PSV: When you have passed Grand de Coi, steer for the east side of Carriacou until PSV bears due east, then head on in, passing well to the south of Mopion, Pinese, and all their surrounding reefs. Keep an eye on current set and compensate if necessary.

A trickier and more dangerous way is to pass between the two little sand cays, Mopion and Pinese. The course from the lee side of Grand de Coi is around 165-170° magnetic, though with current you may have to head considerably more to the east. A bearing of 160° magnetic on the highest peak of Petite Martinique takes you close enough to eyeball your way in. Mopion usually has a small thatch shelter on it. Always sail through the center of the passage, and do not round up too soon, as the reef extends about a quarter of a mile southwest of Mopion. Recently, this has been easier because another small sandbar formed closer to the edge of the reef (see our PSV and Petite Martinique chart). Treat this passage with caution.

Sailing north

From Carriacou to Clifton and Palm: The safest route is to pass to the west of Jack a Dan, and then follow the coast up to Rapid Point. From Rapid Point, aim for the east side of Union, checking on the current set by watching Frigate Island against Union. As you near Union, you should be able to see the reefs between Frigate and Clifton. Do not get too close to these, as the current and wind are setting you down on them. On the other hand, keep an eye out for the Grand de Coi reef to the east. Stay to the west of the beacon that marks this reef (see also Grand de Coi notes, above, under Mayreau).

From PSV to Union: Sail due west till you are on a line between the east coasts of Carriacou and Union before changing course to Clifton. Before the gap closes between PSV and Petite Martinique, edge westward till the finger of land on the western side of Mayreau disappears behind Union Island airport. Pass to the west of the Grand de Coi beacon. Experienced sailors could head out between Mopion and Pinese and then head for the Pinnacle until the finger of land on the western side of Mayreau disappears behind the new Union Island airport, or until the Grand de

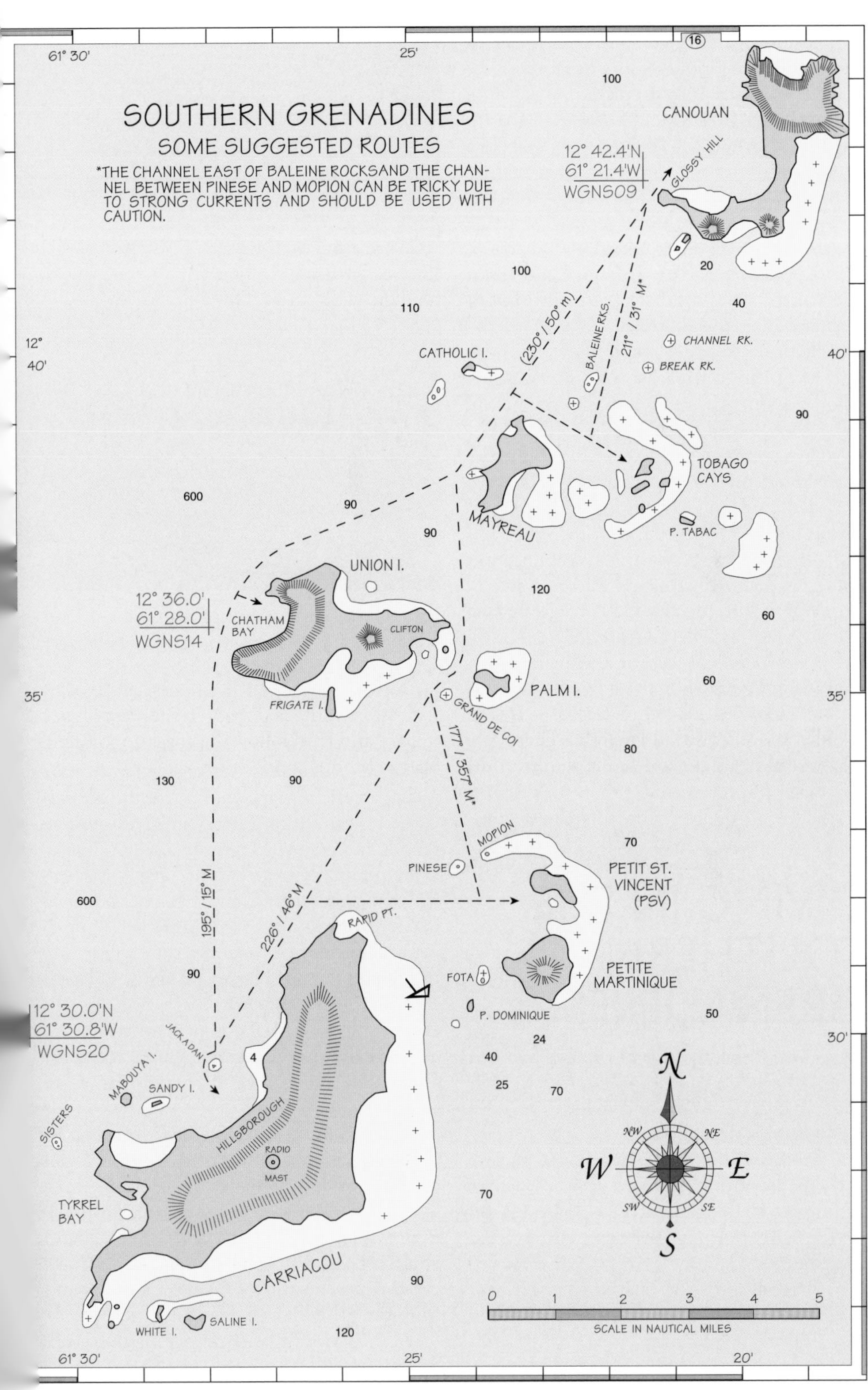
SOUTHERN GRENADINES
SOME SUGGESTED ROUTES
*THE CHANNEL EAST OF BALEINE ROCKSAND THE CHANNEL BETWEEN PINESE AND MOPION CAN BE TRICKY DUE TO STRONG CURRENTS AND SHOULD BE USED WITH CAUTION.
61° 30'
25'
20'
12° 40'
40'
35'
30'
CANOUAN
GLOSSY HILL
12° 42.4'N
61° 21.4'W
WGNS09
(230° / 50° m)
BALEINE RKS.
211° / 31° M*
CHANNEL RK.
BREAK RK.
CATHOLIC I.
MAYREAU
TOBAGO CAYS
P. TABAC
UNION I.
12° 36.0'
61° 28.0'
WGNS14
CHATHAM BAY
CLIFTON
FRIGATE I.
PALM I.
GRAND DE COI
177° / 357° M*
MOPION
PINESE
PETIT ST. VINCENT (PSV)
RAPID PT.
FOTA
P. DOMINIQUE
PETITE MARTINIQUE
195° / 15° M
226° / 46° M
12° 30.0'N
61° 30.8'W
WGNS20
JACKADAN
MABOUYA I.
SANDY I.
SISTERS
HILLSBOROUGH
RADIO MAST
TYRREL BAY
CARRIACOU
WHITE I.
SALINE I.
N
NW
NE
W
E
SW
SE
S
SCALE IN NAUTICAL MILES
0
1
2
3
4
5
16
100
110
600
90
120
60
80
130
70
50
24
40
25
4

St. Vincent & the Grenadines

Coi beacon is identified. Always pass well to the west of the Grand de Coi beacon.

From Palm northwards: Always sail round the lee (west side) of Mayreau. Pass to the west of Grand Col Point, staying well clear of the reef. Then, as you get to the north of Mayreau, stay well east of Dry Shingle (marked by a black and yellow beacon), which extends eastward from Catholic Island.

Approaching the Tobago Cays from the south: Sail round the lee (west side) of Mayreau, then head straight up toward the middle of the Cays. If you are tacking under sail, favor the Mayreau side of the channel when passing Baleine Rocks to avoid the one-fathom shoal to their south. There is a southern entrance to the Cays, but it is tricky and should not be attempted without local knowledge. Many charter yachts have run aground here. However, if you are in the Cays on a quiet day with good reef visibility, you could try leaving by this route to go south.

When leaving the Cays to go north: The safest route is to sail from the anchorage to the north end of Mayreau, then head north after you have passed Baleine Rocks. There is also a channel to the east of Baleine Rocks about a quarter of a mile wide. From the Cays, you have to head just south of the rocks until you reach the channel and then turn north, or you are in danger of hitting the western edge of Horseshoe Reef.

DIVING IN THE SOUTHERN GRENADINES

The normally clear water makes diving in the southern Grenadines wonderful, though currents can be strong, and many dives have to be done as drift dives.

Diving within the Tobago Cays Marine Park (the area from well to the west of Mayreau through to the outside of World's End Reef) is excellent, but you must go with a local dive shop.

One call and a dive boat will come by and pick you up from your yacht in the Tobago Cays, Mayreau, or Union.

Grenadines Dive [VHF: 16/68] is a pleasant, relaxed dive operation in Union Island run by Glenroy Adams from Bequia. Glenroy has many years of experience in this area, knows the sites better than anyone else, and has done much for environmental education in Union, and for the conservation of the Tobago Cays. Glenroy will collect you from your yacht in Union, Mayreau, PSV, or the Tobago Cays. If you are on a big yacht with a large tender and own your own dive gear, Glenroy can supply a knowledgeable dive guide. He will also do private dives. If you are short of ice or have run out of bread, he will happily bring some along on his way out.

Nurse shark at Isle De Ronde , Grenada

Jean-Michel Cousteau Diving is based in PSV. This upmarket operation, where everything is top class, is primarily for PSV guests. They may occasionally have room for additional guests. See also Canouan Dive Center under *Canouan*.

You can still dive on your own in Canouan, Union, and PSV. In Union, you can dive on the outer edge of Newlands Reef, which is very easy from your yacht. In Chatham, you can dive on the northern headland and the coast farther north, and in PSV you can dive on the north side of the reef around Mopion.

Dives within the park include the wreck of the World War I gunboat Purina. It is marked on our chart (page 296). While you can always get some elegant views of large schools of fish framed by pieces of wreckage, this dive does not compare in scenic beauty with the reef dives. As it is only 140 feet long, it is a dive where you don't move much ~ you are already there. Take it easy and get on more intimate terms with the fish and sea creatures, which are abundant. Since the fish are very tame, it is ideal for underwater photography.

Surface current over the wreck can be strong, but at depth it is not usually a problem. I start with a slow exploration to see the layout and to get a feel for the kinds of fish present. Then I examine each part of the wreck, concentrating on the invertebrates and letting the fish come to me as they will.

Diving outside Horseshoe Reef on either side of the small boat passage is pretty, but watch for current, though in this area the current is mostly on the surface. Farther north the current can be very strong, and it is more suitable as a drift dive. Diving is also good on the reef outside Petit Tabac.

Diving in some of the cuts among the reefs between Mayreau and the Cays is spectacular. Discovered by Glenroy, this area is called Mayreau Gardens. If you manage to dive one of these in good visibility, it could turn out to be the dive of your holiday. There is usually a lot of current, so these are drift dives, sometimes so rapid that you come to the surface over a mile from where you went down. You hardly need to fin. The current does all the work while you get wafted through a delightful garden of hard and soft corals, sponges, and fish. My favorite part is on the southern side of the gardens. A sloping reef drops to a sand bottom in 40-60 feet. The reef has a wonderful texture made up of all kinds of corals. Boulder, pillar, and plate corals rise in a variety of intricate shapes. In some areas the sea fans are so large that you can play hide-and-seek behind them. The special luminous quality of the light, typical in the Grenadines, seems to extend below the waves. Massive schools of brown and blue chromis engulf you from time to time, swimming inches from your mask. A few yards away, schools of snapper and jack swim by purposefully creating a flurry of nervousness in the chromis. Angelfish, trumpetfish, large boxfish, and brightly colored parrotfish are there as well.

Purina, Mayreau

Mayreau

Mayreau is rimmed with pristine beaches and offers spectacular views from the hill. It is one of the smaller locally inhabited Grenadines with just one village. Originally the whole island was owned by the Eustace family of St. Vincent, and the inhabitants owned no land. Then land in the village was made available to them, and now much of the island has been sold.

For generations the Roman Catholics were the only religious show in town, with a picturesque little church on the hill. Now, a big new church faces it on the other side of the road, courtesy of one of the Eustace family, offering a livelier approach to the almighty. Apart from this the island is relatively unchanged. Most islanders are happy to see visitors, and indeed yachts are a mainstay of the economy. You can and should walk around the island, up to the village and down the other side, and explore the windward beaches. A road now runs from Saline Bay to Salt Whistle Bay, with many side roads. All the waters around Mayreau are part of the Tobago Cays Marine Park. You must scuba dive with a local dive operation.

SALT WHISTLE BAY

This spectacular bay has a beautiful, sweeping half-moon beach. Many years ago, Tom and Undine Potter built a little hotel here and did an excellent job of being unobtrusive; it is so well hidden in the trees that people who sail in the bay often question whether it is really there. The rooms have recently been renovated and the restaurant and bar are popular.

Enter right in the middle of the bay, as there are reefs to the north and south. The northern reef is about 6 feet deep and not usually much of a problem. The southern reef is

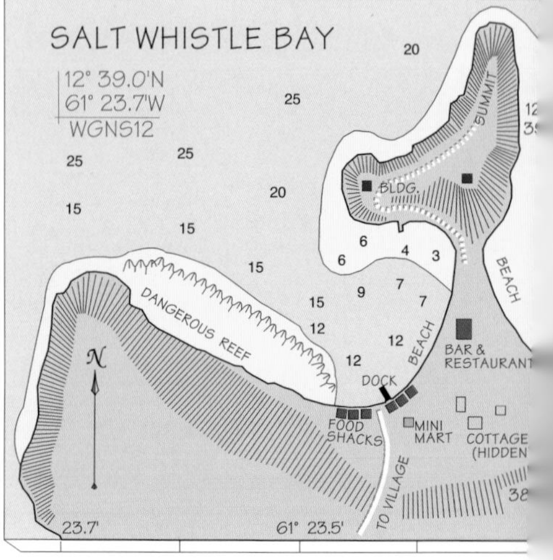

dangerous, because both wind and swells will help drive the inattentive navigator hard onto the coral. Boats often come to grief here, so take care. The holding in the bay varies; good in sand, not so good in the weed which covers much of it. It is very popular and generally very well protected, but northerly swells occasionally make it rolly. There is a dilapidated and roughly patched dock you can use for your dinghy and a mini-mart behind the beach, but no other yacht services. You can also pull your dinghy up the beach. The Tobago Cays Marine Park offers moorings ($60 EC a night, less for longer stays). They are not deep, so it is easy for you to check them.

Just to the east, behind the beach, is another beach on the windward side, where shells, driftwood, and debris wash ashore. Snorkeling on the reefs and rocks in the bay is fair, but usually murky. A road leads to the village from near the dock.

Take the short hike up the hill on the northern point for a great view of the windward reef. Follow the path along the seawall and stay to the right when it splits. It is steep in places and lined with cactus, so could be treacherous in the rainy season.

Restaurants/Ashore

Eating ashore here is easy and good, with

SALTWHISTLE BAY, MAYREAU

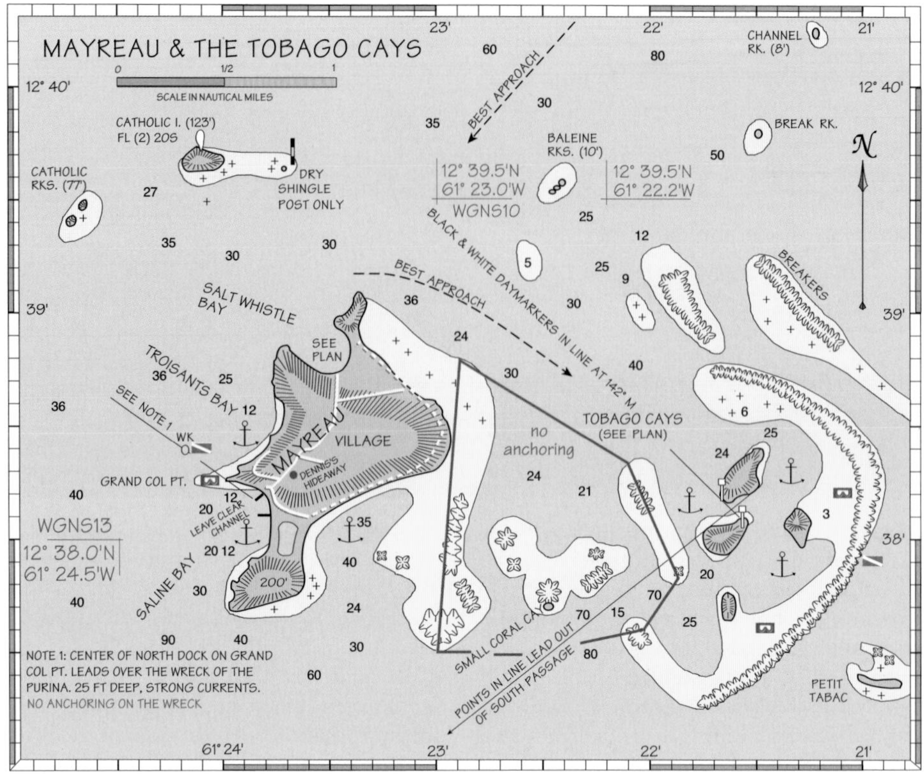

a choice of either tasty local dishes from a string of beach shacks, or more upmarket fare at the Salt Whistle Bay Hotel and Restaurant.

The Salt Whistle Bay Restaurant [$$$$] has a whimsical, woodland atmosphere: the dining area is set in the open among the trees, and each table is built of stone, with its own thatched roof. It is nicely run by Justin from Barbados, who has created a simple but intriguing menu. They serve breakfast, lunch, and dinner, and occasionally have live music and bon fires. Reservations are appreciated.

Kayaks, stand up paddle boards (SUPs), and other watersports are available for restaurant and hotel guests.

On the south side of the dock, simple local restaurants offer tasty seafood meals [$$$] at a moderate cost. Lobster is available and popular in season, as well as fresh fish and conch, with chicken for the pescaphobes.

These include Mama Jean's, operated by Claude and Jean, who also have a restaurant in the village. The Bar Under The Tamarind Tree (a tamarind tree grows right though it) is owned by Rasta Larston. Black Boy and Debbie is a lively place in the middle, Papi's is close by, and Richard's Last Bar Before the Jungle has the best name. Many have WiFi. Choose the one that takes your fancy and enjoy.

In the same area many colorful t-shirts and pareos are for sale, hung out in the breeze along with local handicraft and sometimes fresh fruit and vegetables.

Behind the beach bars is First Stop Mini Mart, a yellow concrete building with a few groceries and essentials. In the red building next door Medina sells cube ice and ice cream.

TROISANT BAY

Troisant Bay lies between Salt Whistle and Saline Bays. It is not as protected as those bays, but is reasonably calm in most conditions. Tribu Resorts are developing this bay as private residences and plan a long dock, beach bar, and restaurant at the southern end of the bay. The seabed is mainly an excellent grass bed, so wait until they put in moorings, as anchors will tear up the grass.

SALINE BAY

Saline Bay has a lovely, long beach. A large electric-generating plant is on the slope overlooking the bay. It has bright lights that shine over the bay at night but, thankfully, you do not hear it from the anchorage.

As you approach Saline Bay from the north, keep to seaward of Grand Col Point. There was a red buoy placed right on the edge of the reef but it was gone in 2018. The reef extends much farther than most people can imagine, so give it a very wide berth. The outer part of the reef is 12°38.25'N, 61°24.14'W.

Saline Bay has plenty of room to anchor, the holding in sand is good, but avoid the weedy areas. Leave a clear channel for the ferries, with room for them to turn. Try to anchor on patches of sand where the holding is good. There are some moorings in the bay, but they are old, so check them carefully.

When cruise ships anchor, Saline Bay does a quick imitation of Coney Island. Luckily the crowds are always gone before nightfall.

Communications/services

Dennis's Hideaway and Combination Cafe both offer internet. Dennis has a desal plant and sells water from the main dock. Call 458-8594 or 492-4417 to make sure he has some. You can tie your dinghy to one of the two docks.

Arthur Roache is a local mechanic and offers general marine services. He can help with diesel, outboard, or electrical problems, and has a shop next to Combination Cafe. Call him at 498-2996.

Ashore

Basic supplies, and sometimes fish, are available in several small groceries. First Stop is the newest and probably has the most, including freshly baked bread. A few handicrafts are available in small shops tucked in

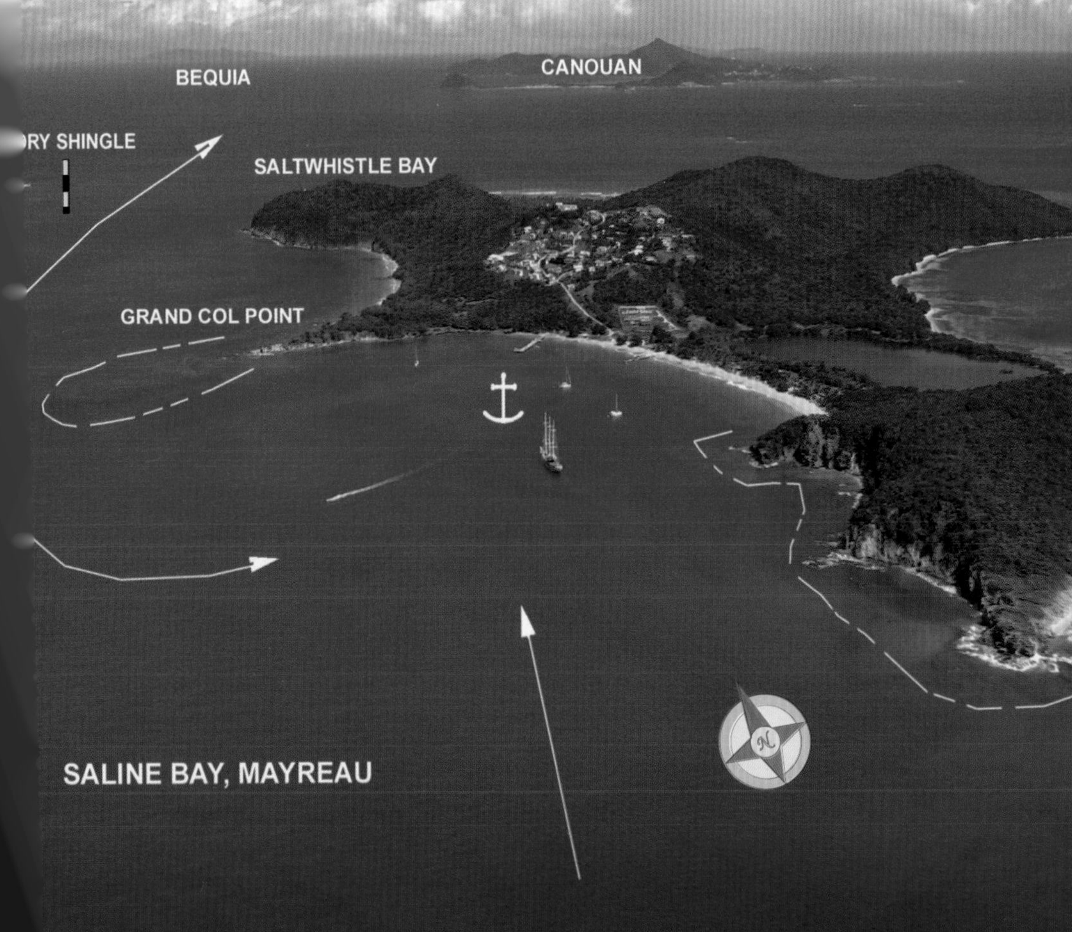

people's houses. Occasionally, a vendor sets up by the roadside.

Yachting visitors support several Mayreau-owned restaurants and a few handicraft and t-shirt outlets ~ all good for the local economy. Reservations for dinner or large groups for lunch are generally appreciated.

Dennis's Hideaway [VHF: 68, $$$] is owned by Dennis, from Mayreau, who used to be a charter skipper. This was the first restaurant here and has the nicest atmosphere, with an open bar and dining area beside a swimming pool and a two-story sunset-view tower. Reservations are appreciated.

Late afternoon is the best time to meet other yachting folk. Dennis has a great flair with guests and when he is around you will get excellent local cooking. Dennis's Hideaway also has a modern guesthouse for rent. Boathouse, a beach bar, is down by his desal plant near the main dock, where he organizes beach barbecues to order.

Almost opposite Dennis is Annie and Alexander's Combination Cafe [$$]. This delightful rooftop bar and restaurant is open for meals from breakfast through dinner. One reader highly recommends the fish sandwich. Alexander was a chef in Salt Whistle Bay for many years. Up the hill, Owens Chill Spa [$] is a grill, bar and pizzeria.

Continue uphill for J & C Bar and Restaurant [VHF: 68/16, $$] on the left. It has the best view of the harbor. It is owned by Jean and Claude and is large enough to take a huge group. Jean and Claude are friendly, make a big effort, and their large portions of fish and lambi are excellent value. They have a water taxi and divide their time between here and Salt Whistle Bay, so reservations are essential.

Robert Lewis "Righteous" is a well-known Rastafarian, and you can groove to Bob Marley and other good sounds and have some good talks with Robert at Righteous & de Youths [$$]. This is the cool hangout for both locals and visitors. The restaurant is an ongoing art form of construction and decoration and is the character spot on the island. Robert is welcoming and friendly, and serves good local food in his ever-changing restaurant. Someone is always there, and they sometimes have live entertainment.

James Alexander has the Island Paradise Restaurant [VHF: 68, $$]. It is well up the hill, with a birds-eye view. This is not a place to come if you are in a hurry, as everything is cooked from scratch, but their Creole fish and curried conch are well worth the wait. They have the biggest sound system on the island, and for those who want to groove to some sounds, they can turn it up after dinner. James has a taxi and can bring you up.

A little higher, on the right hand side of the road, Jenella's Honey Cone [VHF: 68, $] serves good food at a reasonable price. She serves lunch and dinner in a relaxed, open space on the hillside, the perfect place for a rum punch after walking up the hill.

Continue up the hill to an old church and magnificent views of the Tobago Cays.

A walk east from Saline Bay along the salt pond will bring you to a long, pristine beach on the windward side. It is possible to walk north along this beach, almost to the end, then look for the trail, which goes in and out of the bushes. It is unmarked, but easy enough to follow all the way back along the coast to Salt Whistle Bay.

Water sports

Snorkeling on the reef coming out from Grand Col Point is fair, and freediving or scuba diving the wreck of the Purina (max depth of 40 ft) is good and convenient.

WINDWARD ANCHORAGE

There is a pretty good anchorage on the eastern side of Mayreau. It is open to the south and can roll, but is excellent in unusual conditions, when northerly or westerly swells make the western anchorages untenable. Approach from the south in good light and identify the reef that extends east off the southeastern part of Mayreau. Follow this reef in. Be careful of the reefs to the east of the anchorage, as some are hard to see.

The Windward anchorage is within the Tobago Cays National Park protection zone, so no fishing is allowed.

Petit Tabac
Photo by Hannah Morris

The Tobago Cays

The Tobago Cays are a group of small, uninhabited islands protected from the sea by Horseshoe Reef. The water and reef colors are a kaleidoscope of gold, brown, blue, turquoise, and green. Small beaches of white sand blend into luminous clear water. On cloudless nights the stars are cast across the sky like wedding confetti thrown in an excessive gesture of bonhomie. Even squalls can be dramatically beautiful as they approach from afar. The anchorage is, however, open to the full force of the ocean winds, which are sometimes strong.

The best approach is between Mayreau and Baleine Rocks, staying south of One Fathom Bank. Black-and-white day markers help you get the approach right. Petit Rameau and Petit Bateau look like one island for most of the approach. Don't cut corners, lest you land on a coral head.

You can anchor just west of Petit Rameau, in the cut between Petit Rameau and Petit Bateau, to the north or south of Baradel, or between Baradel and the other islands. Shallow-draft yachts can anchor to the east of Baradel. Moorings are available in the Cays for $45 EC a night, but are neither compulsory nor always reliable, so check. They mainly surround the turtle-watching area. Do not anchor between the moorings and the turtle-watching area.

There are strong currents in the cut anchorage, so using a mooring is good.

When heading south from the Cays, it is safest to pass round the lee of Mayreau, though the Cays do have a southern channel (South Exit) that is okay for the experienced when the light is good. Avoid using this southern route as an entrance, as it is hard to find, and many charter yachts have gone aground in the attempt.

Regulations

Tobago Cays is a national park. Park fees are currently $10 EC per day per person, which rangers come to collect. Moorings are available for $45 EC a night. Superyachts should call in advance for advice on where to anchor. Yachts are asked to use holding tanks, as this will keep the water clean for swimmers in what can be a crowded area.

This magnificent park offers the most spectacular anchoring in the Eastern Caribbean. Enjoy, and help others to do so by

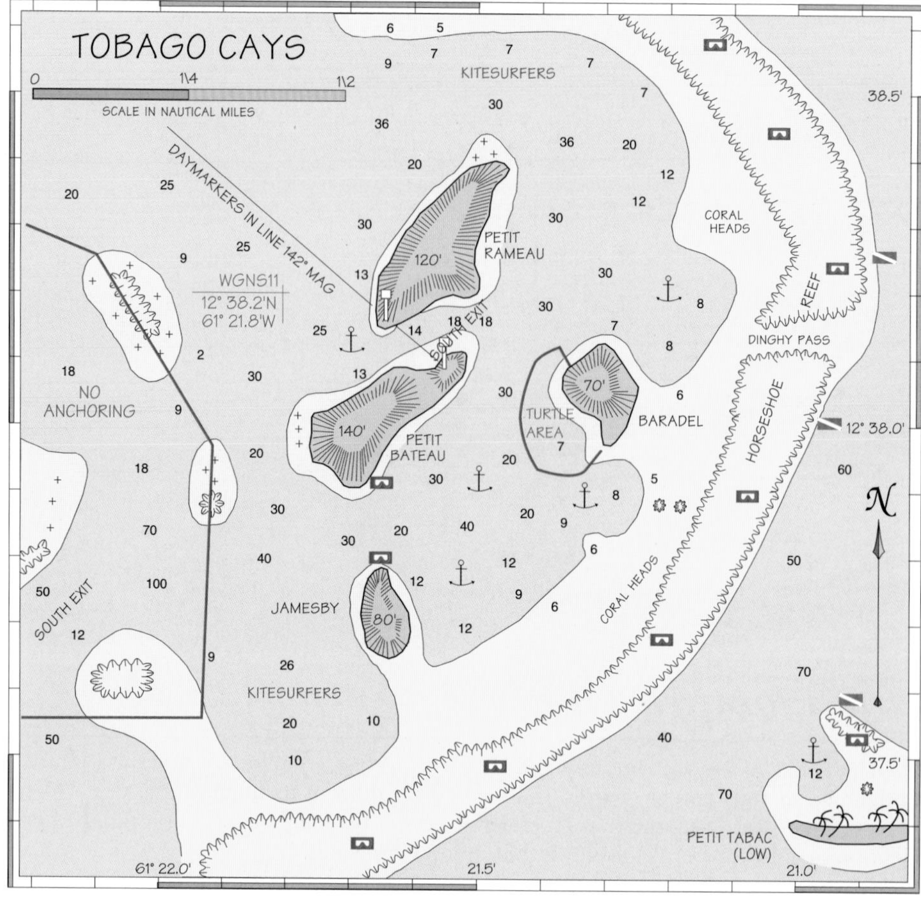

obeying regulations and being considerate.

A 5-knot speed limit is in effect in the Tobago Cays. This applies to all vessels, dinghies, water taxis, and sailing boats. Please obey it and keep a good look out for swimmers. People swim throughout the anchored yachts to the reef, and to the islands. The speed limit precludes water skiing and many water sports. Sail and kite boarders may exceed the speed limit, but only in the area north of Petit Rameau and south of Jamesby.

Enjoy snorkeling and looking at the fish and turtles. They are abundant, because this is a conservation area and no fishing is allowed. You may not collect or harm any kind of sea creature, including the corals. Do not take souvenirs of any kind, not even shells or rocks.

A turtle-watching area has been established around the beach at Baradel. It is marked by a series of linked buoys. If you wish to snorkel here, either anchor your dinghy outside or take it directly (and very slowly) into the beach and pull it up on the sand. No anchoring or drifting with your dinghy is allowed inside this area, and you should not run your dinghy through except to go to and from the beach. Approach turtles slowly, and go no closer than 6 feet. (If you are still and they come closer, that is fine.) Though they look calm and peaceful, they are easily frightened if you chase or try to touch them.

No fires may be made on the beaches, and the vegetation ashore should be left alone.

Do not discharge any oil, chemicals, or other waste into the water or pump your bilges in the park. Avoid using bleach and strong cleaners that get flushed overboard.

Those wishing to scuba dive in the park may only do so with a local dive shop.

Some people get so excited at the beauty of the Tobago Cays that they think the way to complete the experience is to play their

MAYREAU
BALEINE ROCKS
P. BATEAU
P. RAMEAU
JAMESBY
BARADEL
SMALL BOAT PASSAGE
TOBAGO CAYS MARINE PARK
PETIT TABAC

favorite music at top volume for the whole anchorage to hear. Cathartic as this might be for them, it may not be what others want. Keep any noise you make on your boat from music, generators, and windmills low enough that your neighbor cannot hear it.

Anchoring is permitted behind Horseshoe Reef and around the islands in sand only. Adventurous and experienced skippers could sail outside Horseshoe Reef (the approach is easiest from the south exit) and find temporary anchorage in Petit Tabac on sand bottom only. This is strictly eyeball navigation and for calm weather. Even so, it is small and rolly. Yachts should not anchor among any of the reefs between Petit Rameau and Mayreau, except in the anchorage we show directly east of Mayreau.

Ashore

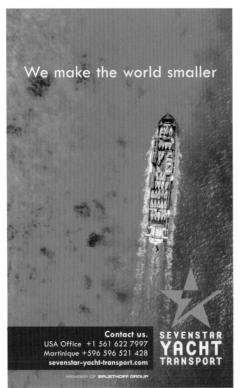

Local boat vendors ply the Cays during the season, selling everything from ice, bread, and lobsters to jewelry. They are a friendly bunch and very obliging if you need them to bring you ice or bread the next day. If you want to be left alone, they will do that, too. They offer great beach barbecues and water taxis to places like Baradel.

Rasta Richard Phillips on Jah Live, Larston Browne of Lordag Velocity 2, Many Man, and Taffy are among the good barbecuers and they are helpful and have been highly recommended.

Rondel Weeks on Mr. Quality is the only authorized vendor selling the Carriacou Fidel Productions art t-shirts. Each one is a painting by a local artist reproduced on a shirt. Felix-Turtle design by Carriacou artist Felix is the most popular - so popular that one vendor has copied the shirts and pretends to be the artist.

Willie, in Free Willie, is among the good and helpful vendors, and Jude has a good water taxi, Bitterz.

Water sports

The snorkeling on Horseshoe Reef is good, though past hurricanes have damaged some hard corals. The reef near the small boat passage is in the best condition. Fish are plentiful and there are lots of turtles. It can be choppy out there, and you will meet current

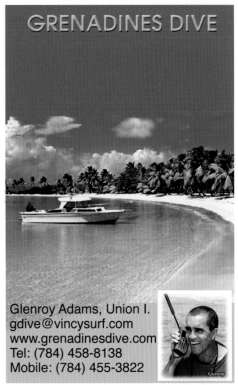

anywhere near the small boat passage. If you have beginner snorkelers on board, the east beach on Petit Bateau (facing Baradel) has some snorkeling that starts in calm, shallow water. The dinghy approach through the reefs is tricky. For turtles, check out the protected turtle area just west of Baradel.

The Tobago Cays are excellent for sailboarding. The designated area for this, when you want to go more than 6 knots, is north of Baradel. Experts can sail out through the small dinghy passage into the ocean.

To go scuba diving contact Grenadines Dive, who will come and collect you from your yacht. Currents can be very strong and most dives are done as drift dives.

Palm Island

Palm Island [VHF:16] was for many years an uninhabited island called Prune Island. John and Mary Caldwell fell in love with it, built a small hotel, and planted palm trees. John was a real character, and his early sailing experiences are outlined in his famous book, *Desperate Voyage*. John had a long and interesting life. After he died, Palm Island was bought by a big hotel group and upgraded to a first-class resort.

The anchorage is off the docks, and holding is fair in 15-20 feet, with a sand bottom. The anchorage can be rolly, so try it for lunch and if you feel comfortable, stay overnight.

You can use the dock for your dinghy, but use a stern anchor to keep it from riding underneath, where it will be damaged. Leave plenty of room for local boats to come onto the outer end and south side of the dock.

Ashore

Palm Island's Casuarina Beach is one of the most beautiful beaches in the Windwards: a gorgeous expanse of golden sand, lapped by translucent turquoise water ~ the ultimate picture-perfect Grenadine beach. When you step ashore, turn right and you will find a boutique that sells essentials, casual wear, and souvenirs.

The main Royal Palm [VHF: 16, $$$$$] restaurant is open for lunch and dinner daily, and the Sunset Grill Beach Bar and Restaurant is open some nights for dinner. It is all pleasant, but geared to the well-heeled in secluded surroundings.

Yachts are welcome to enjoy the beach area around the Sunset Beach Bar and the shoreline to the south. You can walk along Casuarina Beach if you stay fairly close to the water's edge. Please respect the privacy of the hotel rooms and facilities. Reception may be able to arrange a tour for prospective guests.

Union Island

Union is a great island to visit. It stands out from afar with its dramatically mountainous outline. Clifton, the main harbor, is protected by a reef that shows off its brilliant kaleidoscopic colors and patterns as you sail in. If you anchor or take a mooring out near the reef, the water to the east is an expanse of brilliant green-turquoise; jump in the clear, clean water and snorkel on the reef (and watch out for kitesurfers).

Ashore, the main town, Clifton, is charming and colorful, with a picture-perfect market around a green. Union Islanders are welcoming and friendly and there is an excellent choice of restaurants and bars where you can sit outside and watch life in the town. Provisioning is good. The roads and trails offer the best hiking and biking in the Grenadines.

CLIFTON

Clifton is a bustling small port with a cosmopolitan atmosphere, the center of yachting in the southern Grenadines. It has the remnants of a once thriving day-charter industry; the number of tourists flying into the small airport to tour the Grenadines has been drastically reduced by high airport fees.

Those anchored on the reef are treated to great displays of kitesurfing. Union is kept lively and entertaining by various groups of people, and kitesurfing is usually involved. There is no question that Union has become the kitesurfing center of the Windwards.

Jeremie runs the JT Pro Center Kitesurf, the original shop, which is based on the Anchorage Hotel's beach. They have a great beach bar on the beach by the airport, and run lively full moon parties. They also have the Snack Shack (see *Restaurants*) and Salty Girl Boutique (see *Fun Shopping*) in town. Jeremie, his crew, and students are the ones you see doing magnificent displays in the harbor.

Happy Kite is run by Nicolas, based in Gypsea Cafe, and they have a small surf shop in a portion of L'Atelier Turquoise next door. The same family owns Captain Gourmet. They have an on-the-water catamaran base, usually at Frigate Island where they do much of their surfing in the big bay.

Will runs a smaller kitesurfing operation and is probably responsible when you see someone kiting around on foils. You can get in touch with him through La Cabane at Bougainvilla.

Navigation

When approaching Clifton from the north it is necessary to sail halfway over to Palm Island to avoid Newlands Reef. Keep well outside the three red beacons on its outer edge. When approaching from the south, give

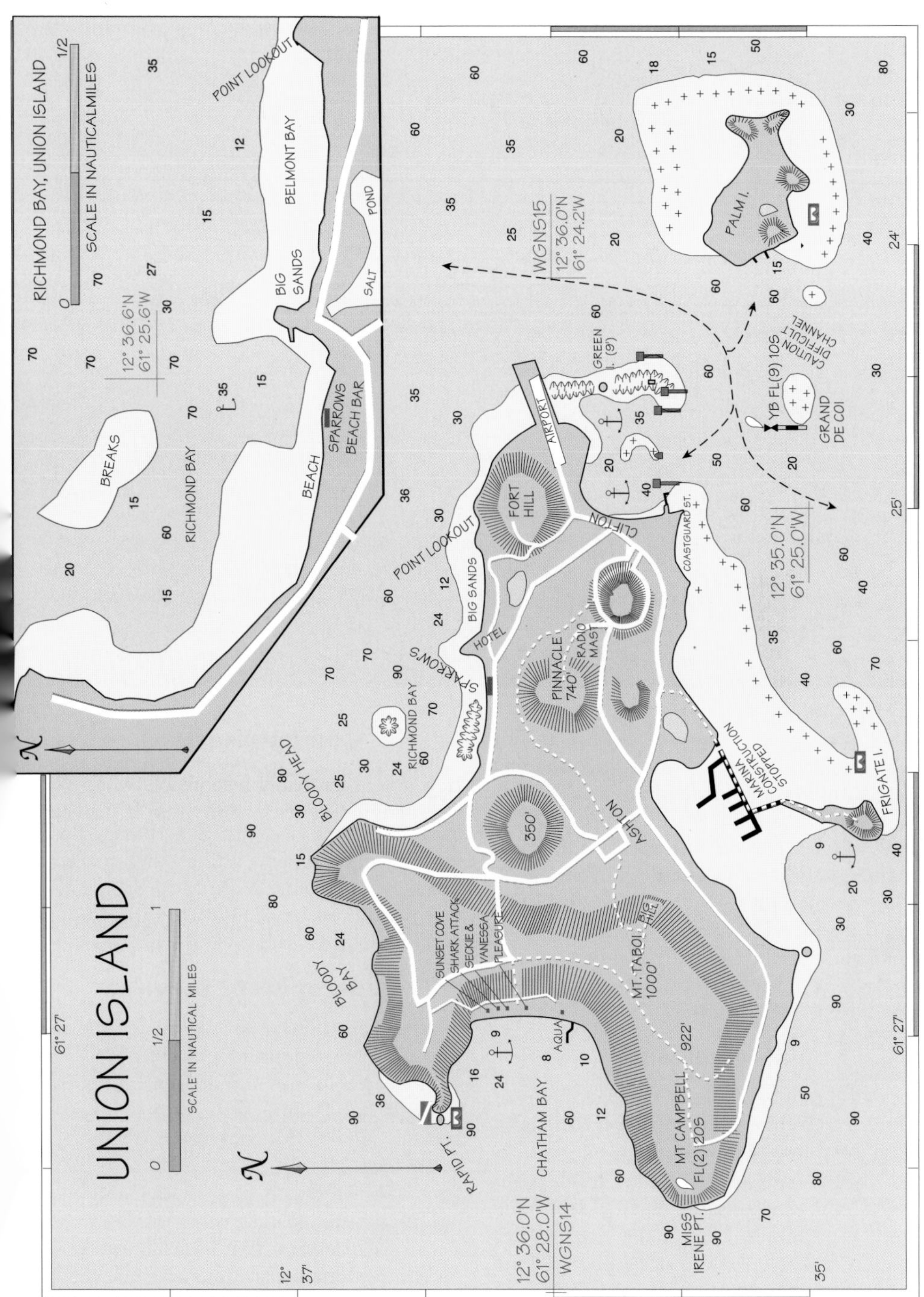

Grand de Coi a wide berth.

Clifton Harbour is protected by Newlands Reef, and it has a small reef in the center. The main entrance is just south of this center reef and marked by red and green beacons. It is possible to sail to the east of the center reef and up behind Newlands Reef toward Green Island. Happy Island, a bar, is a landmark on this reef. The area off the outer reef is a visually great anchorage, but if

CLIFTON HARBOUR

you prefer to be nearer to the action, anchor anywhere off the town. Leave a wide channel with turning room for the ferries.

The Tobago Cays Marine Park (485-8191) has put down 18 numbered moorings for rent, mainly in the shallow water close to the reef. They are marked TCMP and cost $60 EC a night, or $180 EC for four nights. If a local helps you on one, take the ticket he gives you and give it to the ranger when you pay. The boatmen get a third of the fee for helping you.

Regulations

Clifton is St. Vincent's southern port of entry for customs clearance. You can check with customs, then immigration, both in the fishing complex, weekdays from about 0830-1500 (checking in) or 1630 (checking out). You can also clear at the airport; they open from about 0900 and stay open as long as the airport is open, which is often later in the afternoon. They are also open Sundays and holidays. Clear customs as soon as you go ashore. Overtime is charged between 1200 and 1300 and after 1600 on weekdays, on weekends and holidays, and Saturday afternoons.

Communications

You can surf the net and make phone calls at Erika's Marine Services [VHF: 68] or the Internet Cafe above Buffalo Trading. Both have good equipment and are helpful, and both have bay-wide WiFi. Most bars, cafes, and restaurants offer free WiFi. Both Flow and Digicel have offices on the main street.

General yacht services

Bougainvilla has an excellent little enclosed dinghy lagoon and dock, which you are welcome to use, and at some point you will visit the adjoining Waterfront Restaurant and La Cabane. You can also easily use the Anchorage Hotel or the Grenadines Dive dock. Clifton Beach Hotel and Lambi also have docks, not quite as easy to use.

You can leave garbage in the dumpster on the fishing docks, or give it to Lambi's boat for a small fee. Ice is available at Anchorage Yacht Club, Bougainvilla, Lambi, and many rum shops. Unitech fills cooking gas bottles. Lambi also sells gasoline and water from the dock.

Jean-Marc's Bougainvilla [VHF: 16] is a dock with stern-to berthing for about 20 boats. They sell water (they have a desal plant) and ice. It is the home to The Waterfront Restaurant, Mare Blu Boutique, La Cabane sushi and Erika's Marine Services. Wind and Sea charters are based here and do many Grenadines day tours. Air and sea charters are also available.

The Anchorage Yacht Club [VHF: 16] has a 12-berth marina where you can tie stern-to a floating dock, and they can supply water, electricity (220 volts), and ice (block and cube). Fresh croissants, ciabatta, laundry, and showers are usually available. Wholesale cases of water and beverages are available from the hut at the base of the dock.

When Belgian Freddy sold the Big Sands Hotel he bought Clifton's gas station. This has a small dock adjoining Lambi's on its south side and is a good place to get outboard fuel. It is also the best place to buy diesel as it is good clean fuel, not something that arrived on a fishing boat from Venezuela. But, docking is not too easy. You could drop anchor and come downwind bow-to in 7-8 feet of water. They will truck to big boats on the main wharf on demand.

Erika's Marine Services [VHF: 68] is in Bougainvilla; speak to Heather or Chille. Their services include laundry (boat collection and delivery), yacht clearance, and full provisioning. They are travel agents and can book tickets for you. They have a good book swap, can provide water-taxi service, and they will even help you out for cash on a credit card if the ATM is broken. They offer full superyacht service, with agents throughout St. Vincent and the Grenadines, and can arrange a private plane for emergencies.

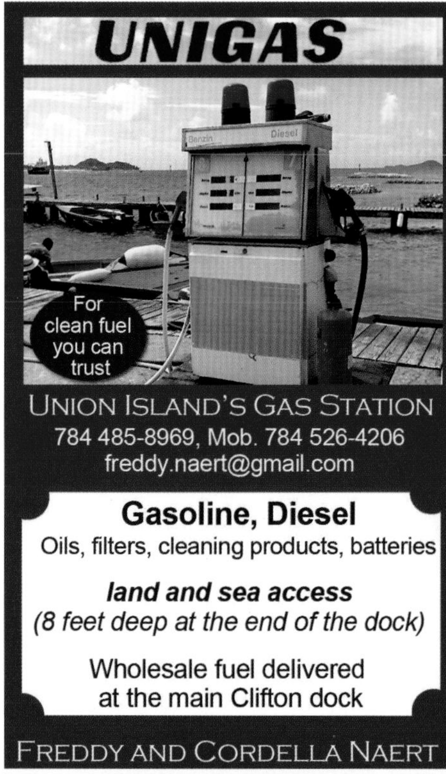

If you need to fly out, check Joy James at James Travel, Eagle's Travel, or Erika's.

Chandlery

Unitech has a chandlery with mechanical and yacht hardware items, and they now carry such things as second-hand equipment and dinghies. They are agents for Yamaha and can sell you a new one or fix the old. Elodie has a boutique corner with lovely hand-painted, ready-to-go fishing lines, hand-crafted soaps, and special coconut oils. These are also available in L'Atelier Turquoise, Mare Blu, and several other stores. Unitech also has a book swap.

Quacy's Marine Tech Services is up a little spiral staircase on main street. He has a good selection of outboard parts along with other accessories. He rents bikes and scooters and fixes outboards and diesels (see *Technical yacht services*).

Technical yacht services

Need something fixed? Quacy was the maintenance manager of a local charter company and now owns Marine Tech Services. He is the local maintenance agent for Horizons Yacht Charters and is good at most boat systems and fixing electrical problems. He will get any make of outboard purring again and keeps many spares. He repairs Yanmar and Volvo inboard diesel engines, can fix general mechanical and plumbing problems, and does welding. He will travel to anyone in need of emergency help anywhere from Canouan to Carriacou. Quacy has mountain bikes for rent as well as scooters.

You will find Laurent at Unitech, just at the beginning of the road to Fort Hill. They repair all kinds of gasoline and diesel motors, including outboards. They weld iron and stainless, and they do fiberglass and electrical repairs. Unitech sells cooking gas and can fill most boat cylinders. If you have torn sails or malfunctioning refrigeration, ask them to point you to the right person.

Almost opposite Unitech, Island Marine Special [VHF: 16] is run by Earl Allen, a good diesel mechanic.

Provisioning

Provisioning in Union is good. The local market is colorful and photogenic. Vendors have an excellent selection of fresh fruits and vegetables in colorful stalls around a green. Don't get so distracted by the market that you forget to look over the road to check out L'Atelier Turquoise and Captain Gourmet.

Bertram and Signa at Island Grown grow much of what they sell in their farm up in the hills, so it is always fresh. They always grow their own lettuce and herbs, but also a lot of other vegetables. Some things are kept cool in the fridge, so if you don't see what you want, ask. These days Jennifer and most other vendors keep well-stocked fridges. Another smaller local market is farther down the road towards Grenadines Dive.

Nicolas and Linda's Captain Gourmet is opposite the market, in the same building as L'Atelier Turquoise (see *Fun shopping*), Gypsea Cafe (*see Restaurants*), and Happy Kite (see *Water sports*). All are owned by the same family, and they have their own dinghy dock.

THE WATERFRONT BAR & RESTAURANT

Simple food, carefully prepared using the best local ingredients

~ Pizzas ~

~ Pastas ~

~ Steak ~

~ Lobster ~

thewaterfrontunion@gmail.com 784-485-6381 / 531-6381

LA CABANE

Sushi and Juice Bar

On the Bougainvilla Dock

Delicious and healthy Juices & Smoothies

100% Natural

Try our Acai Bowls

Sushi Party every Thursday night !

Yoga Classes Tues + Fri 5pm - 6pm

Open: 8.30am -5pm

IT'S ALL AT BOUGAINVILLA

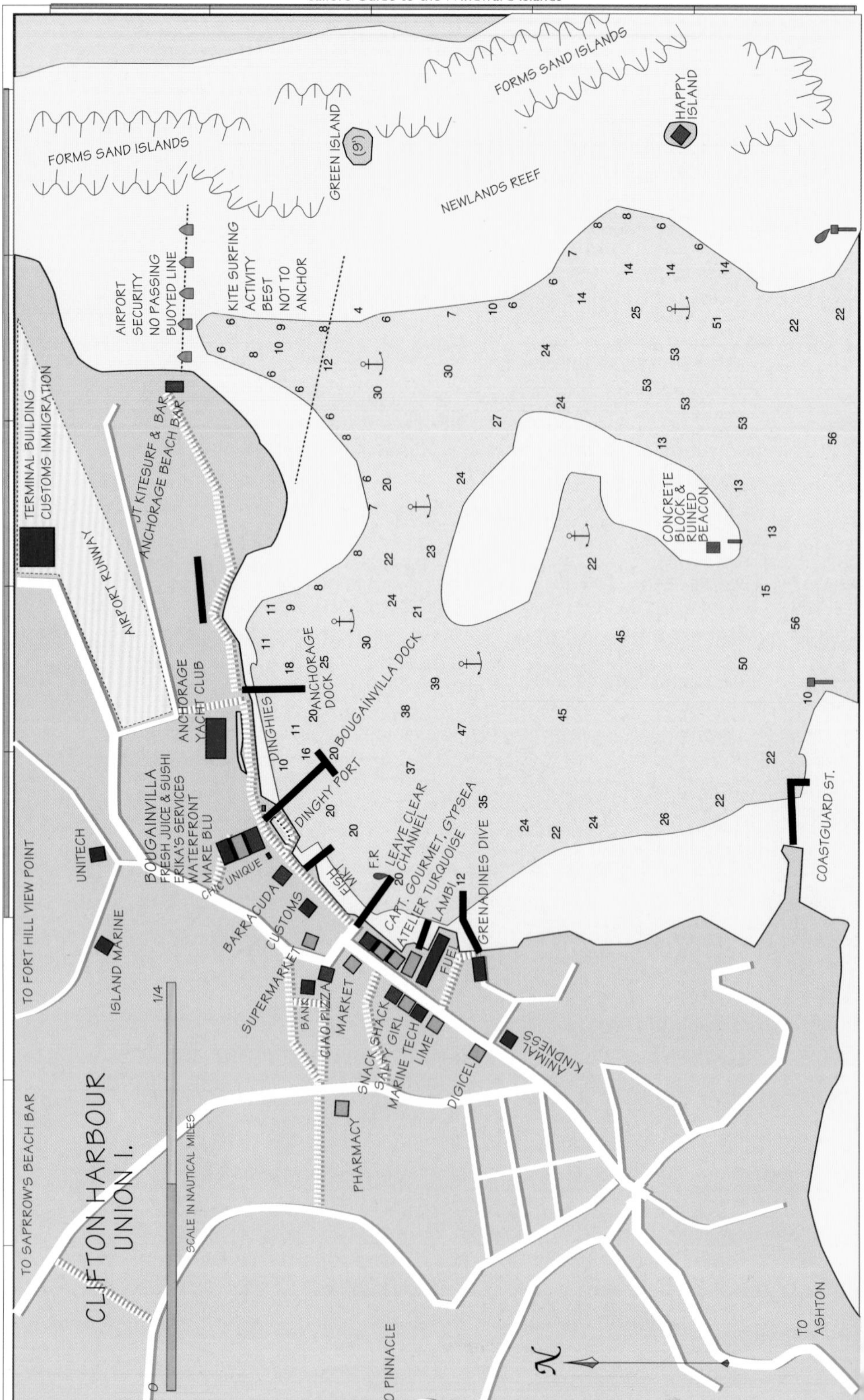

CLIFTON HARBOUR
UNION I.

SCALE IN NAUTICAL MILES
0
1/4

FORMS SAND ISLANDS
FORMS SAND ISLANDS
GREEN ISLAND
(9')
HAPPY ISLAND
NEWLANDS REEF
AIRPORT SECURITY NO PASSING BUOYED LINE
KITE SURFING ACTIVITY BEST NOT TO ANCHOR
TERMINAL BUILDING CUSTOMS IMMIGRATION
AIRPORT RUNWAY
JT KITESURF & BAR ANCHORAGE BEACH BAR
ANCHORAGE YACHT CLUB
ANCHORAGE DOCK
DINGHIES
BOUGAINVILLA DOCK
DINGHY PORT
BOUGAINVILLA
FRESH JUICE & SUSHI
ERIKA'S SERVICES
WATERFRONT
MARE BLU
CHIC UNIQUE
BARRACUDA
CUSTOMS
SUPERMARKET
BANK
CIAO PIZZA
MARKET
FISH MKT
F.R.
LEAVE CLEAR CHANNEL
CAPT. GOURMET, GYPSEA
ATELIER TURQUOISE
LAMBI
GRENADINES DIVE
FUEL
SNACK SHACK
SALTY GIRL
MARINE TECH
LIME
DIGICEL
ANIMAL KINDNESS
PHARMACY
UNITECH
ISLAND MARINE
TO FORT HILL VIEW POINT
TO SAPRROW'S BEACH BAR
TO PINNACLE
TO ASHTON
COASTGUARD ST.
CONCRETE BLOCK & RUINED BEACON
N

Composite of kitesurfer over Happy Island

This great little store has good buys on local Caribbean delicacies like chocolate, coconut oil, coffee, and rum. They sell fresh French bread, pastries, and home made yogurt. They are focused on sourcing and producing fresh, quality local products, and will help provision on request.

The best supermarket in town is The Supermarket, opposite the bank.

Lambi has wine, packaged food, fresh food, pork and beef from Lambi's farm, and general hardware and household goods.

A tiny path runs alongside Snack Shack to Yummy Stuff Bakery and Cafe. This is a great little bakery and sometimes sells out fast, so go early. They also do rotis and other snacks. Otherwise, for French bread, croissants, and Danish, check out Captain Gourmet or the bakery beside Barracuda. There is also a little local bakery opposite the market.

Need pet food or a vet? Check the pet people. These include Susie, Heather from Erika's, and Gary from Union. They have the Animal Kindness Charity (SGAK). They get the fur back on strays, food in their bellies, cut down on random animal procreation, and provide animal education in the local schools. Susie is on first-name terms with every dog on the island. They have had a big impact. Those with kids will want to wander along main street to their center, where you will normally find a pen with some dogs that welcome petting. Those with some time should consider taking one or two for much-appreciated walks. Contributions are always welcome and help pay for vet fees and food, and they welcome

Unique handcrafted Jewelry
Artwork Gift shop
Clifton, UNION ISLAND

Ph:(784) 458 8734
anniefrance@vincysurf.com

CAPTAIN GOURMET
EST. 1998

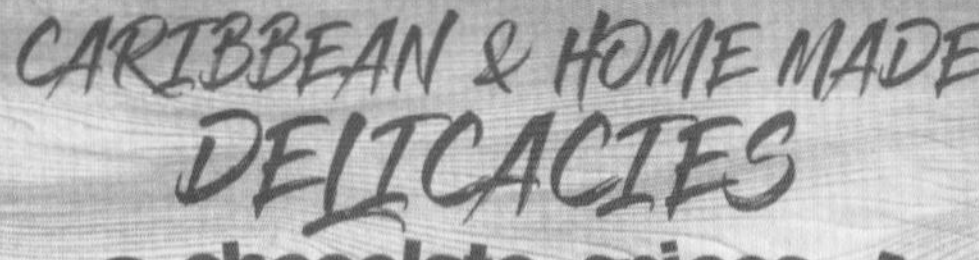

chocolate, spices,
coffee, rum ...

FINE SELECTION OF WINES & CUBAN CIGARS
AND FRESHLY BAKED BREAD!

captain gourmet • +1 (784) 495 86 95

The definition of groovy!

Come to chill and enjoy delicious drinks and food including vegan & vegetarian dishes!

FROM BREAKFAST TO DINNER
7.30 AM TO 10 PM

GREAT VIBES & MUSIC...
SEA VIEW AND HAPPY HOUR!

Connect with mermaids & pirates! (but yes... also free WIFI)

Gypsea Café • + 1 (784) 495 86 95

KITESURF SCHOOL & SHOP

LESSONS - TOURS
RENTALS - REPAIRS
STAND UP PADDLE
YOGA - SUP YOGA

HAPPYKITEGRENADINES.COM

HAPPYKITEGRENADINES@GMAIL.COM +1 (784) 430-8604 / 593-9822

anyone who might provide a prospective new home for one of their orphan pets.

Fun shopping

Union is becoming quite the place for boutiques. Robert and Annie-France's L'Atelier Turquoise (Beads and Art gallery) displays original paintings and local handicrafts and souvenirs. These include locally painted souvenir fishing lines, figures and art from Haiti, and lots more to attract the eye. The main attraction is Annie-France's jewelry, hand made from semi-precious stones, including the lovely larimar stone, and beads. Each delightful item is hand crafted and special. A corner of the shop has surf and beach wear, where you will find hats, sunglasses, and good quality sunscreen.

I have known Charlotte since I first started writing guides, when she ran the Ponton du Bakoua in Martinique. She moved to Union and ran the Anchorage Hotel during its best years. Now she has come out of retirement and opened Mare Blu in The Waterfront restaurant. Charlotte has created a beautiful boutique using artistic design and lighting, so as you come in you have the feeling of entering Aladdin's treasure trove. It is fun to visit and you will find a little of everything: elegant casual wear, hats, art, carvings, ornaments, fancy bags, jewelry, and books, as well as practical stuff like sunblock and flip flops. This is the place to buy postcards and stamps. You can write them over a coffee in The Waterfront and bring them back, Mare Blu will mail them for you.

Zoe's Salty Girl Boutique is next to the Snack Shack, with elegant light clothing, pareos, chic bathing costumes, ornaments, bags, and jewelry. The atmosphere is chic, eye-catching, and full of treasures. She also carries sunblock, sunglasses, postcards, and has a small section of children's toys in the back.

Cynthia Mills has the Chic Unique right next to Bougainvilla. This is not only a shop but a spa for massage and other treatments. If you want an air, sea, or land taxi, just ask here.

Juliet's Colors and Kathy's are in the market and open most days. They stock casual wear, t-shirts, souvenirs, and decorative items, as well as locally made jewelry and metal sculptures. The Clifton Beach Hotel has Sunseekers Shade boutique, with a wide range of casual clothing, souvenirs, and books.

There are several other small stalls and shops for local handicrafts, and many ladies hang out t-shirts for sale in the fish market buildings.

In Clifton heading south, Kandy Cream is the place for ice cream and cake.

Restaurants

Union has some fine restaurants. For a small island, the selection is excellent.

Barracuda [$$] is next to the Bougainvilla complex. It is owned by a very sweet and welcoming Italian couple, Giancarlo and his wife, Tiziana, who is the chef and is helped by locals. Italian cooking, including pasta and pizzas, as well as local food such as rotis are all on the menu. It has a nice atmosphere, wonderful background music, is not too expensive, and the food is tasty. They open from about 1030 for breakfast and stay open until after dinner. They serve food at any time of day, so you can have a really early dinner. Save room for the Italian chocolate cake if they have it, which is more like a mousse

St. Vincent & the Grenadines

and is absolutely delicious. Reservations are recommended.

Marie is originally French, but made Union her home so long ago that it was just about when I started writing guides. She has been involved in several good businesses, but Ciao Pizza [$$] is the best. She cooks excellent fresh fish and seafood specials, homemade pasta, great gazpacho, and, of course, pizza. She opens daily from 1100-2200. Ciao Pizza is in town, opposite the main dock. Sit outside and watch the world go by and use the free high-speed WiFi.

The Waterfront [$$$] is in the Bougainvilla complex, open to the harbor and the breeze, and a perfect little dinghy dock lagoon. This is a great place to hangout, use WiFi, and meet your friends. Bougainvilla is owned by Jean Marc; The Waterfront is run by his daughter Alizee, and La Cabane outside is run by his other daughter Jade. They work together so you can sit outside in La Cabane and get a pizza from The Waterfront, or enjoy La Cabane's sushi indoors.

The Waterfront specializes in lobster, seafood, and pizzas anytime, and for lunch they have lighter fare like pasta and local stews. For dinner you can have fine meat dishes, and by the time this book is available they should have regular live entertainment

La Cabane is a tiny colorful shack on the dinghy dock that produces the best sushi, juices (fruit and/or vegetable), health drinks, and smoothies. They have a covered sitting area around the back, and it is a delight for a fresh juice or light meal. Get your lunch sushi order in in the morning, as they often sell out early.

Bertrand Sailly, brother of Jean-Marc from Bougainvilla, has opened a wonderful hangout called Sparrow's Beach Bar in Richmond Bay by Big Sands, about a mile from Clifton. This is a hot spot in Union: everyone loves it. Getting there is easy, just call the free shuttle bus and they will take you, so you get a mini tour when you visit. It opens for lunch and dinner and is delightful any time of day. Bertrand cold-smokes his own fish, often caught by Sebastien of Grenadines Fishing (see *Water sports*) which is so delicious that he now supplies most of the surrounding hotels. You can ask to buy some to take back on the boat. He prepares raw tuna with a ginger sauce, and it is all served very artistically. They have pastas and salads and fresh seafood, and in the evening they fire up the big barbecue. By day, the energetic will make use of stand-up paddle boards and watersports gear, while the more relaxed crowd will go for the lounges, private gazebos, and the great massage/pedicure/manicure spa, run by Sophie. It is romantic on the beach at night, especially with a full moon, and they often throw parties with live music, especially on Tuesdays. Call for details.

Some captains like to anchor right off the beach here, and I have seen a huge superyacht anchor for lunch. There is a blow-up of the bay on our Union Island chart. The anchorage is weather dependent, best avoided in northerly

swells and northeasters, but wonderful on a calm day. You need to be somewhat adept at spotting reefs. If you approach from the northeast and spot the reef in the middle of the bay, you can pass east of it in 70 feet of water and then come close to the beach slowly. Anchor or pick up one of the two mooring buoys Bertrand has put down.

Gypsea Cafe [$$] is part of Captain Gourmet and is upstairs over the shop. It probably has the healthiest menu on the island - both for you and the planet - as everything is as local and freshly made as possible. It is an atmospheric hang-out with roof beams and gable windows, each with a little balcony. It's a relaxing and artistic space, with views of the street below. This is also the base for Happy Kite. Ask about equipment, lessons, paddle board rentals, and yoga classes. They open in the morning and stay open till after dinner. It is a nice place for a morning coffee and croissant while you catch up on your emails with their WiFi. They serve lunch and dinner with daily specials, all freshly made. They strive for fresh, local ingredients, and almost everything is made from scratch. Vegetarian and vegan options are always available.

The Snack Shack [$$] is a beach bar right on main street (well, the water is just over the road), bringing beach-side relaxing into town and offering a new level of casual chic. Its connection with JT Pro Kitesurf means you are likely to find a relaxed group chilling out here, along with others intently looking at their computers and iPads catching up on the world with the free WiFi. Paninis, smoothies, cappuccino, and ice cream coffee are just a few of the many goodies available from breakfast to dinner. You can arrange your kitesurfing trips here and shop at the attached Salty Girl Boutique.

Exhibit, next to Marie's (opposite the main dock) is Union's new cocktail bar and fusion restaurant [$$]. Owner Sonia is French, and she previously ran establishments in Mayreau and Union before opening Exhibit at the end of 2017. She loves Asian, Caribbean, and international fusion, but also does simpler meals like burgers and spring rolls. Specialty cocktails are always available, and this is the place to go for nice brandy. She opens from 1100 for lunch and dinner, and a breakfast menu is planned.

The cheapest and fastest food is The Local, upstairs opposite the market. For fast food at local prices ignore the menu outside, walk upstairs, and choose from the cafeteria-style dishes.

The Anchorage Yacht Club [VHF: 68], owned by the Palm Island group, is pretty, with a delightful view of the harbor. They have a dinghy dock and a pleasant bar for relaxing. They also have a bar on Kite Beach where you can relax and watch the surfers fly by. They sometimes close in the off season, which will most likely be in August and September.

Lambert is smiling these days, and why not? His Lambi emporium [VHF: 68, $$] consisting of a supermarket, waterfront restaurant, and some rental rooms is going well. Each time I come, his building seems to have crept farther out to sea. The conch shell walls give a rough-and-ready atmosphere. The food is reasonably priced and local, as is the entertainment, with lively steel bands most nights in season. Lambert sells very inexpensive takeaway snacks on the road side.

The Clifton Beach Hotel [VHF: 68, $$], run by Marie Adams-Hazell, has a waterfront location, and its own dinghy dock. The bar is a popular meeting place. After you have finished shopping, try one of their sandwiches. You can also visit for dinner or the occasional jump-up.

For other good and inexpensive local food visit Jennifer's Restaurant and Bar [$] or Lion, opposite the market. Both serve West Indian food at a reasonable price.

If you are anchored near the reef you will notice Janti's Happy Island [$], built on the edge of the reef. Janti is the only man in the Caribbean I know of who built his own island by hand. He used to have a bar in Ashton, but could not find enough customers. He has also worked for tourism, trying to clean up the town. One headache was a huge pile of conch shells left by fishermen on the beach. Janti solved both problems by taking the shells from the beach and using them to build Happy Island. It is perfectly placed for snorkeling by day and for taking a sundowner at night. You can tie your dinghy right outside. This is Union's most informal bar; it is fun and has a lovely view as sunset turns to night. During the high season local kitesurfers often put on a spectacular sunset show.

Transport

Quacy, at Marine Tech Services, rents bikes and scooters, a great way to see the island, which has little traffic and great views at every turn. If you have a cooperative partner, try his tandem bike. He does biking tours as well.

Water taxis will be happy to take you ashore: $10-20 EC one-way for your group, depending on where you are anchored. Eat with Lambi and he will arrange it for free.

For a taxi, try Rosmund Adams (526-4500, not on Saturday). Ask him about the leatherback turtle-watching - this takes place at night from March to August.

Ashore

Hiking and biking will give you views of the island's beautiful turquoise waters, from Clifton to Ashton and Frigate Island and the Grenadines beyond. The road system enables you to bike all over the island. Two obvious viewpoints for walkers are Fort Hill and the road that leads from opposite the hospital back past the Pinnacle and into Ashton. Farther afield, the roads that rise from Richmond Bay to circle round Bloody Bay and Chatham are beautiful, and the road from Ashton to Mt. Campbell has views to the south. Off-road hiking includes the ridge along the western mountain range and, for excellent views, take the well-marked trail to Big Hill, from where the adventurous can rough it up to Mt. Taboi.

The Pinnacle is a tough but sweet climb, with a dramatic, 360-degree, precipitous view at the summit. Looked at from afar, an iguana-like rock lies on the top. The approach is right under the iguana, on the Clifton side of the hill. The best way to do this is to contact Erika's Marine Services and ask them to put you in touch with Bongo, a good local hiking guide, and one of the few who hikes the Pinnacle. Hardy adventurers could try this with a cutlass, after visiting doyleguides.com for detailed directions.

While in Clifton, visit the Tobago Cays Marine Park interpretation center on

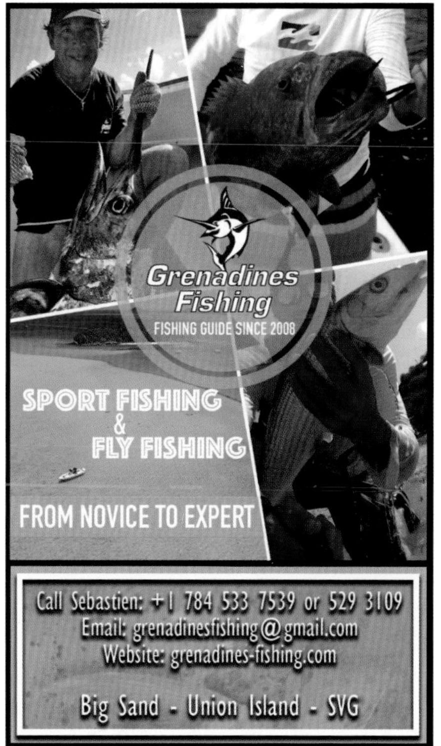

the main square. They have informational brochures, displays on reef ecosystems, and t-shirts for sale. They are happy to answer questions and provide information.

Water sports

You will find information on the dive shops and some dive sites under the Southern Grenadine diving section. Clifton is the base of Grenadines Dive [VHF: 16/68].

Union is a major kitesurf center with two first-rate shops. Jeremie runs the JT Pro Center Kitesurf, which is based in the Anchorage Hotel. They also have the Snack Shack in town, where you can talk kite surfing and book trips. They do a great beach party on full-moon nights, open to all.

Happy Kite is run by Nicolas and based out of Gypsea Cafe. They do much of their surfing in the big bay by Frigate island, where they have a floating catamaran base.

Both shops are top professionals and teach at all levels. Many of their customers are sailors who want to learn to kitesurf or become better. If you are anchored on the reef, or in Frigate Island, you can enjoy a display of kitesurfing prowess most days. Visit their websites: kitesurfgrenadines.com, happykitegrenadines.com

Grenadines Fishing is based out of Sparrow's and run by Sebastien. Originally from Martinique, Sebastien has lived in Union for 30 years and has been a professional fishing guide there since 2008. He specializes in both deep-sea sport and fly fishing for all levels and regularly supplies Sparrow's with fresh fish.

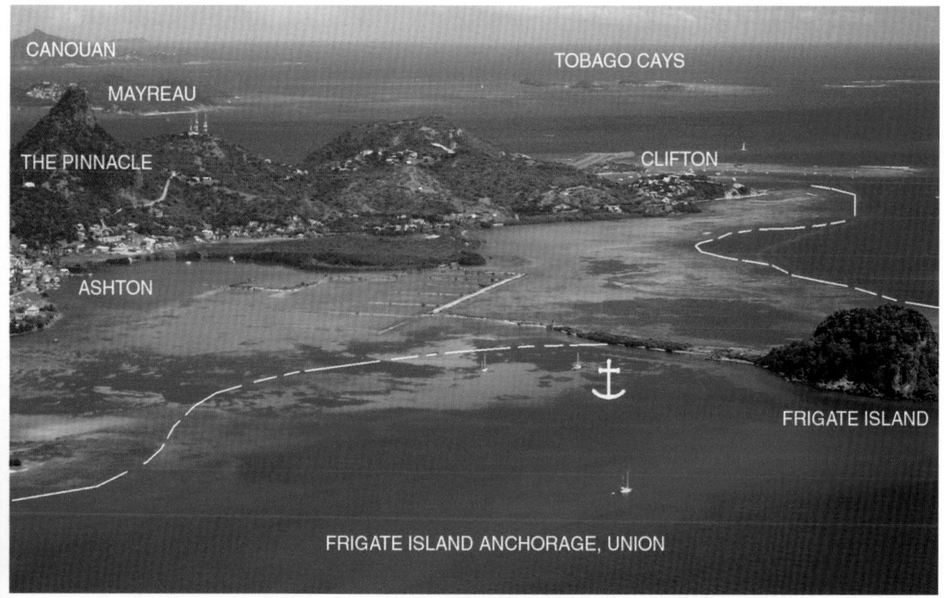

FRIGATE ISLAND ANCHORAGE, UNION

Best of all, on request, Sparrow's will cook up whatever you catch.

Day-charter boats leave most days to visit the other Grenadines. The main operators of the cats are Wind and Sea and Palm Island. There is also Martin's Scaramouche, the lovely Carriacou-built schooner, whose presence enhances the view and is a great addition to any photo of the Tobago Cays.

FRIGATE ISLAND

Frigate Island, although just over a mile from Clifton, is generally quiet and well protected in normal conditions, and exceptionally so in strong northeasterlies. You can anchor in the lee of the island, but enter carefully as the bottom shelves quickly. Construction started on a large development, including a 300-berth marina, but the company went bankrupt and the project stopped. Recently there have been efforts to restore water flow to the area and rehabilitate the damaged ecosystem.

You are within dinghy reach of Ashton, the other town on Union. Ashton is local and delightful, with lower prices than Clifton. It has a good dock where you can leave your dinghy. You will find small restaurants, friendly rum shops, and several small supermarkets.

Walking ashore is pleasant. Those with a head for heights and a firm grip can scramble high up the hill on Frigate Island for a view. For more ambitious hikes, there are Big Hill and Mt. Taboi. There is good snorkeling on the reef on the windward side of Frigate. Be careful of the current.

CHATHAM BAY

Chatham Bay, on the lee side of Union, is a large and magnificent anchorage, with a long sandy beach to the east and a steep headland to the north. While you may not have it to yourself, it is often less crowded than most. Anchor anywhere in the bay. (Just occasionally, you may be asked to move if the fishermen are seine netting.) The wind tends to come over the hills in shrieking gusts. There is a long beach to explore and good snorkeling around the rocks off Rapid Point. The fish life here is particularly rich and attracts all kinds of birds, including pelicans. A rough road leads to the northern headland, and a path leads to the center ridge, and from these,

Chatham Bay

roads go to Ashton or Clifton. The hiking all around is lovely. For a stroll go up to the road, turn left and keep going. Where you have a big grassy field and an overlook of the bay, the road turns into a track. Follow the track and you come to another view point and a cannon post. Jean Marc (Bougainvilla) has mounted the cannon.

Sunday is often popular with locals, who come over for lunch.

Services/Ashore

If you want to avoid Clifton and have not yet cleared in, Seckie will take you by cab and include an island tour at a price that depends on how much you want to do. Sometimes a boat sells fresh bread and ice in the mornings.

At the north end of the beach several master barbecuers compete to give you an entertaining local-style dinner on the beach. For a full meal they charge about $65-100 EC, depending on whether you want fish, chicken, ribs, or lobster. Seckie and Vanessa also sell snacks so you can go in and drink and then have fish 'n chips, roti, or conch fritters. These bars are rough, ready, and lots of fun. Some try a hard sell from their boats. If you want to avoid that, call up in advance and make arrangements.

Seckie and Vanessa are in the pink building with the orange roof, in the middle of the beach. They have a tiny dinghy dock and will look after you well; ask about their beach games. They serve fish, chicken, ribs, and lobster, and a bonfire is often lit after dark. They arrange entertainment for groups and will organize special events like birthday parties. (If you want a real surprise party, set it up in advance.) They are always there in the evening, and sometimes for lunch. For parties of 15 or more they will prepare a full pig roast, and often do smaller pork roasts with live music when they have enough people. Vanessa sells her handmade jewelry; you can ask for a look. They can bring you over from Clifton if you are not anchored in Chatham. If you know this is the place you want to go, call in advance and book, as it will save you a lot of hassle and high pressure salesmanship from others.

Palm Leaf is at the north end and is owned by Jerry, who is sometimes open.

Sunset Cove is next door. They will keep you well entertained and fed with Adelle's chicken, fish, rib, and seafood meals. It is a happening bar and has a very quiet generator so plays music to dance to on the beach in the moonlight. They have WiFi and will do bonfires on request.

Shark Attack was the first to offer beach barbecues here. It was hard work because everything had to come by boat, but he became popular. Eventually, the government put in a rough road. This made life so easy that others saw what he was doing and set up in competition. Shark Attack keeps up his tradition of great barbecues of fish, ribs, and lobster. He does some carvings and has them for sale.

Pleasure, who has hung out at Chatham even longer than Shark Attack, originally sang for him, and now has Pleasure's Bar under a big tamarind tree. It is close by the road and the path that leads to the rest of the island. He and his wife Rosita are pleasant and will cook you fresh fish or lobster, and he is a little less expensive than the others. Pleasure plays guitar and will provide a little music for your entertainment. He also does fine carvings and

Rosita makes art baskets.

Way down at the south end, Antonio has opened Aqua in two wonderful, open, thatched buildings; a bar and a restaurant that are joined by a swimming pool. This is a completely different experience from the others, a lovely boutique resort, comfortable and airy, perfect for when you are beach-barbecued out and want somewhere quiet to relax. Manager Lesia is helpful and they are open for breakfast and a light lunch [$$] of rotis, sandwiches, and grilled fish. The shrimp and lobster rotis are excellent. They open for a gourmet style dinner [$$$$$]. If you come for dinner and need customs clearance they can arrange transport to Clifton for you.

Antonio has built an inventive and artistic dock using giant rocks placed by nature.

(PSV) & Petite Martinique

Petit St. Vincent (PSV) and Petite Martinique lie just a short sail southeast of Union. PSV is part of St. Vincent, and Petite Martinique is part of Grenada.

PSV

PSV (VHF: 16, closed September/October) was probably the first Caribbean boutique hotel. It is a quiet and exclusive resort, where the guests get pampered in secluded stone cottages. Each cottage has a flagpole that

NOTE: MOPION IS A LOW SAND ISLAND WITH A THATCH SHELTER WHICH SOMETIMES GETS WASHED AWAY.

PSV AND PETITE MARTINIQUE

is used to summon room service, which soon appears in a mini-moke. The hotel does well at top Caribbean rates, probably the Caribbean's most successful small hotel.

It was built by the late Haze Richardson, who operated it from its inception until 2007. The island and resort were purchased in late 2010 by Phil Stephenson and Robin Patterson. The new owners have invested heavily in renovating all the buildings and cottages. New additions include the yacht-friendly beach restaurant Goaty's Bar, and a new spa complex.

It is managed by husband and wife team Matt and Annie Semark, along with an excellent local crew. The main anchorage is shown on the chart. The current changes with the tide, and if the wind drops, yachts swing about. The reef off the dinghy dock extends farther than some think.

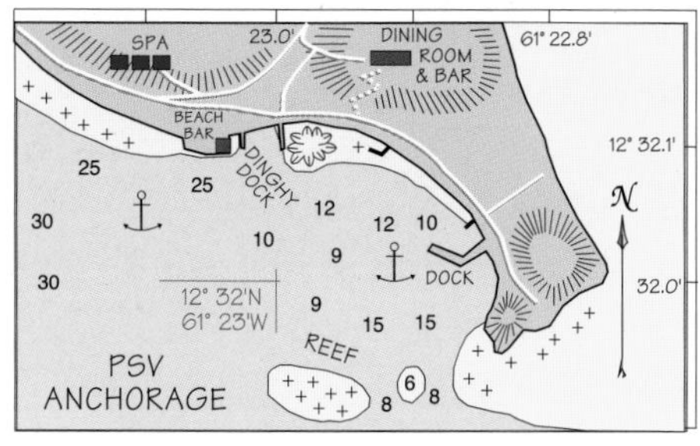

Mopion is a very popular daytime anchorage (see *Water sports*)

Ashore

When you go ashore, keep in mind that this is an exclusive and luxurious resort, so please be respectful. If visitors are to continue to be welcomed, this is essential. Only come ashore by the dinghy dock on the leeward side.

You are welcome to walk along the shore and use the beach from the hotel dinghy dock to the beach bar and boutique. All other areas and beaches are private, for in-house residents only, which include the guest cottages and the western end of the beach, past the beach bar. Private areas are clearly sign posted.

You are welcome to visit the main bar and restaurant upstairs, though smart casual attire is expected (no bathing costumes by day; no shorts or t-shirts for dinner). Reservations are essential for dinner.

The hotel bar, with a view of the bay, is open all day, and it is a pleasant place to take a drink ~ especially those frozen daiquiris and fruit specials they are so good at.

Goaty's Beach Bar is more casual and built with visitors in mind, so shorts, t-shirts and even bathing togs are fine, up until sunset when slacks and a sports shirt or similar attire are appropriate. It is open 1030-2200. Their menu includes tapas, salads, sandwiches, burgers, pizza, pasta, and grilled seafood and meat.

On Fridays, the regular menu closes down and they have a beach barbecue with a steel band. Come for the barbecue or just to listen and visit the bar. On Tuesday night Barracuda's band plays reggae. On many Mondays they have a classic movie night, with a big screen set up in the beach bar.

The spa is open to people visiting on yachts, offering all kinds of massage and beauty or health treatments. Guided island and cottage tours are available on request after 1030. Book by radio, phone, or ask in the bar or office.

If you are longing for a good walk, Petite Martinique is within dinghy range, and if you plan a meal over there you can get a ride over and back.

Water sports

The snorkeling on the surrounding reefs is good. Mopion is an exciting destination for a picnic by dinghy. You can anchor close by as a lunch stop. You can feel your way into anchorages in the reef north of PSV for excellent snorkeling. Pinese makes a fair dive.

PSV is home to Jean-Michel Cousteau Diving. This top-class and upmarket opera-

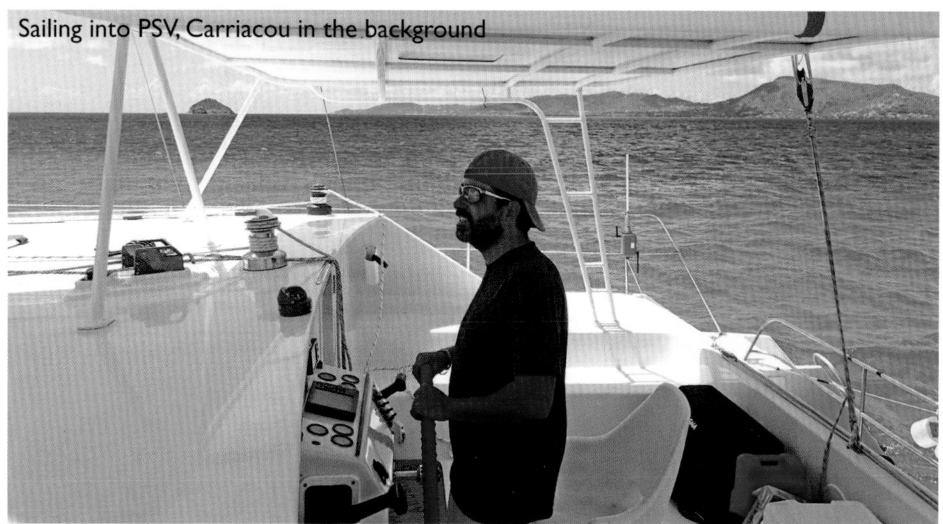

Sailing into PSV, Carriacou in the background

tion is primarily for PSV guests. They may occasionally have room for additional guests.

PETITE MARTINIQUE

Getting tired of all the tourists? Petite Martinique (PM), the northernmost outpost of Grenada, is small and authentic. I love to overnight here, take a long walk, and have a meal ashore. It is a good place to take on water and fuel and look for bargains on beer, liquor, and wine. The inhabitants live by boatbuilding and seafaring (and, in days of old, smuggling). Fishing has always been important, and currently, long-line tuna fishing is very successful. Many vessels lie at anchor and the docks are far busier than the roads. The fancy new houses are recent, but some of the older wooden pitched-roof houses are photogenic, especially at the eastern end of the island. PM is a lot larger than it looks. If you turn right from the dock the road winds round the south side of the island. It is possible to walk all the way around, but the eastern part is a thorny scramble with no real trail. You will find the people here friendly and welcoming, and the island has several shops and a restaurant. For the adventurous explorer and snorkeler Fota and Petite Dominique are within range of a seaworthy dinghy.

If you are coming north from Carriacou, you can clear out and visit PM on your way to Union. Many yachts come directly from PSV or the Grenadines for a quick stop, and it is these yachts that keep the fuel dock and restaurants alive. PM is part of Grenada, but no one is going to sail from PSV to Carriacou to clear in, then sail back to visit PM for a meal or fuel, so many people make an unofficial visit and so far no one has been prosecuted for it. Anchor anywhere off the fuel dock among the other boats. PM can also be visited by a seaworthy dinghy from PSV. You can leave your dinghy on the inside part of the fuel dock, or you can get the Palm Beach Restaurant to bring you over for a meal (see *Shops, restaurants, ashore*).

The holding in PM is in soft mud and not always easy. Use plenty of scope, and if it is blowing hard, use your engine to keep the boat in place to allow the anchor time to sink into the mud before you put strain on it.

The best thing is to eat at the Palm Beach

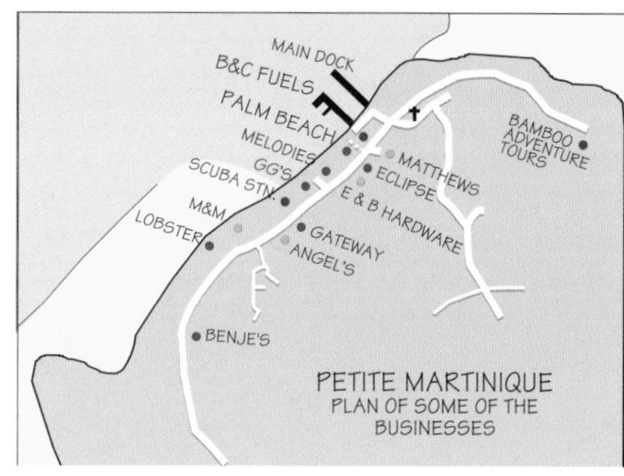

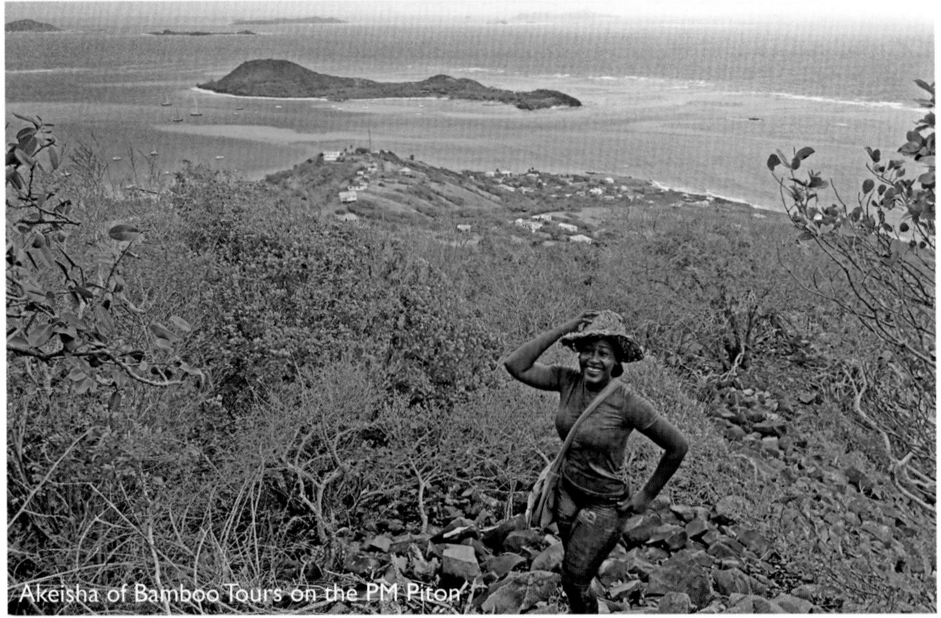
Akeisha of Bamboo Tours on the PM Piton

Restaurant, then you may pick up one of their two free customer moorings off their dock, both marked with their name.

If you do have a problem, a big, shallow (8- to 12-foot deep) patch of easy anchoring sand is clearly visible about half a mile north and a little east of the docks. It is a fair dinghy ride in, but okay.

Communications

Most bars and restaurants have free WiFi for patrons. For a computer, try the resource center above the school, up the stairs beside the road to the main dock.

General yacht services

Glenn Clement and Reynold Belmar own B & C Fuels [VHF: 16, Golf Sierra], the best and most convenient fuel dock in the Grenadines. An easy approach and fair prices have made this the main refueling station for large power yachts, charter yachts, and bareboats. However, currently they are not duty-free. The dock has 16-18 feet of water alongside and you approach it into the wind. They sell high-quality diesel, water, and cube ice.

Chandlery & technical yacht services

E & B hardware is on the left as you walk down the main road heading west. It is upstairs, above Emma's Supermarket, in the same building. Owner Emrol Logan keeps a good supply of resins, cloths, and a little yacht hardware, plus fishing gear, along with general hardware and a lot of plumbing bits. Emrol sometimes repairs outboards. He is often busy, but can probably help repair one in a pinch, along with other mechanical problems.

Shops, restaurants, ashore

Replenish your wine, beer, and liquor lockers and top up on groceries at E & B supermarket or Matthew's Shopping Center at unbeatable prices. Odinga's Millennium Connection is in Matthew's and has stacks of clothes, shoes, jewelry, and more. Adjoining is a gift shop with handicrafts, and a mini-museum.

Palm Beach [VHF: 16, (473) 443-9103, $$] is a very pleasant family restaurant managed by Emmanuel. The setting is perfect: a pretty garden shaded by palms, right on the beach. They serve seafood from the local fishing fleet, with chicken or pork for those who don't like fish, lambi, shrimps or lobster. The food is first-rate, the lobster dishes highly

recommended, but if you prefer the fish, try the lobster bisque as a starter if it is on the menu. Prices are affordable. Palm Beach has two customer moorings and free WiFi. They are usually happy to come to PSV and pick you up from your yacht in their speedboat for lunch or dinner. If you want time to hike, shop, or wander around before your meal you can arrange this with Emmanuel (not always in service). It is a great way to add PM to your PSV visit. There is no charge for this service, but if you are only one or two people, a gas contribution is greatly appreciated.

Close by, Melodies [VHF: 16, "Tasha P Radio"] is a guesthouse, built on the beach. They have a bar and restaurant, but cook meals to advance order only.

Eclipse hosts most of PM's nightlife. They stay open until 2400 most nights, food is almost always available, and they sometimes host karaoke. If you don't see anyone out front, check in the kitchen around back.

There are several other small supermarkets (minimarkets would be a better description), rum shops, and snack shops dotted around the island, along the west-running road. Angel's and M & M are local supermarkets. GG's, Jig's, and Benje's are rum shops and sometimes restaurants.

For an informative walking tour of the island contact Akeisha of Bamboo Adventure Tours. She started as a tour guide in Grenada but relocated to PM years ago with her husband, a local fisherman. She will take you to the top of the Piton, identify birds and medicinal plants, show you interesting volcanic rock formations, and share the island's unique folklore, history, and traditions. If you have questions about the island, she is the one to contact.

Water sports

Francis Logan fills tanks for local fishermen, and he can be found on the beach beside Melodie's. This is not a sports establishment and has none of the safeguards that go with a dive shop, so satisfy yourself that the gear is in order.

Traditional boat building

Grenada & Carriacou

Hillsborough Beach, Carriacou

Carriacou at a glance

Regulations

Carriacou is part of Grenada, and the main customs office for yachts is in Tyrrel Bay at Carriacou Marine, next to the chandlery/mini mart. It is open 0800-1600 Monday to Friday. They also open 0900-1400 on weekends and holidays, when you will pay a reasonable overtime fee. They are on the SailClear system and you can use the office computer on those occasions when their internet is actually working. You can also clear Hillsborough (no SailClear), and by the time this book is published you may be able to clear in at the new Port Authority buildings by Tyrrel Bay Marina.

Monthly customs cruising permits are $50 EC for yachts not exceeding 40 feet; $75 EC not exceeding 60 feet; $100 EC not exceeding 80 feet; and $150 EC for 80 feet or more. You do not pay for months spent in a yard. Crew arriving by plane or from shore pay a $20 EC embarkation fee.

Visitors may not spearfish in Grenada's waters, including around Carriacou and Petit Martinique, and anyone caught doing so will be heavily fined and may be banned from returning to the country. The water surrounding Sandy Island, Sister Rocks, and the mangroves on the northern side of Tyrrel Bay is a Marine Protected Area - The Sandy Island/Oyster Bay Marine Protected Area (SIOBMPA). In these areas, use a park mooring if one is available. The charge for being in the marine park is $25 EC per day for boats less than 50ft; $50 EC per day for boats over 50 ft. There is an additional $1 US per person per visit snorkeling fee. Diving in the marine park must be with a local dive shop, and fishing is prohibited.

Holidays

See *Grenada*. The Carriacou Regatta usually takes place at the end of July. For details check the website:

carriacouregatta.com

Shopping hours

Shops and offices normally open 0800-1600. Saturday is half-day and most places are closed by noon. Banks open Monday to Thursday 0800-1400, and later on Fridays.

Telephones

The easiest way to call is to buy a cell phone or a local SIM. Flow or Digicel are your options. For overseas calls dial 1 for the USA and NANP countries; 011 plus the country code for other countries (see page 19). For collect and credit-card calls, dial 0, then the whole number. When dialing from overseas, the area code is 473, followed by a 7-digit number.

Transport

There are inexpensive ($1.50-$6 EC) buses running to most villages. Taxis are plentiful. Linky Taxi (VHF: 16) is a good driver and is used to working with yachts. Sample taxi rates are:

	$EC
Hillsborough to Tyrrel Bay....	35
Tyrrel Bay to airport..............	40
Island tour (2.5 hours)	200
Mini tour (1.25 hours)...........	100

Rental cars are available (check our directory). You will need to buy a local license, which costs $60 EC. Drive on the left.

Airport tax for international flights is $50 EC, and for flights between Carriacou and Grenada; $10 EC. These are sometimes included in the ticket.

Hawksbill turtle and juvenile drum fish, Sister Rocks

Photo by Scott Wilks

Carriacou

"This is an island with over a hundred rum shops and only one gasoline station." Frances Kay, Carriacou.

Carriacou is enchanting. The inhabitants live by farming, fishing, and seafaring, and must number among the friendliest in the Caribbean. Just about everywhere in Carriacou is of interest, but Windward should definitely be part of your tour, as should the road running from Windward to the north end of the island. Windward is the traditional center of boatbuilding, made famous by the movie *Vanishing Sail*, and it is here that you can see the fishing fleet arrive under sail. If you cannot afford a taxi, take a bus over to Windward and hike. Closer to town, a destination with a great view is the hospital, which sits high on the mountain overlooking Hillsborough Bay.

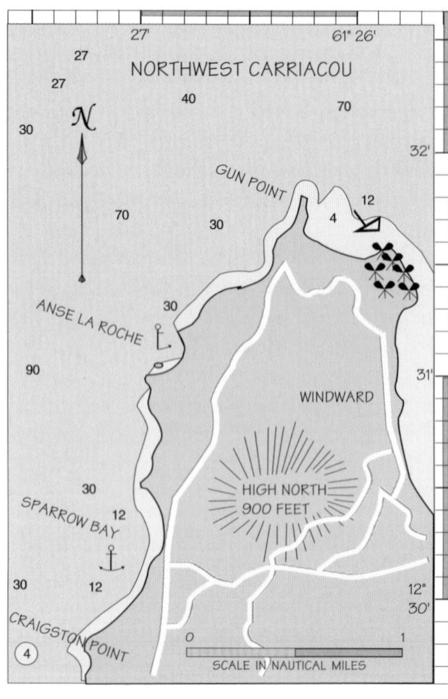

Carriacou has lovely anchorages, pleasant hiking, yacht haul-out facilities, yacht services,

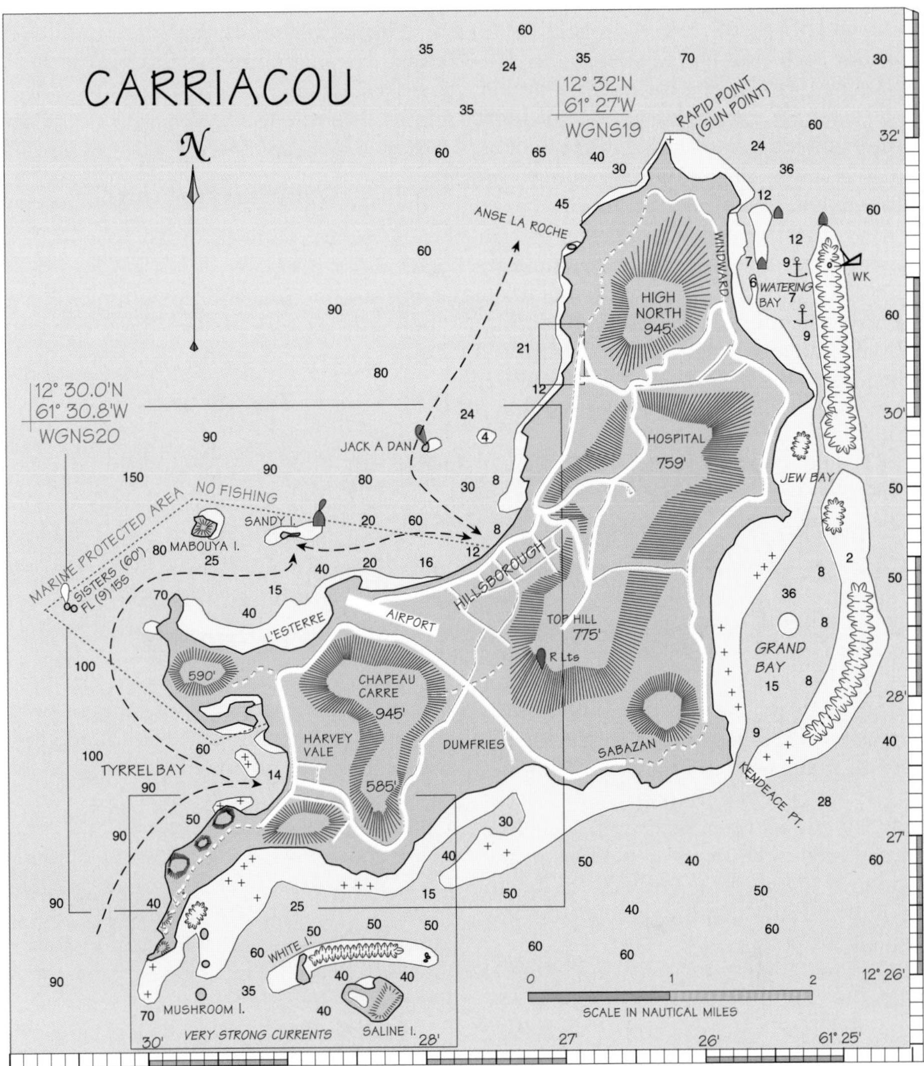

dive shops, and entertaining bars, restaurants, and cafes.

The island has no natural source of water, besides rainwater, which is often in short supply, especially in the dry season. Please be respectful and conserve water when you can.

Navigation

Carriacou is a Carib word meaning "island surrounded by reefs," but do not worry: the approach down the west coast is simple enough. When sailing from the north it is safest to pass to the west of Jack a Dan before heading up into Hillsborough. If you take the trickier route east of Jack a Dan, watch out for the reef, which is about 5 feet deep, roughly one-third of the way between Craigston Point and Jack a Dan. Favor the Jack a Dan side of the channel (but not too close). You can anchor almost anywhere off the town. Hillsborough is a good anchorage except in bad northerly swells, when you will be better off in Tyrrel Bay.

There is a flashing green light on Jack a Dan and a flashing red light on the buoy east of Sandy Island.

Two anchorages north of Hillsborough are worth a thought. Anse La Roche has a perfect beach with a big rock on the south side. It is good for temporary anchorage for a swim and beach visit, or even overnight, but northerly swells will make it untenable. The snorkeling is good. Sparrow Bay is another good anchorage, except during bad northerly swells, but even in moderate swells it will be hard to beach the dinghy. When coming from Hillsborough, pass outside Jack a Dan.

The adventurous might want to poke into Windward and Watering Bay on the northeast coast. You cannot rely on the buoys, but if you eyeball your way in you will find yourself in a vast, fairly protected lagoon. You can explore right down in this lagoon with a draft of 6 feet, but go carefully as it is all eyeball navigation.

HILLSBOROUGH

Hillsborough is a pleasant town built on a lovely beach. As you walk down the main street you catch glimpses of the sea through gaps between the buildings. Hillsborough is a good anchorage, with the Marine Protected Area nearby. You can also visit by hopping on one of the frequent buses that run between Tyrrel Bay and Hillsborough (fare $3.50 EC). You will find good restaurants and shops, a local market, and you can pop into the tourist office for maps and information, including cultural events. There are two ATMs in the middle of town and a Western Union in the Bullen Tours building across from the Republic Bank.

For pets that need attention there is a good non-profit animal hospital, run by Kathy, who brings in qualified volunteer veterinarians from all over the world. If you need attention, Carriacou Health Services (CHS) brings in specialists (including a dentist) on various days of the week and can do tests. They take walk-ins for emergencies, but otherwise call ahead. The local hospital has a commanding view of the bay and Carriacou has a doctor in town.

Regulations

While most yachts clear in Tyrrel Bay, at the time of this writing you could also clear in Hillsborough (this may change when the main port moves to Tyrrel Bay). First check with immigration, by the police station, then visit customs at the base of the jetty. They are not on the SailClear system.

Yachts wanting an agent to handle their clearance can arrange this though Henry Safari Tours of Grenada. He can also arrange a big beach barbecue complete with a band and marquee on Sandy Island.

Communications

Most bars and restaurants have WiFi. If you need a computer, Ade's Dream has an internet room in their office at the back. For phone and fax, try Flow (Cable and Wireless), Digicel, or Ade's Dream.

Transport

Matthew Raymond, aka Linky Taxi [VHF: 16], is a good and reliable cab driver, used to dealing with yachtspeople, and he always carries his phone with him. If you need something done, he can help. Linky also has a select fleet of Jeeps available for rent.

Provisioning

Make a beeline for Patty's Deli. Christine, a Carriacou woman who was brought up in England, is charming and helpful and sells things the other supermarkets do not in her pleasantly cool, air-conditioned shop. Freshly baked French bread, croissants, and other baked goodies come out of her oven around 0800. You will find cold cuts, yogurts, cheeses, frozen meats and fish, good wines, lots of sauces, coffee, and gluten-free items. Visiting Grenadians ask "Why don't we have a store like this in Grenada?"

Christine will also provision bareboats

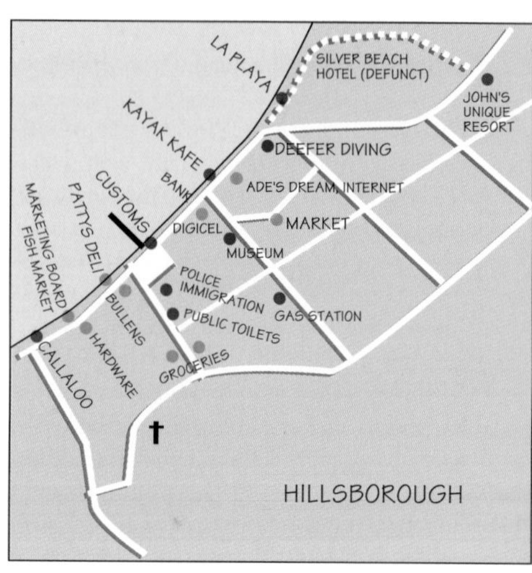

and yachts with a little notice.

Many supermarkets stock essentials, though you will have to visit the market, MNIB, or local street-side vendors for fresh produce. Liquor prices are good. Check Ade's Dream and Bullen's on Main Street. Wander down Church Street to see Kim's Supermarket, A1 Enterprise, and the large Hills and Valley Pharmacy.

Fun Shopping

You can find banks, travel agents, and many quaint, small variety stores, each crammed with its owner's ideas of what sells in Carriacou. If you go round to enough of them you will find a wider selection of products for sale than on many a larger island. Noel's and Dollarman, both on Main Street, carry a good selection of tools and hardware.

Restaurants

Hillsborough has a great collection of restaurants. Kayak Kafe [$$] is bright and cheerful, in a great location, hanging over the beach and looking out to sea. Smoothies and fresh local juice, along with a slice of Carriacou lime pie or banana cake, are always available. The lunch menu includes rotis, sandwiches, wraps, soups, salads, and local fish dishes. Closed Tuesdays, they are otherwise open 0730-1500 for breakfast and lunch. Also for dinner (in season) on Wednesday, Thursday, Saturdays, and Mondays until 2100. Dinner includes fresh fish, lambi, and lobster in season.

La Playa [$], owned by the same people as the Green Roof Inn, is the perfect beach-bar hangout. You can anchor right off and dinghy ashore as long as there are no big swells. La Playa (closed Sundays) is open 1000-1800 (2000 in season). They offer generous hamburgers, fishburgers, soup and sandwiches anytime they are open. It is a perfect place for that sunset drink or as a daytime hangout; try their homemade ice cream. They have live music every Saturday during the season.

Bogles Round House [$$$$] is special and Carriacou's fanciest restaurant. It is a one minute walk from the main bus route, or you can anchor off Bogles (Sparrow Bay)

Grenada and Carriacou

and dinghy ashore, swells permitting. If you have a group of six or more they will provide free transportation from Hillsborough or Tyrrel Bay, or you can take a taxi. The Round House building comes right out of a children's book, with its circular structure and white roof supported by a tree in the center of the room. Whimsical round windows have been made out of old farm implements and wagon wheels. It is so magical you might expect gnomes and wizards to be in attendance.

Roxanne, the chef, spent a few years in the merchant Navy and ended up in the galley of the Onassis yacht. She loves food; her cooking is a fusion of Caribbean and international flavors, she bakes her own bread and makes fresh homemade ice cream. Dinners are elegant, and lunches are simpler. This small place is excellent and popular, so make reservations, especially for dinner. They do a more casual burger night on Wednesdays, plus a popular Sunday roast; reservations are essential. Out of season they close on Wednesdays and Sundays. They have three self-contained cottages for rent at very reasonable rates. They were built by Sue and Roxanne's Father, Kim, who now has the wonderful Crayfish Bay Organic Chocolate Estate in Grenada.

The Jerk Center in town at Laurena II [$] is cheap, cheerful, and serves generous portions of local food. They open around noon and often have live music Saturday nights.

The Mermaid Inn, located on the water just past the fish market, has reopened after many decades of closure, and has taken on new owners who have renovated the Callaloo restaurant [$$$]. Callaloo has a breezy interior, a large deck with a spectacular view overlooking the beach, and a cute little tree house. Open daily 0700 - 2300 for breakfast, lunch, and dinner, it boasts a large menu and serves local and international fare alike. Rooms are available.

Eclipse [$$] is across from Ade's Dream. The dining room hangs out over the beach, with the gentle sound of waves brushing the shore. It serves reasonably priced local food and does takeout.

Cuthbert Snagg [VHF: 16] owns a couple of powerboats to take you on snorkeling trips and expeditions to the offshore islands. He also builds model racing and sailing boats. A good place to meet him is at his bar, Snagg's Place, which is on the beach in front of the big old water tank. On occasion, if the group is right, he will organize a lobster bash or fish cookout.

The Green Roof Inn [$$$] lies about half a mile north of town on the coast. This Swedish establishment is owned and run by Asa and Jonas. They have a small dinghy dock, the restaurant has a nice view, and the bar is open all day. They serve fresh fruit juice and coffee, along with regular drinks. The restaurant opens for dinner; Swedish-trained chefs specialize in international seafood dishes that include local lobster, fish, and lambie.

In the other direction, you can walk 10 minutes towards the airport for a good roti at Annie's Roti Shop, just past the animal hospital and across the road from the beach. She is open from 0730 and does breakfast, lunch, and dinner by reservation. She also rents comfortable wooden beach chairs across the street (free to patrons of the restaurant), which are perfect for a lazy afternoon on the beach.

Ashore

You can use the low part of the main dock for your dinghy, but you may need a stern anchor to stop it from getting mashed up in swells. Use caution on the stairs. The taxi square is at the end of the dock. There is a gas station in town and many youths are willing to fetch ice. The port authority plans to move the main dock to Tyrrel Bay during the life of this guide, at which point the fate of the current dock is unknown.

The museum is worth the short walk and is open 1000 to 1600 Monday through Friday, and 1100 to 1500 on Saturdays. It has an eclectic collection, from Arawak pottery to the island's first telephone exchange. For a taste of local life hang out in the rum shops, you won't have to look too far to find one.

Should you arrive towards the end of July or early August you may witness the famous Carriacou Regatta. The best trading and sailing sloops in the islands are built in Carriacou. Once a year they get together to race on this festive weekend. The boats they build today are unbelievably fast and sweet, and if you are lucky enough to see one sailing into harbor, it is a joy to behold. They are featured in a great movie: *Vanishing Sail.*

Carriacou also has an interesting Maroon Festival towards the end of April: visit carriacoumaroon.com for more info.

Carriacou is one of the last unspoiled islands. One reason for this is that much of the land does not have clear title. However, if you are interested, there are lots overlooking the sea available at Craigston Estates. Contact Renwick and Thompson or Down Island Realty.

Water sports

Diving is very good, with excellent visibility and a big Marine Protected Area. Within the park you must dive with a dive

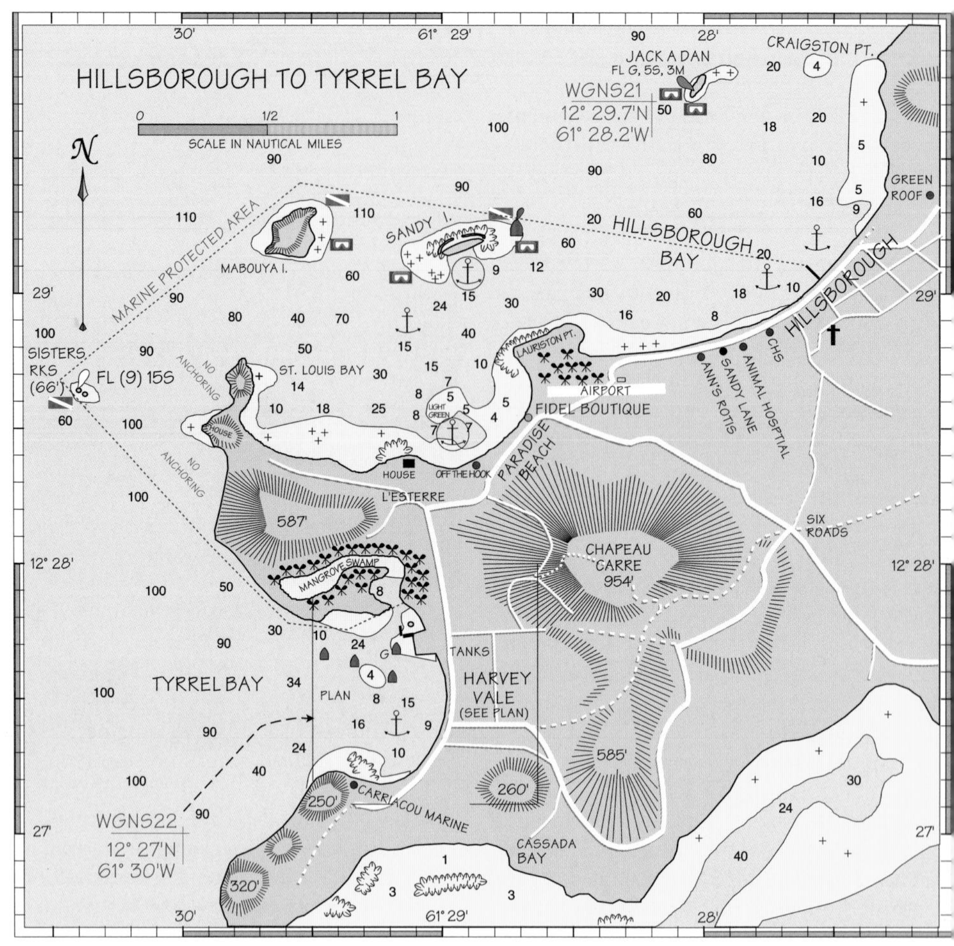

shop, though you are welcome to snorkel on your own. The Sandy Island / Oyster Bay Marine Protected Area (SIOBMPA) has 15 dive sites that are less than a 10-minute boat ride from either Hillsborough or Tyrrel Bay. New dive sites to the north of Hillsborough are being explored.

Sandy Island has a sheltered shallow site that is a favorite with both divers and snorkelers. Other popular sites include Sharky's Hideaway (home to several nurse sharks) and Whirlpool (so called for its champagne-like bubbles, which are caused by volcanic activity), both of which are at Mabouya Island. A reef restoration project and coral nursery was established in the area, although it has currently been put on hold. Sisters Rocks features two sites outstanding for their black coral and masses of aquatic life. Within the SIOBMPA you often see several species of moray eels (green, spotted, chain-link, and chestnut), southern stingrays, nurse sharks, angelfish, a multitude of blennies, and sometimes spotted eagle rays, seahorses, and frogfish.

Deefer Diving is owned by Matt Rideout from England and Austrian/British couple Alex and Gary Ward. They are very welcoming, well-qualified instructors who run a good dive shop with enthusiasm and care. All are experienced PADI master instructors and offer a variety of diving courses, from beginner to instructor, as well as guided dives for those already certified. Snorkelers accompanying divers are always welcome. In June 2017 Deefer Diving launched their purpose-built catamaran, Phoenix, one of the first of its kind to be built on Carriacou. The dive center retains a PADI 5 Star IDC Centre status and remains one of the most qualified dive centres in the Windwards. Like all dive shops on Carriacou, they prefer to go out with small groups, although large groups can be accommodated by prior arrangement.

They open from 0800 to 1700, although bookings by phone and email can be made at any time, and walk-in business is welcome; snorkeling gear is on sale, and equipment rental and tank fills are available. A pick-up service from your yacht in Tyrrel Bay or Sandy Island can be arranged. They do frequent lionfish hunts.

SUP Carriacou is run by Canadian couple Mike and Gwen. They rent good quality inflatable stand up paddle boards, give tours of the coastline and mangroves, and will deliver and pick up from any of Carriacou's beaches. Find them on the road to the airport or give them a call to make arrangements; 404-2653.

SANDY ISLAND AND L'ESTERRE BAY

Sandy Island is nothing but a flawless strip of sand surrounded by perfect snorkeling and diving reefs. Pelicans and seagulls will be your neighbors in this wonderful spot. Across the bay is Paradise Beach, another idyllic anchorage within walking range of both Tyrrel Bay and Hillsborough.

This area is part of SIOBMPA and the daily charge for being in the marine park is $25 EC for boats less than 50ft, and $50 EC for boats over 50 ft. There is an additional $1 US per person per visit snorkeling fee. By the time you read this there should be 22 moorings at Sandy Island and 9 in L'esterre Bay. If none are available and you need to anchor, do so to the west and south of the Sandy Island mooring area, in sand only. Contact the park rangers on VHF: 16 for assistance. Yachts should use holding tanks.

Sandy Island has changed rapidly in recent times. The beach suffered such degradation that all the trees died, but then a hurricane threw up a coral capping, leaving big tide pools and providing the island some protection. Trees planted by locals have thrived and it is now in fine shape. Respect all beach plants and vegetation: they hold the island together.

You can carry 7 feet quite close to the middle of the island, but watch out for the reefs north and south, and the odd shallower spot. There is not much room to drag, so check your mooring.

L'Esterre Bay, with the long and beautiful Paradise Beach, is right opposite Sandy Island. You can pick up a mooring here in 7 -8 feet of water. Head from Sandy towards the white house with the terra-cotta roof on the headland west of Paradise Beach. Skirt the really bright green water, then turn east once past it, and you will be in the best spot. You can also dinghy over.

Ashore

The eastern end of Paradise beach is the home of Sandra's Fidel Productions. This little container-boutique is unquestionably the best in Carriacou. Everything is locally

and artistically made: original calabash art, handmade jewelry, bamboo and coconut craft, Art Fabrik batik, and original paintings and prints. They have a new line of local natural teas, soaps, creams, and oils that they produce themselves.

They also print art on t-shirts: good-quality reproductions from local artists are sold through their website, fidelproductions.com, or in shops up and down the islands. You can find them in a handful of stores in Grenada, as well as Art 'n Beads in Union. In the Tobago Cays, only buy them from Mr. Quality, as he is the only authorised reseller, ensuring the artists receive royalties. Fidel also produce mojos, each an original, using exotic beads from many materials, often accented with gold and silver.

There are several good little bars here, including Joan's [$] next to the boutique. Joan does an inexpensive lunch and will cook dinner on order.

Off the Hook [$$] is much farther down the beach. Part art, part beach bar, part crazy, it is all fun. Off the Hook, with its upper-level and countless corner seats and hammocks, is entertaining to say the least. Curtis Malcolm opens daily, 0900-2300. It is in an open beach area with fishing boats, giving it a pleasant local feel. Curtis's partner Coleen cooks fish, lobster, and lambi, serves good pizza, and claims to have the best fries in Carriacou. Come for live music, barbecue and bonfire on Wednesday nights. They have free WiFi and men can always get a haircut, as Curtis is a professional barber (by appointment only). Dinner reservations are appreciated. This is a good place to leave your dinghy when you want to take a bus, hike, or shop in town. Tyrrel Bay and Hillsborough are both within walking distance, but you may get your feet wet walking on the beach towards Hillsborough. They have affordable accommodation nearby, rent kayaks and SUPs, have a water taxi, do tours, and sell ice and coals.

TYRREL BAY

Tyrrel Bay is huge, well-protected, and very popular with cruisers. The taking of mangrove oysters is no longer allowed, so do not buy any.

Businesses line the waterfront and a road separates them from the sea. The shore was once thickly wooded with manchineel and seagrapes, but most were cut down to increase the visibility between the boats and the businesses. When Hurricane Lenny threw record-breaking swells into the bay it devastated the unprotected shoreline and destroyed much of the road, turning several properties into beachfront real estate. The government then built the big seawall that now lines the waterfront. Thankfully, the trees are now coming back.

Navigation

Tyrrel Bay is deep and wide and easy to enter. Despite this, a surprising number of people manage to run aground. The buoys are rather confusing. Whatever the original color, they end up pelican-guano white on top and rust underneath. Buoys may be added or removed at any time, without notice. There is a reef in the northern part of the bay, towards the center. The deepest channel is to the north of this reef and is marked by three buoys. However, the reef that is most often hit

is along the southern shore. There is a small cul-de-sac in this reef called Bareboat Alley, and people manage to go in here and run hard aground. Two large unlit mooring buoys lie in the middle of the southern channel. It is easiest to enter the bay just south of center. You are not in danger of hitting the northern reef until you are more than halfway across the bay. You can pass closely on either side of the big mooring buoys safely, though keep in mind that buoys should not be relied upon. In the middle of the anchorage there are two small buoys close together, marking a sunken boat, be careful to avoid them. Holding is good if you can find clear sand, but rather poor in the weedy areas.

The northern side of the bay is a Marine Protected Area, with no anchoring, except in the mangrove swamp during hurricane warnings.

If you want a mooring call Carriacou Marine (443-6292). If you accept any other mooring offers, ask anyone else for a mooring, or listen to someone telling you "That mooring no good, try mine," you are likely to have problems.

Regulations

Tyrrel Bay is the main customs station for yacht clearance. The office is open 0800-1600 weekdays and 0900-1400 weekends and holidays. The officers are friendly and Sailclear.com works when they have internet. The office is in Carriacou Marine (see also page 323) and by the time this edition is published there may also be one in the new Port Authority buildings by Tyrrel Bay Marina.

Communications

Carriacou Children's Educational Fund (CCEF), funded by local businesses, is based in the Slipway Restaurant and has free baywide WiFi. Go in to find out how to link up and you will be given an opportunity to make a contribution to CCEF. The Lazy Turtle, Lambi Queen, Gallery Cafe and most other bars have WiFi. The Cruiser's WiFi signal comes from the Lazy Turtle.

General yacht services

Tyrrel Bay Marina has an excellent dinghy dock with large garbage bins at the base. You can also leave your dinghy at Carriacou Marine, Slipway Restaurant, Lazy Turtle, Twilight, the main dock, or beach it. Blue barrel garbage bins are dotted along the main road; try not to overwhelm them.

Carriacou Marine [VHF: 16] is a charming small boatyard and marina. Its fuel dock is open 0800-1730 Monday to Saturday, and 0900-1400 on Sundays. Here you can take on ice, water, and fuel (diesel and gas, both regular and duty-free). If you are after duty-free fuel, this is a good place to buy it. There is only one fuel dock attendant, so be prepared to wait if you arrive at lunch time.

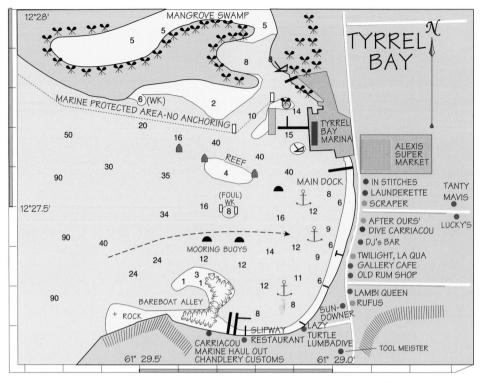

Carriacou Marine has convenient docking, with space for about seven yachts, both on the finger dock and outside of the marine hoist dock.

Yachts are hauled on a 50-ton marine travel-lift. They can take up to 18-foot beam and 8-foot draft at high tide. It is one of the more environmentally friendly yards, with a wash-down catchment to minimise the amount of toxic paint that goes into the sea, and they have vacuum systems to suck up the dust. They can take about 50 boats. Normal opening hours are 0800-1600 Monday to Friday and 0800-1200 on Saturdays.

This yard is excellent for general work and for do-it-yourself jobs. They can provide technicians for most things, including carpentry, electrics, and mechanics. For environmental reasons, they are not currently spraying boats, sandblasting, or encouraging major fiberglass repairs as they lack an enclosed area to contain the fumes and dust.

They have a chandlery, open 0800-1800, with a moderate selection, along with a mini-market. Laundry, showers, and toilets are available for those in the yard, plus a small shop, ice, and rooms for rent for those who prefer to stay ashore. The whole area has WiFi.

Jerome McQuilkin and John Walker have built Tyrrel Bay Marina on the far side of the main dock, the largest development in Tyrrel Bay. There is room for 200 boats ashore to be hoisted by a 150-ton travel lift. Currently there is docking room for a few dozen yachts stern to or alongside, but docks are envisaged for about 180 boats to tie up stern-to once construction is complete. Water and power are available to those hauled out and will become available on the dock during the life of this guide. They aim to be a full-service yard and currently have technicians available to handle welding, antifouling, buffing and polishing, and fiberglass work. Manager Keith Murray is from Trinidad and has experience with everything from yacht construction to launch and delivery.

Gerry owns various tugs and can provide a 24-hour marine emergency service for yachts that go aground or start to sink. He is the right person to contact if you need a hand, as his prices are fair. Call 407-0927 or contact him through Slipway Restaurant.

My Beautiful Launderette, owned by Daniella, is next to the Alexis Supermarket. They will do your wash for you, but if you are obsessive enough to want to do it yourself you can (the price is the same). They have seats where you can sit while your laundry is washing and a book exchange so you will not be bored if you wait. They open 0700-1500 from Monday to Saturday.

Chandlery

Carriacou Marine has a good little chandlery, which is linked to Island Water World, and anything they don't have in stock can usually come on the next ferry.

See also Technical Marine Management in *Technical yacht services*.

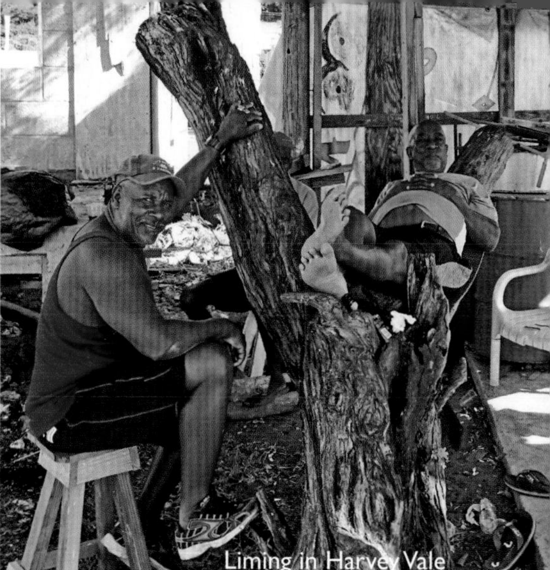
Liming in Harvey Vale

Technical yacht services

In Stitches is an excellent canvas and sail repair shop run by Andy and Jacqui. Andy lives on his yacht, Yellow Bird, and drives an old BMW bike with a sidecar. You can call him on VHF: 16. The shop is ashore, next to Alexis. They are very helpful with all kinds of canvas work, upholstery, sail work (they sell new sails with the Quantum label), and bimini tops. They make very decorative custom flags. Andy does sails while Jacqui does most of the canvas work and runs Jean's Hope Foundation out of Scraper's. They raise funds by selling coffee and souvenirs to help local women access health care, and occasionally host a movie night or walk-a-thon (see Scraper's under *Restaurants*). Check out the Facebook page to see what is coming up.

Paul O'Regan, of Technical Marine Management, is in the Gallery Cafe. He used to manage the boatyard and knows most boat systems. He is a good man to contact for rigging problems and general help. He is a knowledgeable Budget Marine agent and can bring in items from both Budget Marine and Island Water World, same or next day. He has a hotline to Turbulence Sails in Grenada for rigging hardware.

Carriacou Underwater Services is owned and operated by Rob Mcneill and Raquel, a young and enthusiastic couple from South Africa and Canada respectively. Rob was a commercial diver in the BVIs and St. Maarten before relocating to Carriacou. He has a wide range of experience, from beach building and dredging to hull maintenance for large charter companies. They are happy to tackle almost any underwater job, but mostly do search and recovery, mooring inspection and installation, hull cleaning, and video inspections.

Tyrrel Bay is first-rate for welding and fabricating thanks to Dominique [VHF: 16] of Carriacou Aluminum Boats, who does wonders in aluminum, from building a new dinghy to fixing a broken mast. He welds and polishes stainless steel, and biminis are one of his specialties. His wife, Genevieve, sews sails and offers therapeutic massage for bad backs and sore necks. You will find him on his trimaraft workshop, not far from the boatyard.

On the mechanical side, check Manny Work Shop in Carriacou Marine or ask for its owner Immanual Clemment. Immanual is from PM and can fix inboards, outboards, and general mechanical, plumbing and electrical problems. He can also do fiberglass and woodwork. He is good at most everything.

Gus (538-4315) is another good mechanic in the area. He works on inboards, outboards, and electrical. His workshop is around the side of Slipway Restaurant. If you can't find him there, give him a call - he can often help out in a pinch.

Tyrrel Bay has a certified electrician, François Corles, who is also a professional diver. His company is Tall Man Electrics, appropriate for a technician some 2 meters tall. He is French, speaks good English, and is very pleasant to deal with. Look for him on his motor-sailor ketch, Santiago. He can fix any electrical problem, including engines, generators, and other boat systems. If you have a faulty starter or alternator, he can get Al Bernadine in Gouyave to rebuild it. He would be a good person to speak to if you have refrigeration problems.

Transport

Linky Taxi [VHF: 16] is helpful, friendly, and has a good-sized minibus for island tours and shopping trips, backed up by a smaller minibus run by his sister. He is always ready to drive. He can rent you one of his modern Jeeps as well.

Bubbles [VHF: 16] has a fancy, air conditioned bus with spacious seats.

Provisioning

The Alexis family, who own a fleet of

Rufus and his vegetables

boats, recently opened a large American franchise grocery store just south of the new Tyrrel Bay Marina. They have a plethora of frozen and pre-packaged foods, high-end liquor, fresh fruits and vegetables, fresh bread, and ice. A deli counter serves sandwiches, deli meats, and cheeses. Rotisserie chicken is soon to come. Several other little supermarkets along the bay stock a good selection of liquor and beer, along with bread, canned and packaged food, eggs, and chicken. After Ours sometimes has goodies not found in the others. Some also have electronic goods and household supplies. If you don't see what you want, it is worth asking. The store at Carriacou Marine is good for liquor and basics.

La Qua Supermarket [VHF: 16] is run by La Qua and Diana Augustin. They often have fresh eggs and sometimes block ice on hand and, if not, you can get them to order you a block for the next morning. Splash, around the corner from Scraper's, sells wholesale and retail groceries including rum, liquor, and beer, and are the islands one and only Hairoun agent. They are open every day from 0700 to 2200.

Fresh food and produce are sold by Denise in a stall opposite Alexis. She also has a boutique section. Her sister, Donelyn, has another stall, called Empress Elisha Palace, which sells clothing and produce next door. Rufus sells fresh fruit and vegetables every day from his stall at the south end of the bay, across from Sundowners.

Restaurants

The Lazy Turtle [VHF: 16, $$$] is on the waterfront. Dinghy in, tie to their dock, and walk up the steps to the big decks, where you sit looking out over the bay while enjoying the aromas of good cooking. The owners, Sue and Shayne, run a friendly and informal establishment with excellent thin-crust Italian-style pizzas, pastas, and salads, plus a list of specials that are posted on a blackboard. These includes reasonably priced fresh lobster in season, shrimps, lionfish (the fish you can feel good about eating) served in about half a dozen different ways, tuna and more. They bring in live entertainment once in a while, and everyone turns up for the party.

Kate's Slipway Restaurant [$$$], next to Carriacou Marine, is excellent. It is in the original slipway building, complete with a boat in the rafters, planers, routers, and other tools, all left standing but artfully converted to form bars and tables. Service staff greets guest warmly and keeps everyone happy out front, while back in the kitchen Kate cooks like an angel. The menu is posted on a blackboard. The food has a Mediterranean flair, is very good, and reasonably priced with generous portions. They are closed on Mondays and for Sunday dinner (also Thursdays in the summer). Otherwise, they are open 1130-1400 for lunch and 1800-2100 for dinner. Sunday lunch is popular and runs from 1130 to 1400. Tie up your dinghy on the dock right outside.

Gallery Cafe [$$, closed Sundays] is a lovely, cheerful cafe, local art gallery, and craft shop which sells some specialty food items, including gluten-free pasta. They also serve homemade ice cream. It is a friendly place, with WiFi and a book swap, and Sally will make you feel at home. They open at 0800 for coffee and a snack or a full breakfast. They stay open till 1600 (1500 on Saturdays). Come for a healthy lunch-time salad, sandwich, or seafood special between 1200 and 1400. Coffee, iced coffee, teas of all kinds, and baked goodies are always available. The handicrafts are artistically made and local. They include bags, jewelry, clothes, and ornaments.

The Iguana Cafe, at Carriacou Marine [$], is next to customs. It has pleasant covered outside seating and boasts authentic stone-fired pizza. You can also get sandwiches, pastries, good fishburgers, and snacks all day long. In the evening they usually fire up the barbecue, so you can get some chicken or fish.

Sundowners [$], a tiny beachside place between Lambi Queen and Lazy Turtle, is owned by Franky. It opens at around 1630 and stays open, so you can take a sundowner and enjoy dinner. Some Wednesday nights they host a beach bonfire, starting around 1930. They bake excellent bread that you can order in advance.

Scraper's is a small grocery and souvenir shop and is home to Jean's Hope Foundation. They serve tea, coffee, cold drinks, and sell local handmade jewelry and crafts from a corner of the shop. The proceeds go to ensuring that women on the island have access to adequate health care and fund workshops and educational seminars. They host a regular movie night at Tanty Mavis and do Walks for Wellness a couple times a year.

Tanty Mavis [$] is just down the street that leads back from Scraper's and is open every day. Monday to Saturday they serve big local lunch plates for about $15 EC. Ask about dinner.

Across the road, Lucky's Bar [$] is popular with yachtspeople, particularly on Saturday afternoons when she does an affordable afternoon barbecue of chicken, ribs, fish, and conch.

Lambi Queen [VHF: 16, $$] is a cute restaurant with a patio railing made from old barrel planks. The Sylvester family owns it. Edwin goes out fishing, and his son, Sherwin, cooks up the catch in good Carriacou home-style. Nightly happy hour is 1730-1830. They have a party on Fridays, and you can tie up at their small dinghy dock.

The Twilight Restaurant and Bar [VHF: 16, $] has a pleasant, intimate atmosphere; the walls are brightly decorated with paintings, many from local artist, Canute Caliste. Owner and chef Diana Augustin cooks spicy West Indian Creole dishes with fresh fish, lobster, lambi, chicken, and pork. Happy hour is 1800-1900. They have two tables across the road hanging over the beach. They are open every day, except sometimes on Sundays, and sell ice.

Natasha's Bayside Restaurant and Bar [$] sits open to the breeze next door to In Stitches, with one waterfront table across the road. She is often open on Wednesday nights for dominoes. Otherwise, make a reservation.

The Original Rum Shop [$], run by Casana and Timothy, is a great hangout where you can meet people and play dominoes. They sometimes do meals featuring fresh fish, conch, and lobster, but they need about a half-hour notice to get in gear.

After Ours is a handsome building that is a nightclub, conference center, shop, and stage. They open from time to time for occasional music, discos, live bands, and other entertainment.

Painted in bright national colors, DJ's [$] is a bar and restaurant open 1500-2400 daily and serves reasonably priced local dishes. Happy hour is every Friday from 1700-1900. Music tends to be quite loud. There are several other inexpensive hangouts, including Liz's Place [$] which is friendly, and where you can get good local food.

Ashore

The mangrove swamp in Tyrrel Bay is part of the Marine Protected Area. Switch off the dinghy motor and listen to the peace. (Take insect repellent.) You often see herons, and sometimes iguanas. Yachts are not allowed in except during a hurricane warning. Taking oysters is forbidden.

There are plenty of hiking possibilities, including a pleasant trek up Chapeau Carre, the second highest peak on the island, which offers panoramic views. (Hiking instructions are on doyleguides.com.)

Water sports

There is plenty of good diving. All the marine park dive sites are within a 10-minute ride and right off the Sister Rocks is an excellent dive where you find a sloping reef of soft and hard corals, decorated with many sponges. Lots of fish gather here. You are bound to see angelfish and stingrays, and turtles are likely. There are superb dives off Round Island and Kick 'em Jenny, and you can do these on your own, but it is better to go with a dive shop. Here the fish life is outstanding, with sharks, rays, and big pelagic fish. There are 200-foot walls, caves, and many reefs. Since it is a long trip, dive shops do it as a two-tank dive in fair weather only.

Arawak Divers is now Dive Carriacou. They dive almost every day, run PADI courses, snorkel trips, and rent kayaks (a great way to see the mangroves). They teach in English, French, and German, and will pick you up from your boat or run private dive trips. They have three comfortable boats and often do lionfish hunts.

Lumbadive [VHF: 16] is in the same building as the Lazy Turtle and is run by two

Canadians, Diane and Richard, who speak English and French and teach PADI to pro level. They have their own dinghy dock and offer VIP service, so boarding is easy and your equipment is already on board. Any surface intervals include water, fruit or Diane's home-made cookies. Their motto is: "You come as a diver, you leave as a friend." For those that like to hunt, their Friday afternoon lionfish hunts are popular. They offer Horizon, Sunsail and Moorings customers a 10-20% discount.

They will pick you up from your yacht in most Carriacou anchorages and they may catch you with his GoPro camera underwater, or above from his drone.

CASSADA BAY AND SOUTHERN CARRIACOU

The western part of Carriacou's south coast is lovely. It makes for exciting navigation with lots of reefs, rocks, and strong currents, which slice though according to the tide. In our sketch chart we include White and Saline Islands, which offer good dinghy exploration or temporary anchorage. Check our Carriacou to Grenada chart (page 343) for the outer islands, Frigate Island, Long Island, and Boneparte Rocks. Note there is an offshore rock off the northwest part of Frigate Island.

The prospect of cruising in this area has been brightened by the ongoing restoration of Cassada Bay. Joe Walsh is well underway building a restaurant and dock, with plans to dredge and buoy the area in front, and put in yacht moorings. I would advise making sure this has been done before you visit. (Call or check doyleguides.com and our Doyleguides Facebook page.)

Navigation

This area involves extensive eyeball navigation, only go when the light is suitable. As you round Carriacou's Southwest Point, stay clear of the dangerous rock and shoal which extends south about a tenth of a mile. Pass between Mushroom Island and White Island and head up into Cassada Bay. Hopefully, when the dredging is done and the moorings are in, the approach will be obvious. From here we suggest exploring the delightful White and Saline Islands by dinghy.

Waves come around both sides of White Island making the shallow lee side unsuitable for anchoring. However, there is a very small space in the deeper water just to the north of

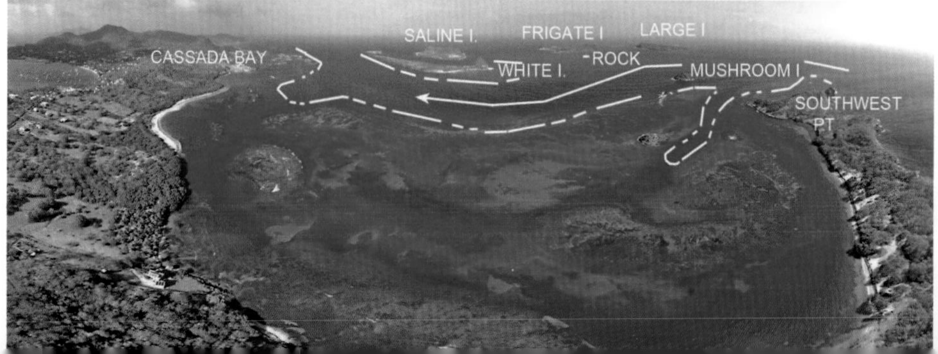

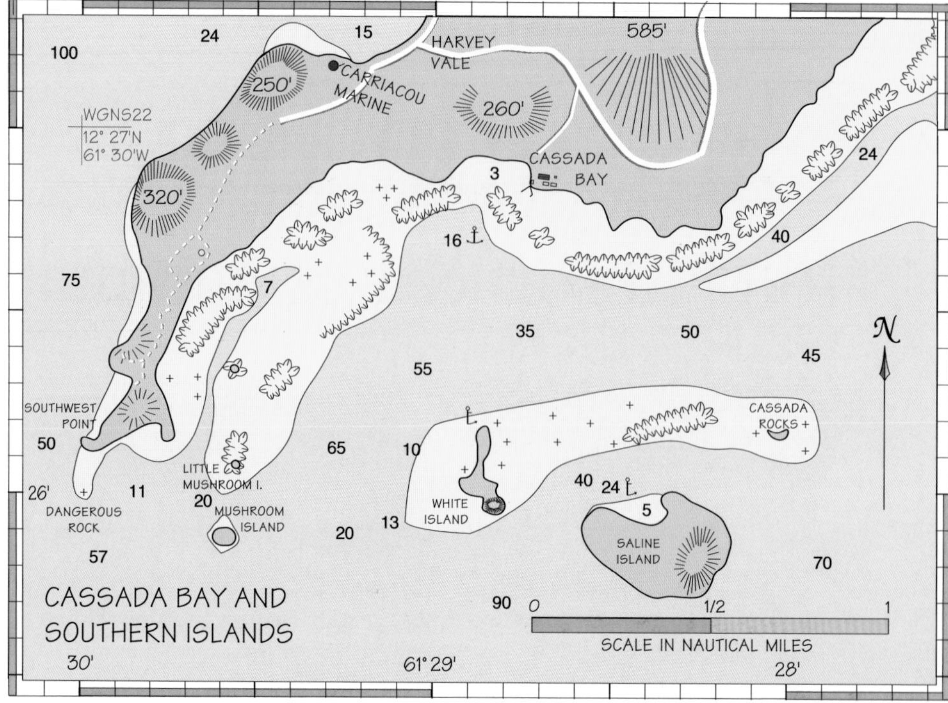

White Island where yachts can find temporary anchorage.

There is no passage through the long reef extending east from White Island to beyond Cassada Rocks, though with care you can get a dinghy though, a little east of White Island, by avoiding the coral heads.

Anchoring in Saline Island is problematic. There is a lovely shallow bay about 5 feet deep, but even if you are shallow enough to anchor here, the holding is terrible, and there is a lovely reef you must not damage in the north eastern part of the bay. Most yachts anchor just outside this shallow bay in 20-30 feet of water in sand. Consider this temporary as it can get very rolly, especially when the tide turns.

Ashore

Cassada Bay Hotel Resort development has built on the foundation of the previous resort, which had been derelict for many years. The restaurant (opening December 2018) sits atop the hill with a pretty view of White and Saline islands. The rooms will be dotted around the hillside and should be available in 2019. The restaurant [$$$$] plans to serve a wide array of fresh lobster from a live tank; from lobster salad and pasta to lobster omelettes. A pizza oven is also planned.

The southwest point of Carriacou has some nice walks. A rough dirt road meanders along the point, passing through farmland and livestock pens along the water, and continues through an interesting, low-laying mangrove area. Follow it to the leeward coast where a foot path runs along the top of the cliff. Ivan, who lives at the very southern tip, has a friendly horse and goat pair that roam free. They are curious, and might approach you, but didn't seem dangerous when we met them.

Water sports

The long reef heading eastwards from White Island makes for an interesting drift snorkel. Start out by Cassada Rocks, jump over and tow your dinghy, letting the current take you down to White Island. You want to do this on the falling tide when the current is flowing to the west. When the rising tide offsets this current the visibility is usually murky.

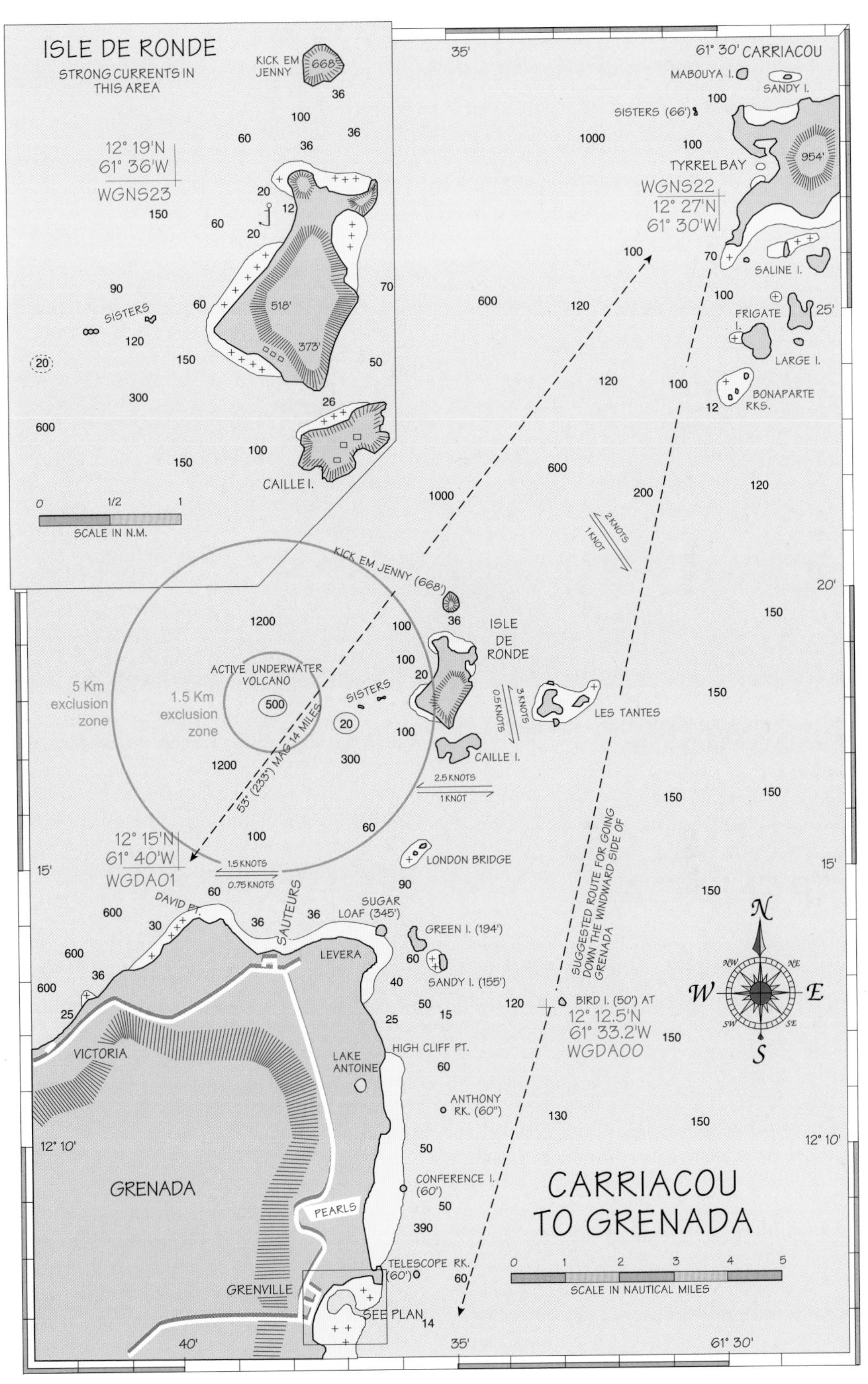
ISLE DE RONDE
STRONG CURRENTS IN THIS AREA
KICK EM JENNY
12° 19'N
61° 36'W
WGNS23
SISTERS
CAILLE I.
SCALE IN N.M.
61° 30' CARRIACOU
MABOUYA I.
SANDY I.
SISTERS (66')
TYRREL BAY
WGNS22
12° 27'N
61° 30'W
SALINE I.
FRIGATE I.
LARGE I.
BONAPARTE RKS.
KICK EM JENNY (668')
ISLE DE RONDE
ACTIVE UNDERWATER VOLCANO
5 Km exclusion zone
1.5 Km exclusion zone
53° (233°) MAG 14 MILES
LES TANTES
12° 15'N
61° 40'W
WGDA01
LONDON BRIDGE
DAVID PT.
SAUTEURS
SUGAR LOAF (345')
GREEN I. (194')
LEVERA
SANDY I. (155')
BIRD I. (50') AT
12° 12.5'N
61° 33.2'W
WGDA00
SUGGESTED ROUTE FOR GOING DOWN THE WINDWARD SIDE OF GRENADA
VICTORIA
LAKE ANTOINE
HIGH CLIFF PT.
ANTHONY RK. (60")
GRENADA
CONFERENCE I. (60')
PEARLS
TELESCOPE RK. (60')
GRENVILLE
SEE PLAN
CARRIACOU TO GRENADA
SCALE IN NAUTICAL MILES

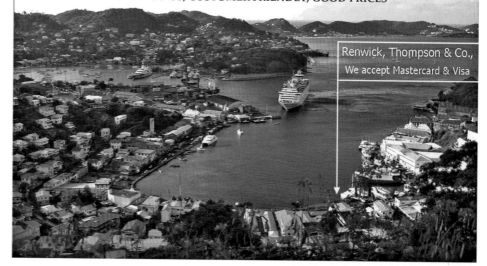

PASSAGES BETWEEN CARRIACOU & GRENADA

None of the islands between Carriacou and Grenada affords good shelter, though Isle de Ronde is okay in fair weather. The anchorage is in the bay on the northern side of the west coast. Try it for lunch, and in settled weather with no swells, overnighting is possible, though you may have to try a few spots to get good holding sand. Snorkeling is excellent off the Sisters (take a dinghy). To explore ashore, I take the dinghy into the northern bay opposite Kick 'em Jenny. About 20 inhabitants live some of the time on the south coast.

Kick 'em Jenny and the Sisters have large nesting-bird populations, and you can see boobies and pelicans, particularly on the Sisters. Beware of the strong currents.

An active volcano that lies about two miles west of Isle de Ronde erupted many times; in 1988, 1989 and 2001. It, too, has been named Kick 'em Jenny, and you certainly will get a big kick if you happen to be on top when it erupts. To prevent this, the Grenada government has declared a 1.5-km exclusion zone around the volcano at all times (not enforced; it is for your own safety). The exclusion zone increases to 5 km when the volcano is rumbling. (For the current status of the volcano, check: uwiseismic.com, or follow the links on doyleguides.com.)

Kick 'em Jenny (the big rock) has the reputation of kicking up a nasty sea as you go north, and this is particularly true if the tide is running east.

When sailing from Grenada to Carriacou, the fastest way is to hug Grenada's lee coast right to the north before heading to Carriacou. Unless the wind is well in the south, take a tack into Sauteurs, as the west-going current is weakest close to the Grenada coast. This will not only get you up faster, but it may keep you outside the 1.5 km volcano exclusion zone.

Grenada at a glance

Regulations

Grenada, Carriacou, and Petite Martinique make up one country, with ports of clearance in Tyrrel Bay, Hillsborough, St. George's, Prickly Bay, Port Louis, Le Phare Bleu, and St. David's Harbour. Entry is on a single page form. In Prickly Bay and Port Louis you can use sailclear.com. Customs charges you for a monthly cruising permit. It is $50 EC not exceeding 40 feet; $75 EC not exceeding 60 feet; $100 EC not exceeding 80 feet; and $150 over 80 feet. There is no charge for months spent in a yard.

You may clear in and out at the same time for stays up to 3 days (72 hours), but you must fill in all the forms for each way.

The port charges an entry fee of $8.10 EC per person, excluding the skipper. You also pay $20 EC per person embarkation tax for those arriving by plane, or who are living ashore. If you want to take a dog ashore, you will need a valid rabies certificate.

Customs hours are 0800-1145 and 1300-1545 on weekdays. At other times you will be charged overtime fees. If you have any questions about yachting, including security, contact the Marine and Yachting Association of Grenada (MAYAG): (473) 416-7135, mayagadmin@gmail.com.

Visitors may not spearfish in Grenada waters or scuba dive without a dive shop in Marine Protected Areas. Collecting or damaging coral and buying lobster out of season are strictly forbidden. (Lobster season is October 31 to April 30.)

Holidays

January 1, New Year's Day
February 7, Independence Day
Easter Friday, Sunday & Monday, April 19-22, 2019; April 10-13, 2020
Feb. 22, Independence Day
May 1, Labor Day
Whit Monday, June 10, 2019; June 1, 2020
Corpus Christi, June 20, 2019; June 11, 2020
Emancipation Day, first Monday in August
Carnival, Second Monday and Tuesday in August
October 25, Thanksgiving
December 25, Christmas
December 26, Boxing Day

Shopping hours

Shops and offices normally open 0800-1200 and 1300-1600. Saturday is a half day and most places are closed by noon. Banks normally open weekdays till 1400 and on Fridays till 1600.

Telephones

Cell phones (Flow or Digicel) are the way to go. For overseas calls, dial 1 for the USA and NANP countries, or dial 011 plus the country code for other countries (see page 19). For collect and credit-card calls, dial 0, then the whole number. When dialing from overseas, the area code is 473, followed by a 7-digit number.

Transport

Inexpensive ($2.50-$6.50 EC) buses run to most towns and villages in Grenada. If you are going a long way, check on the time of the last returning bus. Taxis are plentiful. Sample taxi rates (for four, normal hours) are:

	$EC
Prickly Bay to St. George's	50
Airport to St. George's	50
Airport to Prickly Bay	40
Prickly Bay to Grand Anse	35
By the hour	65
Short ride	25

Rental cars are available (see our directory). You will need to buy a local license, which costs $60 EC. Drive on the left.

Airport departure tax is $50 EC, though it is usually included in the ticket price.

Diving at Isle De Ronde

Grenada

Grenada, a spectacularly beautiful island, has lush green mountains, crystal waterfalls, golden beaches, and the fragrant spice trees that give the island its epithet "Isle of Spice." Come from late January to early March to get the added bonus of seeing the hills ablaze with hundreds of bright orange, flowering immortelle trees: pure magic.

Grenada's history has been lively, with early wars and revolutions. More recently, things got exciting with the transition to full independence in 1974. Most Grenadians felt this was premature, and instead of jubilant celebrations, the island was on strike and in protest. Nonetheless, independence was thrust upon her, and Grenada came of age under the rule of Sir Eric Gairy, a flamboyant and controversial figure who had a very divisive effect on the population. This resulted in the 1979 left-wing coup by Maurice Bishop, who greatly admired Fidel Castro. Bishop attempted to turn Grenada into a socialist state. He improved medical care and education, but he did so at the cost of freedom: anyone who opposed him was thrown in jail, and all independent newspapers were banned.

However, this didn't insulate him from opposition within his own ranks. Second-in-command Bernard Coard, his wife Phyllis Coard, and members of the army took Bishop prisoner in 1983. After a massive crowd freed him an army group executed him along with half his cabinet. At this point, the US, along with Grenada's eastern Caribbean neighbors (the Organization of Eastern Caribbean States), launched a "rescue mission" and were welcomed with open arms. Now, many years later, this is old history, and looking back over these last years Grenada as an independent county has experienced the best, most democratic, and most productive years since it was founded. Grenadians are a warm and hospitable people, exceptionally so once you get off the main tourist route.

From a yachting point of view Grenada has developed rapidly. Haulout facilities are found in St. David's, Prickly Bay, and Clarkes Court Bay. There are Marina facilities in St. George's, Clarkes Court Bay, Prickly Bay, Le Phare Bleu Bay, and Mt. Hartman Bay. St. George's has the big state-of-the-art Camper and Nicholson Port Louis marina, as well as

FISHRIDESWIM
ALWAYS GET WHAT YOU WANT FOR LIFE ON THE WATER.
BUDGET MARINE
Free bus service everySaturday!
I got what I wanted!
BUDGET MARINE
Budget Marine Grenada
True Blue, St. Georges | Grenada | +473-439-1983
*STARTS AT 9:30AM AT WHISPER COVE CALL OUR VISIT OUR FACEBOOK PAGE OR WEBSITE FOR MORE DETAILS.
The Caribbean's
Leading Chandlery
www.budgetmarine.com

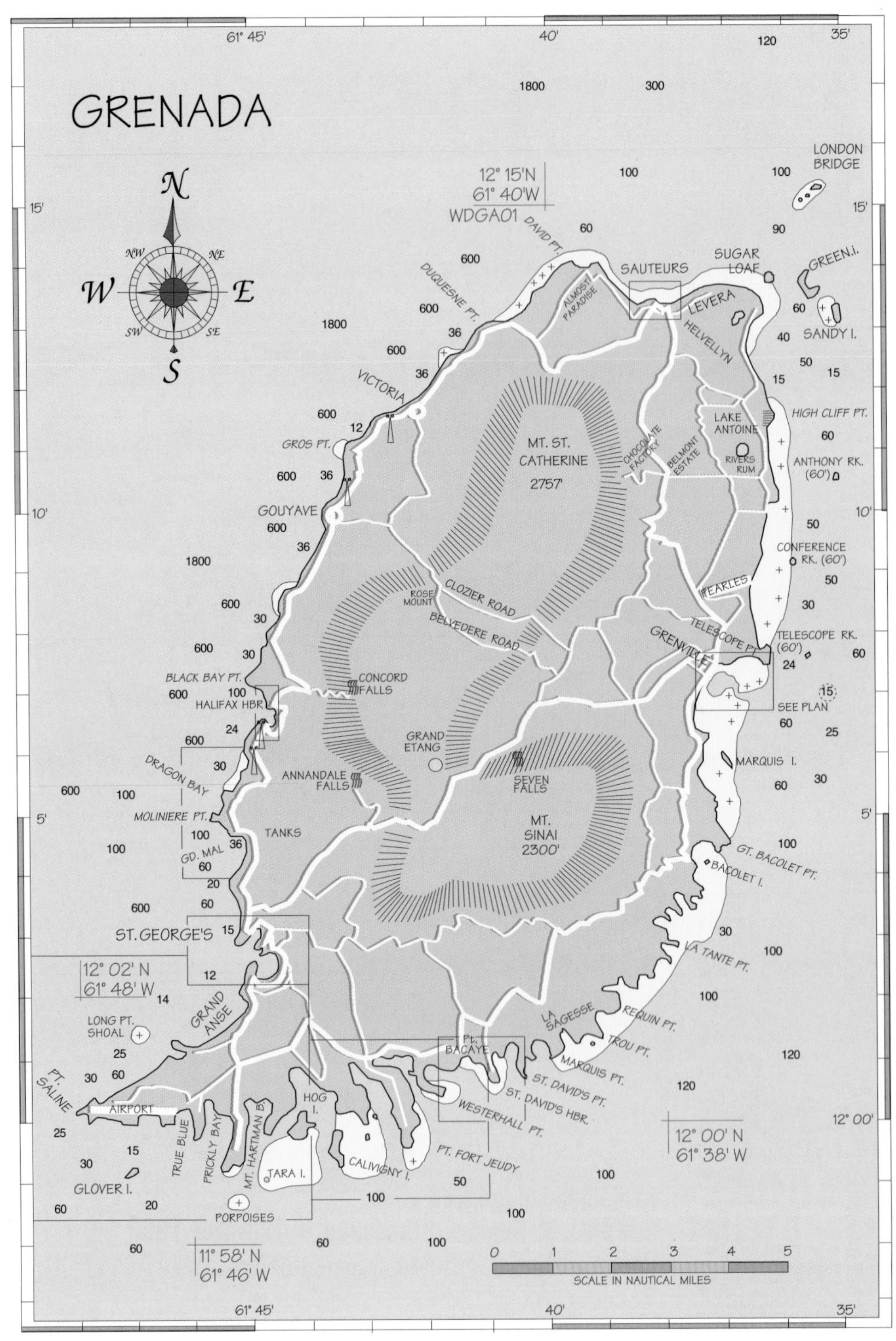
GRENADA
N
S
E
W
NW
NE
SW
SE
12° 15'N
61° 40'W
WDGA01
LONDON BRIDGE
DAVID PT.
SAUTEURS
SUGAR LOAF
GREEN I.
SANDY I.
LEVERA
ALMOST PARADISE
HELVELLYN
DUQUESNE PT.
VICTORIA
GROS PT.
GOUYAVE
MT. ST. CATHERINE
2757'
CHOCOLATE FACTORY
BELMONT ESTATE
LAKE ANTOINE
RIVERS RUM
HIGH CLIFF PT.
ANTHONY RK. (60')
CONFERENCE RK. (60')
PEARLES
ROSE MOUNT
CLOZIER ROAD
BELVEDERE ROAD
TELESCOPE PT.
TELESCOPE RK. (60')
GRENVILLE
SEE PLAN
BLACK BAY PT.
HALIFAX HBR
CONCORD FALLS
GRAND ETANG
DRAGON BAY
ANNANDALE FALLS
SEVEN FALLS
MARQUIS I.
MOLINIERE PT.
TANKS
MT. SINAI
2300'
GD. MAL
GT. BACOLET PT.
BACOLET I.
ST. GEORGE'S
LA TANTE PT.
12° 02' N
61° 48' W
GRAND ANSE
LONG PT. SHOAL
LA SAGESSE
REQUIN PT.
TROU PT.
PT. BACAYE
MARQUIS PT.
ST. DAVID'S PT.
ST. DAVID'S HBR.
WESTERHALL PT.
PT. SALINE
AIRPORT
HOG I.
TRUE BLUE
PRICKLY BAY
MT. HARTMAN B.
TARA I.
CALIVIGNY I.
PT. FORT JEUDY
12° 00' N
61° 38' W
GLOVER I.
PORPOISES
11° 58' N
61° 46' W
SCALE IN NAUTICAL MILES
0
1
2
3
4
5
61° 45'
40'
35'
15'
10'
5'
12° 00'

a yacht club. Three big chandleries now supply yachting gear, and legislation has been passed that encourages yachting by allowing for low-duty supplies, parts, and chandlery for yachts. The yachting act also allows you to clear out at the same time as you clear in, as long as you are not staying more than three days. However, you do have to fill in all the forms twice.

Grenada is host to a few important yachting events as well as smaller club races. Grenada Sailing Week, a week of racing and social events organized by an independent company, is held at the end of January. All entrants are welcome, from serious racing boats to live-aboards. The Grenada Sailing Festival, also known as the Workboat Regatta, is the following weekend. Grand Anse beach is at the heart of the action, where colorful traditional sailing fishing boats launch and finish every race right on the sand.

The Round Grenada race, a two-day event with a stop in Carriacou, is arranged by the Petit Calivigny Yacht Club (PCYC) and normally takes place in August. PCYC also organizes and supplies boats for a match racing every couple of months. It is based out of Le Phare Bleu, and everyone is welcome.

The Grenada Yacht Club organizes other races and Grenada has a strong marine trades association called the Marine & Yachting Association of Grenada (MAYAG) .

The interior

Few islands are as photogenic as Grenada, with mountains, rivers, rainforest, and houses surrounded by flowers. Sometimes, when you are hiking along a river amid nutmeg trees, it has an uncanny resemblance to early pictures of the Garden of Eden. A swim in one of the waterfalls will leave you feeling wonderfully refreshed, your hair and skin feeling extra soft. Concord Falls are in beautiful countryside, and anyone with a spark of adventure should hike the extra half-hour to the upper falls. Seven Sisters Falls are the best, a lovely one-hour hike. You need a guide if you want to make it to Honeymoon Falls, another half-hour from Seven Sisters. Many of the falls are on private land and the owners levy a small charge.

The most beautiful road in Grenada runs from Gouyave to St. Andrew. It has two forks, Clozier is the prettier, and Belvedere the easier. You snake across the heart of Grenada through verdant agricultural land, with lovely mountain views.

Grand Etang is a crater lake, and the Forest Center is close by. You often see monkeys where the buses stop. Trails are laid out so you can wander into the forest. There are wonderful hikes, including one halfway across the island (four hours). The road from St. George's to Grand Etang goes through some lovely forest, and you can include a detour to the Annandale Falls.

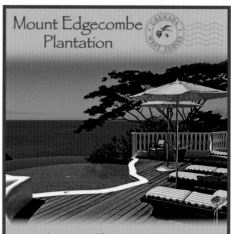

Mt. Edgecombe lies in the hills near Victoria. It is a lovely traditional estate house nestled into 28 acres of fruit trees and flowers overlooking the sea. It makes a special place to stop for lunch on an island tour, and it is delightful enough your tour may stop right there. They have a giant covered verandah for relaxing and eating, and rooms for those that want to stay some days in the country. It is wonderfully peaceful with just the sounds of birds and tree frogs. You will be welcome here, but call in advance and make a reservation; if they are not expecting anyone they may give the chef a day off.

Grenada has several small chocolate factories. The original, The Grenada Chocolate Factory, was the brain child and passion of Mott Green, who loved sailing so much that he delivered chocolate to Carriacou in a tiny beach cat. Sadly, Mott died in an accident in 2013, but the factory has been marching on. Let the high-octane bars (71, 82, and 100 % cocoa) melt in your mouth for a creamy chocolate flavor unlike any other commercial brand. Or try the delicious nibulicious or saltilicious bars. They all make perfect gifts. They have a shop and interpretation center and give tours of the factory daily (except Sundays, no reservation necessary). You can also visit the factories of Crayfish Bay Organic Estate, Jouvay, and Belmont Estate. All give tours for a fee. Belmont Estate is a typical and very picturesque country farm where cocoa beans are grown. Take the tour and they will show how they process the beans.

Crayfish Bay is owned and operated by Kim Russel and his partner Lylette Primell, and is the only single-farm organic certified operation. Kim arrived in Carriacou in 1989 aboard his Collin Archer-style Dutch steel monohull, and is now passionate about socially responsible cocoa production. He designs and builds most of his own machinery, and they give intimate and informative tours upon request.

Grenada now has a week-long chocolate festival in May, founded and organized by the Fielden family of True Blue Bay Resort. Visit their House of Chocolate in St. George's.

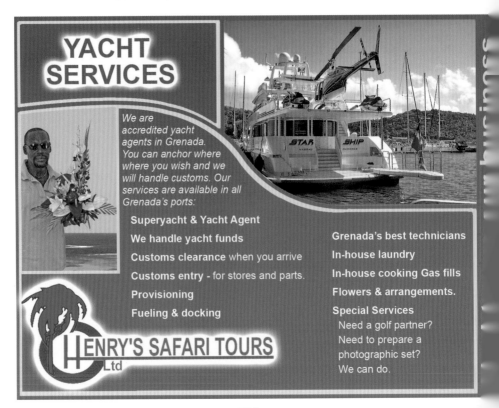

Many years ago I kept an eye on a coconut plantation for a friend. To get there I passed the River Antoine Rum factory, where they made strong white rum called Rivers. I fell in love with this place, which still runs much as it has since the mid-1800s: a giant water wheel crushes the cane, the dry stalks are burned to heat the juice, and large wooden scoops manually move the hot juice from one big cast-iron bowl to the next as it gets hotter (they call these bowls "coppers," as the original ones were made of copper). They now open this rum factory to visitors and give tours for $5 EC, which gets you a full explanation and a taste of the rum. (Ask for the strongest rum, drop a bit of ice in the glass, and watch it sink.) They do not fire up the factory machinery every day, and it is more fun to go when everything is going, so call in advance and ask (442-7109 or 442-4537). The location fits in well with visiting Belmont Estate. Both places serve lunch.

For hiking, Henry's Safari Yacht Services & Tours [VHF: 68], is the best guide. (Note call sign: Henry Safari Tours.) They specialize in hikes and know the trails well, including Seven Sisters Falls. They do turtle-watching tours from May to August, and do ATV (all-terrain vehicle) tours of the island. Most other taxi drivers are reluctant to get their feet muddy, but there are a few exceptions, including Selwyn at Maxwell Adventure Tours, who will hike and keep you happy. There is also Telfor Bedeau (442-6200). No one has hiked more of Grenada than Telfor. You can rent a car and take him along as a guide. He calls himself a driving guide, but he will also hike for an hour or two into some really wonder-

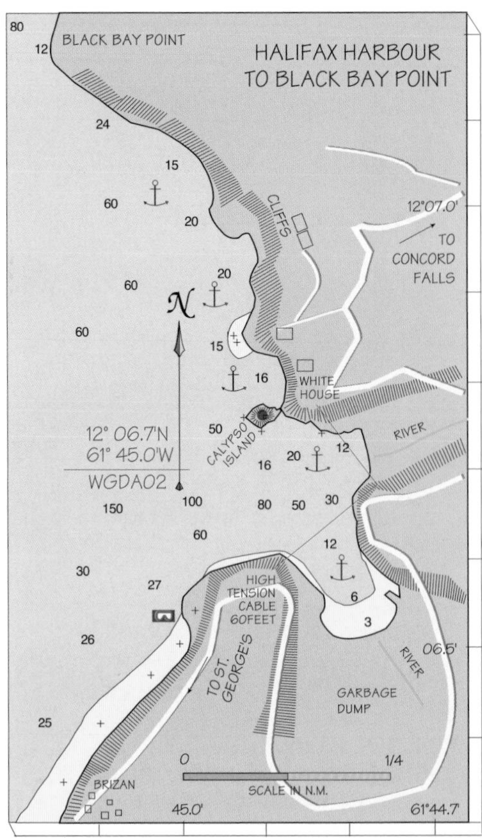

ful places.

Wondering Soles is a new tour and hiking company that aims to give it's guests an authentic experience, away from the traditional tourist attractions. Many of their hikes take you through small villages where you can meet the locals and taste seasonal fruits and juices. Most hikes are within St. George's and include a light lunch (423-0550).

Keep in mind that all Grenada's anchorages are within an easy taxi ride, so wherever you anchor, read about all the anchorages.

Navigation

There is a major light on Point Saline, visible for 18 miles both to the north and south, flashing (2+1) every 20 seconds. There is a lower-elevation (6+1) flashing light on Glover Island, and another at the western end of the airport runway. The lights have not always proven to be reliable.

Grenada uses the IALA B (red right returning) rule. Unless you draw more than 10 feet, you will not normally have to pay attention to the two big-ship channel buoys outside St. George's or use the leading marks.

The west coast of Grenada is steep-to: a quarter of a mile offshore clears all dangers except Long Point Shoal.

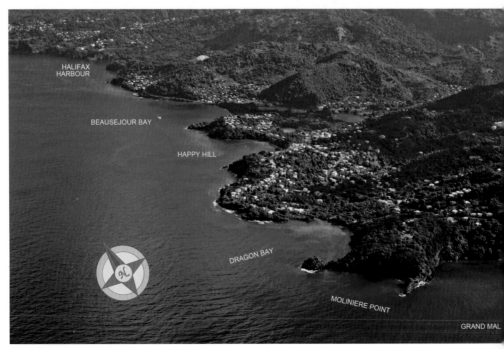

HALIFAX HARBOUR

BEAUSEJOUR BAY

HAPPY HILL

DRAGON BAY

MOLINIERE POINT

GRAND MAL

Some people like to sail down Grenada's east coast. It can be rough, but trolling for fish is usually rewarded. It is only advisable in settled weather. Unless visiting Grenville, stay well off Grenada's east coast. Pass either side of Bird Island, but outside all other islands. Keep well away from the Porpoises as you come along the south coast. They can be difficult to see, especially in the afternoon with the sun in your eyes. Some of the coast lacks landmarks, but you can clearly see Grenada Marine in St. David's Harbour, and look out for the development at Westerhall. Prickly Point has a distinctive saddle shape and a conspicuous house on the headland that looks like a little lighthouse.

Part of Grenada's west coast is a Marine Protected Area and has several lovely anchorages, perfect as a stop for northbound yachts, especially charter yachts that take off after lunch. In the case of northerly swells, Grand Mal and Halifax are the most protected. Anchoring within park boundaries is forbidden, and you should snorkel on park moorings to make sure they are in good shape.

The town of Gouyave, about 8 nautical miles north of St. George's, has a very fancy dock, but it is so busy that it is not practical to use, except maybe to drop someone off.

Sauteurs, at the very northern end of Grenada, has recently constructed a breakwater . It has created a sizeable lagoon suitable for overnighting on your way north, or exploring the many attractions on the northern half of the island (see page 411).

Communication

A repeater on channel 66 international connects all Grenada anchorages. It has a morning cruisers' net at 0730, Monday to Saturday.

HALIFAX HARBOUR

Halifax Harbour, a lovely little bay, was turned into a dump, with port authority wrecks on the inside and the island's garbage on its southern side. It was cleaned up, but has backslid, so you sometimes you get flies and smoke. You can anchor in the bay, but you don't have to. The coast outside from Halifax Harbour to Black Bay Point is perfect for a night stop on your way north or as a destination for a day sail. The snorkeling all around Calypso Island and to its north is excellent.

If you decide to go into Halifax, tuck well in, as the water in the middle is very deep. High-tension cables have been strung across both parts of the bay. On the south side, the lowest wire is about 60 feet above sea level. On the north side, avoid anchoring too close to the low end of the cables. Alternatively, you can anchor anywhere along the shore between Calypso Island and Black Bay Point. Make sure you anchor on sand, not coral. There should be a few moorings; check them carefully if you use one.

An added attraction is Calypso Island, developed by Badre and Karen. Intriguing little wooden steps take you from either side

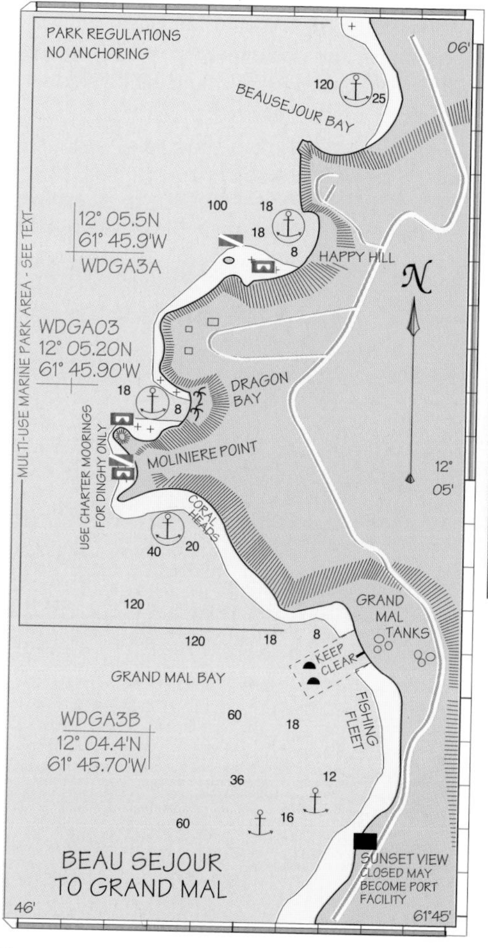

of the island to a variety of sitting areas, with an open restaurant area at the top offering views all around. A watchman stays on the island. Calypso Island and their restaurant are available for special groups. Call 444-3222 to find out what is happening, or check out their website: travelgrenadagrenadines.com.

Regulations

A Marine Protected Area follows the coast from Beausejour to Grand Mal, and one has been proposed for the entire Grand Anse area, around to Point Saline. You will find white yacht moorings in Happy Hill (Flamingo Bay), Dragon Bay, and Grand Mal Bay, just south of Moliniere Point. The rest are for day charter boats and they have priority. These go back by late afternoon, after which using one will not do any harm. The $10 US charge for taking a boat in the park is sometimes collected; make sure you get a receipt. Snorkel on the mooring to make sure it is in good shape, and if you prefer to anchor do so only in the main part of Grand Mal. Personal watercraft are not allowed.

HAPPY HILL

Happy Hill (Flamingo Bay), just north of Dragon Bay, can be very peaceful and is good except in a bad northerly swell. The narrow beach is backed by a hill, and on the hill is a large, old, silk cotton tree. There is good snorkeling and diving on both sides of the bay around the rocks. Anchoring is not allowed; pick up a mooring or dinghy over from Dragon Bay.

DRAGON BAY

Dragon Bay is delightful, with a palm-lined beach and good snorkeling on both sides around the points. It is usually a good overnight spot. Use the moorings.

You can pick up a dinghy mooring just round the corner in Moliniere Point where you can visit Grenada's world-famous underwater sculpture park created by Jason deCaires Taylor. Snorkel off your boat and look for the statues, or hire a guide to make sure you see them all. Arrendell of Sea Tonic Snorkeling & Tours (418-5946) is based in Dragon Bay.

Ashore

Dragon's Bay Bar and Grill [$] is an informal and friendly beach bar owned by Chris Hyacinth and run by Arrendell Antoine when Chris isn't around. It is a perfect place

The Carenage, St. George's

to hang out for dinner and a drink on your way north. It is easily accessible from the moorings in the bay or from those south in Grand Mal Bay. It is open every day. The cook starts around 1400, though you can get food before that. You can eat well on the finger foods they serve, but they will also cook good local seafood if you give them a call (Chris 533-8077; Arrendell 418-5946).

GRAND MAL

Grand Mal is generally a good anchorage. The water is usually clean and the long beach attractive. There are gas storage tanks in Grand Mal and two buoys offshore that are used for unloading tankers. Pipes run out from the small dock to the buoys, so avoid anchoring in this area. Anchor just outside, and a little south of the fishing fleet, or take a mooring on the north side of the bay. It is fairly well protected in northerly swells.

ST. GEORGE'S

St. George's is built on a ridge, with the sea on one side and the protected Carenage on the other. Houses mingle with shrubs and trees, giving splashes of bright color against a background of dark green. From afar, it is as neat and pretty as a picture-book illustration. The historic brick buildings are capped with old "fish scale" tile roofs. The buildings are a reminder of long ago when the profitable journeys were outward bound, laden with rum, spices, and fruit, and returning sailing ships would arrive "in ballast" of bricks.

As you enter the harbor, you see Fort George and the hospital on the left. A little farther in, the channel divides in two: to the left is the Carenage, surrounded by the city of St. George's. To the right is the lagoon and Port Louis Marina. The lagoon is a yachting center, complete with a yacht club, marina, supermarkets, restaurants, and a chandlery. The eastern side, near the chandlery, has been made into a pleasant park along the water, and you will find convenient dinghy docks to help you explore ashore.

Navigation

A large cruise-ship dock has been built and considerable land reclaimed off the Esplanade, north of Fort George, facing west out to sea.

The lagoon has two marinas, or you can anchor outside the harbor, south of the channel. At the time of this writing, the coast from Port Louis to around Point Saline is included in a proposal for a multi-use Marine Protected

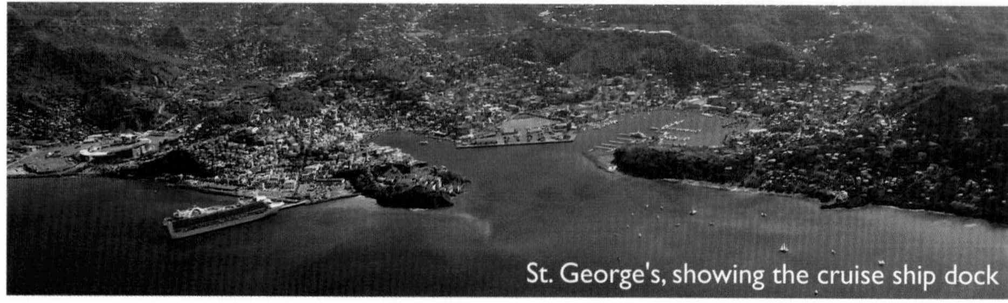

St. George's, showing the cruise ship dock

Area that will limit fishing and anchoring in the area (see *Grand Anse*).

Leave the red buoys to starboard and head on into the lagoon. Most of the lagoon has been dredged to over 15 feet deep, with a few corners that are about 10 feet deep.

If you wish to tie up in the Carenage, call the Grenada Port Authority on VHF: 16. Yachts over 200 tons need a pilot to come here or to Port Louis. Seven entries qualifies you to enter on your own.

No town in the Windwards is completely free of theft. Always lock up the boat and dinghy. The marinas have security.

Regulations

The customs office is in Port Louis. They open weekdays, 0800-1600; weekends and holidays, 0900-1400. They can come to their office outside these hours by request. If you are paying a quick visit and have a lot to do, consider using one of the registered agents:

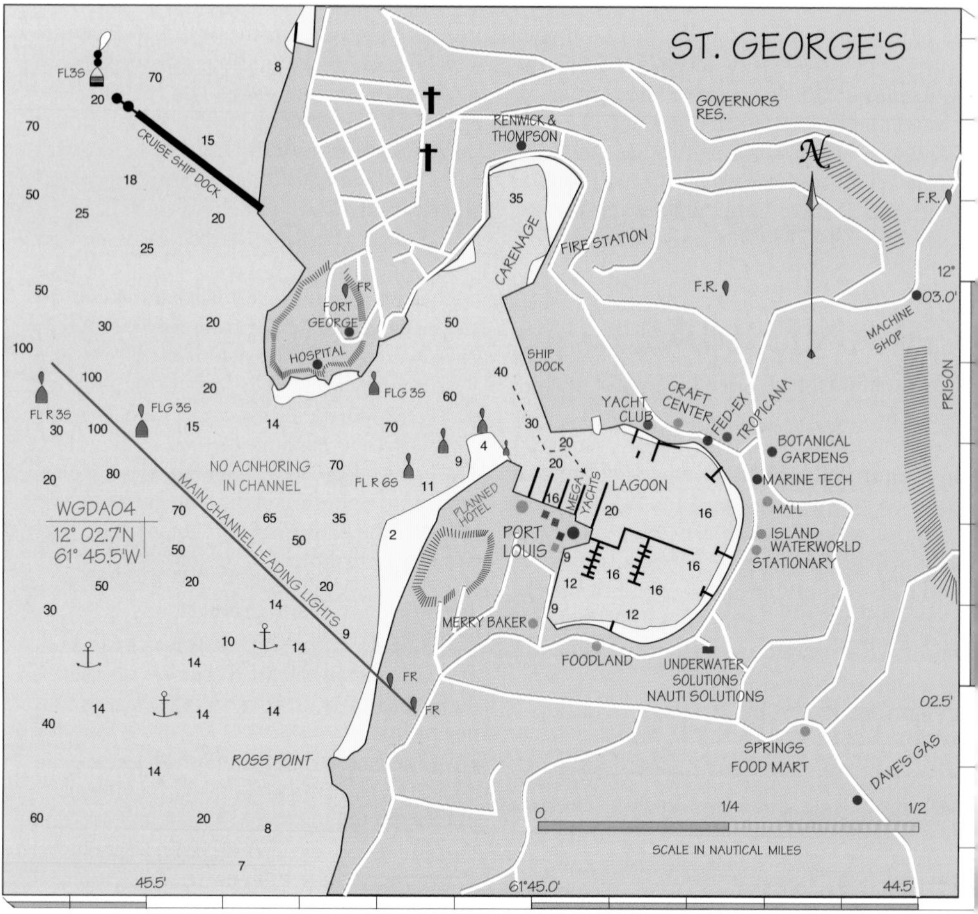

ST. GEORGE'S
CRUISE SHIP DOCK
RENWICK & THOMPSON
GOVERNORS RES.
CARENAGE
FIRE STATION
FORT GEORGE
HOSPITAL
SHIP DOCK
YACHT CLUB
CRAFT CENTER
FED-EX
TROPICANA
BOTANICAL GARDENS
MARINE TECH
MALL
ISLAND WATERWORLD
STATIONARY
MACHINE SHOP
PRISON
LAGOON
MEGA YACHTS
PLANNED HOTEL
PORT LOUIS
MERRY BAKER
FOODLAND
UNDERWATER SOLUTIONS
NAUTI SOLUTIONS
SPRINGS FOOD MART
DAVE'S GAS
NO ACNHORING IN CHANNEL
MAIN CHANNEL LEADING LIGHTS
WGDA04
12° 02.7'N
61° 45.5'W
ROSS POINT
FL3S
FL R 3S
FLG 3S
FL R 6S
FR
F.R.
12° 03.0'
02.5'
45.5'
61°45.0'
44.5'
0
1/4
1/2
SCALE IN NAUTICAL MILES

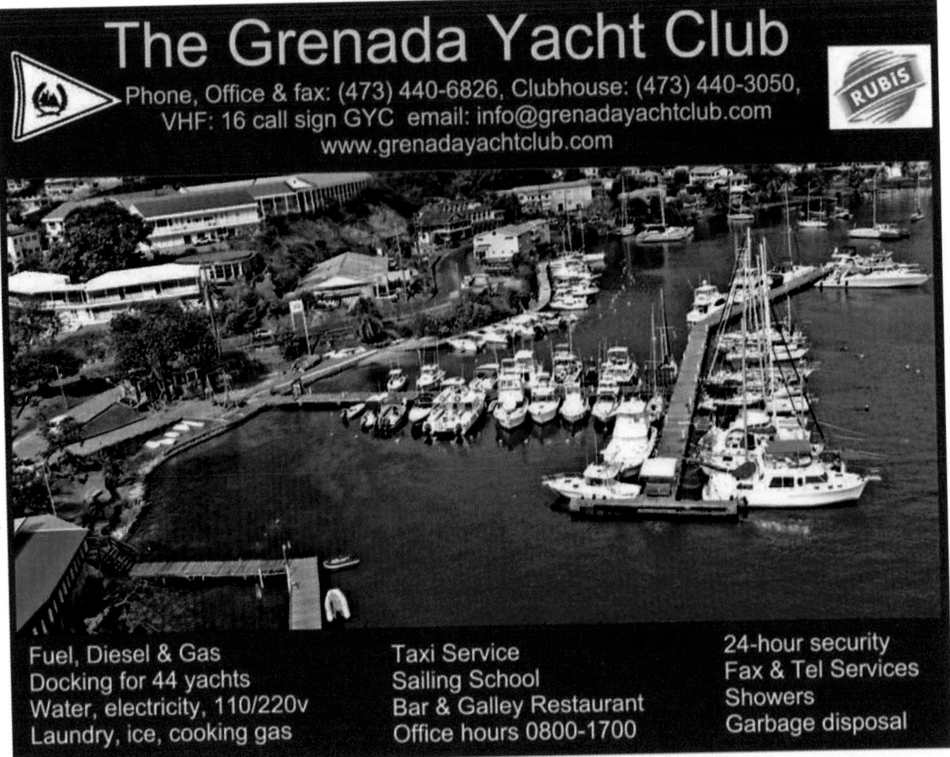

Henry's Safari Yacht Services & Tours or Spronk's Mega Yacht Services. They are on excellent terms with the officers, can often arrange pre-clearance, and they can clear you from anywhere in the island. For visits of up to three days they can arrange your inward and outward clearance at the same time. You can hand your passports and papers over and feel free immediately. It is not very expensive.

Communications

Weather and local information are available on a cruiser's net that operates at 0730 on VHF: 66 international (except Sunday).

Island Water World has WiFi access that covers some of the lagoon. It is free (charity contributions accepted). Other commercial WiFi networks are often available. The marinas have phones and fax. Port Louis has plug-in internet.

The FedEx office is near Tropicana and DHL is in Renwick and Thompson.

Hanky's, near Dr. Isaac on Grenville St. above the market, sells printer ink, tablets, laptops, and computer and phone accessories.

General yacht services

Camper and Nicholson's Port Louis Marina [VHF: 14/16] is a fancy and pleasant marina: very spacious and beautifully gardened. Customers can relax in the swimming pool overlooking St. George's.

The marina includes 10 berths for yachts up to 300 feet long, 16 berths for yachts up to 120 feet long, and over 140 berths for smaller yachts. The dinghy dock is just where the main long dock starts. More dinghy space is available way inside, west of where the inflatable tour boats are moored.

The berths have electricity, cable TV, plug-in internet, and water. The big boat berths have all kinds of voltages at 50 cycles (60-cycle is planned). High speed fuel (duty-free) is planned.

Port Louis has an excellent team. The professional office staff will make sure you have all the help you need. Docks are for sale, they will be delighted to tell you how this works.

Port Louis is home to Dream Yacht Charters, Sunsail, and The Moorings charter companies and Sea Sun Adventures day tours.

The Victory Bar is the place to chill out (see *Restaurants*), and there is a Scotiabank ATM beside the marina office.

The Grenada Yacht Club [VHF: 6/16 "GYC"], includes a modern marina with berthing for about 43 boats and a fuel dock that has both diesel and gasoline. The docks have electricity (110/220-volt, 50-cycle) and water, and the rates are reasonable. The Yacht Club is informal. You can send a fax or get your mail during office hours: 0800-1700 (address mail to Grenada Yacht Club, P.O. Box 117, St. George's, Grenada). Showers, laundry, and garbage disposal are available. Henry Safari picks up empty gas bottles and drops off filled ones on Mondays, Wednesdays, and Fridays. Taxis and other services can be arranged. The Yacht Club bar opens at 0900 and stays open till 2100. The restaurant is open every day and is good (see *Restaurants*). The Yacht Club also runs a sailing school program.

Spronk's Mega Yacht Services is run by Roger and Claire Spronk, who own Bananas (see *True Blue*). They share an office with Sea Sun Adventure in Port Louis marina. They are registered yacht agents and clear yachts in and out, arrange visas, fueling, docking, flowers, travel, taxis, car hire, laundry, crew placement, repairs, flights, and anything else a large yacht could need. The Spronks are building a private marina in Petit Calivigny Bay (see *Clarkes Court Bay*). This will have easy berthing for the largest of yachts, and make a convenient Grenada base. They are excellent at full superyacht provisioning, which means large yachts can be fully provisioned from scratch in Grenada. Their importing business stocks the best quality frozen fish, and they own an 8-acre farm for fresh produce. Where possible, they source locally, but for exotic and special items, they work with all the big international yacht provisioners.

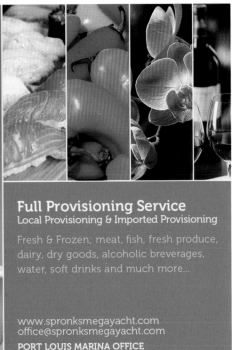

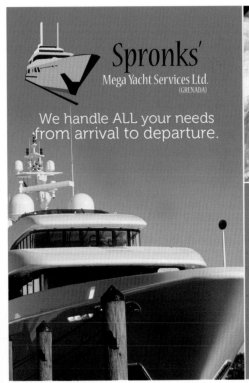

The super-yacht agents work well together. Henry Safari Yacht Services & Tours [VHF: 68], is a superyacht agent who also works well with cruisers. They understand that they have different needs and budgets, which has given them an excellent reputation with everyone. They own the laundry at Port Louis (plus two others), fill everyone's cooking gas cylinders, and have a fleet of taxis, plus Grenada's most colorful service vehicle. They collect and deliver to all Grenada's anchorages.

Henry Safari does customs clearance for yachts and their stores and helps superyachts sort out immigration for arriving crew. Other services include arranging dock space, fuel, technicians, travel, and anything ashore. Henry can arrange full provisioning. They have been in business a long time and know just about anything a yachtsperson may want, and if they don't, they're happy to figure it out.

Bob Goodchild owns Flying Fish Ventures. Bob trained as a boat builder in the UK and is now a marine surveyor and a member of the International Institute of Marine Surveyors (IIMS) and the Society of Accredited Marine Surveyors (SAMS). He can do tonnage measurements and MCA compliance inspections up to Category 2 through his membership in the Yacht Designers and Surveyors Association (YSDA). Bob has been in Grenada for years, is very professional, and a great guy to deal with.

Chandlery

Island Water World has a big branch of their huge and very successful Caribbean marine store (50 years old in 2017), in the lagoon, opposite the marina. They have an excellent range of stock at duty-free prices, including batteries, yacht hardware, winches, electronics, outboards, fishing gear, ground tackle, stoves, charts, and cruising guides. If there is anything you need that they do not have, look at their large catalog, and they can bring items in quickly. On the first Wednesday of the month they run a book/DVD swap and coffee morning for charity, and if you want a run-around bike, they will lend you one for free (there is a deposit).

For electrical items, try ordering from Stephen at Marine Tech's website. Delivery is 5 business days or less, and they will handle clearance and installation. They carry a limited stock of electronics and electrical items in their storefront on Lagoon Road, including LED lights and bulbs, solenoids, regulators for solar panels, and some Raymarine and Garmin electronics. Stephen opens 0900-1700 Monday to Saturday and 1000-1700 Sundays, but is often out working on jobs, so best to call him at 406-1800.

Ace Hardware is on the Maurice Bishop Highway (behind *True Blue*). This is Grenada's best general hardware/car parts/household/gardening store. You can get everything here from a dinghy pump to a new tea kettle. They have another branch in St. George's.

Bryden and Minors stationery store is next door to Island Water World. They sell computers and printers and may have printer ink.

Marine World, on Melville Street opposite the fish market, caters to Grenada's fishing fleet. They stock fishing and snorkeling gear and charts, as well as safety gear and some hardware. Spice Isle Fish House Tackle Shop on the Carenage stocks fishing and snorkeling gear, some electronics, and sells John Deere diesels.

Technical yacht services

Two business specializing in looking after and fixing boats have offices in Port Louis.

Mark and Anita's Island Dreams, with a long-established fine reputation, has a Port Louis office. Mark and Anita Sutton are good people to look after your yacht while you go away. They offer guardianage and owner repre-

sentation at Grenada Marine, and have an office at Clarkes Court, where they can arrange all aspects of yard work. They send regular email status reports. They can also look after your yacht afloat in Port Louis, or assist boats at other marinas, but best discuss that before booking. If you want, they will have your yacht hauled, painted, fueled, launched, and ready to leave when you arrive, and they can book overnight accommodation. Island Dreams also do upholstery and carpet cleaning and they offer gear storage facilities, which is a big help if the interior is being pulled apart. They are the Cruising Association's Honorary Local Representative, and are representatives for Boatshed Grenada for those looking for brokerage.

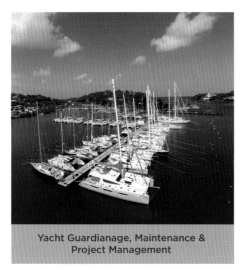

Horizon Yacht Management is owned by James and Jacqui Pascal and this business works well with their charter company, Horizon Yacht Charters, in True Blue. They have a good team of technicians who specialize in maintaining and outfitting yachts while the owners are away. They can repair or install any systems, and can arrange for your haul out and paint job, or oversee any work you may be having done by other contractors. They can also just run a weekly check to make sure everything is okay. With the recent addition of a workshop and office at Clarkes Court Boatyard, they are expanding their operations to suit an increase in demand. Horizon are agents for new Bavaria Yachts, Fontaine Pajot Cats, and offer a full brokerage service, so if you need to sell your yacht or buy a new one, check them out.

Jeff Fisher is the local Neil Pryde Sails representative. He can measure up and quote for a new sail, and advise on re-using any expensive sail hardware you have. He will fit the sail when it arrives.

Grenada Marine (see *St. David's Harbour*) hauls yachts, repairs all boat systems, and sells and installs electronics, engines, watermakers and more. They have an office in Port Louis.

Marine Tech Grenada is operated by Stephen Welsh, an ABYC certified electrician and NMEA certified technician, with over 27 years of experience. Marine Tech supplies, installs, maintains and repairs marine electrical, electronic and refrigeration equipment, most of which can be found and ordered from their website (marinetechgrenada.com).

So whether it's a solar installation, malfunctioning windlass or bow thruster, battery charging issue, engine that won't start or the complete rewiring of your boat, Stephen Welsh is your man. He likes sailing, understands boats, and has an excellent reputation for customer service and getting the job done right, and on time.

The Marine Tech office is located on Kirani James Boulevard (formerly known as Lagoon Road), a 5-minute walk from Port Louis Marina and 2-minute walk from the Grenada Yacht Club. Marine Tech visits most marinas and all anchorages in Grenada, contact them via phone or email.

Royan Joseph has Royan's Marine Services and is a certified welder and fabricator. Together with his wife Valerie, he owns and runs his own large metal workshop, conveniently located so he can reach all the marinas and yards by van quickly. He works with aluminum, stainless, and regular steel using MIG, TIG, and stick welding. Royan and his team can bend pipe, make fancy arches and bimini frames, and do repairs. He offers courtesy pick-up and delivery service and has a mobile welding unit. He is efficient and reliable and small jobs can often be finished the same day.

Turbulence Sails has a location in Port Louis. They handle all sail repairs as well as canvas and cushion work. They are Grenada's main riggers and will come sort out your rig and hydraulic problems. They are a first-rate electronics shop and can fix all your instruments (see *Prickly Bay*).

Brett Fairhead's Underwater Solutions keeps work boats in several harbors, a base in the lagoon, and works all over the island. They are good enough to get asked to do jobs throughout the Caribbean. Brett is one of the Caribbean's most experienced commercial divers and he has done everything from working under ice to underwater welding in the tropics. He trains and works with a team of Grenadian divers who clean yacht hulls and props, remove shafts and rudders in the water, carry out underwater damage survey and repair, do underwater welding, and untangle anchors.

They can undertake salvage work and have a small tug to assist in this. They also do bathymetric depth contour surveys and install pipelines, moorings, and channel markers. They do anything underwater, large or small, and maintain most marina moorings. I trust the moorings they maintain. If you visit their shop, check out the lovely coral-encrusted artifacts they have preserved.

Martin Daniel of Martin Enterprise lives in Molinere and works mainly out of Port Louis and Clarkes Court. He started out polishing and maintaining boats but now does a bit of everything. Call him up (533-3095) and have him come by for a quote.

Other people make boat visits, including Basil St. John, at Lagoon Marine Refrigeration Services, who is good but hard to find, Dexter Hayes (Mr. Cool), at Subzero Air Control, and Michael Cadore (Protech Engineering), who works on fridges, AC, appliances, stoves and many other electrical systems.

Danny's Nauti Solutions is with Underwater Solutions on the lagoon. Danny is good at fixing boats. His wife, Lesley, is excellent at general yacht cleaning. Danny spends most of his time these days doing deliveries, but you might catch him there.

If you need a hand to help with a project, be it going up the mast, maintenance, moving a mooring, or having someone sail with you, Patrick Andrews is very experienced at looking after yachts and sailing them. He will come to you in Port Louis, at the yacht club, in Prickly Bay, or wherever. I have worked with him for years. You can contact him by cell (406-0664/414-1559).

Clarkes Upholstery is run by Vernol

Clarke, who does upholstery and is equally good at canvas work for biminis, covers, and awnings, all at competitive prices. Yachts are about half his business and he will come to measure and fit, not only in St. George's, but in any of Grenada's anchorages.

Sunshine Canvas in Happy Hill does dodgers, cushions, awnings, dinghy chaps, and more, and will visit any of the anchorages.

Tan Tan Sam is excellent for hand varnishing, painting, cleaning, and polishing. Call him on his cell: 403-9904. He often works with Sean Thomas (406-4258/419-7454), who also does good work. Ashley (456-9003) is another good professional, as is Thadius (410-6224), who often works with Island Dreams. These men will work in any marina.

Al Bernadine in Gouyave (444-8016) is a wizard with alternators, starters, and power tools. He has a small machine shop. If you call him he can arrange for you to drop off what you want fixed in St. George's.

Also read about the marine services in the south-coast harbors as most will come to St. George's.

Provisioning

The Merry Baker, owned by Raeanna, is a dreamy home-made bakery just inside the

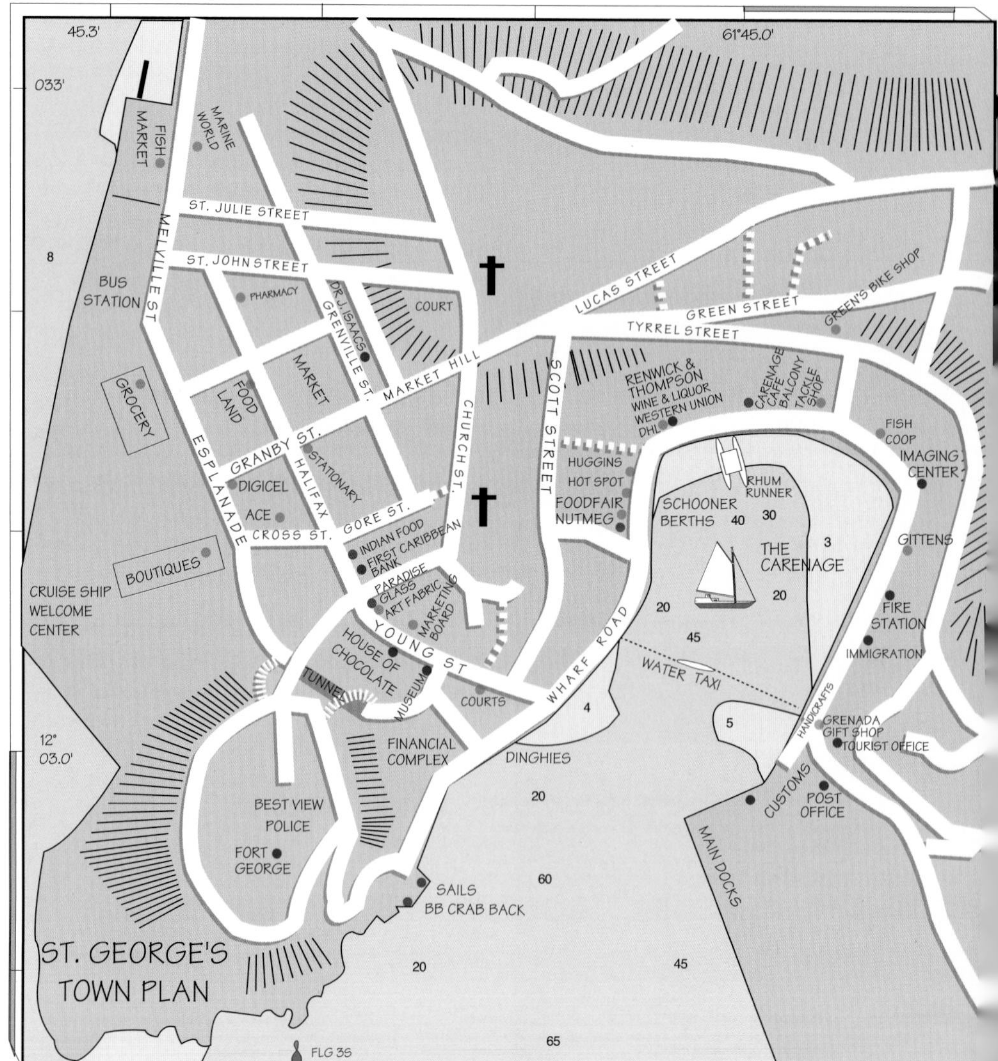

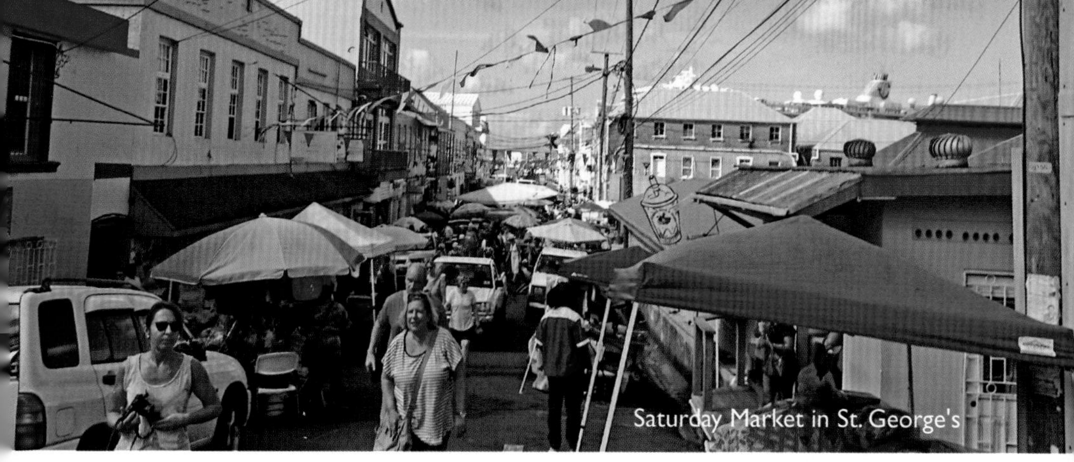
Saturday Market in St. George's

road to the marina. They sell breads, pastries, preserves, and more. Raeanna does excellent inexpensive lunches some days. Thursdays there are rotis, and Friday is the famous build-a-burger lunch. All the sides are put out in a buffet and you help yourself. You can get coffee, soft drinks, and beer. Seating room is outside in a prettily painted patio area. Opening hours are weekdays, 0745-1630, Saturdays, 0800-1300.

St. George's is a first-rate place to provision, with comfortable, air-conditioned supermarkets. Foodland is on the lagoon, has its own dinghy dock, and is often open quite late at night. Foodland has an excellent selection of regular items and a pleasing delicatessen section.

You can dinghy from the lagoon over to town. Take this guide with you; our town map will help. St. George's is a busy place, with plenty of traffic, including buses laden with people and playing loud music, cars, and trucks weighed down with building materials. Sometimes it seems like they are all honking at once. People will shout "taxi!" at you, and vendors may offer fruits from baskets.

On weekdays most shops open from 0800 to 1200 and from 1300 to 1600. Banks are open only till 1500, except Friday, when they open to 1700. The post office is open over lunch, but closed all day Saturday. Most shops close Saturday afternoon and Sunday, though you can still shop (see *Grand Anse)*. The lovely old financial complex, which used to house the post office, has been restored, creating some of the fanciest government offices in the Windwards.

Those wishing to buy wine or liquor should visit Renwick and Thompson's Best Little Liquor Store in Town [VHF: 16, "Rum Runner Base"]. You can tie your dinghy close to the shop. They have a wide selection from all over the world, including about 80 different wines from dozens of good houses.

They are very customer friendly: you can mix wines to make cases for the best deal, and duty-free prices are available with delivery to most marina docks. Allow at least 48 hours for processing. Duty-free has to be delivered after you clear out.

You can transfer money through Renwick and Thompson's Western Union. With increasing bank rates, I often find this to be the most economical way to send money. (They also have a branch in Grand Anse.) You can send many currencies and pay in EC dollars. (It is better not to use US dollars to send US dollars as regulations make them change it to EC first). This is the place to send your DHL packets, and if you are having things shipped in via DHL, Renwick and Thompson offers a full brokerage service to remove any clearance hassle. They provide land and water tours and have an agricultural section where you can find hoses and hose fittings. If you are interested in land on Grenada or Carriacou, they have some of the best for sale.

Food Fair is conveniently close to the water and you can tie up nearby. Food Fair is an excellent supermarket, open weekdays till 1730, except Friday when they are open till 1830. On Saturdays, they close at 0200. They offer charter yachts 3% discount.

The Carenage Hot Spot is between Huggins and Food Fair and carries a good selection of groceries and household items.

They open from 0800 to 2000 during the week, 0600 to 2000 on Saturday, and 0800 to 1400 on Sunday.

Visit the local market, preferably on a Saturday morning. It is a riot of color, where determined ladies under big umbrellas sit amid huge heaps of vegetables. It is one of the most interesting markets in the islands, and you can get fresh produce, spices, and handicrafts. If you need a new watch battery or repair, there is a stall in the market that specializes in this and they can often fix your watch on the spot. The Marketing Board, on Young Street (opposite the House of Chocolate), has some of the best prices on fresh produce, although the range is sometimes limited.

You can usually get a good selection of fresh fish in the fish market.

Henry B, one of the Port Louis Taxi drivers, has an herb farm and can supply fresh herbs, as well as prepared dried herbs for cooking.

Fun shopping

Port Louis has a few boutiques and duty-free shopping. Fidel Productions sells great art t-shirts, commissioned from Caribbean artists, who receive royalties. They stock hand-painted calabash art, Moho jewelry, decorative items, and souvenirs; all are attractive and of good quality. For duty-free items, visit Rouge or Penny's along the megayacht slips.

Young Street, in town, has several attractions. The House of Chocolate is a special place. Part boutique, part cafe, part museum, and all about chocolate. Bright, light, artistic, and interesting, you can see how chocolate is made, from bean to bar, learn about the different kinds of cocoa, and learn about all the benefits of eating chocolate. (Some might surprise you; one study indicated that eating chocolate gives your skin more protection against the sun.) Great coffee, mocha, chocolate brownies, cheesecake, gourmet chocolates, chocolate art and more are on sale. They open at 1000 every day but Sunday. They organize a week-long chocolate festival in May, with trips to chocolate factories, a chance to be a farmer for day, chocolate cooking, and chocolate massage.

Next door the museum, in a lovely old building, is well worth a visit for the small entrance fee. They have excellent cultural events, usually on the second Friday night of the month. Stop by and ask for a program. It includes jazz, good pan, story-telling, and local dance.

A few steps up the hill is Art Fabrik. It is a riot of colorful batik fabrics, clothing, and household items. Batik demonstrations are available on request.

Paradise Glass, atop the Young St. hill, is a small cafe and glass art gallery. Enjoy your coffee surrounded by handmade glass

mobiles, dishes, and jewelry.

With the advent of the cruise ship dock and land reclamation, the focus of tourist shopping has moved into the cruise ship area, where there is a mall of bright and cheerful shops selling everything from fresh juice to jewelry, and tons of souvenirs.

St. George's is a lovely town, with lots of hills to climb and great views. It is best explored when you have plenty of time and no errands. One of the best and easiest is to climb up to Fort George. Nice steps from either side of the Sendall Tunnel take you up and are an alternative to going through the tunnel (though this is to be experienced).

Restaurants

The Victory Bar and Grill [$$$] is the all-encompassing restaurant in Port Louis. Open to the breeze, it is big and informal, with a wide-ranging menu to suit everyone from the admiral to the cabin boy, and the food is very good, as you would expect from the owner Uli, who also has a number of other restaurants (See *Point Saline to Prickly Bay*). You can dine well here on fresh fish and shrimp or the best steak. Or you can get pizza, pasta, salads, burgers, and sandwiches. They open every day and have a good pizza oven in one section. For a more secluded atmosphere, wander into Yolo, adjoining but with a separate entrance. This has a lounge bar and fine restaurant specializing in sushi and Thai cuisine.

The Spout [$$], in the Yacht Club, is on a big deck overlooking the lagoon. It has a friendly, open atmosphere, and is inexpensive and good for lunch or dinner. They are open every day.

Horatio Brizan's Tropicana [$$] on the lagoon is an inexpensive restaurant: cheap enough for any time cooking seems too much of a chore. It is excellent value for lunch or dinner, with a separate and speedy takeout section. If you need a night ashore they have inexpensive rooms upstairs.

In town, the Nutmeg, overlooking the Carenage, is one of the city's older establishments. You don't really know St. George's till you have had lunch at the Nutmeg. They also serve dinner.

For a quick bite you can't beat Karlla and Kaitlyn [$], two Indian ladies who serve delicious, freshly made samosas, pakoras, and doubles out of a small window just down the hill from First Caribbean bank. Prices are very reasonable, and they are there every day but Sunday.

If you follow the Carenage right round town to the end you will come to a restaurant corner. You can tie your dinghy right outside, and these restaurants all have an open view of the harbor. Sails [$$$$] has a wonderful, wide deck, open to the view and the breeze. You can tie your dinghy pretty much onto your table leg. The food is good, using good-quality

Brave cyclists in downtown St. George's

meats and fresh seafood.

Next door Brian and Anna Benjamin's BB's Crab Back [$$$, closed Sunday] serves fancy Caribbean food cooked with a European flair. He sometimes teaches a cooking class. You can tie your dinghy to the railing, but it may need a stern anchor.

Patrick's continues a tradition, started by Mama, of a giant local feast featuring a vast array of local dishes, so you can taste everything one time, a real experience. He is conveniently located across the road from Port Louis.

Transport

The taxi drivers that most often deal with yachts are members of the Marina Taxi Association. They can be found in all Grenada's marinas, including Port Louis, and they set a high standard for reliability and good customer service.

Ashore

Michelle's Spice Isle Retreat Spa is a large and lovely beauty spa in Spiceland Mall. They offer well over 70 procedures and treatments, from sophisticated hairdressing to facials, nails, pedicure, massage, and more. They have a membership plan where you can get a 30-60% discount, and they often have special offers. They sell hair and beauty products. Michelle and her staff are excellent, and the spa is popular, so it is best to book. Stop by and pick up a brochure.

Been in the sun too long? Dr. Jennifer Isaacs is an excellent dermatologist whose office on Grenville Street overlooks the market. It is best to make an appointment, so you will not be waiting in line for hours.

St. George's now has the Spice Isle Imaging Center for any medical tests. They do all kinds of blood tests, MRIs, x-rays, and ultra-sound.

If you have a yen for a few hours in a pretty garden, 600 feet above St. George's is Sunnyside Gardens, open to the public. It costs $10 US a head. Call 406-1381 for directions and to let them know that you are coming.

GRAND ANSE

Grand Anse is what most people have in mind when they think about the Caribbean: a generous, 2-mile sweep of white-gold sand, backed by shady palms and almond trees. A new water taxi and dinghy dock has recently been installed in front of the Spice Market, making it even easier to get ashore. Grand Anse contains a wealth of shops and restaurants and is easily visited by bus or taxi from St. George's or Prickly Bay.

At the time of this writing the coastal waters from Port Louis to around Point Saline are included in a proposed multi-use Marine Protected Area. Designated areas for fishing, yachts, and megayacht anchoring are planned. Anchoring will be forbidden everywhere but where we show in our chart. It is within easy dinghy range of St. George's.

Communications

The Computer Store in Spiceland Mall has everything for cybernuts. They have the widest selection of Mac accessories on the island, do both Mac and PC repair, and even sell drones.

Provisioning

When you get behind the beach, Grand Anse is a big shopping strip lined with malls, from Grand Anse Shopping Center to Excel Plaza. Cars and buses hurtle down the main road with little thought for pedestrians. Stay on the sidewalk and take care when crossing

Grand Anse dinghy and water taxi dock

the road. Grand Anse is good for Sunday shopping; both Real Value and Value Garden are open mid-morning.

The two main supermarkets are Food Fair, in the Shopping Center, and Real Value, in the Spiceland Mall. Food Fair is an excellent supermarket with a big range of products, including fruits and vegetables that are mainly local and refreshed frequently. Charter yachts are offered a 5% discount.

Real Value is like a US supermarket, with the biggest variety, including specialty foods. When a container arrives (usually on Thursdays), you get the widest choice of overseas produce and an excellent deli section. The aisles are wide and everything is attractively displayed in a spacious setting.

Spiceland Mall includes The Wine Shoppe, a good place for retail wines. They open 1000-1900 Monday to Saturday.

Almost opposite Marquis Mall, on the far side of the busy road, is a line of businesses in an area known as Wall Street that includes Gittens Drugmart, a pharmacy, with everything from newspapers to prescriptions, and a couple of banks that have ATMs for Visa or MasterCard. If you need to send money, Western Union is in the Grand Anse Shopping Center.

The Marketing Board runs Value Garden in Excel Plaza. They sell a good selection of local products and produce at the best prices. They have a section run by Meat and Meet, the butcher from Whisper Cove, who works wonders with local meat, and makes sausages and other specialty foods.

When you need fresh flowers, Eleanor Dathorne's Floral Treasures is the place to go. Floral Treasures is on the main road next to Robbie Yearwood's clinic and close to Real Value. She sells mainly local flowers and creates stunning flower arrangements. It is probably best to give her a call, and if you can work out what you want, she will deliver to other bays.

While shopping and eating keep an eye out for Sugar and Spice ice cream. It is made in a tiny factory in Prickly Bay, using fresh local ingredients, from the coconut they grate to chocolate from Grenada's Jouvay Factory. The coffee break is especially delicious, as is the soursop. They now have a storefront in

Spiceland Mall (see *Fun shopping*).

Another local product to look for is "Up in Smoke": top-quality fresh local fish cold- or hot-smoked, depending on your preference. Also, don't forget your Grenada chocolate.

Fun shopping

Grand Anse is an easy bus ride from Spice Island Marine Services or St. George's. This is a wonderful shopping area, with three malls, street-side shops, and hotel boutiques.

If you come by dinghy it is worth checking out the local craft market at the base of the dinghy and water taxi dock. There are a few good bars and restaurants here including Esther's, who makes a great mojito, and local vendors sell spices, beach wear, and other souvenirs.

Food Fair is part of Grand Anse Shopping center where you will find Hubbard's Home Center, Mitchell's Pharmacy [open till 2100], Too Kachi boutique, and Rick's Cafe, [$], which offers local dishes, fast foods, coffee, and a full range of ice creams. Eat them in the pleasant seating area in the mall square.

Spiceland Mall has a host of small shops where you can buy everything from stationery and shoes to clothing and music. You will find a sports clothing and surf store, a big hardware store, a salon and spa, a big American grocery store, an art gallery, Flow and Digicel storefronts, and for refreshments, a fresh food court, good for fresh-squeezed juice and smoothies.

Excel Plaza has Value Garden, the marketing board shop, now doubled in size, a pharmacy, many small shops, plus a small cinema.

Dr. Mike Radix, a GP who has been treating yachtspeople for years, is upstairs in the Grand Anse Mall. He has Lasik to remove problems from aging skin. Behind Spiceland Mall, over the road, is Ocean House, with surgeon and urologist Robbie Yearwood.

Toothache? Grenada not only has good, highly-recommended dentists, they are easily visited in Grand Anse. Many cruisers have been helped by Dr. Roxanne Nedd at the Sunshine Dental Clinic. Her clinic is next door to Excel Plaza, though she has been very busy of late. Two good younger Grenadian dentists, with the most modern equipment, are at Island Dental Clinic, above Gittens Drug Mart. Dr. Tara Baksh trained in the UK and Dr. Victor Samaan trained in the USA. They can do everything from extractions and root canals to complex crowns. Dr. Yaw, a first-rate dental surgeon, has an office opposite North South Wines in Prickly Bay. These days he is only in Grenada occasionally.

Restaurants

A great little Italian quarter has sprung up in Le Marquis Mall. Michael, an Italian with a taste for fish, has Carib Sushi [$$$], a great little Japanese restaurant. On the sushi side, good Oriental chefs use local fish (tuna, dorado, and wahoo), lobster, and lambi, as well as imported salmon, for the best sushi and sashimi. On the cooked side they offer shrimp, vegetable and fish tempura, beef, tuna tataki (lightly seared), and other Japanese dishes. They open for both lunch and dinner, but are closed in between. They have recently added an air conditioned tepenyaki lounge, by reservation only, which is perfect for special occasions.

Maybe because the food is so healthy, you see some good-looking, healthy people here. Their take-out can be handy for charter yachts, whom they often supply with fresh, Grade A cuts of fish.

Next door, Tortuga, an Italian wine bar, is owned by Marco. They serve a big range of wines by the glass or bottle and appropriate food when you want to make a meal of it.

Bella Milano is in the building opposite. You'll see the quaint silver bistro tables, where you can sip your espresso and enjoy pastries and tarts.

Brothers Randy and Dixon have The Clam [$$], in the distinct building on the corner. They serve hefty portions of local food all day, from breakfast through dinner. Take-out is popular, and they will deliver within the area for free. They regularly have oil down, the national dish.

On Grand Anse Beach, Umbrellas [$$] is a perfect beach hangout, open every day except Monday. It is a longish walk down the beach from the dinghy dock, sit under the umbrellas outside, up on the rooftop veranda,

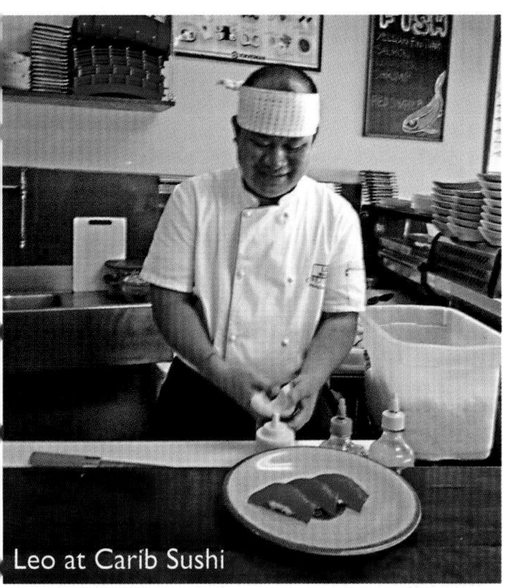
Leo at Carib Sushi

or inside. They have an extensive drinks menu and food to go with it. The emphasis is on salads, sandwiches, burgers, fish, and ribs. Save room for some fancy American-style desserts.

Coconut Beach, a French restaurant [$$$] managed by Scratch, has a superb location on the water's edge on Grand Anse beach. French cuisine has been adapted to local foods.

Saffron Cafe [$$] in Spiceland Mall is local artist Lisa Herrera's latest venture. She serves specialty coffees, desserts, salads, sandwiches, and all day breakfast. Her art adorns the walls, and if you're not in the mood for coffee, they also serve beer, wine, and liquor.

Le Papillion French Creole Cafe [$$] is a short walk towards Morne Rouge from Le Marquis Mall and is excellent for brunch.

The beautiful, but shallow, Morne Rouge Bay is a short ride or healthy walk from Grand Anse. There is a complex here called the Gem Holiday Beach Resort. They run the Fantazia 2001 disco, which is open on Wednesdays for Oldie Goldie night and on Fridays and Saturdays for live music. The restaurant next door serves great rotis.

La Plywood Bar [$] at the head of the beach is famous for their lionfish tacos, which are worth visiting for.

Water sports

Grenada has many dive shops, all keenly competitive and happy to take yachtspeople. Many will collect you from the marinas or docks. All dive shops are PADI or NAUI establishments with all kinds of courses, including introductory courses. We mention just a couple of the Grand Anse dive shops: EcoDive is the most central, right beside Umbrellas. They have on-staff marine biologists and a comfortable, purpose-built catamaran. Aquanauts [VHF: 16] have their main base in True Blue, and a base in Spice Isle Beach Resort. Dive Grenada, run by Phil and Helen, is based at the south end of the beach.

Grenada has a variety of good and interesting dives. For sheer drama you cannot beat the Bianca C, a 600-foot cruise liner that lies in 100-165 feet of water. The wreck is vast, and mainly broken, but there are splendid views up at the bow, and the swimming pool is still intact on the deck. Large schools of small snappers, some midnight parrotfish, and a few barracudas get framed by the wreckage. This is an advanced dive, and most dive shops will insist you do one other dive first.

Flamingo Reef starts just outside of the north end of Happy Hill Bay and continues along the coast toward Dragon Bay. This colorful reef offers a changing seascape as you swim along. There is a balance of healthy hard and soft corals, with a dense, tall forest of waving sea whips, sea rods, and sea fans at the top, on the seaward end. This is the place to look for the flamingo tongues that give the reef its name. Many grunts, squirrelfish, wrasses, parrotfish, and trumpetfish swim along the sloping reef. Large schools of brown chromis pass by. Deeper on the reef you have a chance of seeing large groupers. In the sand are mixed schools of spotted and yellow goatfish, probing the bottom with their barbels.

Dragon Bay and Moliniere Point join together and are the easiest dives to get to with your dinghy. Use one of the park moorings. If you go out from the little bay in Moliniere Point you get to see the underwater sculpture park. These dives have a mix of sand and coral patches, going from shallow water down to about 60 feet. Much of the reef in this shallow area is densely covered with a variety of corals and sponges. When you get to about 30 to 40 feet, you meet a drop-off that goes down another 25-30 feet. Sometimes it is a steep slope, at other times a sheer wall. A few rock outcroppings make for dramatic valleys, and deep, sand-filled gullies are cut into the drop-off.

Boss Reef starts outside St. George's and continues southwest to Point Saline, a distance of at least two and a half miles. It varies in width from 200 to 500 yards. It is possible to do many dives on this reef. Currents are strong here, and it is best done as a drift dive with a dive shop. A popular dive is the middle section, swimming wherever the current takes you. The depth varies from about 30 to 60 feet. The reef rises from the sand to a somewhat level top that is broken by deep gullies and holes that drop down to sand. This is an exceptionally good dive for coral variety. The top is completely covered in an array of corals, all packed close to each other. There are brightly colored fish, with large schools of blue and yellow Creole wrasses, accompanied by blue and brown chromis. Grazing parrotfish and big schools of doctorfish will pass you by on the reef, and you will see schools of smaller grunts and perhaps a large Spanish grunt. Look under corals and in holes for spotted drums.

PT. SALINE TO PRICKLY BAY

When sailing between St. George's and Point Saline, keep well clear of Long Point Shoal. Head west from St. George's and continue till you are on the line between

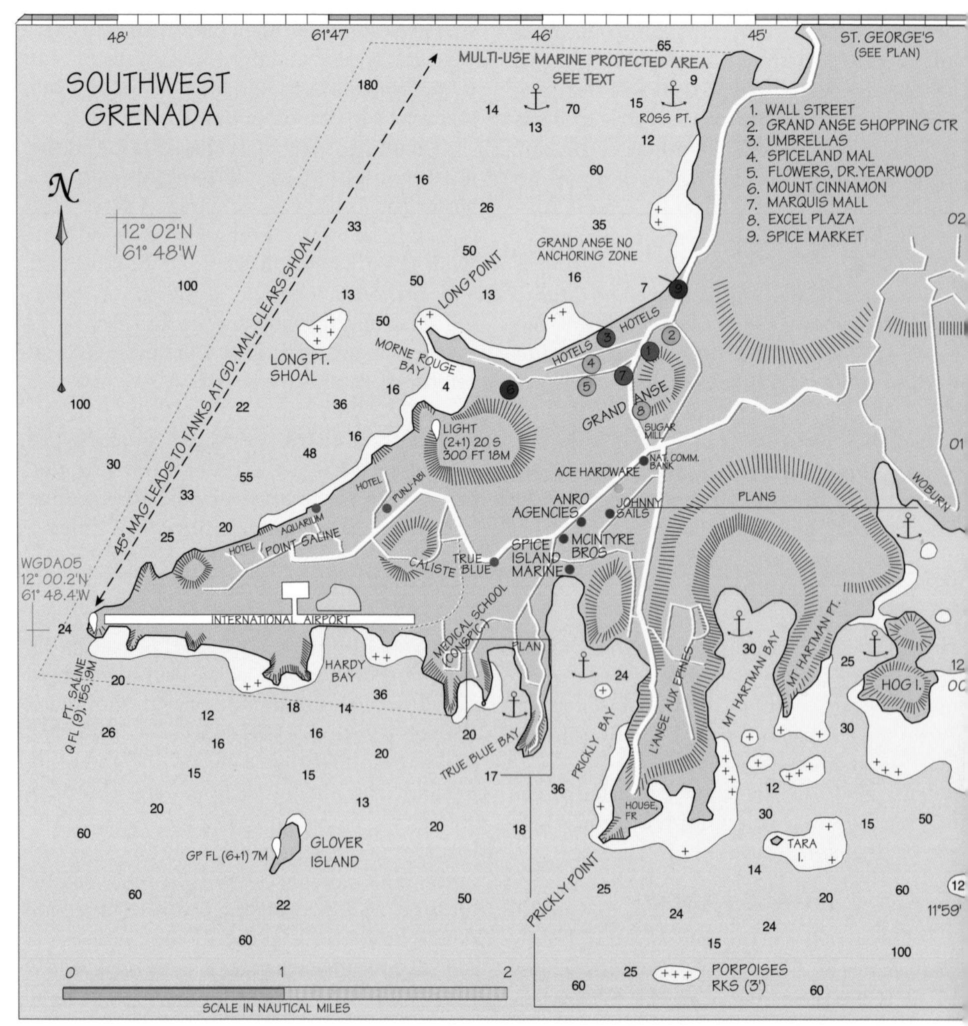

Point Saline and the tanks at Grand Mal, before heading for Point Saline. Reverse this procedure when you return.

Alternatively, coast hoppers may prefer to explore this shore, which has several pretty beaches. You must, however, be very careful of Long Point Shoal, and only approach when there is good light and you can see the reefs. It is possible to eyeball your way inside Long Point Shoal, but don't cut too close to Long Point, as shoals come out about 150 feet from shore. As you round Long Point heading west, you will see the beautiful Morne Rouge Bay, which, unfortunately, is only about 4 feet deep (perfect for multihulls). You can sometimes find lunchtime anchorage just outside Morne Rouge Bay.

As you sail round Point Saline and head toward Glover Island, Prickly Point is the farthest headland that you see. When closer, Prickly Bay is easily identified by all the yachts inside and the handsome houses on the hill. There is plenty of water for most yachts to sail inside Glover Island. There is one good anchorage, just before Prickly Bay, called True Blue. St. George's University and Medical School is on the west side of True Blue; it is conspicuous and looks like a town.

Ashore

Two restaurants lie along the north shore leading to Point Saline. Many people make the effort to visit them, usually by taxi.

Approach Uli's Aquarium Beach Club [$$$$] by taxi or rental car. The setting is spectacular, under some giant rocks that form a headland at the end of an idyllic deserted beach. The architecture has made the most of these features, and the dining room is open to the view on one side and the rocks on the other. They have created interesting corners, with a rock pool and also an open beach bar. The fresh barbecued seafood is excellent, and this is a great place to come for a quiet, romantic, seafood lunch or dinner, or to bring a group and party. The Aquarium Beach Club is popular on Sundays when people come to swim and snorkel. You get to the Aquarium by driving past the airport terminal and looking for the sign on your right. They now offer some of the most gorgeous rooms in Grenada, above the restaurant in their Maca Bana villas.

Punj-Abi [$$$] is Grenada's newest, and only, authentic Indian restaurant. Owner Vajinder teaches at the medical school, and along with his girlfriend Abi, renovated a building along the road to the airport to cre-

ate an airy and welcoming space. The chefs are from Vajinder's home town in India, and the food is flavorful and aromatic. They offer a wide variety of traditional Indian dishes at reasonable prices. Dishes are meant to be shared, and while the mains aren't to be missed, a few starters are often enough for a light lunch. They also do take-out, so you can call in your order from baggage claim and pick it up on your way from the airport.

TRUE BLUE

True Blue is the bay just west of Prickly Bay. It is a beautiful little bay, colorful and clean, and it makes a lovely anchorage. Russ and Magdalena Fielden, owners of True Blue Resort, have spent much time both cruising and working for charter companies, and they love boating customers. A small marina is part of the hotel, and a delightful wooden walkway over the water connects the two.

A distinctive small island is at the entrance. Enter in the middle of the bay between this island and True Blue Point. Go straight up into the bay and anchor inside, take one of the moorings, or tie up at the marina. The water is about 25 feet deep at the entrance to the bay and 13 feet deep up to the outside of the marina. A small surge enters from time to time, when the wind goes south of east. The waves are smaller than in Prickly Bay, but shorter and steeper. This works better for many monohulls, which roll less, but some cats wobble more. If there is a problem, put out a stern anchor to hold you facing out of the bay and into the seas. That will fix it.

If you are anchored in Prickly Bay, everything in True Blue is easily reached if you dinghy to Spice Island Marine Services and take a short walk.

Communications

True Blue has WiFi, you can use the high-speed computer station, and the office will send and receive faxes. Bananas has free WiFi.

Services

Jacqui and James Pascall manage the True Blue Marina and use it as a base to run Horizon Yacht Charters. This is an excellent, owner-run charter company, with bases here and in St. Vincent, making one way charters easy. They have a big range of cats and monos.

Their marina takes about 25 boats and, in addition, they have 15 reliable moorings for rent. The mooring fee is $40 EC per night, with less expensive monthly rates. Mooring is optional, as there is room to anchor. The marina has diesel, water, electricity (110-220 volt, 50 cycles), WiFi, showers, and toilets. You can get propane tanks filled and they will get Henry's Safari to come get your laundry. The office sells ice, cruising guides, and Horizon t-shirts. Jacqui and James will look after you well and help you get any kind of repairs you may need. They look after boats when the owners go away and will undertake major project management. They have offices for this in Clarkes Court Boatyard and Port Louis. They will also arrange a taxi or tour for you.

Spronk's Mega Yacht Services has another location at Bananas. It is run by Roger and Claire. They provision boats and are super-yacht agents. They do customs clearance, arrange docking, find or import parts, organize airline tickets or transportation, and source flowers or anything else (see *St. George's*).

Provisioning/fun shopping

Caul's, in the Container Park, has essentials, including whole coffee beans, beer, wine, liquor, and a variety of imported snacks.

Magdalena, at True Blue Resort, runs Trueblutique, which is small, but packed with a tasteful collection of handicrafts, objects d'art, jewelry, souvenirs, and useful items.

Restaurants

Dodgy Dock [$$$], True Blue Hotel's restaurant, is perched over the bay on stilts, with a dinghy dock. The food is very good and blends Mexican, Caribbean, and European flavors, all made from local ingredients. They have snacks, a full menu, children's menus, daily specials, and in addition to the regular menu, they serve pizzas. They have their own micro-brewery (the third largest brewery in Grenada), and their beer is popular. The nightly happy hour is 1700-1800 with 2-for-1 house drinks, and other drinks discounted.

They have something special almost every night. Monday night is beer and wings specials. Tuesday is Caribbean night with local cooking and a steel band. Wednesday

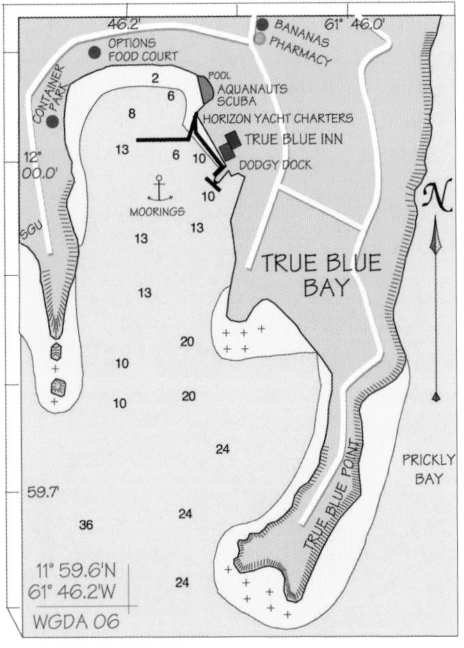

Grenada and Carriacou

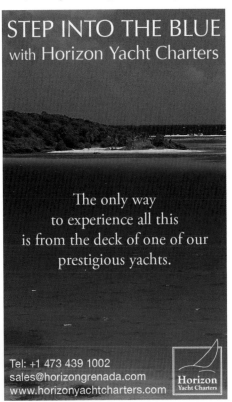

night is street food night; select local vendors are invited in to set up stalls and offer you their local specialties. Thursday features a chocolate-inspired menu. On Tuesday, Wednesday, Friday, and Saturday they have live-music in season. On Sundays they serve a big brunch. Advance reservations are a good idea, especially for a waterside seat. Russ (from the UK) and Magdalena (from Mexico) and their daughter Marie rank among the friendliest of patrons and are especially welcoming to those on yachts.

Their Blue Haven Spa is open to all with three treatment rooms offering massage and beauty care. Of special note are their herbal soaks, using all local herbs, and their chocolate skin treatments using local chocolate. (Magdalena runs the House of Chocolate Museum in town.) They have gentle yoga sessions (with an ocean view) in their fabulous open air, tree top yoga studio. Check their website for a current schedule.

Rooms are available to yachtspeople at special rates. Other facilities include a conference room, children's playgrounds, and two swimming pools. Day passes and packages are available, and are a worthwhile treat.

Esther and Omega run an interactive and entertaining cooking demonstration (including a generous tasting) on Thursdays at 1500 (about $5 US). On Tuesdays at 1750 they have a local rum and chocolate tasting session. Check the special events on their website, including a kid's Easter treasure hunt and Christmas events.

Imaginative in concept, Bananas [$$] was designed by two yachtsmen: Roger, who owns it, and Don, who helped build it. It is a cool restaurant, hangout, and nightspot, with interesting corners and pretty waterways. Bananas has a sports bar with a big TV and free WiFi.

Outside and part of Banana's is Carib Cave [$], Grenada's first wood-fired pizza oven, for excellent pizzas with cold beer. This is also the place for burgers and snacks. Inside, their restaurant has snacks and excellent meals, with good and inexpensive lunchtime specials.

Bananas is Grenada's hot spot, with something always going on for late-night entertainment. They have hosted everything from concerts and magic shows to boxing matches, and their sound-proofed disco and big sports TV screens are a fixture. The easiest way to check out the action is to visit www.bananas.gd.

If you are walking at night from either True Blue or Spice Island Marine Services, take a flashlight, and be cautious on big party nights.

Walk towards the university for more attractions. Options Food Court is a series of small restaurants and bars, each selling something different, including wings, burgers, and ice cream. Tables have free WiFi and power.

Just down the road is the inventively designed Container Park. A popular student hangout, you will find a handful of small bars, restaurants, and cafes, serving everything from burgers and smoothies to specialty desserts. Caul's, a small grocery store, is here and has a variety of imported snacks and candy, some fresh fruit and vegetables, as well as beer, liquor, and wine. Mocha Spoke cafe rents bikes and does cycle tours around the island.

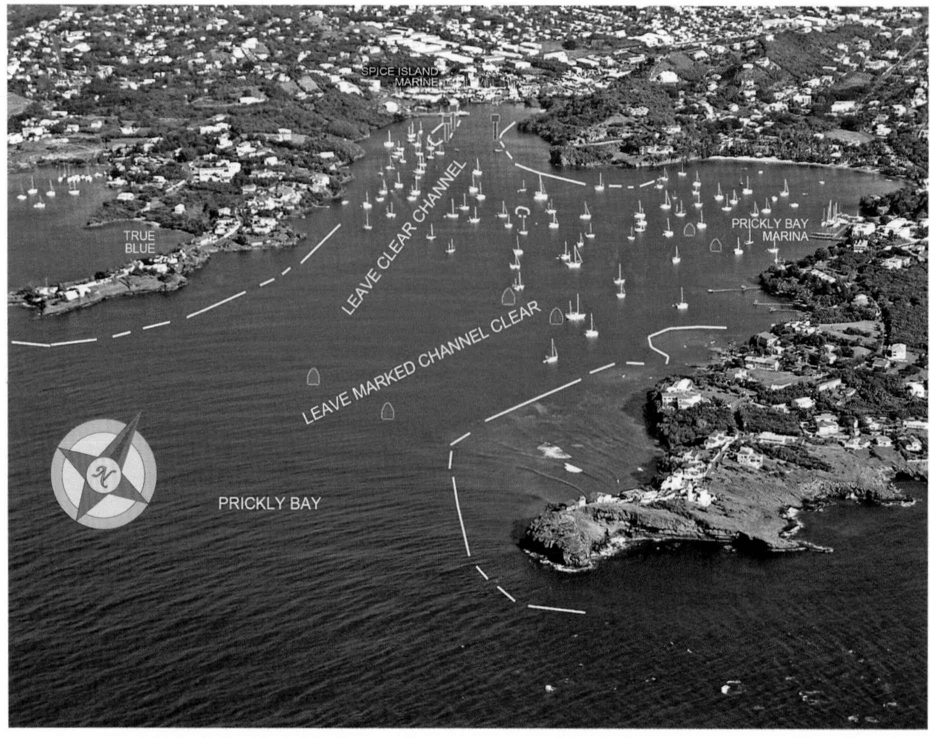

Water sports

True Blue is home to Gerlinde and Peter Seupel's Aquanauts Grenada. This is a PADI 5-star resort and they take people diving, do all kinds of courses, fill tanks, and rent diving equipment to those going on charter. They offer nitrox and rebreather dives and training.

Dinghy up to their dock, or they will collect divers from docks in Prickly Bay. Aquanauts has three large and well-equipped dive boats. Calmer summer weather offers the prospect of exploring special sites off Grenada's south coast, or going to Isle de Ronde.

PRICKLY BAY

(Also known as L'Anse aux Epines, pronounced "Lans O Peen.")

Prickly Bay is pleasant; a well-to-do area of fancy houses, many of which have well-tended flower gardens. At the eastern head of the double-headed bay is a palm-fringed beach. Buildings are overcoming the green areas as people build larger and larger mansions, but you still live with the sound of birds by day and tree frogs by night. St. George's is only 15 minutes away by car, and the airport and Grand Anse are even closer. Spice Island Marine Services is at the western head of the bay, on the True Blue side, and Prickly Bay Marina is in L'Anse aux Epines on the east side of the bay. This makes everywhere from True Blue Bay to Mount Hartman within easy dinghy or walking distance. Buses are plentiful from the True Blue roundabout, at the beginning of the dual carriageway (Maurice Bishop Highway), a short walk from Spice Island Marine Services.

A house at the end of Prickly Point looks just like a small lighthouse. This makes the bay easy to recognize.

Prickly Bay is easy to enter, but don't get careless. There is a reef in the middle, opposite Prickly Bay Marina, that is just deep enough (6 feet) to be hard to see. A second, deeper reef (9 feet) lies a few hundred feet to its west.

Reefs also extend nearly all the way up the eastern shore, and one should give the True Blue headland reasonable clearance. Prickly Bay Marina has put in a marked channel in the middle of the bay. In 2018 one of the outer marker buoys was missing, and the inner-most ones were steel barrels, mostly submerged, with yellow jugs tied to the top. This keeps an entrance channel clear of anchored boats, which can help the big yachts.

Occasional southerly swells can make the bay uncomfortable, though a stern anchor will do much to restore a sense of calm.

Regulations

Prickly Bay is a port of entry, with the customs at Prickly Bay Marina. They normally open every day of the week. Customs officers often have duties on the way in, so they sometimes arrive more like 1000 than 0800. Anchoring is forbidden within 600 feet of the beach, as this area is reserved for swimmers. Small buoys mark the area.

Communications

A cruisers' net operates on VHF: 66 international at 0730 weekdays. It includes weather, local information, and coming events. Channel 66 International is a powerful repeater channel allowed to us courtesy of Leroy Baptiste, Grenada's main communications man. It allows you to join in the net or communicate with other boats all over the island.

Prickly Bay Marina has excellent internet

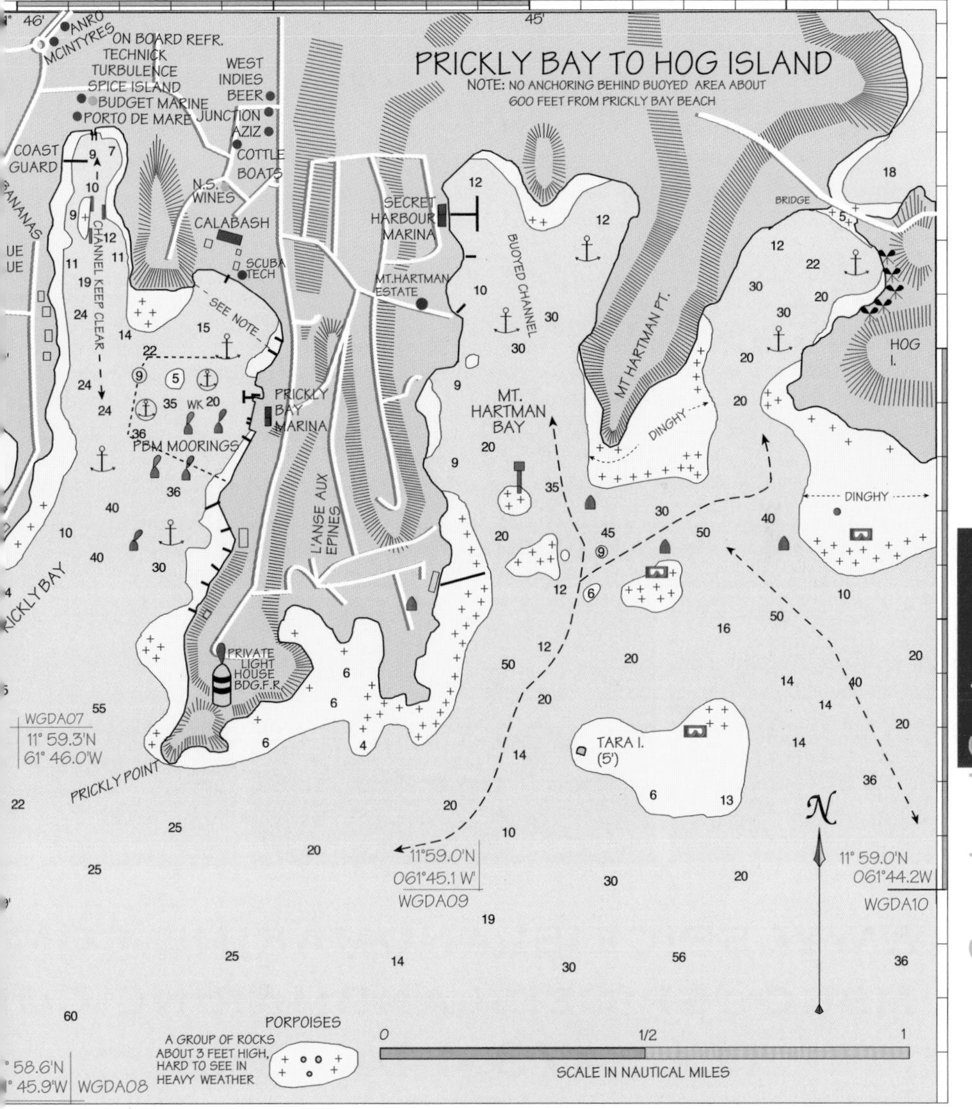

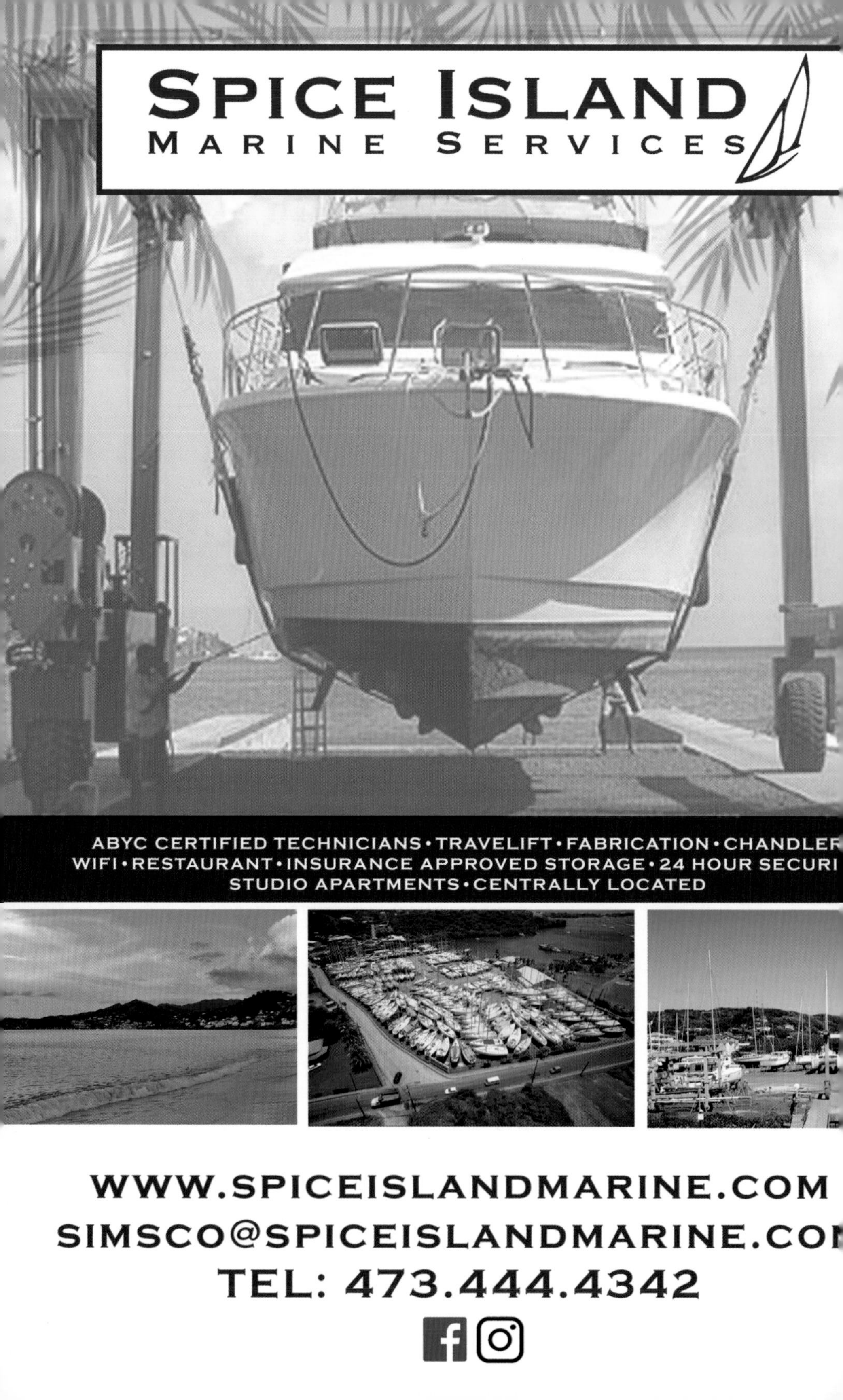

with high-speed WiFi, large benches, and tables equipped with multiple power outlets. Their network covers the docks and the restaurant. If you are farther out in the bay HotHotHot Spot and Cruisers WiFi provide coverage. HotHotHot spot has another base in Clarkes Court Bay and many others up island. Cruisers WiFi covers several Grenada anchorages, including St. George's and the Clarkes Court Bay, and they have stations in Carriacou and Trinidad.

Spice Island Marine Services has WiFi and computers for the use of those on the slip. Other restaurants with WiFi include Porto Di Mare, Bananas, and Dodgy Dock.

Hibiscus flower

General yacht services

Dinghy docks and garbage disposal are available both at Prickly Bay Marina and Spice Island Marine Services. Prickly Bay Marina has fuel, water, and ice. You can bring in the boat or use jerry jugs.

Henry's Safari Yacht Services & Tours [VHF: 68] has on-the-spot laundry and a cooking-gas collection station at the marina, collecting and delivering on Mondays, Wednesdays and Fridays. For emergency service, call them at 444-5313. Spice Island Marine Services has coin-operated laundry machines.

Spice Island Marine Services [SIM, VHF: 16] is a pleasant, orderly boatyard, with room for 200 boats. It is in the northwestern corner of Prickly Bay, on the True Blue side. It is easy to walk from here to all the places we mention in True Blue Bay. It is a family business, owned and operated by Junior Evans. Their travel lift can take boats up to 70 tons and 25-foot beam. At present, yachts of up to 10-foot draft can come in at high tide and they have one 12-foot draft boat they manage to drag in. SIM is the first yard in Grenada to go eco-friendly by recycling wash-down water and removing the harmful solids. They will soon have toilet pump out stations. They have full fire-fighting facilities, security cameras, and a high perimeter fence.

SIM has a hydraulic stacker and a mast crane with mast racks for those storing their masts off the yacht. They have tie-downs for all boats in the hurricane season, and secure cradle berthing is available. The yard keeps cats separate from monohulls. Demand for storage is so high that you cannot get short storage stays during the summer. Their staff includes a team that washes and chocks, does Awlgrip spray painting, osmosis treatment, hull polishing, sandblasting, and antifouling. Their own personnel can do woodworking, electrics, electronics (Raymarine certified) and mechanics (Yanmar agents), mostly with ABYC technicians. They do minor repairs on inflatables, have a bonded warehouse so parts arrive almost duty-free, and an on-site broker.

If you need a place to stay while having work done they have six studio apartments for rent above Budget Marine. Ask at the marina office for details.

Sailmaking and rigging are done by Turbulence; welding and fabrication by TechNick. The yard is secure and kept in excellent order.

Yacht crew can do their own work or arrange it through the yard with their people or, in some cases, outside contractors. The yard has electricity (110/220 volt, 50 cycle), WiFi, and good water pressure. Spice Island Marine Services can look after your yacht while you are away, as well as arrange all the work. While you work life is made easier with showers, toilets, a coin-operated launderette, email (yard customers only), and a waterfront restaurant (see *Restaurants*). Budget Marine chandlery is also based at Spice Island Marine Services.

Prickly Bay Marina [VHF: 16] is a charming, small marina where fresh green lawns are dotted with palms and almond trees. It

has an informal atmosphere and docks for about 25 yachts. They have stern-to docking, showers, electricity (110/220 volt, 50 cycle), diesel, gasoline, water, and ice. Colin the dockmaster is extremely helpful. They have an excellent dinghy dock, new toilets, showers, a mini-mart, and a WiFi-friendly section of the restaurant with power outlets.

They have many moorings in the bay for rent ($18 US a night, less by the month). Check them carefully.

The marina office offers absentee yacht and project management, and they can find someone to fix any boat problem you may have (see *Technical yacht services*).

This marina houses Henry's Safari Laundry, Essentials Mini-mart, Le Boucher, and the Marina Tiki Bar and Restaurant (see *Restaurants*). The owners of this marina have built some very fancy condominiums and plan a bigger marina. Those interested in the condos can ask in the marina or look for Champy Evans.

Superyachts can get any help they need in this area from either Henry's Safari Tours or Spronk's office at Bananas (see *St. George's*).

Chandlery

Budget Marine has a big, duty-free (to foreign yachts) chandlery at Spice Island Marine Services. You will find a good collection of general and technical chandlery, including everything you need for your haul-out and repair. An efficient special-order service brings goods from the parent store in St. Maarten, or directly from the manufacturer. Monthly containers from St. Maarten and weekly deliveries from various vendors keep things in stock. Budget Marine in Grenada is next to the Spice Island Marine Services Boat Yard. Easily accessible by dinghy from Prickly Bay, it is a short walk from True Blue or the main bus route serving the southwest of the island from St. George's. They offer a free weekly bus service, every Saturday, that leaves from Whisper Cove Marina at 0930 and picks up at Nimrod's Rum Shop, Secret Harbour Marina, and Clarkes Court Marina. It also stops at Ace Hardware on the way back. A knowledgeable

Budget Marine agent in Tyrrel Bay, Carriacou (Technical Marine Management) can arrange next-day delivery service from the Grenada store. With 12 locations throughout the region, this chandlery group stocks chandlery that many sailors, fishermen, and pleasure boaters find essential. They currently open weekdays 0800-1700, Saturdays 0900-1400. Bring in your boat papers for the first visit to get the duty-free prices.

Prickly Bay Marina has a small chandlery section in the marina office building and can bring in anything from the Island Water World catalog.

Ace Hardware, on the east side of the dual carriageway from Spice Island Marine towards town, is good for general hardware.

Technical yacht services

TechNick Yacht Services, in the Spice Island Marine yard, is run by Nick, who has years of Caribbean experience but originally came from England. TechNick is the place to come for metal fabrication. Not only does Nick do all the high tech precision work you need, he used to be the Moorings southern area technical manager, so he understands the broader picture of yacht systems and mechanics and will make sure anything he builds for you is going to make sense in the environment in which it is being used. Nick welds and does metal fabrication in all metals using good machining equipment. One of his specialties is the building of arches and supports for dinghies, biminis, and solar panels. Nick is knowledgeable about all boat systems and can often give good advice.

Turbulence Grenada, based in Spice Island Marine Services, has impressive workshops that handle sails, rigging, and electronics. It is owned and run by Richard and Joelle Szyjan, who are French, but have lived in English islands almost forever. They are helped by many excellent local employees. Richard is an experienced rigger and sailmaker (and racing helmsman). He used to prepare maxi boats for major races and is well qualified to advise and handle complete new deck layouts. The store is divided into three sections. The rigging shop is long and well equipped to deal with swaging and all rigging problems up to 16-mm wire, or up to 10-mm rod rigging. They keep materials to make spinnaker poles on hand and can order whole new rigs. They stock all the necessary ropes for running rigging and sheets, as well as the blocks and winches (including electric) to help you get them in tight. They repair big boat hydraulics and are agents for Navtec. They stock and install roller furlers.

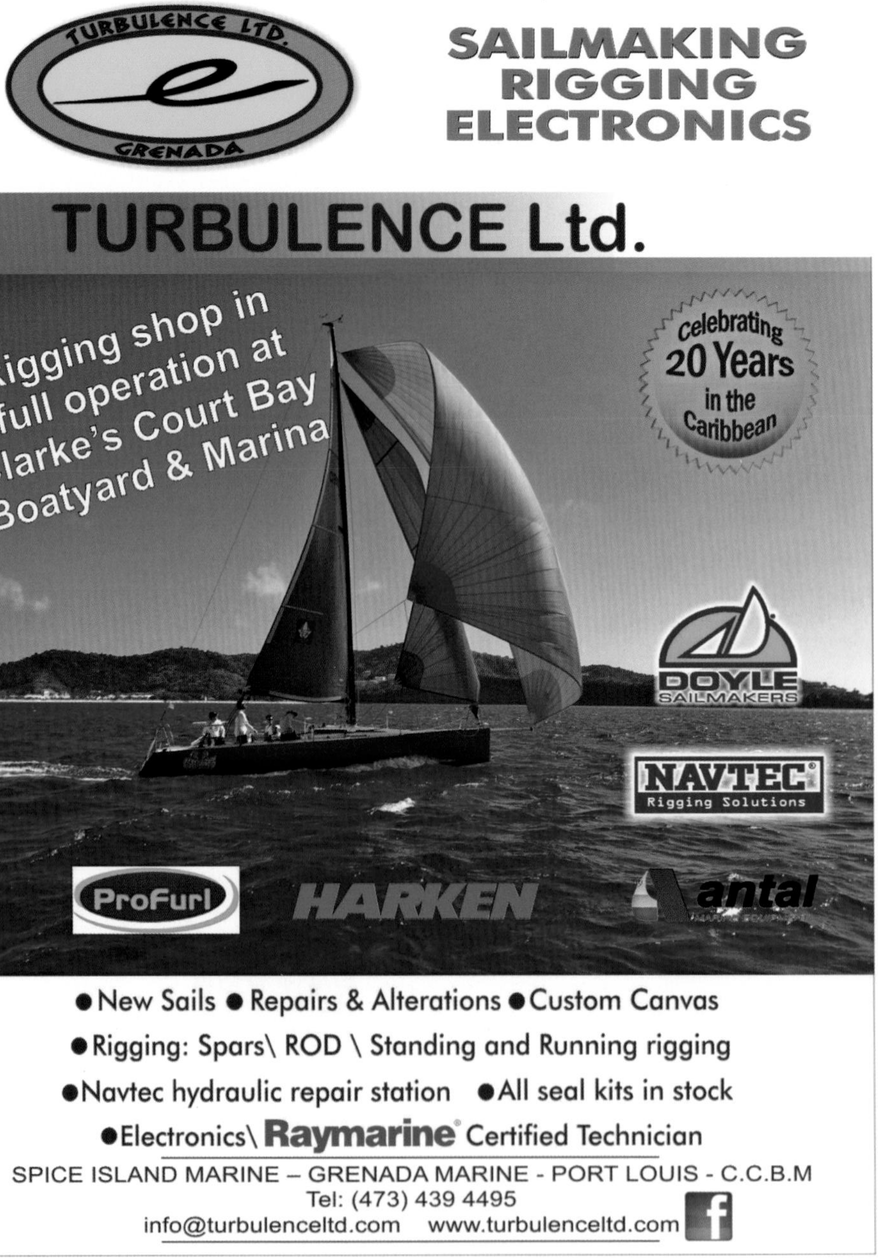

The Turbulence sail loft is large, and they work on everything from sailboard sails to massive mainsails from maxi-yachts. They produce sails themselves under the Turbulence logo, or if you prefer, they are agents for Doyle Sails.

They make biminis from scratch and can tackle other canvas work. Sheldon heads the Turbulence electronics department. They will repair your electronics, whatever the brand, and are agents for Brookes and Gatehouse, Victron Energy, and Raymarine, and they supply and install these brands of instruments and autopilots. All branches of Turbulence are also available at Grenada Marine in St. David's Harbour, where Louis, from Switzerland, is the manager.

On Board Refrigeration (Electrical and Electronics) is run by Oscar Cain. Oscar has experience and qualifications in all three fields, plus hydraulics and mechanics, and is an ABYC master technician. He is a qualified Raymarine technician, has been on the fitting out team of superyachts in Italy and has worked on yachts of all sizes from Antigua to Grenada. You can call him for any electrical/electronic/refrigeration/hydraulic problem. He covers all the major harbors where yachts hang out, from Port Louis to Woburn. He keeps offices in Spice Island Marine and in Woburn. He sometimes runs an "open workbench" where people come with their problems and he solves them and shows them how to fix things. Listen to the net.

Cottle Boat Works is a full marine joinery and carpentry shop. Owner Jim Cottle has been doing marine carpentry since 1972. He sailed to Grenada on his yacht, J. Jeffrey, where he has been repairing and building boats since 1992. Jim has a large, modern shop near The Brewery, full of top-grade machinery. You get to it by taking the left side road just beyond Aziz, and looking on the left. Jim does all his own work, so you can be sure of a good job. He repairs all wood problems and does fine joinery work. Jim can fix dings, burns, and other blemishes in varnish. He keeps a good supply of teak and other hardwoods on hand. Many of his customers come from the large charter yachts. Jim is happy to work on yachts staying in Prickly Bay, Mount Hartman Bay, or St. George's. He can get booked up, so if you have a big job, discuss it with him as far in advance as possible.

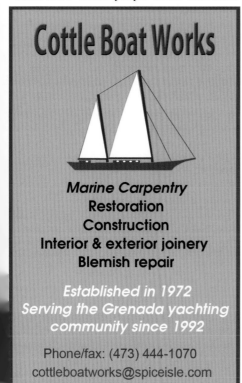

Prickly Bay Marina has a network of trustworthy technicians to call upon. They can fix anything that can be done in the water and undertake all kinds of maintenance, and do it quickly. Many technicians are on hand to maintain the apartments, so refrigeration, mechanical, and electrical repairs are easily done. They scrub boat bottoms, repair dinghies, paint, polish, and service gear.

Anro Agencies, run by Robert Miller, is a classy operation. They are agents for BMW and Mini, as well as Mercury outboards, Mercruiser engines and outdrives, Yanmar and Perkins diesels, and Yanmar marine generators. They sell and install new units, do warranty work, repair broken engines, and will make boat visits. New engines can be bought duty-free from their bonded warehouse and parts may be imported duty-free. They will normally come to any of the Grenada ports to pick up broken outboards. Their shop is a few hundred feet down the road from Spice Island Marine Services, on the Maurice Bishop Highway, the dual carriageway between the roundabouts. They are within easy walking distance of Spice Island Marine Services on the east side of the road. They stock quite a few engine-related accessories in the Quicksilver range and their prices can be quite competitive.

McIntyre Bros., also on the Maurice Bishop Highway, is within easy walking distance of Spice Island Marine Services, next to the roundabout on the east side of the road. They have qualified diesel mechanics and can fix most engines. They are the sales and service agents for Yamaha outboards and can arrange sales to yachts at duty-free prices. They will pick up your Yamaha for repair from most of the marinas. McIntyre rents cars and does island tours (see *Transport*).

Matthew Watton runs Essential Engineering. He lives on a boat and can easily visit yachts in Prickly Bay. He came here eight years ago to work on systems in the Prickly Bay condo complex and now runs his own business and does a good job at a fair rate. He fixes all outboards and inboards, along with gearboxes, sail drives, and the mechanical side of generators. He is also trained in refrigeration, and can do a simple gas top up, but does not carry equipment for more than that. He has an office by the Essentials Mini-Mart at Prickly Bay Marina, but the easiest way to find him is to call 414-7316.

Safe Yachts does guardianage, project management, and runs a water taxi. Owner Denise Simpson lives on a boat in the bay and is active in the local yachting scene. She has seven moorings in Prickly Bay and will look after yachts anywhere in the bay or hauled out at Clarkes Court. Anything she cannot do she subcontracts and supervises. She can arrange to have a boat hauled and serviced in Clarkes Court Bay to be ready for the owner's return. She works with several divers and is a good person to call for a bottom clean or mooring check. If you are leaving your yacht on a mooring during the hurricane season, ask about hurricane precautions.

Tropical Sails & Canvas (formerly Johnny Sails) [VHF: 16/66] is a sail loft just down Dusty Highway, which leads north from Spice Island Marine Services. Johnny's son Douglas has taken over, and the team does excellent work, from sails to canvas and cushions. They also do inflatable repairs.

Ever After Canvas Repair is a small operation based on the yacht Ever After, usually anchored towards the entrance of Prickly Bay. Owners Frank and Julie Turner came to canvas work through a mutual love of horses and leather work, and registered a business in Grenada. They keep enough canvas on board for repairs and small jobs, but if you want an awning, dinghy chaps, cover or bimini, they will help you order, ship, and clear the materials (allow about 10 business days). If you need cushions and cushion covers you can probably find both foam and material at Nabelas on the dual carriageway. All the work is done on a Sailrite machine and they carry lifetime Profilen thread for optimal sun resistance.

Sea Safety Service, whose main business is in Clarkes Court Bay, still have an active shop here, and may keep it going. They do all kinds of inflatable, life raft, and safety gear maintenance and sell the top-quality Zar inflatables (see *Technical yacht services* in Clarkes Court Bay).

Most technicians based in other yards and bays are willing to visit. This includes Marine Tech and Palm Tree Marine.

For computer repairs and IT, try Christian and Anand's ModOne by The Calabash, or The Computer Store in Spiceland Mall (see *Grand Anse*).

Transport

There are some excellent taxi drivers around and they have now organized themselves as the Marina Taxi Association, which covers all the ports in Grenada. It is easy to call Marina Taxi [VHF: 16]. The Prickly Bay branch has a small stand in Prickly Bay Marina. All their drivers are good and one is nearly always available.

If you want to rent a car McIntyre's is close by, will quickly deliver, can provide a local license, and have staff who are used to dealing with yachtspeople. They do excellent hiking and sightseeing tours, including Gouyave's Fish Friday, and they arrange weddings.

Provisioning

People needing to stock up on their wines will be delighted by North South Wines, a short walk from the boatyard, close by the Calabash. They stock wines from all over the world, including Europe, Australia, South America, and South Africa. You can sit in a comfortable atmosphere, discuss your needs, and they can recommend wines for different menus. They have a large enough range to satisfy the superyacht owner as well as those with more modest needs. This is a wholesale outfit, so wines are sold by the case, but they are often willing to mix cases for yachts, and they will deliver to your yacht. If you buy a case of wine and don't want it all at once, they will store it for you in their temperature-controlled rooms. Opening hours are weekdays 0830-1630. They have a retail outlet called The Wine Shoppe in Spiceland Mall (see Grand Anse).

The Prickly Bay Marina shop, Essentials [VHF: 16], is a convenient mini-market open 0800-1600, Monday to Saturday. They have dry goods, a little fresh produce, frozen fish and meat, a good selection of wines and liquor, and the shop is convenient for buying heavy cases of beer, soft drinks, or gallons of spring water. They also sell ice.

A few steps away, Gilles and Frederique's Le Boucher is a French butcher and delicatessen. It stocks meat, fine French cheeses, pates, and a variety of wines. Rotisserie chicken is normally available around noon. The meat is all fresh, but they can freeze it if you ask.

For more than that, take a bus or cab to the malls in Grand Anse (buses go from the True Blue roundabout) or catch one of the regular shopping busses that leave from many of the marinas. They visit multiple grocery and hardware stores and can make additional stops by request and consensus. They generally charge about $15 EC and depart between 0900 and 1100. Listen to the morning net for details.

John Hovan AKA Fast Manacou has competitive prices on a large selection of soda, wine, beer, and water cases, and will deliver to most anchorages, usually the same or next day. He also fills propane and soda stream canisters. Contact him after the morning net.

Restaurants

The Marina Tiki Bar and Restaurant [$$$], right in Prickly Bay Marina, is a favorite yachty haunt. You can get thin-crust Italian pizzas, good meals, and other daily specials that are usually reasonably priced. They have the most popular happy hour in L'Anse aux Epines, from 1700-1800 nightly. Something happens here every night and it is popular with both yachties and medical students. Monday is half-priced pizzas, Tuesday is trivia night, on Wednesdays they have serious bingo with big prizes. Friday is the most popular night, with a steel band from 1800, followed by a big music party. Saturday night varies, and Sunday is movie night. The cruisers net (VHF: 66 international at 0730) gives information about their attractions.

Porto Di Mare [$$] is an Italian restaurant beside Budget Marine. Owner Piero Guerrini is originally from Italy and serves up generous portions of tasty pasta dishes, seafood, and salads. Most popular are their wood-fired pizzas, straight out of a traditional brick oven. In the mornings they serve full English and local breakfasts, and often have a live DJ on Friday and Saturday nights. They are open from 0800 until late, every day but Sunday.

The West Indies Beer Co. Brewery [$$] is a family owned and operated pub and restaurant where Brewmaster Mark is brewing a couple dozen different beers and ciders at any given time. The long wrap-around bar separates the fermentation tanks from the pool table and seating area, where they serve pub-style food from 1200 until late. Thursdays is Salsa music, and they often have live music on Saturdays. Smokers can rent hookahs, and the bartenders are always happy to pour a taster pallet. When you find the ideal beer, you can buy a growler (re-sealable bottle) to take home and get it refilled any time. Their bottles now retail at IGA Supermarket and many bars throughout the island have them on tap.

Next door, Junction [$$] has changed hands and now attracts a more casual, local crowd. It is quite small inside, but a large covered deck creates cozy spaces; there is sometimes live music. They serve simple but tasty burgers, fish, and chicken.

Aziz [$$] started out small but has recently expanded into one of the large buildings beside Junction. He serves a bit of everything, from burgers and Philly cheese steak to lamb and lobster. He's open from 1100 for lunch and dinner every day but Wednesday. The kitchen closes at 2300, but the bar is open later. Both food and drink are reasonably priced, and Aziz says "Every hour is happy hour, you just have to ask." They do take out orders, or, if spending a bit more time, you can rent a hookah from the bar.

Next door, a new Indian restaurant by the same people who have Punj-Abi (see Point Saline to Prickly Bay) should be open by the time you read this.

The Calabash Hotel [$$$$] has a fine, up-market restaurant in a pleasant atmosphere and with excellent food. They prefer you to be dressed fairly smartly, but this is a great choice when you want somewhere special; reservations are essential.

Ashore

You will find tennis courts at the hotels and a golf club in Golflands. Ask for directions. Everything in True Blue is now easily accessible from Prickly Bay; dinghy to Spice Island Marine Services and take the short walk down the road.

There is an easy walk between Prickly Bay and Secret Harbour Marina in Mount Hartman Bay. From Prickly, walk from the marina to the road, turn right and take the first left. When you come to a T-junction, turn right, then the next left.

Water sports

Scuba Tech, a PADI, TDI, and CMAS dive shop, is on the waterfront at The Calabash Hotel. This pleasant shop does all the usual courses, as well as nitrox and rebreather. They also refill tanks and repair equipment. Owner Eveline can teach in English, French, or German, and is a member of the Women Divers Hall of Fame. They dive with small groups on a 32-foot pirogue and visit all of Grenada's sites, including the Bianca C. Divers usually meet at 0830 to gather equipment for a two-tank dive at 0900. If you have gear, they might be able to pick you up from your yacht in Prickly Bay on their way out.

If you are after big fish, ask about the wreck sites south of Prickly Bay. The 170-foot long Hema 1 was sunk in 2005 and is four miles south and 30 meters deep. The 200-foot long King Mitch is six miles south and 37 meters deep. Between the two is Pershia, a small cargo ship that sank in March of 2017.

These wrecks are in open, rough water, so are weather dependent, challenging, and very exciting. They attract nurse sharks, rays, and spadefish, and turtles often drop by.

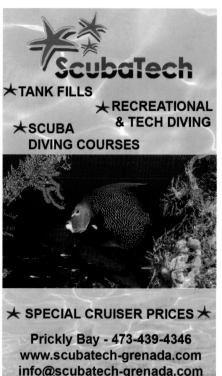

THE SOUTH COAST BEYOND PRICKLY BAY

(See sketch charts pages 379 and 394.)

The south coast of Grenada has beautiful and protected anchorages, some great restaurants, several marinas, a boatyard, and other facilities. A mass of reefs provides interesting, if somewhat murky, snorkeling. The area should be treated with caution: eyeball navigation is essential. On our charts, we have marked as "too shallow" several areas of relatively shoal water (12-15 feet) that extend well offshore. In normal conditions you can sail over these, but when the going gets rough, seas start breaking on them, and they are best avoided. The Porpoises, about half a mile off Prickly Point, awash and hard to spot, are as nasty a group of rocks as you could find to get wrecked on.

The buoyage system, such as it is, is privately maintained, with a lot of markers placed by individuals for their own purposes. My sketch charts include the markers I saw when updating. The current buoys are red-right returning into Mt. Hartman, which may confuse a sailor heading to Hog Island.

Buoys come and go and change position. Markers can be unreliable and, when out of place, dangerously misleading. Visit this coast for the first time in good light and rely on your own navigation skills, not on the buoys. When you know the area and know which buoys are in place, they may be helpful on later visits. The exceptions to this are the buoyed channels into Phare Bleu Marina and Grenada Marine in St. David's Harbour, which are well-maintained. The outer yellow buoy for Phare Bleu is steel, unlit, and a long way out; take care.

Entering Mt. Hartman Bay and Hog Island is tricky and demands attention. The main reefs are easy to see in good light. Two shoals, 6 and 9 feet deep, are not as easy to spot. From Prickly Bay, pass about midway between Prickly Point and the Porpoises. Look out for what was Tara Island and is now a shallow breaking spot. Leave Tara to starboard, passing halfway between it and Prickly Point. Head for Mt. Hartman Point, eyeballing your way through the reefs. For Hog Island, follow the inner reef up to Hog Island, leaving the inside red buoys to port. For Mt. Hartman, pass between the red buoy

and the green beacon. The channel is buoyed to the marina. Do not anchor in the channel.

An alternative is a deeper channel south of Hog Island. For this, approach the western tip of Hog Island on a bearing of magnetic north, and eyeball your way around the reefs as you approach Hog. To leave, pass close by the reef just south of Hog Island, and head out on a bearing of 170° magnetic. In both directions, make sure the current is not setting you to the west. A 14-foot bank lies on the west side of the channel, so deep-draft yachts need to be particularly careful. Last time I passed, two red buoys marked part of this channel.

A repeater on channel 66 international connects all Grenada's anchorages and has a morning cruisers' net at 0730. Buses run between the south coast and St. George's.

MOUNT HARTMAN BAY

Mt. Hartman Bay is deep and well protected (see chart *Prickly Bay to Hog Island*, page 379) with a modern marina. This is a suitable area for dinghy sailing or sailboarding, as there is protected water all the way to Phare Bleu Bay. By land, it is a 10-minute walk to Prickly Bay. (From the marina exit, turn right walk up the hill and round the corner; keep going till you come to a crossroads, turn right again, and then take the next small road on the left. When you come to the next main road, turn right again, and the marina is on your left.)

General services

Secret Harbour Marina [VHF: 16], with 53 berths, has a lovely location in a peaceful bay. Fuel, water, ice, showers, telephone, WiFi, fax, launderette, dinghy dock, 24-hour security, and electricity (110/220/380 Volt, 50 cycle) are among the marina services. They can take any size yacht from the smallest cruiser up to huge superyachts. The maximum draft on the deepest dock is 20 feet, and a yacht of this depth will have to be careful entering the bay. If you have any questions, call or ask Mitra in the office. They will assist you in docking at the marina, or in finding any services you might need. The marina has a swimming pool, tennis courts, a small beach, and lovely self-contained cottages along the waterfront to rent. Each is beautifully appointed and has a delightful balcony over the water. (See also *Ashore*)

There is no customs station, so if you want to come straight here, call Secret Harbour Marina and they can arrange for one of the yacht agents to clear you.

Chris and Chrystal's The Multihull Company and LTD Sailing are based here. They are a branch of the Multihull Company brokerage, and they run a sailing school, LTD sailing (LTDsailing.com).

Technical yacht services

George, a taxi driver whose call sign is "Survival Anchorage," refills propane bottles, looks after yachts when owners are away, helps source parts or other things, and can do underwater work, including hull and prop cleaning. He is willing to do overnight passages for those needing an extra hand. He delivers boats in the Windwards, or helps deliver them farther, and he can act as pilot around the reef-strewn south coast. He has his own yacht and sometimes does day sails or island passages.

Ashore

Sel & Poivre [$$$] restaurant at Secret Harbour Marina is open every day from 0730 until 2100 (2200 on weekends). The newly-renovated location is pleasant, with comfortable cocktail seating, as well as more formal dinner tables. Secret Radio (92.7 FM) is in the middle of the restaurant in a transmitting room of its own. They serve French Caribbean cuisine and their popular happy hour runs from 1600 until 1800 every day. Up the hill is the larger Secret Harbour Hotel, which has also been recently renovated.

George (Survival Anchorage), the taxi driver mentioned in *Services* above, takes people on "Village Life" tours. He will take you to some of the small villages and introduce you to some of his friends to give you an understanding glimpse of village life in Grenada.

Mount Hartman Estate Cave House [$$$$] is an exclusive restaurant within easy walking distance of Secret Harbour. Go through the main hotel and out the other side up to the road. Turn left to the crossroads, then left again, walk up the hill and down again, and you are there. It is a lovely sculpted building with high ceilings and an open view over Secret Harbour. The food is good; but they sometimes close to the public when the hotel is full. It is good for a special night out, but it is not always open and reservations are essential.

HOG ISLAND

North of Hog Island is a huge, protected bay. When you anchor, there will be just a

finger of horizon to remind you that the sea is still there. This is one of Grenada's most popular cruising hangouts. Yachties enjoy the peace and Roger's ramshackle bar that sprawls along a good chunk of the tiny beach. Access to shore is available at Mt. Hartman Bay and Woburn. On Sunday afternoons cruisers get together for a popular barbecue at Roger's Bar.

See pages 379 and 394 (charts) and page 390 for navigation into Hog Island. When you get in, anchor anywhere between Hog Island and the mainland.

A construction company owns Hog Island and Mt. Hartman Estates and development is stalled. So far they have built a bridge to link Hog Island to the shore. (No more sailing yachts through the narrow channel, but you can dinghy through.)

In the land behind Hog, I noticed a lot of grazing horses. I tracked down the owner, Wendell Wilson, who owns Amistad Stables and can take you riding (440-4175/533-8221).

CLARKES COURT BAY

This huge and sheltered bay, with Woburn at its head, has lots of anchoring possibilities: you can explore and find your own spot. It is linked to protected bays to the east and west, offering miles of safe dinghy navigation. This is the home of the huge Clarkes Court Bay boatyard and marina, as well as other marinas and many facilities.

In the old days, big sailing ships would anchor here to take on rum that was brought down the river to the head of the bay by small boat. Calivigny Island lies at the entrance to Clarkes Court Bay. It was privately purchased in 2001 and is now a fancy private island resort for the rich and famous. As part of this development, the deepest part of the entrance channel has been buoyed. These buoys are privately maintained and have proved unreliable. Check for yourself that they are in position. You need to enter fairly close to Calivigny Island to avoid all the reefs and shoals that extend south of Hog Island.

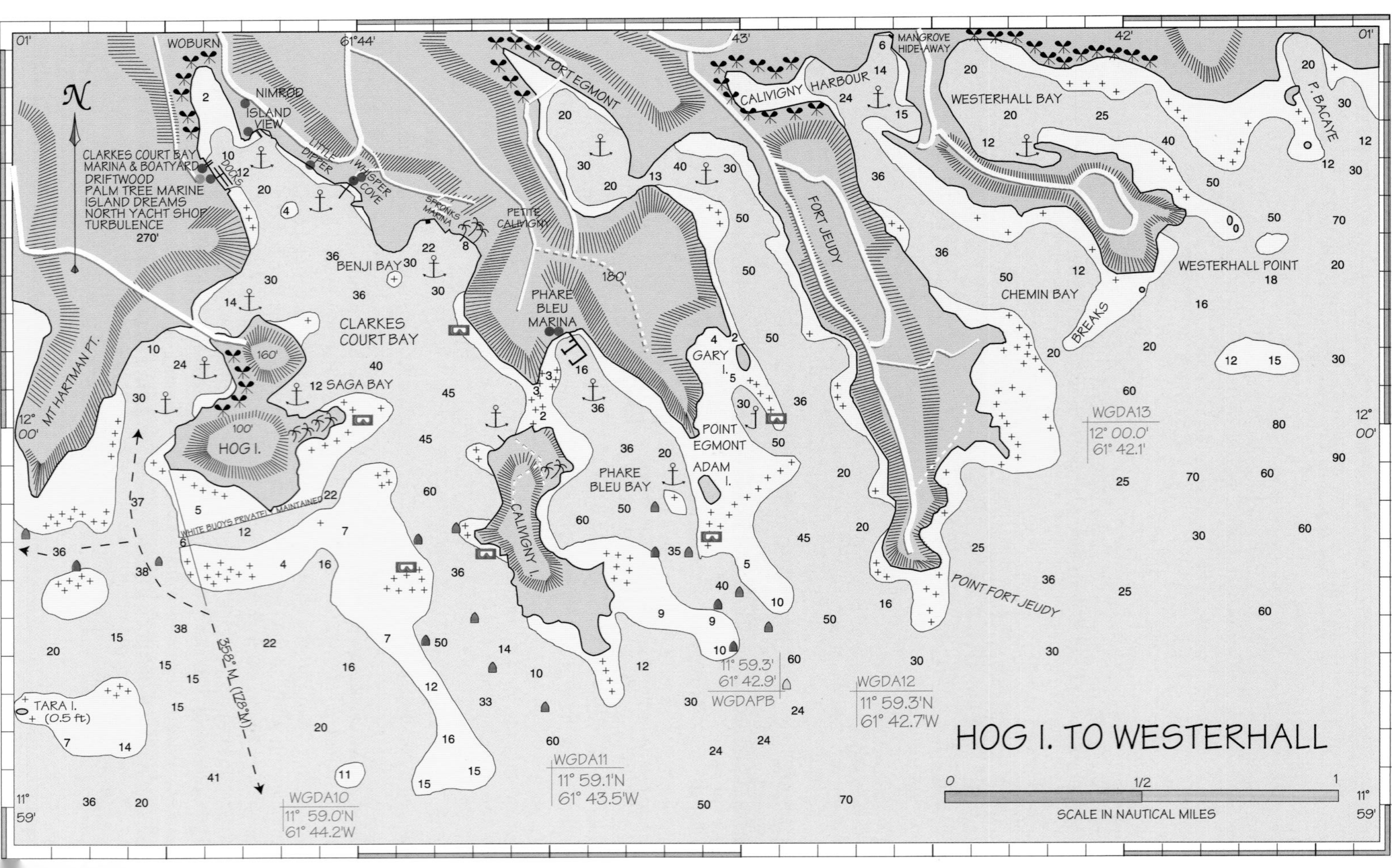
HOG I. TO WESTERHALL
SCALE IN NAUTICAL MILES
0
1/2
1
N
WOBURN
NIMROD
ISLAND VIEW
CLARKES COURT BAY MARINA & BOATYARD
DRIFTWOOD
PALM TREE MARINE
ISLAND DREAMS
NORTH YACHT SHOP
TURBULENCE
270'
DOCKS
LITTLE DIPPER
WHISPER COVE
SPRONKS MARINA
PETITE CALIVIGNY
PORT EGMONT
CALIVIGNY HARBOUR
MANGROVE HIDE-AWAY
WESTERHALL BAY
P. BACAYE
FORT JEUDY
WESTERHALL POINT
CHEMIN BAY
BREAKS
BENJI BAY
CLARKES COURT BAY
SAGA BAY
PHARE BLEU MARINA
180'
160'
100'
HOG I.
MT HARTMAN PT.
GARY I.
POINT EGMONT
ADAM I.
PHARE BLEU BAY
CALIVIGNY I.
POINT FORT JEUDY
WHITE BUOYS PRIVATE, MAINTAINED
358° M (178°M)
TARA I. (0.5 ft)
WGDA13
12° 00.0'
61° 42.1'
WGDAPB
11° 59.3'
61° 42.9'
WGDA12
11° 59.3'N
61° 42.7'W
WGDA11
11° 59.1'N
61° 43.5'W
WGDA10
11° 59.0'N
61° 44.2'W

Once inside, you can anchor almost anywhere that takes your fancy.

One popular anchorage is off Calivigny Island just north of the island, off the beach. The bottom shelves steeply, so make sure you are well hooked. Calivigny Island is privately owned and guarded. The beaches, like all Grenadian beaches, are public. You should not use the dock, go behind the beach, or use any of the owner's beach huts, but you can pull your dinghy on the beach, have your picnic ashore, and swim. Keep it clean. Guards may check you out, but they know the law. One time when we visited two big Labradors came running out and tried to knock us over with their wagging tails, and then lick us to death. We loved it.

You can find good anchorages almost anywhere in the bay. One delightful little anchorage is in Benji Bay, with good snorkeling around the point towards Calivigny Island.

Both Calivigny and Hog are dotted with hardy little frangipani trees. Their leaves fall in the dry season, leaving only sweet-smelling, delicate white flowers.

The Woburn Wind Warriors is a youth sailing group operating from in front of Island View, across from Clarkes Court Marina. Local instructor Shakeem Collins (son of Sep Nimrod, who runs a popular rum shop of the same name in the area) takes an enthusiastic group of sailors out every weekend.

Communications

Clarkes Court Bay Marina has WiFi or plug-in, as does Whisper Cove Marina. Bring your own computer. You can probably pick up Cruisers WiFi or HotHotHot Spot onboard.

General yacht services

Clarkes Court Boatyard and Marina is owned by Kelly Glass and is in the same stable as Blue Lagoon in St. Vincent, and Bequia Plantation House. Kelly has made a large investment to create Grenada's newest major player in the marine industry.

Hauling is done with a 242-ton travel lift which lifts up to 37-foot beam with a 13-foot draft. Some smaller boats are hauled on a trailer, which takes 38-tons with a 6-foot draft. There is room for about 300 boats ashore, and tie downs are available. The haul out is currently fully booked for 2019. A long work dock is already in use, and this, like the rest of the marina, is good for about 12-foot draft. The marina docks are in place, with plenty of space for short and long term visitors. The restaurant, Adrift, looks over the docks.

Facilities in the yard include North Yacht Shop Chandlery, Driftwood wood shop, Waterfall Marine, Turbulence rigging, Palm Tree Marine mechanics, Welding Tec, Sea Safety Service, Caribbean Boat Services, and Island Dreams. You can do your own work, or they will help you arrange it.

Whisper Cove Marina is a small, pleasant, and friendly docking facility between Petit Calivigny and Woburn that is well protected by a groin. It is owned and operated by a Quebecois couple, Gilles and Mary. They have 12 berths for boats up to 60 feet and 10-foot draft, with electricity (220 volt, or 110 volt with a transformer); water comes by a long hose, and showers are on the dock. They have hurricane moorings, and these are available for rent outside the hurricane season (or free if you tie up to one for a meal). They have a laundry machine, WiFi, dinghy dock, the Meat and Meet shop (see *Shopping*), and a bar and restaurant (see *Restaurants*). They look after their customers well, have a bus for airport runs, and organize regular shopping busses for those in the marina and surrounding bay.

Cruisers love their do-it-yourself workshop with its vice, drill press, and other tools. If you need a hand with very simple welding, Gilles may help. You can drop off propane tanks and laundry for Henry's Safari Tours here. Whisper Cove is home to Conservation Kayak (see *Ashore*).

Benji Bay yard is owned by Claire and Roger Spronk of Spronk's Megayacht Services. This is one of the nicest little bays within Clarkes Court Bay. They have moorings available for rent and have a small haul out and typically take just a couple of boats undergoing major projects by the owner, though they can arrange any work. They also run big full moon parties (see *Ashore)* and their bar and restaurant is occasionally open.

Chandlery

In Clarkes Court Boatyard, North Yacht

Whisper Cove Marina

Shop is a big new chandlery run by Matt. He carries a lot of the West Marine range and can bring in anything from their catalog, usually within a couple days.

As the shop is in the yard, his primary approach has been to stock products yachts are going to need. This includes a range of paints and antifouling (including Sea Hawk), glass for repairs, consumables used in preparation, zincs, pumps, hoses, toilets, plumbing, fastener, and safety gear. Zar ribs are available here.

You will find fun stuff here too, including portable fridges and freezers, flags, a great selection of LED bulbs, and a lot of general yacht chandlery. They have a selection of batteries and a trained electrician on staff will answer all your questions.

Pond lily

Budget Marine offers a free weekly bus service, every Saturday, that leaves from Whisper Cove Marina at 0930 and picks up at Nimrod's Rum Shop, Secret Harbour Marina, and Clarkes Court Marina. It also stops at Ace Hardware on the way back.

Sherri owns Wholesale Yacht Parts, a short walk from the dock in Woburn. She can source anything you need from the US, usually at a discounted price, and have it shipped at a discount off the usual FedEx rates. If you want to ship something of your own from the US, she can help. If you are in another island, she can ship direct to you there. She is in the big four-story building right across the bay from Clarkes Court Bay Marina.

Technical yacht services

Sea Safety Service, originally based in Prickly Bay Marina, have their main workshop above the chandlery at Clarkes Court Boatyard. Sarah and Donal Kavanagh from Ireland, along with their skilled team, sell and service life rafts and offer a complete repair service for your tender. They also stock a full range of marine safety equipment. They are agents for high-end Zar ribs from Italy and sell and advise on everything from man overboard systems to life jackets and fire detection systems. They provide professional storage solutions for your tender and outboard while you are away, and will collect and deliver island-wide. They are open Monday to Friday from 0800 until 1600.

Driftwood offers fine yacht woodwork, from fancy joinery to replacing a plank or teak deck. They have a team that does bottom jobs, antifouling, topside buffing, polishing, gelcoat, and glass repairs.

It is owned by Steffen who worked for many years with Chippy in Antigua. He has pulled together a good and reliable team, including Judd Tinius, the well known shipwright and owner of the 1899 classic "Galatea". They work on all sizes of boat and any size job, from completely redesigning and building a yacht's interior, to making a new bookshelf. If a woodworking job involves glass or composite work, they have the skills to do that, which considerably simplifies some jobs. They keep a stock of veneers, including European ones like beech and oak. Their main shop is in Clarkes Court Bay, but that can also work out of St. George's (Lagoon Road).

Island Dreams has a branch in Clarkes

Court Bay Boatyard, with another office in Port Louis. Owners Mark and Anita Sutton look after your yacht while you go away, organizing anything that needs doing at the same time. They can arrange everything from a simple repair to a complete refit. For a more complete description, see *St. George's*.

Mike runs Palm Tree Marine, helped by several Grenadians, including Kevon. This is an excellent place to have all your mechanical, electrical, and refrigeration problems fixed. They work on all brands of inboards, outboards, and generators. They are dealers for Caterpillar, Yanmar, Westerbeke, and Northern Lights, and are equipped for tank cleaning. They are agents for Spectra watermakers and service all makes. They have an efficient mini-machine shop and do steel and stainless welding. Palm Tree Marine has a van for visiting other locations, and their refrigeration department makes boat visits anywhere, but for major mechanical projects, make sure you get them by visiting Clarkes Court Bay.

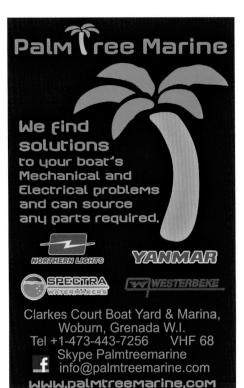

Mango Projects does surveys and looks after yachts. Neil Batcheler, the owner, is a SAMS accredited surveyor who used to work with Flying Fish (see St. George's) and has now set out on his own. He does all kinds of surveys, from condition and insurance to damage and valuation. He is willing to keep an eye on yachts, doing regular checks (but not project management) in Clarkes Court Bay Marina.

Rigging, electronics, and sailmaking are taken care of by Turbulence, who are fast, efficient, and do a good job at a fair rate. They have shops in all of Grenada's yards; more details are given under *Prickly Bay*.

On Board Refrigeration is run by Oscar Cain. Oscar can fix any refrigeration, electrical or electronic problem. He is an ABYC master technician. He keeps an office in the Island View building in Woburn, as well as in Prickly Bay. For a full write-up see *Prickly Bay*.

Francis Hagley from St. David's has been welding for 15 years, 12 in the marine industry. His shop, Welding Tec in Clarkes Court Boatyard, can handle the repair or fabrication of arches, pulpits, pushpits, bimini frames, davits, and everything in between. They weld stainless, aluminum, and regular steel and are very pleasant to deal with.

Royan's Welding shop is close by and he charges no extra to come down, give an estimate and pick up your metal work jobs, or work on your boat with a mobile unit (for a full write-up, see *St. George's*)

Marine Tech does refrigeration, electric, and electronic repairs and installation; they are willing to come over to do work (for full details, see *St. George's*).

Waterfall Marine, from Trinidad, have a branch in Clarkes Court Bay. Waterfall is a company that works with both ships and yachts. It is run by Johan van Druten and Sean Bodden. For yachts they are first-rate at mechanical and electrical engineering, including all prop, shaft, and seal work. They can weld most metals, including stainless and aluminum, and can fix hydraulics. They are one of the few companies to do work on marine jet propulsion drives. They do project management, consulting, and survey work on yachts.

Caribbean Boat Services aim to be a one-stop-shop when it comes to yacht services, repairs, and restoration. They can take care of it all, from fiberglass and gelcoat, to rigging, mast work, mechanical engineering, and woodwork, and provide guardianage while they're at it. They work closely with clients to provide a personalized service and ensure nothing is forgotten or overlooked. Chris has worked in the yacht services industry for over 40 years, and together with his wife they run C.B.S. and live aboard their own boat in the bay.

Shipyard Marine Services is a grouping of several people with an outlet right in the marina. Angus coordinates. Ricardo Moultri does refined sandblasting, fixes outboards, fuel injection, and cleans fuel. Dexter Hays (Subzero) does refrigeration and air conditioning. They have marine contacts in St. Vincent.

There are several general yacht maintenance and repair specialists that work out of Clarkes Court Bay, two of which are Leslie at Hands On Yacht Services and Anderson at AKC. Both do fiberglass, gelcoat, bottom cleaning, and painting.

Rollin' Stitches canvas and upholstery shop is also in the Island View building and owned and run by Karen. She does any kind of canvas work, dinghy chaps, biminis, awnings, bags, and covers. She specializes in upholstery, which most sailmakers do not touch. For new cushions and curtains this is the place to come. She keeps a fair stock of Sunbrella and has a couple of fancy fabric books from which you can choose your interior fabrics. She has a small, informal shop, a pleasant place to pop round and discuss your project.

Shopping

Whisper Cove's Meat and Meet shop is known for the best selection of meat and sausages in Grenada. Gilles Yergeau is a butcher who buys local animals, which he hangs and processes professionally in his modern facility. The result is that you can buy the best cuts of much finer meat than the imports found in the supermarket. He also makes excellent sausages. They can prepare meat to order, so you can get just what you want by cut or portion, and they can freeze it. Quite a number of charter yachts do their meat provisioning here.

Every day, except Sunday, they bake French bread, which is available from 1030,

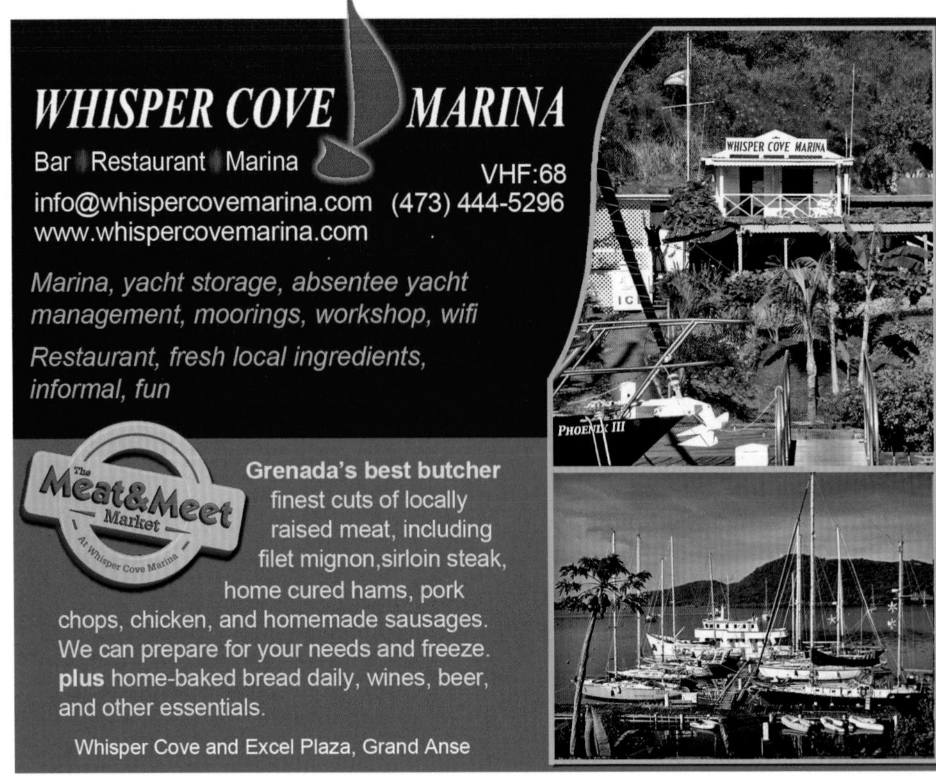

and sell wines, fresh yogurt, and other supplies. The bread sells out quickly, so it is best to call ahead and reserve a loaf. Their main shop is in Whisper Cove, but they have an outlet store in the marketing board's Value Garden in Excel Plaza, Grand Anse.

You can anchor off Woburn or any of the other bays and tie your dinghy to the village dock. Wander up to the road and turn left, you will find a little corner store called Nimrod and Sons Rum Shop, run by Pat and Sep. You can buy ice here, along with bread, fresh chicken, lettuce, a few canned goods, beer, and rum.

There are regular shopping busses that pick up from Whisper Cove, along with many of the other marinas. They visit multiple grocery and hardware stores and make additional stops by request and consensus. They generally charge about $15 EC and depart between 0900 and 1100. Listen to the morning net for details.

Restaurants

Whisper Cove Marina Restaurant [$$$] is a fun French bar and restaurant, family-run by Gilles Yergeau and Mary Caron. They open for breakfast and lunch Tuesday to Saturday. Hearty fish sandwiches, excellent burgers, daily specials, and fresh salads are often on the menu. Wednesday night is pizza night, Thursday night is the popular roast chicken and fries night, and dinner on Friday and Saturday features excellent meat, which they butcher themselves ~ melt-in-your-mouth steak and pork ~ as well as lobster and fresh fish, though they can cater to a vegetarian. They have a popular Sunday brunch buffet starting at 1130, and are often open for special occasions (check the morning cruisers' net). They provide free transport from the other Grenadian anchorages for those wishing to have a meal at the restaurant (call and ask). Bring books for the multi-language book-swap.

Adrift [$$] is a restaurant and cafe in Clarkes Court Boatyard, and is restaurateur Uli Khun's newest venture. Rustic, relaxed, and right on the waterfront overlooking the docks, they are open from 0730 till 2200 every day but Sunday. The breakfast menu features pastries and croissants baked in-house daily, espressos, specialty coffees, and the more traditional English and Caribbean breakfasts. Lunch and dinner are Asian, American, and Italian fusion, and reasonably priced.

Woburn is home to Little Dipper [$], the cutest restaurant in Grenada. Joan, who owns it with her husband, Rock, the taxi driver, has cooked in several fancy restaurants and serves excellent local food inexpensively, making this a special experience and great value. Enjoy the sweeping view out over Hog Island as you taste fresh seafood with a good variety of local vegetables. You won't find a better deal on lobster, fish, or lambi. They open Monday to Saturday, 1000-2200. Their dinghy dock is currently under repair, so tie up at Island View and take the short walk up the hill. Otherwise, Rock can bring you by taxi from Prickly Bay or Secret Harbour at a special rate.

Taffy's at Island Breeze [$, closed Monday], owned by Sue and Colin Wakeman, is a popular yachtie hangout right by the dock. It is not a fancy restaurant. Sue cooks one dish each meal and she does it well. On Mondays, she cooks fish and chips and on Sundays she produces a traditional roast lunch. Other days, Sue wanders out in the morning to see what fresh food is available and decides on the dinner dish accordingly. In season, she opens for lunch and dinner with a cruisers lunch for $20 EC. Taffy's is very popular, so if you do not reserve for dinner, you may not get in (538-0863).

Sep Nimrod runs a popular yachtie hangout on the corner where the road to Island View meets the main road. They have weekly jam sessions and daily lunch specials, check their Facebook page or the morning net for more information.

If you walk down the boardwalk by the dock, you come to Sea Quest, a local bar.

Bob Goodchild, the surveyor (see St. George's), has cottages set in their own private garden, a two-minute walk from Whisper Cove Marina. They are lovely, but on long-term leases. If you are looking to swallow the anchor and move ashore this would be a great option.

Ashore

Roger's Benji Bay hosts a wild and wonderful full moon party (check the date of the next full moon and put it on your calendar). They have a bar, barbecue, and several good live bands. Their dinghy dock is small, so tie it on a long tether to allow room for others.

Conservation Kayak's guided kayak tours give guests an intimate view of the shore, where they learn about mangrove conservation and ecology. Based out of Whisper Cove Marina in lower Woburn, tours range from 2 to 5 hours; no experience is necessary. The longer tours include a stop at an idyllic white sand beach, and include a locally-sourced organic lunch. The tours have become popular and run most days. You need to book in advance.

Transport

The road running through Woburn looks so rough and rural, with the odd chicken wandering over it, that it seems impossible to imagine a bus hurtling by full of smiling faces and big shopping baskets, but it happens all the time. Whichever way it comes, you can catch it to town if you wait around Nimrod's Rum Shop. On the return run, ask for a bus going to "Lower Woburn."

Take it easy on the white rum while you wait, or be prepared to miss the bus.

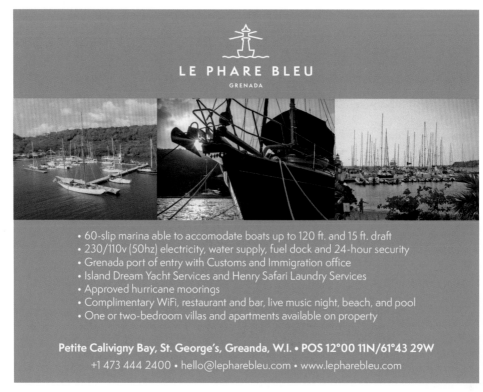

PHARE BLEU BAY

East of Calivigny Island, between Calivigny Island and Point Egmont, is a protected harbor, home to Le Phare Bleu Marina and Boutique Hotel. Dieter Burkhalter and Jana Caniga, the owners, have built a delightful marina and cottage hotel, which has some excellent supporting services.

Entry is down a buoyed channel through the reefs. You have to enter between the shoals that extend south from Adam Island and the shoals that extend east from Calivigny Island. To stay out of trouble, go right up to the outer yellow buoy and follow the markers in from there, red right returning. A couple of boats have tried to cut the corner into the channel and gone aground.

In the channel, there is at least 35 feet of water on your way in. If you are not going into the marina, the best anchorage is in Calivigny Island, a short dinghy ride away.

Petit Calivigny Yacht Club hosts match racing about four times a year at Le Phare Bleu. They supply the boats and anyone can join in. Le Phare Bleu dinghy concerts have become immensely popular with cruisers, who attend in the hundreds. They run about five a year from a barge in the bay. The concert lasts about an hour and is in the late afternoon. The band is on the barge (as is a bar), and dinghies gather all around. Usually Le Phare Bleu has a barbecue afterwards.

Le Phare Bleu also helps organize the Pure Grenada Music Festival, an excellent music festival in the spring.

Regulations

Le Phare Bleu is a port of clearance. Customs are open from 0800-1600 on weekends, and 0900 - 1400 on weekends and public holidays.

General yacht services

Le Phare Bleu is a 60-berth marina (for yachts up to 130 feet), using mainly heavy floating docks. Water and electricity (110/220-volt, 50-cycle), gasoline, and diesel are available. Henry's Safari has a laundry ashore and fills gas bottles (open 0900-1600). WiFi is free to customers and has recently been upgraded (ask for the password). Le Phare Bleu has a good tug, which can help out for rescue and recovery. The marina recycles cans, juice boxes, plastic bottles, and cardboard; please separate. They also have oil disposal.

Restaurants

Le Phare Bleu's The Deck Restaurant ($$$), is in a big high-roofed building open to the breeze. You sit almost on the beach. The pool and lounging area make it a great hangout, they offer a wide-ranging menu, and the food is good. Happy hour is 1700-1830 nightly, a favorite being a six-pack of Carib on ice for $24.50 EC.

The Lightship ($$) is in a lovely, old Swedish lightship alongside the dock. It is a wonderful, casual space with nautical museum overtones (ask to see the engine, built in 1925, which may be one of the oldest boat engines still in active use). They open Wednesday to Friday from 1700 for live music that starts at 2030. They offer tasty bar food: pizzas, burgers, and salads, plus a big beer and wine selection to wash it down.

Ashore

Le Phare Bleu provides a free shopping bus from the marina to various grocery stores and back Friday mornings at 0900, and other days by request. Marina reception can organize car rentals, and Gary Adams, a chiropractor, sailor, and good blues musician (aka Doc Adams), has an office here.

PORT EGMONT

Port Egmont is a completely enclosed lagoon, surrounded for the most part by mangroves. It is quite pretty and makes a first-class hurricane hole. Enter the outer inlet fairly close to Fort Jeudy, keeping an eye out for the reefs that lie near the shore. Fort Jeudy is developed, and there are several prosperous-looking houses on the hill. Anchor anywhere in the inner harbor. Or you can anchor outside, off the little beach at the inner end of

Fort Jeudy, but keep an eye out for the shoal off the northern end of the inlet.

The southwest shore of Port Egmont, from the inner harbor all the way out to Point Egmont, is currently being developed. The inner harbor is Grenada's best hurricane hole. The main people behind this development, Andrew Bierzynski and Geoffrey Thompson, are both local, and, as developers go, have concern for the environment. They have done a magnificent job to this point, with a new bridge over the mangroves and well-laid-out roads that afford lovely views of the bay. If you sail in and fall in love with the place and want to build, contact Renwick and Thompson.

CALIVIGNY HARBOUR

Calivigny Harbour, sometimes called Old Harbour (not to be confused with Calivigny Island), is another enclosed harbor with a fine, palm-shaded beach. It makes an acceptable hurricane hole, though heavy rains can create currents that cause boats to lie sideways to the wind from time to time. The entrance to the outer harbor is between Fort Jeudy and Westerhall Point. You must have good enough visibility to see the reefs off Fort Jeudy. The shoals coming out from Westerhall Point are deeper and harder to see, though they often cause breaking seas. Stay with the devil you can see. Find the reef off Fort Jeudy and follow it into the outer harbor. This entrance can be hairy in heavy winds and large swells, and I would only recommend it to sailors with a lot of experience in reef navigation. When passing into the inner harbor, favor the Fort Jeudy side, as a shoal extends out from the sand spit. Anchor anywhere in the inner harbor. In the deepest recesses of the bay, Mangrove Hide-Away was once a charming little bar and restaurant, but after some legal troubles, is now defunct.

Aubrey's is a bar/restaurant/shop right at the entrance to Westerhall Estate, where you can catch a bus to town. If you turn right at the main road and walk a while, you come to the Coop Supermarket. See also *Petit Bacaye*, which is a fair walk away.

WESTERHALL POINT

Westerhall Point is an attractive housing development, with well-tended grounds, easily seen by walking up from Calivigny Harbour. Westerhall Bay is a protected anchorage if you tuck up in the southeast corner of the bay, behind the mangroves. In rough conditions the entrance is tricky and the exit heads straight into wind and sea. I would suggest anchoring in Calivigny Harbour and walking over to take a look before you attempt this.

Theresa has some nice, very reasonably priced apartments overlooking Westerhall Bay, good for those in Phare Bleu or anywhere on the south coast. Call 443-5779.

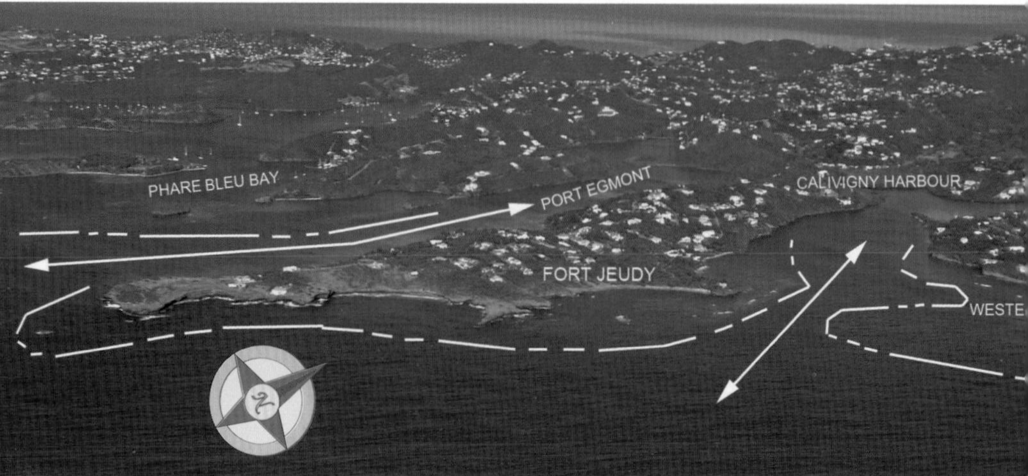

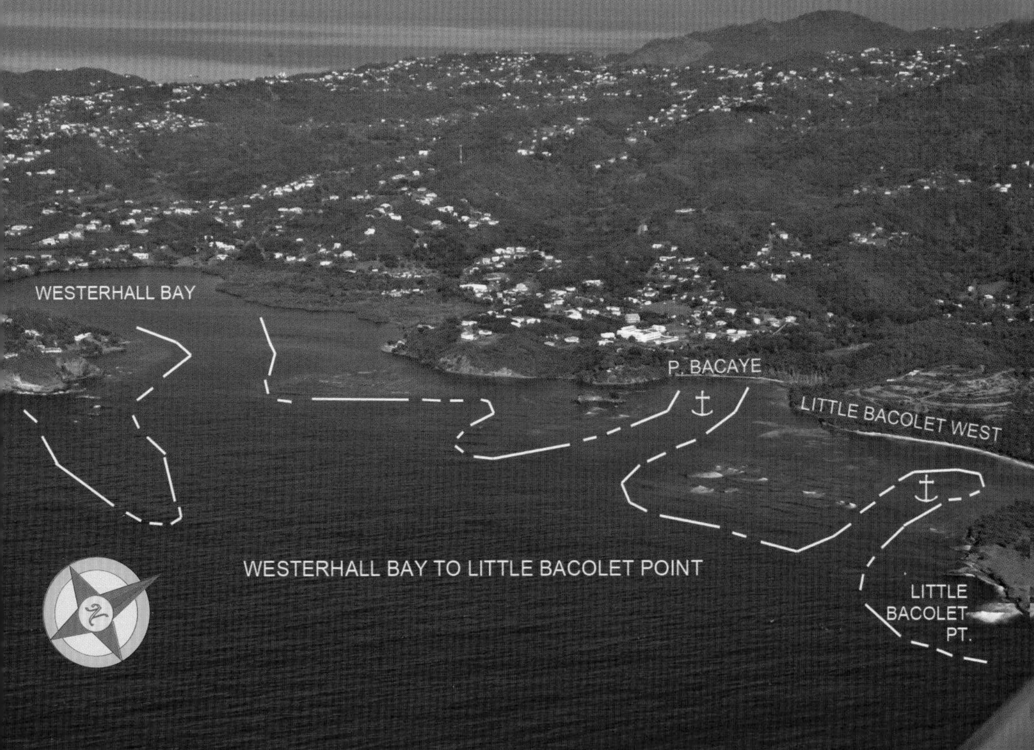

PETIT BACAYE

Petit Bacaye and Little Bacolet West are two nice little anchorages, so small that four boats in either would be a crowd. Space in both is limited enough that I recommend dropping the main before you enter. Petit Bacaye is an idyllic little bay, full of flowers and palm trees, with a little island you can swim to. It has a micro-hotel of the same name [$$, often closed], with a few thatch-roofed rooms, a small bar and restaurant, and a tree top platform in the lovely gardens. If it opens it does so from 1100 to 1800 for lunch and snacks. Take a book, swim, and laze away a day. Entering is strictly eyeball navigation. A visible rock on the western reef helps.

The entrance to Little Bacolet West is narrow: follow Little Bacolet Point and stay just outside the fringing reef. Development has just begun here. This is generally a calm hideaway.

ST. DAVID'S HARBOUR

St. David's Harbour lies 1.2 miles east of Westerhall Point. Many years ago, sailing ships would sail in here to load up on spices and produce bound for Europe. Although never the site of a town, it was an important harbor. It is deeply indented enough to be well protected, and the reefs at the entrance reduce the swells when the trades turn south of east. It can rock a little, in which case a stern anchor to face you out of the bay is a good fix. Wind and current can switch around, so leave far more room between anchored boats than you normally would. St. David's Harbour is a lovely bay with a narrow sandy beach, palm trees, and jungly vegetation crowding down to the waterfront. A pleasant breeze keeps things cool.

Grenada Marine is a haul-out operation for those who want the pleasingly rural atmosphere of Grenada. It is the kind of yard where you can swim right off the beach after work. Owners Jason and Laura Fletcher have 10 acres at the head of the bay and can take up to 250 boats.

The entrance is easy if you approach in good light, provided you have correctly identified the bay. The reef dividing St. David's from Little Bacolet is much harder to see than the one off St. David's Point, so favor the St.

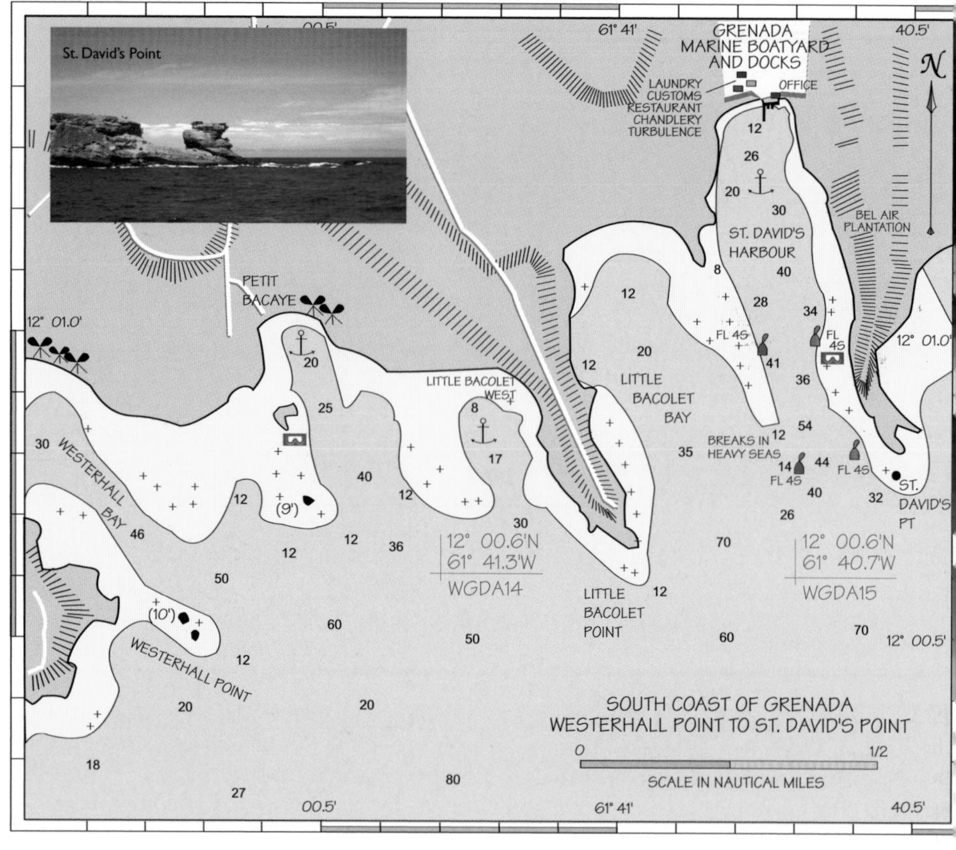

David's Point side of the channel, staying in deep water. Part of the channel is buoyed with red and green markers. They flash about every four seconds. St. David's is well situated if you come down the east coast of Grenada, and it is an easy downwind sail from here to the other south-coast anchorages.

Regulations

St. David's Harbour is a port of entry, with customs and immigration. Customs is there every Monday to Thursday from 0800 to 1600. Immigration will come by appointment anytime during the week.

Communications

Grenada Marine has free WiFi; ask for a voucher at the office or bar.

General yacht services

Grenada Marine [VHF: 16] is a work and storage yard with room for 250 boats. They use a 70-ton Travelift, which is specially designed at 31.5 feet wide to haul catamarans as well as monohulls. Yachts of up to 16-foot draft can be hauled. After hauling, a hydraulic stacking trailer puts yachts close together. Diesel and water are available on the outside of the hauling pier. A 300-foot work dock comes out into the bay, dockage is available, and they offer moorings in the bay.

The office staff is helpful and will make your hauling arrangements, put you at ease, find you a rental car, or help with sending a fax or making a phone call. You can do your own work or use the yard, but cannot hire outside workers. You can do your own laundry in the machines on-site or send it out to be done with Henry's Safari Tours. He will also fill your cooking gas bottles.

Chandlery

Island Water World has a branch of their chandlery here. If you don't find what you're looking for here, ask, as it may be in stock in their larger branch in St. George's. The van from their St. George's location makes deliveries on Monday, Wednesday, and Friday, and you can sometimes catch a ride into town with them. Ask in the store for details.

Technical yacht services

The yard has about 90 employees including technicians that work in fiberglass, spray Awlgrip, and re-gelcoat finishes. They can apply airless-spray antifouling and have metal, woodwork, and fiberglass departments. They have an office in Port Louis and can do some in-the-water installation or work there.

Rigging and sailmaking are run jointly with Turbulence and managed by Louis (rigging) and Martin (sails). They can check out your rig while you go away and do any kind of rigging repair, including a whole new rig. (They share a rod-rigging machine with their larger shop in True Blue.) The sail department does sail construction, repair, and canvas work.

Grenada Marine are agents for Yanmar, Perkins, Volvo, Northern Lights, and ZF drives, along with some watermakers. You can buy these systems though them. They are also agents for Raymarine. Owners and their crew are welcome to do simple jobs like antifouling, brush painting, and removing shafts and underwater systems.

Ashore

Laura's at Grenada Marine [$$] is a restaurant and hangout for technicians, crew, and owners. It is inexpensive, cheerful, and right on the waterfront. They do tasty and hearty food, serve lunch and dinner daily, and are open 0800-2100. They sometimes have live music.

Just a bay to the east is La Sagesse Hotel and Restaurant, a 12-room hotel owned by Mike and Nancy Meranski. It is set in lovely gardens on a gorgeous bay, with one of the longest and broadest palm-backed beaches in Grenada. The handsome main building was put up by the infamous Lord Peregrine Brownlow, who closed beach access to locals, which resulted in a "people's reopening" sponsored by revolutionary leader Maurice Bishop.

The garden, beach, and peace make La Sagesse a perfect antidote to boat work. The room prices are reasonable, especially in the off-season, and, if things are quiet, they offer yachtspeople a 30 percent discount. Lots of cruisers take advantage of it, in part because Mike and Nancy offer a generous free transport service between La Sagesse and Grenada Marine. If you are staying, they will run you over and back whenever you want, and if you are not staying they will happily collect you and bring you over for lunch or dinner.

Their beachfront restaurant is open all day from 0800 till 2100, with informal lunches and romantic fine dining at night. They use fresh ingredients and offer some of Grenada's best seafood. From January until May they do a beach barbecue with live music every Sunday from 1300 until 1600. This is a great escape from the boatyard work. If you have time, you can walk over the hill for lunch.

SOG Foods is on the main road just before the turn off to Fort Jeudy. It is a large, modern grocery store, and they will deliver to Grenada Marine. They open from 0700 until 2300 every day.

When you get tired of work and want a little trip to the country, consider visiting the Laura Herb and Spice Garden, which is a few miles down the road. It is part of an

herb and spice marketing cooperative that sells Grenadian herbs and spices worldwide. They have about eight acres under cultivation in the garden, with well-laid-out trails and sign posted plants. The atmosphere is peaceful, with birds singing in the trees and plenty of shady areas. You pay a $5 EC entry fee and if you ask (you should), they will give you a tour of the garden and explain the plants to you.

GRENVILLE

Grenville is Grenada's second largest town and is well away from the tourist areas. Most basic services are easily found, grocery stores are well stocked, and restaurants serve up hefty portions of local fare. It lies on the east coast of Grenada, a good harbor for skilled reef navigators who want to go somewhere really local. It is not for charterers on a one-week vacation. It is a port of clearance.

Navigation

Grenville is a harbor protected by reefs with wind and sea pushing you in. It is an entrance where you can really get in trouble, should something go wrong. If you are coming from the north you can pass inside or outside of Telescope Rock.

Approach only in the morning with the sun behind. The entrance is a narrow passage between two reefs that are shallow enough to get you in trouble, but deep enough you cannot easily see them. If the buoys are in place it is simple, but they are sometimes missing. Leaving Grenville is best in the afternoon with the sun behind.

The alignment of the church over the buildings below can be helpful; the photo on was taken at the outer entrance. You see the road coming down in front of the church. The channel is over 30 feet deep and the reefs at the entrance are 8-14 feet, breaking in heavy weather. A shallow reef patch lies on the north side, just inside.

Once in the channel, the shallow water is more visible and you should be able to spot

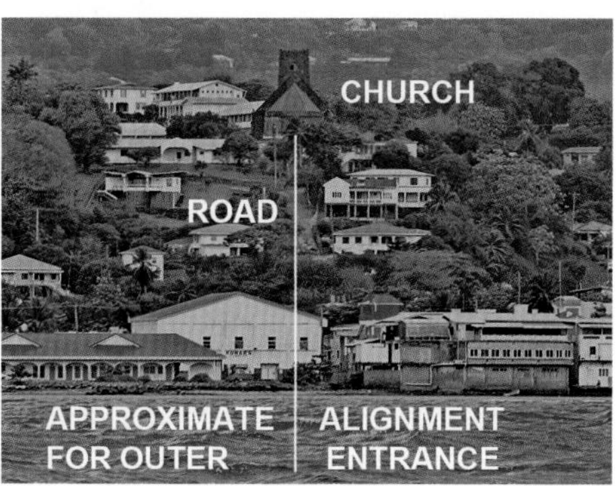

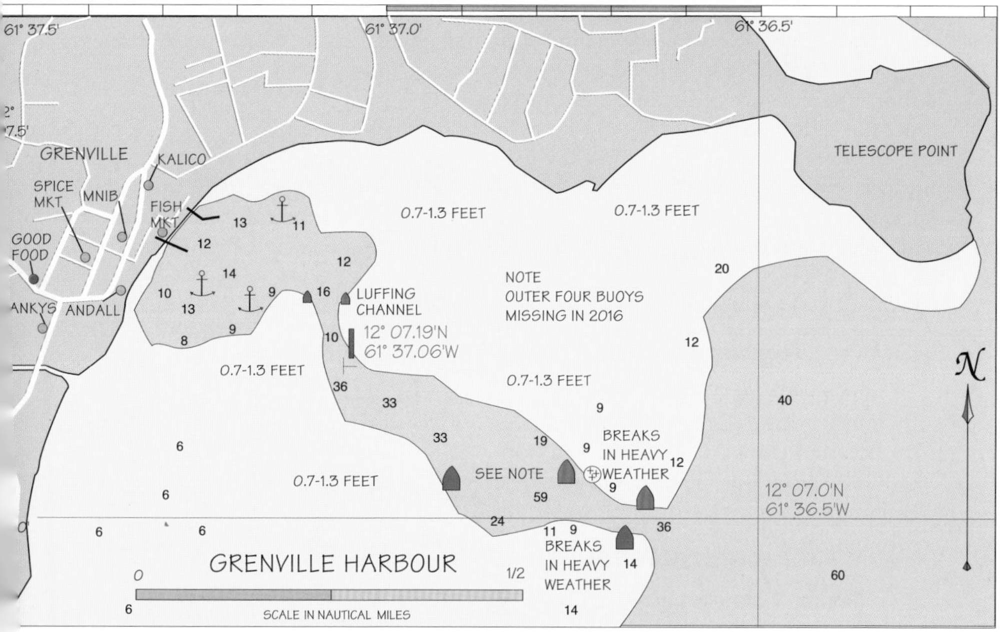

CHURCH
ROAD
APPROXIMATE ALIGNMENT
FOR OUTER ENTRANCE

61° 37.5'
61° 37.0'
61° 36.5'
GRENVILLE
KALICO
SPICE MKT
MNIB
FISH MKT
GOOD FOOD
ANKYS
ANDALL
TELESCOPE POINT
0.7-1.3 FEET
LUFFING CHANNEL
12° 07.19'N
61° 37.06'W
NOTE
OUTER FOUR BUOYS
MISSING IN 2016
SEE NOTE
BREAKS IN HEAVY WEATHER
12° 07.0'N
61° 36.5'W
GRENVILLE HARBOUR
0
1/2
SCALE IN NAUTICAL MILES

Church in Grenville

the rather nondescript beacon well ahead that marks the beginning of the luffing channel. The beacon is on the shoal, not in deep water. Round it turning to starboard. You should be able to eyeball the shallows here, but with luck the inner buoys will be in place. Both are red, but one has a green top. Pass between them and anchor in the basin, leaving plenty of room for any vessels using the main docks.

Boats of yore sailed in and out of this harbor (a few sloops still do), so it can be done, but I don't advise it till you know it well. There is no dinghy dock, and the fishing dock is busy, though fine for a drop off or quick stop. If you want to lock up and leave your dinghy, beaching it north of the fishing dock and locking it to whatever is convenient would be a good option.

Regulations

Grenville is a port of entry, with customs and immigration. Find the offices across from The Marketing Board. They open from 0800 - 1600 Monday to Friday, and generally close over lunch.

Communications

Computer Visioneers is air conditioned and offers sit-down internet access, printing, faxing, and scanning. Find them on the second story of the Grenlec building, on the street north of the Spice Market. The FedEx office is in L.L. Rhamdanny & Co, next to Good Food. Most bars and restaurants provide free WiFi for patrons. For electronics or computer parts and repairs visit Hanky's in the small mall at the south end of town.

Provisioning

There are a few fair-sized grocery stores in town. Kalico, at the north end, just before the main roads merge, carries a good selection of groceries, toiletries, some hardware, and appliances. They are open from 0800-2000 Monday-Thursday, until 2100 on Friday and Saturday, and until 1300 on Sundays. If you are doing early-morning provisioning, Andall's, at the opposite end of town, carries similar stock and opens at 0700 daily. Besides street-side vendors, fresh produce and spices can be found in the main building of the Spice & Craft Market in the middle of town. The Marketing Board (MNIB) sells produce, both local and imported, liquor, and frozen meats and fish. The counter at the back provides baked goods and ready-made breakfast and lunch. They open 0730-1900 Monday to Saturday, and Sundays from 0900-1300. Across from MNIB is the meat market. Visit the fish market vendors every day from 0800 until 1700; 1800 on Fridays and Saturdays. For tools and hardware, check L.L. Rhamdanny & Co.

Restaurants

You will find many local bars and restaurants along the town's main roads. Food is generally simple and inexpensive, and meals often include fish or chicken, rice, peas, and provisions (root vegetables).

Moore's is a sweet little sit down open-air bar and restaurant above Kalico groceries. Owner Claudist serves made-to-order breakfast, lunch, and dinner every day from 0700. The breakfast menu includes sandwiches, wraps, and a local favorite, salt fish and bakes. Lunch and dinner include more of a variety, from pizza to barbecue chicken, rice, pasta, and salad. The Melting Pot, above Andall's, at the opposite end of town, serves up hefty portions of ready-made local fare in addition to baked goods and local juices. They are open from 0800 every day but Sunday.

Ashore

Mt. Carmel falls is a worthwhile nearby attraction. Take a bus heading south to Munich and ask to get off at the Mt. Carmel falls (a 10-minute ride). From the main road, the trail entrance is under the green Mt. Carmel sign and down the concrete steps. This is private land, and you may be asked to pay a small fee. An easy 15-minute hike brings you to a delightful series of pools and falls, great for an afternoon picnic or refreshing swim.

Once at the river, the path splits at a patch of bamboo, where you keep left to get to an impressively vertical wall face of rushing water. Return to the bamboo, cross the river, turn right and follow the path for another few minutes. You will come to a pool beneath a cascading slope, great for swimming and sitting under the falls for a vigorous all-natural back and shoulder massage.

SAUTEURS

Like Grenville, Sauteurs is a historic, rural town. Situated at the very northern tip of Grenada, it seldom sees tourists other than those visiting nearby attractions. The recent addition of a breakwater, intended to protect the beachfront businesses and main street from erosion, has created a lagoon big enough for several yachts. The people of Sauteurs are warm and welcoming, and local businesses are excited to be able to host visiting yachtspeople. The area is largely uncharted, so use caution, but a number of nearby historical and ecological attractions make it a worthwhile stop

Sauteurs jetty

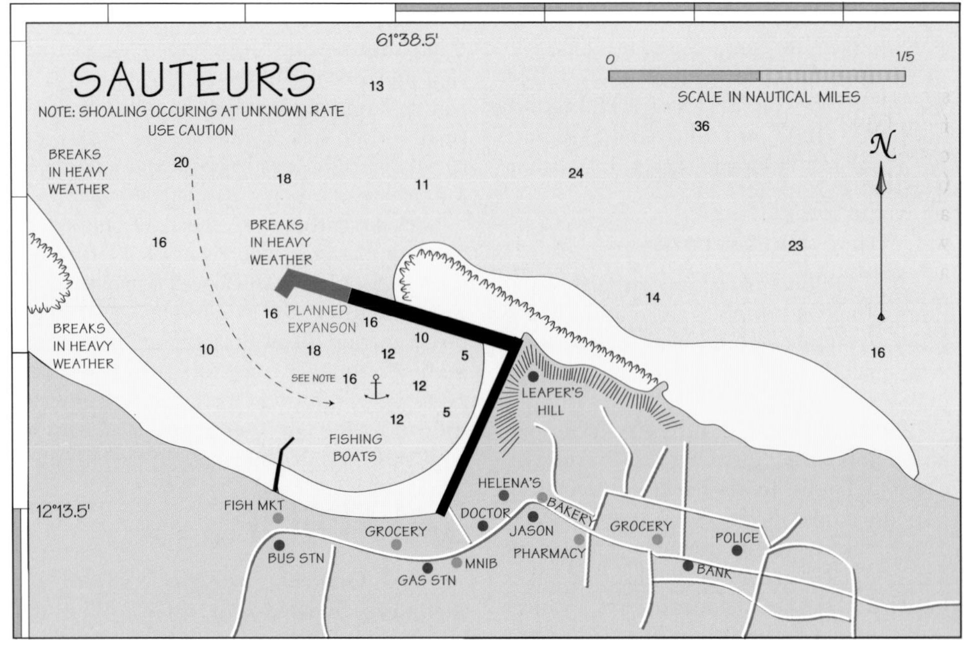

for experienced sailors. The Sauteurs harbor provides a convenient jumping off point for exploring the north of the island, or a stop-over on your way north to Carriacou.

Navigation

Sauteurs has a consistently strong on-shore wind and swell, is only advisable in good weather, and best when you can clearly see the reefs on either side of the entrance. One lies along the shoreline to the west, the other is directly outside and along the breakwater. Both should be easy to avoid. At the time of this writing, heavy seas were causing waves to beak at the end of the unfinished breakwater, although the completed structure should remedy this. There are not yet any channel markers, and although the lagoon was recently dredged to 15 feet, shoaling is still occurring at an unknown rate - use caution. Developers assure that the bottom is all sand, and we found this to be true when we visited. Since the construction of the breakwater, the eastern end of the beach has widened considerably. This may change with continued construction and dredging.

Local fishing boats moor and anchor within the lagoon. Give them plenty of room and be watchful of their moorings, as some are small and hard to see.

Pull your dinghy up on the beach.

Local house

Services

Jason Electrical specializes in appliance repairs and may be able to help with other problems. Find him in the restaurant at the top of the hill. If you have engine problems, he can point you in the right direction.

There are two ATMs, both on the top side of town, as are several pharmacies. New Life Medical Center is on the hill, does blood testing, and has doctors available.

Restaurants & Provisioning

A number of large, well-stocked grocery stores lie along the main road, generally open from 0800 to 1800, with reduced hours or closed on Sunday. The Marketing Board (MNIB) has a large outlet here, almost directly across the street from the base of the breakwater. They have the best selection of fruit and vegetables. For fresh fish, check the fish market at the end of the fishing dock. Availability is erratic and the best time to check is in the morning.

The main road is dotted with rum shops and small restaurants, most selling local dishes for very reasonable prices. Helena's, almost at the top of the hill, is popular and has a few tables on a small balcony overlooking the harbor.

For a great country meal while here or on a day tour, visit Petite Anse [$$$], which has a delightful location, hanging over its own beach, a five-minute drive west of Sauteurs. Phillip and Annie Clift built this boutique hotel after crossing the Atlantic on the ARC and chartering for some years. You can swim in the pool and walk in the beautiful garden, heading down past cottages tucked amid flowers and trees to the beach.

They serve fruits and vegetables from their own garden, fish and lobster from local fishermen, and much of their meat is from local farmers. The restaurant, with its wide ranging menu, is popular with both locals and visitors. They offer yachts their local rate for a weekend escape.

Ashore

Leaper's Hill overlooks the harbor to the west and is one of the island's most popular historic sites. After continuing conflict between French colonists and the indigenous Caribs throughout the early 1600's, the Carib population had been decimated by the French's superior weaponry. The last remaining Caribs sensed a losing battle, and rather than be captured and killed by the French, jumped to their deaths in 1651. To get to the site of this sad occurrence, turn left on the main road from the breakwater and follow the signs up from the top of the hill.

Busses run from 0600 until 2000 and will take you west (the #5) all the way to St. George's, or east (the #9) along two routs - to Hermitage, where you can visit Belmont Estate, or to River Salee, where you can request to be dropped at Levera or Bathway beach for an additional charge. Catch them at the bus terminal at the western end of the main road.

Levera National Park, where leatherback turtles nest between March and August (book a tour in advance 442-2721), is a 1.5-hour walk, or short bus ride away. From here you can hike up to Welcome Rock for a spectacular view of Sugarloaf and the surrounding islands.

The Sulphur Springs, Hermitage waterfalls (a 40-minute hike), River Antoine Rum Factory, Lake Antoine, and Belmont Estate are all worthwhile and a short taxi ride away. Helena, at Helena's Restaurant, can arrange one for you.

If calling a Martinique regular phone from a foreign country dial + 596 596 + 6 digits
If calling a Martinique mobile phone from a foreign country dial + 596 696 + 6 digits

MARTINIQUE EMERGENCY

Ambulance, (0596) 75 15 75

Cosma (Lifeboat) (0596) 70 92 92 VHF: 16

Dr Monique Roussi, Marin (0596) 58 90 16, mroiussi@wanadoo.fr

Dr Deloge, Marin (0596) 74 98 24

Nurse Stephanie Eustache, (0696) 68 39 58/(0696) 27 94 75

Hospital, (0596) 50 15 15

Medical emergency (emergency doctors), (0596) 63 33 33/60 60 44

Police Emergency, **17**

Police headquarters, (0596) 63 00 00

Pompiers (fire department) **18**

MARTINIQUE AIRLINES

Air France, (0820) 820 820, (0596) 55 33 00/33, (0596) 55 33 08

Air Caraibes, (0820) 835 835

Air Canada, (0825) 880 881

American Airlines, (0596) 42 19 19

LIAT, (0596) 42 21 11

MARTINIQUE CHANDLERY FISHING GEAR

Accastiallage Diffusion, 0596) 74 62 12

Akwaba, (0596) 66 67 88, akwaba972@ orange.fr, fishing gear

Caraibes Marine, (0596) 74 80 33, 98, (0696) 27 66 05 contact@caraibes-greement.fr

Carene Shop, (0596) 74 74 80, carene.shop @wanadoo.fr

Clippers Ship, (0596) 71 41 61, clippers-ship@ wanadoo.fr

Coopemar, (0596) 73 37 54, coopemar @ sasi.fr

Intersport, (0596) 63 39 89

Le Grenier du Marin Marin, (0596) 67 98 50, legrenierdumarin@ gmail.com

Le Ship, (0596) 74 87 55, le-ship-martinique@ wanadoo.fr

Littoral, (0596) 70 28 70,

Maxipeche, (0596) 73 37 54,

Polymar, (0596) 70 62 88, polymar@ orange. fr, Baie de Tourelles,

Sea Services, (0596) 70 26 69, seaservices972@orange.fr

W.I.N.D, (0596) 68 21 28, wind@wind-flag. com

MARTINIQUE COMMUNICATIONS

Cyber Base, Customs computer, Les Anses D'Arlet, 0596-68-64-82

Cyber Deli, (0596) 78 71 43

Cyber Base, St. Pierre, (0596) 62-52-31

Marin Yacht Harbour, Blvd Allegre, Le Marin, 97290, Martinique, (0596) 74 83 83, VHF: 09

MARTINIQUE GENERAL YACHT SERVICES

A&C Yacht brokers, (0596) 74 94 02, 0696 73 70 27, acybmichel @wanadoo.fr

Antilles Nautism, (0696) 43 70 11, Power boat brokers

Blanc Marine Marin, 0696 82 65 63, blanc-marine1@gmail.com, laundry

Carbbean Yachts (0596) 74 16 70/ (0696) 23 43 38, stephanie.dupland@ caribbean-yachts.com, brokers

CarenAntilles, Fort de France, (0596) 63 76 74, VHF: 16, carenfdf @wanadoo.fr, haul-out

CarenAntilles, Marin, (0596) 74 77 70, VHF: 73, M. De Lucy (0696) 55 77 03, carenantilles.marin@wanadoo. fr, haul out

DCML, Quai de Tourelles, (0596) 71 74 64, (0696) 44 11 47, dcml.sarl@wanadoo. fr, fuel

Dock Cleaner Ecologique, (0696)-92 62 47, dry dock

DYT Yacht Transport, (0596)-74-15-07, 0696 22 88 13 nadine@ yacht-transport.com

Douglas Yacht Services, (0696) 45 89 75, (0596) 52 14 28, VHF: 09, douglas@yachtservices.fr, super-yacht agent

Eva Yachting, (0696) 29 71 14, evayachting@orange.fr, brokers

Kay Zaza, Grand Anse D'Arlet, (0596) 68 74 22, kayzaza972@ yahoo.fr, laundry

Marin Marina, (0596) 74 83 83, VHF: 09, port.marin@wanadoo. fr

Martinique Dry Dock, (0596) 72 69 40/72 67 48

Surveyor, (Jacques Scharwatt, (0596) 74 02 14, emcscharwatt @wandoo.fr

Somatras Marina, (0596) 66 07 74, VHF: 09, marina3ilets@wanadoo.fr, Anse Mitan, marina

Z'Abricots Marina, (0596) 75 11 57, portduplaisancezab@ cacem.mq.com

MARTINIQUE MISCELLANEOUS

Centre de Decouverte des Sciences de la Terre, (0596) 52 82 42, cdst@cg972.fr

Eau de Tiare, (0696) 37 47 50, (0596) 74 33 57

Distillerie Depaz, (0596) 78 13 14**Fedex**, (0596) 42 41 00

Martinique Yachting Association, (0596) 45 89 75, contact@ martiniqueyachtingassociation.fr

Pre Colombian Museum, (0596) 71 57 05

Tourist Department, (0596)-60-27-73

Zoo Martinique, 0596 52 76 08, info@ zoomartinique.com

MARTINIQUE SAILMAKERS CANVAS CUSHIONS

Manu Voiles, (0596) 63 10 61, (0696) 90 76 33, manuvoiles@ wanadoo.fr

North Sails (Sud Voilerie), (0596) 58 24 69/ (0690) 67 89 98, gavin.dove@north-sails.com

Martinik Voilerie, (0696) 32-70-99, martinikvoilerie@gmail. com wanadoo.fr

Incidences, Marin, (0596) 74 77 47, VHF: 16, incidences.caraibes@wanadoo.fr

Sellerie Marine, (0696) 16 92 35, contact@sellerie-marinej.com

Voilerie du Marin, (0696) 25 94 01, dan.karner@wanadoo.fr

MARTINIQUE TECHNICAL YACHT SERVICES

Alize Composites, glass, gelcoat, paint specialist, (0696)-00-12-34/07 30 75, clippers-ship@wanadoo.fr

Altec Marine, (0696) 28 44 78 machine shop

Antilles Greement, (0696) 50 97 07/29 16 64, antilles-greement@ hotmail.fr

Atelier Sylvestre, (0596) 50 58 91/45 45 56, hydraulics

Azur Spirit, (0696) 50-96-44, Jimy.bouvrais@azur-spirit.com, Boat sales, charters, repair and guardianage

Caraibes Greement, (0596) 74 80 33, cgmar@wanadoo.fr, rigging, electircs

Caraibes Menuiserie (0596) 74 80 33, contact@caraibes-menuiserie.fr

Chalmessin, (0596) 60 03 75/60 03 79, welding & fabrication cooking stoves

Continental Marine, (0696) 29-51-11, Yamaha agent

Debrouilla Marine, (0696) 45 92 20, marine electrics

Diginav, (0596) 74 76 62, diginav@wanadoo.fr, electronics

EM Composites., (0596) 62 91 95, (0696) 23 24 57, glass work and painting

Equniox, (0696) 41-33-33, equinoxalu@gmail.com, welding fabrication.

Caraibes Refrigeration, (0696) 82 24 04, patrice@caraibes-refrigeration.com, refrigeration, aironditioning

Inboard Diesel, (0596) 78 71 96, (0696) 45 95 93, Marin: (0696) 37 35 81 frank@inboarddiesel.com, info@inboarddiesel.com mechanics

Infologeek, (0596) 67 30 53, 0696 71 79 77, contact@infologeek.com

La Survy, (0596) 74 63 63, (0696) 43 07 53, la.survy@wanadoo.fr, inflatables

Madiana Diesel, (0596) 51 16 13, injector pumps & injectors

Maxi Marine, (0596) 63 75 49, Marin (0596) 74 62 12, info@maximarinefwi.com, Mercury, Nani

Mecanique Plaisance, (0596) 74 68 74, Workshop, (0596) 74 72 72, pc.mecaplai @wanadoo.fr, mechanics

Meca Boats, Marin, (0696) 03 74 41, vanille-st@hotmail.com, inboard/outboard repair

Moderne Marine, (0696) 82 40 72, Mercruiser engines

Multi Interventions, (0696) 40 21 94 Electrics, guardianage.

Nautic Froid, (0696) 22 71 13, nauticfroid97290@hotmail.com

Nautic Services, (0696) 45 61 60, nautic.services@hotmail.fr Marin, sandblasting & antifouling

Pochon, (0596) 38-33-45 (0696) 13 91 22, martinique @pochon.com.fr

Propeller Caraibe Services (0596) 63 13 64/(0696) 34 64 10, prop.car.serv@gmail.com

Proto Meca, (0696) 26 09 26, protomeca@hotmail.fr, metal fabrication

Industry Caraibes Services, (0696) 44 45 76, jsolinga@outlook.fr (props and shafts)

Renovboat, (0596) 57 79 28, (0696) 25 01 92, renovboatfwi@gmail.com fiberglass and painting, electrics.

RM Service, (0696) 72 25 44, repairs, maintenance, remservicesnautique@live.fr.

Sarl A2M, (0696) 70 66 25, (0596) 53 74 85, 2m972@orange.fr, metal fabrication

Sea Services, (0596) 70 26 69, rigging

SAV, (0596) 60 03 58, (0696) 25 03 76, domifere@wanadoo.fr, (Johnson and Evinrude)

SMS, (0596) 71 09 31/ (0696) 22 48 70, pleinsud972@wanadoo.fr, boat signs

Tilikum, (0696) 22 79 89/ (0596) 74 67 03, VHF: 16 tilikum@wanadoo.fr,

Tony Crater, (0596) 74 66 60, welding and fabrication

Tony Boats, (0696) 26 55 65 outboards

Yes, (0596) 65 05 24, (0696) 45 29 87, yescaraibes@hotmail.com, electrical

MARTINIQUE TRANSPORT

GD location, (0596) 58 27 89, (0696) 30 09 90, gd location@orange.fr

Madin-Loc,(0596) 74 05 54, madin-loc @ wanadoo.fr

St. Pierre Location, (0596) 78 25 84, (0696) 37 41 71 Saintpierre@saintpierrelocations.com

Jumbo Car, (0596)-74-71 77, (0696) 90 10 67

Velo Club Aosa Cap 110 (0696) 25 34 18, JVLH@orange.f

Vincent Thomas (0696) 07 54 37, taxi. norden.vincent@gmail.com. English speaking, good taxi

Watt Up, (0596) 74 56 51. communication@wattup.fr

MARTINIQUE PROVISIONING

Appro Zagaya, (0596) 74 39 75, (0696) 07 16 29, cathy@appro-zagaya.fr

Champion at Centre Annette, (0596) 74 85 85

Eden Bio, (0596) 74 77 77, biomarine.972@orange.fr

Le Millesime, (0596) 38-74-12/0696 26 33 65, cavemillesime@orange.fr

Port-Apporte, (0696) 25 82 94, contact@port-apporte.fr

Simply (0596) 59 17 13

Vatier, (0596) 70 11 39, impex.vatier@wanadoo.fr

MARTINIQUE FUN SHOPPING

Levalois Racing, (0596) 73 11 96,

Ozar, (0596) 38 44 07, (0696) 29 80 99

Sea Services, (0596) 70 26 69, fine casual clothing including *Saint James*

MARTINIQUE BANKING

Change Caraibes, (0596) 60 28 40/73 06 16

Martinique Change, (0596) 66 04 44

MARTINIQUE RESTAURANTS

Antonio Beach,(0596) 78 17 36,

Aux Poisson D'Or, (0596) 66 01 80,

Bleu des Iles, (0596) 71 73 27, (0696) 30 72 31,

Beach Grill, (0596) 78 34 02

Bistrot des Flmandes, (0596) 50 22 22,

Bolibar, (0596) 50 22 22,

Cercle de Saint Pierre, (0596) 97 59 30,

Fuji Sushi, (0596) 37 99 95

L'Alsace a Kay, (0596) 67 53 65, (0696) 77 68 67, phm. glaciere@hotmail.fr

L'Escale, (0596) 71 52 77. , jonathan.courjon@gmail.com

La Baie, (0596) 42 20 38

La Pause (0596) 52 41 17,

La Table de Marcel, (0596) 67 30 30,

Le Littoral, (0596) 71 58 98/0696-44-20-61,

Le Mayday, (0596) 78 75 24, (0696) 34 50 95,

Le Petibonum, (0596) 78 04 34

Le Reservoir, (0696) 41 83 50/98 71 42

Bidjoul, (0596) 68 65 28,

Copacabana, (0596) 66 08 92,

Delices Caraibes, (0596) 76-96-39, (0696) 81 97 29, delicescaraibes@yahoo.fr

Il Gallo Rosso, (0596) 38 79 57,

Kano, (0596) 78 40 33,

KokoaRum, (0596) 48-02-21

La Manureva, (0596) 66 16 45

l'Annexe (0596) 38-84-77

L'Escapade Marine, (0596)-69 64 26

Le Taj, (0596) 70 33 02,

La Dunnette (0596) 76 73 90,

Le Coco Neg (0596) 76 94 82, coco-neg@wanadoo.fr

Le Grand Bleu (0596) 30 18 03,

Le Mahot (0596) 65 24 38 evelyne.murat@orange.fr

Le Tamaya, (0596) 78 29 09,

Le Vieux Foyal, (0596) 77 05 49 (0696) 29 24 23

Lina's, (0596) 71 91 92,

Mango Bay, (0596) 74 60 89, , mangobay@wanadoo.fr

New Dragon de Chine, (0596),

Numero 20 (0596) 66-02-84, , numero20.martinique@Yohoo.fr

The Yellow, , (0596) 75 03 59. The-yellow@orange.fr

O Ble Noir (0596) 48 12 01,

Shell's, (0596) 66 37 91.

Snack Bar de la plage (0596) 78 80 07,

Ti Payot, (0596) 68 71 78.

Ti Toques, (0596) 74 72 32,

The Crew, (0596) 73 04 14,

MARTINIQUE CHARTER

Autremer Concept, (0596) 74 79 11/ (0696) 43 55 33 info@autremerconcept.com cats, cruisers, racers

Corail Caraibes, (0596) 74 10 76, corail.mart@wanadoo.fr, cat FP

Dream Yacht Caribbean, (0596) 74 81 68, martinique@dreamyachtcharter.com, cats and monos

France-Escales, (0696) 61 17 37, contact@escales-grenadines.com (charter by the cabin)

Punch Croisieres, (0696) 18 14 00, technique@punchroisieres.com, all charter

Regis Guillemot Charter, (0596) 74 78 59, (0696) 17 27 37, contact@regisguillemot.com, catamaran charter

Star Voyage, (0596) 74 70 92, lemarin@starvoyage.com, all kinds of charter

VPM, Port de Plaisance, Marin, 97290, Martinique, (0596) 74 70 10, martinique@vpmestsail.com, all kinds of charter

MARTINIQUE SCUBA DIVING

Alpha plongee, (0596) 48 30 34

Anthinea, (0596) 66 05 26

Case Pilote Diving Club, (0596) 78 73 75/61 60 01

Corail Club Caraibes, (0596) 68 36 36, (0696) 36 40 22 corailclub@ corailclub-caraibes.com

Deep Turtle, (0696) 29 29 11, contact@deepturtleplongee.fr

Espace plongee, (0696) 25 11 90, (0596) 66 01 79,

Immersion Caraibes, (0596) 53 15 43/(0696) 33 40 95, chrisreynier@gmail.com

Kalinargo, (0596) 76 92 98, kalinargo2@wanadoo.fr,

Lychee Plongee, (0596) 66 05 26,

Localize, (0596) 68 64 78, (0596) 68 68 88

Mada Plongee, (0696), 51 60 70, madaplongee@hotmail.fr

Marin Plongee, (0596), 74 05 31, (0696), 83 13 51, marinplongee@ wanadoo.fr

Natiyabel, (0596) 36 63 01

Nautica Antilles, (0596) 57 15 15, F: (0596) 51 85 56

Paradise Plongee, (0696) 34 56 16

Planete Bleue, (0596) 77 08 79, planbleu@ais.mq

Papa D'Lo, (0696) 50 13 68

ST. LUCIA

ST. LUCIA EMERGENCY OFFICIAL

Customs, Castries, (758) 458-4846, 24-hour; (758) 468-4859

Customs, Marigot, (758) 458-3318

Customs, Rodney Bay, (758) 452-0235

Customs, Soufriere, (758) 459-5656

Customs, Vieux Fort, (758) 468-4933/4

Dermmed Clinic, Dr Merlina Joseph, JQ Mal, (758) 452-7546

Mar Medical Center, (758) 453-2552/452-9032, drnega@memberclinic.com

Rodney Bay Medical Center, (758) 452-8621 docb@candw.lc, (multi services)

Tapion Hospital, (758) 459-2000 (multi services)

Kent Glace, (758) 458-0167, glaceassociates@gmail.com-com, dental surgeon

Police Marine, (758) 452-2595, VHF: 16

Marine Emergency, HELP (4357) VHF:16

ST. LUCIA AIRLINES

Air Caraibes, (758) 453-0357

Air Jamaica, (758) 453-6111, 800-538-2942

American Airlines, (758) 454-6777/6779,

American Eagle, (758) 452-1820/453-6019, **BWIA**, (758) 452-3778

LIAT, (758) 452-3051-3

Travel World, (758) 451-7443/453-7521, travelworldslu@hotmail.com, travel agent, car rental, tours

Virgin Atlantic (758) 434-7236

ST. LUCIA CHANDLERY FISHING GEAR

Johnsons Marine Hardware, (758) 452-0299, chandlery, fishing gear

International Inflatables, (758) 450-8622, 715-9671, info@internationalinflatablesltd.com

Island Water World, (758) 452-1222 IWWSLIAN@candwlc, major chanderly

ST. LUCIA COMMUNICATIONS

IGY Rodney Bay Marina, (758) 458-4892/7200

ST. LUCIA GENERAL YACHT SERVICES

Ben's Yacht Services, (758) 459-5457, VHF: 16, Cell: (758) 714-8217/484-0708/721-8500, saltibusb @slucia.com, bensyachtservices@hotmail.com, yacht agent

Cox Co, 758 285 8616, telliot@coxcoltd.com. All superyacht services

Fletcher's Vieux Fort Laundry. 758 454 5936; fletcherdrycleaning@live.com

Harmony Yacht Services, (758) 267-4261/518-0081/ 519-7416 VHF: 16, info@ harmonyyachtservices.com, yacht agent

Ian Dusauzay (Reliant Brokerage), (758) 484-3782/484-3782, rbsbroker@gmail.com

Capella Marigot Resort and Marina, (758) 451-4275/728-9948/9, contact.manager@marigotbaymarina.com, if that does not work: (contact.marinaslu@capellahotels.com)

Destination St. Lucia (758) 452-8531, ulrich@dsl-yachting.com, Yacht brokers

Kessel Marine, (758) 720-0100, kessellc@gmail.com, surveys

Kessel Lisa, (758) 484-0555, lisakessell@gmail.com Customs brokerage

IGY Rodney Bay Marina, (758) 458-7200/4892, VHF: 16, rbm@igymarinas.com

Sud's Laundry (758) 486-0718

St. Lucia Yacht Services (758) 452-5057, VHF: 16, fuel

The Moorings/Sunsail (758) 451-4014/4357/ 285-1270, Boat for sail ex charter.

Chateau Mygo has Marigot docks see *Restaurants*.

ST. LUCIA MISCELLANEOUS

Cocao St. Lucie, chocolate factory (758) 728-3131/459-4401, cocoasaintelucie@gmail.com

Face to Face Day Spa, (758) 452-0394/721-9250, facetofaceconsulting@gmail.com

Forestry Department, (758) 457-1427, forest hikes

National Trust, (758) 452-5005, E: natrust@candw.lc, hikes

Morne Courbaril, (758) 459- 7340/712-5808

Soufriere Marine Management Assn., (758) 459- 5500, Ranger on duty, 724- 6331, Head Ranger cell: 718-1196, 724-6333, manager Michzel Bobb cell:719-0579, VHF: 16, smma@candw.lc,

St. Lucia Golf and Country Club, (758) 450-8522/3, golf@candw.lc

St. Lucia Marine Terminals, (758) 454-8739/42, port authority

St. Lucia Tourist Board, (758) 452-4094, slutour @candw.lc

Tropical Discoveries, (758) 458-9656, sales@tropicaldiscoveries.net

ST. LUCIA SAILMAKERS CANVAS CUSHIONS

Lubeco, (758) 454-6025, allain@candw.lc, Castries branch, (758) 452-3912, fitted sheets and matresses

Rodney Bay Sails, (758) 452-8648, (758) 584-0291, rodneybaysails@hotmail.com Full sail loft

ST. LUCIA TECHNICAL YACHT SERVICES

Caribbean Yacht Services, (758) 484-7614, caribbeanyachtservices@hotmail.com, metal work, engine repair inboard and outboard, refrigeration.

Chinaman, (758) 518-1234, metalwork

Cox Enterprises, (758) 384-2269, glass & paint

Complete Marine Services, (758) 458-3188/485-1141, info@cms-sl.com, yacht/project mangement

Destination St. Lucia (758) 452-8531, Call us on VHF: 72 "DSL" ulrich@dsl-yachting.com, absentee yacht management and repair, all systems

Island Marine Supplies, (758) 450-9879/584-9441, outboard repair, Mariner & Mercury agent.

KP Marine (758) 450-5564/ 454-5568, Yamaha

Liferaft & Inflatable Center, (758) 715 9671, 452-8306, 452-8306, info@liferaftandinflatble.com

Mac's Marine, (758) 452-8061/485-1530, macsmarine@gmail.coom, echotec, Mapi outboards

MarinTek, (758) 484-6031/450-0552, marintek@gmail.com electrical, watermakers, Volvo dealer

Mermaid Marine (Elvis**)**, (758) 488-5291, glass/paint

Pride, (758) 284-7948, woodwork

Prudent Repairs, (758) 384-0825/ 712-9017, refrigeration

Quick and Reliable, (758) 520-5544/584-6544, QRMS44@gmail.com diesel mechanic

Quick Fix Refrigeration, (758) 484-9016

Remy, (758) 450-2000 woodworking, fixing TVs, cds, etc

Regis Electronics, (758) 452-0205, VHF: 09, stlucia@regiselectronics.com

Ryte Weld Enterprises, (758) 450-8019, metal work

Scribble, (758) 718-0224, Jo@scribbledesign.com, boat names, brochures

Tyson, (758) 452-5794/487-5641,

Tony's Engineering, (758) 715-8719 /452-8575, tonysengineering@hotmail.com mechanics

Yacht Services, (758) 718-3888/2781/520-6400, gardiana22@hotmail.com

ST. LUCIA TRANSPORT

Ben's Taxi Service, (758) 459-5457, VHF: 16, Cell: (758) 714-8217/484-0708/ 721-8500, saltibusb @ slucia.com, bensyachtservices@hotmail.com, yacht agent

Mystic Man Tours, (758) 459-7783/455-9634, info@myticmantours.com

Soufriere Water Taxi Assn., (758) 459-7239/5500, VHF: 16, richie@candw.lc

Theresa Taxi., (758) 384-9197/458-4444 (Vigie)

Taxi Service Marigot, (758) 451-4406, VHF: 16

Sixt RMB, (758) 452-9404, car rental.

Winson Edward Taxi, (758) 584-1183/520-5231, Vieux Fort

ST. LUCIA BANKING

CITS, (758) 452-1529, American Express agent

ST. LUCIA PROVISIONING

Chateau Mygo (Marigot Bay), (785) 451-4772/724-7335, VHF: 16, info@ chateaumygo.com

Crown Foods Ltd, (758) 452-0531/285-4197, kevincrownfoods@candw.lc

Glace Supermarket, 758 452-8814/0514/8179, Cell: 484-1415, glaceg@candw.lc

Eroline Foods, (758) 459-7125/5299, F: (758) 459-7882

Flower Shack, (758) 452-0555, mail@flowershack.net

Market Place (The), marketplacestlucia.com

MariGourmet, (758) 451-4031

Super J Supermarkets, (758) 457-2000

ST. LUCIA FUN SHOPPING

Bagshaw's, (758) 452-6039

Caribbean Perfumes, (758) 453-7249, caribperfumes@candw.lc

Handicraft Center, (758) 459-3226

La Place Carenage (758) 452-7318, slaspa@candw.lc

Sea Island Cotton Shop, (758) 452-3674

The Art Boutique, (758) 452-8071, caribbeanart@ candw.lc

Zaka Art Cafe, (758) 457-1504/384-2925/384-5859, zaka-art@yahoo.com

ST. LUCIA RESTAURANTS & ACCOMMODATION

Anse Chastanet, (758) 459-7000,

BB's (The), (758) 452-0647,

Big Bamboo (758) 455-9171/724-8681,

Big Chef Steak House (758) 450-0210, bigchefsteakhouse@gmail.com

Cafe Ole, Boardwalk Bar, (758) 452-8726,

Capella Marigot Bay, (758) 458-5300, res.marigotbay@capellahotels.com

Chateau Mygo, (785) 451-4772/724-7335, VHF: 16, info@ chateaumygo.com,

Coal Pot, (758) 452-5566, xavier@cand.lc,

Doolittles, (758) 451-4974,

Elena's (758)-458-0576,

Fire Grill (758) 451-4745, firegrillstlucia @ gmail.com

Harbor Club, (758) 731-2900/458--2201, info@theharborclub.com

Hassy's Waterfront Bay, (758) 460=9713,

Hummingbird Resort, (758) 459-7232/721-7995/717-3503, VHF 16, Fax: (758) 459-7033, hbr@candw.lc,

Jacques Waterfront Dining, (758) 458-1900, , cathy@ jacquesrestaurant.com,

Jambe de Bois, (758) 452-0321, VHF:16, , btipson@candw.lc

JJ's Restaurant & Bar, (785) 451-4076, VHF: 16,

Kimatrai, (758) 454-6328, , info@ kimatraihotel.com

La Haut, (758) 459-7008,

Ladera Resort (Dasheen), (758) 459-6623, dasheen@ladera.com.

Landings Beach Club, (758) 458-7375,

Mango Bay, (758) 4485-1621/458-3188, judith@marigotbay.com, accommodation

Fond Doux, (758) 459-7545/8/7790, fonddoux@cqndw.lc,

Orlando's, (758) 459-5955,

Pink Plantation House, (758) 452-5422,

Pirate Bay, (758) 727-9898, ulrich_augustin@hotmail.com,

Rituals Sushi, (758) 458-4334,

Spice of India, (758) 458-4234/716-0820, info@spiceofindiastlucia.com,

St. Lucia Yacht Club, (758) 452-8350, VHF: 16,

Still Estate (The), (758) 459-5179, (758) 459-7301, duboulayd@ candw.lc, ,

Stonefield Estate, (758) 453-3483, 453-0394,

Sugar Beach Resort, (758) 456-8000, viceroyhotelsandresorts.com/sugarbeach@ thejalousieplantation .com, .

Tapas on the bay, (758) 451-2433,

Ti Kaye, (758) 456-8101/03, Ti Manje, (758) 456-8118, info@ tikaye.com

Villa des Pitons, (758) 459-7797,

Winsdjammer Landing, (758) 452-0913

Zaika, (758) 459-2452/ 45-zaika, (758) 488-2777, zaikathetaste.slu@gmail.com,

Zaka Cafe, (758) 457-1504/384-2925/384-5859

Zoe's, (758) 455-9411,

ST. LUCIA CHARTER

Bateau Mygo, (758)-458-3947, VHF: 16, kite cruises, bareboat, day, skippered

BBC Yachting, (758) 716-7610/ 458-4643, bbcyachting@ live.com, bareboat, skippered, day charters

Destination St. Lucia Box 2091, Gros Islet, St. lucia, W.I. Call us on VHF: 72 "DSL" Telephone: (758) 452-8531, Fax: (758) 452-0183, destsll@ candw.lc, all charter

Caribbean Yachting, (758) 458-4430 Fax: (758) 452-0742, Ben@ candw.lc

The Moorings, 758-451-4357, mooring@ candw.lc, all kinds of charter

ST. LUCIA SCUBA DIVING/WATERSPORTS

Action Adventure Divers (AA) (758) 459-5599, 485-1317

Dive Saint Lucia, (758)-451-3483, info@ divesaintlucia.com

Buddies Scuba, (758) 450-8406

Island Divers, (758) 456-8101, diving @ tikaye.com

Iyanola Dive Adventures, (758) 584-5642/720-2017, scuba@ianoladiveadventures.com

Scuba St. lucia, (758) 459-7000, VHF: 16

Windward Island Gases, (758) 452-1514/1339

ST. VINCENT

ST. VINCENT EMERGENCY

Customs Kingstown, (784) 456-1083

Customs Chateaubelair, (784) 485-7907

Customs Wallilabou, (784) 491-1849 (Cesar)

Immigration Wallilabou, (784) 527-6398 (Phillips)

Customs Blue Lagoon, no number

Emergency, 999 - fire, police, medical

Maryfield Hospital, (784) 457-8991/1300, private hospital

Police, (784) 456-1185

Police Chateaubelair, (784) 458-2229

ST. VINCENT AIRLINES

American Eagle, (784) 456-5000,

Air Martinique, (784) 458-4528, 456-4711,

LIAT, (784) 457-1821,

SVG Air, (784) 457 5124, svgair@ vincysurf.com, air charters

ST. VINCENT CHANDLERY FISHING GEAR

KP Marine, (784) 457-1806, kpmarine @ vincysurf.com

ST. VINCENT COMMUNICATIONS

Computec, (784) 456-2691, sales@ computecsvg.com

see also Barefoot and Blue Lagoon Marina under General Yacht Services

ST. VINCENT GENERAL YACHT SERVICES

Bay Central, (784) 527-3298, 431-1899, water, washing machines

Barefoot Yacht Sails, (784) 456-9526, VHF: 68, barebum@vicysurf.com, sailmake, moorings

Blue Lagoon Marina and Hotel, (784) 532-8347, 433-4826, VHF: 16/68, Bluelagoon@ kgroup.vc

Charlie Tango, (784) 458-4720, 493-2186, 593-1882, info@ charlietangotaxi.com, moorings

Ottley Hall, VHF: 68, haul out

Sam Taxi Tours, (784) 456-4338, 528-3340, F: (784) 456-4233, VHF: 68/16, sam-taxitours @vincysurf.com, Bequia, 458-3686

Sam, Union, 494-4339, shipping, customs clearance

St. Vincent Yacht Club, (784) 457-2827, stvincentyachtclub.com

Wallilabou Anchorage, (784) 458-7270, VHF: 68, $$, water

MISCELLANEOUS

Dept of Tourism, (784) 457-1502/1957,

Cumberland tour guides, Suzanne, (784) 454-9236, Marsden, (784) 497-3516, Abbey, (784) 531-0237

Montreal Gardens, (784) 432-6840

Richmond Vale Academy, (784) 491-9761, 526-5729, 530-5501, info@richmondvale.org

ST. VINCENT TECHNICAL YACHT SERVICES

Barefoot Marine Center, (784) 456-9334/9526, VHF: 68, barebum@vincysurf-surf.com, sail loft, diesel repair. Electronics dept, electronics@barefootyachts.com

Horizon Yachs, (784) 456-9395, info@horizonstvincent.com

Howard's Marine, (784) 457-4328, VHF: 68, mechanics, inboard and outboard, haul-out

Nichol's Marine, (784) 456-4118, VHF: 68, starter motors and alternators

Oscar's Machine Shop, (784) 456-4390

ST. VINCENT TRANSPORT

Fantasea Tours, (784) 457-4477/5555, info@ fantaseatours.com

HazEco Tours, (784) 457-8634, hazeco@ vincysurf.com

Ivan Oliver Taxi, (784) 529-1222, 458-4303, VHF: 68,

Harold Taxi, (784) 493-3779, VHF: 68,

Sam Taxi & Tours, (784) 456-4338, VHF: 68/16, sam-taxi-tours@ vincysurf.com,

ST. VINCENT BANKING

CITS, (784) 457-1841, Amex agent

ST. VINCENT PROVISIONING

Gonsalves Liquor, (784) 45-1881, F: (784) 456-2645, gon-liq@vincysurf.com

Greaves C. K., Kingstown (784) 457 1074, Fax: (784) 456-2679, Arnos Vale, 458-4602, ckgreaves@ vincysurf.com

Lagoon Marketplace, (784) 430-3797

ST. VINCENT RESTAURANTS & ACCOMMODATION

Beachcombers, (784) 458-4283, F: (784) 458-4385, beachcombers @ vincysurf.com, $$$

Beach Front Restaurant, (784) 458-2853, VHF: 68/16, $$$

Bungalow, (784) 456-6777, VHF: 68/16, $$$

Beni, (784) 593-9143, VHF: 16, benett@ vincysurf. com, $$

Driftwood, (784) 456-8999, $$$

Flow Wine Bar (784) 457-0809, cell: 494-0869, & **Flowt Beach Bar** (784) 456-8435, $$, andrewwilliams@ flowwinebar.com

Grand View Grill, (784) 457-5487, $$

High Tide, (784) 456-6777, hightide@ vincysurf.com, $$$

Mareyna Bar and Grill, (784) 457-5233, $$

Mariner's Hotel, (784) 457-4000, French Veranda Restaurant (784) 453-1111, $$$$

Marsy Beach Bar, (784) 458-2879/ 430-8437, VHF:16, $$

Mojito, (784) 530-2791/496-6352, $

Paradise Beach Hotel, (784) 457-4795,info@paradis-esvg.com, $$$

Pirate Grill, (784) 495-5758, $

Rock Side Cafe, (784) 456-0815/430-2208, $$, rosimorgan@ vincysurf.com

Surfside Restaurant, (784) 457-5362, $$

The Loft, (784) 458-4308, $$$$

Wallilabou Anchorage, (784) 458-7270, wallanch@vincysurf.com, VHF: 68, $$, wallanch@gmail.com

Wilkie's Restaurant, (784) 458-4811, $$$$, grandview @vincysurf.com

Young Island Resort, (784) 458-4826, VHF: 68, $$$$$

ST. VINCENT CHARTER

Barefoot Yacht Charters, (784) 456-9334/9526, VHF: 68, Email:barebum @ vincysurfsurf.com, all kinds of charter boats.

Dream Yacht Charters, Blue Lagoon, (784) 451-1525, 494-4321, mtaylor@ dreamyachtcharters.com, all kinds of charter

Horizon Yacht Charters, (473) 439-1002, Info@horizonstvincent .com, all kinds of charte

ST. VINCENT SCUBA DIVING

Dive St. Vincent, (784) 457-4948, VHF: 68

Indigo Dive, (784) 493-9494, info@ indigodive.com

Serenity Dive, (784) 528-8030, serenity-dive@hotmail.com

BEQUIA EMERGENCY

Police, (784) 458-3211

Customs, (784) 457-3044, VHF: 16

Imperial Pharmacy, (784) 458-337

Bequia Hospital, (784) 458-3294, VHF: 74

Patrick Chevailler, (784) 458-8829, 529-0422, palmdoc@ vincysurf.com

BEQUIA CHANDLERY FISHING GEAR

Dockside Marine, (784) 457-3005, docksidemarine.bq@ gmail.com

Lulley's Tackle Shop, (784) 458-3420, lulley@ vincysurf.com

Piper Marine, (784) 457-3856, 495-2272. VHF: 68

BEQUIA COMMUNICATIONS

ACS, (784) 458-3967, 454-9519, DHL and computer store

Bequia Technology Center, (784) 458-3045, info@bequiatech.com

Fedex, Solana's, (784) 458-3554,

Maria's Cafe, (784) 458-3116, mitchell1@ vincysurf.com

RMS, (784) 458-3556, VHF: 16/68/10, rms@ vincysurf.com

BEQUIA MISCELLANEOUS

A Caribbean Wedding, (784) 457-3209, 528-7444

Bequia Land & Home, (784) 458-3116, 533-0677, bequialandandhome @vincysurf.com

Bequia Photo Action, (784) 529-5005, 492-3725, VHF: 77, bequiaphotoaction@ gmail.com, photographer

Caribbean Compass, (784) 457-3409

Caribbean Woods, (784) 457-3000,caribwoods@vincysurf.com

Grenadines Island Villas, (784) 529-8046, 455-0696, islandvillas@ mac.com

Kenmore Henville, (784) 457-3212, 529-5005, VHF: 77, marine photograher

Old Hegg Turtle Sanctuary, (784) 458-3245/3596, oldhegg@ vincysurf.com

Patrick Chevailler, (784) 458 8829, 529 0422, palmdoc@ vincysurf.com

Serenity Day Spa, (784) 533-4005, serenity_dayspa@yahoo.com

BEQUIA GENERAL YACHT SERVICES

African, (784) 593- 3986,VHF: 68, yacht management, deliveries, moorings, provisioning

Bequia Marina, (784) 495-0235, 431-8418, capt.waterdog@gmail.com VHF: 68, docking, water

Daffodil Marine, (784) 458-3938, 496-5819, VHF: 67,daffodil_harris@yahoo.com, water, fuel, laundry

Lighthouse Laundry, (784) 458-3084,VHF: 68, laundry

Miranda's Laundry, (784) 530-6865,VHF: 68, laundry

Papa Mitch, (784) (784) 458-3116, laundry

BEQUIA SAILMAKERS CANVAS CUSHIONS

Allick Sails, (784) 457-3040, 458-3992, VHF: 68

Bequia Canvas, (784) 457-3291, VHF: 68, bequiacanvas@gmail.com

Grenadine Sails, (784) 457-3507/3527, VHF: 16/68, gsails@vincysurf.com

BEQUIA TECHNICAL YACHT SERVICES

Caribbean Diesel, (784) 457-3114, 593-6333, VHF: 68, mechanics, fuel polishing

KMS Marine Services, (784) 530-8123, 570-7612

Piper Marine, (784) 457-3856, 495-2272. VHF: 68, rigging, F: 68, mechanics

SVG Yacht Services, (784) 530-8300, john@sailgrenadines.com

BEQUIA TRANSPORT

Admiral Transport, (784) 458-3348, admiraltrans@vincysurf.com

Challenger Taxi Service, (784) 458-3811, VHF: 68, challenger-taxi@ yahoo.com

De Best, (784) 458-3349, 530-4747, VHF: 68, friendshipgapt @ vincysurf.com

Gideon Taxi, (784) 458-3760, 527-2092, VHF: 68, gideontaxi@vincysurf.com, taxi, rentals

Handy Andy, (784) 458-3722, VHF: 68, rentals

BEQUIA FUN SHOPPING

Bequia Bookshop, (784) 457-3008, bequiabookshop@hotmail.com

Claude Victorine, (784) 458-3150, claudevictorine @ vincysurf.com

Oasis Gallery, (784) 497-7670, oasisbequia@gmail.com

Patrick Chevailler, (784) 458 8829, 529 0422, palmdoc@vincysurf.com

Solana's, (784) 458-3554, solanas@vincysurf.com

Whaleboner, (784) 458-3233,VHF: 68

BEQUIA PROVISIONING

Bequia Foodstore (784) 457-3928

Doris Fresh Foods, (784) 458-3625, VHF: 68

Knights Trading (784) 458-3218, knightstrad @ yahoo.com

Linas, (784) 457-3388

Nature Zone, (784) 458-3793

Mama's, (784) 457-3443

Maranne's Ice Cream, (784) 458-3041

Select Wines, (784) 457-3482

Virginie's Gourmet Catering, (784) 458-8829, 493-0696

BEQUIA RESTAURANTS & ACCOMODATION

Bequia Beach Hotel, (784) 458-1600, info@bequiabeach.com

Coco's Place, (784) 458-3463, VHF: 68, $$

Colombo's, (784) 457-3881, $$

Dawn's Cafe, (784) 492-6508, $

De Reef, (784) 458-3412/3484, $

Fig Tree, (784) 457-3008, figtree@vincysurf.com, $$

Firefly Hotel Bequia, (784) 488-8414/458-3414, $$$$$

Frangipani, (784) 458-3255, VHF: 68, $$$, info@ frangipanibequia.com

Gingerbread Hotel, (784) 458-3800, $, info@gingerbreadhotel.com

Jack's, (784) 443-9054, 458-3809, 529-4692, $$$

Keegan's Beachside, (784) 458-3530, VHF: 68, keegansbequia@yahoo.com, $$

Kingsville Apartments, (784) 458-3404/3932

Laura's, (784) 457-3779, $$

La Plage, (784) 458-3361, $$

Mac's Pizzeria, (784) 458-3474, VHF: 68, ,beqvilla @vincysurf.com

Maria's Cafe, (784) 458-3116, mitchell1@vincysurf.com, $$$

Open Deck, (784) 455-3962, VHF: 68, $$$$$

Papa's, (784) 455-5463/457-3443, $$$

Plantation House, (784) 434-9333, $$$$

Porthole, (784) 458-3458, $$

Sugar Reef, (784) 458-3400, info@sugarreefbequia.com

Tantie Pearle's, (784) 457-3160, $$

Whaleboner Inn, (784) 458-3233, VHF: 68, whalebonerbequia @ hotmail.com $$

BEQUIA CHARTER

Island Time Holidays, grenadines@vincysurf.com

Sail Grenadines, (784) 533-2909, 530-8300, info@sailgrenadines.com

Sail Relax Explore, (784) 457-3888, 495-0886/9

Tradewinds Cruise Club, (784) 457-3407, info@ tradewindscruiseclub.com

BEQUIA SCUBA DIVING

Bequia Dive Adventure, (784) 458-3826, 496-4754, VHF: 68, adventures@vincysurf.com, dive shop

Dive Bequia, (784) 458-3504, 495-9929, VHF: 68,16, cathy@divebequia.com, dive shop

MUSTIQUE MISCELLANEOUS

Mustique Moorings, (784) 488-8363,VHF: 16/68

Horse riding, (784) 488-8316

Berris Little (Slick) (784) 527-9043

Mustique Company, (784) 488-8424

Airport, (784) 488-8336

Doctor,(784) 488-8353

MUSTIQUE SHOPPING

Coreas, (784) 488-8479

The Purple House, (784)- 528-8788 boutique, elegant wear

MUSTIQUE RESTAURANTS & ACCOMMODATION

Basil's Bar,(784) 488-8350,VHF: 68, $$$$

Cotton House, (784) 456-4777/8215 VHF: 68, cottonhouse@vincysurf.com $$$$$

Firefly Mustique, (784) 488-8414, VHF: 10, stan@ fireflymustique.com, $$$$

The View, (784) 488-8807/532-2421, $$

MUSTIQUE SCUBA DIVING

Mustique Watersports, (784) 488-8486, VHF: 16/68

CANOUAN COMMUNICATIONS

Tamarind Bay Hotel, (784) 458-8044

CANOUAN GENERAL YACHT SRVICES

Glossy Bay Marina, (784) 431-2825, 434-3791

John's Marine Services VHF: 16, cell: (784) 593-0875, moorings, water, fuel, ice

Marcus Marine Services VHF: 16, (784) 492-3230, 458-8375, moorings, water, fuel, ice

CANOUAN TECHNICAL YACHT SERVICES

Gazimo Marine Service (784) 491-1177, gazimo.marine@gmail.com

CANOUAN TRANSPORT

Gazimo Mule Rental (784) 491-1177, gazimo.marine@gmail.com

Phyllis Taxi, (784) 593-4190

CANOUAN HOTELS/ RESTAURANTS

Pink Sands Club, (784) 431-4500, $$$$$

Sea Grape, (784) 495-7601, $$

Tamarind Bay Hotel, (784) 458-8044,VHF: 16, info@tamarind.us, $$$$

The Mangrove, (784) 482-0761/593-3364, VHF:16/68, $$

CANOUAN SCUBA DIVING

Canouan Dive Center, VHF: 16, (784) 528-8073, info@canouandivecenter.com

MAYREAU RESTAURANTS & ACCOMODATION

Dennis's Hideaway, (784) 458-8594, VHF: 16/68, $$$

Honey Cove, (784) 572-0671, $$

Island Paradise, (784) 458-8941/8562/3442, VHF: 68, $$

J & C Restaurant, (784) 458-8558, VHF: 16/68, $$

Owen's Chill Spa, (784) 496-4972, $$

Righteous & de Youths, (784) 458-8203, VHF: 68, $$

Salt Whistle Bay Restaurant, (784) 493-5286, hello@saltwhistlebay.com, $$$

MAYREAU PROVISIONING

First Stop, (784) 458-8325

MAYREAU TECHNICAL YACHT SERVICES

Arthur Roache, mechanic, (784) 498-2996

PALM ISLAND

Palm Island VHF: 16, Tel: (784) 458-8824, Fax: (784) 458-8804

UNION ISLAND EMERGENCY

Customs, (784) 458-8360

Health Center, (784) 458-8339

UNION AIRLINES

Eagle Travel, (784) 458-8179, eagtrav@vincysurf.com, VHF: 68

UNION COMMUNICATIONS

Erika's Marine Services, (784) 485-8335, 494-1212, F: (784) 485-8336 VHF: 68, info@erikamarine.com

Internet Cafe, (784) 485-8326

UNION MISCELLANEOUS

Happy Kite, (784) 430-8604, 458-8734, happykitegrenadines@gmail.com

JT Pro Center Kitesurf (784) 527-8363, info@kitesurfgrenadines.com

Tobago Cays Marine Park, (784) 485-8191, 527-3855, info@tobagocays.com

Southern Grenadines Animal Kindness (784) 485-8287

UNION GENERAL YACHT SERVICES

Anchorage Yacht Club, (784) 458-8221, VHF: 16/68, stay@unionanchorage.com, docking, laundry

Bougainvilla, (784) 458-8878/8678, laquarium@ vincysurf.com, VHF: 16, docking

Erika's Marine Services (784) 485-8335, VHF: 68, info@erikamarine.com

Unigas (784) 485-8969, 526-4206, naert@gmail.com

UNION TECHNICAL YACHT SERVICES

Island Marine Special, (784) 458-8039, VHF: 16, mechanics

Marine Tech Services, (784) 526-8510, 432-4208, VHF: 16, marinetechsev@gmail.com, all yacht systems, mechanical and electrical

Unitech Marine Services, (784) 458-8002, 530-5915, unitech@vincysurf.com, VHF: 16, mechanics & glass work

UNION TRANSPORT

Marine Tech Services, (784) 526-8510

432-4208, VHF: 16, marinetechsev@gmail.com, Bike rental and tours

UNION RESTAURANTS & ACOMMODATION

Anchorage Yacht Club, (784) 458-8221, VHF: 16/68, $$$$

Aqua, (784) 430-4654, $$$$

Barracuda, (784) 458-8571/527-5163, giancarlotiezzi@gmail.com, $$$

Big Citi, (784) 458-8960/494-8424, $

Ciao Pizza, (784) 430-5006, $$

Clifton Beach Hotel, (784) 458-8235, VHF: 68, $$$

Exhibit, (784) 496-8977, $$

Gypsea Cafe, (784) 495-8695, $$

Janti's, (784) 455-3611, happyisland@unionisland.com $

L'Aquarium, (784) 430-4088/458-8678, caribbeadelicacy@yahoo.com, $$$

La Cabane, (784)434-6704, $$

Lambi, (784) 458-8549, VHF: 68, $$$

Limelite Bar, (784) 485-8486, $

Pleasure, (784) 593-1989, $$

Shark Attack, (784) 527-2694/2691, sharkattack2006@ hotmail.com, $$

Sparrow Beach Bar, (784)-458-8195/593-1713, free shuttle, 454-1888, info@grenadinesislandestates $$$

Seckie & Vanessa, (784) 531-6965/530-5913, VHF: 16, njide12@hotmail.com, seckietours@gmail.com, $$

Sunset Cove, (784) 497-8543, 593-1660 $$

Snack Shack, (784) 458-8652, $$$

Waterfront, (784) 531-6381, $$$

UNION FUN SHOPPING

Clifton Boutique, (784) 458-8235

Driftwood Boutique, (784) 434-0764

L'Atelier Turquoise, (784) 458-8734, anniefrance@vincysurf.com

Mare Blu, (784) 494-8880

UNION PROVISIONING

Captain Gourmet, (784) 495-8695, VHF: 08 (USA) capgourmet@vincysurf.com

Island Grown, (784) 532-2914, 529 0935

UNION CHARTER

Sail Grenadines, (784) 533 2909, In UK, 800-321-3801, katie@sailgrenadines.com

Wind and Sea, Union I., Bougainvilla, T: (784) 458-8678/8678, windandsea@ vincysurf.com

UNION SCUBA DIVING

Grenadines Dive, (784) 458-8138, 455-3822, VHF: 16/68, E: gdive@ grenadines-dive.com

PSV RESTAURANTS & ACCOMODATION

Petit St. Vincent Resort VHF: 16, (784) 458-8801, $$$$, Jean-Michel Cousteau Diving, 784-458-8984

GRENADA, CARRIACOU & PM

PETITE MARTINIQUE GENERAL YACHT SERVICES

B&C Fuels, (473) 443-9110, Fax: (473) 443-9075,BandCfuels@gmail.com, VHF: 16, "Golf Sierra" fuel, water

PM COMMUNICATIONS

Millenium Connection, (473) 443-9243, ieshodinga@yahoo.co.uk

PM CHANDLERY TECHNICAL SERVICES

E&B Hardware, 473-443-9086

PM RESTAURANTS & ACCOMMODATION

Palm Beach, (473) 443-9103, VHF: 16, emmanuel.palmbeach@ygmail.com, $$

Melodie's Guest House, (743) 443-9052/9093/9108,

Seaside View, (473) 443-9007

PM SHOPPING

Matthew Shoppng Center, (473) 443-9194

Millenium Boutique, (473) 443-9243

CARRIACOU EMERGENCY

Customs, Tyrrel B. 443-9379/6100 Hills. (473) 443-7659

Hospital emergency, 774

CHS, (473) 443-8247, chscarriacou@gmail.com

Carriacou Animal Hospital, (473) 443-7177

CARRIACOU AIRLINES

LIAT, (473) 443-7362

Bullen, (473) 443-7468/7469, Fax: 443 8194, travel agent

CARRIACOU MISCELLANEOUS

Isle of Reefs Tours, (473) 404-0415, allison@isleofreefstours.com

SUP Carriacou, (473) 404-2653, 416-2054, supcarriacougrenada@gmail.com

CARRIACOU GENERAL YACHT SERVICES

Bullen, (473) 443-7468/7469, Fax: 443 8194 vbs@spiceisle.com, duty free fuel

Carriacou Marine, (473) 443-6292/6940, 533-8927, info@carriacoumarine.com

My Beautiful Launderette, (473) 403-6606, 419-3357

Tyrell Bay Marina, (784) 443-8417, 416-6805, info@tyrellbaymarinacarriacou.com

CARRIACOU SAILMAKERS CANVAS CUSHIONS

In Stitches, (473) 443-8878, 406-4117, VHF: 16, asmelt@gmaill.com

Sling's Uphostery, (473) 403-4416

CARRIACOU TECHNICAL YACHT SERVICES

Carriacou Underwater Services, (473) 416-6854, 459-0159, contactcusi@gmail.com

Dominique Wer (473) 407-1151, VHF: 16, aluminum & stainless (Genevieve's therapeutic massage)

Hezron Wilson Refrigeration, (473) 443-6212

Manny Workship (473) 416-1169, 406-9460

Paul O Regan, (473) 416-5491, rigging, chandlery, general help, T.M.M.carriacou@gmail.com

Tall Man Electrics, (473) 403-6505

Tool Meister, (473) 445-8178, tmmachine @spiceisle.com, machine shop, mechanics

CARRIACOU TRANSPORT

Ade's Dream, (473) 443-7317, adesdea@spiceisle.com, car rentals

Bubbles Turtle Dove Taxi, VHF:16, (473) 407-1029, 443-7194

Cuthbert Snagg, (473) 443-8293, bikes, marine eco-tours

Linky Taxi Service, Tel: (473) 443-7566, Cell: (473) 406-2457, 416-5358, VHF: 16,

CARRIACOU RESTAURANTS & ACCOMMODATION

Ade's Dream, (473) 443-7317/8636/7, adesdea@spiceisle.com

After Ours', (473) 443-6159

Anne's Roti Shop, (473) 443-6761, $

Bayside Bar and Restaurant (473) 443-8008, $$

Cassada Bay, (473) 443-8946, cassadabayresort@gmail.com, $$$$

Callaloo, The Mermaid, (473) 443-8286/554-3340, mermaidcarriacou@gmail.com, $$$

Gallery Cafe, (473) 443-7069, gallerycafe@outlook.com, $$$

Iguana Cafe, (473) 443-6292, VHF: 16, carriyacht@ spiceisle.com, $

Kayak Kafe, (473) 443-6523, sallyandjinger@yahoo.co.uk, $$$

La Playa, (473) 443-9399, $$

Lambi Queen, (473) 443-8162/406-4122, VHF: 16, $$

Lazy Turtle, 473-443-8322, VHF: 16 lazyturtlewi@gmail.com $$$

Le Petit Conch Shell, (473) 443-6174/7233 $$

Lucky's, 473-456-5151, $

Off the Hook, 473-533-4242, $$

Slipway Restaurant, (473) 443-6500, info@slipwayrestaurant.com, $$$$

Sundowners (473) 533 3430, $$

The Green Roof, (473) 443-6399, greenroof@ spiceisle.com, $$$$

Twilight, (473) 443-8530, VHF: 16, $$

CARRIACOU FUN SHOPPING

Fidel Productions, (473) 435-8866/415-0710, 443-6185, 443-7366

CARRIACOU PROVISIONING

Ade's Dream, (473) 443-7317, F: (473) 443-8435, adesdea@spiceisle.com

After Ours', (473) 443-6159

Alexis Supermarket, (473) 443-8530

Bullen, (473) 443-7468/9, VHF: 16 vbs@spiceisle.com

Patty's Deli (473) 443-6258, shop@pattysdeli.com

Splash (473) 419-1497

Twilight, (473) 443-8530, VHF: 16

CARRIACOU DIVING

Deefer Diving, (473) 443-7882, VHF: 16, info@deeferdiving.com

Dive Carriacou (473) 443-6906, VHF: 16, info@divecarriacou.com

Lumbadive Ltd., (473) 443-8566, 457-4539, VHF: 16, dive@lumbadive.com

GRENADA EMERGENCY/ OFFICIAL

Emergency: police/ coastguard 911

Customs, Port Louis, (473) 440-3270

Customs, Prickly Bay, (473) 444-4509,

Customs, St. George's, (473) 440-2239/2240

Customs, Phare Bleu Marina, (473) 443-3236

Coastguard, 399

Dr. Mike Radix, (473) 444-4855, 443-4379, emergency: 443-5330

Dr. Jennifer Isaacs (dermatology), Grenville St. St. George's, (473) 440-3963, jenniferjapalisaacs@gmail.com

Robbie Yearwood (surgeon), Ocean House, Grand Anse (afternoon) (473) 444-1178, ho: (473) 444-5624, rosbrad@spiceisle.com

Hospital, (473) 440-2051

Police, 911,

Port Authority, (473) 444-7447, VHF: 16, port

St. George's School of Medicine, (473) 444-4271

Spice Isle Imaging Center, (473) 444-7679, 415-2754, 405-4557, images@spiceisle.com

True Blue Pharmacy, (473) 444-3784

St. Augustin Medical Clinic, (473) 440-6173-5, staugms@spiceisle.com, private hospital.

Sunsmile Dental Clinic, (473) 444-2273

Island Dental Care, (473) 437-4000, islanddentalcare @ yahoo.com

GRENADA AIRLINES

American Airlines, (473) 442-2222

British Airways, (800) 744-2997 (local 800)

BWIA, (473) 444-1221-2/4134

LIAT, (473) 440-2796-8,

GRENADA CHANDLERY FISHING GEAR

Budget Marine, 473-439-1983, budmargd@spiceisle.com

Marine World, (473) 440-1748

Island Water World, (473) 435-2150, 435-2152, Grenada Marine: 443-1028, sales@ islandwater-world.com

North Yacht Shop, (473) 432-1201, info@northyachtshop.com

Wholesale Yacht Parts, (473) 458-6306, 763-8387, Miami: (305) 454-2971, sherri@wholesaleyachtparts.com

Spice Island Fish House Tackle Shop, (473) 435-0189

GRENADA COMMUNICATIONS

Grenada Yacht Club, St. George's, Grenada, (473) 440-3050, VHF: 16

Fedex, (473) 440-2206

Mod 1, LAE, (473) 232-4000, 800-4000, computer repairs

Onsite Software Support, Marquis Mall, (473) 444-3653

Renwick & Thompson, (473) 440-2198/2625, renthom@spiceisle.com, Western Union & DHL agent

Spice Island Marine Services, P.O. Box 449, St. George's, Grenada, (473) 444-4257/4342, VHF: 16, simsco@spicislandmarine.com

GRENADA GENERAL YACHT SERVICES

Bob Goodchild Surveys, (473) 443 5784, 407 4388, surveyor@flyingfishventures.com

Caribbean Boat Services, (473) 534-4931, 416-4931, info@cbs-grenada.com

Clarkes Court Haul out and Marina, (473) 439-3939, 405-2739, info@clarkescourtmarina.com

Grenada Marine, (473) 443-1667, Port Louis 444-1667, info@grenadamarine.com, haul out

Grenada Yacht Club, (473) 440-3050, VHF: 16, gyc@spiceisle.com, marina, fuel

Henry's Safari Tours, (473) 444-5313, F: (473) 444-4460, info@henrysafari.com, VHF: 68, laundry, yacht agent

Horizon Yacht Management, 473-439-1000, 535-0328, info@horizongrenada.com. marina, moorings

Island Dreams, (473) 443-3603, 415-2139, VHF: 74, info@islandreamsgrenada.com, absentee yacht project management

Le Phare Bleu Marina & Resort, (473) 444-2400, 409-7187, marina@lepharebleu.com

Prickly Bay Marina, (473) 439-5265, info@pricklybaymarina.com, VHF: 16, marina, fuel

Port Louis Marina, (473) 435-7431/2, dockmaster (24-hour) (473) 415-0820, VHF: 14, reservations@cnportlouismarina .com

Rock Taxi, (473) 444-5136, VHF: 16, absentee yacht management

Secret Harbour Marina (473) 444-4449, VHF: 16,71, secretharbour@spiceisle.com, marina, fuel

Spice Island Marine, (473) 444-4257/3442, Cell: (473) 407-4439, simco@spiceislandmarine.com, haul-out

Spronk mega yacht Services, (473) 435-6342, 534-3688, 534-6342, office@spronksmegayacht.com

Survival Anchorage, (473) 443-3957, 459-3502, VHF: 16, georgespice1@hotmail.co.uk, gas refills

The Multihull Co, (473) 440-1668

Whisper Cove Marina, (473) 444-5296, , info@whispercovemarina.com.

GRENADA MISCELLANEOUS

Caribbean Horizons, (473) 444-1555/3944, info@caribbeanhorizons.com

Conservation Kayak, (473) 449-5248, info@conservationkayak.com

Crayfish Bay Organic Estate, (473) 442-1897, crayfishbayorganics@gmail.com

Grenada Board of Tourism, (473) 440-2279/2001, 415-2556, gbt@spiceisle.com

Grenada Chocolate Factory, (473) 442-0050, info@ grenadachocolate.com

Grenada Golf Club, (473) 444-4128

Hankey's, (473) 435-0101, 443-0505, computer parts and services

Jouvay Chocolate, (473) 437-1839

Marlin Master, (473) 405-3056, info@marlinmaster.com, fishing tours

MAYAG, (473) 443-1667, mayagadmin@gmail.com

Peter Evans, (473) 444-3636, cell: (473) 441-7864, real estate & yacht broker

River Antoine Rum factory, (473) 442-7109, 442-4537

Sunnyside Gardens, (473) 440 1588, 456-5096, 406-1381

Spice Island Retreat Spa, (473) 231-6167, info@spiceislandretreat.com

Wondering Soles, (473) 423-0550, info@wonderingsolesgrenada.com

GRENADA SAILMAKERS CANVAS CUSHIONS

Clarke's Upholstery, (473) 414-1827, vlarkupholstery@ hotmail.com

Ever After (473) 423-6499, julesandfrank@gmail.com

Neil Pryde Sails, (473) 537-5355

Rollin' Stitches, (473) 420-6010, 534-7290, rollinstitches@gmail.com

Sunshine Canvas (473) 534-6866/7217, sunshinecanvas2003@gmail.com

Tropical Sails & Canvas, (473) 456-7486, 457-5856, tropicalsailsandcanvas@gmail.com

Turbulence, Grenada (473) 439-4495, 405-8380 turbsail@spiceisle.com

GRENADA TECHNICAL YACHT SERVICES

AKC Yacht Maintenance, (473) 449-1906, akcyacht@gmail.com, fiberglass and general

Anro Agencies, (473) 444-2220/4269, info@anroagencies.com,

AJS Enterprises, (473) 440-0192, yacht names

Albert Lucas, (473) 440-1281, machine shop

Cottle Boat Works, (473) 444-1070, cottleboatworks@ spiceisle.com, shipwright

Dave's Gas Service, (473) 444-5571,davidbenoit@ spiceisle.com, stoves

Driftwood, (473) 459-1493, driftwoodgrenada@gmail.com, woodwork

Essential Engineering, (473) 414-7316, essentialengineeringgrenada@gmail.com, VHF: 68, All engines, outboartd and inboard.

Hands On Yacht Services, (473) 420-4129, handsonyachtservices@gmail.com, fiberglass and general

Horizon Yacht Management, 473-439-1000, 535-0328, info@horizongrenada.com

Lagoon Marine, (473) 440-3381, refrigeration

Mango Projects, (473) 536-2319, survey@mangoprojects.gd, surveyor

Martin Enterprise, (473) 536-3231, 449-4772, 533-3095, martinenterprise11@gmail.com

Marine Tech Grenada, (473) 406-1800, marinetechgnd@gmail.com

McIntyre Bros, (473) 444-3944/5/3911, 535-0030, macford@spiceisle.com, mechanics inboard an outboard

Miguel Irala, (473) 533-4851, miguelirala41@gmail.com, electronic engineer

Nauti Solutions, (473) 416-7127/7537, svmagnum@hotmail.com, mechanics

On Board Refrigeration Electrics and Electronics, (473) 456-8339, 420-3041, 21gunzchrome@live.com

Palm Tree Marine, (473) 443-7256, 407-2783, info@palmtreemarine.com, mechanics

Protech Engineering Services, (473) 403-6371, 538-3080, mncadore@gmail.com

Royan's, (473) 537-0816, 406-0894, VHF: 68, royanwelding@hotmail.com, royanjoseph44@gmail.com, metalwork

Safe Yachts, (473) 410-0241, VHF: 68, admin@safeyachts-grenada.com, absentee yacht/ project management, sewing, cleaning.

Sea Safety Service, (473) 538-8099, donal@seasafetyservice.com, liferafts, dinghy sales and repair

Sipyard Marine Services, (473) 405-4767, 444-4767, 407-2727, smsgrenada@gmail.com

Subzero Air Control, (473) 440-4072, 409-9376, refridge/ac

TechNick, (473) 405-1560, technick@spiceisle.com, welding, fabrication

Tan Tan Sam, 1-473-403-9904, 444-5190, varnish, paint, polish.

Turbulence, (473) 439-4495, St. David's: (473) 443-2517, turbsail@spiceisle.com, rigging, electronics

Ultimate Filtration, (473) 440-6887, Cell: (473) 407-4989, outboards, fuel tank cleaning

Underwater Solutions, (473) 456-3927, brettfairhead@ yahoo.com

Waterfall Marine, info@waterfallmarine.com

Welding Tec, (473) 420-6509, weldingtecgnd@gmail.com

GRENADA TRANSPORT

Marina Taxi Association, (473) 444-1703, VHF: 16, taxi

K&J Taxi (473) 409-9621, 440-4227, VHF: 16, kjtours@ genada-explorer.com

Grenada Adventure, 473-444-5337, 473-535-1379, adventure@spiceisle.com

Henry's Safari Tours, (473) 444-5313, F: (473) 444-4460, safari@ spiceisle.com, VHF: 68

Maxwell Adventure Tours, (473) 444-1653, cell: (473) 406 4980, VHF: 68

McIntyre Bros, (473) 444-3944/5, (473) 444-2899, macford@spiceisle.com

Rock Taxi, (473) 444-5136, VHF: 16/10

Survival Anchorage, (473) 443-3957, 459-3502, georgespice1@hotmail.co.uk

Telfor Bedeau (473) 442-6200, guide

Y&R Car Rentals, (473) 444-4448, Y&R@ spiceisle.com

GRENADA BANKING

CITS, (473) 440-2945, AmEx agent

National Commercial Bank (The), (473) 444-2265, (473) 444-5501, ncbgnd@spiceisle.com

GRENADA FUN SHOPPING

Ace Hardware/Napa, (473) 440-5090

Fidel Productions, (473) 435-8866

House of Chocolate, (473) 440-2310, info@houseofchocolategnd.com

Penny's, (473) 420-6775, 439-9523

Too Kachi, (473) 439-0938

Yellow Poui Art, (473) 440-3001, yellowpoui@ spiceisle.com

GRENADA PROVISIONING

Best Little Liquor Store in Town, (473) 440-2198/2625, VHF: 16 "Rhum Runner base", renthom @ spiceisle.com

Carenage Hot Spot (473) 439/435-4558

Essentials, (473) 444-4662

Fast Manacou, (473) 410-5151, VHF: 68, johnhovan@gmail.com

Food Fair, (473) 440-2588, hubbards@spiceisle.com

Foodland, (473) 440-1991

Floral Treasures, (473) 444-2832, floraltreasuresgrenada@gmail.com

Le Boucher, (473) 456-3232, leboucher.inc@gmail.com

North South Wines, (473) 444-1182, 439-9463, info@northsouthwines.com

Merry Baker, (473) 435-6464, merrybakery.gd@gmail.com

MNIB (marketing board), St. George's, 440-1791

Spronk's Provisioning, (473) 407-3688, 444-4662, F: (473) 444-4677

The Wine Shoppe, (473) 444-1182, nst. wines@ spiceisle.com

Phare Bleu Mini Mart, (473) 443-4232

See also **Spronk Megayacht Services and Henry Safari Tours** in *General Yacht Services*

GRENADA RESTAURANTS & ACCOMMODATION

Adrift, (473) 231-4567, adriftbar473@gmail. com, $$

Aquarium, (473) 444-1410, aquarium@ spiceisle.com, $$$

Bananas, (473) 439-4662, (473), F: (473) 444-4677, $$

BB's Crab Back, (473) 435-7058, bbscrab-back@hotmail.com $$$

Bella Milano, (473) 410-6912, 537-4362, bellamilanogrenada@ gmail.com, $

Calabash, (473) 444-4334, $$$$$

Carib Sushi, (473) 439-5640, spiceisle@ caribsushi.com, $$$

Clam (473) 459-0930, 449-2528, $$

Coconut Beach, (473) 444-4644, $$$

Dodgy Dock, True Blue, 473-439-1377, $$$

Dragon Bay Hideaway, 473-533-3077/231-0808, kelelectric@hotmail. com, $

Taffy's, (473) 538-0863, VHF: 16, $$

Junction, (473) 420-1086, $$

Laura's, (473) 443-1064/1667 ext. 224, lauras@grenadamarine. com, $$

La Sagesse, (473) 444-6458, 409-0887, lasagesse@spiceisle. com, $$$$

Little Dipper, (473) 444-5136, VHF: 10/16, $$

Mango Cottage, (473) 407-4388, mangocot-tagegrenada@gmail. com, accommodation

Mount Hartman Estate, (473) 407-4504, reser-vations@ mount hartmanbay.com, $$$$$

Nutmeg, (473) 440-3654, $$

Patrick's, (473) 440 0364, 449-7243, $$

Petite Anse, (473) 442-5252, info@petiteanse. com, $$$

Petit Bacaye, (473) 443-2902, $$

Porto Di Mare (473) 423-2235, maktoub@ mac.com, $$

Punj-Abi, (473) 420-0202, restaurant@punj-abi.com, $$

Rose Mount, (473) 444-8069, $

Sails, (473) 440-9747, 405-7609, sailsinc13@ gmail.com, $$$$

Sel & Poivre, (473) 435-4439, $$$

Spout, Grenada Yacht Club, (473) 440-3050, VHF: 16, $$

Tiki Bar, Prickly Bay Marina, (473) 439-5265, $$

Tropicana Inn, (473) 440-1586, $$

True Blue Bay, (473) 443 8783, windward@ truebluebay.com, VHF: 16, $$$

Umbrellas, (473) 439-9149, $$

Victory Bar/ Restaurant, (473) 435-7263, $$$

Yolo, (473) 435-7263, $$$$

GRENADA DIVING

Aquanauts, (473) 444 1126, VHF: 16, aqua-nautsGDA@gmail.com

Dive Grenada, (473) 444 1092, info@ diveg-renada.com

Eco Dive, (473) 444/407-7777, dive@ ecodiveandtrek.com

ScubaTech, (473) 439-4346, 457-6317, info@ scubatech-grenada. com

GRENADA CHARTER

Dream Yacht Charters, Port Louis, (473) 440-8800, 536-1187, cats monos, skippered bare.

Horizon Yacht Charters, True Blue, (473) 439-1000, 535-0328, toll free: 1-866-463-7254, info@horizongre-nada.com, all kinds of charter

Footloose Charters, (473) 440-7949, 440-6680, footloos@ spiceisle.com, VHF: 16, yacht agent

John Clement, (473) 406-2064, johnclem-ent80 @hotmail. com johnclement08 @ yahoo.com

TUI Marine (The Moorings and Sunsail), (473) 6661/2, 405-8633,

OTHER BUSINESSES OF INTEREST

AB Inflatables, see Budget Marine, Grenada

Doyle Sailmakers, 6 Crossroads, St. Philip, Barbados, (246) 423-4600,

Floatinator, www.floatinator.com

Power Boats, (868) 634-4303, VHF: 72 pbmfl @powerboats. co.tt

Peake Marine, (868) 634-4427/3

Seajet 038 Taisho, The new ecofriendly antifouling that works. See WIND, Martinique

INTERNATIONAL CHARTER

Ed Hamilton, (207) 549 7855, all kinds of charter

Sunsail, (888) 350-568, sunsail.com, all kinds of charter

The Moorings, (888)952-8420, sales@ moorings.com

INTERNATIONAL YACHT SALES

Boatshed, (473) 415-2138, 443-3603, anitasutton@boatshed-grenada.com

Multihull Co, +1-215-508-2704, Info@ multihullcompany.com 207)

General Index

CRUISING GUIDE TO THE VIRGIN ISLANDS
By Nancy & Simon Scott
19th Edition, 2017-2018
ISBN 978-0-9978540-0-8
6 x 9, 350 pp. **$34.95**

Completely reesigned and updated style, with more Virgin Island photography and full color detailed anchorage charts, these guides have been indispensable companions for sailors and visitors to these islands since 1982. Includes a free 17 x 27 color planning chart, with aerial photos of some of the anchorages. Covers the Virgin Islands including all the U.S. and British Virgin Islands!

- GPS co-ordinates for every anchorage
- Anchoring and mooring information and fees
- Customs, immigration and National Park regulations
- Particulars on marina facilities and the amenities they offer
- Water sports-where to go and where to rent equipment
- Shore-side facilities, restaurants, beach bars, shops, provisions, internet connections

Post hurricane updates available at www.cruisingguides.com

SAILORS GUIDE TO THE WINDWARD ISLAND
By Chris Doyle and Lexi Fisher
19th Edition, 2019-2020
ISBN 978-0-9978540-7-
6 x 9, 430 pp.
$34.95

Revised and updated for 2019-2020, this guide features detailed sketch charts based on the authors' own surveys, and aerial photos of most anchorages. It also includes clear and concise navigational information. By far the most popular guide to the area, it covers the islands from Martinique to Grenada, with dazzling scenic photography, unsurpassed onshore information, sections on exploring, provisioning, water sports, services, restaurants and photography. Information is linked to the authors' website where you can download town maps, GPS waypoints from the sketch charts, and obtain links to local weather, news and more.

CRUISING GUIDE TO THE NORTHERN LEEWARD ISLAND
Chris Doyle
2018-2019
ISBN 978-0-9978540-3-9
6 x 9, 288 pp **$31.95**

The Cruising Guide to the Northern Leeward Islands covers the islands of Anguilla, St. Martin & Sint Maarten, St. Barts, Saba, Statia, St. Kitts, Nevis, Redonda, and Montserrat. This guide is an essential tool for all cruisers sailing this region. Chris Doyle spends months sailing these islands to update each edition. Included are over 100 up-to-date color sketch charts, full color aerial photos of most anchorages, island pictures, and detailed shore-side information covering services, restaurants, provisioning, travel basics and island history. Information is linked to the author's website where you can download the GPS waypoints given in the sketch charts, learn of essential updates, print town maps, and obtain links to local weather, news, and businesses. A free 17 x 27-inch waterproof planning chart of the northern and southern Leeward Islands is now included in each edition! *Post hurricane updates are available on www.doyleguides.com

CRUISING GUIDE TO THE SOUTHERN LEEWARD ISLANDS
Chris Doyle
2018-2019
ISBN 978-0-9914550-6-5
6 x 9, 324 pp **$31.95**

The Cruising Guide to th Southern Leeward Islands cove the islands of Antigua, Barbud Guadeloupe, Marie Galante, th Saintes, and Dominica. This guide is an essential tool fo all cruisers sailing this region. Chris Doyle spends mont sailing these islands to update each edition. Included a over 100 up-to-date color sketch charts, full color aeri photos of most anchorages, island pictures, and detaile shore-side information covering services, restaurant provisioning, travel basics and island history. Informatic is linked to the author's website where you can downlo the GPS waypoints given in the sketch charts, learn essential updates, print town maps, and obtain links local weather, news, and businesses. A free 17 x 27-in waterproof planning chart of the northern and southe Leeward Islands is now included in each edition! *Po hurricane updates are available on www.doyleguides.co